FOUNDATIONS OF LANGUAGE

THE MACMILLAN COMPANY
NEW YORK · BOSTON · CHICAGO
DALLAS · ATLANTA · SAN FRANCISCO

MACMILLAN AND CO., LIMITED
LONDON · BOMBAY · CALCUTTA
MADRAS · MELBOURNE

THE MACMILLAN COMPANY
OF CANADA, LIMITED
TORONTO

Foundations of Language

by *Louis H. Gray*

PROFESSOR OF COMPARATIVE LINGUISTICS
IN COLUMBIA UNIVERSITY IN THE
CITY OF NEW YORK

New York

The Macmillan Company

1939

Published September, 1939

PRINTED IN THE UNITED STATES OF AMERICA

To
My Wife
Florence Ridley Gray

PREFACE

Il n'y a pas de faits indépendants; chaque catégorie de faits reste inintelligible, tant qu'on s'enferme dans une étude spéciale, car elle est liée à d'autres, qui en sont la raison d'être. On doit isoler les faits pour les constater, les rapprocher pour les comprendre. (Henri Delacroix, *Le Langage et la pensée,* second edition, Paris, 1930, p. 77.)

THIS book has had its origin not only in many years of technical study of language, but in practical experience of the needs of students in the classroom, in questions asked by lay friends and acquaintances, and in letters read in the daily press or received from many enquirers personally unknown. It is an attempt to answer the problems raised by specialist and layman alike, to summarise the present state of linguistic knowledge, to set forth certain hypotheses which seem not wholly improbable, and to draw boundaries between what is generally accepted, what may fairly be inferred, and what is at present utterly unknown. It is not planned for the technical linguist alone, or merely for students in secondary schools, colleges, or universities who may be interested in language, but also for the cultivated public in general who may desire to know something of a phenomenon without which thought itself would be well-nigh impossible (cf. pp. 93–97).

These pages deal with language as a whole, not with this or that language or with this or that linguistic group. Words are quoted from some two hundred languages, and forms and grammatical categories are cited from tongues spoken in every part of the globe; yet beneath this outward multiplicity and, very frequently, apparent contradiction, underlying unity must ever be traced. The aim has been to present, so far as our present state of knowledge permits, an encyclopaedic compendium of linguistics in a single volume; and, since Indo-European is the branch most studied, to give, at the same time, an introduction to Indo-European linguistics as a whole, for which no up-to-date manual in English exists.

Though all are not general linguists, and though Indo-Europeanists are rare, a few Classicists still remain, and many study French, Italian, or Spanish, English or German. These latter students have constantly been borne in mind; and every effort has been made, so far as space permits, to explain the various phenomena which present themselves in the languages commonly studied. Had it been possible, citations would have been made only from them, but so closely are they interwoven with others, less known, that such restriction quickly proved impracticable.

Special stress has been laid throughout on precise definition of technical terms. Great haziness here exists in the minds of most, but vagueness of definition brings with it vagueness of thought: a return to Scholastic exactitude is desirable. These definitions and technical terms, as well as cardinal principles, are indicated by *italics*, even at the risk of impairing the aesthetic appearance of the page; and particular care has been taken to give examples to illustrate every statement made. So conflicting are the explanations of many linguistic phenomena, and so rapid and revolutionary are the changing theories of the intensive study of language at the present time, that I have found myself obliged, in a general compendium, to make what seemed to me a wisely conservative choice, and to appear more dogmatic than I really am.

Objection may be made that linguistic psychology is less fully discussed in this volume than in some other manuals on language. After careful consideration, I have become convinced that I should leave recondite problems of psychology to the psychologists — *ne sutor ultra crepidam;* my last here is linguistics, not psychology; and I venture to think that in Chapter IV I have given full value to the influence of thought on language so far as language itself is concerned. I commit myself neither to a vitalistic nor to a mechanistic theory of language, but I can at least say that mechanistic philosophy seems to me (and to others of higher competence here than I) to be not without grave flaws. So far as I am here concerned, the problem is philosophic rather than linguistic.

The standard adopted throughout for the pronunciation of English is that of the public schools in Southern England. English spelling is dictated by historical reasons in themselves: *honour* is from Anglo-French *honour,* and only indirectly from Latin *honore*[m] as *honor* would imply; and *catechise* is from French *catéchiser,* and only indirectly from Late Latin *catechizo* (itself borrowed from Greek *κατηχίζω)* as *catechize* would suggest (cf. p. 348). Since I am convinced that Indo-European bases were originally disyl-

labic (cf. p. 159), I have reconstructed them as *bhere- ' bear ',
etc., rather than the more conventional *bher-, etc. Latin quanti-
ties have seldom been marked except where necessary for etymological reasons; and Greek and Vedic Sanskrit accents have been
indicated in phonetic transcription as stress, though tonic accentuation would technically have been more accurate (e.g., τομός ' a
cut ' as [tomōs] rather than [to'mos]; cf. p. 63). The injunctive
(p. 210) is scarcely a true mood, but simply the tenseless aorist
used as a future; and the Latin 'faciō (pp. 63, 233) was merely the
unaccented base *dhē- (cf. Greek τί-θη-μι) in the zero-grade *dhə-
(cf. pp. 65–66), so that 'vir 'facit ' the man makes ' was originally
*'u̯iros dhək̑eti. For the pronouns *so-, *to- (pp. 175, 192), E. H.
Sturtevant (Language xv [1939], 11–19) has proposed an origin
different from that which I suggest. The following works came
to my attention after the plating of the book: H. Hirt, Haupt-
probleme der indogermanischen Sprachwissenschaft (ed. H. Arntz,
Heidelberg, 1939); M. Wehrli, Neue Karte der Völker und
Sprachen Europa's (Bern, no date); the first part of S. Pop's
Atlasul lingvistic romîn (Cluj); A. N. Tucker, The Eastern
Sudanic Languages (London, 1939); A. Dauzat, Toponymie
(Paris, 1939); and the Revue des études indo-européennes
(Bucharest, 1939, sqq.). A revised edition of Les Langues du
monde is being prepared.

No formal bibliography has been given. Instead of a long list of
titles with no suggestion of their values, which even a technically
trained linguist is sometimes puzzled to decide, it has seemed better
to record the principal relevant books with some indication of their
particular importance as regards their specific subjects after the
various language-groups in Chapters XI and XII and in the chapter on The History of Linguistics (Chapter XIII).

My thanks are due to many who have aided me in preparing
this volume: to the late Dr Frederick Tilney and to Drs Foster
Kennedy, William H. McCastline, and Kenneth M. Lewis for
examining the section on the brain (pp. 89–93), and to Dr Paul R.
Neukirch for reading the manuscript as a whole; to my colleagues
at Columbia, Dean George E. Pegram for revising the pages dealing with the physics of sound (pp. 45–46), and Professors David
Eugene Smith for the mathematical formula of the word (pp.
159–160), Gardner Murphy for criticising Chapter IV on Language and Thought, and Robert M. MacIver for similar help in

Chapter V on Language and Society; to Professor Robert J. Menner of Yale University for clarifying the problem of the origin of Anglo-Saxon (pp. 346–347) ; to Mr Hans J. Uldall of Vedbæk for his criticisms of my definition of the word (pp. 146–147) ; to Professor Daniel Jones of the University of London for his permission to reproduce Figures 4, 5, and 7 from his *Outlines of English Phonetics,* and to the Librairie O. Doin et Fils of Paris for allowing me to reproduce Figure 8 on the language-centres of the brain.

I must also acknowledge my debt to my students, whose questions, comments, and criticisms have been of much value. In a very real sense, the volume is inspired with the principles of my lamented *quasi-maître* M. Antoine Meillet and my confrères of the Société de Linguistique de Paris, to whose Gallic profundity of thought, divinatory intuition, and clarity of expression I owe much. To the Publishers and Printers I am grateful for their courtesy, skill, and patience in a task which must at times have been sorely vexing. To my wife I owe a gratitude transcending words. A constant inspiration, an unsparing critic, she has from the first given beyond her strength in correcting manuscript, in reading proof, and in every form of aid that her technical skill and training could afford.

Louis H. Gray

Columbia University
in the City of New York,
22 June, 1939.

TABLE OF CONTENTS

ARBITRARY SIGNS AND
DIACRITICAL CHARACTERS

The following omissions are here intentionally made: Greek letters; characters of the International Phonetic Alphabet (pp. 58–59) ; those whose phonetic value is obvious in French, Spanish, Italian, German, Latin, etc., or is sufficiently indicated in the text; some, especially in American Indian, which occur only once or twice, and for whose value special grammars dealing with the languages in question should be consulted; and certain signs whose pronunciation is quite dubious (e.g., $a̜$, $ǵ$, $ř$, $š$).

: $=$ in relation to
$<$ $=$ comes from; is derived from
$>$ $=$ becomes; develops into
/ $=$ varies between
$\sim$ $=$ is similar to, but not identical with; is contaminated with
* $=$ hypothetical reconstruction (see pp. 3, note; 440)

Accented vowels *(á,* etc.) in Anglo-Saxon, Old Icelandic, and Irish denote long vowels *(á* $=$ [aː], etc.) ; so also *â,* etc., in Old High German, Old Frisian, and Old Saxon

$_̨$ under a vowel *(u̜,* etc.) in Balto-Slavic denotes nasalisation *(u̜* $=$ [ũ], etc.)

A tilde over a vowel denotes nasalisation in Portuguese; over a vowel, nasal, or liquid in Lithuanian, low-rising intonation (e.g., $ỹ =$ [‚iː])

Small superior letters (e.g., *centuᵐ, katbuⁿ*) indicate that the sounds which they represent were pronounced extremely short, and under certain conditions were either dropped or survived only as nasalisations; in Avestan, a small superior vowel (e.g., *bavaⁱti, haᵘrva-)* denotes an infection-vowel (cf. p. 313)

' in Semitic $=$ [ʔ]
' in Semitic $=$ [ʕ]
$à$, etc., in Lithuanian $=$ ['a]
$ä$ in Tokharian $=$ [ə]
$å$, $å̊$ in Avestan and Swedish $=$ [ɔ], [ɔː]
ai in Gothic $=$ [e]

xiii

aṁ in Sanskrit = [ã]

aú in Gothic = [u]

c in Armenian and Balto-Slavic = [ts]; in Sanskrit = [tʃ]

č in Iranian, Armenian, and Balto-Slavic = [tʃ]

c̣ in Armenian = [tsh]

č̣ in Armenian = [tʃh]

ch in Anglo-Saxon, Lowland Scots, Irish, Welsh, and Slavic = [x]

c'h in Breton = [x] or [ç]

ḍ, ṭ, ṇ in Sanskrit and Semitic = [ḍ], [ṭ], [ṇ]

δ in Semitic = [ð]

ė in Lithuanian = [eː]

ě in Slavic = [ɛ]

ei in Gothic = [iː]

γ in Semitic = [ɣ], as does ʒ in Proto-Teutonic

gk, gg in Gothic = [ŋk], [ŋg]

h in Sanskrit = [ɦ]

ḥ in Sanskrit = [h]; in Semitic = [ħ]

ḫ in Semitic = [χ]

ẖ in Semitic is silent

í in Oscan = [i̯]

i̯ in Proto-Indo-European = [j]

ĭ in Slavic = extremely short [i]

j in Albanian, Gothic, Balto-Slavic, etc. = [j]; in Armenian = [dz]; in Sanskrit and Arabic = [dʒ]

ǰ in Avestan and Armenian = [dʒ]

l̥ in Proto-Indo-European = [l̩]

ḷ in Sanskrit = [ḷ]

m̥ in Proto-Indo-European = [m̩]

ṉ in Tamil = English semi-retroflex [n]

n̥ in Proto-Indo-European = [n̩]

ǫ in Lithuanian = [oː]

ø in Danish = [œ]

r̥ in Proto-Indo-European = [r̩]

ṛ in Sanskrit = [r̩]; in Hindī = [ɽ]

ṙ in Armenian = [ʀ]

š in Semitic, Iranian, and Balto-Slavic = [ʃ]

ṣ in Semitic, Sanskrit, and Tokharian = [ṣ]

ś in Sanskrit and Tokharian = [ṣ]

sch in Dutch = [sk]

sz in Hungarian = [s]

ṭ in Avestan = [ṭ] (?)

þ in Teutonic = [θ]

u̯ in Proto-Indo-European = [v]

ŭ in Slavic = extremely short [u]

ú in Oscan = [o]

x in Iranian and Slavic = [x] or [ç]

χ in Semitic = [x]

y in Welsh = [y], [ə]; in Lithuanian = [iː]; in Old Church
Slavic = [ɨ]

ý in Anglo-Saxon = [yː]

ŷ in Welsh = [yː]

z in Hittite and Old French = [ts]

ž in Avestan and Slavic = [ʒ]

FOUNDATIONS OF LANGUAGE

CHAPTER I

General Survey of Language and of Linguistics

Subject and method of the science of language — the name of the science — its place among other sciences — its relation to physiology and physics — phonation and audition — mental and physiological aspects — its relation to literature, to national consciousness, and to the history of civilisation.

LINGUISTICS, or the science of language, deals with the history and scientific investigation of language whether one studies a phenomenon common to all mankind, or examines the resemblances and differences between languages belonging to a given linguistic family (cf. pp. 301–303), or to sub-groups of such a family, or investigates an individual language or one or more of its dialects.

We may, for example, seek to know how language has affected man's mentality, and how his mentality has affected his language; or how the meaning of words has changed as his civilisation has changed; or how language has influenced his consciousness of belonging to a given social group; or wherein the Indo-European and Semitic languages resemble or differ from each other; or what are the relations of the Indo-European or of the Semitic languages among themselves; or what are the history and characteristics of English, or of any of its dialects (e.g., Kentish, whether in itself or in comparison with Suffolk or some other English dialect).

So far as the data accessible permit, linguistic method must be essentially historical in its assemblage of material, which it must gather with the utmost fullness possible, and without preconceived theories. Only after such unprejudiced collection of data may it safely seek to compare and to contrast the phenomena which have been found; and only then may it endeavour to draw deductions or to make generalisations. Each resemblance and each contrast

1

must carefully be considered from at least two points of view: (1) as an individual phenomenon; and (2) as a part of a complex whether of the language immediately concerned, or of a group of kindred languages, or of language as a whole. In very many instances, particularly in case of languages whose history is known only in scanty measure (e.g., the great majority of the American Indian languages), this can be only a counsel of perfection, since the data are too meagre to afford a basis for more than the most tentative of interpretations; but it should invariably be followed so far as circumstances permit.

It must always be borne in mind that equal attention must be given to resemblances and to differences in linguistic phenomena; dissimilarities are as truly characteristic as are similarities, and a single apparently aberrant form (e.g., *went* as the past tense assigned to *go*, or the series *am* : *was* : *been*, or *was* : *were*) may be of more real value than a hundred seemingly regular types (e.g., *come* : *came; love* : *loved*). Again, outward similarity or even identity of form does not necessarily imply essential and historical unity; widely differing origins not infrequently lead, through varying evolutions, to results which are superficially identical, as in the three English words *sound*, which in the meaning of ' a passage of water connecting seas, lakes, etc. ', is cognate with Old Icelandic *sund* ' strait ', in the connotation of ' healthy ' with German *ge-sund* ' healthy ', and in the signification of ' noise ' is derived from French *son*, Latin *sonus* ' noise '. It becomes necessary to be thoroughly versed in the history of each language studied, and to know what rules have governed its sounds, forms, and arrangements of words before one can render a scientific judgement upon any of the phenomena which it presents. Only when such knowledge has been gained for a number of languages, is it possible to formulate principles valid for their comparison or for their differentiation. It is worse than useless to form any opinions of general application to language from, say, the phenomena of Modern English or Modern French alone.

When these general principles have been thoroughly understood, the specific function of linguistics is, for the most part, investigation of the phenomena of languages belonging to cognate groups (such relationship being established by methods to be set forth later; cf. pp. 301–303) to determine their historical development and mutual relations, and to discover, if possible, why these phenomena assume the forms in which they actually appear, whether at one particular stage or in a series of stages. The special method is comparison and contrast of such cognate languages, and, if need be, comparison or contrast with non-cognate groups, so as to ascertain their characteristics and their resemblances or differences according to certain laws which may be deduced empirically, and then formulated to interpret the linguistic phenomena under consideration. If, for instance, one has such a series as English *(he) bears*, Old Icelandic *berr*, Gothic *baíriþ* ['beriθ],[1] Old High German *birit*, Old Irish *berid*, Modern Irish *bheir* [ver], Latin *fert*, Greek φέρει ['phere:], Armenian *berē*, Old Church Slavic *beretŭ*, Sanskrit *bhárati*, one may, by comparing and contrasting these forms in accordance with phonetic correspondences (pp. 74–83), determine why they are here alike, and there unlike, and may perceive how they can all be derived from an hypothetical pre-form *'*bhereti* or (more probably) *'*bher$_e$ti*.

The science thus outlined is conventionally termed, for the most part, ' comparative philology ' in English-speaking countries, but this designation is open to grave objections. In the first place, it lays undue emphasis on comparison of linguistic phenomena, whereas differentiation is equally important. By comparison, the zoologist determines that the lion and the tiger belong to the cat-family; by differentiation, through knowledge of the historical processes of evolution and through actual observation, he determines what peculiar characteristics demarcate the one species from the other. A more serious objection to the term lies in the fact that ' philology ', strictly speaking, denotes not only the study of language, but also of literature and of all the civilisational phenomena of a people or of a group of peoples as given in written records. This meaning is preserved in the English term ' classical philology ' as well as in French *philologie*, German *Philologie*, etc. The terms ' linguistics ' (French *linguistique)* or ' science of language ' (German *Sprachwissenschaft)*, on the other hand, are

---

[1] Characters in brackets refer, in linguistic works, to the signs employed in phonetic alphabets, in this volume, to the *International Phonetic Alphabet*, Fig. 6, found on pp. 58–59. By means of this alphabet, *which should be thoroughly learned by every student of linguistics,* the actual pronunciation, or at least a very close approximation to it, may be acquired, additional characters being devised if necessary. An asterisk * indicates that the form before which it is placed is hypothetically reconstructed and has not thus far been found in any written or spoken record.

free from danger of misinterpretation. Of these, 'linguistics' seems preferable as being briefer and equally descriptive.

The precise position of linguistics among the sciences is a matter of dispute, due, in great part, to its somewhat composite nature. It must be said at once that it is not an exact science in the sense that mathematics and chemistry are exact; the human factor in it is too strong to permit it to be merely mechanical in operation. Neither is it a purely empirical science, like modern psychology or philosophy, or like anthropology or the social sciences, since strict laws may be deduced for all the more important phenomena which language presents, so that it is possible to predict in great measure what will be the given form of a given word in a given language. It is, in fact, a combination of two main factors hard to reconcile and often in conflict: physical, or mechanical; and mental, or psychological. It seems, on the whole, to take a place among the historical sciences, especially as its method of procedure is essentially the same as in investigation of any problem of history, both in its collection and comparison of material, and in its prognostication of the future, so far as one may legitimately forecast the probable future from the known facts of the past.

Linguistics does not, however, stand in isolation from other sciences, but, as one of the most important developments of the human race, it is intimately connected with many of them, casting new light upon them, and receiving indispensable illumination from them. Language is much more than a mere vehicle for communication of thought. Before a single sound can be uttered or heard, both physiology and physics are involved. The interaction of the highly complicated mechanism of the organs of speech (from the glottis to the oral and nasal cavities) and of hearing (the ear) demand a general acquaintance with the anatomy of these areas, although the linguist is not obliged to possess the exact knowledge of these areas which the surgical specialist in the throat, mouth, and ear must have; and physiological processes which, because of their constant use and repetition, become so familiar as to pass unnoticed are found to be almost incredibly complex when studied by the X-ray or the laryngo-periscope. Physics is involved by the fact that the sounds of a living being's voice, like all other sounds, produce vibrations which impinge on the ears of the auditor.

From the physical point of view, communication of thought by means of speech consists of *phonation* (the utterance of sounds by the speaker) and *audition* (the hearing of sounds by the listener). The part played by phonation is too obvious to need discussion; the rôle of audition is sometimes overlooked. Yet so important is audition that one will scarcely be far wrong in maintaining that, in the great majority of cases, slowness or rapidity of linguistic change throughout the history of language, both as a whole and in the various specific forms of speech, has been largely conditioned by accuracy or inaccuracy of audition (cf. pp. 83–87). The current view, which tends to regard language merely as a means of phonation, seems dangerously incomplete. Phonation is only half of language; a speaker requires a hearer; audition is at least as necessary as speech; the relation of the two is reciprocal and complementary; and linguistic phenomena cannot properly be understood without equal attention to both factors. As things have been from time immemorial, one hears a sound before one attempts to speak it; and then one endeavours to reproduce it as accurately as one can. In the case of persons whose phonational and auditory apparatus are normal, this ability of reproduction is not conditioned by the mechanical structure of the organs concerned, for these are not essentially different in any race or in any part of the world.

It is a linguistic commonplace that any sound whatever which any normal human being is able to hear or to utter can, so far as the vocal apparatus is concerned, be reproduced with mechanical exactness by any other normal human being whomsoever; it is simply a matter of correct adjustment of the vocal apparatus. If one who says he cannot pronounce a given sound is intelligently taught by one who knows the correct position of the phonational organs for the utterance of that sound, and if he has the requisite patience and ability to adjust the organs concerned, he will be perfectly able to reproduce the sound in question. On the other hand, it very frequently happens that a sound accurately heard and accurately reproduced in childhood or during a sufficiently long sojourn in the area of its vernacular utterance is so utterly forgotten when the speaker changes his residence to a region where the sound in question is never, or at best very seldom, heard that he honestly believes that he cannot reproduce it. As a matter of fact, physically he can do so, and return to the old area will very probably restore the supposedly lost ability, perhaps without his even noticing it. The real cause of his fancied incapability is merely that he has forgotten, through long disuse, how to adjust his vocal apparatus to reproduce the sound; and, probably, the situation is complicated, through the same desuetude, by the fact that his audition no longer catches the sound exactly.

One must remember that, however excellent the mechanism of the human ear, it is far from being so accurate a recorder of sound as some machines invented by man. Most valuable assistance in gaining a deeper knowledge of the mechanism of sound and audition is given by apparatus especially designed to record, reproduce, and transmit speech; and here the linguist must acknowledge his indebtedness especially to three inventions for artificial conveyance of the human voice: the telephone, the phonograph, and the radio, for whose further improvement intensive researches both practical and purely scientific are constantly being made. It is by no means impossible that these investigations may revolutionise many of the older theories of phonetics, and may place this study on a new and surer basis.

The importance of audition as a linguistic factor receives vivid illustration in cases of deafness. Even if only partial, this often involves mispronunciations; while total deafness, especially if congenital or contracted in childhood, generally involves total loss of intelligible speech, not because the ' deaf-and-dumb ' patient cannot speak (for he practically always can, as certain famous cases prove), but simply because he cannot hear sounds, and so does not know how to utter them.

The production of speech is the function of the vocal apparatus — the larynx, throat, oral and nasal cavities, tongue, teeth, and lips. The mechanism and inter-working of this apparatus are highly complex; and very slight changes of position often give rise to differentiations of the sounds produced, as in [s] in contrast to [θ] (e.g., English *sin* : *thin*). Spoken sound thus produced may be defined as a current of air given resonance and modification during its passage from the lungs to the atmosphere beyond the lips or nostrils (the reverse is relatively rare; cf. pp. 45, 57, 406–407). During this progress, the sound, like any other, causes vibrations in the air which impinge on the auditory apparatus of the hearer. Only in case of abnormality of the vocal or of the auditory apparatus is there inherent abnormality in the process of speaking or hearing, i.e., of reproducing or receiving more or less artificially sounds normally uttered or heard with almost mechanical accuracy. Such abnormalities are of great interest to the linguist in that through their negative characteristics, and through the adjustments and devices to which the abnormal subject must resort to reach his closest possible approximation to the normal, they afford a valuable check upon observations of the normal processes in speech and hearing. It thus becomes necessary for the linguist to know by what processes the various sounds are produced; next, he should learn how to co-ordinate his own vocal apparatus so as to produce the sounds in question; and then he will be in position not only better to understand the data of his own science, but also to correct speech-defects, and even trifling errors of pronunciation, in others due to faulty placement of the vocal organs.

Behind the vocal and auditory apparatus, conditioned by physics and physiology, lie mental and psychological processes. Generally speaking, the function of language is the conveyance of thought. In its non-physiological aspect, it is the result of unnumbered centuries of effort to express facts and ideas. Various means, not always compatible, have been adopted to fulfil the purpose desired by all speech. Consequently, languages are expressions of underlying psychologies which characterise them, delimit them, and often actually hamper them; while they, in turn, characterise, delimit, and perhaps hamper the psychologies of their speakers. Thought, which is psychological in essence, and language (the oral expression of thought), which is physiological in operation, are by no means co-extensive, still less co-incident. From this point of view, one may define language as the endeavour to express the mental by the physical or, what is really an equal paradox, to connote the intangible by the tangible.

Language is inherently conservative in its structure. Formed in earlier periods, when conditions of life and thought were far less complex, this structure strongly tends to remain stable, and change takes place only after overcoming stout resistance. Even then, except in vocabulary (cf. pp. 126–136), there is little modification in more than details, with the result that no language is a perfect instrument which can render each and every concept of the speaker. ' Thoughts too deep for words ', ' words fail to express ', and the like are no idle phrases in their essence, but indicate a state of affairs which one may lament, but can remedy only more or less inadequately (cf. p. 15). But on the other hand, the necessity of expressing ideas, especially those which, previously unknown, arise in course of time, has led to the invention of new forms which, often in widely differing ways, seek, frequently with great ingenuity, to connote the new concepts, e.g., in the case of the future tense cf. pp. 20–21). From this point of view, language is a check on thought which regulates, even if it often hampers, the expression of ideas by compelling them to assume some degree of formulation, and thus of clarity.

Just as certain principles are common to language as a whole, while individual language-groups and individual languages have their own linguistic characteristics, so the human race as a whole seems to possess certain psychological principles in common, even though each race (using this term in its common, non-scientific sense) apparently has certain individual psychological characteristics. If this be true, to know a language intimately is to know at least something of the mentality of those who speak it, always remembering that thought and word constantly affect each other, whether by broadening and extending or by narrowing and constricting. Language and psychology are inherently connected, and some knowledge of psychology must be presupposed in any real study of the principles of language. Indeed, two of the great divisions of language — syntax (the relation of words to each other) and semantics (the development of the meaning of words) — are psychological in nature (pp. 105–106, 144–145, 224, 249).

The psychology of language presents two aspects: that of the speaker and that of his audience; and these psychologies must be so nearly alike that the speaker's thought, when expressed in words, shall be intelligible to his hearer or hearers in the sense which he seeks to convey, or misunderstanding and confusion will result. If, from the psychological side, the speaker is presenting ideas of which the hearer has insufficient elementary knowledge, or if these ideas are such that his hearer's mentality is so repelled by them that he refuses even to discuss them or to consider them, there is no real understanding between speaker and hearer, even though the former may utter his words perfectly, and the latter may hear them perfectly. Turning to the physiological side, we find an analogous situation. If the hearer's audition fails to convey to his brain the meaning intended by the speaker's words, or if the speaker's vocal organs fail to produce sounds intelligible to the auditor, communication of thought is impaired or even rendered impossible. Again, the speaker may enunciate perfectly, the auditor may earnestly desire to comprehend, and the vocal apparatus of the one, like the auditory apparatus of the other, may be physiologically flawless; but if the part of the hearer's brain concerned with audition is impaired, his understanding of the words spoken will be imperfect in proportion to his mental defect. In the speaker, lack of co-ordination between his brain and his vocal apparatus may make his words meaningless, or even contrary to what he intends and endeavours to say. Severe cases of mental disturbance in the functions of speech and hearing call for the attention of the alienist, whether in themselves or as symptoms and concomitants of other forms of mental disease.

Language is much more than merely physical, physiological, mental, and psychological. It is, for example, a vehicle of literature; and in this aspect of it, it would appear that one can neither have a truly profound appreciation of literature without deep knowledge of the possibilities, niceties, and inherent qualities of the language in which the literature in question may be written, nor can one create literature of the highest type without such knowledge. It is equally impossible truly to translate from any one language into any other language without such knowledge of both the languages concerned; otherwise, either the content or the style of the original will not be faithfully represented in the translation; and in the majority of such renderings, both content and style suffer alike.

It is impossible, furthermore, to have a complete understanding of any individual language without knowledge of its history. Only in this way can one perceive the reasons for its grammatical structure, for the shadings of meanings of its words, for its modes of expression (and particularly its idioms), for its possession of certain elements and its lack of others, or for its virtues and its faults as compared with other languages. Such knowledge, to be at all adequate, involves scientific acquaintance (and, if possible, practical acquaintance) with other modes of speech. The wider such knowledge, the better, since not merely languages immediately cognate, but even those totally unrelated, help in the understanding of any individual language through their similarities and (very often even more) through their dissimilarities.

Language may also be an important political factor, particularly in the creation and maintenance of national consciousness;

and while it has no inherent connexion with race (even using this term in its general and quite non-scientific sense; cf. pp. 115–117), so interwoven in popular consciousness have race and language become that even the best ethnographic and linguistic maps are practically, if not absolutely, identical.

Perhaps the most valuable service rendered by the study of language, at least from the point of view of general culture, is the light which such study casts on the history of a people and on their spiritual, mental, and material civilisation. Through scientific investigation of the etymology of terms for various religious, ethical, and intellectual ideas, or for many words denoting concrete objects or the non-human beings which surround man, it is very frequently possible to determine the views associated with these ideas, objects, and beings in the times before history began to be recorded. Study of the changes of meaning found in many such terms, whether by generalisation or by restriction, and sometimes by radical change of content, is an indispensable tool in tracing the evolution of human thought and of human civilisation. Not infrequently, linguistic investigation is the sole means of determining the earlier history of a people, who, otherwise vanished from an area, are known once to have inhabited it, or at least to have impressed themselves upon it, because of words in their language which still survive there, even if only in place-names.

We must, wherever possible, examine the entire vocabulary of a language from this same point of view. What of its words are an inheritance from the forefathers? What words has it borrowed? From whom did it borrow them? Why did it borrow them, and into what categories do such borrowings fall? The answers to such questions often enable us to reconstruct history when all other sources are lacking. It is scarcely an exaggeration to say that the study of language, from this point of view, is to a knowledge of the spiritual and mental development of man what archaeology is to that of his material evolution or embryology to that of his physical evolution. Just as the palaeontologist reconstructs the extinct beasts and birds, fishes and reptiles, which roamed the earth in pre-historic periods, often having but a few fragments of bones or scanty fossils to guide him, and just as the geologist can determine the earlier configuration of the world from evidence which to the untrained mind is meaningless, so the linguist can trace — and he alone in absence of material and tangible data — the history of man's long and toilsome development in thought. He is the mental archaeologist who supplements the work of the archaeologist who deals with actual objects once used by man; and often, through his knowledge of the meanings of words, he can make valuable contributions toward the restoration and reconstruction of periods anterior to those from which material remains survive.

CHAPTER II

What is Language ?

Definition of language; its general, specific, and special connotations — symbolism of language — *langage, langue,* and *parole* — verbal and acoustic images, significant and sign — soliloquy and hyperendophasia — formal and functional aspects of language — 'early' and 'late' in linguistic usage — complexity and simplicity of forms and functions, their possible evolution — synchronic, diachronic, and panchronic grammar — standard languages and dialects — isoglottic lines — rise, fall, and re-creation of dialects — patois, *parler,* technical languages, argot, slang — living and dead languages — rise and fall of languages illustrated by Latin and Romance — international languages, real and artificial — mixed and creolised languages — insoluble problem of origin of language — monogenesis or polygenesis — questions of linguistic progress or degeneration, of superiority or inferiority — theories of spread and relationship of languages — number of words in a language an idle question — rhythm and style not part of linguistics.

IN approaching the study of any subject whatsoever, it is necessary to define, with the utmost precision possible, the terms employed; to delimit the divisions and subdivisions of the subject; and to determine not only what the subject includes, but also what must be excluded from consideration. Unless this be done, vagueness and confusion are bound to result; terms will be used in varying senses, different aspects will be intermingled, and extraneous matter will be introduced. This necessity frequently involves, in linguistics as in many other fields of investigation, an analysis of components which is admittedly artificial. Here the linguist is in the position of the chemist. If the nature of the compound, whether linguistic or chemical, is to be known, it must be separated into its elements; only then does it become intelligible and more than a mere phenomenon. The phenomenon may be very interesting in itself, and it may possess high practical value; but its full interest and importance can be discerned only after exact analysis and re-combination.

One may, then, attempt to define language as follows. (1) In its broadest and most general sense, language may be said to be any means of expressing emotional or mental concepts by any living being or beings whatsoever, and of communicating them to, or receiving them from, other living beings. (2) In its specific and usual sense, language is such expression and communication to or from human beings by means of speech and hearing, the sounds uttered or heard being so combined in systems evolved, conventionalised, and recognised by common usage at any given period in the history of the human race within a given community or within given communities that they are mutually intelligible to all approximately normal members thereof. (3) In special and derived senses, the term may be applied to other means of expression and communication between human beings, as by gestures, signals, carved or written symbols, and the like, or even to sentiments supposed to be conveyed to or between human beings by means of inanimate objects.

The first part of this triple definition gives due recognition both to the gestural and to the vocal expression of emotions, and to more or less reasoned processes whereby the non-human being communicates with his fellows or with human beings. Even superficial observation of animals, birds, and some insects shows that certain gestures and vocal sounds are associated with specific emotions and desires. Animals in particular become able to associate gestures and sounds made by their masters with simple commands, invitations, or prohibitions; and close observers, in turn, soon learn to comprehend most of the limited language of animals and birds.

Unless the term is expressly qualified otherwise, ' language ' is used in linguistic as in popular parlance only in the specific and usual sense of the second part of our definition, i.e., as an ' expression and communication to or from human beings by means of speech and hearing '. The cardinal element of this sentence is that the sounds of language are ' combined in systems evolved, conventionalised, and recognised by common usage '. These words imply, in the first place, that language is, at any given period, the result of previous processes of evolution and is, at the same time, destined to undergo further change. No language remains perfectly static in its spoken form, and even its written form almost always changes, though usually far more slowly than its spoken type.

Only when a language has become dead, i.e., has ceased to be vernacular, does its form become unchanging. This is the case, for example, with Classical Latin, Classical Arabic, and Classical Chinese. The rate of change varies widely in different languages; thus, Lithuanian has remained extremely conservative, while English has changed radically, although even Lithuanian shows marked deviations from what scientific reconstruction shows it must once have been. In the relative rate of such change, non-linguistic factors (notably those of a historico-political nature) have very frequently played a dominant rôle. Classical Arabic, for instance, spoken in an area isolated from great trade-routes, remained remarkably true to what must have been the common Proto-Semitic type. Hebrew, in a region traversed by many peoples, and Akkadian, the language of Semites who had travelled far from the homeland, and who came in contact with speakers of other and unrelated tongues, underwent radical changes at a very early date. Certain isolated modern Himalayan dialects of the Sino-Tibetan family are much more archaic than the Tibetan of the seventh century A.D.; and this, in turn, is less changed than the Chinese of the sixth century B.C. The reason here is that Tibetan was exposed to contacts with other languages of Central Asia far more than was the case with the inhabitants of the lonely valleys of the Himalayas, while China was, from very early times, in even greater contact than Tibet with peoples of other speech.

In the second place, language is a system of recognised conventions. This had already been maintained by Aristotle (384–322 B.C.) and by the Epicureans, whereas the Stoics held that words and their meanings existed through some inherent necessity, conflicting theories which had been raised by Plato in his *Kratylos*, and which were debated for centuries (cf. pp. 278, 423, 427–428). With the development of linguistics, the view that words and their meanings are purely conventional has become universally acknowledged. There is no intrinsic reason why the English word *tree*, for instance, should denote the object which it does, except that among English-speaking peoples it is recognised as having the meaning which it bears. Among those speaking other languages, *Baum* (German), *arbor* (Latin), δένδρον (Greek), *crann* (Irish), *'derevo* (Russian), *mēdis* (Lithuanian), *kùoks* (Lettish), *caŕ* [tsaʀ] (Armenian), *darakht* (Persian), *vṛkṣa-* ['vṛkʃa] (Sanskrit), *'ēṣ* (Hebrew), *'īlānā* (Syriac), *šarjatuⁿ* [ʃardʒatŭ] (Arabic), *aghaj* [aʁadӡ] (Turkish), etc., have the same connotation as English *tree*.

From this it follows that language is essentially symbolic; i.e., it is a physical and external manifestation of a non-physical (emotional, intellectual, spiritual) and internal state, an endeavour to represent materially what is essentially immaterial. Since this endeavour can scarcely ever be fully realised except in the most trivial and banal aspects of life, a considerable amount of confusion results in the relations between external manifestation and internal state: the content and meaning of the symbol may undergo profound changes while the symbol remains the same, or the symbol may be modified or entirely replaced while its content and meaning continue to be unaltered (cf. pp. 19–21). It is for this reason that one frequently is at a loss to find just the right word to express one's precise thought, and why it is often impossible to discover the term which exactly conveys the idea to be transmitted with the delicate shading which the speaker desires to give (cf. p. 7). ' Words fail me ', ' I don't know how to say it ', and the like, are no idle phrases, but are themselves symbols (even if often unconscious symbols) of the inherent difficulty, if not of the actual impossibility, of expressing the immaterial by the material. From this point of view, language becomes part of the philosophical problem of symbolism; but the inference is plain that the immaterial is as real as the material. Normally the symbolism of language is unconscious, so that neither the speaker nor the hearer is aware of it; but under special stress, as when an attempt is made to suppress one language in favour of another, or to revive one language in opposition to another, language becomes a vital and conscious symbol of, e.g., nationalistic consciousness (cf. pp. 117–119).

The word ' language ' is ambiguous in that it includes at least three distinct aspects which must be carefully distinguished, and which are best differentiated by the French terms *langage, langue,* and *parole* (' language ', ' tongue ', and ' speech '). ' Language ' *(langage),* in this specific and restricted sense, is the entire complex of phenomena associated with human vocal and auditory communication of emotions and ideas; it comprises each and every one of these phenomena from the first babblings of the infant and the most rudimentary forms of human speech to the most highly developed types of man's utterance; it includes all the connexions

with physiology, psychology, history, etc., already noted; it apper-
tains simultaneously to the individual and to society.

Langue ('tongue'), as distinguished from *langage* ('language'), is a specific form of speech which (to quote from the definition given above) has been so 'evolved, conventionalised, and
recognised by common usage at any given period in the history of
the human race within a given community or within given communities that they are mutually intelligible to all approximately normal members thereof'. It is in this sense that we speak of the
English language, the French language, etc. From this point of
view, language appears primarily, if not exclusively, as a social
phenomenon. Except in the rarest instances, an individual can
neither create it nor noticeably modify it; and to learn its use is a
long and arduous task, as is evident from observation of the normal
infant's efforts to acquire it; or from the process of re-education in
curable types of aphasia; or (in perhaps the majority of cases)
from the difficulty experienced in learning a language which is not
one's mother-tongue.

If language be essentially symbolic, it follows that both *langage*
and *langue* are representations of ideas by means of phonation and
audition. In the speaker's mind a concept arises which he wishes to
convey to his auditor or auditors in such fashion that they will
understand it in the sense which he desires. This concept is termed
the *signified;* and in the speaker's mind it sets up a *verbal image*
which, according to the language used by the one about to speak, is
expressed vocally by a complex of sounds (e.g., *tree, Baum, arbor,*
etc.). This complex, as giving expression to the concept, or signified, is its *significant.* The utterance of this significant produces a
word (see p. 146) which is the *sign* of the signified. If this sign
arouses in the hearer a corresponding *acoustic image* (the second
aspect of the significant), and if this acoustic image evokes a concept, or signified, in the auditor, the chain is complete, and the
hearer comprehends what the speaker says. This process is roughly
indicated on Fig. 1. If the sign calls forth no acoustic image and,
consequently, no concept on the part of the hearer, as when a
language is employed or words are used which the hearer does not
understand, or in cases of paraphasia, where some other word is
uttered instead of the one conventionally used for the concept intended, other signs must be substituted (e.g., *crann, 'derevo,* etc.)
until one of them arouses an acoustic image in the hearer's mind.

From this point of view, *language is essentially correspondence of signified and sign.*

In this connexion, we may note what may seem superficially to be an exception to our definition of language as communication between two or more individuals, namely, soliloquy, or talking to one's self. In the small child, and very often in the adult, soliloquy appears to be little more than a mere outward and vocal expression of thoughts without need or desire for response on the part of others. But we also seem to have, besides an inheritance of infantile ego-centrism (cf. p. 94), a temporary self-division of an individual into a dual personality: as one person he speaks; as another he hears. Soliloquy is very frequently an endeavour to clarify the individual's thoughts by translating them into audible speech, as is implied by colloquially terming soliloquy ' thinking aloud '; i.e., the individual is seeking (however unconsciously) to ensure harmony between concept and verbal image on the one hand and acoustic image and concept on the other through the connecting bond

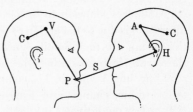

FIG. 1. Interrelation of Speaker and Hearer. C, Concept (Signified); V, Verbal Image (Significant₁); P, Phonation; S, Sign (Word); H, Hearing; A, Acoustic Image (Significant₂).

of the word or sign. Essentially the same purpose may be gained by orally propounding a train of thought to another individual whom the speaker knows to be only slightly interested in the ideas expressed, or even quite ignorant of their purport, but who serves, with what patience he can muster, as a visible *terminus ad quem* for the words of the speaker, who is in reality (as he himself usually well knows) his own auditor.

Soliloquy frequently degenerates, through force of habit, into utterance of the merest banalities. While one may rationally speak aloud to imaginary hearers, as in rehearsing a formal address, soliloquy may also be associated with hallucinations, just as, through pathological excitation of the auditory centres, one may believe that he hears words addressed to him by invisible beings (or perhaps by visible beings, if visual hallucination be added in his special case). Here we deal with the pathological state known as *hyperendophasia*, in which verbal images (usually unconscious or subconscious) are morbidly linked with acoustic images with such abnormal acuteness that the patient is convinced that he actually hears what he, it would seem, has unconsciously spoken to himself. This condition, which we may term (to coin a word) *monacousis,* is the auditory counterpart of the pathological forms of the phonational soliloquy.

The third aspect of language as a whole is *speech* or *parole.* This is, in essence, the individual side of language, the sum total of the processes whereby one individual expresses, and another comprehends, emotions and concepts formulated according to the conventions of a particular *langue* understood by both. It is, in other words, the individualistic aspect of *langage* in contrast with the social aspect of *langue.* While *langue* is static in itself, any historical survey shows it to be in a state of change (cf. p. 13). Such alteration is due to the action of *parole;* i.e., the individual modifies the group. He modifies it, however, so imperceptibly, except in those rare instances where he is a personage of unusually outstanding importance in his community, that his fellows are unaware of any change, and, usually, he himself is equally unaware that he has made even the slightest innovation. It would seem that if such modification takes place, the community as a whole must already have a general, though unconscious, tendency toward change in the direction indicated by the alteration. The broad principles governing linguistic changes appear to be as vague and as unpredictable as those which control many other phenomena of society, such as modes of dress, fashions in etiquette, types of thought, and the like. In all these, as in language, the individual and the community constantly act and counteract upon each other (cf. pp. 82–87).

The third part of our definition of language, dealing with gestures, carved or written symbols, and the like, is obviously concerned almost exclusively with *langage* rather than with *langue* or *parole.* Gesture-language is a well-nigh universal means of communication between those who do not hear or speak each other's *langue,* especially interesting and well-known examples being the sign-languages of Trappist monks, of deaf-mutes, and of the Plains Tribes in North America. Similarly, the beginnings of the alphabet in pictographs, as in American Siouan ' winter-counts ', or in the initial stages of Egyptian hieroglyphics, in the most primitive periods of Chinese and Sumerian scripts, and perhaps in Mayan and Hittite hieroglyphs, are essentially attempts to convey emotions and ideas from one person to another without the aid of vocal utterance. All writing and reading fall within this category: they are not language in the proper sense of the term.

The case seems to be rather otherwise in respect of what we have termed ' sentiments supposed to be conveyed to or between human beings by means of inanimate objects '. When we speak of the murmuring brooks, the whispering trees, the voice of Nature, the message of the stars, and the like, we regard such phrases as merely figurative and poetical. So they are, from our modern point of view; but we must remember that poetry is in its very essence highly conservative; and investigation of the more primitive stages of human thought will soon reveal a period when brooks, trees, Nature, and stars were believed to speak in languages of their own, though these, like the languages of the gods, might not be understood by man. Birds, beasts, and reptiles were also supposed, and in some areas are still supposed, to speak in their own tongues, of which man may gain knowledge by magic or by other supernatural means.

Besides the distinctions drawn (pp. 4–6) between the linguistic aspects of physiology and psychology, and between phonation and audition, one must differentiate rigidly between the formal and the functional sides of language. In language, a single form may have several functions, and the same function may be expressed by several forms, these phenomena being almost invariably due, wherever historical data are sufficient to warrant judgement on the matter, to amalgamation of more than one form or of more than one function. Here the process must be comparison of simpler and later forms with those that are earlier and more complex, or of later and more complex functions with those that are earlier and more simple.

To cite a single form with several functions, we may consider the Latin ablative, which has three general connotations: ' from ', ' with ', and ' in ' (e.g., *magno me metu liberabis* ' you will free me from great fear '; *certantes pugnis, calcibus, unguibus, morsu denique* ' fighting with fists, heels, nails, finally with teeth '; *premit altum corde dolorem* ' he presses the pain deep in his heart '). From the purely Latin point of view, these connotations can only be registered; they are irreconcilable and inexplicable so far as Latin alone is concerned. If, however, we compare Latin declension with

Sanskrit, we find that the Latin ablative is a combination, through phonetic change, of what Sanskrit retains in separate forms as an ablative, an instrumental, and a locative (e.g., Sanskrit *dắnād*, *dắnā* [Vedic], *dắne* for **dōnōd*, **dōnō*, **dōnoi* as contrasted with Latin *dōnō* ' from, with, in a gift ' [cf. Old Latin *Gnaivōd* ' from Gnaeus ', *Romai*, Classical Latin *Romae* ' at Rome ']). In Greek the situation is even more involved, for in that language the ablative has vanished (except for a few isolated instances in the dialects) and has come to coincide in form with the dative. Here, then, a subsequent identity of form (technically termed *syncretism;* see pp. 201–202) together with a retention of the meanings of forms originally distinct has given the form a series of incompatible connotations.

For an example of the same function expressed by several forms, we may consider the so-called future tense. The earliest stages of Indo-European had no future (see p. 212), but as need arose to express future time and, consequently, to denote such a tense, a number of devices were adopted in various areas. Divergent as such devices were, they have now lost all trace of their primary meanings and are regarded as mere indications of futurity. Thus we have, in English, *I shall do, he will do* (i.e., ' it is my duty to do ' [cf. German *ich soll tun*], ' it is his will to do ' [cf. German *er will tun*]) ; in Modern Greek, θà δένω (Classical δήσω) for θέλω ἵνα δένω ' I wish that I may bind ' = ' I shall bind '; in South Tosk Albanian, *de të kem* ' he (or, it) wills that I have ' = ' I shall have '; in French, *je ferai* ' I shall make ' (i.e., *faire* [*j'*]*ai*, literally, ' I have to make ' = Vulgar Latin *facere habeo;* cf. an Old Latin version of St. Mark xiv. 27: *omnes vos scandalizari habetis* = Vulgate *omnes scandalizabimini* ' all ye shall be offended '); contrast the meaning of the formally identical English *I have to do* = French *j'ai à faire);* in Modern Pontic Greek, χà δένω for ἔχω ἵνα δένω ' I have that I may bind ' = ' I shall bind '; in Old Church Slavic, *ne imamĭ piti* ' I do not have to drink ' = ' I shall not drink ', and *xošteši sę jěviti* ' thou art going to manifest thyself ' = ' thou wilt manifest thyself ' = French *tu vais te manifester;* in German, *ich werde tun* ' I am becoming (so as) to do ' = ' I shall do '; in Latin, *amābō* ' I shall love ' (originally, apparently, as in German) or *faciam* ' I shall make ' (originally a voluntative, or wishful, subjunctive ' may I do! '); in Sanskrit, *kariṣyắmi* ' I shall do ' (originally a desiderative, or desireful, present, ' I desire to do ')

or a verbal noun with the copula (e.g., *datắsmi* ' I am a giver ' =
' I shall give '); and in Slavic, the present of a perfective verb
(cf. pp. 203–208; e.g., Old Church Slavic *damĭ* ' I shall give ';
cf. English *I give to-morrow*).

These amalgamations of several forms into a single function and
these representations of a single function by various forms show
that *forms are expressed grammatically, and functions psychologically*. It thus becomes obvious that, while form and function
are amalgamated in the mind both of speaker and of hearer, historically they are of very divergent origin; and if their combination is to be understood, their components must first be analysed
and then considered separately. Such careful analysis will clear
up many problems in language which at first glance appear hopelessly confused and irrational.

That the earlier forms are the more complex, and the later the
more simple, while the reverse holds true for the functions, where
the earlier are the simpler, and the later the more complex (p. 19),
appears to hold good as a general principle, although at least
apparent exceptions are not unknown. We must bear in mind
that ' earlier ' and ' later ' are here to be taken as referring to
stages of development, not to chronological dating. Thus the
Lithuanian spoken to-day is shown, by comparison with the other
languages of the Indo-European linguistic family, to be earlier in
this sense than Greek even of the Homeric period, many centuries
B.C.; and the most archaic Hebrew known is, roughly speaking,
on the same linguistic stage as the modern Arabic dialects, and is,
consequently, later than the Classical Arabic of the Qur'ān. The
forms of Latin and, in even greater measure, of Lithuanian and
Sanskrit are far more complex than those of English; but even the
earliest Sanskrit, the language of the Rigveda (which was completed by 800 or 500 B.C., and whose earliest portions are dated by
various scholars between 2000 and 1500 B.C.), perhaps the most
complicated of all the Indo-European family, seems simple when
compared with many languages of other present-day linguistic
groups, e.g., Finnish, Turkish, African Bantu, and numerous
American tongues. While, for instance, one can say in any Indo-
European or Semitic language simply, ' the man is ill ', trusting
that the context will indicate or that the hearer will know what
particular man is suffering, in American Indian Kwakiutl (spoken
in part of British Columbia) one must say something like, ' that

invisible man near me, I am told, lies ill on his back on the floor of the absent house away from you ', or, ' this visible man near me, I know, lies ill on his side on the skins in the present house near us ', etc. Nor can he merely ' lie '; he must ' be in a lying position ' or ' be lying on his back, his face, his side, on the floor of the house, on the ground, on a pile of things ', and the like.

At the stage in which languages of the Kwakiutl type historically present themselves, this complexity of form apparently arises from the necessity of expressing concepts in definite and unmistakable terms. More or less absence of power of abstract thought seems to be implied; little can be left to the imagination; the function of each form must be complete in itself. With the progress of thought on the psychological side, and with the wearing down of forms through phonetic decay on the grammatical side, forms coalesce and their multiplicity decreases, unless the creation of new devices comes to be felt necessary for continued or increased clarity of expression. Consequently, the functions of the remaining forms become increasingly complex, but, thanks to greater power of abstract thought, they are fully intelligible both to speaker and to hearer.

There is some evidence which may be construed as implying that the more or less complex systems of forms, or inflexions, were preceded by a stage in which vocables were employed in a vague and most general sense without the precise meaning which inflexion gives them; and some of the forms which may be reconstructed by the comparative scientific method for Indo-European in its prehistoric stages seem to warrant such inference (cf. pp. 38, 150–154). This would imply progress from the vague and undefined to the specific and detailed, thence to the generalised, and, finally, to the abstract. On the other hand, two *caveat*s must be entered. In the first place, only two of the many linguistic families (Indo-European and Semitic) are known for a sufficient period of time to give any adequate idea of their historical development, and only the former is sufficiently large or has become sufficiently diversified to permit of wide-sweeping inferences. All the rest are either too isolated (e.g., ancient Etruscan, modern Basque and Japanese), or are found in too scanty remains (ancient Sicel in Sicily and Lemnian), or are known only from comparatively recent date (Dravidian only from the earliest reference to it in the seventh or eighth century A.D.; American Indian, African, and Polynesian solely from the arrival of Europeans in their areas). They offer, therefore, practically no evidence whatever of their earliest stages; the best that we can do is to compare the data which they afford either with the phenomena presented by the historic forms of Indo-European and Semitic or with their reconstructed pre-historic types.

In the second place, the most primitive languages are themselves, even in their simplest recorded forms, the results of long evolutions. Languages are known to have diverged widely from their earliest forms; only minute and painstaking investigation reveals that, for instance, English, Russian, and Armenian are derived from the same primitive stock. Chinese, which has remained practically unchanged in its literary forms for centuries, and which during all that time has presented characteristics which one would almost inevitably deem primitive, is generally regarded as having passed through a stage of inflexions, i.e., of distinct forms for cases, numbers, persons, tenses, etc. (cf. p. 390), somewhat like that of Modern English as compared with Anglo-Saxon, which itself had undergone profound changes which become evident when it is compared with the cognate Gothic.

In considering language one must distinguish carefully between its grammatical forms and psychological functions as contrasted with its vocabularies. The vocabularies may contain words taken from many different sources; and the meanings of words may change with changing culture or environment. Forms are practically never borrowed (cf. p. 129); and functions show borrowing only in rare instances, chiefly in consequence of slavish translation from other languages, as in the Gothic and Syriac versions of the Bible. Vocabulary must not, then, be confused with grammar in its aspects either of form or of function.

Study of language may be either *synchronic* or *diachronic*. Synchronic grammar deals with a language at a given period in its development; diachronic grammar traces the evolution of a language throughout its history. It is not only possible but necessary, wherever data permit, to have a purely presentational grammar of a given language at a given stage (e.g., for the Homeric, Classical, Hellenistic, Byzantine, or Modern periods of Greek), or even for a single author who has written in it, as for Chaucer or Shakespeare in English. Synchronic grammar is the only type suited for practical study of a language, particularly in the elementary stages of that study; and such is rightly the type of the conventional grammars of individual languages. Indeed, where the history of a language is unknown, it may be the only type possible. On the other hand, if one is to have a thorough grasp of English, Latin, Greek, or any other language, it is necessary, wherever conditions allow, to have a survey of the language in question from its earliest recorded stages to its latest, e.g., from Anglo-Saxon or the Homeric period to the present day for English or Greek, or from Archaic Latin (whose earliest monument is a Praenestine fibula with four words, dating from the seventh century B.C.; cf. p. 332) to the end of the Vulgar Latin period, probably in the eighth century A.D.; while for any real knowledge of French, Italian, or any other Romance language, one must know the linguistic history from the earliest emergence of Latin to the present time. At some given point, synchronic and diachronic grammars intersect, as, e.g., a grammar of Chaucer and a grammar of English as a whole. A true diachronic grammar can be constructed only on the foundation of a series of synchronic grammars.

Through comparison and contrast of synchronic and diachronic grammars, it should be possible, at least in theory, to construct a *panchronic* grammar, thus giving a scientific basis for a knowledge of *langage* as distinct both from *langue* and from *parole*. Practically, this means exclusion of what is peculiar to any *langue* or group of cognate *langues* and to every *parole*. The components of such a panchronic grammar, which may technically be termed *general grammar*, will be few in number; we shall have little more than sounds arranged in complexes which we may term vocables (we cannot yet speak of parts of speech, as nouns, verbs, etc.), which, in turn, are combined in concept-expressing groups which we may call sentences. From these elements the various individual *langues* have developed their multitudinous types; but *why* they have so evolved is a problem as yet unsolved. Granted the beginning, we can usually see *how* they have developed; and, except for the interference of alien *langues* or of such non-linguistic factors as political, economic, or military conditions, we find that a *langue* normally evolves along lines fairly well defined.

If we examine the area of any language, we shall find that speech is by no means uniform throughout, but that divergencies range all the way from almost imperceptible variations to complete unintelligibility. Not only different sub-areas, but also differ-

ent strata of society or different professions, very often have characteristic features of pronunciation, forms and arrangements of
words, and vocabulary, so that one may frequently say that such-
and-such an individual is from such-and-such a district within the
language-area, or belongs to such-and-such a social level, or
follows such-and-such an occupation. We must, accordingly, distinguish between *standard language (literary* and *colloquial), sub-
standard language, dialect, patois, professional language* (or
special language), slang, and *argot* (or *thieves' cant);* and it will
also be necessary to consider just what one means by the terms

living and *dead* languages and
mixed and *creolised* languages,
and to consider the place of
artificial languages (or *auxiliary world-languages)* within
the scheme of language and
society.

Since, from the scientific
point of view, a *standard language* (the current meaning of
' language ' in such phrases as
' the English language ', etc.)
is nothing more than a *dialect*
which has gained supremacy
over its fellows for some reason which is almost invari-

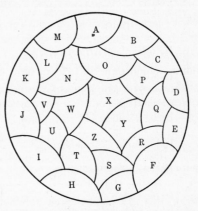

Fig. 2. Evolution of Dialects and
Languages in an Hypothetical Language-Area **A.**

ably non-linguistic, we must begin our survey with the *dialect.* Let
us suppose a series of dialect-areas A .... Z, as in the accompanying scheme, which, combined, make up the territory of a language **A.**

Here the dialects will normally differ in proportion to their distances from one another. The dialect of O, for instance, will be
intelligible within the areas A, B, C, P, X, N; P, in areas B, C, D,
Q, X, O; T, in areas Z, S, H, I, U, W; etc.; O and T, connected
by X and Z, will be less mutually intelligible; A and H, mutually
intelligible only with difficulty, if at all. Certain features of any
one of the dialects will be common to some of the rest (perhaps
to all), and certain other features to some others, so that it will be
possible to draw upon a map lines indicating at least the approximate boundaries of these features. These lines will be *isophonic,*

isotonic, isomorphic, isosyntagmic, or *isolexic* according as they indicate identical sounds, tones, inflexions, syntax, or vocabulary. Such lines are termed *isoglottic lines* or *isographs.* Far from co-inciding throughout, they cross and intertwine with a complexity which thus far defies any attempt at systematisation. How complex isographs may be will be evident from the following list of some of them in the principal Indo-European language-groups:

Vocalism	Celtic, Italic, Armenian	$o > o, u$
	Celtic, Teutonic	$i > i, e;\ \ e > e, i;\ \ u > u, o$
	Celtic, Slavic	$\bar{o} > \bar{a}$
	Teutonic, Baltic, Albanian, Indo-Iranian	$o > a$

Consonantism	Indo-Iranian, Armenian, Albanian, Balto-Slavic	gutturals > sibilants
	Indo-Iranian, Balto-Slavic	s after $i, u, k > \check{s}$
	Greek, Iranian, Balto-Slavic	$tt > st$
	Celtic, Italic	$tt > ss$
	Irish, Baltic	$\underset{\circ}{n} > in$

Morphology	Indo-Iranian, Armenian, Greek	presence of augment (cf. p. 151)
	Indo-Iranian, Tokharian, Hittite, Italic, Celtic	verb-forms in -*r* (cf. pp. 218–219)
	Italic, Celtic	genitive singular in -$\bar{\imath}$ (cf. p. 196)
	Italic, Celtic, Teutonic	preterite = aorist $\frown$ perfect (cf. p. 214)
	Teutonic, Balto-Slavic	dative-ablative plural in -*m*-
	Indo-Iranian, Armenian, Greek, Italic, Celtic	dative-ablative plural in -*bh*

(cf. p. 199)

The dialects of a given area will, as a rule, be recognisable as belonging to a common group by the average speakers of the various dialects within the area in question. About this language-area **A** are other language-areas **B, C,** etc., each similarly composed of its own dialect-areas. The speakers within these areas **A, B, C,** etc., will be conscious that they do not speak the same language, although on the frontiers they may be bilingual (or even multi-lingual), i.e., able to speak the languages of both (or all) the adjacent linguistic areas.

It is impossible to draw exact lines of demarcation between either dialects or languages, for at their frontiers they merge imperceptibly one into another unless great natural barriers intervene, as when the Channel and the North Sea form an absolute

boundary between English and French, Flemish, Danish, and Norwegian. Within Great Britain, on the other hand, it is impossible to
say precisely where English ends and Welsh or Scots Gaelic begins,
or where the English dialect of Somerset is to be demarcated from
the dialects of Gloucestershire, Wilts, Dorset, and Devon. By colonisation oceans may be crossed, as in the spread of English and
French to North America and of Spanish and Portuguese to South
America; or wide areas may be traversed, as in the case of the
entrance of the Uralic Hungarian into Indo-European Central
Europe, of Latin into what is now Rumania, of the extinct Celtic
Galatian into the centre of Asia Minor. Here, however, we are
dealing with historic, not linguistic, factors.

Returning to our language-area **A,** let us suppose that three
dialect-areas, say N, S, and U, become, for some non-linguistic
reason, more important than the others: N, for instance, is an
important religious centre; S is situated at the junction of important roads; U is the favourite seat of the ruler of the region.
The importance of these areas will tend to make their dialects
correspondingly more important than those of the other areas.
People will flock to them from the surrounding areas and even from
the borders of the whole region; the dialects of N, S, and U will be
considered worthy of imitation, and the others will tend to decline
in prestige. Suppose, further, that the commercial importance of
S becomes such that the ruler makes it his capital rather than U;
then the religious rulers will probably also tend to gravitate
thither, with the result that S finally becomes the chief centre of
the entire dialect-area. Its dialect will thus come to be regarded
as *the* dialect of the whole region and will be the *standard language,* while the others will tend to become less and less important.
This is precisely what has happened in France. Parisian French has
become standard through purely non-linguistic factors; Parisian
French is intrinsically no better than that of Picardy, except in so
far as it has been cultivated more carefully; had the course of history been different, the standard French might have been that of
Amiens, the capital of Picardy.

The standard language thus evolved will not be entirely uniform, but will have certain stratifications. At the one extreme will
be the highest classes who will use the language in the form regarded as the best; at the other extreme, the lowest classes who
will speak in a fashion regarded as the most slovenly. Between

these extremes will be various intermediate grades; and throughout the language-area as a whole there will be a general regional
standard, tinctured more or less with survivals of old dialectic
differences. With the use of literature and the development of
formal systems of grammar, the standard language in its highest
types may tend to develop two forms. People seldom speak just as
they write, otherwise their conversation is apt to be dubbed bookish
or their writing colloquial; and, to complicate the situation, literature tends to be conservative in diction, while speech constantly
changes in greater or less degree. The letters of Cicero are far
different in diction and style from his orations, and his actual conversation was doubtless unlike either, while he scarcely used the
same style of colloquial speech in talking with his equals and in
giving orders to his inferiors. In standard language we must, then,
distinguish between *literary standard, colloquial standard, sub-
standard*, and *regional standard*.

Meanwhile, what becomes of the dialects? They survive for a
long time, and may, when the importance of their areas warrants,
receive more or less recognition, and even literary development.
Generally speaking, however, they steadily decline in dignity, until
they are spoken only by the lowest strata of society within the
language-area; their use may even be discouraged as a mark of
ignorance; those who still speak them may seek both to drop them
themselves and to induce their children not to use them; and the
young, learning more or less of the standard language, may re-
proach their elders for continuing to speak dialect. In such cases,
the upper strata of the lower classes will seek to use their best
standard language when talking with the speakers of that standard, though their speech is sub-standard in the sense that it contains many words and sounds that are dialectic; but in conversation with those of their own class they employ only their own
dialect.

Where mass-education, extensive intercommunication, military
conscription, touring, radio, and other assimilatory processes are
operative, dialects tend increasingly to become mere *patois* (dialects spoken more and more impurely by only the lowest classes)
and to disappear, while the population as a whole tends more and
more to speak nothing but the standard language. On the other
hand, forces exist which tend to preserve dialects and even languages, notably, a romantic desire to preserve something of the

good of the past, and, even more, nationalistic or regionalistic pride. In certain dialect-areas efforts have been made to create standard languages as an aid to the survival of the linguistic area concerned. Here either a given dialect is taken as the standard, or the elements of the various dialects regarded as best are selected and combined to constitute the standard. Thus Eire has adopted the dialect of Munster as the standard; in Brittany the standard is an amalgam of the three chief dialects most closely akin (Trégorois, Léonard, and Cornouaillais; Vannetais, because of its divergencies, remains apart; cf. also pp. 117–119).

When for some reason the prestige of a standard language declines, renewed formation of dialects may take place. This is illustrated with peculiar clarity by the history of Greek. In its early records, Greek is represented by four principal dialect-groups (each with sub-divisions) : Attic-Ionic, Central or Aeolic, Arcado-Cyprian, and Western (cf. p. 328). With the rise of Athens to political and literary supremacy, Attic became the standard language to such a degree that ' Greek ' in the popular mind still means only Attic. This, with slight modifications, was the language of all the Greek world from Alexander the Great to Justinian, or from the end of the fourth century B.C. to the middle of the sixth century A.D.; and the ancient Greek dialects vanished. Throughout this Hellenistic period, there was but one Greek, the *Koiné* (' Common ') ; and from then until the fall of Constantinople in 1453, we have the Byzantine period, with a standard language which forms the transition to Modern Greek. With the Turkish conquest this unity was broken, and dialectic fission began, continuing to the present day despite the development of a double standard, literary *(Katharévusa,* ' purifying ') and colloquial *(Dhēmotiké,* ' popular '). One must note that these modern Greek dialects, which fall into two broad categories, northern and southern, are not descended from the ancient, but only from the Koiné, the one exception being Tsaconian, spoken in a small area on the western shore of the Gulf of Nauplia, which retains strong traces of its origin in ancient Doric.

Whatever may be the purely practical objections, economic, commercial, etc., against dialects, from the scientific point of view their disappearance is lamentable. It is, indeed, quite untrue that dialects invariably preserve older sounds, forms, syntax, and vocabulary than their standard languages; and only the incurably romantic or the very ignorant would allege that the speech of certain isolated mountainous areas in the United States speak Elizabethan English or that the *parler* of French Canada is the language of the reign of Louis XIV. Nevertheless, it is true that dialects conserve much old material which has disappeared from the standard language; and in their divergencies from it and from each other the linguist may find clues to the development of the language as a whole. We may safely say that *no investigation of a language can be considered complete without the most exhaustive study possible of all its dialects.*

Just as the dialects of a given language have evolved from a common source, so related languages are themselves, in the last analysis, simply dialects derived from a single stock. Exactly as one may trace the dialects of France, Italy, Spain, Portugal, and Rumania, together with the French, Italian, Spanish, Portuguese, and Rumanian standard languages, back to a common colloquial Latin, one may term Latin itself an Italic dialect, like its ancient cognates, Oscan, Umbrian, Volscian, etc. Latin, Greek, Irish, German, Russian, Armenian, Sanskrit, etc., and their kindred, though now popularly ranking as separate languages, each with its own dialects, are, in like manner, only dialects from a common origin which, scientifically reconstructed by comparative processes, is called Indo-European (cf. pp. 74, 226). The languages of South India (Tamil, Telugu, Kanarese, etc.), with their dialects, are dialects of an hypothetically reconstructed Proto-Dravidian; and the Semitic languages (Hebrew, Arabic, Aramaic, Akkadian, etc.; cf. p. 360) have evolved from an hypothetical Proto-Semitic. Research may yet show some of these great language-groups to be mutually related, though such kinship cannot now be demonstrated (cf. pp. 302, 366–367, 369, 372–376, 378–384, 388, 392–393, 397, 399, 403, 406, 407, 417).

Dialects (using the term in its conventional sense) normally tend to sink lower and lower in the social scale, and finally to disappear in favour of a standard language. On these lower levels they are often termed *patois,* though the line of demarcation between a dialect and a patois is as tenuous as that between a dialect and a language. The term *parler* is practically synonymous with dialect, but is free from the somewhat pejorative connotation often associated popularly with the latter. Even in the highest forms of a standard language a very real type of dialectic fissure exists, the *technical* (or *professional*) language. Many trades, occupations, and professions have a terminology of their own: the farmer, the mechanic, the herdsman, the hunter, the seaman, the student, the physician, the lawyer, the priest, the scientist each has a special technical vocabulary which may be intelligible to those of other occupations only in small part, so that it becomes necessary to draw up technological dictionaries for various occupations. These technical languages differ from the corresponding standard languages only in vocabulary, not in phonology, morphology, or syntax.

Special languages of much linguistic interest have been developed by the criminal classes, such languages (technically termed *cant* or *argot)* differing from other technical vocabularies in that they are deliberately intended, for obvious reasons, to be unintelligible to the non-initiate. They resemble the rest in that they consist mainly of semantic changes (i.e., in specialisation of the meaning of a term which commonly has another connotation) and include many words borrowed from other languages, especially from foreign argot. Only in a few instances do they actually change the forms of words, as in the relatively recent French *loucherbème* and *javanais,* the former of which makes the first letter of a word the last, adds a slang termination, and prefixes *l* to the whole, as in making *boucher* ' stop up ' into *l-oucher-b-ème;* while the latter intercalates a syllable *(al, ar, em, oc,* etc., and especially *va* for *av,* from *Java)* in a word, e.g., *ce-va-st si-va-mple e-va-t faç-av-ile* ' c'est simple et facile '.

Differing from technical languages in dignity, rather than in essence, is *slang.* Here again the characteristics are (1) borrowing from foreign (and often very obscure) sources (e.g., English *cheese* in such phrases as ' he's the big cheese ' from Anglo-Indian *cheese* from Hindūstānī-Persian *čīz* [tʃiːz] ' thing ') and (2) semantic developments, usually of a whimsical or sarcastic nature (e.g., French *douloureuse* ' mournful, painful ' = ' bill '). For the most part, slang is highly ephemeral; what is very slangy at a given time usually becomes meaningless within a few years. Nevertheless, a fairly large number of slang words prove to fill a gap in the vocabulary of the standard language which leads to their gradual adoption by the higher classes of the speakers of the language in question. Occasionally they displace words of the highest type, a notable example being French *tête* ' head ' from Latin *testa*

' earthen pot ' which has utterly ousted (except in technical meanings) the word *chef,* derived from Latin *caput* ' head ', *tête* itself
being replaced in slang by such terms as *bobine* ' spool ', *fiole*
' phial ', and the like (cf. Sanskrit *kapála-* ' skull ', originally meaning ' dish '; *testa* is used in Latin as early as the end of the fourth
century A.D. in the sense of ' skull '; in Argentina the native word
mate ' gourd ' is used by Spanish-speakers to mean ' head ' especially as a term of irony; cf. p. 262). Investigation of slang is,
etymologically and semantically, one of the most interesting and
most difficult of all linguistic tasks.

Just as dialects may become of minor importance as compared
with one of their number which rises in dignity and ultimately is
elevated to the rank of a standard language, so languages themselves may cease, more or less gradually, to be spoken and may
vanish as living speech, being entirely superseded by some other
language. Of many languages only a few words have been preserved by grammarians or travellers. Thus, we have some words of
the American Indian Beothuk of Newfoundland, but not enough
material to form even a skeleton grammar of their language; the
Greek lexicographer Hesychios (fifth century A.D.?) records scattered words of dialects and languages otherwise wholly unknown
(cf. p. 425) ; from the New Testament (Acts ii. 8–11, xiv. 11) we
know that in the first century A.D. Parthian, Median, Elamite, Cappadocian, Pontic, Phrygian, Pamphylian, Cretic (probably Eteo-
Cretan [cf. p. 383], since ordinary Cretan was simply a Greek
dialect), and Arabic were spoken; and that Lycaonian was a living
language, though not a word of it has survived. It is safe to say
that the number of languages dead and vanished is far greater,
from the times when speech began, than the number of those
which are living or which, if dead, are still remembered.

Some languages have died within comparatively recent times:
Gaulish was spoken in the fifth century A.D.; the Baltic Old Prus-
sian lingered until the seventeenth century, and the Celtic Cornish
until the first half of the nineteenth. Other languages are moribund
at the present day, such as the Celtic Manx and certain North
American Indian languages along the Pacific coast. On the other
hand, some languages seem to have taken a new lease of life, like
Lithuanian and Lettish. But if Gaulish was replaced by Latin;
Old Prussian by German; Cornish, Manx, and American Indian by
English; or if Lithuanian, Lettish, and Irish, like Hebrew in

Palestine, have experienced a revival, all these changes are due to non-linguistic causes. The stern laws of superior civilisation, economic advantage, military conquest, and the like, have enabled the strong to triumph over the weak; or else a pride in race and nationality has aroused a spirit which dares to defy these laws, with what final success only the future can tell, even though, in the light of the past, the prognosis can scarcely be termed favourable.

When a language ceases, for any reason whatever, to be vernacular, i.e., when it ceases to be spoken by the great majority of persons within its area, it is said to be *dead;* if it is spoken, it is termed *living.* It is quite true that a language may long survive as an instrument of communication among certain classes (notably among the learned or for the offices of religion) ; and this has been the fortune of Hebrew and Aramaic, of Ethiopic, of Classical Armenian, and of Old Church Slavic, and of Latin and Sanskrit. Such survival is purely artificial; the language in question is rigidly restricted to its old forms (and usually even to its old vocabulary), and the processes of change operative in all languages actually spoken cease.

Whether a given language or dialect shall live or die seems to depend, in the last analysis, not so much upon economic laws and the like as upon that imponderable sentiment or emotion which constitutes, on the one hand, will that it shall live or, on the other, indifference to its fate (which practically means its death). This will or this indifference must, it would appear, come from the speakers of the language or dialect themselves; interference by governing powers seems only to change indifference into resistance of one kind or another. The Gauls surrendered Gaulish for Latin, not because they were under any compulsion to do so, but simply because they regarded Roman civilisation and literature as superior to their own (cf. p. 138) ; the German attempt to suppress French in Alsace-Lorraine led only to stubborn attachment to French as a symbol of lost independence; the endeavours of the Government of Eire to constrain the Irish to revive their dying language seem at present not wholly successful. The Welsh, on the other hand, free from either encouragement or discouragement from without, quietly maintain their language, whereas in Scotland, under precisely similar external conditions and with an analogous geographical situation, Gaelic is moribund (cf. pp. 137–139).

In one linguistic area, that of Latin and its successors, the modern Romance languages, we can trace the actual course of development in an almost unbroken line from the Praenestine fibula of the seventh century B.C. to the present day. Here we perceive how the dialect of the single small area of Latium, with Rome as its capital, gradually superseded, with the increasing political supremacy of Rome, all other languages spoken in the Italian Peninsula, not only the entirely unrelated Etruscan and the remotely cognate Messapic, Venetic, and Ligurian, but also the closely kindred Oscan and Umbrian. Later we see Latin spread *pari passu* with the Empire; we have monuments of it in every period and every part: popular literature (represented, for example, by Plautus and Petronius), one invaluable record of the diction of a highly cultured man (Caesar), technical and artificial literature (as in Cicero's writings), an enormous mass of material in poetry and prose more or less standardised, and — of especial value for linguistic purposes — thousands of inscriptions of every sort, style, and period which, despite attempts to be literary, give priceless indications of Latin as actually spoken by all strata of society. What we here find, even in the inscriptions from all parts of the Roman Empire, is a language essentially the same; one would expect marked differences, for instance, between popular inscriptions in Italy, Gaul, Spain, and Dacia, but they seem scarcely to exist. From a fair number of similarities between the Latin of Plautus and that of late writers in non-Classical and Vulgar Latin (e.g., Apuleius and Gregory of Tours), and from the evidence of the vocabulary, we seem entitled to suppose that the language of the people was not the same as the somewhat artificial literary style.

Latin we find replaced by languages and dialects sprung from it, beginning with the famous Old French Oath of Strasbourg A.D. 842, and represented by the successive Old, Middle, and Modern stages of Romance, especially Italian, Spanish, Portuguese, French, Provençal, Catalan, Rhaeto-Romanic, and Rumanian, each with many dialects. By that time Latin had become a dead language, however long it may have been artificially preserved as an international language for the learned and as the ecclesiastical language of the Roman Catholic Church.

But — and here comes the reason for the ' almost ' in an otherwise ' unbroken line ' — we have no direct evidence for the steps from Latin to Romance. Since the Latin of the inscriptions shows a language practically uniform throughout the Empire, we know neither the genesis nor the development of the Latin dialects which must have given rise to the divergencies existing in the various Romance tongues to-day; and we are ignorant even of the approximate periods at which Latin ceased to be vernacular, and when the Romance languages began. The most we can say is that they had been developing long before they appear in documents as distinct dialects. Greek and Sanskrit, with their modern descendants, show a history even longer than that of Latin, the former from the Homeric period (about 800 B.C.), the latter from the time of the Rigveda, whose oldest hymns are conventionally supposed to date from about 1500 B.C.; but in both of them the links in the chain of their development are less evident than in the case of Latin (cf. pp. 298, 314–315, 327–329, 332–334, 337).

We have spoken of Latin as an international language. For this purpose, had it been freed from the slavish adherence to Cicero imposed upon it by the Renaissance, it might have been even better adapted than it actually was. From the practical point of view, men speaking languages mutually unintelligible need to know some one language in common if they are to communicate profitably with each other, even though this language be not necessarily intended to supplant their own vernaculars, but simply to serve as an auxiliary international language. Political and economic factors have, in fact, made certain languages international. Greek spread with the domination of Greece; Latin long survived the downfall of the Roman Empire, and was only gradually superseded by new national tongues; French is pre-eminently the international language of diplomacy and of the higher strata of European and of some Asiatic society; the use of English is rapidly increasing as the international vehicle of trade and commerce; Classical Arabic serves as a similar medium for the learned literature of the Muhammadan world; in Negro Africa (i.e., in the areas south of the Sahara), Haussa, belonging to the Nigero-Chad group (?), is the international language of trade.

Repeated efforts have been made to go beyond this state of affairs, and to create an artificial auxiliary international language to be used throughout the world. Here belong, notably, Volapük, Idiom neutral, Langue bleue, Universal, Esperanto, Ido, Latino sine flexione, Novial, Gloro, etc. All these have been constructed because of a conviction that existing languages are too complicated and too irregular, and also because of the very obvious fact that no one existing national language could be elevated to the position of a universal world-language without arousing insuperable nationalistic prejudices on the part of all other tongues of wide areas and recognised importance. A grave defect (though perhaps unavoidable) is that every international language thus far proposed has been based essentially upon Latin and upon the vocabulary of the Latin-Romance world, so that for all outside that world, whether in Europe, Asia, Africa, the Americas, or Oceania, acquisition of any one of them would be tantamount to learning a language of a type hitherto more or less unknown. Knowledge of the phonology and morphology would be fairly easy to gain; but the vocabulary would remain hopelessly alien. Even if the language proved more than a pleasing theoretical exercise and actually became vernacular, it would either remain static, since it seems to allow little scope for further grammatical evolution, or it would suffer dialectic fission, although it might well become the vehicle, not merely for the affairs of every-day life, but of a true literature.

Taken all in all, the outlook for the success of a purely artificial and created language does not seem promising — the theory may be laudable, and the grammatical schemes proposed of high order; but the practical difficulties appear at present to be insurmountable. Languages are evolutions, not creations. The simplest plan for an international language would seem to be the revival of Latin, which has already proved its competence for this purpose, which has no regionalistic connotations except those which may be alleged against the artificial systems proposed (all of them being derived from it), and which has demonstrated its capacity to adopt words from other languages and to express with exactness concepts of every type. Given a uniform pronunciation, and modelled on the Latinity of the Vulgate (Ecclesiastical Latin) rather than on that of the Classics, there seems little reason to doubt that such a language would amply meet all contingencies that might arise.

A type of quasi-artificial language has evolved in certain areas, especially under economic conditions, the *mixed language*. Such a language is normally formed by amalgamating the vocabulary of one language with the grammatical system of another (or, if the vocabulary is drawn from several languages, with the grammatical system of one of them), the system in question being simplified to the utmost degree possible. As a means of communication no mixed language has ever advanced beyond the rather rudimentary stage of expressing more than the simplest and most obvious facts and needs of every-day life. The best known of this type are *Pidgin English* (i.e., ' Business English '), essentially an English vocabulary adapted to Chinese phonology and with the Chinese grammatical system; *Sabir,* a mixture of French, Spanish, Italian, Greek, and Arabic, which serves as a *lingua franca* for the Mediterranean ports; *Broken-English,* an amalgam of English and African spoken in Sierra Leone and Liberia; *Beach-la-Mar,* a much-corrupted English used in the western islands of the Pacific South Seas; and the extinct *Chinook Jargon* of the north-west Pacific coast of the United States, an extreme simplification of Chinuk mixed with English and neighbouring American Indian languages.

Under special conditions, a mixed language may become more than a mere means of communication between traders, sailors, etc., and may be adopted as the normal mode of speech when persons originally using mutually unintelligible languages remain, unlike traders and sailors, in permanent contact with each other. In such cases the languages are termed *creolised,* examples being the *Taki-Taki* (or *Ningre Tongo)* and *Jew Tongo,* both based on English and spoken as a vernacular by the descendants of African slaves in Dutch Guiana; the *Gulla Negro* of parts of the islands and seaboard area of South Carolina; and, in great measure, the *Afrikaans* of South Africa, a mixture of African vocabulary with an extremely simplified Dutch grammar. Mixed and creolised languages must not, however, be confused with bilingual or multilingual regions where two or more languages exist amicably side by side without intermingling. A particularly interesting instance of this linguistic situation is found in the Lesser Antilles. Originally held by the Arawak, who had come from South America, these islands were conquered by the Karib, also from South America, who expelled or killed the Arawak men and married the women, with the result that women and children continued to speak Arawak, and men, Karib. Another case is represented by the Indian drama, where the King and the Brāhmans speak Sanskrit, while all the other characters employ various Prākrits (Middle Indian popular dialects) according to their several stations, the whole doubtless reflecting actual conditions at an Indian Court, each understanding the other's dialect, but speaking only his own. In such a city as Brussels, a question may be asked in French, and answered in Flemish.

Of special interest in this connexion is *Gypsy*. Originally the language of some tribe in north-west India, and ranking as a Modern Indian dialect, it has been carried wherever Gypsies have migrated (cf. p. 316). Its vocabulary is strongly tinctured and augmented by those of the peoples among whom they have come; and its grammatical system, primarily Modern Indian in type (and thus akin to such important languages as Hindūstānī; cf. p. 316), shows all grades of alteration by those of the peoples who have been the Gypsies' more or less unwilling hosts. In Armenia, the Gypsies have adopted Armenian phonology and morphology, but have retained their own vocabulary; among the English Gypsies, on the other hand, we can trace the steady degeneration of a language with its own systems of grammar and vocabulary into a creolised dialect with Gypsy words and an extremely sub-standard English. Finally, among the great majority of English and American Romani, the language has become an English approaching more and more nearly the standard type with an ever-diminishing number of Gypsy terms, many of those which survive serving chiefly as cant to prevent non-Gypsies from understanding what is being said.

The beginning of language, whether of *langage* or of *langue*, is beyond our ken. Whatever be the antiquity of the human race, we have no actual knowledge of language earlier than about 4000 B.C., the period of the oldest Sumerian documents of the Lower Euphrates valley (cf. p. 378). Even that date must be relatively late in the history of mankind, and it is clear that language had already had a long course of evolution behind it. Every language and every language-group is evidently the result, even in its earliest known stage, of centuries if not of millennia, of development.

Generally speaking, the older the form of a language, and the more primitive its structure (using the word ' primitive ' in its conventional sense, as contrasted with the equally conventional term ' developed '), the more complex its grammatical structure appears to be (cf. pp. 19, 21, 22). It would seem, on the whole, that language in its earliest stages was a system of vocables (cf. pp. 24, 154) denoting, on the one hand, vague generalities and, on the other hand, definite concrete objects; that other vocables denoting relationship of time, space, and the like came to be added to them (agglutination; cf. p. 300) ; that, in very many languages, these relational vocables lost their distinct forms and became inseparable from the vocables to which they were attached, thus giving rise to inflexion; and that these inflexions often tend to disappear and to be replaced by relational vocables of the analytic type (cf. pp. 300–301). Whether this hypothesis (or, rather, guess) be true or false, existing languages give no clue whatever as to how language arose.

If we are unable to affirm that the earliest men could speak (except in the sense that animals and birds can speak), no skeletal remains thus far found show any evidence that they could not. Anthropology throws no light on the problem, and it is equally vain to seek for hints in the babbling of the infant or in his endeavours to speak. The infant evidently has acquired, through inheritance from countless generations, an innate tendency to utter sounds of a certain type just as various species of animals, birds, and insects tend to utter their own distinctive sounds; and this process is obviously assisted, in infants, animals, birds, and insects alike, by imitation of their elders. In essaying to talk, moreover, the infant is constrained to adopt a current form of language both by constant correction from those about him and by the very practical necessity of conforming, at least in general principle, to their speech.

Theoretically one might suppose that if a group of new-born children were rigidly isolated from hearing a word of any language whatever, they might evolve a speech of their own. At least three experiments of this type have been tried. Herodotos records that the Egyptian king Psammitichos thus secluded two children, whose first utterance was *bekos*, which was identified with the Phrygian word for ' bread '. Emperor Frederick II (1194–1250) made a similar experiment, but the infants died before producing any intelligible sounds; and James IV of Scotland (1488–1513) is said similarly to have interned two children, who, he determined, ' spak very guid Ebrew '. It would obviously be impossible to reach any conclusion unless a considerable group could be so isolated for many generations, a course of procedure which is out of the question for several reasons. It is true that very young children tend to form so-called ' little languages ' of their own; but these, when very closely examined, appear to be nothing more than extreme deformations of the language spoken in their surroundings.

Many theories have been proposed to account for the origin of speech. It has been supposed to arise from onomatopoeia (sound-imitation; cf. pp. 275–276), as when a child calls a sheep *baa-baa* or a locomotive *choo-choo* (the bow-wow theory); or from some mystic harmony between sound and sense (the ding-dong theory); or from ejaculations of pleasure, surprise, contempt, etc. (the pooh-pooh theory); or from reflex vocal utterances after strong physical exertion (the yo-he-ho theory). Language has been traced by some to primitive rhythmic chants and to singing (the sing-song theory); and by others to sounds produced by the vocal organs when half-consciously imitating the movements of the body in performing some activity (the ta-ta theory). Finally, man is often supposed to have become able to originate language when, in contradistinction to the higher primates, he is alleged to have learned to walk upright, thus so altering the contour of his brain that the evolution of the language-centres (cf. pp. 89–91) was rendered possible. From other points of view, psychologists of different schools and representatives of the various social sciences have essayed to solve the problem with the qualifications of imagination and enthusiasm rather than with those of patient investigation of the data and history of language itself.

None of the guesses here summarised can find a place in scientific linguistics. Although some of them may be regarded as suggesting possible factors in the origin of language, human speech is too complicated to be explained from any single source; and the further the strictly scientific linguist investigates it, the more complicated it is seen to be. For the present, the whole question of the origin of language must be ruled out of the sphere of scientific consideration for lack of evidence. This does not mean that solution of the problem would not be highly desirable, for it would be; but the best we now can do is to entertain a pious hope that some day data may be found on which to build an hypothesis of true scientific worth.

Neither do linguistic data afford any evidence as to whether language was monogenetic or polygenetic in origin, i.e., whether it arose from a single source or from several sources. The extreme diversity of such linguistic families as the Indo-European, American, etc., between which no genetic connexion can as yet be traced, would seem to imply a polygenetic origin; but, on the other hand, the differences now existing between languages of the Indo-European group, e.g., between Sanskrit, Irish, Armenian, Russian, and English, whose genetic relationship has long been scientifically established, appear to give fair ground for arguing by analogy that, during the millennia of the development of language, all the linguistic stocks may have evolved from a single source. The problem may well be bound up with the further question, quite outside the linguist's domain, as to whether the human race was monogenetic or polygenetic.

If speculation as to the origin of language must be excluded from linguistics, two other questions frequently raised seem equally outside its province: whether languages progress or degenerate, and whether some languages are better or worse than others. From the strictly linguistic point of view, the most that can reasonably be said in answer to the first question is that languages change with the requirements of those who speak them; but change may be for the better in some respects and for the worse in others. In certain regards, English, for example, may be considered more progressive than the Indo-European from which it has sprung, notably in its greater simplicity. In certain other regards, e.g., in its loss of more than one delicate *nuance* of meaning which Indo-European had, and which English could ill afford to surrender, one might justifiably regard it as degenerate, even though it endeavours, by more or less clumsy devices, to revive those lost shadings.

It is equally impossible to affirm categorically that one language is better or worse than another. Generally speaking, each language, or at least each language-group, may have certain advantages over others, but these advantages are only too often counterbalanced by disadvantages. One may have personal preferences, but personal preferences are not safe guides. So long as a language fulfils the needs of its speakers and can expand to meet new conditions as they arise, it is good; when it can no longer satisfy their requirements, it is bad, no matter what may be its excellencies from a purely theoretic point of view.

To account for the spread and relationship of languages, two main hypotheses have been advanced, both, it is true, primarily for the Indo-European group, but, in principle, equally applicable to all others. These are the *pedigree-theory (Stammbaumtheorie)* advanced by August Schleicher in 1866 and the *wave-theory (Wellentheorie)* proposed by Johannes Schmidt in 1872, the latter, with some modifications, still serving as the basis of the genealogical system of classification now adopted by all serious linguists (cf. pp. 301–302).

According to the pedigree-theory as outlined by Schleicher in the accompanying cut (Fig. 3), branch-languages sprang from a parent stock, from these smaller branches grew, and from the latter

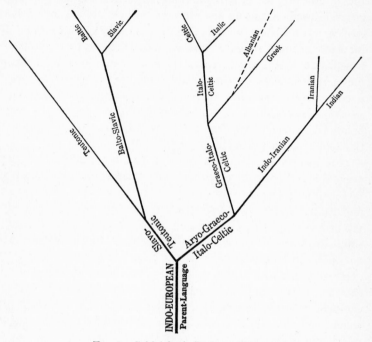

Fig. 3.   Schleicher's Pedigree-Theory.

sub-dialects bifurcated. Thus, for example, the Italo-Celtic group (Latin, Irish, etc.; cf. p. 335) split off from Indo-European; Italic and Celtic from Italo-Celtic; Latin, Oscan, Umbrian, etc., from Italic, and Irish, Welsh, Cornish, etc., from Celtic; French, Italian, etc., from Latin, and the dialects of Munster, Leinster, Connacht, and Ulster from Irish; Picard, Berrichon, etc., from French, and Donegal Irish, etc., from the dialect of Connacht. It was soon found that these clean fissures did not correspond to the evidence of history, and Schleicher's explanation yielded place to Schmidt's.

This maintains that the Indo-European languages sprang indeed from a common centre, but that they owe their evolution into independent entities not to abrupt fission, but to a wave-like spread from that centre. Consequently, adjacent areas are more alike than are those which are widely separated, and, generally speaking, the differences increase in proportion to the distances between linguistic regions (cf. p. 25). The wave-like advance of languages also explains the irregular distribution of isoglottic characteristics (cf. p. 26) just as, in a rising tide, waves advance in the same general direction, but no one wave, in its overlapping progress, is exactly symmetrical with its predecessor. Perhaps we may go further, and may roughly compare languages, when once established, to opposing currents in a river or strait, where the general limits of each current are generally definable and where the major portion has free flow, but where the edges intermingle and conflict so that exact boundaries cannot be drawn. When, on the other hand, a language disappears, the process is like that of an ebbing tide, not of sudden extinction.

This theory is not unassailable, it does not explain each and every phenomenon involved, and it ignores the non-linguistic factors of history which have affected the rise and fall of languages and dialects, but it seems to be the best general working hypothesis yet proposed for the problem as a whole. It must be modified by supplementary theories, such as the *peripheral hypothesis* recently advanced by Antoine Meillet for the Indo-European group, where, observing that the Italic and Celtic languages at the western extreme of this linguistic area possess certain characteristics in common with the Indian and Iranian groups at the eastern extreme, and that these characteristics are nowhere found in the intervening area, he suggested that Italo-Celtic on the one hand, and Indo-Iranian on the other, broke away from the parent Indo-European stock before any of the rest.

The linguist is often asked how many words a given language has, a question which cannot be answered with any degree of exactness. One may, indeed, count the number of words in the best dictionaries of that language; but when this has been done, obsolete words must be deducted and neologisms must be added, as well as the argot which practically every language possesses, to say nothing of the new words which are constantly being formed on the analogy of old, even though these may not gain recognised status in the vocabulary. One may determine, for example, that Shakespeare uses x words, Sir Walter Scott y, and Rudyard Kipling z; but this does not mean that Shakespeare or Scott or Kipling knew or used only so many in actual speech. It is equally impossible to determine the extent of the vocabulary of an individual. The stock of words of an educated man is doubtless much larger than that of one who is illiterate; but both of them know many more words than they habitually use, and both will instantly recognise the meaning of countless words that they have never heard before. Are such words part of their personal vocabularies, and so of the *langue* which they speak?

Whatever the value of such questions may be, they are scarcely linguistic in the strict sense of the term. In like manner, one must exclude from linguistics proper all consideration of rhythm (including the so-called *Schallanalyse*) and literary style, except in so far as such factors may influence the phonology, accentuation, morphology, syntax, or semantics of the language or languages under consideration at the time. Apart from the special conditions just noted, all these are problems of rhetoric and stylistics, not of linguistics.

CHAPTER III

Phonetics and Phonology: The Physiological Aspect of Language

The physics of speech-sounds — functions of the vocal organs in the production of speech — pitch, intensity, timbre — anatomy of the vocal apparatus — sounds in isolation: classification of sounds according to (1) place and (2) manner of production — difference between consonants and vowels — classification of vowels and diphthongs — International Phonetic Alphabet — relative lengths of sounds — phonemes and tonemes — accent: tonic and stress, free and fixed — strong and weak forms — quantitative and qualitative vowel-gradation — vowel-gradation as an inflexional element in Teutonic — sounds in combination within a word: assimilation, dissimilation, metathesis, epenthesis, and prothesis — change of sounds because of contiguity of words — mechanical and psychological classifications of all these changes — change of phonemes in the course of centuries as shown in Modern English from Proto-Indo-European — systems of phonetic correspondences, their method of construction, their lack of mechanical necessity, and their cardinal linguistic importance — the temporal and spacial nature of correspondence-systems — how to distinguish and date borrowed words by these systems — apparent violations of them due to borrowing, existence of factors previously undiscovered, analogy, and dialect-mixture — the Laws of Grimm and Verner for Teutonic — linguistic change — reasons assigned for it — its reason probably mainly auditional — progress of linguistic change in the individual and in the community — influence of colonisation on linguistic change.

COMMUNICATION by means of speech depends upon the physics of sound, a disturbance of air which starts from some vibrating body, and upon the physics, physiology, and psychology of hearing. The vibrations constituting the source of voice or speech are set up by forcing air from the lungs through the trachea into the larynx (with or without vibration of the vocal cords), and then through the pharynx and mouth (frequently in co-operation with the nasal cavity), over the tongue and past the teeth out beyond the lips and nose as sketched in the accompanying cut (Fig. 4). In very rare instances, the process is the reverse, i.e., there is inhalation instead of exhalation, as in the Hottentot-Bushman clicks (pp. 57, 406). From the vibrating air in the mouth and nose, sound-waves spread in all directions through the surrounding air, travelling with a speed of about 1200 feet per second. In their spreading progress, these waves diminish in magnitude or loudness; and coming to solid objects, they may be either reflected or absorbed in varying degrees. The movement of any small portion of air is a to-and-fro motion through only a minute distance; but as the waves pass by, this small motion is repeated many times a second. The number of vibrations per second is termed the *frequency,* and is determined by the source. Upon this frequency depends the quality of sound called *pitch.*

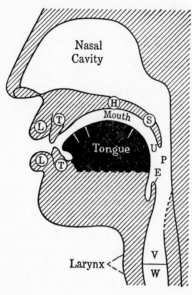

L = Lips. T = Teeth. H = Hard Palate. S = Soft Palate. U = Uvula. P = Pharynx. E = Epiglottis. V = Vocal Cords. W = Wind-Pipe.

Fig. 4. Sketch of the Vocal Organs (from Jones, *An Outline of English Phonetics,* fourth edition, Cambridge, 1935, Fig. 1, p. 14).

Speech, like other complex sounds, may be analysed into vibrations of many different frequencies. The human ear can hear sounds of frequencies ranging from a few vibrations per second to perhaps 20,000; clear speech utilises between 90 and 10,000, although speech which has no wider range than from 200 to 2000 may be fairly distinct. Four-fifths of the energy of speech is in frequencies below 1000 per second, but distinct articulation depends mainly on frequencies above that number. (The pitch of B above middle C on the piano is approximately 1000 per second.) The higher frequencies arise chiefly from the consonant sounds.

Since the tongue aids in forming the various characteristic sounds, whether by positive action, as in the case of the dentals, or by mere quiescence, as in the case of the labials, it may divide the pharyngo-buccal cavity into two parts, whose relative sizes change with every alteration of the lingual position. The resonances of these two chambers are further influenced by the size of the opening between them, determined by the distance between the highest point of the tongue and the roof of the mouth; and by their outlet, determined by the size and shape of the opening between the lips. When the tongue is entirely quiescent, as in the case of the labial vowels ([o], [u]) and consonants ([p], [b]), there is but a single cavity from the pharynx to the lips. Besides the pharyngal and buccal resonance-chambers, we may also have a third, the nasal cavity, formed by lowering the velum, or soft palate, either partially, so that the current of air passes through the buccal and the nasal chambers simultaneously, producing nasalised sounds (e.g., in French *mon* [mɔ̃]); or entirely, so that the air-current finds an exit only through the nasal chamber, in which case nasal sounds result (e.g., [n], [m]).

We may describe the production of a sound in terms of (1) the horizontal position of the tongue, (2) the vertical position of the tongue, (3) the position of the lips, and (4) the position of the soft palate, to which must be added (5) the position of the vocal cords.

A sound, whether vocal or other, is not actually so simple as this. It is, in reality, a compound, whose stronger portion normally has sound-waves of lower frequency and, consequently, of greater length. This portion, termed the *fundamental,* determines the pitch of the sound as a whole. The other components are the *overtones,* which are usually higher in pitch (and so shorter in wave-length) but less in *intensity.* When the frequencies of the overtones are exact multiples of the frequency of the fundamental, they are harmonic, and produce *tone;* otherwise they are inharmonic, and give *noise.* The combination of fundamental and overtones, with their varying frequency and intensity, gives the resultant sound its *timbre* or *quality.* The intensity depends primarily on the amplitude of the sound-waves, which diminish with the square of their distance from the sound-centre, and which are also modified by the density or rarity of the air through which they pass, as well as by the character of the obstacles which they may encounter. In the case of vocal sounds, the nature of these obstacles in the phonational apparatus varies: the tongue, soft palate, and epiglottis dampen them, while the hard palate and the teeth sharpen them, exactly as non-vocal sounds are differently affected according to whether they strike against hard, dry surfaces, or against those which are soft and moist.

The speech-organs proper are the *larynx*, the *pharynx*, and the *buccal* and *nasal cavities*. The *larynx* is set immediately on top of the trachea, or windpipe, and is formed by the ascending succession of the cricoid, arytenoid, and thyroid cartilages, capable, through muscular control, of great mobility. From the linguistic point of view, the functions of the larynx centre in the *vocal cords*, two fleshy lips running from front to back on either side of the interior of the larynx, which are attached in front to the thyroid cartilage, and at the back to protruding bases of the arytenoid cartilages, the space between these cords being termed the *glottis*. The vocal cords are highly elastic. When they are completely relaxed, as in ordinary breathing, the breath passes freely between them through the glottis, and no sound is produced. When they are held tense, with resultant closure of the glottis, and air from the lungs is forced between them, they are set in vibration. Sounds so produced are termed *voiced;* those produced without vibration (i.e., with the vocal cords lax and the glottis open) are called *voiceless*. This vibration in the production of voiced sounds may clearly be perceived either by pressing the front of the thyroid cartilage (the Adam's apple) between the finger and thumb, or by closing both ears. In the former case, voiced sounds show a tremor, and in the latter case a buzzing, neither of which is felt in the production of voiceless sounds, as in the voiced [b], [d], [z] as contrasted with the voiceless [p], [t], [s].

Above the vocal cords are two similar folds of mucous membrane termed the *false vocal cords*, which play no part in normal phonation. If air is only very feebly expelled through the cartilage-glottis (the space between the arytenoid cartilages), the vocal cords being in contact, but without vibration, the result is *whisper*. Midway between voice and whisper stands *murmur*, in which the tension of the vocal cords is reduced to a minimum, the voice being accompanied by the friction-sound of the breath passing through the glottis.

Above the larynx, and separated from it by the *epiglottis*, which folds over the glottis during deglutination, thus protecting it from admission of food or drink, and also providing a bridge from the mouth to the oesophagus, is the *pharynx*. Formerly regarded as of little phonological importance, it is now known to modify the laryngal tones by changing its shape, and, consequently, its resonant effects, during the pronunciation of vowels; while, because of its fleshy substance and moist surface, it seems to exercise a muffling effect upon vowel-quality. It is apparently the place of utterance of the *pharyngals* found in the Arabic 'ayn [ɢ] and *ḥ* [ħ].

The glottis itself is the place of formation of the voiceless plosive (cf. pp. 50–51) termed the *glottal stop* or *glottal catch* [ʔ], produced by the vocal cords in exactly the same way as [p] is formed by the lips. The glottis is closed, and is then released with a sudden explosion, the effect resembling a very weak cough. It is frequently heard before initial vowels when the speaker hesitates, and between vowels, as *papa a à aller à Arles* [papa ʔa ʔa ʔale ʔa ʔarl]. It does not occur in Standard English, although it is found in some of its dialects, especially before [t], e.g., [kʌʔin] for *cutting;* and it is a distinct phoneme in Danish (e.g., [moʔr] ' murder ', but [moːr] ' mother ') and in Semitic (Hebrew *'alef,* etc.). Two other glottal (or laryngal) sounds of importance are represented by the *h*'s of English *how, ahoy* [hau, ə'ɦɔi], unvoiced and voiced respectively.

The *buccal cavity,* or mouth, may be described, so far as speech-production is concerned, as a resonating chamber lined with mucous membrane. It possesses projecting hard formations (the teeth) and has between its upper surface (the roof of the mouth, the hard and soft palates, and the uvula) and its floor a large mass of extremely mobile muscular matter (the tongue), which is hinged at the back to the pharyngal wall, while the front of the cavity is formed by two fleshy and muscular masses with an opening between them (the lips). The mouth is the area in which the majority of speech-sounds are given distinctive form, a highly complex rôle being played by the tongue, whose changing position very materially alters the proportions of the whole buccal cavity (cf. p. 46). The principal sounds formed in this cavity are termed, from back to front, *uvular, velar, palatal, alveolo-palatal, palato-alveolar, retroflex, dental and alveolar, labio-dental,* and *bilabial.*

Uvulars are produced by approximating the back part of the tongue to the uvula, the fleshy tip of the soft palate (velum). They are comparatively rare in European languages, though the uvular *r* [ʀ] is present in the French *r grasseyé,* in North German and Danish, and in the Northumbrian ' burr '; and something similar to the corresponding voiceless plosive may be found in such English words as *caw* [qɔː] if the initial sound be produced as far back as possible.

Velars are pronounced by placing the back part of the tongue against the velum, or soft palate, as in English *can, get, sing* [kæn, get, siŋ]; German *noch,* Spanish *jabón, gente* [nɔx, xa:'βo:n, 'xente]; North German *Wagen* ['va:γṇ]. Approximation of the front part of the tongue to the hard palate produces *palatals,* e.g., the plosives in dialectic French *cuer, Gyeu* [ce:, ɟø] for the standard *tuer, Dieu;* the nasal in French *montagne,* Italian *ogni,* Spanish *año* [mɔ̃'taɲ, 'oɲɲi,'a:ɲo]; the lateral in Italian *egli,* Spanish *allá* ['eʎʎi, aʎ'ʎa:]; and the fricatives in German *ich,* English *you* [iç, ju:].

We may omit, as only sporadic in West European languages, the *alveolo-palatal* and *retroflex* plosives, the latter, a marked feature of Sanskrit and the Prākrits, as well as of Modern Indian and Dravidian, also being termed *cacuminal* and, by Sanskrit grammarians, *cerebral.* Alveolo-palatals are produced by articulating in the area between the alveolus (the ridge just behind the upper gum) and the front part of the hard palate; and retroflexes by curling the tip of the tongue back and upward toward the hard palate and then releasing it sharply.

Palato-alveolars are exemplified in the English sibilants [ʃ] and [ʒ], as in *shell, pleasure* [ʃel, 'pleʒə(r)]. *Dentals* and *alveolars,* formed respectively by the tongue approximating the tips of the teeth (as in French) or the alveolus (as in English), are represented by [t], [d], [n], [l], [r], [θ], [ð], [s], and [z], as in *tot, dot, not, lot, rot, thin, then, seal, zeal. Labio-dentals* are made by the lower lip touching the upper front teeth, as [f] and [v] in English *fit, vivid;* and *bilabials* by the action of the lips alone, as [p], [b], [m], and [w] in English *pet, bet, met, wet.*

As regards *manner* of production, in contradistinction to *place,* the sounds thus far discussed may be classified as *plosives, nasals, lateral, rolled, fricatives* (and *affricates),* and *sibilants* (the latter usually grouped together with the fricatives). *Plosives* (also termed *occlusives, mutes, stops,* or *explosives)* are characterised by complete closure of the air-passage at some point of their pronunciation, followed by complete opening of that closure. Properly speaking, there are three stages in the enunciation of any plosive: (1) *implosion,* when, preliminary to the utterance of the sound, the buccal closure is made; (2) *retention,* while air from the lungs is stored behind the point of closure; and (3) *explosion,* when the closure is immediately and fully opened, and the air stored up is released. One may further describe these three stages from the phonational and the acoustic point of view respectively as (1) *articulatory* — closing, closure, and opening; or as (2) *auditional* — on-glide, silence (or buzz, in the case of voiced sounds), and off-glide (or pop).

The *point* of closure is usually supposed to determine the character of the plosive (velar, dental, labial, etc.); but it seems more accurate to say that this character is due, rather, to the *relative position* of the particular speech-organs involved, the back part of the tongue with the uvula and soft or hard palate forming uvulars, velars, and palatals; the fore part of the tongue, alveolars and dentals; and the lips, labials and bilabials. The presence or absence of vibration of the vocal cords determines whether the plosive is *voiced* or *voiceless* (cf. p. 48). The explosion may also be accompanied by a tiny puff of breath, thus producing *aspiration*, as in the frequent pronunciation of *pit* as [phit]. Besides the voiced and voiceless plosives, we also find *devoiced plosives* or *lenes*. These are formed by weak exhalation of unaspirated voiced plosives, with a resultant feeble articulation which produces an effect midway between voiced and voiceless, with the result that to the unaccustomed ear they seem to be now the one, now the other; e.g., a devoiced [b] may be heard as either [p] or [b], whereas in reality it is neither, but is a separate sound [ḅ] appearing as a distinct phoneme (cf. pp. 61–62) in a number of languages, e.g., South German. Examples in English, where devoiced plosives are only sporadic, are the pronunciation of *bulb* halfway between [bʌlb] and [bʌlp], i.e., [bʌlḅ], or of *heads* halfway between [hedz] and [heds], i.e., [hedẓ]. This devoicing would seem to underlie the evolutions of plosives so characteristic of modern Western Armenian as contrasted with Eastern, which phonetically represents the earlier stage. Thus, the Eastern and Classical Armenian proper name *Tigran*, borrowed from an hypothetical Old Persian **Tigrāna-* (Τιγράνης in Herodotos), appears in Western Armenian as *Dikran*, showing not only a shift of [g] to [k], doubtless through an intermediate devoiced stage [ǧ], but also of [t] to [d]. This example shows that, in addition to devoiced plosives, we must assume *invoiced* plosives or *fortes* [ḳ, ṭ, p̣], thus having the two series [k] > [ḳ] > [g] and [g] > [ǧ] > [k], although, as a matter of fact, the acoustic value of [ǧ] is identical with that of [ḳ].

Nasals are formed by complete closure of the buccal cavity while the velum is lowered to permit escape of air through the nostrils; the chief forms are [ŋ] (velar), [ɲ] (palatal), [n] (dental and alveolar), and [m] (labial), as in English *king* [kiŋ]; French *cygne* [siːɲ], and English *nail, mail.*

Laterals are produced by blocking the centre of the buccal air-passage, with one or both edges of the tongue left free, thus forming an open space or open spaces between the tongue and the back teeth. The principal types are [l] (dental and alveolar) and [ʎ] (palatal), as in English *lot;* Spanish *calle* ['kaʎʎe], Italian *toglio* ['toʎʎoː].

Rolled sounds (all of the *r*-type) are made by rapidly tapping either the front of the tongue against the ridge of the teeth, or the uvula against the back part of the tongue, thus giving the rolled lingual [r], the flapped lingual [ɾ] (pronounced by a single tongue-tap), the rolled uvular [ʀ], and the retroflex flapped [ɽ].

Fricatives (also called *spirants*) are formed by so narrowing the air-passage that the air expelled from the lungs produces an audible friction. Of these there is a great variety, a voiceless and a voiced fricative corresponding to each of the plosives, the difference between a fricative and a plosive lying essentially in the fact that the fricative is the result of constricting the air-passage, while the plosive is due to complete closure of that passage (cf. p. 50). The principal types of fricatives are as follows: *glottal,* as in English *habit, inhabit* ['hæbit, in'ɦæbit]; velar, as in German *Loch,* Spanish *mujer, gemir* [lɔːx, muːˈxeːr, xeːˈmiːr], North German *mögen* ['mœɣn̩]; palatal, as in German and Lowland Scots *licht,* English *yet* [liçt, jet]; dental and alveolar, as in English *thick, this, deed* [θik, ðis, diːd]; labio-dental, as in English *fan, van;* and bilabial, as in colloquial German *Schwester* [ʃøestr̩], Spanish *saber* [saːˈβeːr].

One of the characteristics of a plosive is complete opening of a previous closure of the buccal cavity at some point (p. 50). If this opening, instead of immediately following the explosion of the plosive, is made slowly, air-friction results, and the plosive becomes combined with a fricative or sibilant. Thus arise such series of *affricates,* or *semi-plosives,* as [kx, ts, tθ, tʃ, dz, dʒ, pf], as in Swiss German *kchind* [kxind̩]; German *Zeit* [tsait]; English *eighth* [eitθ] and *church* [tʃəː(r)tʃ]; Armenian *jet* [dzet]; English *judge* [dʒʌdʒ]; German *Pferd* [pferd̩]. That the sounds represented by English *ch* in *church* and by *j* in *judge* are palato-alveolar affricates and not simple plosives is shown by rapid pro-nunciation as a single sound-group of such word-combinations as *that shows* [θætʃouz] and *said Jean* [sedʒã] (compare also the vulgar pronunciation of *did you* as [didʒuː]).

Sibilants, though usually classed together with fricatives, are distinguished from them in that the air-current does not pass directly through the constricted air-passage, but proceeds along a groove down the middle of the tongue, narrow for the dental and alveolar, and wide for the alveolo-palatal. Each of these divisions has both voiceless and voiced types; to the dental and alveolar sibilants belong [s] and [z], as in English *false, falls* [fɔːls, fɔːlz] ; and to the palato-alveolar, [ʃ] and [ʒ], as in English *ship, seizure,* French *jour* [ʃip, 'siːʒə, ʒuːr].

The sounds thus far considered are conventionally termed *con-sonants,* because of a popular belief that they can be uttered only in combination with a type of sound known as *vowels,* which alone are supposed to be capable of pronunciation by themselves, defi-nitions which were already given by the Greek grammarian Diony-sios Thrax (second century B.C.; pp. 424–425). These statements are far from correct, for all consonants can be uttered by them-selves whether they are *static* (or *continuant*), i.e., can be held continuously without changing quality (notably nasal, lateral, rolled, fricative, and sibilant sounds, e.g., [m], [n], [l], [r], [f], [v], [s], [ʃ]) ; or are *kinetic,* i.e., cannot be so held (plosives, affri-cates, and flaps, e.g., [p], [b], [ts], [ɾ] in Spanish *pero*). The dis-tinction between consonants and vowels must evidently be sought elsewhere than in the current definition. If we consider the series [t], [d], [n], [l], [r], [ð], [z], [i], we find that the first is characterised by an abrupt explosion without vibration of the vocal cords, the second by similar explosion with such vibration, the third by diversion of part of the air-stream to the nasal cavity with vibration, the fourth by blocking the centre of the buccal cavity with the tongue with one or both of its edges left free (also with vibration), the fifth by tapping the tongue against the alveo-lus or the uvula against the tongue with vibration of the vocal cords, the sixth by friction with vibration, the seventh by causing the air-current to pass through a groove in the centre of the tongue with vibration, and the eighth (the vowel) by permitting the air to pass through the buccal cavity in a more or less constricted passage, but with no such obstruction as would cause complete stoppage or friction.

We may define a vowel as *a sound produced by passage of air through the buccal cavity without any stoppage, obstruction, or constriction giving rise to audible friction or interruption;* and a consonant as *a sound characterised by audible friction or interruption due to stoppage, obstruction, or constriction of the air in passing through the buccal cavity.* The definition of a vowel is negative rather than positive; and the precise line of demarcation between the vowel and the consonant is none too sharp. The essential phonetic difference between them is one of sonority; *on the whole, vowels are more sonorous than consonants* (cf. p. 80).

Functionally vowels form peaks of syllables (see pp. 146–147), as in *tan, ten, tin, ton, tun, in-or-di-nate.* Nasals, laterals, and rolls may similarly serve as syllabic peaks, so that they function either as consonants or as vowels, as [m] in *mad schisms* [mæd sizm̩z], [n] in *new heavens* [njuː hevn̩z], [l] in *low apple-tree* [lou æpl̩triː], [r] in *real buttermilk* [riːl bʌtr̩milk]; and it is worth noting that the alphabets used in writing Sanskrit have special characters for [l] and [r] when used as vowels. In the terminology of Indo-European linguistics such an [m] and [n], [r] and [l] are called *sonant nasals* and *sonant liquids* respectively. Like ambiguity attaches to the sounds known as *semi-vowels,* represented in English by *w* [w] and *y* [j], and in French by *o* in the combination *oi,* as in *roi, loi* [rwa, lwa], as well as by the voiced counterpart of [j], [ɥ], seen in the combination written *ui,* as in *lui, puis* [lɥi, pɥi]. From the point of view of articulation, [w] and [j] are vowels, short forms of [u] and [i]; from the point of view of function, they are vocalic before consonants and finally, as· *pound, point* [paund, pɔint]; *thou, day* [ðau, dei] *(y* in the latter word is merely a mode of writing *i,* and Middle English actually spells it *dai);* they are consonantal initially, between vowels, and after consonants, as *wait, yet* [weit, jet]; *await, royal* [əˈweit, ˈrɔjəl]; *twelve, onion* [twelv, ʌnjən].

The so-called English long *a, o,* and *i* are really diphthongs, and not long vowels at all, as in *came, home, time* [keim, houm, taim].

The classification of vowels is much more disputed than is that of consonants, but three main factors in vowel-production appear to be (1) the height of the tongue (e.g., *heat* [hiːt] as contrasted with *hat* [hæt]); (2) the part of the tongue raised (e.g., *heat* [hiːt] as contrasted with *hut* [hʌt]), and (3) the position of the lips (again [hiːt] : [hʌt]). According to the height of the tongue, we distinguish between *close, half-close, half-open,* and *open* vowels; according to the part of the tongue raised, between *front, back* (also termed *palatal, velar; slender, broad; bright, dark),* and *central;* and according to the position of the lips, between *spread, medium,* and *rounded.*

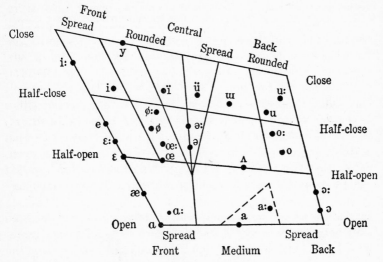

FIG. 5. Vowel-Quadrilateral.

The number of vowels is practically unlimited, but eight *cardinal vowels* may be distinguished as ' having known acoustic qualities and known tongue and lip positions ' (Daniel Jones)—[i, e, ε, a, ɑ, ɔ, o, u]. Their tongue-positions may be roughly plotted as an irregular quadrilateral (Fig. 5) whose four angles indicate respectively close front [i], open front [a], open medium [ɑ], and close back [u]. Between these come the four intermediate cardinal vowels [e, ε, ɔ, o], between half-close and half-open front, at half-open front, nearly open back, and midway between half-close and half-open back respectively. From the entire number of possible vowels, we may select twenty-seven as of general importance, considering them from top to bottom of each compartment of this same diagram (Fig. 5). Of this number, English has only twelve, [iː, i, e, æ, ɑː, ɔː, ɔ, uː, u, ʌ, əː, ə].

Midway between close and half-close, front, spread or medium [iː] — English *peat* [piːt].

Nearly half-close, front, spread or medium [i] — English *pit* [pit].

Midway between half-close and half-open, front, spread or medium [e] — English *pet* [pet].

Nearly half-open, front, spread or medium [ɛː] — French *père* [pɛːr].

Half-open, front, spread or medium [ɛ] — French *mettre* [mɛtre], German *Bett* [bɛt], first part of English diphthong in *pair, pear* [pɛə(r)].

Midway between half-open and open, front, spread or medium [æ] — English *pat* [pæt].

Nearly open, front, spread [aː] — French *page* [paːʒ], German *fahren* ['faːren].

Open, front, spread [a] — French *patte* [pat], German *Strasse* ['ʃtrasə], first part of English diphthongs in *time, pyre* [taim, pair], *pound, town* [paund, taun].

Close, front, rounded [y] — French *lune* [lyn], German *über* ['ybr̩].

Rather more than half-close, front, rounded [øː] — French *Meuse* [møːz].

Intermediate between half-close and half-open, front, rounded [ø] — French *peu* [pø], German *schön* [ʃøn].

Nearly half-open, front, rounded [œː] — French *peur* [pœːr].

Half-open, front, rounded [œ] — French *neuf* [nœf], German *zwölf* [tsvœlf].

Nearly half-close, central, spread or medium [ï] — Russian *syn* ' son ' [sïn], Welsh *bryn* ' hill ' [brïn].

Nearly half-close, central, rounded [ü] — Lowland Scots *biuk* [bük].

Midway between half-open and half-close, central, spread [əː] — English *bird* [bəː(r)d].

Nearly half-open, central, spread [ə] — English *salad, along* ['sæləd, ə'lɔŋ].

Rather less than half-close, back, spread [ɯ] — Scots Gaelic *iollach* ' shout ' ['ɯlʌk].

Half-open, back, spread [ʌ] — English *but, rub* [bʌt, rʌb].

Nearly close, back, rounded [uː] — English *cool, rude* [kuːl, ruːd].

Rather less than half-close, back, rounded [u] — English *pull, good* [pul, gud].

Rather more than half-close, back, rounded [oː] — French *côte* [koːt], German *wohl* [voːl].

Midway between half-close and half-open, back, rounded [o] — Italian *corte* [kortə].

Rather more than half-open, back, rounded [ɔː] — English *caught* [kɔːt].

Nearly open, back, rounded [ɔ] — English *want, dog* [wɔnt, dɔg].

Nearly open, back, medium [ɑː] — English *father* ['fɑːðə(r)], French *pâle* [pɑːl].

Open, back, medium [ɑ] — French *pas* [pɑ].

Diphthongs, or combinations of two vowels into a single syllable (cf. pp. 146–147), present no new principles, so that it suffices here to note that Standard English has nine [ei, ou, ai, au, ɔi, iə, ɛə, ɔə, uə], exemplified respectively in *came* [keim], *home* [houm], *night* [nait], *house* [haus], *noise* [nɔiz], *beer* [biə(r)], *fair* [fɛə(r)], *more* [mɔə(r)], and *poor* [puə(r)].

This survey by no means exhausts the number of possible sounds. There are, for instance, *nasalised vowels*, as in French *mon* [mɔ̃]; and many modifications of consonants, such as *palatalised* (e.g., Irish *te* [ţe] ' hot ', in some dialects even [tʃe]; *velarised* or *pharyngalised* (e.g., the final sound of English *little, feel* ['litɫ, fiːɫ]); *ejectives* (plosives with a simultaneous glottal stop); *clicks* (produced with closed glottis, so that the air can pass only from some part of the mouth or nose to a place above the vocal cords, thus constituting an *inverse sound*, practically inspiratory in contrast to the usual expiratory types [cf. pp. 45, 406–407]); *labialised fricatives* (e.g., [ʊ] for [θ], uttered with marked lip-rounding); and *labio-velars* ([kp, gb], etc.); but full discussion of these falls, rather, within the scope of grammars of the languages in which such sounds occur or within the domain of treatises on phonetics as a special science.

The consonants and vowels, with their various modifications and their length, stress, and pitch, are tabulated as follows in the *International Phonetic Alphabet* given on pp. 58 and 59.

In hundredths of a second the approximate durations of the principal English phonemes are as follows:[1] for all dentals, .094; for all velars, .105; for all labials, .113; for voiceless plosives, .12; for voiced plosives, .088; for nasals, .146; for lateral and rolled, .122; for fricatives, .112; for sibilants, .134; for short vowels, .228; for long vowels, .318; for diphthongs, .323; for all consonants, .118; for all vowels and diphthongs, .29; and for all sounds, .2.

Sounds are seldom uttered as isolated elements except in such simple ejaculations as *oh!, ah!* [oː, aː]. They are, therefore, practically always more or less modified by other sounds with which they stand in contact, and these conditions affect, *inter alia*, their *length*. All vowels and all continuant consonants may be either *long* or *short;* and this length or shortness may be of varying degrees with the two extremes of *under-short* (notably [ə] as in

---

[1] For a thorough discussion, see E. A. Meyer, *Englische Lautdauer = Skrifter utgifna af K. Humanistiska Vetenskaps-Samfundet i Uppsala,* viii. part iii (1903).

THE INTERNATIONAL PHONETIC ALPHABET.

(Revised to 1932.)

CONSONANTS

	Bi-labial	Labio-dental	Dental and Alveolar	Retroflex	Palato-alveolar	Alveolo-palatal	Palatal	Velaral	Uvular	Pharyngal	Glottal
Plosive	p b		t d	ʈ ɖ			c ɟ	k g	q ɢ		ʔ
Nasal	m	ɱ	n	ɳ			ɲ	ŋ	ɴ		
Lateral Fricative			ɬ ɮ								
Lateral Non-fricative			l	ɭ			ʎ				
Rolled			r						ʀ		
Flapped			ɾ	ɽ					ʀ		
Fricative	ɸ β	f v	θ ð s z ʃ ʒ	ʂ ʐ	ʃ ʒ	ɕ ʑ	ç j	x ɣ	χ ʁ	ħ ʕ	h ɦ
Frictionless Continuants and Semi-vowels	w ɥ	ʋ	ɹ				j (ɥ)	(w)	ʁ		

VOWELS

	Front	Central	Back
Close	(y ʉ u)	i y ɨ ʉ	ɯ u
Half-close	(ø o)	e ø ə	ɤ o
Half-open	(œ ɔ)	ɛ œ ɞ	ʌ ɔ
Open	(ɒ)	æ a	ɑ ɒ

(Secondary articulations are shown by symbols in brackets.)

58

OTHER SOUNDS.—Palatalized consonants: ƫ, ᶁ, etc. Velarized or pharyngalized consonants: ł, đ, ʑ, etc. Ejective consonants (plosives with simultaneous glottal stop): p', t', etc. Implosive voiced consonants: ɓ, ɗ, etc. ř fricative trill. σ, ʓ (labialized θ, ð, or s, z). ʖ, ʓ (labialized ʃ, ʒ). ʇ, ʗ, ʖ (clicks, Zulu c, q, x). l (a sound between r and l). ʍ (voiceless w). ɪ, ʏ, ʊ (lowered varieties of i, y, u). ɜ (a variety of ə). ɵ (a vowel between ø and o).

Affricates are normally represented by groups of two consonants (ts, tʃ, dʒ, etc.), but, when necessary, ligatures are used (ʦ, ʧ, ʤ, etc.), or the marks ⁀ or ͡ (t͡s or t͜s, etc.). ɕ, ʝ may occasionally be used in place of tʃ, dʒ. Aspirated plosives: ph, th, etc.

LENGTH, STRESS, PITCH.— ː (full length). · (half length). ˈ (stress, placed at beginning of the stressed syllable). ˌ (secondary stress). ‾ (high level pitch); _ (low level); ˊ (high rising); ˏ (low rising); ˋ (high falling); ˎ (low falling); ˆ (rise-fall); ˇ (fall-rise). See *Écriture Phonétique Internationale*, p. 9.

MODIFIERS.— ~ nasality. ˳ breath (l̥ = breathed l). ˯ voice (s̬ = z). ˙ slight aspiration following p, t, etc. ˌ specially close vowel (ẹ = a very close e). ˛ specially open vowel (ę = a rather open e). ̫ labialization (n̫ = labialized n). ̪ dental articulation (ṯ = dental t). ˙ palatalization (ż = ʒ). ˔ tongue slightly raised. ˕ tongue slightly lowered. ˒ lips more rounded. ˓ lips more spread. Central vowels ï (= ɨ), ü (= ʉ), ë (= ɘ), ö (= ɵ), ɛ̈, ɔ̈. ̩ (e.g. n̩) syllabic consonant. ̯ consonantal vowel. ʃ variety of ʃ resembling s, etc.

59

FIG. 6.

the man [ðə mæn]) and *over-long* (quite rare, e.g., in a prolonged *ah!* [aːː]).

So far as English is concerned, the following general principles may be laid down.[1] Short vowels are generally shorter before voiceless than before voiced consonants (contrast *bit* with *bid* [bit, bid]). Similarly, long vowels are shorter before voiceless than before voiced consonants or when final (contrast *seat* with *seed* or *sea* [siːt, siːd, siː]). They are also shorter before a nasal or lateral followed by a voiceless consonant (contrast *learnt* with *learn* or *learns; fault* with *fall* or *falls* [ləː(r)nt, ləː(r)n, ləː(r)nz; fɔːlt, fɔːl, fɔːlz]) ; and likewise in stressed syllables immediately before an unstressed syllable (contrast *leader* with *lead* ['liːdə(r), liːd]). In unstressed syllables they are shorter than in stressed (contrast *audacious* with *August* [ɔː'deiʃəs, 'ɔːgəst]). Consonants are longer after short vowels than after long vowels or diphthongs (contrast *sin* with *seen, sign* [sin, siːn, sain]) ; liquids are longer before voiced than before voiceless consonants (contrast *bald* with *fault* [bɔːld, fɔːlt]) ; and in emphatic utterance consonants following stressed vowels may even become over-long, so that *splendid!* may be pronounced [splenːːdid].

Generally speaking, consonants require less time for their utterance than semi-vowels or vowels; plosives, in the rising order of dentals, velars, and labials, less than any other type of consonants, and voiced plosives less than unvoiced. Fricatives stand between plosives and sibilants; and dental fricatives are shorter than labial. Like the plosives, voiced fricatives and sibilants are shorter than voiceless; and sibilants are shorter than laterals and rolled, which, in turn, are shorter than nasals. In respect of vowels, the order of increasing length is short, long, and diphthongs.

Sounds may also be grouped in order of *sonority*, or *carrying power*, the decreasing sequence here being open vowels, close vowels, rolled, laterals, nasals, voiced fricatives and sibilants, voiceless fricatives and sibilants, voiced plosives, and voiceless plosives.

Thus far we have seemed to imply that speech-sounds are produced each in one way; but, as a matter of fact, this is far from being the case. The great majority of these sounds may be formed in several positions; and observation by X-rays shows that the

[1] See D. Jones, *Outline of English Phonetics*, fourth edition, Cambridge, 1934, §§862–885, from which these examples are taken.

same subject frequently employs different positions in repeating utterances of what is heard by the observer as the same sound. It would appear that the acoustic properties of a speech-sound are due to the same general relational position of the vocal organs concerned within the same general area. Thus, the dental [t] is produced essentially by the explosion following the breaking of the contact between the tongue and the front teeth or the roof of the mouth, the range being approximately A–C in Fig. 7, where A represents the normal position for the French [t], B, for that of the English [t], and C, for that of the retroflex [t] found in Sanskrit and in modern Indian languages of the Indo-European group. A [t] produced at either A or C would sound strange to the English ear, as would one produced at either B or C to the French ear, but even [t] would not render it difficult for either an Englishman or a Frenchman to know that, for example, *two* (or *too, to)* and *tout* (all pronounced [tuː]) respectively were intended.

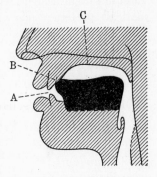

FIG. 7. Tongue-Positions for [t].

In Sanskrit, on the other hand, [t] must not be confused with [t], since *natá-* [nata], for instance, means ' bent ', but *nata-* [naṭa] denotes ' actor, dancer '. Similarly, one may confuse the dental [l] and the velarised [ł] in English without causing uncertainty of meaning to the hearer; but this is not true in Polish, for example, where *los* means ' fate ', but *łos* ' moose-deer '. Here [l] and [ł] distinguish two words of entirely diverse origin and meaning; in English, the difference of sound is merely a matter of position, [l] being used before vowels, and [ł] finally and before consonants, as in *loaf* [louf], *jelly* ['dʒeli], *bell* [beł], *people* [piːpł]. A sound which may have one or more shadings, but which is regarded as a unit in a given language, the shadings there being considered unimportant, is termed a *phoneme;* thus, in the illustrations just cited, [t] is a single phoneme in English and French, as is [l], but Sanskrit has the phonemes [t] and [t], and Polish the phonemes [l] and [ł]. Generally speaking, the number of phonemes in any one language scarcely exceeds two score.

The exact nature of the phoneme is disputed. It is variously regarded as (1) a mere grouping of sounds that are conditionally determined, on the one hand, by the position and movements of the speaker's vocal organs in producing the sounds in question, and, on the other hand, by the acoustic effect produced on the hearer (' phonetics '; the London and French schools); or (2) as a point in the psychological pattern (' phonology '; Edward Sapir and the Prague school); or (3) as a point in the linguistic (grammatical) pattern (' phonematics '). According to the second and third theories, the actual sounds are regarded as realisations of a non-physical norm, while the first theory considers the sounds themselves as constituting the phoneme.

In addition to phonemes, one must also consider *tonemes*, i.e., cases in which the pitch of utterance is a necessary characteristic. These are a marked feature in Swedish and Norwegian, e.g., Swedish *anden,* which, pronounced with a high tone [ˉandən] means ' the wild duck ' *(and-en);* but with a high-falling ['andən], ' the spirit' *(ande-n).* In English, many compound words borrowed from French consisting of a preverb (commonly, but erroneously, called a preposition in this connexion) and a base-word, and serving either as a noun (or adjective) or as a verb, are distinguished in their use as the one or the other by a difference of stress-accent. If the word in question is used as a noun or adjective, it receives its stress on the preverb; if it is used as a verb, it is stressed on the base-word, as 'address (noun) : ad'dress (verb) ; 'perfect (adjective) : per'fect (verb), so that I can ad'dress a letter to an 'address, but I cannot per'fect what is already 'perfect.

The rôle of tone is an essential factor in certain languages of Asia and Africa. Thus, the standard dialect of Chinese (Mandarin) possesses four tones (high level, high rising, low rising, and low falling), and these tones are essential to denote the meaning of the groups of phonemes to which they are attached (cf. p. 391). The group *fu,* for instance, pronounced with the high level tone denotes ' man, husband '; with the high rising, ' fortune, happiness '; with the low rising, ' prefecture '; and with the low falling, ' rich '. By subdividing each of these into a higher and lower, the dialect of Fo-kien (near Canton) has eight tones. The Tai of Indo-China, related to Chinese, has ten: natural, grave (deep bass), straightforward (midway between the first two), high, and emphatic (abrupt and explosive), each pronounced with the lips either partially closed or open. Hottentot has three tones, and

Duala, belonging to the Bantu group, also three, e.g., *mba* with the high tone means ' I '; with the low, ' cloud '; and with the rising, ' yam '. Essentially the same phenomenon is present in the two chief Indo-European languages which indicate tonal accent, Vedic Sanskrit and Greek. Thus Greek τομός [to'mos] means ' cutting, sharp ', but τόμος ['tomos] means ' a cut, a slice '; πάθη ['pathe:] means ' suffering, pain ', but βολή [bo'le:] means ' the act of hurling '; μητροκτόνος [me:tro'ktonos] means ' slaying one's mother ', but μητρόκτονος [me:'troktonos] ' slain by one's mother '; λιθοβόλος [litho'bolos] ' hurling stones ', but λιθόβολος [li'thobolos] ' pelted with stones ', just as Sanskrit *rājaputrá-* [ra:dʒaput'ra] means ' son of a king ', but *rájaputra-* ['ra:dʒaputra] ' having a king as a son '.

Tone is one of the two chief forms of *accent*, which appears either as *tonic* (or *musical* or *pitch)* or *stress* (or *expiratory)*. Tonic accent is, generally speaking, of four types: acute (high pitch), grave (low pitch), high-falling (conventionally called circumflex), and low-rising, which may be represented musically by ♩♩♩♩. Thus Greek τομός is pronounced [tomōs], but τομὸς [tomǫs], and τομῶν [to'mo:n]; in Lithuanian, which alone among Indo-European languages continues to observe this distinction, *būdas* [‚budas] ' custom ' is written, musically ♩♩♩, and *lángas* ['langas] ' window ' is ♩♩♩.

While tonic accent is characterised by pitch of voice, i.e., by frequency of vibration, stress-accent is marked by intensity of vibration and by muscular energy of the articulatory organs involved. Vedic Sanskrit and Classical Greek were, at least predominantly, languages with tonic accent; English, like Classical Sanskrit and Modern Greek, is essentially a language with stress-accent. Broadly speaking, stress-accent, as the historical evidence of languages shows, preserves the vowel upon which it falls. Vowels in unstressed syllables tend either to be weakened or to disappear (cf. p. 283), with the result that consonants formerly separated are brought into contact, with frequent modifications or even simplifications of the consonant-groups thus formed. The Latin verb *facio* ' I make ', for example, was originally accented, when accented at all (cf. pp. 232–233), on the first syllable. When it was compounded with a preverb, e.g., *de*, the stress fell upon the latter, with the result that **'defacio*, for instance, became **'deficio*. Later, the accent was shifted, but the altered vowel was retained, whence the

Classical Latin form *de'ficio* ' I unmake, fail '. In such doublets as Latin *'calidus* : *'caldus* ' warm '; *'dominus* : *domnus* ' master ', we see entire disappearance of an unstressed vowel *(syncope)*.

In Latin *officīna* ' work-shop ' beside the older *opificīna* from a still earlier **'opi-facīna* we observe a change of *p-f* to *ff* after loss of a vowel; and in Latin *pōnō* ' I put ' for **poznō* from **posnō* from **'(a)po-sinō* (cf. the perfect passive participle *positus)* we note the simplification of a consonant-group felt by Latin-speakers to be awkward. Here, too, belong such forms as Latin *ager* ' field ' (with *e* secondarily developed) for **'agr(o)s* (cf. Gothic *akrs*, Old High German *ackar*, English *acre*, and especially Greek ἀγρός [ag'ros], Sanskrit *ájras* — note the divergency of accent between the Greek and Sanskrit words).

We must distinguish between *free* and *fixed* accent, the former falling now on one syllable in the inflexion of a word, and now on another, as Sanskrit *páda* ' foot ' (accusative) but *padás* (genitive) ; Greek πόδα : ποδός; Russian *'materi* ' mothers ' (nominative) : *mater'ei* (accusative) ; Lithuanian *rankà* ' hand ' (nominative) : *rañkos* (genitive). Latin, Celtic, and the Teutonic languages (including English) have fixed accent; but there is evidence to show that originally this was not the case, as when, for example, the interchange between *s* and *r* in English *was* : *were* finds its explanation in an earlier accentual difference between Proto-Teutonic **'u̯esa* and **u̯ēs'm̥* (cf. Anglo-Saxon *wæs* : *wǽron*, and see pp. 79–81).

Word-accent must not be confused with *sentence-accent*, which appears to be influenced in the main by the meaning of the sentence as a whole, and which, like the order of words in the sentence, is essentially governed, at least in part, by psychological considerations (cf. pp. 232, 238–240). A word of any length has several accents, but only one of them is the *main accent;* the others are *secondary*. The place of the secondary accent or accents appears to be conditioned principally by considerations of rhythm, which vary in different languages, though the interval between accents, whether primary or secondary, is scarcely more than two or three syllables, as in English *antilatitudinarianistically* [ˌænti̩læti̩tuː din̩ærjan'istik̩æli].

A further result of stress-accent is the presence of *strong forms* of words beside *weak*, the former normally being stressed and retaining their full meaning, the latter normally unstressed and with weakened connotation. The weak form usually differs from the strong either in the length of its vowel or in the vowel itself, or in the omission of a sound, whether vocalic or consonantal. Only words of very common use have these double forms *(lento-* and *allegro-forms)*, as *she* in *it is she* [it iz 'ʃiː] as contrasted with *she says* [ʃi 'sez] ; French *mon sieur* [mɔ̃ sjœːr] ' my lord ' as contrasted with *monsieur* [məsjø] ' Mister ', this English word itself weakened from *Master* as *Miss* and *Missis* are from *Mistress*.

Weak forms occasionally appear in inflexion, as in the Romance future (e.g., French [*vous*] *viendrez* ' you will come ' from Vulgar Latin *venire habetis;* cf., with separation of the components, Old Spanish *venir vos edes* : Modern Spanish [*os*] *vendréis)* and in the Modern Greek future (e.g., θὰ δένω [θa ðenoː] ' I shall bind ', where θά stands for θέλω ἵνα [θeloː ina] ' I will, I wish ', and χὰ δένω [xa ðenoː] in the Pontus dialect of the same language, where χά is for ἔχω ἵνα [exoː ina] ' I have in order that I may [bind, etc.]'; cf. p. 20). Weakening is also a marked feature in place-names, as *Lyon* from Gallo-Roman *Lug(u)dūnon* ' stronghold of Lug '. The same principle of allegro-forms is seen in such pronunciations as ['windm̩] for *Wymondham* in Norfolk ('Wígmunds hám [village]'), ['tʃʌmli] for *Cholmondeley* ('Céolmunds léah [grove]') in *Cheshire* (itself shortened from *Chestershire)*, and ['sisətr̩] for *Cirencester* in *Gloucestershire* [glɔːstr̩ʃiːr], *Gleawcestrescír* in Anglo-Saxon. On the other hand, the pronunciation [dʌn'liːri] for *Dún Laoghaire,* the seaport of Dublin, is not an allegro-form, but the normal Irish pronunciation of the proper name anglicised as *Leary* (cf. p. 284).

Nowhere are the importance and the operation of stress-accent more clearly shown than in the phenomenon known as *vowel-gradation* (or *ablaut, apophony)* in Indo-European and (at least in the author's opinion) in Semitic. In a base we distinguish four main grades: *normal, prolonged, reduced,* and *zero,* which are characterised by the quantity of the vowel as conditioned by the presence or absence of stress-accent. Thus for *e* and its diphthongs *ei̯, eu̯, eə̯* (the treatment of *o* is analogous; for *ə̯* see pp. 445–446) we have the grades:

P(rolonged)	ē	ē̯i̯	ē̯u̯	ē̯ə̯ > ē (?)
N(ormal)	e	e̯i̯	eu̯	eə̯ > ē
R(educed)	ͤ	ͤi̯ > ī	ͤu̯ > ū	ͤə̯ > ē
Z(ero)	0	i	u	ə

Broadly speaking, the *normal* grade is found under the main accent (e.g., Latin *'pedem,* Greek πόδα ' foot ' [accusative]). The *prolonged* grade occurs under the accent when an unaccented vowel or a consonant originally following the accented syllable has disappeared (e.g., Latin *pēs,* Doric Greek πῶς ' foot ' [nominative] for **ped-s,* **pod-s);* in other words, it is lengthening to compensate for the loss of a phoneme. A *reduced* grade is found either (1) in the first syllable of a word when the accent originally followed at an interval of at least one syllable from it (e.g., Latin *patris* ' of a father ' from **p_et'res* from **p_et_e'res;* cf. Greek πατρός), or (2) in a middle syllable before the accent when preceded by a long syllable, i.e., by one with a long vowel or a short vowel followed by two consonants, as Gothic *haírdeis* ['herdiːs] ' shepherd ' from *herdiyas from Indo-European **ḱerdh_e'i̯os,* but *harjis* ' army ' with zero-grade from Indo-European **qor'i̯os.* The *zero*-grade comes (1) immediately after the accent when a short syllable precedes (as in the Gothic *harjis* from **qor'i̯os* just cited); (2) in the first syllable of a word when the accent follows immediately (e.g., Sanskrit *tatá-* ' stretched ' from **tn̥'to-;* cf. the Sanskrit present *tanóti,* Latin *tendit* ' stretches ', *tenuis* ' thin '); and (3) in a middle syllable before the accent, as in Latin *patris* just cited. This is the theory at its simplest; and it is evident from such forms as *patris* from **p_et'res* from **p_et_e'res* that every zero-grade must have developed from a reduced grade, actual evidence of this being seen, for instance, in the co-existence of Sanskrit *hatá-* ' smitten ' from the zero-grade **gʷn̥-'to-* beside *ghātá-* from the reduced grade **gʷh_en_e-'to-,* or in Avestan *ptā* ' father ' (and even *tā)* beside *pitā* from **pə'tē.*

Gradation lies for the most part in the period before the evolution of the various historic languages; and analogy (see pp. 106–114) has played so levelling a rôle that much confusion has resulted. The details are only too often highly obscure, but the main principles are fairly certain and explain much that otherwise would be hopelessly obscure and apparently merely capricious.

Beside this type of gradation, termed *quantitative,* there is another, called *qualitative,* which concerns an alternation of *e* and *o.* This appears in such words as Greek λέγω ' I say ' (originally unaccented; cf. pp. 232–233) : λόγος ' word '; τρέφω ' I nourish ' : τέτροφα ' I have nourished ', τροφή ' nourishment '; λείπω ' I leave ' : λέλοιπα ' I have left '; Latin *tego* ' I cover ' : *toga* ' covering, mantle', cognate with German *decken* 'to cover', *Decke* 'covering' : *Dach* 'roof' (literally, 'cover' from Proto-Teutonic **doʒoz); Gothic *giutan* 'to pour' : *gaut* 'he poured' (Gothic *iu*, *au* = Indo-European *eu*, *ou);* Lithuanian *vežù* 'I go' : *vážis* 'sledge'; Old Church Slavic *tekǫ* 'I run' : *tokŭ* 'stream, flow'. Qualitative alternation is usually explained as showing *e* in unaccented syllables, and *o* in accented; but it may be due, rather, to a difference of aspect, the grade in *e* being imperfective and that in *o* perfective (cf. p. 213).

In the Teutonic languages gradation has become an inflexional element or morpheme (see p. 150) in the past tense of the strong (or irregular) verbs, as in English *choose, chose, chosen; sing, sang, sung.* This may be illustrated by the series:

LANGUAGE	FIRST SINGULAR PRESENT	FIRST SINGULAR PRETERITE	FIRST PLURAL PRETERITE	PAST PARTICIPLE
Modern English .	choose	chose	chose	chosen
Middle English. .	chēse	chēs	curen	chōsen
	(chōse)		(cǫren)	(chēsen)
Anglo-Saxon . . .	céose	céas	curon	coren
Old High German	kiusu	kôs	kurum	gi-koran
Gothic	kiusa	kaus	kusun	kusans
Sanskrit	jóṣi	ju-jóṣa	ju-juṣúr	juṣṭá-
	(second sing.)			

Here, by the operation of Verner's Law (see pp. 79–82), the accent, preserved in Sanskrit and retained in Proto-Teutonic (but lost in the historic Teutonic languages), has caused an alternation of *s* and *r* in Anglo-Saxon and Old High German *céas* and *kôs* as contrasted with *curon coren, kurum, gi-koran* (the one surviving instance in Modern English is *were* as contrasted with *was).* At the same time, the presence or absence of accent affects the vocalism. Under the accent we find the normal grade; when the accent falls on the following syllable, the one preceding has the zero-grade (cf. p. 66), so that the Indo-European series was something like **'ĝeusō, *ĝe'ĝeusa, *ĝeĝu'sr̥(s), *ĝus'to-.*

This explanation holds good for all irregular verbs of the Teutonic group; and it further follows that the Teutonic strong preterite is in large part developed from the Indo-European perfect, though with admixture of the Indo-European aorist, very much like the Latin perfect, which also shows an amalgamation of Indo-European perfect and aorist forms (cf. p. 214). On the other hand, comparison of the Modern English with the Anglo-Saxon forms just given shows that analogy (see pp. 106–114) has created a false uniformity. Of *chosen* the exact Modern English representative would be *chorn*, and of *we chose*, *we churn*.

The fact that phonemes are normally uttered in groups very often causes more or less drastic modification of one or both of the sounds involved, notably in *assimilation, dissimilation, metathesis, epenthesis*, and *prothesis*. *Assimilation* is the process whereby one phoneme is harmonised with another, either by being made identical with it, or by being given common characteristics, an example of the first being Latin *annus* ' year ' from *at-nos* (cf. Gothic *aþn);* and of the second, Latin *actus* ' act ' for *ag-tos* (cf. Latin *agō).* Italian has here gone still further and has completely assimilated the combination so that *actus* becomes *atto*, the complete series being *gt* > *ct* > *tt*. The former of the types of assimilation is frequently termed *accommodation,* and the latter is more specifically called *equalisation.* Assimilation may, further, be either *progressive*, when the first phoneme modifies the second, as in Latin *collis* ' hill ' from *col-nis* (cf. Lithuanian *kálnas);* or *regressive*, when the second modifies the first, as in Latin *annus*, already quoted; or it may be *reciprocal,* when the modification is mutual, as in Sanskrit *ruddhá-* ' obstructed ', from *rudh-'to-*. In Indo-European languages, assimilation is most frequently of the regressive type.

In the words just cited, the assimilation is *contiguous;* i.e., the phonemes affected are in juxtaposition. There is also *incontiguous* assimilation (or *dilation)* of phonemes not juxtaposed, both progressive (very rare) and regressive. The word for ' five ' shows both these types in different Indo-European languages. The reconstructed pre-form of this word is *penqʷe,* preserved in Sanskrit *páŋca* ['paɳtʃa], Armenian *hing,* and Lithuanian *penkì.* Progressive assimilation is seen in Gothic *fimf,* Old High German *finf, fimf* (the second with regressive assimilation of *n* to *m* before a labial; Old High German *funf,* Modern German *fünf* are not from the same grade of the base as *finf),* Anglo-Saxon *fíf,* and English *five* from an older *finf.* Regressive assimilation appears in Latin *quinque*, Old Irish *cóic*, Breton *pemp;* had there been no assimilation, we should have had in Gothic *finh, in English *fi [fai], in Latin *pinque, in Old Irish *óic, and in Breton *emp.

The examples of assimilation just given concern consonants, but vowels play an equally important part. Progressive vocalic assimilation (relatively rare) is seen in Vulgar Latin *salvaticus* beside the Classical *silvaticus* ' wild ', the Vulgar form being retained in Italian *salvatico* beside *selvatico* as well as in Old French, Middle English *salvage*, Modern French *sauvage*, English *savage*. Regressive assimilation of vowels is much more frequent. This is a marked feature of Teutonic, notably in the German ' umlaut ', as German *Gast* ' guest ' : plural *Gäste* = Old High German *gast* : *gesti* = Gothic *gasts* : *gasteis* [gasti:s] from Proto-Teutonic *gasts : *gastiiz from Indo-European *ghostis : *ghosteies (cf. Latin *hostis* ' enemy ' : *hostes)*, as well as in Celtic, e.g., Old Irish *fer* ' man ' : *fir* ' of a man ' : *fiur* ' to a man ' (cf. Latin *virum, virī, virō)*. While vocalic assimilation is predominantly regressive in the Indo-European languages, it is more usually progressive in certain other linguistic families, notably in some of the Uralic group (e.g., Hungarian εmber-nεk ' to the man ', but *mådār-nåk* ' to the bird ') and in Altaic (e.g., Turkish *tash-lar-dar* ' in the stones ', but *el-ler-der* ' in the hands '; *gel-ir-im* ' I come ', but *gül-ür-üm* ' I laugh ').

The reverse of assimilation is *dissimilation*, where phonemes originally identical or possessed of common characteristics are differentiated; and, like assimilation, it may be either *progressive, regressive,* or *reciprocal;* and either *contiguous (differentiation)* or *incontiguous* (dissimilation proper). Contiguous dissimilation of identical phonemes is very rare, but the Indo-European combinations *tt(h), dd(h),* whether regular or assimilated from still earlier *dt(h),* become in certain languages first affricates *(t^st*[*h*], *d^zd*[*h*] ; cf. pp. 52–53) then *st, zd,* as Avestan *hasta-* ' seated ' from the hypothetical series **s_et^s'to-.* < **s_et'to-* < **s_ed-'to-; dazdi* ' give ! ' from **d_od^z'dhi* < **d_od-'dhi.* Regressive assimilation appears in the Sanskrit equivalent of Avestan *hasta-, sattá-,* and progressive in Latin *ob-sessus;* Greek μαζός [maz'dos] ' breast ' beside μαστός from an hypothetical series **m_ad^z'do-* < **m_ad'do-* < **m_ad-'to-* (contrast, with regressive assimilation, the equivalent Sanskrit *mattá-* ' drunk '). Regressive contiguous dissimilation is seen in such words as Spanish *alma* ' soul ', Provençal, Catalan *arma*, Old

French *arme*, Modern French *âme* (from **alme)* from Latin *an(i)ma* (note also the metathesis in Old Friulian *amna*, and the intricate development of Piedmontese *ambra* from **amra* from **arma*, with successive regressive assimilation, metathesis, and insertion of a glide-consonant for greater ease of pronunciation). Incontiguous dissimilation is much more frequent than contiguous. The regressive type appears, for instance, in Vulgar Latin *cinque* ' five ' (whence Italian *cinque*, Spanish *cinco*, French *cinq*, etc.) beside the Classical *quinque* already considered from another point of view (pp. 68–69). The progressive type occurs, for example, in Spanish *mármol* ' marble ', English *marble* (itself dissimilated from French *marbre* with a glide-*b)* from Latin *marmore^m*, while an Italian dialectic form *nálbare* shows a double regressive dissimilation, plus a dissimilation of *m* to *b*. Reciprocal dissimilation, or interchange of phonemes (termed *inversion* when contiguous, and *metathesis* when incontiguous), appears in such words as Spanish *palabra* ' word ' and dialectic Italian *palora* beside Standard Italian *parola* (French *parole)* from Latin *parabola* (whence English *parable* through the learned French *parable),* itself borrowed from the Greek παραβολή; or Modern Irish *béarla* [be:rla] ' language ' (particularly ' English ') : Old Irish *bélrae.*

A noteworthy form of incontiguous dissimilation is seen in the operation of Grassmann's Law (so named from Hermann Grassmann, who formulated it in 1863), whereby one of two original aspirates (usually the first) in the same base must be de-aspirated. Thus, a base of the type of **dheg^uhe-* ' burn ' must appear either as **deg^uhe-* or as **dheg^ue-*, as in Sanskrit *ni-dāghá-* ' heat, summer ', Greek τέφρα ' ashes ' as contrasted with Sanskrit *dhakṣyáti* ' he will burn ', Greek θέπτανος ' enkindling '. Because of the loss of original aspiration in the other Indo-European languages, the actual working of this law is visible only in Greek and Sanskrit, as Greek θρίξ ' hair ', but genitive τριχός [θriks, tri'xos] from a base **dhriĝhe-;* Sanskrit *dugdhá-* ' milked ' (for **dugh-'ta-* by reciprocal contiguous dissimilation), but *ádhukṣat* ' he milked ' (for **'adhug-s-at)* from a base **dheuĝhe-.*

Dissimilation not infrequently causes entire disappearance of one of the phonemes concerned, as dialectic Greek γίνομαι ' I become ' beside Classical γίγνομαι ['ginomai : 'gignomai] (progressive) or Vulgar Latin *propius* ' proper ' beside Classical *proprius* (regressive). Vocalic dissimilation appears in contiguous position especially in the phenomenon of *diphthongisation,* or the resolution of a long vowel into two short ones, as in German *Bein* [bain] or English *bone* [boun] as contrasted with Anglo-Saxon *bán* [baːn] or Dutch *been* [beːn]; or in the vulgar English pronunciation of *baby* as [baibi].

Dissimilation may also cause the disappearance of one of two identical consonants *(haplology),* as in Latin *sēmodius* ' half-modius ' for **sēmi-modius,* or French *idolâtre* (whence English *idolater)* from Latin *īdōlolatres* (itself borrowed from Greek εἰδωλολάτρης).

Combinations of phonemes felt to be awkward in pronunciation may be separated by vowels or consonants to make utterance more agreeable, this phenomenon being termed *epenthesis* or *paraptyxis;* though it should be noted that ' awkwardness of pronunciation ' and ' ease of utterance ' are concepts which differ widely in different languages, and even at different periods within the same language. Italian, for instance, like Latin, does not object to the initial combination of *s* with another consonant; Spanish and Old French regard such a combination as awkward and prefix *e;* Modern French objects even to *esp,* and drops *s* in the combination, as in Latin *spatha* ' sword ' (borrowed from Greek), Italian *spada* : Spanish *espada,* Old French *espée* : Modern French *épée.*

Instances of consonantal epenthesis are Latin *sumptus* ' taken ' for **sumtus* (compare the present *sumō),* or Greek ἀνδρός [an'dros] ' of a man ' for **ἀνρός* [an'ros] (compare Sanskrit *náras)* and the *b* in Piedmontese *ambra* for **amra.* Vocalic epenthesis appears in Italian *biasimare* ' blame ' from Old French *blasmer* (Modern French *blâmer)* or in such English vulgarisms as *chiminey, umberella, elum;* and it gives rise to an important class of nouns in Hebrew (the ' səghōlates ') of the type of *keleβ* ' dog ' as compared with the equivalent Arabic *kalbuⁿ.*

As just noted, a vowel may be prefixed to a word beginning with a combination of consonants *(prothesis),* particularly when the first is *s,* this being especially marked in French and Spanish, as Spanish *escribir* ' write ', Old French *escrire* (Modern French *écrire)* from Latin *scribere.*

Thus far we have considered only sounds within an individual word, but assimilation and metathesis (though not dissimilation, epenthesis, or prothesis) are frequent when words are linked together, the process being called *sandhi* (' combination '), the term employed for it by the native Sanskrit grammarians. This is seen, for instance, in the alternation of ' strong ' and ' weak ' forms, such as the English *she* in *it is she* [it iz ʃiː] as contrasted with *she says* [ʃi sez] (cf. p. 65). Sandhi is regular in Greek in such combinations as 'εφ' ἵππῳ [eph'ippoː] ' on a horse ' for [e'p 'hippoː], in Sardinian *una gosa* ' a thing ' (cf. Italian *una cosa)* beside *sas cosas* ' the very things ', and Irish *an tobar* [ən thʌbər] ' the well ' beside *mo thobar* [mʌ hʌbər] ' my well '. A remarkably clear case of sandhi alternation is found in the Old High German writer Notker of St. Gall (about A.D. 1000), who changes initial voiced plosives to voiceless at the beginning of a sentence or clause (e.g., *tír ist uuóla chúnt* ' dir ist wohl kund '), or after a final voiceless plosive of a preceding word, as *únde demo gólde* ' und dem Golde ', but *tes kóldes* ' des Goldes '.

Sandhi is regularly expressed in written form only in Sanskrit, as in *rǎjǎha* ' the king said ' for *rájā ǎha; ityǎha* ' thus he said ' for *íti ǎha; náro jayati* ' the man conquers ' for ['narɔ: dʒayati] for ['naraz dʒayati], but *nárah pacati* ['narah patʃati] ' the man cooks ', *náras trasati* ' the man is terrified '. The voiceless plosive in the first example becomes voiced before the following voiced plosive by regressive assimilation (Sanskrit has no [z]). Similarly we have *agnír jayati* ' fire conquers ' beside *agnís tapati* ' fire heats ' and *agníh pacati* ' fire cooks ', where *r* represents the sonant [z] just as in the Latin genitive plural *equārum* ' of mares ' as compared with Oscan *egmazum* ' of things ' and Sanskrit *tǎsām* ' of those ' (feminine). Sometimes a lost consonant is restored in sandhi, as in Sanskrit *tǎn* ' those ' (accusative plural masculine), but *tǎms ca* [tãːs tʃa] ' and those ' (cf. Cretan τονς, Doric τως [tons, toːs], Gothic *wulfans* ' wolves ').

Not infrequently false sandhi causes addition or loss of an initial phoneme in a word. Thus in English *an adder* is for Middle English *a nadder* (cf. German *Natter); an apron* is for Middle English *a napron* (cf. French *naperon* ' large cloth ', English *napery); Spanish *la reata* ' the tie-rope ' becomes in American English *the lariat* and in the Acadian French of Louisiana *l'ariate*. Quasi-sandhi occasionally appears in erroneous assimilations and metatheses between contiguous words, as *paster noster* for *pater noster*, and especially in the type known in English as ' Spoonerisms ' (cf. p. 105) after an Oxford don traditionally said to have been peculiarly liable to make them, usually with absurd results, as ' what is more cold than to hug a half-warmed fish to one's bosom? ' instead of ' a half-formed wish ', or ' riding a well-boiled icicle ' for ' a well-oiled bicycle '; or, for French, ' le père de Marie ' instead of ' le maire de Paris '.

These modifications fall, generally speaking, into two broad categories. Progressive assimilation and dissimilation, and epenthesis, are essentially *mechanical,* since the position of the organs of speech for the production of one of the phonemes concerned affects and alters that normally taken for the production of the other. In regressive assimilation and dissimilation, and in metathesis, the process is *psychological,* for in the utterance of groups of sounds thought is ahead of pronunciation, with the result that the utterance of a sound contemplated takes place prematurely and then, in case of assimilation or dissimilation, mechanically affects another phoneme.

The phonemes which we have been discussing, whether isolated or in combination, do not remain constant, but undergo modifications of many kinds in the course of the history of a given language-group, individual language, or dialect. The pronunciation of standard modern English, for example, for which the average speech of the educated classes in Southern England is taken as the norm, is by no means the same as that of Anglo-Saxon (the vowels, in particular, have undergone a radical transformation), or of the Middle English of Chaucer, or of the early Modern English of the Elizabethan period, or even of the time of Alexander Pope. The present-day English of Somerset, as spoken by the educated classes, differs widely from that of the uneducated, and to some degree from that of the educated in Lancashire or Edinburgh; while the vernacular of the uneducated varies so widely that the speech of Cornish fishermen conversing among themselves is unintelligible, in great part, to one who knows only Standard English, and the dialect of the Cornish fisher would be meaningless to a farm-labourer from Aberdeenshire. The English spoken in the United States differs more or less from Standard English, especially in pronunciation; and there are also marked divergencies within the United States. Nevertheless, all these varieties can be traced back to a common source.

The dialects of Modern English, as well as those of Middle English and Anglo-Saxon, come, ultimately, from a language of the Teutonic group acclimatised in England (cf. p. 347). This language was once a dialect developed from a language which may be reconstructed from the historic tongues, and which is conventionally termed *Proto-Teutonic*. Proto-Teutonic was one of several dialects (others being Proto-Italic, Proto-Celtic, Proto-Slavic, Proto-Indo-Iranian, etc.) which may similarly be reconstructed; and these, in combined reconstruction, give a family known as Proto-Indo-European, itself already existing with dialectic differences in the pre-historic period. It is thus possible to trace the genealogy of the great mass of the Modern English vocabulary and grammatical forms in unbroken line to a period of unknown antiquity, but at least earlier than 2000 B.C. (cf. pp. 305–310).

Efforts of increasing scientific accuracy are being made to link the reconstructed Proto-Indo-European with other linguistic families, notably, on the one hand, with Uralic (represented by Finnish, Hungarian, etc.) and, on the other, with Semitic (Hebrew, Arabic, etc.), and so, through Ancient Egyptian (a Hamitic language, cognate with the Semitic group), with the great Bantu linguistic stock of Central Africa; but these endeavours can as yet scarcely be regarded as convincing (cf. pp. 366–367, 369, 406). Some idea of the wide ramifications of English words, and of their long history, may be gathered from our discussion (pp. 99–105, 252–255) of *Tues-day, god, Os-car, timber, -thorpe, -wick* (in place-names), *booth, hall, hell, house, yard, thatch,* and *deer*.

If we examine a number of groups of words having either identical meanings or, as is more usually the case, meanings which may reasonably be traced to a common basal signification, we find that one series shows both certain differences and certain resemblances in phonemes, while another reveals differences and resemblances which are entirely unlike those of the first group. In both groups, however, it will be found that the differences and resemblances in question are regular, each for the group concerned, so that one may set up *systems of correspondences*.

As an example we may take a word widely current in the Indo-European languages, represented in English by the numeral *ten*. This appears in the Teutonic group in Modern English dialects as [tæn], [tin], [tən], etc.; in Anglo-Saxon as *tíen, týn;* in Old Saxon as *tehan;* in Old Frisian as *tian;* in Dutch as *tien;* in Old Icelandic as *tío;* in Swedish as *tio;* in Gothic as *taíhun* [tehun]; in Old High

German as *zehan*, Modern German *zehn* [tseːn]. In Latin the group is represented by *decem*, whence the Romance series of Italian *dieci*, Engadine *diesch*, Friulian *dis*, French *dix*, Provençal *detz*, Catalan *deu*, Spanish *diez*, Portuguese *dez*. In Greek the form is δέκα ['deka], and in Albanian *dhjetë;* in Irish *deich* [deç], and in Breton *dek*, for the Celtic group; for the Baltic and Slavic groups we have Lithuanian *dẽšim-t*, Old Church Slavic *desę-tŭ* [desět], Russian *desjati*, Czech *deset*, etc.; in Armenian *tasn*, and in Tokharian *śäk;* in the Indo-Iranian group Sanskrit *dáśa*, Avestan *dasa*, Modern Persian *dah*, Afghān *las*, etc. From these forms the hypothetical *ˈdek̑m̥ is reconstructed as being one from which all the words here listed *can* (not *must)* be derived (cf. p. 282). An examination of these historic forms, to take only two of the phonemes involved, reveals the following correspondences in the principal groups of Indo-European:

English *t* = Gothic *t* = German *z* [ts] = Latin *d* = Greek [d] = Irish *d* = Lithuanian *d* = Slavic *d* = Armenian *t* = Sanskrit *d* = Indo-European *d.*

English *(h)* = Gothic *h* = German *h* = Latin *c* = Greek [k] = Irish *ch* [x] or [ç] = Lithuanian *š* [ʃ] = Slavic *s* = Armenian *s* = Sanskrit *ś* [ṣ] = Indo-European *k.*

If correspondences of this type be found to exist regularly (as in English *tear* = German *zehren* = Greek δέρω ' flay ' = Breton *darn* ' piece ' = Lithuanian *diŕti* = Old Church Slavic *derǫ* = Armenian *teŕem* ' flay ' = Sanskrit *dar-* ' split ' : English *hound* = German *Hund* = Latin *canis* = Greek κύων ['kyoːn] = Irish *cú* = Lithuanian *šuõ* = Sanskrit *śván-* ' dog '), they are said to constitute a *phonetic law. The establishment of such laws and operation in accordance with them are the very foundations of all sound linguistic investigation.* The term ' phonetic law ' is not altogether happy, especially as no idea of necessity is implied by ' law ' in this particular connexion; nor is an alternative ' phonetic rule ', which has been suggested, appreciably better. Phonetic law is best defined as *a factual statement of a regular correspondence or set of correspondences found by empirical observation and comparison to exist, under like circumstances or conditions, between a given phoneme within a given area at a given period in the history of a given language-group, language, or dialect and a parallel phoneme (or parallel absence of phoneme) at another period or at different periods within such group, language, or dialect, or in different members of the language-group, whether at the same period or at different periods.*

By far the best term to replace ' phonetic law ' is *(phonetic) correspondence,* which denotes the facts observed without expressing any opinion as to their origin. This latter question is an entirely separate problem, whose solution must be sought, if it can be discovered, in physiological phonetics. To investigation of the underlying reasons for phonetic change or for the absence of such change far too little attention has thus far been devoted. Most comparative linguists are not scientifically trained in physiological phonetics (though there seems to be no reason why they should not be), and few physiological phoneticians have any deep knowledge of linguistics. Obviously, it is not enough merely to record such correspondences as [t] = [ts] = [d] or [h] = [k] = [ʃ] = [ş] = [s]; knowledge of the *cause* of these correspondences is, in reality, more important in every respect than the mere statement that they exist.

We may safely say that English *t* corresponds to German *z* [ts], Latin *d,* etc.; and, knowing the correspondences for the other phonemes involved, one would naturally reconstruct from English *two* both Old High German *zwâ* and Latin *duo.* Yet there is no inherent compulsion whereby [d] = [ts] = [t]; it is possible to proceed from a voiced plosive [d] to a fricative [ð] (not represented historically in this group), to an affricate [ts], and finally to a voiceless plosive [t]; and it is fair to assume that such was the actual process. This evolution, however, was not obligatory, else [d] must invariably have become [t]. That is by no means the case, for [d] remains unchanged in Greek, Latin, Celtic, Balto-Slavic, etc.; and in Semitic [d] remains constant, but Syriac, in addition, has developed [d] from [ð], which has become [z] in Hebrew, while Arabic retains [ð] (e.g., Hebrew *zāβah* ' slaughter ', but Syriac *dəβah,* Arabic *ðabaha,* Proto-Semitic **ðabah-,* as contrasted with Hebrew *dālāh* ' draw water ', Syriac *dəlā,* Arabic *dalā,* Proto-Semitic **dalau-).*

We may elucidate by examples some of the salient portions of the definition of a correspondence as just set forth. First, we observe that a given correspondence is operative only within a given area. The development of Indo-European [d] to [t], for instance, occurs only in Armenian, Gothic, and Low Teutonic, and its further evolution into [ts] solely in High German; while Indo-

European [k] remains unchanged only in Greek and Latin, becomes a glottal fricative [h] in Teutonic, a velar fricative [x] in Irish, and various types of sibilants (palato-alveolar, dental [alveolar], and palatal or palatalised [ʃ, s, ş]) in Lithuanian, Slavic and Armenian, and Sanskrit respectively.

The principle that a correspondence operates only during a period of longer or shorter duration may be seen, for instance, by comparing the Old High German words *pfâl* (Modern High German *Pfahl*) 'stake' with *falo* (Modern High German *fahl*) 'fallow, yellow'. Comparison of the latter with such cognates as Latin *pallidus* 'pallid, pale', Greek πολιός, and Sanskrit *palitá-* 'grey' shows that the regular correspondence of an original *p* in Teutonic is the labio-dental fricative *f*, so that, since *pfâl*, Anglo-Saxon *pál*, English *pale, pole* are cognate with Latin *pālus*, 'stake', we should expect Old High German **fuol* (Modern **[fu:l]*), Anglo-Saxon **fól*, English **[fu:l]*. The reason why we have *pál* and *pfâl* rather than **fól* and **fuol* is that these words are not, like *falo*, etc., direct derivatives from Indo-European, but are borrowed from Latin *pālus*. The correspondence of High German *pf* to Low German *p* shows, moreover, that *pfâl* was borrowed *during* the specifically High German shift of *p* to *pf*, i.e., some time between the first and the end of the seventh century (cf. p. 82). On the other hand, such a High German borrowing as *paradîsi* 'paradise' (first recorded in the eighth century) from Latin *paradīsus* is shown by its *p* instead of **pf* to have been taken over *after* the Old High German development of *p* to *pf* had ceased to be operative.

Similarly, the English doublets *pale* and *pole*, both borrowed from Latin *pālus*, are shown by their vocalisation to have been taken at different periods; *pole* is directly descended from Anglo-Saxon *pál* (cf. Anglo-Saxon *bán* : English *bone*, p. 71); *pale* entered after the Norman Conquest as borrowed from French *pal* from Latin *pālus* (cf. pp. 131–132). From these examples it becomes clear that apparent divergencies from regular correspondences are explicable in some instances as borrowing from a common source. Observation of conformity with, or divergence from, the correspondences involved may afford evidence, in the case of borrowed words, as to the date and chronological order of such borrowing.

Certain other instances of apparent violation of phonetic correspondences must also be considered. One of these we have already seen in the operation of Grassmann's Law (p. 70); and another, which long vexed linguists, is solved by Verner's Law, whose operation may be illustrated by the two English words *brother* and *father*. The principal cognates of these, so far as we are at present concerned, are Anglo-Saxon *bróðor*, Modern German *Bruder*, Old High German *bruoder*, Gothic *broþar*, Sanskrit *bhrátar-* : Anglo-Saxon *fædar*, Modern German *Vater*, Old High German *fater*, Gothic *fadar*, Sanskrit *pitár-*. The normal correspondences for Indo-European *t* in Anglo-Saxon and High German are [θ] and [d] respectively, as in Sanskrit *tráyas*, Latin *trēs*, Gothic *þreis* [θriːs], Old High German *drî*, Modern German *drei*, Anglo-Saxon *þrí*, English *three*. For *father* we should, then, expect Anglo-Saxon **fæþar*, Gothic **faþar*, Old High German **fader*, Modern German **Vader;* only English *father* is in accord with the regular correspondences. When we examine the Sanskrit series *bhrátar-* and *tráyas*, as contrasted with *pitár-* (cf. also Greek φράτηρ as contrasted with πατήρ), we observe that in *pitár-* the accent immediately follows the *t*-phoneme, whereas in the first series it precedes. It is precisely the accentuation which causes the apparent irregularity, study of numerous other words coming under this general category establishing the truth of this principle. Accordingly, before we assume that correspondences show exceptions to the norm, we must seek to know whether some other factor, operating under definite conditions, may not be the cause of the apparent irregularities, which thus become fully explicable. The error has lain, not in the operation of normal correspondences, but in ignorance of all the factors involved.

Our words for *brother* and *father* reveal yet another type of irregularity which they share with *mother*. As Anglo-Saxon *fædar* and *módor* show (cf., for the latter, Sanskrit *mātár-* [the accentuation of Greek μήτηρ ['meːteːr], Doric μάτηρ is not original]), Old High German *muoter*, Modern German *Mutter)*, we should have in English **[fædə(r)]* and **[muːdə(r)]* (cf. Dutch *vader, moeder* [muːdər]) instead of *father* and *mother;* the [d] has been changed to [θ] on the analogy of the regular [θ] in *brother*. We must, therefore, bear in mind the possible working of analogy (cf. pp. 106–114) with words of kindred meaning (as *father, mother, brother)* or of similar formation (as *weather* [Anglo-Saxon *weder*, Modern German *Wetter*] : *whether* [Anglo-Saxon *hwæðer*, Gothic *hwaþar*, Old High German *hwedar*, Sanskrit *katará-* ' which of two? ']).

We have just seen that we should expect in English the forms
*[fɑdə(r)] and *[muːdə(r)] instead of *father* and *mother;* and
these forms actually occur in English dialects, for dialects often retain old and regular forms which have been distorted in standard
speech through the operation of analogy. Thus, the ungrammatical
and vulgar English type *they makes* is really a survival of the regular third person plural in the Northern dialects of Middle English
(Northern *makes,* Midland *maken,* Southern *maketh;* cf. the
famous motto of William of Wykeham, ' Manners maketh man ').

Yet another reason for apparent exceptions to regular correspondences lies in mixture of dialects of the same language (cf.
p. 128). A very noteworthy instance of this is found in Modern
German. By Grimm's Law, instead of *Kuh* [kuː] ' cow ', the form
actually found, we should expect *[kxuː], as corresponding to
Sanskrit *gau-* ' ox, cow ', English *cow;* and, similarly, *ke-pären,* as
corresponding to Sanskrit *bhar-* ' carry ', English *bear,* instead of
ge-bären, the form actually in use. In the southern, or Alemannic,
area of German speech, we find precisely the forms that we should
' lawfully ' expect, e.g., Tyrolese *kchu* [kxuː] and Old High German *ki-peran* beside *gi-beran.* Standard High German, based on
the dialect-type of Middle Franconia (cf. p. 349), stands midway
between true Low Teutonic (represented, for instance, by Dutch
and Anglo-Saxon) and true High Teutonic (as seen, for example,
in Modern Swiss German).

The Teutonic languages are characterised by the operation of
one of the best-known of all phonetic correspondences, Grimm's
Law, which is supplemented by Verner's Law. The combined
Grimm-Verner Law is so important in itself, and illustrates so
admirably the whole principle of phonetic correspondence, that it
merits somewhat detailed discussion. This correspondence-system
affects the Indo-European voiceless, voiced, and voiced aspirate
plosives *p, t, k(u); b, d, g(u); bh, dh,* and *g(u)h (k, g,* and *gh* here
representing a coalescence of Indo-European $\hat{k}$, *q;* $\hat{g}$, g; and $\hat{g}h$, gh
respectively) and the sibilant *s;* and the treatment of the internal
voiceless plosives (unless preceded by *s* or by a fricative) and of
the sibilant differs, by Verner's Law, according as the Indo-
European accent immediately precedes the plosive or sibilant in
question, or follows it (cf. pp. 78, 82). Before giving the underlying
principles of this Teutonic ' sound-shift ', as it is frequently called,
it may be advisable to cite examples of it.

	INDO-EUROPEAN	SANSKRIT	GREEK	GOTHIC	ANGLO-SAXON	MODERN ENGLISH	OLD HIGH GERMAN	MODERN GERMAN
p	*pə'ter-	pitár-	πατήρ	fadar	fæder	father (dialectic fader)	fater	Vater
	*sep'tm̥-	saptá	ἑπτά	sibun	seofon	seven	sibun	sieben
t	*¹bhrāter-	bhrātar-	φράτηρ	broþar	brōðor	brother	bruoder, pruoder	Brüder
	*pə'ter-	pitár-	πατήρ	fadar	fæder	father (dialectic fader)	fater	Vater
k	*ḱm̥'tom	śatá-	ἑ-κατόν	hund	hund-red	hund-red	hunt	hund-ert
	*eḱo'no-	īśānd-	Oscan aík-dafed(?)	aigin	ágen	own	eigan	eigen
s	*sep'tm̥	saptá	ἑπτά	sibun	seofon	seven	sibun	sieben
	*snu'so-	snuṣá	νυός		snoru		snur(a)	Schnur
b	*sleube-		Latin lūbricus	sliupan	slūpan	slip	slupfen	schlüpfen
d	*de/ome-	damáyati	δαμάω	ga-tamjan	tam	tame	zam	zahm
g	*¹ḡe/oneu-	jā́nu-	γόνυ	kniu	cnéo	knee	kniu	Knie
bh	*bhere-	bhárati	φέρω	ga-baíran	ge-beran	bear	gi-beran, ki-peran	ge-bären
dh	*dhugh(ə)'ter-	duhitár-	θυγάτηρ	daúhter	dohtor	daughter	tohter	Tochter
gh	*ɥe/oǵhe-	váhati	ὀχέω	ga-wigan	wegan	way	wegan	be-wegen

If we tabulate the sound-shifts by phonemes in their probable chronological order, we have the following results:

	Indo-European		Proto-Teutonic		Low Teutonic		High Teutonic	
Voiceless Plosives	[p]	> "	[Φ]	= "	[Φ]	= "	[Φ]	⎫ Grimm's Law
	[t]	> "	[θ]	= "	[θ]	= "	[d]	
	[k]	> "	[x]	= "	[h]	= "	[h]	
	[s]	= "	[s]	= "	[s]	= "	[s]	⎭
Voiceless Plosives	[p]	> "	[Φ]	> "	[β]	= "	[b]	⎫ Verner's Law
	[t]	> "	[θ]	> "	[ð]	= "	[t]	
	[k]	> "	[x]	> "	[ɣ]	= "	[g]	
	[s]	> "	[z]	> "	[r]	= "	[r]	⎭
Aspirated Voiced Plosives	[bh]	> "	[β]	> "	[β]	= "	[p]	
	[dh]	> "	[ð]	> "	[ð]	= "	[t]	
	[gh]	> "	[ɣ]	> "	[ɣ]	= "	[k]	
Voiced Plosives	[b]	> "	[p]	= "	[p]	= "	[pf]	
	[d]	> "	[t]	= "	[t]	= "	[ts]	
	[g]	> "	[k]	= "	[k]	= "	[kx]	

In other words, Indo-European voiceless plosives became the corresponding fricatives in both Low and High Teutonic if they were labials or gutturals and were immediately preceded by the accent (Grimm's Law); but if they were dentals, the Low Teutonic fricatives became the corresponding voiced plosives. If the accent did not immediately precede, the voiceless plosives developed, through the voiceless fricative stage, into the corresponding voiced fricatives in Low Teutonic (Verner's Law); and these (except in the case of dentals, which were devoiced) evolved in High Teutonic into the corresponding voiced plosives. The aspirated plosives became voiced fricatives in Proto-Teutonic, and then developed in Low Teutonic into voiced plosives, which were devoiced in High Teutonic. Finally, the Indo-European voiced plosives were devoiced in Proto-Teutonic, and remained so in Low Teutonic, but were further developed into affricates in High Teutonic, though the guttural shows this only in certain Alemannic dialects (especially in Swiss German; cf. p. 79).

The process here roughly outlined is not easy to fix chronologically, but it seems most probable, on the whole, that the first sound-shift took place by degrees in the centuries preceding the Christian era, while the second would seem to have reached practical completion by the eighth century A.D. (cf. p. 310). The phenomenon is not without counterparts elsewhere, notably in Armenian, where, since the eleventh century, voiced and voiceless plosives have interchanged places, so that the Ancient and Eastern Armenian proper name *Tigran*, for instance, is represented in Western Armenian by *Dikran* (cf. p. 51). Irish shows certain analogous developments; and comparison of proper names in Biblical Hebrew with their transcriptions in the Septuagint suggests some similar evolution. Nowhere, however, has the process been carried through so completely as in Teutonic.

No principle of linguistics has aroused more controversy than that of the rôle of phonetic correspondences. In its crassest form, this principle has been enunciated as ' phonetic laws (we should now say, " phonetic correspondences ") know no exceptions '; on the other hand, some scholars deny that there are any regular phonetic correspondences worth considering (cf. pp. 443–444, 423–424). A survey of language as a whole seems, however, to justify the following conclusion: *phonetic correspondences, as we have defined them* (pp. 75–76), *operate without exception save when we have to deal with* (1) *borrowing of words of various types* (cf. pp. 77, 125–136) ; (2) *the existence of other correspondence-systems either yet unknown or active only under special conditions* (cf. pp. 70, 77–78) ; (3) *analogy* (cf. pp. 78–79, 106–114) ; (4) *dialect-mixture* (cf. pp. 79, 128) ; (5) *onomatopoeia* (cf. pp. 275–276) ; or (6) *rhyme-words* (cf. pp. 113–114). Any other working hypothesis appears destined to resolve linguistics into a congeries of meaningless guesses, and to open the way to unbridled fantasies. We must also bear in mind that *only exact phonological correspondences (with the modifying factors just noted) enable us to determine either the connexions or lack of connexions of languages and dialects with each other so as to classify them, or to explain and understand their development, whether parallel or divergent, from their common source or sources. Phonology is the very foundation of all scientific linguistics.*

Sounds change according to regular correspondences; but *why* do they change? Many hypotheses have been advanced to answer this question. It has been alleged that geographical conditions account for much: the consonant-shifting so characteristic of Alemannic High German and of Armenian has been supposed to be due to the mountainous areas in which they are spoken; but this explanation fails, for instance, in the languages of the American Indians of California or of the Great Plains. Modifications of the vocal organs have been supposed to cause phonetic change: prognathism has been invoked to explain the absence of *f* in Basque (probably the modern representative of a dialect of ancient Iberian; cf. p. 377) and the change of initial *f* to *h* in Spanish, except, chiefly, before *ue* (cf. *hacer* ' make ' : Latin *facere;* but *fuego* ' fire ' : Latin *focu^m;* up to the fourteenth century *f* was written, e.g., *facer,* but the pronunciation of this initial is uncertain). We have seen, however (p. 5), that the vocal organs are essentially the same throughout the world, and that pronunciation of phonemes is conditioned rather by the general relative position of the organs concerned than by the exact point of formation of the sounds (pp. 60–61). The most that we can say here is that extremely marked divergencies, whether natural or acquired (e.g., by extraction of teeth or by insertion of permanent labrets for aesthetic reasons), might cause slight variations in the enunciation of sounds; but, except in specific instances, the explanation seems entirely unconvincing.

Economy of effort has also been assigned as the cause. So far as the various phenomena of assimilation, dissimilation, etc., and the tendency to weaken or drop unaccented vowels are concerned (cf. pp. 64-66, 68–71), this may not infrequently be a contributing factor; as a main cause it appears to be negligible. The sub-stratum theory has also been evoked to solve the question. The Teutonic consonant-shift, in particular (pp. 79–82), has been explained as due to the influence of the speech (vanished before the historic period) of some pre-Indo-European people upon that of a conquering section of Indo-Europeans whom we call Teutons from their Celtic appellation, *teuto-* ' people ' (cf. Gothic *þiuda* ' people ', German *Deutsch* ' German ', English *Dutch* ' Hollander ') ; the nasalised vowels of French and Portuguese have been supposed to have been due to the Gauls on whom Latin was imposed, etc. We shall consider the problem of sub-strata in another connexion (see pp. 136–137) ; here it must suffice to say that it scarcely explains phonetic change as a whole. Even granting the premisses for Proto-Teutonic or for Franco-Portuguese, this theory offers no explanation of the changes which have taken place in the various Teutonic languages since the Teutonic conquest, or for the subsequent development in either French or Portuguese. Equally unsatisfactory is the view that language-mixture has been the cause of phonetic change. It is true that on a language-frontier, as between German and French, the sounds of the one may affect those of the other; but in all essentials this theory is that of the sub-stratum hypothesis, and seems open to the same objections.

The Mendelian Law of biology has likewise been brought to bear on the problem. According to this, phonetic traits would be inheritable like purely biological features, and would be governed practically, if not entirely, by the same laws. This law may briefly be stated as follows: half the offspring of two parents will share the characteristics of both; one quarter will reproduce the characteristics of only one parent; the remaining quarter, only those of the other. The complexity thus arising in a series of generations may readily be imagined. Besides this action, which may be termed the normal operation of Mendel's Law, there are also sudden mutations (or sports) whose genesis is very imperfectly understood, and also instances of atavism, in which one or more of the offspring harks or hark back to some more or less remote ancestor. The question of principle involved appears to be whether aptitudes of phonational type are inheritable; but on the whole, the applicability of the Mendelian Law to the problem of sound-changes seems at present highly doubtful.

The most obvious factor in phonetic change appears to lie in more or less imperfect auditional imitation (cf. pp. 5–6). As soon as the child begins to acquire language, he imitates the phonemes of the persons who surround him; and in the highly formative period of his earlier years, he seeks to reproduce the utterances of an ever-widening circle. Unless an individual lives within a very circumscribed area, this process of imitational assimilation may continue until late in life. Such change of pronunciation may be unconscious, as when the individual resides for a considerable period in an area whose general pronunciation is unlike that of his original habitat; or it may be deliberately acquired by intentional imitation of the pronunciation of those regarded as superior in station or education; and we must also reckon with the existence of purely individual traits. Each man's pronunciation is, therefore, a composite of pronunciations heard from others; but he, like those about him, is restrained from excessive vagaries of speech by the general conventions governing his milieu.

The ear, however, is not an infallible instrument (cf. pp. 5–6); and the individual's reproduction of sounds is not precisely the same as the pronunciation of his fellows, and still less an exact replica of that of his parents, even though he imagines it to be identical, and though his divergencies may be so slight as to escape notice on the part of his auditors, who are more concerned with the matter of his speech than with his pronunciation, provided the latter be what is regarded as normal.

In the course of generations, phonetic change reaches a stage in which the pronunciation differs so radically from that of another more or less early period that the phonetic systems would be mutually unintelligible if speakers of the two periods could come into contact. Thus the pronunciation, and also the grammatical forms, of Old, Middle, and Modern French, or of Old, Middle, and Modern German are widely divergent, though the generations which have succeeded each other have doubtless been unaware of any noteworthy change. If moreover, speakers of a common language become geographically separated and have little or no communication with each other, the resulting communities will tend, in course of time, to develop differing phonological modifications which may ultimately become so great that members of one community may have considerable difficulty in understanding those of another, or may even not understand each other at all.

Normally, the speech of one area is readily intelligible to the inhabitants of the areas immediately adjacent; but the difficulty of mutual comprehension increases, as a rule, in proportion to distance from a given speech-centre, as may be seen in such areas as Germany, Italy, and India. This is the underlying cause for the rise of the dialects (cf. pp. 25–28). Again, colonisation, especially over-seas, leads to greater or less speech-differentiation. This appears with striking clearness in the United States and in French-speaking Canada, both of which were founded by colonisation. In what are now the United States, this was effected by several waves of immigration, each bringing, in consequence of the diverse provenances of its components, a mixture of English dialects; and on their new soil these amalgams developed further changes, represented, for example, by what may roughly be called the New England and Southern types of American English.

In French Canada, the colonists brought with them a mixture of dialects of the north, west, and centre of France, but, cut off by political events from the mother-country after the middle of the eighteenth century, new dialectic differences have evolved. These are not such as to cause the Acadian and the Québecois to have any difficulty in understanding each other; but, on the other hand, the divergency between Canadian French and Standard French has become so great that a Parisian would scarcely understand a speaker of pure Canadian *parler,* the difficulty being due only in small measure to vocabulary or grammar, but almost wholly to the phonetic changes in the two dialects in the last two or three centuries. In like manner, Afrikaans, the Dutch spoken by the Boers of South Africa, has diverged so widely from its parent that it has well-nigh become a separate language.

On the whole, the auditional theory seems best to explain the cause of phonetic change. It would also appear that linguistic and dialectic areas have certain *trends,* i.e., in a given area phonology (pronunciation) tends to change in this direction or in that, though

why or how these tendencies arise is as yet uncertain. The problem
is further complicated by non-linguistic factors, notably by the
shifting predominance of now one, now another dialect, whether
social or regional, according to changing political, economic, or
religious conditions, and the like (cf. p. 27).

CHAPTER IV

Language and Thought: The Mental Aspect of Language

The language-areas of the brain — other-brainedness — linguistic types of aphasia — languages of the insane — desirability of an adequate psychology of language — thought and instinct in relation to language — thought prior to language — process of acquisition of language by the child and by the adult — necessity of formulation of thoughts in speech — exophasia and endophasia — emotive and intellective language — creation and loss in development of language — development of thought and evolution of concepts illustrated in Indo-European by the history of words for 'god' and 'house' — true meaning of 'knowledge of a language' — the rôle of psychology in linguistic analogy — categories of linguistic analogy in modification of words, of phonology, of morphology (types of French *aimer* and *devoir,* inflexion of the word for 'foot', levelling in Teutonic verbs, noun-inflexion, e.g., English plurals, formatives) — graphic analogies — syntactic analogies — rhymewords.

THOUGHT is indispensable in language, since without thought on the part of speaker and hearer alike it is impossible to formulate sounds or combinations of sounds intended by the one to convey certain meanings and recognised by the other as bearing those connotations. There is a further dichotomy within the individual himself; as the simplest conversation shows, every person is sometimes a speaker and sometimes a hearer, so that language combines motor and sensory aspects, being, from this point of view, *essentially a correspondence of the motor and sensory systems of the brain.*

Language is, therefore, inseparably connected with psychology as well as with anatomy; but among the countless problems of psychology hotly debated by its various schools, the linguist must restrict himself to a single question: What is the relation between language and thought? Even here, in the present state of knowledge, it seems doubtful whether more than tentative conclusions can be reached; and it would appear that the linguist will be wise in taking thought, as well as language (cf. pp. 38–41), for granted. As yet, he can scarcely hope to find the origin either of the one or of the other.

In the brain, the areas especially concerned with language, i.e., the centres governing audition, phonation, and vision, were formerly localised very precisely, though it now seems probable that no exact boundaries can be drawn, since in minor lesions the functions of these areas may be taken over by neighbouring portions of the cortex. Although we can now safely speak only of general regions for audition, etc., the older theory still retains some value if liberally construed; and the approximate general regions in question are shown in the accompanying Fig. 8 with its explanatory caption.

According to the classical anatomists, the *glosso-kinaesthetic* area, which governs speech-utterance, is situated, in right-handed individuals, in the cortex of the posterior part of the third frontal convolution of the left hemisphere of the brain (in left-handed individuals it lies in the corresponding part of the right hemisphere). The *audito-kinaesthetic* area, controlling speech-hearing, is in the first left (or right) temporal convolution. In the Sylvian fissure between them is a triangular group of convolutions (the *gyri longi)* called the Island of Reil, which, in the opinion of many investigators, forms their connecting link. With both these areas and the Island of Reil is closely involved, from the linguistic point of view, the associational part of the brain, governing memory and lying in the *gyrus angularis*. All these areas are connected by commissures, or bands of nerve-tissues, and for reading and writing they co-operate respectively with the *visual* and *cheiro-kinaesthetic* areas, the one situated in the upper parietal lobule, and the other in the foot of the second frontal convolution.

In cases of total destruction of one or more of these areas, prognosis for recovery is extremely grave if such destruction involves the left areas of a right-handed individual or the right areas of a left-handed person. The only exceptions to this rule would seem to be where the patient has a strong trend towards *other-brainedness*, as when a right-handed individual comes from left-handed stock, or a left-handed person from right-handed stock, in which cases hereditary tendency may permit the uninjured lobe to take over the functions of the one destroyed. In childhood, it would appear, both lobes are equally active; but with the normal development towards either right- or left-handedness, language-activities seem to be evolved practically only in the single corresponding area, left or right respectively.

The rôle played by the language-areas of the brain receives negative illustration in various forms of aphasia, which may arise from many causes, such as cerebral lesions, traumatic neuroses, toxic

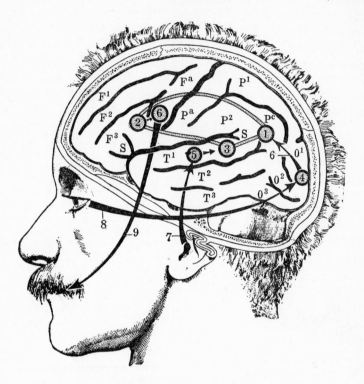

FIG. 8. Classical Scheme of Language-Centres in the Brain (from L. Testut and O. Jacob, *Traité d'anatomie topographique*, 3rd ed., Paris, 1914, i, Fig. 84).

F^1, F^2, F^3, F^a: first, second, third, and upper frontal convolutions. P^1, P^2, P^a, P^c: first, second, and upper parietal convolutions, and upper parietal lobule. O^1, O^2, O^3: first, second, and third occipital convolutions. T^1, T^2, T^3: first, second, and third temporal convolutions. S: Sylvian fissure.

1. Visual image-centre. 2. Articulate language-centre (Broca's centre). 3. Auditive image-centre (Wernicke's centre). 4. Visual sensory-centre. 5. Auditive sensory-centre. 6. Motor language-centre. 7. Audition, passing from ear to auditive sensory-centre (5) as noise, comprehended at auditive image-centre (3). 8. Written or printed word, passing from eye to visual sensory-centre (4) as image, comprehended at visual image-centre (1). 9. Phonation, passing from articulate language-centre (2) to motor language-centre (6), then to mouth.

conditions, prolonged worry or fatigue, and the like. Lesion of the motor-area (2, Fig. 8) produces *motor-aphasia* (Broca's aphasia). Here the patient understands words heard or read, but cannot repeat them and does not speak voluntarily, although he can write from dictation and can copy. Lesion of the auditive centre (3, Fig. 8) results in *word-deafness* (Wernicke's aphasia). The patient does not understand words spoken, but does understand words read. The effect of lesion of the visual centre (1, Fig. 8) is *word-blindness*, in which the patient understands words heard, but not those read; he can write, but cannot read what he has written or control its accuracy in any way. Lesion of the graphic centre causes *agraphia*, in which the patient understands words heard or read; he can speak intelligibly and can repeat what he has heard or read, but cannot copy or write at dictation. Lesion of the associational centre results in *associational aphasia,* marked by inability to co-ordinate sounds or characters as normally uttered, written, and understood. Clinically pure cases of any of these types are extremely rare, if they ever occur; practically all show every grade of complication of two or more of them.

All grave cases of aphasia involve general lowering of the mental level; the power of symbolism, which underlies all language (p. 15), decays; and the patient is subject to progressive weakening of memory. Different types and stages present phenomena of much linguistic interest. The patient may be unable to pronounce a given word, but may be able to indicate the number of its syllables (cf. pp. 146–148) ; he may forget his vocabulary in a definite order, as when he loses first his memory for proper names, then for specific and concrete terms, next for common nouns, and, last of all, for other parts of speech. He may, for example, be unable to say *wine,* but will use *good, red,* or the like when he wishes to denote it, a fact which may possibly help to confirm the theory (cf. pp. 22, 150–154) that words were at first vague and general in connotation, evolving specialised meanings only by degrees.

A discussion of aphasia naturally leads to some consideration of the *language of the insane,* a subject which has received comparatively little study, and practically none from linguists. We may omit, as of small linguistic interest, the gibberish of the insane, which recalls the meaningless sounds uttered by infants, apparently for the mere pleasure of hearing sounds *(lalling),* or logorrhoea without thought or comprehension *(psittacism),* or verbal automatism of the type of *farizitocéricia, fandizitorfé, forsiaozé, dorsüssitirtousoréta, sirropé, cériporéalessio*, etc. On the other hand, we have records of a few cases of true *glossolalia*, or creations of language by the insane, in which the patient utters sounds which he feels to be full of meaning, but which he can seldom repeat when asked to do so. A particularly interesting case of a highly developed language of this type is afforded by a paranoiac who invented ' Salisjeur ', his term for what he called ' Excellenzsprache ' when speaking to the common herd. An analysis of it, however, shows that it was based on German, his native language, and on French, his acquired tongue. The case-history of Mlle J ... reveals that she had read widely in books containing foreign and exotic terms, this reading being reflected in her language by such words as *tschario, moemdiana, ariotoebilium, manaés, aéda, davidiapulom, aprovia, astraerideo, arés, adula, atrobois, abitam*, etc. (repeated, on request, by an entirely different series of vocables). The celebrated ' Martian ' of the Genevan medium Miss Smith (who was not a mental case) was clearly based on her native French. The conclusions reached by Dr. Michel Cénac after his careful study of insane languages (*De certains langages créés par des aliénés*, Paris, 1925) are well worth quoting in this connexion:

' This language [true glossolalia], more or less well organised according to the mental level of the patient, is governed by grammatical rules which are simply more or less poor copies of those of current languages known to him. The words are neologisms fabricated by him. They are generally few in number and represent either ordinary words deformed or twisted from their meaning, or (and chiefly) vocables formed wholly anew. ... True glossolalia appears especially as a logical, co-ordinated, and voluntary effort, whose effective cause must be sought in the need for compensation felt by schizoid, schizomaniac, and schizophrenic patients.'

Like statements seem to apply to languages supposed to be invented by children: in every case where accurate data are available, they are found to be more or less drastic deformations of the vernaculars spoken around them.

From the strictly linguistic point of view, far more study would seem to be desirable in the fields of aphasia, insane languages, and the languages of children. Here the psychologist and the alienist should work in close co-operation with the linguist; and wherever pathological conditions exist, accurate case-histories are a prime requisite. The results of such investigations would, in all probability, be of much value for a knowledge of the underlying principles of language. It is not, however, on the pathological side alone that such research should be made, but on the normal side as well; and we shall scarcely go far wrong if we say that *one of the most urgent needs of the science of language to-day is a thorough treatment of linguistic psychology.* This is a task much easier to set than to perform, for it demands an equally intensive training in psychology and in linguistics, not merely in two or three important languages or in one or two of the great linguistic families, but in the entire realm of language. Such a task probably transcends the powers of any one man, so that collaboration seems the only method possible. Many attempts have been made to write psychologies of language, but almost exclusively either by linguists inadequately trained in psychology or by psychologists with insufficient knowledge of linguistics, and only too often in both camps to refute or to defend some preconceived theory. Practically the only exception to this rather sweeping statement known to the writer is Henri Delacroix's masterly *Le Langage et la pensée* (second edition, Paris, 1930), but even this, its author would doubtless have been the first to say, by no means exhausts the possibilities of its theme.

In considering the relation between language and thought, we may roughly define thought as a purposive mental adjustment of means to ends, and in all but the most rudimentary modes of thought we may restrict this adjustment to non-immediate ends. This seems to be the cardinal distinction between the thought of man and of non-human living beings, although in certain cases, as in long migrations of birds over the same course during long series of years, the test of non-immediacy seems scarcely valid. Here we come into contact with instinct, which we may perhaps define as elementary thought which, through constant repetition under given circumstances, has become subconscious and quasi-automatic. This seems implied by the instinctive aspect of vocabulary as contrasted with its intellective aspect, since, under stress, certain types of aphasics can pronounce words which they are ordinarily unable to utter; and since observation of aphasia in general shows that the higher and voluntary aspects of a function suffer more than those which are lower and automatic.

Whether thought precedes speech, or whether speech or the capacity of speech is a prerequisite of thought, is still a moot problem; but the bulk of evidence seems to be in favour of the priority of thought. This appears to be borne out by observation of the process of learning to speak a language. Here much attention has justly been devoted to study of the efforts of the infant and child to acquire the language of those about him. He begins with meaningless babblings and ejaculations indicative of desires, which adults around him interpret just as they do those of non-human beings, except for sentimental meanings which they may read into them; by a long process of trial and error he gradually gains a vocabulary — first of a vague and general kind, next of simple individual objects and needs; and, then, by degrees, he acquires some notions of the elements of grammatical relations; he passes through an ego-centric stage in which he speaks to himself, whether alone or in the presence of others, with no purpose of conveying thought to his companions and with no heed to their replies (cf. p. 17); and, as he grows older, he becomes increasingly able to command language in its higher functions, i.e., as an abstract and symbolic expression of emotions and thoughts subject to his intention and will.

Language has thus passed, like thought itself, from immediate to non-immediate adaptation of means to ends; but the problem is gravely hampered in its initial stages by the difficulty, if not the impossibility, of entering, in any adequate measure, into the thought of the child, and by the facts that the adult has forgotten the mental development through which he has passed in infancy and childhood, and that the child, in learning to speak, is guided, checked, and stimulated by the adults around him. For the most part, facility in learning either a single language or several languages simultaneously is greatest in the formative stages of the individual, when a language extremely difficult for an adult to acquire is mastered without apparent effort by the child, who may also speak with ease a number of languages of wholly different structure and vocabulary if in contact with those to whom such languages are vernacular.

The process of acquisition of a new language by an individual who has reached maturer years is also instructive in this regard. Exact observation is complicated here by the fact that the individual in question has already been affected by learning one language, however little he may remember of the processes whereby he gained that knowledge. Nevertheless, if one who has consciously and deliberately acquired a speaking command of at least one language in addition to his original speech carefully examines the stages through which he has passed, he will normally find the process to have been somewhat as follows. He first learns the names of simple objects and activities, and, along with this, he finds that he must avoid certain sounds present in his own language and must learn to make others hitherto unknown to him. He endeavours to imitate those speaking the language he is learning; and they correct any of his noticeable divergencies from their own speech. Gradually, the new language ceases to be felt as new; the use of the proper sounds and inflexions becomes more and more automatic; he is no longer obliged first to formulate in his native language what he wishes to say, or to translate back into it what is said to him. Very frequently, the acquired language so becomes part and parcel of him that he involuntarily thinks in it and finds it affecting his original speech; he may even come to speak his native language with difficulty or may forget it entirely, although in the latter case, since it is retained subconsciously, it can be regained with comparative ease.

Whether it be a child or an adult who is learning a language, there will be periods of apparent regression due to various causes (mental fatigue, interference of other interests, and the like) ; but there will also be periods when the outward rate of progress astonishes the observer and, in the case of an adult, the learner himself, since, more or less unconsciously, thought has been at work and has finally reached the stage of correlation.

The influence of speech on thought is very great; and it seems safe to say that any novel idea remains more or less vague in the thinker's mind until it has been expressed, whether to himself or to others, in speech either uttered or internal. If one can pursue a complicated train of reasoning without conscious speech, or if an idea suddenly flashes on the mind in finished form apparently with no previous thought on the matter, this must be because both the subject of that reasoning and the methods of ratiocination are so familiar that they have become automatic and quasi-instinctive to the thinker. If, on the other hand, the matter is really new to the thinker, he may feel obliged to formulate it in speech, either mental or oral, even though he have no auditor. If this be true of all complex and highly abstract ratiocination, as any close observer may see from considering his own mental and linguistic processes, even the simplest phrases, now become quasi-automatic, must once have been preceded first by a general concept, and then by a careful verbal formulation. Many words and phrases constantly used may become so conventional that they automatically evoke conventional responses, sometimes with awkward results if the circumstances are not equally conventional.

If reflective thought is conditioned by language, and is largely dependent upon it, do we think in speech? Scarcely at first. The initial form of a thought seems to be vague and nebulous; it is then mentally phrased in somewhat indefinite shape; only as it becomes necessary so to clarify the thought that its content shall be unmistakable does speech itself come into play. It is for this reason that in oral formulation of a complex thought a speaker will frequently hesitate for 'just the right word'. The same conditions are seen very clearly in translating from one language into another; the concept common to both languages involved is grasped, and then the phraseology peculiar to the one is completely transformed into that characteristic of the other, a process which, with sufficient practice, becomes quasi-automatic. In sum, the more complicated the thought, the greater the need of exact expression in speech.

There are two broad types of language, one vocal and audible *(exophasic)*, and the other non-vocal and inaudible *(endophasic)*. Endophasic speech, in turn, is of two kinds: conscious, when one silently formulates words and phrases in one's mind; and subconscious, when such formulation is quasi-automatic. Observation both of the child and of an adult learning a new language strongly suggests that endophasia, at first conscious and then subconscious, precedes exophasia, as is shown by unexpected utterances of words and phrases which a casual observer would suppose unnoticed or forgotten by the speaker, or even unknown to him. It would likewise seem that subconscious endophasia is closely connected with linguistic memory, i.e., the great mass of one's vocabulary is stored up in memory, whence the words and phrases required are evoked by the stimulus of concept and translated either into conscious endophasia or, at least apparently, directly into exophasia. Conscious endophasia seems strictly necessary solely when the matter requiring formulation is really new to the thinker. That reading involves endophasia is clear from the fact that those who read with difficulty often move their vocal organs to form the words read, but without utterance, i.e., without exophasia; in the case of those who read with ease, endophasia doubtless also exists, though with them it is subconscious.

Language may further be divided into *emotive* and *intellective (langage effectif* and *langage logique)*, a division already implied in our definition of language as expression and communication of emotional or mental concepts (p. 13). While emotive and intellective language are normally interwoven in all degrees of complexity, the essential difference between the two seems to be that emotive language seeks an immediate end, intellective language one that is not immediate. The language of non-human beings as well as of children in their earlier stages of speech is emotive, as is much of the speech of adults. If, however, the speaker's purpose be the communication of some idea which does not seek an immediate and tangible result, but which endeavours to influence his auditor's conduct or thought towards some future course, his language becomes intellective. Nevertheless, not only does emotive language precede intellective in stage of development, but it persists as a vital component in language of the severest intellectuality. The dryer-than-dryest-dust scholar expounding a most arid hypothesis is filled with emotional fervour for it; he chooses, to the best of his ability, language which shall be convincing; he seeks to win his auditor or his reader to his own point of view; his language is really emotive as seeking an immediate result, and its intellectivism is more seeming than real.

As thought and civilisation become increasingly complex, language must enlarge its content to express new concepts and new inventions; it must be adaptive if it is to survive as a vital force. This it may do in several ways. It may expand its vocabulary, as by evolving new connotations for its words (see Chapter IX) or by borrowing words from other languages (see pp. 126–128) ; or it may invent new forms to express new shades of meaning. Thus the Romance languages have created the definite past (derived from the Latin perfect) to denote a single act in past time in contradistinction to the imperfect (from the Latin imperfect) expressing repeated action in the past, and as distinguished from the perfect (a new creation whose initial stages are seen in Classical Latin itself) connoting action performed in the past but existing in completed form in the present (cf. pp. 205, 211–212, 215).

On the other hand, creation may be counterbalanced by loss. Here it is difficult to escape the conviction that fine distinctions between forms become worn down, not only through phonetic decay, so that forms originally quite distinct become outwardly identical (e.g., Greek ἔφερον, either first person singular imperfect active, ' I used to carry ', or third person plural imperfect, ' they used to carry ', from Indo-European *'e-bherom and *'e-bheront respectively), but also because of sheer slovenliness on the part of the speakers. Here belong, for instance, the loss, in the spoken language, of the French distinction between the definite past and the imperfect (though the former is still retained in writing and in formal speech), the increasing obsolescence of the English subjunctive, and the neglect of its nice distinction between I shall : you will in the future (cf. p. 20). It does not seem pedantic to regard such losses as retrogressions, for they blur shades of meanings which might well be kept. In Latin, apart from the context, one does not know whether vidit means ' he saw once ' or ' he has seen ', but one does know that videbat means ' he saw repeatedly, he used to see '; and, similarly, in colloquial French il voyait means ' he used to see ', but il a vu denotes both ' he saw once ' and ' he has seen '; only il voyait, il vit, il a vu ' he used to see, he saw once, he has seen ', as in written French, are perfectly clear in connotation.

The development of thought and the evolution of concepts as reflected in language are vividly illustrated by the changing meanings of many words of high value for the history of civilisation (cf. pp. 10–11). As examples of this we may take two sets of terms in the Indo-European languages, one denoting a spiritual concept of supreme importance, and the other a material object of absolute necessity. If one speaks or reads French or consults a French dictionary, one finds that the word for ' God ' is Dieu, and that the one for ' house ' is maison. So far as the linguistic consciousness of the speaker of either French or English is concerned, this is perfectly correct; but the question arises whether, by examining the history of the various terms for ' God ' and ' house ' throughout Indo-European, we can determine their original meanings and thus know what ideas they primarily conveyed to those who spoke and heard them.

While these Indo-European languages possess words derived from some base (cf. pp. 150–152, 159) common to at least their most important members for ' father ', ' mother ', ' cow ' (cf. pp. 132–133), ' wolf ', ' three ', and ' tooth ', and perhaps a few others, in the overwhelmingly greater part of their vocabulary no such widespread correspondences exist, e.g., for ' man ', ' hand ', ' daughter ', ' dog ', or ' one ', although the Indo-Europeans certainly had men, hands, daughters, and dogs, and knew the unit. We need feel no surprise, then, if we find no common Indo-European terms for either ' God ' or ' house '; and we perceive that the absence of a common designation in the Indo-European period for a given concept or thing by no means necessarily implies the non-existence of that concept or thing at that period. The *argumentum e silentio* is notoriously fragile (cf. p. 305).

The significations of the bases for the concept God in the Indo-European linguistic groups are plain in most instances. Leaving out of account the Armenian *astuac,* whose etymology is not yet determined, ánd the Albanian *zot* (also meaning ' lord, master '), whose precise origin is uncertain, the words for ' God ' fall into seven main groups, plus some isolated terms.

(1) Latin *deus,* Old Latin *deivos* ' god ', Oscan **deívaí** ' goddess ', Sanskrit *devá-* ' god ' (contrast the meaning of the cognate Avestan *daēva-* ' demon '), Greek δîos ' divine ', Old Icelandic *tívar* ' gods ' (poetic and archaic), Old Icelandic *Týr,* Anglo-Saxon *Tíg, Tí(w)* (cf. English *Tues-day* translating Latin *Martis dies,* French *mar-di),* Old High German *Zio,* Gaulish *Dēvo-gnātā* ' god-born ', Old Irish *día,* Lithuanian *diēvas,* Old Prussian *deiw(a)s* ' God '. These words are but part of a large group, in which are two divisions whose meaning is significant in the present connexion. One of these denotes ' sky ' as in Sanskrit *dyaú-* (the Vedic combination *Dyaús pitár* ' Father Sky ' recurs in the Greek vocative Zεû πάτερ and in the Latin *Iuppiter,* Archaic Latin *Diēspiter)* and Latin *divum;* and the other means ' day ', as in Latin *diēs,* Armenian *tiw,* Old Irish *dia* ' day ', Sanskrit *divā* ' by day ', and Greek ἔν-διos ' midday, in the sky '. The Indo-European base is **deiǎ-* ' shine, bright '; and the group evidently stresses the gods as ' shining ', plainly regarding them as divine beings of the bright sky.

(2) Greek θεός ' god ', Latin *fērālis* ' relating to the dead ', Gaulish *dusius* ' unclean spirit, incubus ', Cornish *dus, diz* ' devil ', Middle High German *ge-twās* ' ghost ', Lithuanian *dvasià* ' spirit, breath ', Lettish *dvēsele* ' breath, soul, life ', Old Church Slavic *duchǔ* ' breath, spirit '. All these come from the Indo-European base **dheuese-* ' breathe, breath ' (though the Greek word may be connected, rather, with the following group), and among their

many cognates they number Latin *bēstia*, Gothic *dius*, Anglo-Saxon *déor* (with a specialised meaning in English *deer*), Old High German *tior* ' animal ' (cf. pp. 252–255). This group seems to conceive of the deities as spirits or, perhaps, as connected with the cult of the dead.

(3) Armenian *dik'* ' (false) gods ', cognate with Old Latin *fēsiae*, Latin *fēriae* ' holidays, festivals ', *fēstus* ' festal ', Latin *fānum*, Oscan **fíísnú** ' temple ', Sanskrit *dhiṣṇya-* ' mindful, attentive ', from an Indo-European base **dhēse-* apparently meaning ' respect ', so that the divinities would here be regarded as ' reverend '.

(4) Gothic *guþ*, Old Icelandic *guð*, *goð*, Anglo-Saxon, English, Old Saxon, Old Frisian *god*, Old High German *got* ' god '. This group is restricted to Teutonic, and it is noteworthy that in Gothic, Old Icelandic, and Anglo-Saxon it is neuter in gender (plurals *guda*, *goð*, *godu*; cf. pp. 185–186) when referring to the gods of the heathen. The word is masculine when denoting the Christian God, and is always so in Old Saxon, Old Frisian, and Old and Middle High German (the plurals of the latter two being *gota*, *göte*) as it is in Modern High German, though here with the neuter plural *Götter* (when we find the masculine plurals *gudas*, *guðir* in Anglo-Saxon and Old Icelandic, these merely translate the Ecclesiastical Latin plural *dii*). The group is most probably derived from **ĝhu'tom*, the neuter passive participle of the Indo-European base **ĝhau̯e-* ' call upon, invoke ' (cf. Sanskrit *hav-* ' call, invoke ', Old Irish *guth* ' voice, word ', Lithuanian *žavĕti* [ʒav'jeːti] ' conjure, bewitch ', Old Church Slavic *zvati* ' call '), although some prefer to connect it with Sanskrit *hav-* ' sacrifice ', Greek χέω ' pour ', Phrygian ζευμαν ' spring ' from the base **ĝheu̯e-* ' pour '. The group seems to have meant primarily ' the (collectivity of that which is) invoked ' (cf. also p. 185) rather than ' the (collectivity of the) poured-out-to '.

(5) Latin *nūmen* (neuter) ' nod, command, indication of divine will, divinity ', cognate with Greek νεῦμα ' nod, expression of will, command '. Restricted to Latin, so far as our present evidence goes, this represents a very primitive form of religion; as in the case of the group of **ĝhu'tom* just considered, no personality is attributed to the deity; there is merely a belief that some divine, super-human power exists, petition is made to it, and some simple phenomenon following this petition is taken to be the divinity's answer.

(6) Gothic *ansis* ' demigods ', Runic *ansagui* ' divine ', Old Icelandic *áss*, Anglo-Saxon *ós* ' god ' (surviving in proper names, as in English *Os-car)*. The group is of very uncertain origin. It has been explained as cognate with Gothic *ansts* ' grace, favour ', Old Icelandic *ást* ' affection ', Anglo-Saxon *ést*, Old High German *anst*, *unst* ' grace ' (cf. Modern German *G-unst* ' favour, grace '), or with Gothic *ans*, Old Icelandic *áss* ' beam ' (cf. the Irminsul, pillar-gods worshipped by the pagan Germans), or with Sanskrit *ásu-* ' breath ', *ásura-* ' spirit, demon ', Avestan *ahura-* ' lord ', and ultimately with the group of Sanskrit *an-* ' breathe ', Latin *anima* ' soul ', *animus* ' breath ', etc. Of these three hypotheses, the third seems the least likely, for the Sanskrit form should not be accented on the first syllable if for ***ņsura-;* unfortunately, the base-meaning both of *ansts* and of *ans* is unknown.

(7) Avestan *baγa-*, Old Persian *baga-* ' god '. This isolated group must be compared with Sanskrit *bhága-* ' dispenser, gracious lord, patron ', and it regards the deity as the ' apportioner ' (cf. Sanskrit *bhaj-* ' to apportion '). Here, too, belongs the group represented by Old Church Slavic *bogŭ* ' god ' (cf. *boga-tŭ* ' rich ', *ne-bogŭ* ' not rich, wretched '), though whether this is genuinely Slavic or is borrowed from Iranian is not wholly clear, a statement which is equally applicable to the Phrygian Βαγαιος, an epithet of Zeus.

A few isolated terms may also be noted for the sake of completeness. Khotanese *gyasta, jasta* ' god ' : *gyaysna* ' sacrifice ' is cognate with Avestan *yaz-*, Sanskrit *yaj-* ' to sacrifice ' (cf. Avestan *yazata-* ' being to whom sacrifice should be made, worshipful being ') ; Agnean *ñkät*, Kuchaean *ñäkte* ' god ' is of doubtful origin, though the suggestion has been made that it was borrowed from Greek ἄναξ ' king '; and the Italic group of Marrucinian *aisos* (nominative plural), Paelignian *aisis* ' gods ' (dative plural), Umbrian *erus* ' to the gods ' (?), connected with Oscan **aisusis** ' by sacrifices ', Umbrian *esono-* ' sacred ', Volscian *esaristrom* ' sacrifice ', and Illyrian *iser* ' holy ', was borrowed, in all probability, from Etruscan *aesar* ' god ', recorded by Suetonius and confirmed by Hesychios, who gives αισοι as the Tyrrhenian (i.e., Etruscan) word for ' deities '.

When these terms are examined, they are seen to be purely descriptive epithets of divine beings, and only one of them, the group of *deus*, is really widespread. Originally, they were what we should now call adjectives rather than nouns, a matter of considerable

importance in investigating the nature of the parts of speech (cf.
p. 169). If ever there actually was a primitive Indo-European
word for ' god ', it would seem to have been *deiṇos ' the bright
one ' because of the occurrence of its derivatives at the geographical extremes of this linguistic family (Sanskrit devá-, Old Irish
día; cf. p. 453). If this was the case, it is possible that, when once
the term had been crystallised to mean ' god ', other words were
substituted for it because of the frequent tabu of utterance of
divine names (cf. pp. 263–265). When several terms are used for
' deity ' by a single group, as in the case of the Old Icelandic guð,
tívar, and áss, there is not merely a distinction in meaning (cf. the
basal significations of the Iranian ahura- and baga-, or of the
Latin deus and nūmen), but also a difference in use. In the Old
Icelandic group, áss is applied especially to the gods of the most
ancient cycles, and tívar is poetic and archaic; only guð is commonly employed. It is clear that the divine beings were already
regarded as animate since the terms denoting them are masculine
(i.e., animate; cf. pp. 184–187) in gender, the only exceptions being
the neuter (i.e., inanimate) Latin nūmen and the Teutonic group
represented by Gothic guþ, English god.

Turning to the material side of the history of civilisation as illustrated by linguistics, we infer that to the Indo-Europeans the
house was, among other things, a ' building '. This is the connotation implied by Latin domus, Sanskrit dáma-, Avestan dəmāna-,
nmāna-, Armenian tun, Greek δόμος, Old Saxon timbar, Old Frisian
timber, and Old Church Slavic domŭ ' house ' (cf. also Swedish
tom-t ' ground, place, site ', Lithuanian dim-stis ' yard, estate ')
from the Indo-European base *deme- ' build ' (cf. Greek δέμω
' build '), with an earlier meaning ' fit, join ' (cf. also Old Icelandic
timbr, Anglo-Saxon, English timber, Old High German zimbar
' timber ', i.e., originally, ' building-wood '); the Anglo-Saxon word
means ' house ' as well as ' timber '). The same concept underlies
the group of Oscan tríibúm, Old Irish, Old Breton treb, Welsh tref
' dwelling ', Lithuanian trobà ' building, house ', connected with
Old Icelandic þorp, Anglo-Saxon þorp, þrop ' farm, hamlet ', Old
High German dorf ' village ', and Latin trabs ' beam ' (with the
Anglo-Saxon word compare the English place-name type of Swan-
thorpe [also Swanthrope in the fourteenth century] ' thorp of the
swineherds '; English names with this second component are usually Danish in origin).

The house was also regarded as a ' dwelling-place '. Thus we have the group of Greek οἶκος, Sanskrit *viś-, vésman-*, Avestan *vaēsma-* ' house, abode ', Latin *vīlla* ' country-house, farm ' and in Vulgar Latin ' village ' from **ueik̂-sla*, Lithuanian *viḗš-pat(i)s* ' lord ' (literally, ' house-master '; cf. Sanskrit *viś-páti-*), connected with Latin *vīcus* ' village ' (from **ueik̂os;* borrowed in Middle Irish *fích*, Old High German *wîch*, Anglo-Saxon *wíc;* cf. such English place-names as *Hard-wick* ' Flock-Town ' [*Heordewican* about 1067], *Nor-wich* ' North-Town '), Gothic *weihs*, Old Church Slavic *vĭsĭ* ' village '.

A group of similar type is represented by Albanian *banë* ' dwelling, dilapidated house ', Messapian βυριον ' house ', Old Icelandic, Anglo-Saxon *bú*, Old High German *bû*, *pû* ' dwelling ', Modern German *Bau* ' building ', Old Icelandic *búð*, Old Danish *bóþ* ' dwelling ' (borrowed in English *booth)*; Old High German, Old Icelandic, Anglo-Saxon *búr* ' hut, room ' (English *bower*, Lowland Scots *byre* ' cow-stall '; from Old High German, Old French borrowed *buron* ' hut '), Anglo-Saxon *botl* ' dwelling, house ' (cf. the English place-names *Bootle, Har-bottle* [*Hyr-botle* in 1245] ' Hireling-Town ', *New-bald* [*Niu-botle* in 963], *New-bold, Newbottle* ' New-Building ', etc.), Middle High German *būde* ' hut, tent ', Old Irish *both* ' house ' (whence Lowland Scots *bothie)*, and Lithuanian *bùtas* ' house '. From this point of view, the house is an ' abode '; and the widespread group finds further cognates in Gothic *bauan* ' dwell ', Anglo-Saxon *búan* ' dwell, build ', Old High German *bûan*, Modern German *bauen* ' build '. Ultimately it is from the Indo-European base **bheu̯e-* ' become ', represented, for instance, by Sanskrit *bhav-*, Greek φύομαι, Latin *fuī*, Old Church Slavic *byti*, English *be*, and especially, in the present connexion, by Sanskrit *bhavana-* ' house '.

Much the same idea recurs in the group of Sanskrit *vắstu-*, Agnean *waṣt*, Kuchaean *ost* ' house ' (cf. Sanskrit *vas-* ' dwell ', and Greek ἄστυ ' city ', Arcadian and Locrian ϝαστος ' citizen ') ; while Gothic *razn*, Old Icelandic *rann* ' house ' (cf. English *ransack*, borrowed from Old Icelandic *rann-saka* ' house-search '), Anglo-Saxon *ærn, ern* ' secret place, house ', Old Frisian *fiā-ern* ' cattle-stall ' are cognate with the group of English *rest*. The same semantic development is seen in French *maison* ' house ' from Latin *mansionem* ' abode ' (cf. Latin *maneō* ' remain ').

A third important group regards the house as ' a place of refuge or concealment ', as from weather or from enemies. Here we may note, first, the type of Sanskrit śā́lā ' house, building, hall, shed ', Greek καλιά ' hut, barn ', Latin cella ' storeroom, small room, hut ', Old Icelandic höll, Anglo-Saxon heall, Old High German halla (borrowed in French halle, whence English hall) ' hall ', all connected with Greek καλύπτω, Latin cēlō, Old Irish celim, Old High German helan, Modern High German hehlen ' hide, conceal ' (cf. also Gothic halja, Old High German hella, Modern German Hölle, Anglo-Saxon, English hell, all meaning primarily ' hiding-place ', hence ' darkness ', and so ' place of darkness '; cf. ' darkness ' in this sense in the New Testament, e.g., Matthew viii. 12) from the Indo-European base *k̑ele- ' hide, conceal '.

A group meaning ' covering ' is found in Gothic, Old Icelandic, Anglo-Saxon, Old High German hūs (English house, Modern German Haus) from *qū-so-, *qū-dh-so-, or *qū-t-so; and in Old High German hutta (Modern German Hütte), borrowed in Old French hutte, from which comes English hut from *qu-t-i̯ā or *qu-dh-i̯ā. All these are cognate with Anglo-Saxon hýdan, English hide, Greek κεύθω, Sanskrit skav- ' hide ', Latin ob-scūrus ' dark '; and are akin, among many other words, to Old Icelandic skáli ' hut, bedroom ', skjól ' shelter ', dialectic Norwegian skyggne ' hut, granary ', Armenian çiw ' tiling, roof ', Middle Irish cú(i)l ' nook, corner, cellar ', and Lettish uz-kude ' cellar ', all derived, with various determinatives, from the widespread Indo-European base *(s)qeu̯e- ' cover '.

Another type of house was originally made of wickerwork. This construction is implied by two groups: first, that of Latin casa ' house ' from *qat-i̯ā (Italian and Spanish casa, French chez) from the base *qate- ' weave ', which perhaps reappears in Old Irish cathir ' city '; and second, that of Sanskrit gṛhá- ' house ', Avestan gərəδa- ' house of evil beings ' (borrowed in Uralic, e.g., Votyak gurt ' dwelling-place, village '), Gothic gards ' house, palace, praetorium ', Old Icelandic garðr ' courtyard, house ' (borrowed in English garth and in such place-names as Asken-garth-dale), Anglo-Saxon geard ' house, yard ', Old Saxon gardos (plural) ' house ', Old High German gart, Modern German Gart-en, English yard, gard-en, Phrygian gordum, and, probably, Old Church Slavic gradŭ ' city ' from the base *gheredhe- ' weave '.

Among minor groups, mention may be made of Latin aedes

'house' (originally 'hearth'); cf. the use of French *foyer* 'hearth' in the sense of 'home'), cognate with *aestas* 'summer', *aestus* 'fire, heat', Greek αἴθω 'burn', Old Irish *áed* 'fire', Old Icelandic *eisa* 'embers', Anglo-Saxon *ád*, Old High German *eit* 'funeral pyre'; of Prākrit and Pāli *ghara-* 'house', akin to Greek χόρτος 'enclosed place', Latin *hortus* 'country-seat, garden', *co-hors* 'enclosure, court', Old Irish *gort* 'garden, field', Hittite *gurtas* 'citadel' from the base *ĝhere-* 'surround, comprise'; and of Old Irish *tech*, Old Welsh *tig*, Modern Welsh *tŷ*, Old Cornish *ti* 'house', Old Breton *bou-tig* 'cow-stall', connected with Greek (σ)τέγος, (σ)τέγη, Latin *tectum* 'roof, house', Old High German *dah*, Modern German *Dach*, Lithuanian *stógas* 'roof', Sanskrit *sthag-*, Greek στέγω, Latin *tegō* 'cover' (cf. also Old Icelandic *þak*, Anglo-Saxon *þœc*, English *thatch*) from the base- *(s)t(h)ege-* 'cover'. The exact etymology of some terms is uncertain, e.g., of Old Church Slavic *chramŭ* 'house' and of Lithuanian *namaĩ* (plural only), Lettish *nams* 'house'.

Investigations of this type may be extended to include not only the various aspects of thought and civilisation, but also fauna, flora, topography, and the like; and the same method will be found to hold good for Semitic and all other language-groups so far as their respective data permit useful conclusions to be drawn.

It would appear that even closely related languages differ in their inward spirit even more than in their outward form. Herein seemingly lies the chief difficulty in learning a language. Knowing a language is much more than possessing a thorough acquaintance with its grammatical forms, or than being able to read or translate it perfectly, or than having an ability to speak it fluently according to the rules of its best authorities (cf. p. 129). One may be amply qualified to do all this, and yet not really know the language so spoken or read. To possess true knowledge of a language is to feel it an integral part of one's self; it must not be 'foreign' in any sense. Like all other things connected with man, whether physically, mentally, or spiritually, language either grows or decays; it never stands still.

Psychology is the foundation of two of the five great subdivisions of linguistics — syntax and semantics (Chapters VIII, IX); it plays a part in certain phonological phenomena, notably in the anticipation of sounds with resultant transposition, as in Spoonerisms (cf. pp. 72–73), and is the cause of popular etymologies (pp. 270–272). Its rôle, however, comes perhaps most strikingly to the fore in its operation as the basis of one of the two chief types of linguistic change, *analogy*, the tendency to modify a less usual sound, form, or word so that it may agree in type with one that is more common and which is taken, rightly or wrongly, as a model.

So important in linguistics is analogy that its principal types and their practical effects must be considered here in some detail, especially as it is the chief process by which new words are coined as need for them arises (cf. pp. 148–149). In nature, it is quasi-proportional (though not proportional in the strict mathematical sense of the term), and may be represented by the formula $T : T' = c : x$, where T and T' denote two type-forms associated with each other in the linguistic consciousness of the speaker, and c an actually existing form which the speaker regards as of the same type as T, and from which he creates a new form x on the model of T'. Thus for the verb *move* he rightly makes the preterite and the past participle *moved* on the analogy of such verbs as *love (T) : loved (T')* $=$ *move (c) : x;* but if he similarly creates *drived* for the past of *drive* (as the ignorant occasionally do), he is wrong, not because of his method, which is correct, but because he has taken the wrong model for $T : T'$ instead of the right one, the type of *ride (T) : rode (T')* $=$ *drive (c) : drove (x)*. The type of formation *move : moved* is *true analogy;* that of *drive : drived, false analogy*, but it is the false analogies which are, in point of fact, of major linguistic interest.

The operation of linguistic analogy falls into a number of categories. The first of these, *likeness of signification with diversity of form*, combines into a single unit certain elements of totally dissimilar forms of words possessing more or less kindred meaning, thus giving rise to portmanteau words (see p. 150) of the type of *bruncheon, parabrella*. Then comes *affinity of signification and diversity of form*, where words falling within certain semantic categories undergo analogical changes. This type is particularly characterised by change of grammatical gender, e.g., French *été* ‘ summer ’ is masculine, though its source, Latin *aestate^m*, is feminine, because of the masculine gender of *hiver* ‘ winter ’, *automne* ‘ autumn ’, and *printemps* ‘ spring ’ (Latin *hibernum [tempus], autumnum [tempus], primum tempus*, all neuter).

Analogy due to *contrast of signification with partial likeness of form* is operative when words of opposing *(polar)* meaning are linked by some similarity of form, as English *female*, which, appearing in Middle English as *femel(e)* from Old and Modern French *femelle*, has changed its second *e* to *a* under the influence of *male*. Similarly, Latin *meridialis* ' relating to mid-day ' becomes *meridionalis* through the influence of *septentrionalis* ' relating to the north ', construed as *septentr-iōnālis* instead of the linguistically correct *septentriōn-ālis;* Late Latin *senexter* ' left ' (Classical Latin *sinister)* on account of *dexter* ' right '; Old Latin *ningulus* ' no one ' on account of *singulus* ' single '; Greek μείζων ' greater ', whose true form is seen in Ionic and Arcadian μέζων from *μεγιων, on account of χείρων ' worse, inferior '; English *neither* for *[noːðər] from Anglo-Saxon *náwðer* on account of *either* from Anglo-Saxon *ǽgðer;* French *ouvrir* ' open ' by contamination (see p. 257) of Latin *aperīre* ' open ' with *cooperīre* ' cover ', and *rendre* ' restore ' by contamination of Latin *reddere* ' restore ' with Vulgar Latin *prendere* (Classical Latin *prehendere)* ' take '.

Resemblance of form suggesting possible resemblance of signification is the prime factor in popular etymologies of the types of English *bridegroom* from Anglo-Saxon *brýdguma* ' bride's man ' through the influence of the common word *groom;* Modern High German *Sündflut* ' deluge ' from Old High German *sin(t)-vluot* ' universal flood ' under the influence of *Sünde* (Old High German *sunta* ' sin '; see pp. 270-271). *Resemblance of form may also suggest possible likeness of function.* Thus English *pleasure* from French *plaisir* should be *pleasir, but has its ending changed to -ure on the analogy of *measure, nature* (from French *mésure, nature),* etc., and the same is true of *leisure* (Middle English *leiser,* Old French *leisir,* Modern French *loisir).* Similarly, English *tardy* (French *tardif)* is influenced by *hardy* (French *hardi); and *syllable* for *syllabe* (French *syllabe,* Greek συλλαβή) has had its ending changed because of such words as *parable, constable,* etc.

Analogy affects not only words and their formatives, as in the examples just given, but also their phonology, morphology, syntax, and semantics. As instances of phonological analogy we may cite Greek ἧσται ' sits ' for *ἦσται (cf. Sanskrit *áste)* with initial [h] on the analogy of the synonymous ἕζεται (cf. Sanskrit *sídati,* Latin *sedet,* English *sits);* Heraclean Greek ηοκτω, Elean ὀπτō ' eight ' for Attic ὀκτώ (cf. Sanskrit *aṣṭaú,* Latin *octō,* Gothic *ahtau,* Old

High German *ahto*, Anglo-Saxon *eahta*, English *eight)* with [h] and [pt] respectively on the analogy of ἑπτά ' seven ' (Sanskrit *saptá*, Latin *septem*, English *seven)*; Greek ἡμεῖς ' we ' for *ἡμεῖς (Sanskrit *asmá-*, Homeric ἄμμες) with [h] by analogy with ὑμεῖς ' ye ' (Sanskrit *yuṣmán)*. Such phonological levelling is the cause of the normalisation of many inflexions, e.g., in the present of such a French verb as *aimer* ' love ' as contrasted with that of *devoir* ' owe '.

LATIN	OLD FRENCH	MODERN FRENCH	LATIN	MODERN FRENCH
ámō	aim	aime	débeō	dois
ámās	aimes	aimes	débēs	dois
ámāt	aime	aime	débēt	doit
amắmus	amons	aimons	debḗmus	devons
amắtis	amez	aimez	debḗtis	devez
ámānt	aiment	aiment	débēnt	doivent

Another interesting example is found in the inflexion of the word for ' foot ' in Greek, Latin, and Old High German compared with its Proto-Indo-European forms as shown on p. 109.

Here Greek has normalised the vocalism [o] throughout; Latin, [e]; and Old High German, [oː]; the Sanskrit vocalism *(pád, pắdam* [the latter by analogy with the nominative instead of *páda]*, *padás, padé, padắ, padí)* is ambiguous, since Sanskrit *a* stands for Indo-European *a, e, o, a, e, o;* the zero-grade *bd-* from *pd-* appears in Sanskrit *upa-bdá-* ' rattling noise ', Avestan *fra-bda-* ' before the foot ', and Greek ἔπι-βδα ' day after a festival '.

The Teutonic verb shows similar analogical formations, as in German *ich war* by analogy with *wir waren*, where Old High German, like English, retains the earlier form *was;* Modern English *they sang* instead of *they sung* (still found in dialects) by analogy with *he sang* (Middle English *sang, sunge, sang; sungen;* cf. Modern German *wir sangen* after *ich sang* as contrasted with Old High German *ih sang*, but *wir sungum)*, and *he found* instead of *he fand* (still existing in dialects) by analogy with *they found* (Middle English *fand, founde, fand; founder.)*.

	PROTO-INDO-EUROPEAN	GREEK	LATIN	OLD HIGH GERMAN	PROTO-TEUTONIC
Nominative singular	*péd-s, *pōd-s	πώς (Doric) < *ποδ-ς	pēs < *péd-s	fuoz	< *fōt-s
Accusative "	*péd m̥, *pōd-m̥	πόδα	pedem < *pédim	fuoz	< *fōt-um
Genitive "	*pₑd-ós, *pₒd-ós, *bd-ós < *pd-ós	ποδός < *παδ-ός	pedis < *pad-és	fuozes	< *fat-éz
Dative "	*pₑd-eí, *pₒd-eí, *bd-eí < *pd-eí	(lacking)	pedī < *pad-eí	(lacking)	
Instrumental "	*pₑd-ṓ, *pₒd-ṓ, *bd-ṓ < *pd-ṓ	(lacking)	(lacking)	fuozu	< *fat-aí
Locative "	*pₑd-í, *pₒd-í, *bd-í < *pd-í	ποδί < *παδ-í	pede < *pad-í	fuoze	< *fat-í

This process has led in Modern English to a change of many verbs from the strong to the weak conjugation, e.g., *glide* : *glided* = Anglo-Saxon *glídan* : *glád; creep* : *crept* = *créope* : *créap* ([kreːp : kroːp] still preserved in dialects); *help* : *helped* = *helpe* : *healp* ([olp, oːp] still found in dialects); *knead* : *kneaded* = *cnede* : *cnæd* ([nad, ned, nod] still preserved in dialects); *bake* : *baked* = *bace* : *bóc* (obsolete Lowland Scots [buk]); *sow* : *sowed* = *sáwe* : *séow* (*siu* still found in dialects). Much more rarely, English weak verbs have become strong, as *ring* : *rang* = *hringe* : *hringde* (*ringed* still preserved in dialects); *wear* : *wore* = *werie* : *werede* (*weared* still found in dialects); *strive* : *strove* (*strived* still preserved in dialects) from Old French *estriver* on the analogy of such words as *drive* : *drive; stride* : *strode.*

Nouns likewise often show the effects of analogy. Thus, the genitive of Greek δράκων ' dragon, serpent ' should be *δράκονος (cf. the feminine δράκαινα), but actually is δράκοντος by analogy with present participles of the type of λύων : λύοντος ' loosing'; and Latin *arbor* ' tree ', *labor* ' labour ', *vapor* ' vapour ' should be *arbos, labos, vapos* (forms which actually occur), but receive their -*r* from non-nominative cases *(arboris,* etc.), where an intervocalic *s* is regularly changed to *r* in Latin. Doublets (cf. pp. 134–135) like English *shade* : *shadow, meed* : *meadow* are due respectively to original nominative and non-nominative cases (Anglo-Saxon *sceadu* : *sceadwe, mǽd* : *mǽdwe),* as are French *pâtre* : *pasteur* ' shepherd ' (Latin *pástor* : *pastóre^m),* Old French *cuens* : *conte* ' count ' (Modern French *comte,* Latin *cómes* : *cómite^m).* In German, the umlaut of the plural, properly found only in -*i*-stems (e.g., *Gast* : *Gäste* ' guest[s]', Old High German *gast* : *gesti;* cf. Latin *hostis),* has been extended to other stems, as *Wolf* : *Wölfe* ' wolf ' (Old High German *wolf* : *wolfa), Bruder* : *Brüder* ' brother ' (Old High German *bruoder* : *bruoder).*

In English, the genitival -*s,* originally only in masculine nouns, has been extended to the feminine, e.g., *cow's, mare's, lady's* (Anglo-Saxon *cú, myran, hlǽfdigean).* The old genitive still survives in the compound *Ladyday* ' day of (the Annunciation of our) Lady ', 25 March (cf. *þe leafdi riwle* ' the Lady's rule ' in the *Ancren Riwle* [about 1210] and Chaucer's *in his lady grace* ' in his lady's grace ') as contrasted with *Lord's Day,* and also in *Monday, Fri-day, Sun-day* = Anglo-Saxon *Mónan-dæg, Frig-dæg,*

Sunnan-dæg, as contrasted with *Tues-day, Wednes-day, Thursday* = Anglo-Saxon *Tiwes-dæg, Wódnes-dæg, Þúres-dæg*, as well as in the Modern German types of *Regierungs-art* ' mode of government ', *Unabhängigkeits-erklärung* ' declaration of independence ', etc. In Modern English, all weak plurals have disappeared except *oxen* and the archaic *hosen* (Anglo-Saxon *oxan, hosan*). Double plurals are seen in Standard English *children* (Anglo-Saxon *cild : cildru* [neuter gender like German *Kind : Kinder*], Middle English *childre, childer, children* [*childer* preserved dialectically]), *brethren* (Anglo-Saxon *bróðer : bróðru*, Middle English *breðere, breðeren*), and *kine* (Anglo-Saxon *cý*, preserved in modern dialectic [kai], Middle English *cí, cý, cýn, cíen*). The strong plural has practically ousted all others in Modern English, e.g., *books* instead of *[bi:k] (Anglo-Saxon *bóc : béc;* cf. *foot : feet* [fi:t] = Anglo-Saxon *fót : fét); nuts* instead of *[nit] (Anglo-Saxon *hnutu : hnyte*). New singulars have been created in such words as *cherry, pea, riddle, burial* because of the mistaken idea that *cherries*, etc., are plurals, whereas they are really singulars (Vulgar Latin *cerasea, cerisia*, French *cerise;* Anglo-Saxon *pise : pysan; rǽdels : rǽdelsas; byrgels : byrgelsas); and a few old plurals have become singulars, as *chess* (Old French *eschecs*, plural of *eschec), invoice* (French *envois*, plural of *envoi), quince* (Old French *coins*, plural of *coin*, Modern French *coing), truce* (Middle English *tréwes*, plural of *tréwe*, Anglo-Saxon *tréowa : tréowan).

Formatives are often extended analogically to words to which they do not properly belong, e.g., the Romance adverbial ending *-ment(e)*, for example, in French *récemment* ' recently ', which does not mean ' with a recent mind ' any more than the English *recently* signifies ' with a recent body ' (cf. p. 161). In this latter word we have a hybrid formation (cf. p. 148), in this case, a Teutonic suffix with a Latin-Romance base, as is also true of English *easy* (French *aise* ' ease ') and *noisy* (French *noise* ' quarrel ') in contrast to the legitimate *mighty* (cf. German *mächtig*). Similarly, the Romance formative *-able*, Latin *-ābilis*, correctly found in *amiable* (French *aimable*, Latin *amābilis*), is analogically extended to Teutonic words, as *lovable;* English *egotism* beside the correct *egoism* receives its *-t-* from such words as *despot-ism, nepot-ism*, and *tobacconist* for *tobaccoist* its *-n-* from words like *pian-ist, organ-ist*.

Occasionally one finds *graphic analogies,* as in English *could* for **coud* on the model of *should, would* (Middle English *schólde, wólde,* Anglo-Saxon *sc[e]olde, wolde,* as contrasted with Middle English *couðe, coude,* Anglo-Saxon *cúðe); foreign, sovereign* modelled on words like *reign* (Middle English *forein,* Old French *forain,* Vulgar Latin **forānus;* Middle English, Old French *soverain,* Mediaeval Latin *superānus;* but Old French *reigne,* Modern French *règne,* Latin *regnum); delight* on the model of *light,* etc. (Anglo-Saxon *léocht,* Lowland Scots and German *Licht,* but Old French *delit); whole* and *whoop* by analogy with *who,* etc. (Middle English *hal,* Anglo-Saxon *hál,* Middle English *houpen,* Old French *houper;* but Anglo-Saxon *hwá); island* and *aisle* on the model of *isle* (Anglo-Saxon *ígland,* Old Icelandic *eyland,* Middle English *iland;* Old and Modern French *aile,* Latin *ala;* but Old French *isle,* Modern French *île,* Latin *insula).*

Once in a while, spelling or misspelling permanently affects pronunciation, as in the name of the island of *Iona* instead of the earlier *Ioua,* found in the seventh century in Saint Adamnán's life of Saint Columba.

Syntactic analogies are seen in such constructions as French *le père donne au fils* ' the father gives to the son ' on the model of *le père envoye au fils* ' the father sends to the son ' (Vulgar Latin *pater donat ad filium* on the model of *pater mittit ad filium),* a type found in Latin at least as early as Plautus, *hunc . . . ad carnuficem dabo* ' I'll give this fellow to the hangman '. This process is often aided by the loss of inflexion *(deflexion;* cf. p. 301), whereby, for example, the dative and the accusative coincide in form. So in English one says *the father gives a book to the son* or *the father gives the son a book* as contrasted with the German *der Vater giebt dem Sohne ein Buch;* and the same ' to '-construction is found in Irish and sometimes in Modern Greek (e.g., Old Irish *as du-Christ as-immaircide in salm-so* ' that it is to Christ that this Psalm is appropriate ', Modern Greek ἔδωκε τὴ βούλα στὸ παιδί ' he gave the signet-ring to the boy '). Here, too, would seem to belong the distinction in Spanish, etc., between the animate and the inanimate object of the types *el hijo ama á su madre* ' the son loves his mother ', but *leo un libro* ' I read a book ' (pp. 188, 246), as well as the type of Latin *nocet fratri* ' he injures his brother ', for which Vulgar Latin has the type *nocet fratrem,* while French *il nuit à son frère* represents **nocet ad suum fratrem* or **nocet ad suo fratri* (cf. the eleventh-century Spanish type *decepit ad suo germano* = *engañó á su hermano* ' he deceived his brother ').

Under the head of analogy we may also consider *rhyme-words*, i.e., words changed either in form, so as to rhyme with words of analogous or even diametrically opposed meaning; or in signification, because they already rhyme with words possessing certain group-connotations. Thus, Latin *nectō* ' bind ', for which one would expect **nessō* from **ned-tō* (cf. Oscan **nessimas** ' nearest ' from **ned-tṃmo-*, Latin *nōdus* ' knot '), has, in all probability, been made to rhyme with *plectō* ' plait ' (cf. Greek πλέκω ' plait ', πλεκτή ' coil ', German *flechten* ' braid ') and *flectō* ' bend ' (of uncertain etymology). Sanskrit *áśru-* ' tear ' (Lithuanian *ãšara)* and Greek δάκρυ mean the same and rhyme, but there is no etymological connexion between them. Originally, *áśru-* apparently denoted ' bitter ' (cf. Latin *ācer* ' sharp ' and the phrase ' bitter tears '), and δάκρυ (Old Latin *dacruma*, Latin *lacrima*, Old High German *zahar*, Modern German *Zähre*, English *tear;* cf. p. 128) was probably at first ' biting ' (Sanskrit *daś-*, Greek δάκνω ' bite ', Old High German *zangar* ' biting ', and the phrase ' biting tears '), so that the pair would seem to have influenced each other as rhyme-words.

Similarly, Modern German *strecken* ' stretch ' (Old High German *strecchan*, Anglo-Saxon *streccan*, English *stretch)*, a denominative verb from Old High German *strac* ' straight, rigid ' (Modern German *stracks* ' straightway, directly ', Anglo-Saxon *strœc;* cf. English *straight*, Anglo-Saxon *streht*, literally, ' stretched ', the perfect passive participle of *streccan)*, has been influenced in meaning by its rhyme with the synonymous *recken* (Old High German *recchen*, Anglo-Saxon *reccan*, Gothic *uf-rakjan* ' stretch out ', cognate with Latin *rectus*, German *recht*, English *right*, literally, ' stretched '). English *mash*, properly meaning ' mix, mixture ' (cf. Lowland Scots *mask* ' infuse ', *mask-fat* ' brew-vat ', *mashlin* ' mixed grain ', German *Maische* ' brew-mixture ', *Mischmasch* ' medley, hodge-podge '), and with its old signification surviving in *sour-mash, beer-mash*, etc., has become practically synonymous with the rhyming but unrelated *smash*, the idea of violent action being aided by such rhyme-words as *clash, crash, dash, (s)lash, (s)plash, rash, flash, hash, bash*, etc. The *a* in Latin *aper* ' boar ' and *aries* ' ram ', for which one would expect **eper* and **eries* (cf. for the former Anglo-Saxon *eofor*, German *Eber*, Old Church Slavic *veprĭ;* and for the latter Umbrian **erietu** ' ram ', Greek ἔριφος 'kid', Old Irish *heirp,* Modern Irish *fearb* 'deer'), has probably been taken from that in *caper* 'goat' (Greek κάπρος 'boar', Old Icelandic *hafr* 'goat'). It would appear that there were a considerable number of rhyming bases in Indo-European itself, such as *$sqele-$: *$sp(h)ele-$ 'split', *$qerte-$: *$u̯erte-$ 'turn', *$u̯reĝe-$: *$bhreĝe-$ 'break', *$dhreughe-$: *$leughe-$ 'tell falsehoods', *$tere-$: *$bhere-$ 'rub, bore', *$ĝele-$: $ḱele-$ 'be cold', *$gleu̯e-$: *$sleu̯e-$ 'be slippery', and the like.

CHAPTER V

Language and Society: The Social Aspect of Language

No inherent relation between language and race — language an important factor in nationalistic and regionalistic consciousness — political aspects of language — minority-languages — language as an instrument in investigation of the historical evolution of thought and civilisation — connexion of language with history — linguistic geography — place-names, street-names, and church dedications — migrations reflected in place-names and vocabulary — composite nature of vocabulary — dialect-mixture — additional requisites for thorough knowledge of a language — categories of components of the vocabulary of a language: native and foreign (naturalised and alien) words, reasons for borrowing and criteria for distinguishing between the categories — translated borrowings — re-borrowings — the problem of linguistic sub-strata — independent identical developments — results of conflict of languages — relation of linguistics to literature — the problem of translation — linguistics and literature not antagonistic, but mutually complementary.

SINCE language is much more than an individual phenomenon, and since its whole complicated mechanism serves almost exclusively as a means of communication not only between members of the same community, but also between communities often widely separated, it has its social side, so that one of its many aspects may very properly be termed *social linguistics*. Until recently, this aspect has received insufficient attention, but its importance must be fully recognised if the scope of linguistics and its proper place among the sciences are to be truly estimated.

In the first place, one idea still too widely prevalent must be dissipated, namely, that there is any inherent connexion between language and race. To define race with scientific accuracy seems impossible; but, broadly speaking, the term appears to denote a community, however large, which considers itself sprung from a common stock, and thus to possess a certain blood-affinity. How inexact this feeling is becomes evident upon even superficial examination, and its inexactitude becomes increasingly apparent with deeper study. A strong popular conviction exists, for example, that there is a French race, but this race is, in reality, a mixture of many races: of prehistoric peoples who may themselves have been amalgams of still earlier races; of Celts (likewise doubtless amalgams) in the east who invaded parts of what is now France from the fourth century B.C. onwards; of Ligurians in the south-east and of Iberians in the south-west; of Teutonic tribes who swept through the eastern half in the fifth century A.D. and gave the name ' France ' to the whole region; of Mediterranean peoples in the south; of Scandinavians in the part still called Normandy in the north; and, from the fourth century A.D., of a new Celtic immigration from Britain into the area since known as Brittany. Although a certain amount of regionalism still persists (e.g., among Normans, Bretons, and Provençals), all these totally different stocks have long been welded into one. These statements regarding the French race seem to hold true of all other races; it is doubtful whether a pure race (i.e., one unmixed with others) exists.

One of the strongest factors in the process of amalgamation here outlined is possession of a common language, and dialectic variations form but minor barriers to the feeling of underlying unity. So important is this factor that, as a matter of fact, ethnographic (i.e., racial) maps (cf. pp. 449–451) are based on linguistic evidence, so that a given map is at the same time both linguistic and ethnographic unless it deals explicitly with one side or the other. Thus, a map of isoglottic lines, as of the representation of Latin c [k] by c [k] or ch [ʃ] in French (e.g., Latin castellum : Picard and Norman castel [whence English castle] : Old Île-de-France chastel, Modern French château), would be only linguistic (cf. pp. 25–26) ; one showing the distribution of brachycephalic, meso-cephalic, and dolichocephalic (short-headed, medium-headed, and long-headed) peoples would be purely ethnographic.

Another proof of the lack of any inherent connexion between race and language lies in the fact that individuals ethnologically the furthest apart have no inborn difficulty in acquiring each others' languages. If a Japanese infant of Japanese stock from time immemorial were placed, before it had learned to talk, in surroundings wholly French, it would speak French like a native of France; and in later years would not only have as much difficulty in learning to speak Japanese as any Frenchman, but would almost certainly speak it with a French accent. This phenomenon actually takes place on a large scale among Negroes in areas where the predominant language is English, French, or Spanish. Their ancestors spoke various African languages mutually unintelligible, belonging to different linguistic stocks, and wholly unrelated to any of the tongues of Europe. Brought as slaves to the New World, where their native languages were unknown, they were forced to adopt English, French, or Spanish. These they spoke at first in creolised form (cf. p. 37), and gradually, as circumstances permitted, they advanced to substandard types of them. Given favourable conditions of environment and education, their descendants speak flawless English, French, or Spanish; they learn the African languages of their ancestors no more easily than the white man; the whole thing is a matter of environment, not of race.

That possession of a common language, as of a common religion, of a common type of civilisation, of common economic interests, etc., is a powerful factor in creating a feeling of community is obvious, just as differences in these regards give rise to a feeling of disunity. Those who are either ignorant of the language spoken by the great majority of the community, or who speak it only with difficulty, feel, with good reason, more or less isolated. Language thus becomes an important element in creating and enhancing nationalistic consciousness. That neither unity of race nor unity of language is inherently necessary for such consciousness is strikingly demonstrated by Switzerland, which is inhabited by speakers of French, German, Italian, and Rhaeto-Romanic, all four officially recognised as of equal standing; but Switzerland is indubitably a nation and a state with a strong national consciousness.

Generally speaking, however, each nation, like each race (using this term in its vague, popular sense), desires to have a language of its own; and this desire not infrequently gives rise to a nationalistic or regionalistic consciousness so intense as to lead to separatistic movements. Thus we find agitations for Breton and Catalan in France and Spain, where governmental pressure has been exercised to discourage and smother them, if not to suppress them summarily. In Eire, an intensified nationalism has given rise to a determined effort to revive the Irish language, now little spoken outside the Gaeltacht along parts of the west coast. In Iran, a similar movement has caused a tendency to banish from the vocabulary all Arabic and Turkish words as reminiscent of alien conquerors, a procedure which would be parallel to an English resolve never again to use a word borrowed from another language; and Turkey has recently embarked on a similar course, seeking to employ, so far as possible, only words regarded as purely Turkish. One of the linguistic results of the World War has been the rise to national importance of three languages which the Imperial Russian Government had endeavoured to suppress, Lithuanian, Lettish, and Esthonian in three new republics along the Baltic coast.

That a nation should desire to have its own language is readily intelligible, for language is then a symbol, and symbols are — rightly enough — of far more spiritual worth than most mere material facts. When, then, there is either interference with freely speaking a given language or dialect, or an endeavour to enforce its use, much more than linguistic factors is at stake. What had been a mere matter of convenience of communication becomes a symbol, and the whole problem of personal freedom becomes involved. It is equally intelligible that a conquering power should desire its new territory to adopt the conqueror's speech, both for practical convenience and as a mark of absorption. If at heart the conquered area retains its own individuality and inwardly battles against such absorption, it naturally resents adopting the conqueror's tongue. Whatever it may outwardly do under compulsion, it inwardly clings only the more firmly to its own speech, as witnessed in resistance to German efforts to impose their language on Alsace-Lorraine or to Italy's endeavour to enforce the use of Italian in the territories awarded to her from Austria in consequence of the World War.

That such measures may constitute unjustifiable oppression is expressly recognised in the various Minority Treaties drawn up at Paris after that War, all of which contain the phrase: '[The country concerned] undertakes to assure full and complete protection of life and liberty to all inhabitants of [the country concerned] without distinction of birth, nationality, language, race or religion '. Other clauses secure to racial, linguistic, and religious minorities ' adequate facilities ' [' facilités appropriées ' in the French text] for the use of their language, either orally or in writing, before the courts; provision is made for the use of minority languages in primary schools in towns and districts where a ' considerable proportion ' of such minorities reside; and ' in particular they shall have an equal right to establish, manage and control at their own expense charitable, religious and social institutions, schools and other educational establishments, with the right to use their own language and to exercise their religion freely therein '.

Minority-languages may thus be not merely linguistic in interest, but may also constitute political problems of all degrees of importance. In principle, it seems highly doubtful whether governmental interference either for or against a language or dialect is politically wise except in so far as some one or more of them may be necessary for the conduct of official affairs. Unless approved by the great majority of the governed, prohibitions and commands alike arouse resentment rather than willing obedience; and a policy of linguistic *laissez faire,* so far as possible, would seem to be most expedient. Only when a minority-language becomes a means for violent subversive political activities does governmental action appear to be justifiable. Speakers of minority-languages are subject, by the very constitution of society, to certain social and economic disadvantages. Left to themselves, such persons will either remain static, with correspondingly continuant disadvantages; or they will, if ambitious, become bilingual and perhaps will ultimately discard their minority-language altogether in favour of the prevailing tongue. Examples of the first type are the German colonies along the Volga in Russia, dating from the reign of Catharine the Great; of the second, a very large proportion of the Welsh; of the third, an increasing area of the Scottish Highlands, where Gaelic is steadily yielding place to English, while in Cornwall the old Celtic vernacular has utterly disappeared. In none of these areas has there ever been the slightest attempt to interfere with language; and in none of them is there any language-problem of more than purely linguistic interest. It is only in regions where linguistic minorities feel themselves aggrieved, whether this feeling be justified or not, that such problems arise (cf. p. 117).

We have already seen (p. 10) that language is an indispensable agent in studying the history of civilisation; and we have also sought (pp. 98–105) to trace the development of terms now meaning ' God ' and ' house ', seeking to know what were the earlier ideas associated with the Divine Being or divine beings, and what houses primarily meant to those who gave them their various names. Here comparative religion and archaeology mutually illuminate linguistics and receive illumination from it.

The methods already applied to two categories are equally valid, wherever the existence of data permits, for the entire range of man's activities and interests, both in relation to himself and to all the human and non-human world which surrounds him. We thus learn what ideas he associated with religion, with agriculture, with the chase, with whatever he made; the way in which he viewed animals, birds, and reptiles; his concepts of human relationships and of his own anatomy; something even of his own abstract thought. It seems no exaggeration to say that *investigation of the evolution of thought and civilisation from their oldest knowable forms to the present day is incomplete without the most thorough linguistic knowledge possible.* We must remember always that the names of things are, in origin, descriptive terms (cf. p. 169), and that they were given, in the first place, simply because they were regarded as appropriate. To understand them, we must consider them, not from our own modern point of view, but from that of the far earlier stage of thought which created them. It is perfectly true that, even with our best efforts and with all the knowledge at our command, many of them will baffle us; but the large number of terms which we can explain by the methods of sound etymology show that our failure is due to the relatively scanty material at our disposal, not to any lack of validity of the principle itself.

Linguistics is also intimately connected with history and geography. We know from history that the Galatians of Asia Minor, to whom St. Paul addressed one of his Epistles, were Celts, and the scattered words of Galatian preserved in Classical writers are identical with those of the ancient Celtic language of Gaul. Geographically, if we study the distribution of the Teutonic cognates of the English word *ten* (pp. 74–75, 281–282), we see that they fall into three classes: Low Teutonic (English *ten*, Anglo-Saxon *tíen*, *týn*, Old Frisian *tian*, Dutch *tien*, Old Saxon *tehan*, Gothic *taíhun);* Scandinavian (Old Icelandic *tío*, Swedish *tio*, Norwegian *ti);* and High Teutonic (Old High German *zehan*, Modern German *zehn).* It thus becomes evident, first, that English is part of the Low Teutonic group, and, second, that it is more closely related to Scandinavian than to High Teutonic. Historically we know that the Anglo-Saxons migrated from the Low Teutonic area (cf. p. 347) ; and though practically all the Gothic that we have is from Thrace, now part of Greece (portions of a translation of the Bible by the Arian bishop Wulfila in the fourth century), and from the Crimea (a vocabulary of the sixteenth century), the language alone would show that the Goths also had migrated from Low Teutonic regions.

Such observations bring us into contact with *linguistic geography,* a science which is rapidly being developed and which is casting new light upon the history of the human race, especially as it frequently tells of events which took place long before our written records begin, and of which we should otherwise be wholly ignorant. Linguistic geography has two divisions: *synchronic,* which shows the present distribution of languages and dialects, and of isoglosses, isophones, etc. (cf. pp. 25–26) ; and *historical,* which, particularly by the study of place-names and the like, shows how linguistic areas have arisen, expanded, contracted, or disappeared in the course of centuries.

Synchronic geography may be reduced to maps, which usually coincide with those termed ethnographic (cf. p. 116). It is possible to draw up language-maps of the world, though only in the broadest outlines because of our inadequate knowledge not only of many languages, but even of a number of linguistic families, and of individual languages together with their dialects; or we may show the distribution of a given grammatical formation or of terms for given beings and things in a given area. We may, for example, prepare maps of the Indo-European, Semitic, or Dravidian linguistic families; or of the various representations of the Latin termination -*ācus* in French place-names (e.g., *Sabiniācus* '[estate of] Sabinius': *Savignac, Savignat*[*s*], *Savigné, Savigny, Savigneux, Sévignac, Sévignat, Sévigné, Sévigny,* etc.) ; or of the words for ' mare ' *(jument, ega, cavala)* in France; or of linguistic conditions in such areas as Belgium or Switzerland. When we have maps for a series of periods, we may graphically determine the historic sequence of changes in linguistic areas, and may thus have the rudiments of a *diachronic* linguistic geography. Unfortunately, accurate linguistic statistics over any considerable period of years are available in only a very few areas. Even with the best of statistics, delimitation of linguistic boundaries can be only approximate (cf. pp. 26–27) ; here we are in like case as for economic maps of the distribution of wheat, iron, forests, and the like.

Historical linguistic geography operates in the main by investigation (1) of place-names to trace the migrations, expansions, contractions, etc., of peoples speaking given languages, and (2) of the vocabulary of a given language or set of languages to determine under what influences the speakers of that language or set of languages have come.

Let us first consider place-names, including street-names and, in many cases, church dedications. In Japan, at the present time as for many centuries past, the Ainu, who are believed, from their physical characteristics, to have migrated from Europe in the Stone Age, have been restricted to one of the Kurile Islands (Shikotan), the southern half of Sakhalin, and the northernmost island of the Japanese Empire (Yezo); but study of the place-names of the Empire shows that at one time the Ainu were at least as far south as Tokio. A place-name like *Leipzig* is indicative of the fact that it was founded by Slavs (cf. Russian *'lipa'* ' linden-tree '); and the ancient name of Isakchea, some sixty-five miles from the mouth of the Danube, *Novio-dūnon* (' New Fort '; cf. such names as *Newcastle)*, is evidence of a Celtic origin. Place-names in Greece like *Korinthos* and *Lindos*, inexplicable in Greek, are proved by those of similar formation in Asia Minor to be Asianic. In Scotland, names of the type of *Aber-deen* and *Inver-urie*, some seventeen miles apart, show two Celtic strata; both *aber* and *inver* mean ' river-mouth, estuary, harbour, bay ' (from **ad-ber-* and **eniber-* respectively), but the one is British Celtic (cf. such place-names as Welsh *Aber-gavenny)* and the other Irish Celtic (cf. Middle Irish *Inbir-dáile*, now Ennereilly, County Wicklow; cf. also Middle Irish *inbir*, Modern Irish *inbhear* [invær]; in Modern Irish *abar* means ' marsh ', and Cornish *aber* is glossed by ' gurges ' [' whirlpool ']). Thus we have evidence of the former presence of British Celts in an area from which they were later expelled by Irish Celts who invaded what is now Scotland from the fifth century of our era onward. So also in the United States, American Indian names of places and rivers *(Onondaga, Mississippi,* etc.) attest languages of peoples who formerly dwelt there; and the race of the earliest or most prominent earliest citizens of many a place is shown by its name, as *Boston,* Massachusetts, from Boston, England; *New Rochelle,* New York (settled by French Huguenots), from La Rochelle, France; *Swedesboro,* New Jersey, established by Swedes; *Bismarck,* Dakota, founded by German admirers of the ' Iron Chancellor '.

In examining place-names, history must always be consulted as far as possible. The name of *Lincoln,* Nebraska, is superficially identical with that of Lincoln, England; but only superficially. The English city-name is derived from the Roman Lindon Colonia ' Pool-Colony ', a hybrid of the Celtic word for ' pool ' (cf. Welsh *llyn,* Old Irish *lind, linn,* and the Irish place-name *Dublin* ' Blackpool ') and the Latin term for ' colony '. Before the creation of surnames in the modern sense of the word, persons from that city might be termed ' John, etc., of Lincoln ' and then ' John Lincoln '. From some family so called a President of the United States was descended, and a new city was named in his honour. We must also observe that place-names, through constant use, frequently assume allegro-forms (cf. pp. 64–65), so that determination of the original forms, unless we have historical data on the subject, becomes very difficult, and too often impossible. Few would divine, for instance, that the earliest known form of *Vienna* (French *Vienne)* was *Vindo-bōna* ('City of Vindos' or 'White City'?), and that the French city of *Vienne* has a totally different origin (Gaulish *Vienna*, of unknown meaning). How complicated the history may be is shown by the city-name *York*. Originally called *Eburācon* (with the *b* pronounced [v]), probably meaning '(Estate) of Eburos ', its name was changed by popular etymology to *Eofor-wíc* (' Boar-Town ') in Anglo-Saxon; this was adopted by the Scandinavians as *Iorvík*, which later became *Iork* and was re-adopted in English as *York*. Of many place-names, even of well-known cities, the origin is still either obscure or very uncertain.

The names of streets, etc., in old cities furnish similar information as to local geography. The city of Senlis in France, for example, originally the capital of the Gaulish tribe of Silvanectes (probably meaning ' Property-Protectors '), contains, of course, perfectly banal street-names (rue de Paris) and those commemorating noteworthy events in the town's history (rempart des Otages) or the sites of important buildings long vanished (porte Saint-Rieul, from the church of Saint Regulus or Saint Rule). In addition to these, one finds reminiscences of early Teutonic invaders (e.g., a ' lieu-dit ' *Marigaut* ' Sea-Goth, Viking ' [?]) and of pre-Roman Celts *(rue Bellon),* while the little river *Nonette* bears a pre-Celtic name given by a people whose language has vanished. One of the Senlisian street-names is a particularly interesting instance of popular etymology (cf. pp. 270–272). The *rue Saint-Yves-à-l'Argent* has a number of variants running back to the fifteenth century, such as *Sainctisme Alargent, Sanctissima Argentea* (1414), etc. On the face of it, this ' Saint Yves at the Silver ' or ' Most Holy Silver (street?)' is absurd. Saint Yves, the patron of lawyers, is essentially a Breton, not a French, saint; and, as many a Breton carving shows, he repulses the wealthy client with his bag of money, but welcomes the honest suitor in rags.

Study of the street-name and its variants seems to indicate that its source was a Gaulish phrase *senti-sama argentea* ' great silver buckle ' (for the formation cf. Gaulish *Rigi-samos* ' Greatest King, Most Kingly ', an epithet of Mars) ; the Old Irish hymn of Broccán in honour of Saint Brigit actually mentions her *sét argait* ' silver buckle ', and her Latin life similarly speaks of her *sentis argenta*. The analogy of very many French street-names (e.g., the Parisian *rue de l'Arbre Sec* ' Dry-Tree Street ', whose old inn-sign of the dry tree may be seen to-day in the Musée Carnavalet) shows that it doubtless received its designation from an inn whose sign was a large silver buckle. Similar mutilations are of frequent occurrence; the Parisian *rue Gît-le-Cœur*, popularly supposed to mean '(here) lies (buried) the heart ', for instance, does not commemorate some romantic tragedy, but the very prosaic fact that a certain Gui-le-Queux (' Guy the Cook ') lived there at least as early as 1215. Old farm-names and field-names may be of equal interest. At Dorchester in Oxfordshire, for example, there is still a farm called *Bishop's Court*, though Dorchester has not been an episcopal see since 1092 until recently (1939) ; and *Lepers' Croft* remains to-day in Aberdeen, Scotland.

More remotely connected with linguistics, yet not altogether divorced from historical linguistic geography, is consideration of the dedications of many old churches, which frequently refer to historical events. Thus, the church of Saint-Séverin at Paris is on the site of the saint's hermitage, and his well still exists in the church. In the Celtic area, churches of early Celtic dedication point to the fact that they were actually founded by the holy men whose names they bear; it was only later that churches were dedicated in memory of saints formally canonised and without personal connexion with the sites. Accordingly, when we find old dedications to the same Celtic saint in Brittany and in Wales or in Cornwall or in them all, we have evidence of the actual migrations of the holy man in question (the early Celtic saint was a man of exceptional piety, not necessarily canonised by the Church Catholic) ; and this material is at once of linguistic and of historical value. In certain old cities we may even see from church dedications the approximate boundaries of the differing races which once inhabited them. In Dublin, for instance, a line may fairly be drawn between the Irish and the Danish parts of the city (Saint Patrick's Cathedral there is an Irish foundation; but Christ Church Cathedral is Danish) ; and a similar demarcation may be made in Exeter between Celtic and English (e.g., Saint Petrock's as contrasted with Saint Olave's). For even the amateur linguist, a walk or a ride through a country or a ramble through a city's streets, with observation of the names as he passes, reveals a past often centuries older than any remains that he may see, however ancient.

Our cursory survey of place-names has shown that the same area has not always been occupied by the same race. This diversity of race is reflected in the diversity of linguistic elements in the vocabulary, and sometimes even in the grammar, of any given language, for vocabulary is as mixed as is race. Linguists are, therefore, devoting increasing attention to the problem of *linguistic sub-strata* (cf. pp. 136–137). A survey not only of history but of the evidence of archaeology and of the place-names derived from diverse languages shows at once that peoples have never remained stationary. Leaving out of account seasonal migrations and re-migrations of many nomadic tribes for the purpose of securing the best pasturage for their flocks and herds, one must reckon with traders and merchants, whose numbers have always been comparatively few, but whose cultural influence was and is very considerable, as evidenced, for example, by the well-known trade-routes which permitted the interchange of commodities from China and India with those of Greece, Italy, and Gaul.

The most important migrations were those destined to result in conquest and permanent occupation of alien territories, such as the barbarian invasions in the declining years of the Roman Empire, even as Rome herself had expanded from the small area surrounding a little city on the Tiber to become mistress of the world. When one nation conquers another, neither victors nor vanquished remain the same as they were before; and material conquest does not necessarily mean moral conquest. Rome crushed Greece by force of arms, but the captor sat at the captive's feet to learn, a fact which is linguistically evident in the number and the character of the words in the Latin vocabulary borrowed from Greek.

Further to the north, Scandinavians and Danes made invasions which carried them to the Baltic lands, to Britain, and to Ireland, in all of which linguistic traces of their presence remain: in Russia, the very name of the country is not Slavic, but is derived from the Scandinavian tribe of Rus, who there established their supremacy; in England, we find, for example, *Whitby* 'White Village' from Old Icelandic *hvítabýr,* and in Ireland, *Leixlip*

'Salmon-Leap' from Old Icelandic *laxhlaup*. Another group went to what is now northern France, where they subdued a region still known as *Normandy* 'Land of the Northmen' (cf. such Norman place-names as *Vittefleur* for **Vittefleud* 'White Gulf' [with *-fleur* instead of **-fleud* by popular etymology with French *fleur* 'flower'] : Old Icelandic *hvítaflóð)*. There they lost their Scandinavian speech, even though it was still spoken at Bayeux as late as the twelfth century, and adopted a form of Old French. From Normandy, in 1066, they conquered England; and for a time Norman French was the language of the Court and of the aristocracy, while Anglo-Saxon and the nascent Middle English remained the tongue of the common people. Gradually Norman French waned until English became supreme, the whole process carried on with neither constraint nor resistance on either side. To this day, the vocabulary of English retains clear evidence of the old conquests of the people by Scandinavians, Danes, and Gallicised Normans, to say nothing of marks of the earlier Roman conquest in the vocabulary of Anglo-Saxon itself (e.g., *flit,* still used in Lowland Scots in the sense 'move from one residence to another' : Norwegian *flytte,* Old Icelandic *flytja,* Swedish *flytta* 'move'; *skirt, shirt* : Danish *skjorte,* Old Icelandic *skyrta,* as contrasted with Anglo-Saxon *scyrte,* Middle English *schirte; guise* from Old French *guise* from Old High German *wîsa,* Modern German *Weise* 'manner' [English *guise* is thus a doublet (cf. pp. 134–135) of *wise,* 'manner', and *skirt* and *shirt* are likewise doublets]; *street* : Anglo-Saxon *strǽt* from Latin [*via*] *strāta* 'paved [way]').

The vocabulary of every language of which we have adequate scientific and historic knowledge is highly composite. Thus, the 5,140 words recorded in Gustav Meyer's *Etymologisches Wörterbuch der albanesischen Sprache* (Strassburg, 1891), may be classified as follows:

LANGUAGE		NUMBER		PERCENTAGE	
Genuine Albanian		430		.0837	
Borrowed from Romance . . .			1420		.2762
" " Slavic			540		.1051
" " Modern Greek . .			840		.1634
" " Turkish	3,980		1180	.7743	.2296
Uncertain		730		.142	
	5,140			1.00	

Similarly, the 1,940 Classical Armenian words listed in Heinrich Hübschmann's *Armenische Grammatik* (Strassburg, 1897) fall into the following categories:

LANGUAGE	NUMBER		PERCENTAGE	
Genuine Armenian	438		.2258	
Borrowed from Middle Parthian .		686		.3536
" " Modern Persian and Arabic		171		.0881
" " Syriac		133		.0686
" " Greek	1,502	512	.7742	.2639
	1,940		1.00	

Finally, a survey of the 9,902 rubrics in Wilhelm Meyer-Lübke's *Romanisches etymologisches Wörterbuch* (second edition, Heidelberg, 1919; the last edition, 1935, does not differ sufficiently to make re-calculation worth while) gives the following very rough approximation of the various elements in the Romance vocabulary:

LANGUAGE	NUMBER		PERCENTAGE	
Latin	6,337		.6399	
Classical		5,275		.5327
Ante-Classical		41		.0041
Ante- and post-Classical		32		.0032
Mediaeval		989		.0999
Place-names	86		.0087	
Personal names	56		.0056	
Onomatopoetic words	151		.0153	
Borrowed words	3,007		.3036	
Greek		656		.0662
Celtic		239		.0241
Teutonic		1,680		.1697
Iberian (including Basque) . . .		56		.0056
Oriental		376		.038
Various	48		.0049	
Unknown or uncertain	217		.022	
	9,902		1.00	

Among the words classed as ' unknown, uncertain, various ', etc., in the various standard etymological dictionaries, a good number are evidently survivals from non-Indo-European languages which have otherwise utterly vanished before the conquering Indo-European tongues — languages vaguely termed Alpine, Mediterranean, Asianic, and the like.

Similar lists might be drawn up for Teutonic, etc., and for such individual languages as French, Spanish, or English; and all of them would reveal a vocabulary at least equally composite. We must also bear in mind that the vocabulary of a given language contains not only words borrowed from other languages, but also those taken from its own dialects. Thus, Latin has two words for ' red ': *rūfus* and *ruber*, but comparison with the cognates, e.g., Sanskrit *rudhirá-*, Greek ἐρυθρός, Lithuanian *raũdas*, Old Irish *ruad*, Gothic *rauþs*, German *rot*, and English *red*, shows, when the Latin and Osco-Umbrian correspondences are known, that only *ruber* is genuinely Latin, whereas *rūfus* was borrowed by Latin from Osco-Umbrian. In like manner, Latin *bōs* ' ox ' should be **vōs*, since initial Indo-European gᵘ becomes u in Latin (cf. *vīvus* ' living ' from Indo-European **gᵘīu̯os* : Sanskrit *jīvá-*, Lithuanian *gývas*, Old Church Slavic *živŭ*, Gothic *qius*, English *qui-ck)*; but, in reality, the word is not Latin at all, but is a dialectic form found in Umbrian **bum** ' bovem ' (cf. Oscan **bivus** ' vivi '). So, again, Latin *lacrima* ' tear ' should be *dacruma*, a form actually found in Old Latin (cf. Greek δάκρυ, Gothic *tagr*, Anglo-Saxon *téar*, English *tear*, Old High German *zahar*, Modern German *Zähre*, Indo-European **daḱru-;* see p. 113). It is really a Sabine word, in which an original [d] seems regularly to have become [l]. French *siffler* ' to whistle ', as contrasted with Latin *sibilare*, is ultimately derived, not from Latin (like the corresponding Spanish *silbar* [with metathesis; cf. p. 70]), but from an Osco-Umbrian equivalent which must have existed, but which is not recorded in our rather meagre texts of those languages. The unhappy fate of the Ephraimites who did not know how to pronounce the palato-alveolar voiceless sibilant, and so said *sibbóleθ* instead of *šibbóleθ* (Judges xii. 6), shows the presence of dialects among the Israelites.

Less usually, syntactic constructions are borrowed, such as Swiss German *er ist kränker als du nicht denkst* = French *il est plus malade que tu ne le penses* (' he is more ill than you think ') ; and Esthonian (of the Uralic family) has invented a future and a

passive on the German model by using *sāma* ' become ' in imitation
of the German *werden* (e.g., *ta sāβ tulema* = *er wird kommen*
' he will come '; *sē sāβ tehtuδ* = *es wird getan* ' it is done ').
Morphological borrowings are excessively rare. The American
Indian Wishram (of the Chinuk stock) has apparently taken
its system of postpositive particles from the neighbouring Shahaptin group (e.g., *-ba* [*-pa*] ' in, at ' : *-pa* ' in '), and Afghān (an
Iranian language) seems to have borrowed its causative in *-av-*
from the specifically Indian type in *-pa-* (e.g., *kšal-* ' to draw ',
kšavul ' to make draw '; cf. Sanskrit *dádāti* ' he gives ', *dāpayati*
' he makes give ').

Acquisition of a thorough knowledge of a language is not easy
(cf. p. 105) : one must know not merely the linguistic side, but
must also be acquainted with the entire history of the people who
speak or spoke it. Migrations, conquests, commerce, occupations
of every sort, geography, religion, law, intellectual level, and all
associations and contacts with other peoples are reflected in language. On the specifically linguistic side, one must know not only
the history of the changes in sounds, forms, meanings, and arrangements of words of the language one is investigating, but must also
be sufficiently versed in the languages which have exercised noteworthy influence upon it. To illustrate this in the case of English,
one should know not only Anglo-Saxon, Middle English, and Old
French (especially Old Norman), Latin, and Greek, but also
Gothic and Low Teutonic (particularly Old Icelandic, Dano-
Norwegian, Old Frisian, Old Saxon, and Dutch), with at least
some acquaintance with Celtic, and considerable knowledge of the
various English dialects, both of the Middle and the Modern
periods. Finally, one should have at least a general familiarity with
Indo-European linguistics in general to place the specific phenomena of English in their proper setting. Analogous statements
hold good for French, German, Russian, Armenian, Sanskrit,
Hebrew, or any other language whatever so far as accessible
data permit.

The vocabularies of all languages of which we have scientific
knowledge are divided into two great categories, which we may
term *native* and *foreign*. *Native* words are those which belong, as
far back as we can trace them in history, to the linguistic stock
which still speaks them. Thus, a native English word is one which,
by its phonology and morphology, may not only be traced back to

Anglo-Saxon as the most ancient historical form of English, but must also, by the same characteristics, have formed part of the linguistic stock of Teutonic generally. Such a word may actually be present in the extant remains of Anglo-Saxon, though we must bear in mind that these written records, like those of all other languages, contain only a portion of the vocabulary of the language as spoken; or it may be reconstructed by scientific linguistic methods. In either case, the phonology and morphology must conform to the rules of Modern English, Middle English, Anglo-Saxon, and general Teutonic in the order named. It is in view of these requirements that we say that *ten* is a native English word, but that *pole,* though it appears in Anglo-Saxon as *pál,* is not, while its doublet *pale,* though appearing in Middle English, is also borrowed (cf. pp. 74–77). By these same criteria we distinguish native from foreign words in the vocabulary of any language; and these methods determine the classifications which we have given (pp. 126–128) for Albanian, Armenian, and Romance.

Foreign words are those whose phonology (morphology is here only very rarely concerned) shows that they have come from other linguistic stocks or areas in consequence of political, military, religious, economic, or other contacts, so that we may fairly infer, for example, from purely linguistic evidence, that the Teutonic peoples learned of paved roads only from the Romans, since their word, represented by German *Strasse,* Dutch *straat,* Anglo-Saxon *stræt,* English *street,* is obviously borrowed from Latin *(via) strāta* ‘ paved (way)’; were they native words, they would have the forms **Storte* in German and **stord* in the rest from a Proto-Teutonic **sturþō* from Indo-European **st$_e$r$_e$'tā.*

From the point of view of social linguistics, a study of the relations between the native and the foreign words in the vocabulary of a language, and, still more, of the types and categories of the words borrowed, reveals both the extent and the nature of the intercourse between the borrowers and the lenders; and it very frequently shows, what in many respects is still more important, the relative grades of civilisation of the peoples concerned. We may regard it as an axiom that each and every word borrowed is taken over for a reason which seems good and sufficient to the borrower. The chief of these reasons are two in number. First, the term taken over represents a concept or thing previously unknown (at least consciously) among the people borrowing it (e.g., *bishop,* a religious dignitary who had had no counterpart among the pagans previous to the spread of Christianity to their lands; *tobacco*, unknown in Europe before the discovery of America). Second, a word is very frequently taken over because the people from whom the loan is made are felt to possess a superior civilisation, with the result that their vocabulary is regarded as more elegant. The native equivalent is then considered less dignified, and sometimes as actually coarse, so that it tends to be used only by the lower classes and sometimes disappears, at least from written speech (e.g., *spit* : *expectorate;* Middle English *ém* ' uncle ', Early Modern English *eme* [cf. the proper name *Eames* and German *Oheim*] as compared with *uncle* from French *oncle,* Latin *avunculus).* On the other hand, a word borrowed from the lower race, and used originally by the inferior classes of the borrowing people, sometimes rises in dignity till it supplants the equivalent term of the higher civilisation (e.g., the supersession of Latin *equus* ' horse ' in Romance by the Vulgar Latin *caballus* ' nag ', Italian, Portuguese *cavallo,* Spanish *caballo,* Catalan *caball,* Old Provençal *cavals,* French *cheval,* all, like Greek καβάλλης, Albanian *kal,* Irish *capall* [also ' nag, mare '], Manx *cabbyl,* Welsh *ceffyl,* Cornish *kevil,* Middle Breton *caual, caffal,* Old Church Slavic *kobyla* ' mare ', borrowed from some Mediterranean or Danubian language, long since vanished except for such traces of the pre-Indo-European period; cf. pp. 262, 269).

Foreign words are divided into two categories, *naturalised* and *alien,* the latter being more usually termed *learned. Naturalised* words are those which have been so thoroughly incorporated into the language which has borrowed them, and which are so commonly used there, that they are no longer felt to be foreign. So completely are they absorbed that they undergo the regular phonetic correspondences operative for native words both at the time of their borrowing and subsequent to it; but they are not subject to correspondences which may previously have governed the borrowing language and then ceased to operate. Thus we term Anglo-Saxon *pál,* English *pole,* a naturalised word from Latin *pālus* because its phonology shows that it was borrowed from Latin after the Teutonic changes *p* to *f* and *ā* to *ū* (cf. p. 77) had ceased to operate, but while the change of Anglo-Saxon *á* [a:] to Middle and Modern English *ō* [ou] was still in force. Its doublet *pale,* borrowed from French *pal,* and this, like Anglo-Saxon *pál,* also from Latin *pālus,* was taken over by English *after* this change of *á* to *ō* had ceased to be effective.

Learned words are those which are consciously and deliberately borrowed (such as the majority of modern scientific terms) to express new concepts or things (e.g., *relativity, telephone, hydrochloric)*, and which retain their foreign impress with only such changes as may be absolutely necessary to adapt them to the grammatical structure of the language to which they are admitted; sometimes, indeed, they retain the inflexion of their original languages (e.g., *radii* as the plural of *radius)*. To this group we may also assign *translated* words, i.e., those created to denote concepts or things received from other languages, but formed, not by *borrowing* the words themselves, but by *translating* the foreign terms into the language which adopts them (e.g., German *Fern-sprecher* ' distance-speaker ' = English *tele-phone; über-setzen* = Vulgar Latin *translatare*, whence English *trans-late;* cf. pp. 135–136).

One or two examples of each of these categories will serve to give practical illustration of the principles here set forth.

(1) Native words. — English *cow* (dialectic [ku:, ḳau], etc.), Anglo-Saxon *cú*, Old Frisian *kû*, Old Saxon *kô*, Dutch *koe* [ku:], Old Icelandic *kýr*, Swedish *ko*, Old High German *kuo*, Modern High German *Kuh* [ku:]; Latin *bōs* (English learned loan-word *bov-ine)*, Umbrian **bum** (accusative), Italian *bove*, Logudoresian *boe*, Engadine *bouf*, Friulian *bo*, Old French *boef* (English learned loan-word *beef*, re-borrowed in French *bif-stek)*, Provençal *buou*, Catalan *bou*, Spanish *buey*, Portuguese *boi*, Rumanian *bou;* Old Irish *bó*, Welsh *buw-ch*, Old Cornish *bu-ch*, Old Breton *bou-tig* (' cow-house '), Modern Breton *buc'h* [bux]; Old Church Slavic *gov-ęždĭ* (probably something like [govēꝫdï]), Russian *gov-jádo*, Ukrainian *hovádyna*, Bulgarian *govédo*, Slovene *govędo*, Serbo-Croate *gòvedo*, Czech *hovado;* Lettish *gùovs;* Greek βοῦς, Doric βῶς [bo:s], Modern Vernacular βούδι [vu:ði] βόδι, βοίδι; Armenian *kov;* Avesta *gau-*, Modern Persian *gō, gāv*, Afghan γwā, Balōčī *gōk*, Kurdish *gā*, East Ossetic γog; Sanskrit *gau-*, Prākrit *gaüa-, gāa-*, Bengalī *gāvī*, Hindī *gāī, gāv*, Gujarātī *gāe, gāy*, Kāśmīrī *gāv*, Siṁhalese *gava, go, gā*, Welsh Gypsy *gu-ruv*. This is one of the relatively few words which have representatives in nearly all the divisions of the Indo-European group of languages (cf. pp. 98–99), and it may be regarded as an Indo-European term, even though one scholar considers it a very primitive borrowing

from a Sumerian (and, hence, non-Indo-European) word *GU(D)* ' cow '. The entire group may be derived from an hypothetical Proto-Indo-European form *g^{u}ou-*.

A certain number of native words in English find cognates, so far as now known, only in other members of the Teutonic group. Here belongs, for instance, the group of English *drink*, Anglo-Saxon *drincan*, Old Saxon *drinkan*, Dutch *drinken*, Old Frisian *drinka*, Old Icelandic *drekka*, Swedish *dricka*, Norwegian *drikke*, Gothic *drigkan* [driŋkan] (in Gothic *gk* and *gg*, by an orthography imitated from the Greek γκ and γγ, are [ŋk, ŋg] ; cf. p. 284), Old High German *trinkan*, Middle and Modern High German *trinken* (Italian *trincare* and French *trinquer* ' drink a toast ' are borrowed from Middle High German). That this group is truly native is shown by the characteristic Scandinavian *kk* for *nk*, and by the Low Teutonic *d* corresponding to High Teutonic *t*. In other terms, the word has evolved in each of the Teutonic languages according to the specific correspondences governing each of them; and all of the forms may be derived from an hypothetical Proto-Teutonic *drenkan*. Further than this, we can say nothing; we may reconstruct a Proto-Indo-European base *dhre(n)g(h)e-*, but nothing outside Teutonic implies its existence. A number of guesses have been made to explain the group, but all lack plausibility.

The only two hypotheses which can reasonably be advanced seem to be either *(a)* that the base has vanished from all the Indo-European languages except Teutonic, the rest having representatives of the Indo-European base *pōie-*, e.g., Sanskrit *pāti* (with a curious reduplicated form *pibati*, which recurs in Latin *bibō* for *pibō* [whence French *boire*, Italian *bevere*, etc.] and in Old Irish *ibid* ' drink ye ! '), Aeolic Greek πώνω, Old Church Slavic *piti;* or *(b)* that some form like *drenkan* was part of the language of those whom the Indo-European invaders found already settled in the area (subsequently called Teutonic) when they conquered it — that the group is, in other words, not Indo-European at all, but a survivor of a language utterly vanished except for a few such scanty vestiges. Many of the commonest English words are of most uncertain origin, as *dog, cat, flag;* some of them, e.g., *cat*, we find widely spread, but only as loans from one language to another; of their etymology (i.e., of their history) and of their original source we know nothing.

(2) Foreign words: *(a)* Naturalised. — An excellent illustration

of this type is the English word *bishop*, which, though borrowed
from another language to express a new dignitary, previously unknown, has long been felt by those who use it to be essentially an
English word, and which has undergone at least one characteristic
English sound-change, i.e., that of *sk* to *sh* (cf. Anglo-Saxon *scip* :
English *ship*). With the rise of Christianity, Latin used the term
episcopus as a direct borrowing, or learned word, from the Greek
ἐπίσκοπος, originally meaning ' overseer, supervisor, superintend-
ent '. As the domain of Latin Christianity spread, we find the
Latin loan-word borrowed widely in naturalised forms: Anglo-
Saxon *bisceop*, Old Saxon, Swedish *biskop*, Dutch *bisschop*
[biskop], Old Icelandic *biskup*, Old High German *biscof*, Modern
High German *Bischof;* and, in other branches, Italian *vescovo*,
Sicilian *vispiku* (with metathesis of *k* and *p*), Logudoresian *pis-
kamu*, Engadine *ovaisk*, Friulian *veskul*, Spanish *obispo*, Portuguese *bispo*, Catalan, Provençal, and Old French *evesque*, Modern
French *evêque;* Old Irish *epscop*, Modern Irish *easbog*, *easpog*
[æspʌg] (with metathesis), Breton *eskop*, Welsh *esgob;* Albanian
upeshk, *üpeshkup*, *ipeshkvë*, *peshkop*, *pespëk*. Where, however,
it was still felt to be a foreign word, there was close adherence to the
original form, as Gothic *aípiskaúpus* [episkopus], Old Church
Slavic *jepiskupŭ* (but Czech *biskup*, etc., borrowed from German).
Bishop still retains its original meaning in one passage of the
English Bible (1 Peter ii. 25), ' the Shepherd and Bishop of your
souls ' (cf. *bishoprick* Acts i. 20 = *office* Psalms cix. 8). *Priest*
likewise is borrowed from the naturalised Old French *prestre*
(modern *prêtre)* from Latin *presbyterus*, which is a learned borrowing from Greek πρεσβύτερος ' elder '.

The adjective meaning ' relating to a bishop ', on the other
hand, was introduced solely as a learned word, and since it has
always borne a connotation scarcely likely to be used by the
common people, it has retained its foreign guise, as English
episcopal, German, Danish, Swedish *episkopal*, French *épiscopal*,
Spanish, Portuguese *episcopal*, Italian *episcopale;* and, similarly,
the various forms of the adjective meaning ' relating to a priest ',
English *presbyterian*, etc.

(b) Alien. — This type, e.g., *episcopal*, *presbyterian*, is termed
learned (or alien) as contrasted with the naturalised category of
bishop, *priest*, etc. Hence we have in English and in many other
languages what are called *doublets* (sometimes *triplets*, *quadrup-*

lets, and even a few *quintuplets),* i.e., pairs (or more) of words derived at different periods from the same foreign source, but one of them naturalised, and the other (or others) retaining an alien guise. Of these, the naturalised term is usually employed by the people as a whole, who believe it to be of native stock, while its meaning, like that of a genuinely native word, often comes to cover much more than its primary scope. The alien (learned, unnaturalised) word is normally used only by the educated classes, and solely with a technical and restricted meaning. In course of time even an alien word, though still unnaturalised, may so change its connotation that one or even more words may be borrowed from the same foreign word which has already furnished both a naturalised and an alien word. Thus we may quote for English such doublets (giving first the naturalised and then the alien form) as *caitiff, captive; court, cohort; fashion, faction; human, humane; pale, pallid; pity, piety; poison, potion; treason, tradition; palsy, paralysis; blame, blaspheme.* More rarely, we find triplets: *gentle, genteel, gentile; leal, loyal, legal; reason, ration, ratio; sir, sire, senior; spice, specie, species; shrub* (a sort of drink), *syrop, sherbet* (all ultimately from Arabic *šaraba* 'to drink'); more rarely quadruplets: *jaunty, gentle, genteel, gentile;* and, still more rarely, quintuplets: *desk, dish, dais, disc, discus* (cf. also pp. 257–258).

(c) Translations. — Sometimes a word borrowed from another language is not taken over either in its naturalised or in its alien form, as in *bishop* and *episcopal,* but is translated literally into the language borrowing it, as in German *Fern-sprecher* : English *tele-phone;* German *über-setzen* : English *trans-late,* already cited (p. 132). English examples are *gospel* (Anglo-Saxon *god-spell,* Old Saxon *god-spel,* Old High German *got-spel),* literally ' good tidings ', a direct translation of Latin *evangelium,* a learned borrowing from Greek εὐ-αγγέλιον ' good message ' (whence the learned English *evangelical,* etc.) ; and *elder* (as a church official in certain Protestant communions), translating the *presbyterus* cited above (p. 134), and thus really a doublet of *priest.* German is particularly rich in such translations, e.g., *Bauch-redner* ' belly-speaker ' : Latin *ventri-loquus* (whence the learned English *ventriloquist),* *Durch-messer* ' through-measure ' : Greek διά-μετρος (learned English *diameter),* *Nas-horn* ' nose-horn ' : Greek ῥινό-κερως (learned English *rhinoceros),* *zwie-back* or *zwei-back* ' twice-cooked ' :

French *bis-cuit* (learned English *biscuit*); for French, one may cite such words as *presqu-'île* ' almost-island ' : Latin *paen-insula* (learned English *peninsula*).

It is also possible for words to be borrowed by one language from another and then to return, in more or less altered form, to their source. Thus, English *budget*, now meaning ' official financial statement ', but originally ' little bag ' (e.g., in Shakespeare's mention of a tinker's ' sow-skin budget '), borrowed from Old French *bougette* ' little bag ', has been re-borrowed by French in its technical English sense. On the other hand, English *riding-coat* was taken over by French as *rédingote*, and has come back to English as *redingote*, a garment as changed from its original shape as is the name itself. Again, German has borrowed *Spion* ' spy ' from Italian *spione*, French *espion*, themselves formed from German *spähen* (Middle High German *spëhen*) ' to spy ', so that German *Spion* and *Späher* are doublets.

These manifold categories of native, naturalised, alien, and translated words show the stratification present in all languages so far as we have any adequate scientific knowledge of them. Many words, even such a common and widespread term as *wine*, for which no etymology is known, and which cannot be derived from any Indo-European base, are apparently survivors from vanished languages of whose grammar and affinities we know absolutely nothing (cf. pp. 128, 133). Many linguists go still further, and believe that languages wiped out by conquerors, except for scattered words, have modified, not merely the vocabulary (this much scarcely admits of doubt), but also the sounds, forms, and word-order (phonology, morphology, and syntax) of the languages which have succeeded them. Thus, certain phenomena of Armenian phonology (notably the numerous affricates) have been supposed to be due to the linguistic systems of the non-Indo-European peoples of the Caucasus (e.g., Georgians) with whom they have been in contact for centuries; and the syntax of Old Irish, differing in many respects from that of other Indo-European languages, has been explained as due to a non-Indo-European sub-stratum, possibly the Berber of North Africa, a language of Hamitic stock (cf. pp. 84, 366).

However attractive the hypothesis of sub-strata may be, and however plausible its theoretical foundation, strengthened by the demonstrable existence of ethnological sub-strata, it seems scarcely safe as yet to give it full credence, except in the domain of vocabulary. We know, for the most part, little or nothing of the sub-strata; and it is at least significant that both the phonological and the syntactic phenomena which appear, at first glance, alien, and hence explicable only on the theory of sub-strata, seem, when more closely investigated, to be even more readily interpreted by the physiological developments of phonetics and the psychological evolutions of syntax and semantics. This does not mean that the sub-stratum theory is to be rejected, for it may yet prove of value; but in our present state of knowledge, it seems more prudent to view it with much caution, and to use it only as a working hypothesis when all other methods fail.

The problem is further complicated by the fact that we are often unable to determine whether similar or identical phenomena appearing in different areas are the result of development from a common stock, borrowing from a common source, or independent parallel evolutions. Here the maxim *si duo faciunt idem, non est idem* (' if two make the same, it is not the same ') must constantly be borne in mind. Both in English and in Persian *bad* means ' evil '; but the words have absolutely no genetic relation, and the outward identity is merely fortuitous. Again, Modern Romance and Modern Greek alike form the superlative of the adjective from the conjunction of the article with the comparative, as ὁ σοφώτερος : *le plus savant* (literally, ' the wiser '), as contrasted with the Classical Greek superlative σοφώτατος, Latin *sapientissimus*. Here, striking as is the parallel, historical investigation quickly shows that the similarity is due to independent identical development, not to any common source.

As the course of history shows, when dialects or languages meet, a conflict results with varying consequences. Either one language or dialect may suppress the other, even though the conquering language or dialect incorporates into its own vocabulary a larger or a smaller number of words from the vocabulary of the conquered; or the two, after more or less stress and strain, exist side by side. The outcome of the conflict depends, as so often in linguistic history, upon non-linguistic factors, and, in the last analysis, practically always upon the will of the speakers of the languages concerned (cf. p. 33). We may illustrate the principles involved by four examples: the Roman conquest of Gaul, the Norman conquest of England, modern Switzerland, and modern Belgium.

At the time of the Roman conquest of Gaul, the level of the civilisation of the Celtic peoples living there was far inferior to that of Rome, and, what was still more serious from the linguistic point of view, they had evolved neither a literature nor a feeling of unity. They speedily assimilated the higher civilisation of their conquerors, which had been enhanced by amalgamation with the still richer civilisation of Greece; and, less ripe both politically and intellectually, they voluntarily abandoned their language, of which only a few loan-words and the like survive (e.g., French *alou-ette* ' lark ', *banne* ' hamper, basket ', *braies*, ' trousers ', *changer* ' change ', *chemise* ' shirt ', *char* ' waggon ', *chouan* ' owl ', *tonne* ' tun ', *vouge* ' billhook ' : Gaulish *alauda, benna, braca, camb-iare, camisia, carros, cavannos, tunna, vidubion;* and also *quatre-vingt* ' eighty ', apparently on the basis of such Celtic phrases as Old Welsh *petwar-ugein(t)*, Modern Welsh *pedwar ugain*, Old Cornish *padgwar iganz*, Breton *pevar-ugeñt*, Middle Irish *cethri fichit* ' four twenties ').

When the Normans, who had in Normandy almost entirely surrendered their originally Teutonic (Scandinavian) tongue under the pressure of the much higher Romanic civilisation of which they had conquered a part by force of arms, invaded England and militarily overcame it, they found a state of affairs very unlike that which the Romans had met in Gaul. England had passed from the stage of a congeries of tribes, and had become, first, a heptarchy of kingdoms, and, finally, a monarchy; while its civilisation was at least equal to that of the invaders. England accepted the Norman conquerors only under the compulsion of *force majeure* and saw no reason to abandon her own civilisation, including her language. In a relatively short course of time, she absorbed Normans and Norman-French into Englishmen and English, preserving little of Norman civilisation but what she considered superior and worth adopting, including the large number of borrowed words which, side by side with its native vocabulary, have made English so peculiarly rich in its delicate synonyms (cf. p. 126). This wealth comes to the fore very notably in the *Book of Common Prayer* (e.g., in the Exhortation to Confession in Morning and Evening Prayer, the Romance words being italicised: ' to acknowledge and *confess* ', ' not *dissemble* nor cloke ', ' *assemble* and meet together ', ' *pray* and beseech '; cf. also ' *mortify* and kill ', ' *perceive* and know ', ' *power* and might ', where the corresponding prayers in the Roman Missal have simply ' mortifica ', ' videant ', and ' virtutum ' respectively).

Where two or more languages are practically equal in political, economic, and intellectual prestige, they normally continue side by side with little change of linguistic frontiers. This is excellently illustrated by the language-boundaries in Switzerland, where the confines of French, German, Italian, and Rhaeto-Romanic have remained essentially unchanged for centuries.

Where, on the other hand, a language, though possessed of such political, economic, and intellectual prestige, is inferior in one or more of these respects to a neighbouring language, it normally tends to yield to its rival unless reinforced by some other powerful factor, such as regionalistic consciousness (cf. pp. 117–119). This finds illustration in Belgium, which is linguistically divided (not counting Walloon, a Romance dialect) between French and Flemish. The latter is a dialect of Dutch, whose importance is too evident to need emphasis, and whose existence is guaranteed by the political entity of Holland. The Flemings, akin to the Dutch both racially and linguistically, and with points of view differing in many respects from those of the French, have long striven vigorously against the advance of the French language in Belgium. Officially, Belgium is bilingual, public documents and the like being required to appear both in French and in Flemish. Nevertheless, the friction between the two races, with language as the symbol, still continues and finds only too many parallels elsewhere (cf. p. 117), contrasting quite unfavourably with conditions in Wales, likewise divided between two languages (Welsh and English), but with peaceful relations between them.

Social linguistics also has at least an indirect connexion with literature and appreciation of literary style. The term literature covers so much that any precise definition of it becomes well-nigh impossible; but a survey of what the verdict of the world's best judgement has finally dignified as true literature, from Homer and certain portions of the Bible and the Rig-Veda to the present day, would seem to indicate that it must have at least two qualities: on the subjective side, subject-matter which is of permanent appeal to the human mind; on the objective, diction which expresses this subject-matter with the greatest accuracy, delicacy, and beauty possible in the particular language employed as the vehicle of thought. The employment of banal, inaccurate, or incoherent language in writing or speaking betrays a banal, inaccurate, and incoherent mind; and more than a little of what has an ephemeral acclaim as literature is really of pathological interest only. True literature is like true painting, true architecture, or any other production of true art: the more closely and the more rigorously it is examined, the more delicate and the more beautiful it becomes, not merely subjectively, but also objectively.

From the point of view of expression, one might almost define literature as ' the collocation of just the right words to give the exact shade of meaning which the author wishes to convey '; and the more complete the writer's technical knowledge of the language in which he writes, the better is his style, though such knowledge must not be displayed, or the result is pedantry, as in such pathological movements as the Euphuistic period in English literature. If, instead of original composition, a person translates from one language into another, the difficulty of the task is more than doubled; the knowledge requisite for writing in one language must be supplemented by an equally exact knowledge of each delicate shading in another, and the meaning in the one must be transposed into the other. Translation from or into languages so nearly akin as English and French or German is by no means easy; exact rendering from or into such utterly dissimilar languages as English and Hebrew, or English and American Indian, African, or Polynesian, etc., is practically impossible.

Probably the best translation in English, and certainly by all odds the most careful, is the Authorised Version of the Bible, which has rightly become one of the greatest classics of the language. Yet neither it nor its Revised Version exactly reproduces the full connotation of its Hebrew or even of its Greek original; and the same statement holds true of the most important early versions of the Bible, Greek for the Old Testament, and Latin and Armenian for both the Old and New. Each brings out certain shades of the original according to its own genius; each fails in certain others. To gain any approximation to the true meaning of the author of any part of the Bible, one must consult the original; and even then one's knowledge of Hebrew and of Greek must be supplemented by thorough linguistic acquaintance with the Semitic languages generally and with all the history of the Greek language.

Perhaps the only time when one feels that he can make a truly satisfactory translation is when he is beginning a language and knows little about it. 'The horse is grey' can be translated into French or German without trouble, but in Irish the word which ordinarily means 'green' must be used for a grey horse or a grey eye *(glas*, not *liath* [liːə]). Except in the rarest of instances, there are only two types of translation: a wooden version which mechanically reproduces the original without regard to its native shadings or literary style; or a more or less periphrastic rendering which represents the spirit rather than the letter of its source. Indeed, so soon as one has advanced beyond the first rudiments of a language, one begins to paraphrase: French *il y a* ('it has there') and German *es giebt* ('it gives'), where *a* and *giebt* are really impersonal (cf. pp. 229–230, 246–247), are in essence equivalent in meaning to, but not translations of, English *there is (are)*. Persian has such a wealth of synonyms, both native and Arabic, that it is often possible to translate a passage of English literature into it in several ways, each of which is equally correct according to the translator's interpretation of his original; and in Hindūstānī and Urdū, where Sanskrit and Turkish words are used as well as Persian and Arabic, the possibilities of different, but equally correct, versions are further increased.

Broadly speaking, a translation should seek to reproduce the precise meaning of the original, so far as the genius of the two languages permits, even at the expense of strict literalness (except, of course, in purely scientific translations where no attempt is made to show more than the grammatical structure of the language, as in grammatical versions of American Indian); words designedly ambiguous in the original should be translated with corresponding ambiguity, for the translator's business is to reproduce, not to interpret or to explain; and, in poetry, every effort should be made to retain, so far as possible, even the rhythm of the original language. In view of the difficulty of the task, the wonder is not that there are so few really satisfactory translations, but that there are as many as one finds!

From the strictly technical point of view, the linguist is only too often obliged to deal with what is anything but literature in the conventional sense of the term. Many of his most important sources can scarcely be termed literary: dry annals of petty kings; sepulchral inscriptions; legal codes; the Catechisms of Martin Luther, our chief source for our too scanty knowledge of Old Prussian; folk-tales, though these frequently have some human interest; more or less fragmentary vocabularies of languages otherwise lost, as of ancient Macedonian and the Gothic dialect of the Crimea; glosses on the margins of Biblical texts (e.g., for Old Irish and Old High German).

Though the lack of human interest be true, if the linguist blinds himself to another fact, that the purpose of language is to communicate thought to others; if he treats language merely as a cadaver for linguistic dissection; if he deliberately ignores the beauty of living speech, whether oral or written, he is guilty of a grave scientific sin. He must not rest content with dictionaries and grammars, except when other material is absolutely unobtainable. Too many fancy that when they have read a grammar of such-and-such a language, have collected a number of words of its vocabulary, and have stumbled through a few pages of its texts, they can speak with authority upon it. The linguist must know, so far as material permits, the literature, the religion, the law, the history, the archaeology, and all else accessible regarding the peoples who spoke or speak the languages with which he deals; and this knowledge must be neither superficial, hostile, nor contemptuous, but as profound and as sympathetic as possible. Like a good actor, he must seek to throw himself into the spirit of the speakers of those languages, and to become, at least for the moment, one of them, looking at their languages from their point of view, and ignoring his own.

On the other hand, the *littérateur* should constantly remember that language has a material, almost a legalistic, element which must receive due recognition lest his flights of fancy carry him away. Each, then, must at once both inspire and curb the other; neither can accomplish his best possible end without the other's constant aid and restraint. If the student or the writer of literature refuses to consider the delicate and complicated mechanism of the language or languages which he reads or writes, if he is ignorant or contemptuous of the historical development of words and forms and their arrangements, if he cares only that a word please his ear by its sound regardless of its meaning, if he capriciously distorts words and meanings, he wilfully sunders himself from that which will give him a deeper and keener appreciation of literature, whether he reads and criticises it, or seeks to produce it.

When we find those who regard themselves as *littérateurs* decrying the value of rigid linguistic training as mere juggling with sounds and forms; or when we see, as is too frequently the case, those who profess to be linguists regarding students and writers of literature as nothing more than shallow aesthetes, slaves of mere subjective impressions, and governed only by the sensuous impressions of style (whatever that vague term may mean), we may safely say that neither is a complete master of his trade. Between true literature and true linguistics there is no conflict; the real linguist is at least half a *littérateur*, and the real *littérateur* at least half a linguist.

CHAPTER VI

Morphology: The Parts of Speech

The five divisions of the structure of language — phonology vital for all scientific linguistics — definition of morphology — the nature of the word and of the syllable — how new words are coined — clipped words — components of the word — base and inflexion — problem of the origin of inflexion — possible traces of a pre-inflexional stage in Indo-European — structure of the inflexionless Aranta of Central Australia — transition from the inflexional to the analytic type of language — full and empty words — the determinative — the morpheme — some Indo-European determinatives — bases originally chiefly disyllabic in Indo-European and Semitic — formula for a word — proper and improper compounds — distinction between compounds and non-compounds — productive components of proper compounds — categories of proper compounds — improper and separable compounds — parts of speech — necessity of replacement of their conventional classification by one based on morphology and history — origin of the conventional classification — the interjection not properly a part of speech — division of parts of speech into nominal and verbal — nouns and adjectives not essentially different — close connexion between nouns and verbs — nouns arise from adjectives, both descriptive in origin (epithetologues) — relation between adjectives and verbs — adverbs, prepositions, and conjunctions — grammatical differences between pronouns and epithetologues — deictic character of pronouns — categories of pronouns — the pronoun of the third person originally demonstrative, not personal — possessive pronouns originally identical with the genitive case of the epithetologue — relatives, interrogatives, and demonstratives — plural of pronouns — gender of non-personal pronouns — connexion of the feminine singular with the neuter plural and the sex-denoting feminine demonstrative pronoun — neuter and broken plural epithetologues with singular verbs — late origin of grammatical feminine gender — chronological order of development of pronouns — numerals — character of verbs — epithetologues and verbs developed from a single category of onomatorrhemes — the epithetologue historically prior to the verb — all parts of speech perhaps developed from a single source.

LANGUAGE, as we have seen in the third and fourth chapters on phonetics and phonology and on the relation of language to thought respectively, has two aspects: physiological or mechanical, and psychological or non-mechanical. When we come to study the actual structure of language, which constitutes the domain of linguistics in the strict sense of the term, we find that each of these aspects has two sub-divisions: *phonology* and *morphology* for the mechanical side; *syntax* and *semantics* for the psychological; and in addition to these, there is a fifth subject of investigation, *etymology*, which is essentially historical in character.

Phonology is the linguistic study of the system of sounds found in a given linguistic family as a whole, or in a given division of the same, or in a given language or dialect of such a division. The results of that study appear as systems of correspondences obtained and formulated by the method outlined on pp. 74–83. Since accurate phonology is the very foundation of all exact linguistics, the first step of the linguist should be to draw up a list, as complete as possible, of correspondences between the language or languages with which he is dealing and some other group or members of a group (e.g., between Modern English and Anglo-Saxon, between Anglo-Saxon and some other Teutonic language or languages or with Proto-Teutonic, or between it and other members of the Indo-European linguistic family and with Proto-Indo-European; cf. pp. 75, 281).

Phonology must not be confused with *phonetics*. The latter deals with the physical and physiological (vocal and auditional) properties of sounds in themselves; the former, with the rôle which sounds play in individual languages or groups of languages. The phonetic value of [b], for instance, depends upon its mode of phonation by the speaker and upon the acoustic effect which it produces upon the auditor, i.e., upon its value as a phoneme (cf. pp. 61–62); its phonological value is dependent upon its historical origin and development; a Teutonic [b], for instance, may come either from an Indo-European [bh], as in English *brother* : Sanskrit *bhrǎtar-*, or, by Verner's Law (pp. 78–82), from an Indo-European [p], as Gothic and Old High German *sibun* (Modern German *sieben*, English *seven)* : Sanskrit *saptá*, Latin *septem.*

Morphology, the subject of this chapter, is based immediately upon phonology and deals with the grouping of individual sounds into sound-complexes which are regarded by all who speak, hear, or read the language or languages having those complexes as possessing definite, and purely conventional, meanings (cf. pp. 14–15); in other terms, *morphology deals with the forms and formation of words.*

So far as the great majority of languages is concerned, a *word*

may be defined, with Antoine Meillet, as ' the result of the association of a given meaning with a given group of sounds susceptible
of a given grammatical employment '; or, as the present writer
would put it, ' a complex of sounds which in itself possesses a
meaning fixed and accepted by convention '. A word is the smallest
thought-unit vocally expressible, and is composed of one or more
sounds, combined in one or more syllables.[1]

The definition of a *syllable* has been much debated and is none
too easy, especially as its limits are not the same in all languages.
Essentially it consists of a vowel or of a continuant (cf. pp. 53–54)
either alone or in conjunction with one or more consonants, e.g.,
English *o'* [ɔ], *too* [tuː], *top* [tɔp], *stop* [stɔp], *stopped* [stɔpt],
hmp! [hm̩p], *shh!* [ʃː]. This vocalic or continuant element constitutes the *syllabic peak*, i.e., the element of greatest sonority in
the sound-complex, whether the other components be pure consonants or merely continuants (e.g., in English *ran*, though *r* and *n*
are continuants and possessed under certain circumstances of
vocalic value, the sonority of *a* is superior to that of either of
them). In case of a diphthong (cf. pp. 56–57), the sonority of one
of the vocalic elements is superior to that of the other, but the
sonority even of the second is superior to that of the pure consonants or of the continuants, as in English *roam*, whose relative

---

[1] The author is indebted to his friend, Dr. Hans J. Uldall, for the following
criticism in a letter of 16 January, 1935: the definition of a word given in
the text, he writes, ' seems to me all right for European languages, as far as
I know them, and apart from such anomalies as an *-ism*, which are really also
words; but it will not hold for other languages of a different structure. When
you have either an agglutinating language or a polysynthetic one [cf. p. 300]
(not that I love those terms, but they will do), where the individual elements
are phonetically strong and reasonably unvarying, your definition fits the
element (stem, affix) better than the syntactic unit formed by a string of
such elements. There are languages, I still maintain (and Maidu [spoken in
north-eastern California] is one of them), in which the word as such is not
a relevant unit of analysis. I think I can best explain what I mean by telling
you how it is in Maidu. There I can split the sentence up into units which
each play a syntactic role (subject, object, etc.); these syntagms can be
defined as a group of elements terminating in an inflexional ending expressing either mood, case, or connection. But they are not words in the conventional sense, because the constituent elements are very strong and absolutely
invariable, and because an element that forms part of a syntagm may at the
same time form part of a phrase in which the syntagm does not enter; e.g.
[(*wɛntin is*)-*wɔːt'ɔ*]-*m* "(he) told (them) to live well " : *wɛn-ti-n* " well "
is an independent syntagm (as shown by the connective ending -*n*) qualifying
is- " to live ", but not *is-wɔːt'ɔ-m* " told to live ", so that *is-* is both a member of the syntagm *is-wɔːt'ɔm* and of the phrase *wɛntin is-*. This means, as

sonority may be graphically expressed as [rōu̯m] or ['roum] ; such a syllable is bipeaked.

In words of more than one syllable, the syllabic peak of some one syllable (which one, depends upon the accentual system of the language concerned) receives an accent which still further increases the sonority of its vocalic element; the vocalic element of the less stressed syllables has what may roughly be termed normal sonority; and that of syllables entirely unstressed, reduced sonority, e.g., English *hatefullest* would be something like [hēi̯t-fʌl-lₑst]. The sonority seems to be entirely relative; but whatever the relation of the various syllabic peaks to each other, each peak apparently remains more sonorous than the consonants accompanying it.

However difficult the definition of the syllable may be, it is very significant that it is a real entity in speech-consciousness. Cases of aphasia are reported in which the patient, though unable to pronounce a given word, taps with his finger or moves his vocal organs precisely as many times as the word contains syllables. Not only are English blank verse and the sonnet-form based upon the number of syllables in a verse, but the same statement holds true of very early poetry, e.g., in the Rigveda, the Avesta, and the most primitive types of Greek verse as preserved, in part, in the choruses of the drama, etc. After the pictographic stage of writing

I see it, that the functions of the word in our languages are divided between two different units in Maidu: the grammatical element (especially the stem) and the composite syntagm. Furthermore, this formal difference corresponds exactly to a difference in the distribution of meaning: each grammatical element (apart from the formative endings) has a definite meaning corresponding very well to that of our words, while the syntactic function and its meaning is carried by the syntagm.

' All this, naturally, makes a difference to the definition of the parts of speech as well. The elements can be divided into two main groups: nouns (i.e., substantives, adjectives, pronouns, numerals) and verbs on the basis of their ability to combine among themselves: the verbal elements combine very readily, the nominal elements only within very narrow limits. On the next plane we get syntagms with case-endings (which may be composed of verbal elements) and syntagms with mode-endings (which may contain noun-stems) plus a third class ending in connectives; the connective endings are on the same plane as the case- and mode-endings, they serve to combine both, for instance, two subjects with the sentence-verb (predicate) common to them both, and two verbs to the subject common to them both. Finally, on the last plane, we have the categories of rank. So you see that the characteristics of the word, as we know it, are shifted about considerably and redistributed in a way that is very puzzling until you have gotten used to it. After I have seen this, you can imagine that I am very shy of defining a " word ".'

(seen, for instance, in hieroglyphic Egyptian, traceable in early Chinese, and probably present in Mayan hieroglyphs), apparently came syllabic script. This is found, for example, in the native ancient Cyprian writing, in the Sanskrit alphabet, and in the Sumerian, where each character represents a syllable, not a sound. If, for instance, I wish to write the Sanskrit word *nábhas* ' cloud ' in the ordinary Dēvanāgarī script, I use only three characters: one for *na*, one for *bha*, and one for *sa*, indicating by a special sign that *sa* here has no vowel (that it is, in other words, non-syllabic, and is to be pronounced merely *s)*. So far as the evidence of the earliest inferable forms of hypothetically reconstructed Indo-European and Semitic bases goes, it would appear that, at least in these language-groups, the syllable consisted of a single vowel or of one or more consonants plus a single vowel, this being still more evident when the base is augmented by determinatives (cf. pp. 156–159).

How words arose, and how they came to have meanings, are questions involved with the insoluble problem of the origin of language itself (see also pp. 38–41). New words are constantly coined, but these are almost invariably compounds of old elements and are made according to recognised methods, though often strongly affected by analogy with words of more or less similar meaning. This is particularly the case with the majority of scientific terms, e.g., *arteriosclerosis* ' hardening of the arteries ', from Greek ἀρτηρία ' artery ' and σκλήρωσις ' hardening ' from σκληρός ' hard '.

This type of formation is linguistically correct, both elements being drawn from the same language. There are, however, many formations, linguistically unjustifiable, whose components are taken from different languages. Such words are termed *hybrids*, such as *acidosis* ' excess of acidity ', from Latin *acidus* ' sour ' plus the Greek termination -ōsis, or *electrocute* from Greek ἤλεκτρον ' amber ' (electricity having been discovered by rubbing amber) plus -*cute* from Vulgar Latin *executāre* ' to execute ' (itself a late denominative formation from Latin *ex[s]ecūtus* ' punished '). The whole word is modelled on the analogy of *execute*, misinterpreted as *exe-cute* instead of the correct division *ex-[s]ecute*, probably by popular etymology (see pp. 270–272) with Latin -*cutiō* ' strike ' for *quatiō*, seen in *per-cutiō, con-cutiō, dis-cutiō, ex-cutiō*, etc. Occasionally a coined word is vaguely affected by some term of more or less similar sound and meaning, as *gas*, invented by the

Brussels chemist van Helmont (died 1644) under the influence of
Greek χάος ' chaos ', which also meant ' air ' in the technical language of mediaeval alchemists (in Flemish *g* is [ɣ], the voiced
plosive corresponding to the Modern Greek χ [x]), whence such
hybrids as *gasometer*, etc.

The process of creation of true new words can seldom be stated
definitely for lack of precise evidence, but at least two examples
are known with certainty. Part of the first stanza of the nonsense-
verses of ' Jabberwocky ' in ' Lewis Carroll's ' *Through the Looking
Glass* is carefully explained by the author himself:

> ' 'Twas brillig, and the slithy toves
>   Did gyre and gimble in the wabe;
> All mimsy were the borogoves,
>   And the mome raths outgrabe'.

' *Brillig*,' Alice is told by Humpty Dumpty, ' means four o'clock
in the afternoon — the time when you begin *broiling* things for
dinner. . . . *Slithy* means lithe and slimy. . . . You see it's like a
portmanteau — there are two meanings packed up into one word.
. . . To *gyre* is to go round and round like a gyroscope. To *gimble* is
to make holes like a gimlet. . . . *Mimsy* is flimsy and miserable
(there's another portmanteau for you). . . . *Mome* I'm not certain
about. I think it's short for " from home ".' Concerning the origin
of the rest of the obscure vocabulary, Humpty Dumpty is dis-
creetly silent.

The other certain example of a coined word is *kodak*. This was
invented by George Eastman in 1888, and its genesis was described by Eastman himself in a published interview as follows:
' I devised the name myself. A trade-mark should be short, vigorous, incapable of being misspelled to an extent that will destroy
its identity and — in order to satisfy trade-mark laws — it must
mean nothing. . . . The letter " K " had been a favorite with me —
it seems a strong, incisive sort of letter. Therefore, the word I
wanted had to start with " K". Then it became a question of trying
out a great number of combinations of letters that made words
starting and ending with " K ". The word " Kodak " is the result '.

In recent years, words have been formed from the initial sounds
of groups of words, e.g., *Anzac* from A(ustralian and) N(ew)
Z(ealand) A(rmy) C(orps), *Nabisco* from Na(tional) Bis(cuit)
Co(mpany), *Hapag* from H(amburg-)a(merikanische) Pa(ket-
fahrts)g(esellschaft) ; but these have small linguistic interest.

Portmanteau-words, or *blends,* of the type of *bruncheon,* a combination of *br(eakfast)* and *(l)uncheon,* are due to a fusion of words of separate origin with a general meaning somewhat similar, other instances being *parabrella,* a contamination of *para(sol)* and *(um)-brella,* and *snerpent,* a confusion of *snake* and *serpent.* Passing mention may be made of *clipped words* like *bus* for *omnibus, cab* for *cabriolet, mob* for *mob(ile vulgus)* ' fickle crowd ', *bike* for *bicycle, Bart's* for *St. Bartholomew's Hospital,* and such vulgarisms as *vet* for *vet(erinary surgeon), doc* for *doctor,* and the like.

In Indo-European and Semitic, as in many other linguistic families, historical evidence shows that a word *must* consist of at least two parts: *base* and *inflexion* (also termed *semanteme* and, popularly, *root,* the element containing the general meaning of the word; and *morpheme,* the element which gives definite form to that meaning), e.g., Latin *agimus* ' we perform ' = *agi-* (base) plus *-mus* (inflexion). This *base,* obtained by abstracting the inflexional element, can be used alone in only two instances: as the second singular active imperative of the verb *(age* ' perform! ') or as the vocative singular of the noun *(domine* ' master! '), both mere exclamations. The inflexion can never be employed independently; *-mus,* for example, cannot be used in isolation to mean ' we '. By taking such bases of individual words in various languages of a given group, and by comparing them with corresponding bases in all languages possessing them, with strict attention to all the phonetic correspondences involved, one reconstructs an hypothetical Indo-European (or Semitic, etc.) base; e.g., the Indo-European base of the Latin base *agi-* may be reconstructed as *$a\hat{g}e$-*. Such a base is the form from which a given historic word *may* be derived, not *must* be, for only too often words are ambiguous in derivation, i.e., they may as plausibly be derived from one given base as from another (cf. pp. 290–293). Many linguists distinguish between *roots* and *stems* (thus, *ag-* would be the root of *agimus,* and *agi-* its stem) ; but the distinction seems unnecessary, since both, upon analysis, are seen to be merely different grades (cf. also pp. 65–66) of the same base. Equally needless appears to be the *radical* which some scholars distinguish as the invariable part of a given word, as *act-* in Latin *actor* ' performer ' for *$ag-tor$-*.

The meaning of the base is general and vague; it is neither verb nor noun nor any other part of speech. To become one, it must

receive, in the majority of languages, an *inflexion*, an element also
meaningless in itself, at least in the historic period and so far back
as our powers of reconstruction go, such as the Latin -*mus* just
cited. The rôle of inflexion is to denote the various relations of
nouns, pronouns, verbs, etc., as Latin *amōr* ' love ', *amōr-is* ' of
love ', *amōr-ī* ' for love ', *amōr-e* ' by love ', *amōr-es* ' loves ', *amōr-
um* ' of loves ', etc., or *am-ō, amā-s, amāt* ' I love, thou lovest, he
loves ', etc. Indo-European inflexions are mostly affixed, as in the
examples just given; but they may also be prefixed. Here, prefixes
of the type of Sanskrit *a-ricat*, Greek ἔ-λιπε, and Armenian *e-likʻ*
' he left ' (only with monosyllabic forms in Armenian) are termed
augments; those of the type of Sanskrit *da-daú*, Greek δέ-δωκε,
Latin *de-dit*, and Gaulish δε-δε ' he has given ' are called *reduplica-
tions.* Prefixed inflexions are very common in Semitic and some
other language-groups, as in Arabic *ya-ktub-u* ' he will write ',
ta-ktub-u ' thou wilt write ' as contrasted with *katab-a* ' he has
written ', *katab-ta* ' thou hast written '.

If one contrasts the radical of the Latin nominative *amōr* with
the genitive *amōris*, or the English verbal *(I, we, ye, they) bear*
with *(thou) bearest, (he) bears*, one would, at first glance, incline
to doubt the statement that inflexion is an indispensable part of a
word. When, however, one compares *amōr, amōris* with such cognate formations as Latin *pēs, pedis*, or English *bear* with Gothic
baíra [bera], *baíram, baíriþ, baírand* : *baíris, baíriþ*, one sees that
amōr is for *amōr-s just as *pēs* comes from an earlier *ped-s, and
that the English verb-forms have likewise lost their inflexions (contrast Old High German *hilfu, helfames, helfet, helfant* : *hilf(i)s(t),
hilfit* with English [*I, we, ye, they*] *help* : *helpest, helps)*. In such
cases, a word is said to have *zero-inflexion;* and one must bear in
mind that in linguistics, as everywhere else, absence of a characteristic is as truly distinctive as is its presence. Synchronically (cf. pp.
23–24), it may be true to affirm that English is, in the main, an
inflexionless language; diachronically, it may be described, from
this point of view, as a language possessed in great measure of
zero-inflexions. *Final judgement upon languages must be based, so
far as evidence permits, upon diachronic, not upon synchronic,
considerations.*

What, then, shall we say of such a language as Chinese, which
has no inflexions? Is it a language without inflexion, or one with
zero-inflexion? Lack of evidence forbids definite answer, but

though it was formerly regarded as a most primitive language of the pre-inflexional stage, many Sinologists now incline to the opinion that it has reached a still higher stage of zero-inflexion even than English; i.e., that it was once highly inflected, but has now lost its inflexions (cf. p. 390).

This brings us to the problem of the *origin of inflexion*. For this question no certain answer has yet been found; the best that we can thus far do is to weigh the probabilities suggested by the mass of material as a whole, remembering always the gaps in our knowledge and the dangers inherent in any argumentation from analogy. Bearing all this in mind, there seems to be some evidence, especially from the so-called primitive languages, that inflexional elements are mutilated survivals of words once independent, but later agglutinated to the base. This comes out very clearly in such examples of verbs as the following, taken from linguistic families as far apart as Africa and America:

(1) Vaï (of the Nigero-Senegalese group):

m-fa ' my father '	*n-do* (for *m-ro) ' I say ' (i.e., ' my say ')
i-fa ' thy father '	*i-ro* ' thou sayest ' (i.e., ' thy say ')
a-fa ' his father '	*a-ro* ' he says ' (i.e., ' his say ')
mu-fa ' our father '	*mu-ro* ' we say ' (i.e., ' our say ')
wu-fa ' your father '	*wu-ro* ' ye say ' (i.e., ' your say ')
an-fa ' their father '	*an-do* (for *an-ro) ' they say ' (i.e., ' their say ')

(2) Maipure (Orinoco sub-division of Arawak):

nu-ani ' my son '	*nu-nawa* ' I see ' (i.e., ' my see ')
pi-ani ' thy son '	*pi-nawa* ' thou seest ' (i.e., ' thy see ')
ani '(his) son '	*nawa* ' (he) sees ' (i.e., ' [his] see ')
wa-ani ' our son '	*wa-nawa* ' we see ' (i.e., ' our see ')
e-ani ' your son '	*e-nawa* ' ye see ' (i.e., ' your see ')
ni-ani ' their son '	*ni-nawa* ' they see ' (i.e., ' their see ')

In the noun the evidence is far less clear. Nevertheless, there is some reason to suppose that the various case-endings may have been at first independent full words which gradually, through constant use in stereotyped positions and fixed meanings became empty (cf. p. 155) and are so worn down that their original significations have long since disappeared. This was apparently the case, for example, in the Tibetan and Dravidian linguistic families, and it is clearly seen in such instances as the Uralic Hungarian locative of the type of *kēz-bɛn* ' in the hand ', where *-bɛn* was

originally the adverb *bɛnn* ' within ', itself the locative of *bēl*
' interior '. The same statement holds true of the instrumental,
dative, and ablative formatives in Āhom (of the Tai group), *tāng*
' with ', *tī* ' place ', *luk(-tām)* ' place ' (e.g., *tāng khân* ' with a
cudgel ', *tī po kam* ' to my father ', *luk-tām Kāshmīr* ' from Kāshmīr '). Similarly, the Modern Persian accusative singular of the
type of *šāh-rā* [ʃɔːhrɔː] ' regem ', which in Old Persian would be
**xšāyaθiyahyā rādiy* ' for the King's sake ' (cf. Old Persian
avahyarādiy ' therefore ', Old Church Slavic *cego radi* ' therefore '), where *-rā* is now a mere case-ending, is evidently in origin
a collocation of two separate words. For reasons which will be
explained later (pp. 192–194, 195–198), these observations do not
necessarily hold good for the nominative, accusative, and genitive
cases.

Instances like those just quoted are rare, and it is quite uncertain how far sweeping conclusions may be drawn from them. The
Semitic verb seems to show agglutination of the base with pronouns (e.g., Arabic *'an-ta* ' thou ' : *ta-ktubu* ' thou wilt write ',
katab-ta ' thou hast written ') ; but if ever a similar condition prevailed in Indo-European, all traces of it have long vanished.
Attempts have frequently been made to connect the first personal
ending in *-m-* (e.g., Sanskrit *ásmi*, Armenian *em*, Greek εἰμί
[eːˈmi], Latin *sum*, English *am* — the lone survivor of this type in
English) with the pronoun of the first person singular (e.g.,
English *me*). This explanation breaks down in the second person
(Sanskrit *bhárasi*, Armenian *beres*, Gothic *baíris* [beris], English
beares-t), for the pronoun of the second person in Indo-European
is characterised by a dental, not by a sibilant (Sanskrit *tvám* [i.e.,
tu-ám], Armenian *du*, Latin *tu*, English *thou* — in Attic Greek
σύ [sy] the *s* is not original, the dental being preserved in the
Doric form τύ).

Traces of a pre-inflexional stage possibly survive in Indo-
European. Such would seem to be the case notably in prepositions
like *apo ' from ' (Sanskrit *ápa*, Greek ἀπό, Old High German *aba*,
Gothic *af*, English *of*); in the numerals from ' five ' to ' nineteen '
(cf. p. 177), which appear to have had no inflexion in Indo-
European (though ' eight ' seems to be a dual: Sanskrit *aṣṭaú*,
Greek ὀκτώ, Latin *octō*, Gothic *ahtau*), as **septḿ̥* (Sanskrit *saptá*,
Greek ἑπτά, Latin *septem*, Gothic *sibun*, English *seven*); and in
such verb-forms as Hittite *esa* ' sits ' (contrast Sanskrit *áste*,

Greek ἧσται), *kisa* ' becomes ', Sanskrit *(a)duha* ' he milked ', *aiṣa*
' he ruled ', and possibly passives like Sanskrit *ákāri* ' was made '
(cf. pp. 171, 219–220). It may even be that such forms were originally not what we should term verbs, but were, rather, verbal
nouns, so that *esa, (a)duha,* and *ákāri* primarily meant '(there is)
a sitting, (there was) a milking, a making '.

Despite the paucity of really cogent evidence, one may not be
wholly unjustified in suggesting that the earliest languages knew
only inflexionless words; that certain of these words (notably
verbs and pronouns, nouns and other nouns, or nouns and prepositions) became closely associated, much as in the English types
I see, homeward, of children, etc.; and that some of these (especially the pronouns and certain nouns) suffered such wear from
frequent and stereotyped usage that only the slightest vestiges of
them remained if, indeed, any traces whatsoever of their original
form survived. The result was inflexion as we see it in Latin, etc.

In this connexion, particular interest attaches to a study of one
of the most primitive languages known, the rapidly vanishing
Aranta of Central Australia, by the Indo-Europeanist Alf Sommerfelt of Oslo (cf. pp. 399, 449). This language is of extremely
simple phonemic structure, having, in reality, only the three
vowels [a], [i], and [u], the semivowels [w] and [j], the plosives
[p], [t], and [k] (apparently, rather, [p], [t], [ḳ], or [ḅ], [ḍ],
[g̣]), the affricate [tʃ], the nasals [m], [n], and [ŋ], and the
liquids [l] and [r]. Aranta can express only actions and states,
but not things, except in so far as they can be regarded as actions
or states; e.g., *aranga* ' paternal grandfather ' is, in reality, *(a)ra*
' being before ' plus *nka* ' carrying or being at a distance '; *tara*
' two ', really *ta* ' bursting out, becoming visible ' plus *ra,* i.e.,
' being visible (and) being before '; *mara* ' good ', *ma* ' giving
more ' plus *ra; nala* ' that one ', *na* ' sitting, existing ' plus *la* ' going
in '; *albuka* ' he returned ', *(a)lba* ' curving within, returning ' plus
ka ' cutting off ' (i.e., ' ceasing ') ; *tukala* ' he beat ', *(a)tu* ' beating ' plus *ka* plus *la; atuala* ' in the man ', *(a)tu* plus *wa* ' being
more ' (i.e., a man is a superior fighter) plus *la.*

It is thus evident that Aranta has neither parts of speech nor
inflexions, but that it forms its words by a simple juxtaposition of
bases; and it knows no subordinate clauses (cf. p. 234). Some idea
of its structure may be gained by analysing a sentence meaning
' that man there, who returned yesterday, beat the boy ' *(atua*

nala nana tmurka albuka worana tukala ' man that there yesterday returned boy beat ') : ' beating-more *(atua)* existing-going-in
(nala) existing-existing *(nana)* yesterday-cutting-off *(tmurka)*
returning-cutting-off *(albuka)* boy-being *(worana)* beating-cut-
ting-off-going-in *(tukala)'*. So meagre is the language that it is
frequently impossible to determine the meaning of its words without knowledge of the circumstances under which they are spoken,
further assistance frequently being given by accompanying gestures; but it would seem that its entire vocabulary is essentially
epithetologic in character (cf. p. 169).

When inflexion has once definitely begun, we can trace its evolution fairly well. Inflexional terminations steadily tend to lose
their values and to undergo such deformation as frequently to
drop *(deflexion;* cf. pp. 152, 237, 301), the inflexions of verbs being
replaced by pronouns, and those of nouns by prepositions. Here we
pass from the inflexional to the analytic type of language (cf. pp.
300–301), although even languages predominantly analytic, such
as English, still preserve more or less inflexion (e.g., *who : whom;
he : him; father : father's : fathers : fathers'; I come : thou com-
est : he comes).* Speaking in most general terms, language may, in
many particulars, be said to develop in cyclic form.

Transition from the inflexional to the analytic type may be
traced historically with especial clarity in the development of
Romance from Latin, e.g., French *je vois* = Late Latin *ego
video* = Classical Latin *video; j'ai vu* = *ego habeo visum* = *vidi;
de monde* = *de mundo* = *mundi,* where *je, ai,* and *de* no longer
mean ' I ' (emphatic), ' possess ', and ' from ', but simply indicate
the first person singular, the perfect, and the possessive respectively. The exact French equivalent of Classical Latin *ego video*
would be *moi, je vois,* but that of *video,* merely *je vois.* Not infrequently, such a word preserves traces of its original complete signification, as English *of* in *ten minutes of five* (i.e., ' ten minutes from
five '; cf. French *cinq heures moins dix,* and such cognates as Sanskrit *ápa,* Latin *ab,* Gothic *af* ' from '), and the archaic *wisdom is
justified of* (i.e., from) *her children.* Adopting technical terms employed by Chinese grammarians, words of this type are frequently
called *full* when they retain their complete and distinct meanings,
and *empty* when they degenerate into mere indicators (e.g., English
have is full in *I have a book,* but empty in *I have had a book).*

Many words consist simply of a base plus an inflexion, such as

Latin *pēs* (from **ped-s)* and *agi-mus* cited above. Besides these, there are others, much more numerous, which contain another element (sometimes more than one such element), normally inserted between the base and the inflexion, which modifies or determines the meaning of the base in some manner or other. This element is called a *determinative*. Thus we have in Latin, from the Latin base **can-*, such a series as *can-ō* 'I sing', *can-t-ō* 'I sing loudly', *can-t-it-ō* 'I sing repeatedly', *can-t-ill-ō* 'I sing softly '; or from the Latin base **horre-*, *horre-ō* 'I shudder', *horre-sc-ō* 'I begin to shudder', where *-t-* and *-sc-* specify and limit the *type* of action denoted by the base. Similarly, from the Latin base **amā-* ' love ' we have such a series as *amā-re* 'to love', *amā-ba-m* 'I used to love', *amā-v-ī* 'I have loved', *amā-tūr-i-ō* 'I wish to love', *amā-tu-s* 'loved', *amā-bili-s* 'lovely', *amā-bili-tāt-is* 'of loveliness', *amā-nt-is* 'of one loving', *amā-tōr-is* 'of a loving man', *amā-tōr-iu-s* 'relating to a lover', *amā-trīc-is* 'of a loving woman', *amā-si-u-s* 'lover', *amā-si-uncu-lu-s* 'dear little lover', *amī-cu-s* 'friend', *amī-ci-ti-a* 'friendship', *amī-c-āli-s* 'friendly', *amī-c-ōsu-s* 'rich in friends', *am-ōr-is* 'of love', *am-ōr-ā-bundu-s* 'loving', etc.; and some of these, such as *amā-bili-tāt-is*, *amā-tōr-iu-s*, *amā-si-uncu-lu-s*, *amī-c-āli-s*, *amī-c-ōsu-s*, and *am-ōr-ā-bundu-s*, have more than one determinative.

In Indo-European, determinatives are normally placed after the base, but to this rule there is at least one exception, the nasal infix *-n-*, as in Sanskrit *yu-ná-k-ti*, Latin *iu-n-g-it*, Lithuanian *jù-n-gi-a* 'yokes' as contrasted with Sanskrit *yugá-*, Latin *iugum* 'yoke' (cf. Greek ζεύγ-νυ-μι 'I yoke' : ζυγόν 'yoke'); Hittite *ni-nin-k-anzi* 'they raise' : Sanskrit *nā́śati* 'attains', Old Church Slavic *nes-ti* 'to carry'; Greek τυ-γ-χ-άν-ω 'hit, chance upon' : τύχη 'chance, fortune'; Old Irish *-boi-n-g*, Sanskrit *bha-ná-k-ti* 'breaks' : Armenian *beki* 'I broke' (present *bekanem)*, *bek* 'broken'; English *spri-n-g* : Sanskrit *sprh-aya-ti* 'makes eager', Greek σπέρχω 'set in motion'; English *sta-n-d* : Sanskrit *tí-ṣṭha-ti* 'stands'. In Semitic, infixation is common in the verb, as Arabic *iq-ta-raba* 'cause oneself to come near, approach' from the base *qariba* 'be near'.

Determinatives may also be prefixed to the base. This is a regular process in Semitic, for instance, as in Arabic *ma-ktab-uⁿ* 'writing-place', *ta-ktīb-uⁿ* 'to teach writing' from the base *kataba* 'write'; and especially in the verb, e.g., Syriac *sa-rheβ* 'hasten' (base *rahaba*), Hebrew *hi-qrīβ* 'bring near' (base *qariba*), Arabic *ta-'arraba* ' behave like an Arab' (base *'araba*), Hebrew *ni-χtaβ*, Arabic *in-katab-a* ' be written ', *'a-ktab-a* ' cause to write ' (base *kataba*). It is even possible to have a combination of several prefixed determinatives, as in Mishnāic Hebrew *ni-š-ta-'bēδ* ' become a slave ' (base *'abada*).

All these various modifiers of a base — inflexions, determinatives, prefixes, infixes, affixes, etc. — are classed together as *morphemes* (cf. p. 150), a term extended to include the various prepositions, pronouns, etc., which serve as substitutes for inflexion in analytic languages, as *of* and *we* in English *of love* and *we perform* as contrasted with Latin *amōr-is* and *agi-mus*.

The meaning, or at least the effect, of some determinatives is known. Thus Indo-European

-ent- or *-ont-* gives a base the force of a present active participle (e.g., Latin *fer-ent-is* ' of one carrying ', Gothic *baír-and-s* ' carrying ').

-to- gives the force of a past passive participle (e.g., Latin *amā-tu-s*, English *love-d*).

-i̯es-, *-i̯os-*, *-is-* give comparative force (e.g., Sanskrit *svā́dī-yas*, Latin *suāv-ior*, Old High German *suoz-ir-o*, Modern High German *süss-er*, English *sweet-er*).

-(i)i̯o- means ' relating to ' (e.g., Sanskrit *pítr-ya-*, Latin *patr-iu-s* ' relating to a father ', perhaps connected ultimately with the relative pronoun **i̯o-* and with such forms as the Homeric genitive λύκοιο ' of a wolf ' for **λυκοσ-ι̯ο* [cf. p. 196]).

-no- often has the force of ' made of ' (e.g., Latin *aē-nu-s* ' brazen ' for **ai̯es-no-s* [cf. Latin *aes*, Sanskrit *áyas-* ' metal ']; English *braze-n*, *silver-n*).

-is-qo- (a compound determinative, whose first component is identical with the comparative *-is-* already mentioned) has relative and diminutive significations (e.g., Gothic *mann-isk-s* ' human ', English *mann-ish;* Greek ἀστερ-ίσκο-ς ' little star ', borrowed in English *aster-isk*).

-tor- or *-ter-* denotes an agent or actor (e.g., Sanskrit *dā́-tar-*, Latin *da-tor* ' giver ', *ōrā-tor* ' speaker ', *amā-tor* ' lover ').

-tu- is abstract in force (e.g., Sanskrit *mán-tu-* ' counsel ', Latin *ad-ven-tu-s* ' a coming to '; Latin *por-tu-s*, Old High German *fur-t*, English *for-d* ' passage '; Gothic *dau-þu-s*, English *dea-th*).

Among verbal determinatives we may note *-n-* and *-sk-* as denoting the point from or to which action proceeds, so that they characterise terminative verbs (Sanskrit *yu-ñ-ja-ti*, Latin *iu-n-g-it* ' starts to put a yoke on and carries the process through ' [cf. pp. 156, 207]; Sanskrit *gá-ccha-ti* [for **gṃ-ske-ti*], Greek βά-σκε

' starts to go and keeps on going '; Latin *crē-sc-ō* ' I grow ', *nā-sc-or*
' I am born '; Gothic *þri-sk-an*, Old High German *dre-sk-an*,
Modern High German *dre-sch-en*, English *thre-sh)*. Semitic likewise possesses determinatives. Thus we have Hebrew *śūr* (for
**śa-ụa-ra)*, Arabic *na-šara*, *wa-šara* ' saw ' (base **śara)*; Hebrew
yā-'aṭ ' cover ', *'āṭ-āḥ* ' wrap oneself ' (base **'aṭa)*; Hebrew
hā-laχ ' go, come ', Arabic *la-'a-ka*, *'a-laka* ' send ' (base **laka)*;
Hebrew *'ā-naq*, *nā-'a-q* ' groan ', Arabic *naqqa* ' croak ' (base
**naqa)*.

It would also appear that Indo-European had the infixes -*ǝe*-
(i.e., [ħe]; cf. pp. 65, 445–446), -*ịe*-, and -*ụe*-. Only thus can
we explain such forms as Latin *regis* ' thou rulest ' : *rēgis* ' of
a king ' : Old High German *reichen* ' reach ' from **reĝe-*, **re-ǝe-
ĝe-*, and *re-ịe-ĝe-* respectively, or Middle Irish *serg* ' illness ',
Lithuanian *sir̃gti* ' to be ill ' : Gothic *saúrga*, Old High German *sorga*, *sworga* ' anxiety ', Sanskrit *sūrkṣati* ' heed ' from
**serge-* : **se-ụe-rghe-*. The base **(k̂)sele-* ' beam, board ' shows
an extraordinary complexity in this regard. From the simple
**(k̂)sele-* we have Anglo-Saxon *sealma* ' couch ', Old Lithuanian
šalma ' long beam '; from **(k̂)se-ǝe-le-*, Albanian *gjollë* ' plate for
cattle-salt ' (from **(k̂)sₑǝle-); from **(k̂)se-ịe-le-*, Lithuanian *sýlė*
' trough ' (from **(k̂)sₑịle-); from **(k̂)se-ụe-le*, Greek *ξύλον* ' wood ',
Lithuanian *šùlas* ' pillar, post ', Anglo-Saxon *syll* ' sill ' (from
**(k̂)sule-)*, Greek *σέλμα* ' ship's deck ', Old High German *swelli*
' threshold ' (from **(k̂)sụele-)*, Gothic *sauls* ' pillar ' (from
**(k̂)soule-)*, Anglo-Saxon *sȳl*, Old High German *sûl*, Modern Ger-
man *Säule* ' pillar ' (from **(k̂)sₑule-); and from **(k̂)se-ụe-ǝo-le-*,
Lithuanian *súolas* (from **(k̂)suole-)*.

The infixes -*ịe*- and -*ụe*- apparently gave a relative sense to the
words in which they were infixed, and the former may be identical
in origin with the relative pronoun **ịo-* (Sanskrit *yá-*, Phrygian
ιος, Greek *ὅς)*, which is perhaps seen in certain case-forms (cf.
pp. 195, 196) ; -*ǝe*- seems to have had the force of completeness or perfectivity. This appears to be borne out not only by
such perfect tenses as Sanskrit *sedúr*, Latin *sēdērunt*, Gothic
setun ' they have sat ' beside the presents *sátsi*, *sedeō*, *sitan*
(from **sₑ-ǝ-de-* as contrasted with the present **sede-)*, but also
by such epithetologues (cf. p. 169) as Sanskrit *bhārá-* ' burden ',
Greek *φώρ*, Latin *fūr* ' thief ', Old High German -*bâri* ' bearing '
beside *bhárati*, *fert*, *birit* ' bears ' (from **bhe-ǝe-re-* as contrasted

with *bhere-), or the type of Sanskrit mānavá- ' human ' : mánu-
' man ' (i.e., relative to man as an entirety). It would accordingly
appear that the conventional base-types *xēce-, *xeice-, *xeuce-
were originally *xe-ǝe-ce-, *xe-ie-ce-, *xe-ue-ce-, made by infixation in a primary *xece-.

The force of the vast majority of determinatives, however, has
long since been lost; all that one can say is that they must have
modified the primary base-meaning in some way; and it may well
be that in many cases it is they that cause the bases to have meanings which, at least at first glance, seem to diverge widely from
their original connotations. A survey of the material as a whole
appears to militate against the view, still popularly held, that
Indo-European bases were originally monosyllabic, and that
Semitic bases were triliteral. It would seem, on the contrary, that
*at least the great majority of both Indo-European and Semitic
bases were originally disyllabic* (e.g., *dhere- ' hold ', *laka ' go ').
When determinatives were added to such bases, those which had
originally been disyllabic assumed trisyllabic form (e.g., *qeue-
' bend ', as in Avestan fra-kava- ' fore-humped, pigeon-breasted ';
*qeue-qe-, as in Sanskrit ku[ñ]cati ' makes crooked '; *qeue-ge-,
as in German hocken ' squat '; *qeue-pe-, as in Lithuanian kaũpti
' heap up '; *qeue-be-, as in Latin cubāre ' lie down '). With compound determinatives, one may have bases with four or five syllables. If, then, one includes all the determinatives of a given base,
the number of derivatives from it will often be, at first glance,
incredibly large, as in the case of *dheue- ' blow ' (pp. 253-255).

In the light of all this, it seems possible to draw up a formula
for a word in any inflected language somewhat as follows, W
standing for ' word ', B for ' base ', $_kI$ any number of ' inflexions ',
from zero onward, at the beginning of the word and $_kI'$ any number of ' inflexions ', from zero onward, at its end, D for ' determinative ', and Σ the sum of all terms following it:

$$_kI + \overset{0}{\underset{m}{\Sigma}}D + B + \overset{0}{\underset{n}{\Sigma}}D' + {}_kI' = W$$

This is the formula for a simple word. There are, however,
several types of word which are *compound*, i.e., compounded of
more than a single base, only one of which bases is inflected. The
formula for such a compound differs from that for the simple word

only by allowing for the additional bases, each of which may have its own determinatives, so that it becomes:

$$_kI + \underset{m}{\Sigma D} + B + \underset{n}{\Sigma D'} + \underset{p}{\Sigma D''} + B' + \underset{q}{\Sigma D'''} + \cdots + _kI' = W$$

As examples one may cite Latin *arti-fex* ' craft-maker, artisan ' (two components), German *Eisen-bahn-fahr-preis* ' iron-road-journey-price, railway fare ' (four components), Sanskrit *sakala-nīti-śāstra-tattva-jña-* ' all-conduct-textbook-essence-knowing ' (five components).

Formally, compounds fall into two types: *proper* and *improper*. The proper compound inflects only the last member, so that the genitives of the words just cited are *arti-ficis* (not **artis-ficis* or **artis-fex*), *Eisen-bahn-fahr-preises*, and *sakala-nīti-śāstra-tattva-jñasya*. In the improper compound, at least two of the bases are inflected, as Latin *ius-iurandum, iuris-iurandi* '(of an) oath ', *res-publica rei-publicae* '(of a) commonwealth '. Proper compounds date from a very early linguistic period; improper compounds result from a relatively late amalgamation of two or more words to express a single concept. Thus *ius iurandum* ' a right to be sworn to ', because of frequent juxtaposition of the two words with a combination of their meanings, came to signify ' oath ', just as *res publica* ' public affair ' developed the meaning of ' commonwealth '.

The ultimate test of distinction between a compound and a non-compound is purely semantic: has, or has not, the word-combination acquired a special and distinct connotation? If I mean to speak merely of a ' public affair ', I say *'res 'publica* as two words (i.e., a non-compound), but if I talk of the technical entity known as the ' commonwealth ', I pronounce *res'publica* as one word (i.e., a compound). There is practically the same difference of meaning between Latin *'res 'publica* and *res'publica* as between English *'black 'berry* (any berry of black colour) and *'blackberry* (a special sort of berry). I can even say, without any realisation of its literal absurdity, that ' a blackberry is red when it is green ', but I cannot rationally say that ' a black berry is sometimes green and sometimes red ' — a black berry can only be black. So far as English is concerned, accent often distinguishes between a compound and a combination of two or more words, as *'black 'berry* but *'blackberry, for'get-me-not* (a flower; cf. German *Ver'giss-mein-nicht)* but *for'get 'me 'not.*

Compounds are normally written as one word, which is what they really are, as Latin *armiger, iusiurandum, respublica,* German *Eisenbahnfahrpreis,* Sanskrit *sakalanītiśāstratattvajña-.* In English, the components are frequently either connected by hyphens or written as two or more words, as *verb-form, protection of minorities treaty, destructive insect and pest act advisory board* in contrast to the type of *blackberry.* Linguistically speaking, whether compounds are written as one word, as words joined by hyphens, or as separate words is immaterial; each of the types just cited is an equally valid compound; and the elaborate, and often irreconcilable, rules laid down for the use of the hyphen in English are largely of typographical interest only.

If one of the components of a compound possesses so general a meaning that it readily admits of combination with a considerable number of words, it may become *productive,* i.e., it may become a regular formative element. Here belong such components as

English -*kind* ' sort ', e.g., *man-kind, woman-kind, cattle-kind.*

English -*ly,* German -*lich,* which originally meant ' body ' (cf. Anglo-Saxon *líc,* Old High German *lîh,* Modern High German *Leiche* ' body, corpse '), as Anglo-Saxon *heofon-líc,* English *heaven-ly,* Old High German *himil-lîh.*

English -*dom,* German -*tum,* originally signifying ' relation, condition, status ' (cf. Anglo-Saxon *dóm* ' judgement, meaning ', English *doom,* Old High German *tuom* ' judgement '), as Anglo-Saxon *hǽðen-dóm,* English *heathen-dom,* Old High German *heidan-tuom,* Modern High German *Heiden-tum.*

English -*head,* -*hood,* German -*heit,* primarily meaning ' nature, state ' (cf. Anglo-Saxon *hád,* Old High German *heit),* as Anglo-Saxon *cild-hád,* English *child-hood,* Old and Modern High German *kind-heit;* Anglo-Saxon *préost-hád,* English *priest-hood.*

German -*bar* ' bearing, possessing ', as *frucht-bar* ' fruitful ', *furcht-bar* ' fearful ' (this English -*ful* is a similar component, identical with the independent word *full).*

Romance -*ment(e)* as an adverbial formative, originally signifying ' with such-and-such a mind ' (cf. Latin [Catullus] *obstinata mente* ' with an obstinate mind, obstinately '), as French *obstiné-ment,* Italian *ostina-mente,* Spanish *obstinada-mente* (cf. also Old French *humle et dolcement* ' humbly and gently ', Modern Spanish *clara, concisa y elegantemente* ' clearly, concisely, and elegantly ').

Latin -*igāre* for *-*ag-āre* (cf. *ag-ere* ' to perform '), as *navi-gāre* ' to work a ship, navigate ', *liti-gāre* ' to work the law, litigate '.

Whether some of the determinatives discussed above had their origin in such formations as these, but have become so worn down

both in form and meaning that their primary shapes and significations have long since been lost is a question which may fairly be
raised, but cannot as yet be answered.

Compounds fall into four main categories: *copulative, determinative (dependent, descriptive,* and *appositional), possessive,* and
iterative.

Copulative compounds (often called *dvandvas* ' two [and] two ',
the term employed by native Sanskrit grammarians, who were
the first to discuss them) consist of two or more nouns as mere
enumerations, such as Sanskrit *Indra-Vāyǘ* ' Indra (and) Vāyu ',
jaya-parājayau ' victory (or) defeat ', *aśva-vanara-gaja-vṛka-
siṁha-makara-haṁsa-matsya-narās* ' horse(s), monkey(s), ele-
phant(s), wolves (or, wolf), lion(s), crocodile(s), swan(s), fish,
(and) men (or man) '. Except for numerals from ' eleven ' to ' nineteen ', *dvandva* compounds are relatively rare outside Sanskrit,
although a few examples are citable, such as Greek νυχθήμερον ' a
night (and) a day ', γλυκύ-πικρος ' sweet (and) bitter, bittersweet ';
Latin *reci-procus* ' going backward (and) forward ', *su-ove-taurilia*
' sacrifices of a pig, a sheep, (and) a bull '; Anglo-Saxon *suhter-
(ge)fœderan* ' uncle (and) nephew '; Middle Irish *brat-gaⁱsced*
' mantle (and) armour ', *gorm-gel* ' blue (and) white '; Lithuanian
plaũč-kepeniai ' lungs (and) liver '; Old Church Slavic *bratŭ-sestra*
' brother (and) sister '; colloquial French *Monsieur-(Ma)dame*
' Mister (and) Mistress '; colloquial English *two-three times.* For
the numerals compare English *four-teen,* German *vier-zehn,* Latin
quatuor-decim, Sanskrit *cátur-daśa* as contrasted with Greek
τετταρεσκαίδεκα ' four and ten '.

Determinative compounds fall into three sub-groups, dependent,
descriptive, and appositional, their common characteristic being
that in them all a noun or an adjective is compounded with a preceding noun, adjective, or adverb which qualifies or determines it.
In the *dependent* compound, often termed *tatpurusha* ' his man '
from the Sanskrit grammarians' designation of the type, the prior
component or components stands or stand in some case-relation to
the final member, as Sanskrit *deva-sená* ' army of gods ', *pādō-
daka-* ' foot-water ' (' water for the feet '), *ātma-sama-* ' self-
equal ' (' equal to one's self '), *mad-viyoga-* ' me-separation '
(' separation from me '), *grāma-vāsin-* ' village-dwelling ' (' dwelling in a village '), *nagara-gāmin-* ' city-going ' (' going to a city ') ;
Greek ψυχο-πομπός ' soul-sending ' (' sending a soul or souls '),

δορί-κτητος ' spear-taken ' (' taken by a spear '), ἱππο-μάχος ' horse-fighting ' (' fighting on horse[back]') ; Latin *iũdex* for **i̯ous-dex* ' law-speaking, judge ', *crē-dõ* for *cred-dhõ ' I put-faith, believe ', *anim-advertõ* for *animum advertõ* ' I mind-turn, notice ' (cf. p. 229), *monti-vagus* ' mountain-wandering ' (' wandering on the mountain[s]') ; and improper compounds like *aquae-ductus* ' water-conductor ' (' conductor of water '), *iure-consultus* ' law-versed ' (' versed in law '), *sacrõ-sanctus* ' sanctity-holy ' (' holy with sanctity ') ; Gothic *faíhu-geigan* [fehu-giːgan] ' to money-desire, covet ', *wein-drugkja* [wiːn-druŋkja] ' wine-bibber '; English *man-hating* ' hating men ', *man-hater* ' hater of men ', *man-hated* ' hated by men '.

Descriptive compounds (often called, from the name given them by the native grammarians, *karmadhãraya*, a term of obscure meaning, but apparently signifying ' action-establishing ') are those in which the first component, acting either as an adjective or as an adverb, qualifies the second. Here belong, for example, Sanskrit *nīlotpala-* ' blue-lotus ', *sú-kṛta-* ' well-done ', *dvi-já-* ' twice-born '; Greek ἀκρό-πολις ' high-town, citadel '; Latin *angi-portus* ' narrow-street, alley '; French *rouge-gorge* ' robin red-breast '; Gaulish *Novio-dũnon* ' New-Fort '; Gothic *midjun-gards* ' middle-dwelling, world '; Old High German *junc-frouwa* (Modern German *Jungfrau)* ' young-lady '; Lithuanian *júod-varnis* ' black-crow, raven '; Old Church Slavic *dobro-godŭ* ' good-time, fit occasion '.

In *appositional* compounds one component is explanatory of another, and, except for absence of inflexion of the first member, such compounds are, in reality, nominal sentences (cf. pp. 228, 230–232), English *man-servant,* for instance, being equivalent to ' a man (is) the servant ' (in the primitive period, neither the copula nor the article existed). As examples we may cite Sanskrit *rãjarṣi-* ' king-sage ' (a king who is also a sage), *nara-siṁha-* ' man-lion ' (a man like a lion), *jaya-śabda-* ' the word " conquer " '; Greek ἰατρό-μαντις ' physician-seer ' (a physician who is also a seer) ; Gothic *þiu-magus* ' servant-boy ' (a boy who is a servant), Old Church Slavic *konje-človĕkŭ* ' horse-man, Centaur ' (a horse who is also a man), English *man-mountain* ' a man like a mountain '.

Possessive compounds (also called by the native Sanskrit grammatical term *bahuvrīhi* ' much-riced, possessing much rice ') result, in the main, from the transformation of a compound noun into an adjective with the meaning ' possessing (or possessed of) so-and-so ', e.g., Sanskrit *anyá-rūpa-* ' other-formed ', *an-antá-* ' un-ended '; Greek ῥοδο-δάκτυλος ' rose-fingered ', ἄ-παις ' child-less '; Latin *magn-animus* ' great-minded ', *capri-cornus* ' goat-horned ', *in-animus* ' life-less '; Gothic *hrainja-haírts* ' pure-hearted '; Old Church Slavic *črĭno-vlasŭ* ' black-haired '; and such English words as those just given as translations — *un-ended, great-minded,* etc.

Iterative compounds are formed by repetition of the base, or even of an inflected word, to give emphatic or distributive force to the whole. This type is relatively rare, though one may cite such examples as Sanskrit *prá-pra,* Greek προ-πρό ' forward-forward, ever forward ', Sanskrit *uttarottara-* ' higher (and) higher ', *páñca-pañca* ' five-five, five each ', *dáme-dame* ' in-house-in-house, in every house ', *píba-piba* ' drink-drink! '; Latin *quis-quis* ' who-who, whoever '; colloquial French *très-très-très joli;* English *goody-goody.*

A special type, whose origin is not wholly certain, is formed by that of English *mar-plot, cut-throat,* etc. Here the first component is felt to be verbal, and the second nominal, the conventional explanation being that this prior member is an imperative singular (e.g., *cut-throat* would mean ' cut the throat! '). It seems more probable, when examples are studied in all the Indo-European languages in which the type is found — it is very rare in Slavic and Lithuanian, and appears not to occur in Celtic or Teutonic, the type of English *cut-throat* being merely imitated from that of French *coupe-jarret* — that we are here dealing either with a mere base or with an active participle. This is apparently implied by such examples as Sanskrit *trasá-dasyu-* ' fright-foe ' (proper name), Greek ἀρχέ-κακος ' start-trouble ', Latin *verti-cordia* ' turn-heart ' (an epithet of Venus), *posci-nummius* ' want-money, avaricious '; French *garde-robe* (borrowed in English as *ward-robe),* *porte-monnaie, attrape-mouche,* etc. The underlying reason for this type, which is none too common, seems to be stress of the verbal rather than of the nominal portion of the compound.

Improper compounds, of which we have already given some examples in passing, do not differ in principle from the proper, so that they scarcely need detailed discussion. By their substitution of inflexion for true composition, as in Sanskrit *dhanaṁ-jayá-* ' booty-winning ', Greek Πυλοι-γενής ' born in Pylos ', Latin *aquae-ductus, sacrō-sanctus,* Gothic *baúrgs-waddjus* ' city-wall ' instead of *dhana-jayá-, *Πυλο-γενής, *aqua-ductus, *sacri-sanctus, and *baúrg-waddjus respectively, French gendarme 'constable', sabot-de-Vièrge ' ladyslipper ', English leg-of-mutton sleeve, they betray their comparatively recent origin. At least equally late are the separable compounds, in which the components are not conjoined. This type (technically known as tmesis) is especially frequent from the early historic period onward in compounds of verbs with preverbs (less correctly termed prepositions in this use [cf. pp. 170–171]), as in Early Latin ob vōs sacrō ' I implore you ' as contrasted with obsecrō vōs, Sanskrit á tvā viśantu ' may they enter into thee ', Greek ἡμῖν ἀπὸ λοιγὸν ἀμῦναι ' to ward off plague for us ', Lithuanian pa-mums-dĕk ' help us ' (instead of *áviśantu tvā, *λοιγὸν ἀπαμῦναι, *padĕk mums), German ich setze es zusammen ' I put it together ' as contrasted with ich habe es zusammengesetzt (cf. also English to uswards as contrasted with towards us). Occasionally we even find the linguistic monstrosity of separation of a determinative from its base, as when the early Roman poet Ennius wrote (for metrical reasons) cere-comminuit-brum ' he crushed his skull ' instead of cerebrum comminuit.

So soon as we begin to study the structure of any language, we perceive that the various words which constitute its vocabulary exercise distinct functions, that there are, in other terms, what are called parts of speech. Thus, certain types denote actions or states of being (run, exist); others indicate things or ideas (mountain, goodness); others describe actions or states, things or ideas (slowly, well; high, sincere), etc. These categories, conventionally termed verbs, nouns, adverbs, adjectives, etc., are not necessarily the same in all language-groups or even in all members of the same group; so that the definition of, e.g., a verb which fits a given category so termed in Indo-European or Semitic may not be applicable in American Indian, Polynesian, or Chinese.

At this point, we must recall the distinction between form and function (see pp. 19–21), and, discarding the conventional arrangement of the parts of speech founded on function, we must seek to classify them according to form, i.e., according to morphology viewed in the light of historical development. This classification alone seems to meet the requirements of scientific linguistic principles, and it appears to be applicable to the majority of languages. Some, such as Chinese, at least in the historic stages, do not distinguish between nouns and verbs, etc., and so would appear to militate against this principle; but whether such exceptions to the general rule are due to a very rudimentary linguistic stage, or are the result of long series of successive simplifications, can be determined only after long and impartial study, the difficulty of decision being augmented, if not made insuperable, by the paucity of historical evidence in the greater number of such languages.

Conventional grammatical terminology was established, in the main, by the grammarians of Greece, notably in the summary of Dionysios Thrax (second century B.C.; cf. pp. 424–425). From the Greeks it was adopted by the grammarians of Rome, and even by those of Armenia and Syria, passing from the latter to the Arabs, and from them to the Jews. Constructed primarily for Greek, this terminology was made to apply not only to Latin, but also to all mediaeval and modern Indo-European languages and even to the Semitic group. For Indo-European, this was not seriously incorrect; but it was scarcely applicable to Semitic, and, what was far worse, especially in the pre-scientific period, the grammatical systems of all sorts of languages, American Indian, African, Polynesian, Australian, etc., were forced into the same Procrustean bed. A more intelligent understanding prevails to-day, so that each language and each language-group is now judged on its own merits in all scientific linguistic work.

The parts of speech are conventionally reckoned as eight in number: nouns, pronouns, adjectives, verbs, adverbs, prepositions, conjunctions, and interjections; but scientifically this arrangement is so inexact as to be quite misleading.

In the first place, we must exclude the *interjection* from the parts of speech. The true interjection, of the type of English *O!*, *ouch!*, *humph!*, *hello!*, *whoa!*, is nothing but a reflex vocal activity, devoid of any linguistic significance and possessing merely psychological or affective value; such false interjections as *stop!*, *murder!* are nothing but verbs or nouns employed elliptically (e.g., *stop!* = *stop where you are!; murder!* = *murder is being done!*, or the like; cf. p. 230). From the strictly linguistic point of view it is important to observe that true interjections neither possess nor ever have possessed, so far as we can tell, any inflexion whatever.

The true parts of speech may be divided provisionally into two classes: *nominal* (nouns, adjectives, adverbs, prepositions, conjunctions, and pronouns) and *verbal* (verbs). The reason for the seeming preponderance of the first class is that no clear line of demarcation can be drawn between nouns and adjectives, or even pronouns, while adverbs, prepositions, and (probably) most conjunctions are originally nothing more than stereotyped cases of nouns or adjectives. These various parts of speech we may now take up in the order given at the beginning of this paragraph.

Dionysios Thrax laid down what is still the conventional definition of a *noun:* ' A noun is a part of speech with cases, denoting a thing or an act — a thing, such as " stone "; an act, such as " education "; termed both common and proper — common, such as " man, horse "; proper, such as " Sokrates "; and five [characteristics] accompany a noun: genders, species [primary and derived], forms [simple, compound, and derived from compounds, i.e., secondary compounds], numbers, cases '. It is noteworthy that Dionysios makes no mention of the *adjective* among his parts of speech, but classifies it as the derived species, the noun proper being the primary species. Here he is essentially correct: *grammatically* (i.e., in form) *there is no essential difference between a noun and an adjective;* the distinction is purely functional, the noun denoting the name of an animate being or of an inanimate thing or idea, and the adjective (or epithet, as Dionysios calls it) serving to express some modification of the concept conveyed by the noun. So far as such inflexional languages (see pp. 300–301) as Indo-European and Semitic are concerned, *we may define the noun and adjective as words characterised by inflexion, if inflected at all, for case,* since they share with the verb inflexion for number and (not infrequently) gender (cf. p. 190).

Another point of much historical importance is that the great majority of nouns (including adjectives) and verbs alike may be traced back in these languages (and even more clearly in a number of other linguistic groups) to identical bases as reconstructed with due observance of the relevant phonetic correspondences (cf. pp. 74–83), and these bases evolve, by processes of specialisation according to morphological correspondences, into the noun-group on the one hand, and into the verb-group on the other.

The close connexion of the noun and the verb has already been implied in the discussion of such parallels as Vaï *mu-fa* ' our father ' with *mu-ro* ' we say ' and Maipure *wa-ani* ' our son ' with *wa-nawa* ' we see ' (cf. p. 152). The Semitic atelic (commonly called imperfect; cf. pp. 204–205) seems to be of similar origin, so that, for example, Arabic *katabta* ' thou art in a state of having written ' (conventionally translated ' thou hast written ') probably meant at first something like ' thy (being) writer '. In Middle and Modern Persian a perfect tense has been created (cf. p. 214) on this model; thus *kardam* ' I have done ' is really the perfect passive participle of the neuter gender plus the possessive personal pronoun in the genitive singular, as is shown by Old Persian *ima tya manā kartam* ' hoc (est) quod mei factum (est)' = ' this (is) what (is) my deed ' = ' this (is) what I have done ' (Modern Persian *īn [ast] kih kardam)*.

In Hupa (of the Athapascan stock, spoken in California) many verbs in the third person present active or passive are used as nouns (e.g., *nañya* means both ' it comes down ' and ' rain '; *willoiᵉ* ' it has been tied ' and ' bundle '), as also in Malayo-Polynesian (e.g., Javanese *turu* ' sleep ' and ' to sleep '; Fiji [Melanesian] *mate* ' death ' and ' to die '; Samoan [Polynesian] *'ofu* ' clothing ' and ' to dress '). In Kwakiutl (spoken on the coasts of British Columbia and of north-western Washington) ' all stems seem to be neutral, neither noun nor verb; and their nominal or verbal character seems to depend solely upon the suffix with which they are used, although some suffixes are also neutral. . . . A division of words into verbs and nouns has taken place, both being fairly clearly distinguished by suffixes. We find, however, that syntactically the distinction is not carried through rigidly; nouns being treated with great ease as verbs, and verbs as nouns. It must be added here that the forms of the pronouns as attached to the noun and as attached to the verb are distinct ' *(Handbook of American Indian Languages*, i, 441, 443).

In Eskimo the verb is merely a sub-class of the noun, so that ' he sees me ' would be, literally, ' my-being-seen-by-him-is ' (cf. pp. 200, 220) ; the Basque verb is really a pronominal expression of the subject plus the copula plus the locative of a noun of action, as *n-a-kar-su* ' thou carriest me ', literally ' I am in-being-carried by thee '. In most of the Dravidian languages, spoken in the southern half of India, the verb ' can be characterized as an inflected noun of agency. The Dravidian verb in this respect distinctly differs from the real Indo-European verb, which simply denotes the action done by the subject, and from the Tibeto-Burman verb which can be described as a noun of action without any reference to subject or object, both of which must be indicated by means of other words. The Dravidian verb is half adjective and half noun, denot-

ing as it does the subject as the doer of the action in question '
(Linguistic Survey of India, iv, 295; e.g., Telugu *mēmu vanṭa
chēsē-vāra-mu* = ' we cookery-doers-are ' = ' we cook '; in Tibeto-
Burman ' I go ' is, literally, ' my-going ', and ' I strike the man ' is
' by-me man striking' as contrasted with Latin *coquimus* ' we-
cook, *eo* ' I-go ', *virum ferio* ' man I-strike ').

The intimate relationship, and even the ultimate identity, of the
noun and the adjective are clearly shown in such abstracts or collectives as *the beautiful, the true, the false, the good,* which are
practically synonymous with *beauty, truth, falsehood, goodness.*
We may go even further. Taking such words as English *serpent*
and *reptile,* which we term nouns, their Latin originals *serpens* and
reptile show that they were, rather, what would popularly be
called adjectives, both meaning ' creeping, crawling '. Indeed, the
conventional explanation is that words meaning ' beast ' and ' animal' are to be understood when using them, that, e.g., Latin
serpens stands for *serpens bestia.* This seems to be a learned and
rationalising interpretation, and appears to be not only needless,
but also incorrect. If we examine the great majority of nouns whose
etymology we can trace back to an Indo-European base, we find
that, like *serpent* and *reptile,* they were primarily *descriptive*
words, as in the case of the English word *beaver,* which, when compared with its many cognates, is seen to be derived from an Indo-
European base **bhere-* ' brown ' (cf. pp. 249–250).

Originally *there were neither nouns nor adjectives, but only descriptive words. Grammatically, nouns and adjectives are identical; their functional differentiation, whereby nouns became names
of beings or things, and adjectives words modifying nouns, was a
later development, even though it appeared before the dawn of
history.* Instead of the adjective being derived from the noun, the
noun would seem to be derived from the adjective if we are to rely,
as it would seem that we must, on the term descriptive as a characteristic common to them both. We may, accordingly, group them
together as *epithetologues* (' epithet-words ').

In many languages the adjective frequently assumes verbal
form, particularly when it serves as a predicate, as in ' *the land is
broad* '. Thus we find in Hupa *tcūwindas* ' he was heavy '; in Maya
keel-kan ' is cold, snake ' = ' cold snake '; in Japanese *yokatta* ' it
was good ' *(yoi* ' good ') ; in Hebrew *qāṭōn* ' be small '; in Arabic
kabura ' be large '; and in the languages of West Africa any part

of speech used in a qualifying sense must be considered a verb
unless there is conclusive evidence to the contrary. In Indo-
European this phenomenon is comparatively rare, though it is
occasionally found in denominative verbs, as in Latin *albeō* ' be
white ', *superbiō* ' be proud '.

Very little investigation is needed to show that the *adverb* is
only a stereotyped form of some case of the epithetologue (in the
historical period, of the adjective). Thus Latin *falsō* ' falsely ' and
cārē ' dearly ' are evidently old Latin ablatives (cf. Old Latin
meretōd ' justly ', *faciluméd* ' easily '), whereas Latin *facile*
' easily ' is the neuter singular of *facilis*. Similarly Teutonic adverbs of the type of Gothic *galeikō*, Old Saxon *gilîko*, Old High
German *gilîcho*, Modern German *gleich* ' likewise ' are originally
ablatives in *-ōd* like Old Latin *meretōd*, while the corresponding Anglo-Saxon *gelíce* is an ablative in *-ēd* like Old Latin
faciluméd; and Gothic, Old High German *filu*, Modern German
viel ' very, much ' are precisely similar in formation to Latin *facile*.
Some Teutonic adverbs are old genitives, as Gothic *gistradagis*
' to-morrow ', *nahts*, Anglo-Saxon *nihtes*, Modern German *nachts*
' at night ', Modern English *homewards* as contrasted with the
accusatival *homeward* (Anglo-Saxon also has both *hám-weardes*
and *hám-weard;* cf. Modern German *heim-wärts;* cf. pp. 198, 268).

Prepositions are less obvious at first glance, and their very name
is misleading, though its origin may be traced as far back as the
πρόθεσις (' a placing in front ') of Dionysios Thrax. The preposition
and the adverb were originally the same, and this feeling still survives in such English phrases as *to see through a thing* and *to see
a thing through*. Clear examples of nouns in case-forms used as
prepositions are not uncommon, e.g., French *chez* ' at the house of,
in, among ' (probably from a Vulgar Latin locative **casae); Old
French *lez* [lets] ' beside, near ' (Latin accusative *latus* ' side ';
cf. Vulgar Latin *latus se* ' by his side '), still retained in such place-
names as *Sart-les-Spa* ' Sart-near-Spa '; and Latin *exempli gratia*
' for (the sake of) example '.

Linguistic reconstructions help us to see in many prepositions
early cases no longer obvious. Thus we clearly have old locatives
in English *in* (Anglo-Saxon, Gothic, Old and Modern High German, Latin *in* [Archaic Latin *en*], Greek, ἐν, ἐνί from **en, *_eni;
cf. Ogam Irish *ini-gena*, Old Irish *in-gen* ' in-born girl, daughter ',
Gaulish *Eni-genos);* Latin *ob* ' at, about, for, instead of ' (Greek

ἐπί ' upon ', Sanskrit adverb ápi ' moreover ', from *ₑpï, *opi);
Latin per ' through ' (Sanskrit pári, Greek περί, Modern German
ver-loren ' lost ', from *pₑri, *peri); English over (Anglo-Saxon
ofer, Old High German ubar, Modern German über, Latin super
for *uper [the initial s being by analogy with sub ' under '], Greek
ὑπέρ [the initial h here also of secondary origin], Sanskrit upári,
from *upₑri, uperi); Latin ante, Greek ἀντί, Sanskrit ánti ' before '
(Anglo-Saxon and-swaru, English an-swer, Modern German Ant-
wort ' reply ', from *anti; Hittite has the cognate adverb hanti
' before ' as the dative-locative of the noun hanza ' front ', which
was in actual use) ; and an old dative is probably seen in Latin prae
' before ' from *prai.

Certain prepositions appear to date from a pre-inflexional period
(cf. pp. 152–154), since they seem to be simple base-forms (cf. pp.
150–151), notably English of (Gothic af, Old High German aba,
Modern German ab, Greek ἀπό, Sanskrit ápa ' from ' from *apo).
Most, however, became fixed in form at too early a date to permit
of exact analysis.

The same statement holds true of conjunctions, though the origin
of some of them is fairly evident. Thus Indo-European *ₑpi, *opi,
which we have just studied as a preposition in such words as Latin
ob, appears as a conjunction in Armenian ew ' and '; Indo-European *eti, *oti (a locative like *ₑpi, etc.) ' out over ', and hence also
' away from ', gives rise not only to the Greek adverb ἔτι ' moreover ' and to the Old Church Slavic preposition otŭ ' from ', but
also to the Latin and Gothic conjunctions et, iþ ' and '; from *ei,
the locative singular of the demonstrative pronoun *e-, comes
Greek εἰ [e:] ' if ' and perhaps also Old Church Slavic i ' and, also '
(both, originally, ' in that case ') ; and from a similar demonstrative locative *sei comes Latin sī ' if ' (Old Latin sei) and, with the
particle -ce, sic ' so ' (Old Latin seic), originally likewise meaning
' in that case '.

Sometimes a pronoun may develop into a conjunction, as English
that and German dass in such constructions as he says that it is so,
German er sagt, dass es wahr ist, or in Old Persian tya in mātya
mām xšnāsātiy tya adam naiy Bardiya amiy ' that one may not
know that I am not Smerdis '. Here the original force of that, etc.,
is clear : it was the direct object of the verbs of knowing, saying,
etc., and the following phrase of indirect discourse was primarily
an appositional phrase explaining what the that was. Thus the

earliest meaning of such a sentence as *he says that it is so* would seem to have been ' he says that (thing), (namely) " It is so " ' (cf. also *he says it is so* = ' he says: " It is so " '). Similar constructions appear in Latin *quod* ' which ' (e.g., Terence, *gnatus quod se adsimulat laetum* ' knowing that he pretends to be happy '; Petronius, *dixi quod mustella comedit* ' I said that the weasel ate them '; Vulgate, *et vidi quod hoc quoque esset vanitas* ' and I saw that this also was vanity '; cf. French *il dit qu'il est vrai* ' he says that it is true '), in Greek ὅτι ' whichsoever ' (e.g., λέγει ὅτι γράφει ['lege: 'hoti 'graphe:] ' he says that he writes '), and in Avestan *yaṯ* ' which ' (e.g., *taṯ ahmāi jasaṯ āyaptəm yaṯ hē puθrō us-zayata* ' that boon came to him that a son was born to him '), etc.

We appear to be wholly justified in considering adverbs, prepositions, and conjunctions as stereotyped forms of adjectives or of nouns, and likewise correct in grouping nouns and adjectives together under the category of epithetologues.

The *pronoun* likewise falls within the nominal category; but its ancient conventional definition, ' a word used for or instead of a noun ', from which it derives its name (Latin *pronomen*, Greek ἀντωνυμία), while functionally accurate enough, is linguistically inadequate. Grammatically, the pronoun is identical with every other epithetologue in being inflected for case; but it differs in certain noteworthy respects. In the first place, it cannot be reduced to bases primarily nominal and verbal at the same time, but solely to those which are pronominal only, except in sporadic instances like Italian *eglino* ' they ' beside *egli*, with *-no* taken from the third person plural of the verb (e.g., *parla-no* ' they speak '). In the second place, its inflexions are sometimes so different from those of the epithetologue that they appear to be irreconcilable with them, as in the nominative plural masculine **toi*, **tei* ' those ' (Sanskrit *té*, Gothic *þai*) in contrast to the nominal **aĝrōs* ' fields ' (Sanskrit *ájrās*, Gothic *akros)*, or in the Sanskrit dative singular *máhyam* ' to me ' for **méĝh-i-om* in contrast to *padé* ' to a foot ' for **p₀d-eí*.

The oldest Indo-European personal pronouns lacked number in the grammatical sense of the term; they had, instead, separate bases for the singular and plural which are still retained by their descendants, as in Sanskrit *ahám, tvám*, English *I, thou*, but *vayám, yūyám* : *we, ye*, where the number is indicated, not by the inflexion, but by the base (cf. also the Sanskrit ablatives singular,

dual, and plural *mát, tvát* : *āvát, yuvát* : *asmát, yuṣmát* ' from
me ', ' from thee ' : ' from us two ', ' from you two ' : ' from us ',
' from you '). It is also noteworthy that the pronoun of the first
person (but not of the second) shows two separate bases both in
the singular and in the plural, as in Latin *egō, mē* : English *I, me* :
Sanskrit *vayám, asmán* : English *we, us*, the one being the base for
the nominative, and the other for all the rest.

Semantically, pronouns differ from nouns in that they are essentially *deictic*. They do not designate persons, things, concepts, or
qualities in general (as do the nouns *man, stone, thought, goodness*), but, without limitation to any single category of ideas, they
denote a specific individual or specific individuals of any category
(e.g., *I, we*, any individual person, concept, or thing, or plurality
thereof, regarded as acting or being; *that, who*, any individual
person, concept, or thing, or plurality thereof, to or of whom or
to or of which some predication is made).

Pronouns fall into two groups: (1) *personal pronouns*, referring
to *(a)* the speaker or speakers; *(b)* the person(s), concept(s), or
thing(s) spoken to; or *(c)* the person(s), concept(s), or thing(s)
spoken of; and (2) *non-personal pronouns*, a category including a
number of sub-classes, of which the more important are *demonstratives* (e.g., English *this, that*, Latin *hic, iste, ille), relative*
(e.g., English *who*, Latin *qui), interrogative* (e.g., English *who?*,
Latin *quis?), indefinite* (e.g., Latin *quis-quis* beside the relative
qui and the interrogative *quis),* and *possessive* (e.g., English *my,
mine*, Latin *meus, tuus)*. In Indo-European, the personal pronouns
show no gender, though certain other language-groups, such as
Semitic, have separate forms for the masculine and feminine of
the second person (e.g., Arabic *'anta, 'anti* for the singular, and
'antum[u], 'antunna for the plural) ; the non-personal pronouns
are inflected for gender as well as for number and case. Some languages, on the other hand, do not show separate bases, but merely
pluralise the singular, e.g., Semā, of the Nāgā group in North India
(ngi, ngi-ko; nā, nā-ko ' I, we; thou, ye ').

In Indo-European, as in a number of other linguistic families,
only the first and second persons possess true personal pronouns;
the pronoun for the third person is, in reality, a demonstrative
which, unlike the true personal pronouns, is inflected for gender.
In Sanskrit, Greek, and Latin, for instance, the only way of denoting the pronoun of the third person is by using *sá, sā́, tád; ὁ, ἡ, τό*

[ho, he:, to] ; *ille, illa, illud* (or *iste, ista, istud)*, literally meaning
' that person or thing ', and sometimes developing into the definite
article, as in French *le, la;* Italian *il* or *lo, la;* Spanish *el, la;* English *the* as contrasted with Latin *ille, illa,* Sanskrit *tá-d* (in Greek,
ὁ, ἡ, τό serve both as a demonstrative and as the definite article).
The triple series of demonstratives seen in Latin *hic* ' this ', *iste*
' that nearer ', *ille* ' that farther ' recurs in Armenian *ay-s, ay-d,
ay-n* (cf. Latin *ce-do* ' here ! ', Greek τό, Lithuanian *añs* ' that ').

The non-personal pronouns may be simplified considerably from
the conventional classification which we have given above (p. 173).
The possessive is, in origin, just the same as the genitive case (cf.
p. 197) ; the relative, interrogative, and indefinite are, in Indo-
European, of identical source (e.g., English *who, who?, who-ever);*
and the demonstrative forms a class by itself. In some other linguistic families we find a different state of affairs in that the relative may be identical with the demonstrative, as in Wiradyuri
(South Australian) *ńina dibilain ńana ńindu bala-buni* ' this bird
this thou killedst ' (cf. German *dies ist der Vogel den du tötetest)*
or Bari (of the Nilo-Equatorial group) *ńun lo a-togwé liń* ' God
that hath-created all '; or there may be no relative whatever, as
Maya *le uinik qainaki kimi* ' that man sang, he died ' = ' the man
who sang died '.

Sometimes the plural is made by adding the plural of the third
personal (or demonstrative) pronoun to the noun-form which
serves for singular and plural alike, as in Mafōr (of the Papuan
group) *snūn* ' man ', *snūn-si* ' men ' (literally ' man-they '), Dinka
(Nilo-Abyssinian) *dźoṅkor* ' horse ', *dźoṅkor-ke* ' horses ' (' horse-
those '), Encounter Bay (South Australian) *bāmi* ' girl ', *bām-ar*
' girls ' (' girl-they '), Āhom (Tai group) *po* ' father ', *khau-po*
' fathers ' (' they-father '), Maya *nik* ' flower ', *nik-ob* ' flowers '
(' flower-they ').

As these examples imply, the pronoun may have a plural while
the noun has none, as in Bāṛā of the Bodo family of North India,
where the noun shows no distinction for singular and plural, whereas the pronoun does *(āng, zang; nang, nang-sŭr; bī, bī-sŭr;* note
here the significant difference in the formation of the plural of the
second and third persons as contrasted with that of the first) ; or
the plural of the pronoun of the first and second persons may be
formed in a way wholly unlike that of the noun, as in Santālī
(Muṇḍā group) which, as contrasted with the nouns, e.g., *apāt*

' father ', *apāt-kīn* ' two fathers ', *apāt-kō* ' fathers ', has inclusive and exclusive forms for the first person plural (cf. p. 182) :

iñ ' I '	*alaṅ* ' I and thou '	*aliñ* ' he and I '	*abo(n)* ' we and you '	*alä(n)* ' we, not ye '
am ' thou '	*abän* ' ye two '		*apä(n)* ' ye and they '	
ach' ' self, he '		*akīn* ' they two '		*akō* ' they '

Linguistically the pronoun is far more important for a knowledge of the history of language and of the evolution of inflexion than its present rather modest position among the parts of speech would seem to imply. We may even say that *the pronoun is, in all probability, the grammatical source of the categories of number* (cf. pp. 172–173) *and gender, and of the distinction between the active case (i.e., the nominative) and the inactive cases (i.e., all the rest;* cf. pp. 192–201).

Both for case and for gender, the importance of the pronoun emerges with special clarity in the demonstrative pronoun represented by the bases **so-* and **to-* in Sanskrit, Greek, and Gothic:

	SANSKRIT			GREEK			GOTHIC		
	Masculine	Feminine	Neuter	Masculine	Feminine	Neuter	Masculine	Feminine	Neuter
Nominative	*sá(s)*	*sā́*	*tád*	ὁ	ἡ	τό	*sa*	*so*	*þat-a*
Accusative	*tám*	*tā́m*	*tád*	τόν	τήν	τό	*þan-a*	*þo*	*þat-a*
Dative	*tásmāi*	*tásyāi*	*tásmāi*	τῷ	τῇ	τῷ	*þamma*	*þizai*	*þamma*

Here we observe, for case, that the two active forms (the nominative male and female) are marked off from the inactive (all non-nominative cases except the neuter nominative) by different bases: **so-* and **to-* respectively (cf. pp. 192–201).

As regards gender the argument is somewhat less simple. If, however, we consider certain languages, such as Latin, which have in the noun what is conventionally termed *grammatical gender,* and in the pronoun what is equally conventionally called *natural gender* (e.g., Latin *locus* ' place ' [masculine], *fuga* ' flight ' [feminine], *iugum* ' yoke ' [neuter] : *iste, ista, istud* 'yon [man, woman, thing]'), we see that their neuter nominative plural coincides in form with the feminine nominative singular (e.g., Latin *ista fuga* ' yon flight ' : *ista iuga* ' yon yokes '), a phenomenon which will receive fuller elucidation in connexion with a consideration of the problem of the origin of gender (pp. 183–190). We observe, moreover, that the neuter plural and the feminine singular frequently have exactly the same force, i.e., that of a collective noun (e.g., Latin feminine singular *familia* ' family ', literally ' the collectivity of *famuli* ', i.e., of ' household retainers, etc.', as contrasted with the neuter plural *servitia* ' the collectivity of servants '; cf. French *le service* in the same sense; so also Latin *opera* appears both as a feminine singular and as a neuter plural; cf. likewise such feminine singulars as French *feuille*, Italian *foglia*, Spanish *hoja*, Portuguese *folha* ' leaf ', from the Latin neuter plural *folia)*.

In certain languages the neuter plural governs a verb in the singular, notably in Greek (e.g., τὰ οἰκήματα ἔπεσεν [ta oi'ke:mata 'epesen] ' the buildings fell '), Avestan (e.g., *sax^vārō yā zī vāvərəzōi* ' plans which have been carried out '), Modern Persian (e.g., *kārhā bi-ṣabr bar-āyad* ' affairs succeed through patience '), Vedic Sanskrit (very rarely, e.g., *ákāri ta indra gótamebhir bráhmāṇi* ' prayers were made to thee, O Indra, by the Gotamas '), and (also very seldom, sometimes through Greek influence) Vulgar Latin (e.g., *ea vitia difficiliter vincitur* ' those faults are overcome with difficulty '). In Arabic, the broken plural (really a feminine singular collective) regularly takes its verb in the feminine singular (e.g., *qālati 'l-yahūdu* ' the Jews say ' [really, ' Jewry says '], *ta'kulu 'ṭ-ṭayru* ' the birds were eating ' [really, ' birddom was eating ']).

The Indo-European termination of the feminine singular of the sex-denoting pronoun was evidently identical in form with that of the collective neuter plural noun. Since, however, such a pronoun as *ista* meant ' yon female ' (and also ' yon things '), a word of the type of *familia*, in origin doubtless a neuter plural, came to be regarded, because of the coincidence of terminations, as a feminine singular.

The process may be summarised thus: the neuter plural (originally collective) type of **iugā, *iugə* ' yokedom, yokes ' (Vedic *yugá*, Greek ζύγă, Latin *iuga)*, having its termination identical in form, though not in origin, with that of the true feminine singular pronoun **sā* 'that female' (Sanskrit *sá*, Doric Greek ā̆ [haː], Attic ἡ [heː], Gothic *so)*, developed into the grammatical feminine type of **bhugā*, **bhugə* 'flight' (Doric Greek **φυγā*, Attic φυγή, Homeric φύγă-δε 'to flight', Latin *fuga;* cf. Sanskrit *sénā* 'army').

Under the influence of the true feminine **sā* were coined feminines of the type of **eḱuā* 'mare' to **eḱuos* 'stallion' (Sanskrit *áśvā*, Latin *equă* : *áśvas, equus;* cf. Greek ἀδελφή 'sister' : ἀδελφός 'brother' = Sanskrit *sagarbhā* : *sagarbhos)*. How late, relatively speaking, such formations are is shown by the fact that exactly parallel words are none too common. Along with Sanskrit *áśvā*, Latin *equă* one would expect in Greek **ἵππη* beside ἵππος, but here we actually find for the feminine ἡ ἵππος, as in *Odyssey* iv, 635–636, ἵπποι δώδεκα θήλειαι 'twelve female horses'; ἡ ἵππος also means 'cavalry' (e.g., ἵππος ἄλλη χιλίη = English 'another thousand horse'). In like manner we find in older Latin such combinations as *lupus femina* 'female wolf' (Ennius) beside the grammatically later *lupa; Fortunae Iovis puero primigeniae* (inscription) 'to Fortune, firstborn child of Jove'.

Surveying language as a whole, the bulk of purely linguistic evidence seems to give some justification for the inference that *the personal pronoun is the most primitive of all the parts of speech, earlier even than the epithetologue; and that of these pronouns, the one for the first person was the earliest.* The relative would appear to be derived sometimes from the interrogative and sometimes from the demonstrative; and in any case, as its absence in many languages shows (compare also the English type of *the man I saw* beside *the man whom I saw* or *the man that I saw)*, it is of late origin, indeed, the latest of all. The irreducible minimum of pronominal classes seems, then, to be: personal, interrogative, and demonstrative.

Among the epithetologues we may also reckon the *numerals* (cf. p. 202), which appear sometimes as nouns and sometimes as adjectives, Indo-European originally having adjectives for the cardinal numbers from 'one' to 'nineteen', and Semitic for 'one' and 'two'; but nouns in Indo-European from 'twenty' on, and in Semitic from 'three' on.

Beside the epithetologic category stands another, the verbal, which consists solely of verbs (cf. p. 166). The *verb* is defined by

Dionysios Thrax as ' a word without cases, indicative of tenses and persons and numbers, denoting an act or state. And eight [characteristics] accompany the verb: moods, voices, species [primary and derived], forms [simple, compound, and derived from compounds], numbers, persons, tenses, conjugations '. If we compare this definition with that of the epithetologue (see p. 167), we observe that Dionysios says that epithetologues and verbs possess certain characteristics in common: numbers, forms, species, and connotations of things and acts or of states and actions. They differ, on the other hand, in that the epithetologue has cases and genders; while the verb has no cases, but possesses tenses, persons, moods, voices, and conjugations. In some languages, however, verbs have gender, and epithetologues may express tenses and voices, while the moods and conjugations of the verb find close parallels in various types of formation of the epithetologue (cf. pp. 190, 203, 221–223). *We may, then, define the verb as a word characterised by inflexion, if inflected at all, for person.*

The verb and the epithetologue alike (excepting pronouns and practically all numerals) are, for the most part, traceable to identical bases which in themselves belonged to neither category, but contained the germs of both (cf. pp. 150–151, 167). It would seem that we are justified in grouping epithetologues and verbs into a single category which we may term *onomatorrhemes* (coined from Greek ὄνομα ' noun ' and ῥῆμα ' verb '). This classification tacitly implies that the two categories have a common origin. In historical development, there seems to be good reason to believe that the verb came into being later than the epithetologue; and even superficial observation shows that the child, in learning to speak, begins with epithetologues (especially nouns, pronouns, and adjectives), not with verbs.

Despite serious difficulties in details, such as the impossibility, in our present state of knowledge, of tracing any connexion between the personal endings of the verb and the case-endings of the pronoun in Indo-European (cf. p. 153), we seem not wholly unjustified in provisionally holding, as a working hypothesis in the light of the sum total of evidence accessible, that *all the parts of speech have developed from a single source.*

CHAPTER VII

Morphology: The Grammatical Categories

Number: forms and probable chronological order of development — gender: natural and grammatical; its source in animism; original meanings of genders; tendency of neuter to disappear in the noun; distinctions between animate and inanimate gender; gender in non-Indo-European languages — case: origin of the term; the number of case-forms in Indo-European; grammatical and relational cases; cases in non-Indo-European; syncretism — numerals — verbs: basal meaning; persons; aspect in Indo-European and non-Indo-European; mood; tense (development of tenses; suppletion; decline of the tense-system; re-creation of tenses; non-Indo-European tenses); voice (meaning: evolution of the passive from the middle and from the impersonal) — infinitives, participles, and gerunds.

EPITHETOLOGUES and verbs are characterised, according to Dionysios Thrax (pp. 167, 177–178), by certain *grammatical categories,* notably by number for them both, by gender and case for the epithetologue, and by person, (aspect,) mood, tense, and voice for the verb.

Number, common to the epithetologue and to the verb alike (cf. p. 203), has, in the more developed languages, two divisions, while many possess three: singular, plural, and sometimes dual. The *singular* denotes either a single being or thing, or a group of beings or things regarded collectively (as *hand, mankind*); the *plural* more than one being or thing (or, in languages possessing the dual, more than two beings or things) regarded as individuals, collectivity being expressed by the singular (e.g., Latin *latrones,* originally ' individual thieves ' as contrasted with *latrocinium* ' band of thieves ') ; and the *dual,* two beings or things (Sanskrit *áśvau,* Greek ἵππω ' two horses '; Old Irish *fer* ' two men '; Gothic, Old Icelandic, Anglo-Saxon *wit* ' we two '; Lithuanian *vilkù,* Old Church Slavic *vlŭka* ' two wolves '; Arabic *sāriqāni* ' two thieves ').

That *the singular was, chronologically, the earliest number and, in all probability, originally the only one,* is strongly suggested by linguistic evidence as a whole (cf. pp. 172–173). In Indo-European and Semitic, the singular and plural are distinguished by special inflexions (e.g., English *thief* : *thieves;* Latin *latro* : *latrones;* Arabic *sāriquⁿ* ' thief ' : *sāriqūna* ' individual thieves ', as contrasted with the collective singular with plural force, *thiefdom, latrocinium, surrāquⁿ* ' thiefdom ', *saraqatuⁿ* ' thieves, thievery '). Many language-groups present formations radically different; and even in Indo-European the inflexional system of the plural of the epithetologue is less developed than that of the singular.

Very frequently the same form is used for singular and plural alike, as in North American Kwakiutl, Tübatulabal, and Haida; in Siouan only animate beings have a plural, while its personal pronoun sharply differentiates the two numbers in the first person, is identical for both in the second, and is very imperfectly delimited in the third. Like Siouan, the Dravidian Malto of India has no plural for the neuter, and in Dravidian generally the same neuter form often serves for both numbers. Similarly the Australian Dippil and Lake Macquarie languages, the Central American Nahuatl and Totonak, the South American Arawak and extinct Yunkan Mochika, etc., show no distinction between the singular and the plural.

Occasionally the plural is formed by reduplicating the singular, as in Hebrew *pīɸīyōθ* ' cutting edges ' beside *pīyōθ;* Japanese *kuni* ' country ' : *kuni-guni* ' countries '; Bushman (South Africa) *tu* ' mouth ' : *tu-tu* ' mouths '; Malay *dūri* ' thorn ' : *dūri-dūri* ' thorns '; Tsimshian (northern British Columbia) *māl* ' canoe ' : *mmāl* ' canoes '; Sumerian *KUR* ' mountain ' : *KUR-KUR* ' mountains '; and certain languages add the plural of the third personal pronoun or of the demonstrative to form the plural of a noun-form which in itself serves both as singular and as plural (p. 174).

The plural is often made by combining a word meaning ' many, all, people ', and the like with the singular, as in Gurung (of the Tibeto-Burman family) *āba-mae* ' father-many ' = ' fathers ', *naki-jaga* ' dog-all ' = ' dogs '; Ibo (of the Nigero-Camerun group in Africa) *ātur-m nīle* ' sheep-my-all ' = ' all my sheep '; Mare (Melanesian) *re nodei ṅome* ' the totality-man ' = ' the men '; Tahitian *mau taata* ' heap-man ' = ' men '; Nahuatl (Central America) *miek tetl* ' many-stone ' = ' stones '.

Besides the plural, many languages have a dual, as in Indo-European, e.g., Sanskrit *sá vŕkas* ' that wolf ', *táu vŕkau* ' those two wolves ', *té vŕkās* ' those [more than two] wolves '. As a number consciously recognised, the dual appears in Indo-European in

Sanskrit, Avestan, Old Persian, Old Irish, Gothic (here only in the pronoun and in the verb), Lithuanian, Old Church Slavic, Sorbian (moribund), and Slovenian. It is, however, a decaying category, as is clearly shown by its history in Greek; in Latin, there are only four certain survivals: *duo* ' two ' (cognate with the one Modern English remnant *two)*, *ambō* ' both ', *octo* ' eight ', and *vī-gintī* ' twenty ' (for *duī-kṃtī* ' two tens '); and Anglo-Saxon seems to possess it in the two nouns *nosu* '(two) nostrils ' and *doru* '(two leaves of a) door '. In Semitic, only Classical Arabic maintains the number in full vigour (e.g., *sāriquⁿ*, *sāriqāni*, *sāriqūna* ' thief, two thieves, [more than two] thieves '); in the rest of the group, e.g., in Hebrew, it survived solely in words denoting natural pairs and in a few stereotyped phrases (e.g., *kənāφayyim* ' wings ', *yōmayyim* ' two days '; cf. Akkadian *šaptān* ' two lips ', *rīšān* ' two heads '; Rās Shamrah *THMTM* ' two deeps ', *MSBTM* ' tongs ').

Members of many other linguistic groups likewise possess a dual as well as a plural, sometimes both in nouns and in pronouns, sometimes in pronouns only, never in nouns alone. To the first class belong, for instance, the Tibeto-Burman Limbū and the Muṇḍā group (both in India); the Uralic Vogul, Ostyak, Lapp, and Samoyede; Aleut; and the North American Maidu and Eskimo. The second class, which is far more widespread, includes the Tibeto-Himalayan Kanāwᵃrī and Manchāṭī and the Nāgā Angāmi (all in India), the North American Chinuk, and the Central American Maya, and the Talamank-Barbacóa Kuna, of South America, as well as Polynesian, Melanesian, and most Australian languages. It may be symptomatically significant that in the Assamese Lhōtā the dual is well developed in the pronoun, but is only rudimentary in the noun.

The statement is frequently made that, besides the singular, dual, and plural, a trial and even a quadrial number may be found, i.e., not only ' I, we two, we (more than two)', but likewise ' we three ' and ' we four '. This trial number is regarded as peculiar to the Melanesian linguistic group, as in the dialects of Ysabel, Kwamera, Paama, Ambrym, Nogugu, and the Bay of St. Philip and St. James for the trial, and in those of Gao (one of the Solomon Islands), Duke of York Island, and the Gilbert Islands for the quadrial, similar formations being found also in certain dialects of the Central Australian Aranta group. When they are examined, however, they are seen to be merely the plural plus the numerals

for ' two ', ' three ', and ' four ' (e.g., Ysabel *gita* ' we ', *ro gita*
' two-we ', *tolu gita* ' three-we '; the quadrial is analogously formed
wherever it occurs). Grammatically, it is obvious that Ysabel, for
instance, really has only a singular and a plural *(inau* ' I ', *gita*
' we '), and that we are no more justified in calling *tolu gita* a trial
than we are in so terming English *we three* (we might equally call
we nine a nonal number).

Many languages carefully distinguish in the pronoun (especially
in that of the first person dual and plural) between *inclusive* and
exclusive forms, i.e., between ' we two ' = ' I and thou ' (inclusive)
and ' I, but not thou ' (exclusive), as in Santālī, of the Muṇḍā
family in India (see p. 175). In Limbū and some other complex
pronominalised languages of the Tibeto-Burman group (cf. p.
394) we find for the first person such elaborate series as *angā* ' I ',
ān-chī ' I and thou ', *ān-chī-gē* ' I and he ', *ānī* ' I and you ', *ānī-gē*
' I and they ', *chī* here being apparently an old dual suffix, and *nī*
the suffix of the plural. Similar categories are found in the Dravidian languages of India, in Melanesian generally, in North
American (Kwakiutl, Chinuk, Siouan, Fox, etc.), and in Central
American (Chipanek, Mískito, etc.).

As regards the chronological sequence of these three numbers,
there seems to be good reason to suppose that the plural is later
in origin than the singular and is, indeed, derived from it (cf. pp.
172–173, 174–175, 180). For the dual, evidence conflicts. In Bunān,
one of the complex pronominalised languages of the Tibeto-
Burman group, the plural is evidently derived from the dual, as
gyi ' I '; exclusive dual *hing,* inclusive *erang;* exclusive plural *hing-
ji,* inclusive *erang-ji, erang-zhi;* and in Lai, of the Central Kuki-
Chin family (also in India), the plural of the pronoun appears to
be, in reality, a dual *(nang* ' thou ', *nan-nī* ' ye ' : *rang* ' horse ',
rang-nī ' horse-two '; usual plural, *rang rwēl* ' horse-herd ' [?]).
In the Melanesian Mare, each number of the second personal pronoun has a distinct base *(nubo, hmeňo, buhnidže),* as have the
Australian Lake Macquarie *(nin-toa, bula, nura)* and the North
American Coos *(ṇ-; îs-* [inclusive], *xwîn* [exclusive]; *lîn).*

In Semitic, the dual seems to have been formed by inserting *a*
between the stem and the termination, and the plural by lengthening the termination of the singular (e.g., Arabic *sāriquⁿ* ' latro ',
sāriqaⁿ ' latronem ' : *sāriqāni* ' duo latrones ' : *sāriqūna* ' [plus
quam duo] latrones '). In Indo-European, the series appears to

have been, for the nominative, -s in the singular, -ŏ(u), -ĕ(u) in
the dual, and -s in the plural (e.g., Sanskrit *vŕkas*, Greek λύκος,
Lithuanian *vil̃kas*, Latin *lupus*, Gothic *wulfs* ' wolf ' from *ul̥-qᵘos,
*ul̥-pos; Sanskrit *vŕkau*, Greek λύκω, Lithuanian *vilkù* ' two
wolves ', Latin *duo* ' two ' from *ul̥qᵘŏ[u], *d[u]u̯ŏ[u] ; Sanskrit
vŕkās, Gothic *wulfos* '[more than two] wolves ' from *ul̥qᵘŏs,
*ul̥pŏs, Oscan **Núvlanús** ' citizens of Nola '). Here, on the whole,
the dual seems to be independent of the singular and of the plural
alike.

While Indo-European shows seven case-forms (exclusive of the
vocative; cf. pp. 191–192) for the singular and six for the plural,
it has only four for the dual, one of which (the genitive) seems to
be derived from the singular, and another (the locative) from the
plural. This difference in the number of case-forms, together with
the steady decay and final loss of the dual in many languages, may
be interpreted in two opposite ways. Either (1) it was an extremely
primitive number which came to be regarded as unnecessary, so
that it survived only in vestiges; or (2) it was very late and never
developed beyond a comparatively rudimentary stage. The bulk
of evidence from a survey of all linguistic data seems to indicate
that *the dual was somewhat later than the singular, but older than
the plural*, so that the former of the two hypotheses just mentioned
is perhaps the more likely. The antiquity of all three numbers,
however, is attested by the co-existence of words in Indo-European
and Semitic for ' one ', ' two ', and ' three ' in singular, dual, and
plural forms respectively: *oinos* (and other terms), *d(u)u̯ŏ(u),
*tre̯i̯es, and *'aḥadu, *θinai, and *θalāθu respectively, as repre-
sented, for instance, by Old Latin *oinos*, Latin *ūnus, duo, trēs*, and
Arabic *'aḥaduⁿ, iθnāni, θalāθuⁿ*.

To *gender*, which occurs especially in the epithetologue, though
certain languages possess it in the verb as well (cf. p. 190), some
consideration has already been devoted (pp. 175–177). In such
great linguistic families as Indo-European and Semitic, there are
three genders — masculine, feminine, and neuter; and in them the
system as a whole may be divided into the two types of natural
and grammatical gender. In *natural gender*, as found in English,
Armenian, and Modern Persian, for example, animate beings and
inanimate things are classified as masculine, feminine, or neuter
according to their sex or lack of sex *(man* is masculine, *woman* is
feminine, and *town* is neuter). In *grammatical gender*, which is

found in the great majority of languages, this is by no means necessarily the case. Sometimes the sex-classification is found in obvious cases, as when, in Latin, *vir* ' man ' is masculine, *femina* ' woman ' is feminine, and *oppidum* ' town ' is neuter. But in Latin *fluvius* ' river ' is masculine, and *stella* ' star ' is feminine; while in German *Weib* ' woman ' is neuter. In Latin and Greek the words for ' sun ' are masculine *(sol, ἥλιος)*, while those for ' moon ' are feminine *(luna, μήν)*; but these conditions are reversed in German and Lithuanian, the sun being feminine *(Sonne, sáulė)* and the moon masculine *(Mond, měnuo)*. At first glance, there seems to be no rational basis for grammatical gender; and one of the greatest practical difficulties in mastering a new language is learning the gender of its nouns.

Languages possessing grammatical gender usually denote it by the inflexion of the nominative. Thus, in Latin, nouns of the second declension ending in -*us* are normally masculine (e.g., *equus* ' stallion '), and those of the same declension ending in -*um* are neuter (e.g., *dōnum* ' gift '), while those of the first declension ending in -*a* are feminine (e.g., *equa* ' mare '), a distinction clearly shown in adjectives of the type of *bonus* ' good ' (masculine), *bona* (feminine), *bonum* (neuter). Beside these, one finds certain very old nouns which have the same termination for both masculine and feminine, such as Latin *pater* ' father ' (masculine) : *māter* ' mother ' (feminine). It would seem that we must postulate an earlier stage in which (as was still the case in Hittite) there were but two genders, *animate* and *inanimate*, the former comprising all living beings or things regarded as living, and the latter not only all things considered inanimate, but also animate beings regarded as sexless because of their physical immaturity. The neuter is, furthermore, the gender of the vague, indefinite, impersonal, and general, as contrasted with the masculine and feminine, which are definite and endowed with personality.

The chief source of grammatical gender seems to lie in animism, a type of earlier thought which holds that conscious life and will exist in many of what we call lifeless things, which are not merely acted upon, but which themselves act with purpose and intention. Traces of this widespread primitive belief are evident in linguistics, which here confirms the evidence gathered by anthropology and comparative religion. When Longfellow speaks of ' the murmuring pines and the hemlocks ', or when one says that ' the roaring river carries away the bridge which crosses it ', we regard the phrases as poetic or as mere figures of speech. Now they are; but in reality they are survivals of a stage of thought in which the trees were actually supposed to murmur, the river to roar and to carry away, and the bridge to cross as living and sentient beings (cf. p. 19). Some such notion would seem to have caused *fluvius* ' river ' and *pons* ' bridge ' to be masculine in Latin. The ' pine ' and the ' hemlock ', on the other hand, are feminine in Latin *(pīnus, cicūta)*, doubtless because, like other trees (Latin *arbores*, also feminine), they are productive, and so, animistically, are regarded as female. But if trees are female, as being life-giving, what they produce is neuter; thus, *mālus* ' apple-tree ' and *pirus* ' pear-tree ' are feminine, so that the ending -*us* was originally neither masculine nor feminine, but animate; but their fruits, *mālum* ' an apple ' and *pirum* ' a pear ', are neuter.

Frequently the same concept is expressed by different grammatical genders, as when the word for ' tree ' is sometimes neuter (Greek δένδρον, Russian '*derevo)*, sometimes feminine (Latin *arbor*, Avestan *van-*, Breton *gwezenn* [but the cognate Middle Irish *fid* is masculine]), and sometimes masculine (Sanskrit *vrkṣá-*, *taru-*, *druma-)*. Here the reason must lie in the fact that the tree was sometimes regarded as a mere lifeless, sexless, inanimate thing (neuter), sometimes as a female (feminine, passive) living producer, and sometimes as a male (masculine, active) living producer. Thus one may explain such doublets as the two Latin words for ' river ': the masculine *fluvius* originally connoted the river as an active agent, while the neuter *flūmen* expressed primarily a mere collectivity of a passive mass of water. So, again, the most primitive Latin term for ' god ' (see pp. 100, 102) is the neuter *nūmen*, a mere ' nod ' as a manifestation of Divine will and, hence, the vague collectivity well expressed in the abstract sense of English *divinity*. Beside *nūmen* stands the active and concrete *deus* ' god '. Primarily this was used both for gods and for goddesses, like the older use of ὁ θεός and ἡ θεός ' the god, the goddess ' in Greek; and traces of this early usage survive in Latin poetry, which, like all true poetry, is inherently conservative of old forms and of old concepts, as when Vergil employs *deus* both of Venus and of Alecto. Latin adjectives of the third declension like *levis* ' light ' have only animate and inanimate forms *(levis* masculine-feminine, *leve* neuter) ; and the same phenomenon reappears in the

Homeric ῥοδοδάκτυλος Ἠώς [hrodo'daktylos eː'oːs] 'rosy-fingered Dawn ', where in form the noun is feminine, but the adjective is masculine (i.e., active).

When the feminine gender has once become established (see pp. 175–177), female beings or things regarded as such are put in this new category, so that in Latin *dea* ' goddess ' appears beside *deus* ' god ', as does Greek θεά beside θεός, in harmony with Nature's own division of living beings into male and female. Even neuters may be endowed with sex and may thus be regarded as male and female, e.g., Latin *Venus,* the love-goddess, whose name originally meant nothing more than the abstract idea of ' loveliness, desire ' (Sanskrit neuter *vánas-).* Here, too, belongs the German masculine *Gott* ' God ', whose equivalents in Gothic, Old Icelandic, and Anglo-Saxon are masculine when referring to the Christian God, but neuter when denoting pagan deities; not, it would seem, because a heathen god was a mere thing, but because the term originally connoted a vague general idea, probably ' the (collectivity of that which is) invoked ' (cf. pp. 100, 102). The Christian God, on the other hand, is from the beginning, as the Bible shows, a definite Person, so that the distinction between Anglo-Saxon *god* ' god ' (neuter) and *God* ' God ' (masculine) is much the same as that between the Latin neuter *nūmen* and the masculine *deus* (with the later feminine *dea).* A further noteworthy category of the neuter is the *diminutive,* e.g., German *Mädchen* ' girl ', *Fräulein* ' miss ', *Männlein* ' manikin ', the underlying idea being that the individual denoted by such terms is immature, i.e., has not yet proved to be animate by producing offspring, just as in English an infant is often designated as ' it '.

Significance likewise seems to lurk in the fact that the accusative singular of the masculine is identical in form with both the accusative and the nominative singular of the neuter of Indo-European -*o*- stems as in the Latin second declension (e.g., masculine accusative *servum* ' slave ' : neuter accusative *oppidum* ' town ', as contrasted with the nominatives *servus* and *oppidum).* If it be true that there is good reason to regard the nominative as the active case, and the accusative as the non-active or passive (pp. 192–193), we may suggest that *the masculine (and, later, the feminine as well) was primarily the animate, concrete, and active gender, while the neuter was the inanimate, vaguely general, and passive gender.* We have also seen (pp. 175–177) not only that the feminine singular is closely connected with the neuter plural, and that it is, at least in Indo-European, a relatively late formation, but also that it may owe its very origin to its identity of form with the sex-denoting feminine pronoun.

The fact that the feminine and the neuter have the idea of passivity in common may explain such phenomena as the Teutonic neuter for the word for ' woman ' seen in Old Frisian, Old Saxon, Anglo-Saxon *wîf* (English *wife*), Old High German *wîb*, Modern German *Weib* (feminine in Middle High German) as contrasted with the feminine in Gothic *qens*, Old Saxon *quân*, Old Icelandic *kván*, Anglo-Saxon *cwén*, ' woman, wife ', English *queen* (Latin *mulier* ' woman ', on the other hand, like *māter*, is purely animate in gender, and only naturally feminine). It is interesting to note that the conclusions here reached on strictly linguistic evidence had already been attained in principle by the author of the fourteenth-century *Grammatica speculativa* (formerly ascribed to Duns Scotus) : ' the masculine gender is the mode of indicating a thing in its property as agent *(sub proprietate agentis)*, the feminine . . . in its property as passive *(sub proprietate patientis)*, the neuter . . . in its property as neither, [but] indetermined and [applicable] to either indifferently '.

Occasionally, as in the case of the German word for ' God ', which is masculine in the singular, but neuter in the plural *(Gott : Götter)*, a word may be of one gender in the singular and of another in the plural. Thus we have Latin *locus* ' place ', plural *loci* ' individual places ' beside *loca* ' regions, places in general '; *digitus* ' finger ', Vulgar Latin *digita* beside *digiti*, whence Italian *il dito : le dite* beside *i diti*. The same word may have more than one gender, e.g., Old Latin *frons* ' forehead ' as masculine beside the Classical feminine; *dies* ' day ' is both masculine and feminine; and the double gender of *finis* ' end ' is still represented in Spanish *el fin* (masculine) as contrasted with French *la fin* (feminine) ; or a word may have one gender in one language while its cognate in another language of the same family has another. Thus Latin *via* ' way ' is feminine, but Gothic *wigs*, German *Weg*, and Anglo-Saxon *weg* (= English *way)* are masculine; Latin *nĭdus* ' nest ' is masculine, but German and Anglo-Saxon *nest* are neuter; Greek θόλος ' vault ' is feminine, but Old Church Slavic *dolŭ* ' pit ' and Old Icelandic *dalr* ' valley ' are masculine, and Gothic *dal*, German *Tal*, and Anglo-Saxon *dœl* (= English *dale)* are neuter.

Of the three genders, the neuter shows a tendency to disappear in the noun, although it is found, together with the masculine and feminine, in Old Indo-Iranian (Sanskrit, the various Prākrits, Avestan, and Old Persian), Greek, Italic (Latin and Osco-Umbrian), Ligurian (Lepontic), the Baltic Old Prussian, and throughout Slavic. It has vanished from Modern Indian Sindhī, Pañjābī, and Hindī, which have only masculine and feminine, while Bengalī and Oṛiyā have no grammatical gender whatever; from Iranian Afghān; from British Celtic (Welsh, Cornish, and Breton) and from Modern Irish; from the Romance languages; and from the Baltic Lithuanian and Lettish. Hittite has no feminine, but only masculine and neuter (i.e., animate and inanimate). Nevertheless, there are traces of a former existence of the neuter and of grammatical gender generally in a number of languages where they are no longer found as distinct categories, e.g., in the type of Armenian *amaw* ' with a year ' : nominative *am* (cf. Sanskrit *sámā)* for the feminine; and, for the neuter, the type of Armenian *gelumn* ' twist ' : Latin *volūmen* ' roll '); Breton *tra* ' thing ', which is feminine in the singular, but masculine in the plural *(ann dra* ' the thing ' : *tri zra* ' three things ') ; and the Lithuanian type of *měnas* ' art ' (masculine) : Sanskrit *mánas-*, Greek μένος ' mind ' (neuter).

A number of languages distinguish between an animate (masculine or feminine) and an inanimate (neuter) in such constructions as Latin *occisus gladio* ' slain by a sword ', but *occisus ab hoste* ' slain by an enemy '; Spanish *el hijo ama á su madre* ' the son loves his mother ' (and personifications like *amo á mí patria* ' I love my country '), but *leo un libro* ' I read a book ' (cf. pp. 112, 246), a construction found likewise in Sicily and in South Italy, as well as in some Rhaeto-Romanic dialects. Rumanian, since the seventeenth century, has used *pe* = Latin *per* in the same way; Old French employs *de* to mark the genitive denoting a thing or a class, but the genitive without a preposition when referring to a specific person (e.g., *la cort de roi* ' the royal court ', but *la cort le roi* ' the court of the [specified] king '; cf. p. 245) ; Old Church Slavic uses the genitive as the objective case for animate, but the accusative for inanimate, as *vĭzljubiši Gospoda Boga svojego* (genitive) ' thou shalt love the Lord thy God ', but *vŭzŭmi lože tvoje* (accusative) ' take up thy couch '; many modern East Armenian dialects, such as those of Erivan and Erzerum, make the accusative of nouns denoting inanimate things coincide in form with the nominative, while that of nouns denoting animate beings is in the genitive-dative; Modern Persian distinguishes in the plural between animate and inanimate (e.g., *mard-ān* ' men ', but *gul-hā* ' roses ').

If the problem of gender be viewed in the light of the principles here set forth, it is seen to have a perfectly valid reason for existence, granting, as we must grant if we are to understand its true nature, the premisses and the logic of earlier animistic thought; and its very intricacies and apparent inconsistencies furnish clues of much value in studying the evolution of human thought.

Gender in non-Indo-European languages may here be treated very briefly, since they present little in principle that is not found in Indo-European, their evidence both confirming and being confirmed by what has already been given. Semitic, in the historic period, possesses only two genders, masculine and feminine (e.g., Arabic *maliku^n* : *malikatu^n* ' king : queen '), but some old nouns and adjectives are clearly only animate (e.g., Arabic *'abu^n* ' father ', *'ummu^n* ' mother ' = Hebrew *'āß, 'ēm;* Arabic *ḥāmilu^n* ' pregnant ') ; and occasionally the same word may be either masculine or feminine (e.g., Hebrew *dereχ* ' way, road '; *lāšōn* ' tongue '). The question may even be raised whether the distinctive Semitic feminine sign *-t-* was not originally a characteristic of the inanimate, and whether the *-a-* preceding it may not primarily have been identical with the accusative (or passive) singular of the masculine (or active) gender (e.g., Arabic *maliku^n* ' rex ', *malika^n* ' regem ' : *malik-a-t-u^n* ' regina ').

The Dravidian languages distinguish between beings endowed with reason and all others, terming their designating nouns ' high-caste ' (high-caste male and high-caste female) and ' casteless ' respectively. Here Tamil, Malayālam, and Kanarese have separate suffixes for male and female in the singular, but not in the plural; Telugu, Kurukh, Malto, and Kōlāmī use the casteless (neuter) for the feminine singular; while Kui and Gōṇḍī employ the casteless for both feminine numbers. A similar classification prevails in the Caucasian languages, the subdivisions ranging from three in Abk'az (rational male, rational female, irrational) to four (e.g., in Andi, rational male, rational female, animals and many inanimate objects, other things), six (e.g., Ingush and Chechen), and even eight (e.g., T'ush).

The distinction between animate and inanimate underlies the

system of the demonstrative pronouns in the Muṇḍā family in India, and is seen in the African Zande or Nyamnyam of the Ubangi group (also only in pronouns), as well as in the American Cherokee, Fox, Ponka, and Maya. In the American Iroquoian the division is between higher and lower, and in the African Māsai (of the Nilo-Equatorial family) between great and strong as contrasted with little and weak. In the American Chinuk the neuter may denote an indefinite individual (e.g., *ikā'nax* [masculine] ' the chief ', but *Lkā'nax* [neuter] ' a chief '), the neuter here having indicated, until recently, both the indefinite singular and the indefinite plural. Some language-groups, notably the Semitic, show gender in the verb, e.g., Hebrew *yiχtōβ* ' he will write ', *tiχtōβ* ' she will write ', *tiχtōβ* ' thou (masculine) wilt write ', *tiχtəβī(m)* ' thou (feminine) wilt write '.

In certain other languages we find what are termed classes rather than genders. Thus in the Melanesian Isai we have two classes, the first comprising names of parts of the body, relationships, things closely associated with their possessors, and some nouns of place used as prepositions; the second including all other nouns, though with many subdivisions distinguished by possessive nouns. Classes are likewise present in the North American Haida, where objects are classified as long, slender, round, flat, animate, full of, material, branching, and the like; and perhaps in the American Chibcha Talamank and Melchora. In Ēmpeō, a dialect of the Nāgā-Bodo sub-group in India, the plural has classes (e.g., *minā-mī* ' men ', *godōm-dūng* ' cows ', *jingbāng-jīō* ' trees ', *mi-kēdā* ' fires ') ; and the African Bantu family has from seventeen to twenty-three classes. It is not quite certain whether these classes can properly be termed genders. They appear to suggest, rather, the determinatives of Indo-European (see pp. 156–158), though the problem requires much further investigation.

We turn next to a consideration of *case*, i.e., to the form of an epithetologue which indicates its relation to another word either by means of an empty word (cf. p. 155) or by means of an inflexional termination (cf. pp. 151–155; contrast English *to man* with Latin *virō*). The word ' case ' has a history that is not without interest. Derived, through French, from Latin *casus*, itself a translation of Greek πτῶσις ['ptoːsis], it means, literally, ' a fall ' (cf. German *Fall*, Russian *padežǔ* ' case ', literally ' fall '), because the cases were regarded as ' falling away ' from the nominative, the ' direct ' or ' straight ' case *(ὀρθή, εὐθεῖα [πτῶσις])*. As this suggests, one case was considered to be original, the nominative or noun-case *par excellence (ὀνομαστική, nominativus;* cf. *ὄνομα, nomen* ' name, noun '). The Sanskrit grammarians termed case *vibhakti-* ' separation, distinction, modification ' as being a modification of the bare stem-form.

The *number* of case-forms varies widely, twenty-three being ascribed to Georgian (of the South Caucasian family), but only one each to Modern French, Italian, Spanish, etc. In all, we may reckon the number as at least thirty-six, of which Indo-European has eight (originally, perhaps, nine or even ten), and Semitic three (with clear traces of a fourth). Some of these are, in reality, compound cases, i.e., they are made by adding one case-termination to another, as in Vogul *εü-püänə-n-ət* ' with his children ' = the adessive *εü-püänə-n* ' near his children ' + the locative *εü-püänə-t* ' in his children '; Kichua (Peruvian) inessive *yayappi* ' in what is the father's ' = the genitive *yaya-p* ' father's ' + the locative *yaya-pi* ' in the father '; and possibly Indo-European ablatives of the types of Sanskrit *mukhatás* ' from the mouth ', Latin *funditus* ' from the bottom ' = the ablative ending *-t* + the genitive ending *-o/es*. Of the eleven cases in Uralic, for example, only six are simple in this sense, the remaining five being compound.

This wealth of cases, apparently arising from the need for exact definiteness often felt in earlier stages of language (cf. pp. 21–22), evolved, it would seem, from the addition of empty words (cf. p. 155) to the epithetologue proper. This appears to be true in the Dravidian and Tibeto-Burman linguistic families; and the elaborate system found in North Caucasian is clearly relatively late in development. Ultimately the problem is involved with that of the origin of inflexion in general (cf. pp. 151–155).

For a practical consideration of case we may best begin with a survey of the Indo-European system, particularly as represented by Sanskrit, the language most conservative in this regard; and we may restrict ourselves to the singular, as being the most primitive number (cf. p. 179). Here we find eight cases (originally, possibly, nine): nominative *(yajñás* ' worship, sacrifice '), accusative *(yajñám)*, dative *(yajñáya* for **yajñái-a* ' for sacrifice '; the most primitive form appears, e.g., in Old Latin *duenoi* = Classical *bonō*, Avestan *vəhrkāi* ' to a wolf ' = Greek λύκῳ = Lithuanian *vilkui)*, genitive *(yajñásya* ' of sacrifice '; cf. Homeric λύκοιο ' of a wolf ' for *λυκοσιο), locative (yajñé ' in sacrifice '; cf. Greek οἴκοι ' in the house, at home '), ablative (yajñât ' from sacrifice '; cf. Old Latin meretōd ' from merit ', facilumēd ' most easily '), instrumental (Vedic yajñā ' with, or by, sacrifice '), and vocative (yájña ' O sacrifice! ').

From these cases we may at once drop the vocative, which is a mere base-form used as an exclamation (cf. p. 150), and so is the epithetologic counterpart of the imperative of the verb (see p. 209). The true cases seem to fall into two categories, nominative and accusative on the one hand, and dative, genitive, locative, ablative, and instrumental on the other; the first category we may term grammatical, and the second relational (cf. pp. 194–201).

The nominative case is conventionally defined as the case of the subject of the verb, and the accusative as the case of the direct object of the verb (e.g., filius patrem amat ' the son loves the father '). It would seem more exact, however, to define the nominative as the active case and the accusative as the non-active (passive is here too strong a term). This view seems to be sustained by the demonstrative pronoun (see p. 175), which appears to distinguish sharply not only between animate and inanimate gender, but also between the active (nominative) case and the inactive cases (neuter nominative and all non-nominative cases), as is shown by the masculine and feminine nominative Sanskrit sá(s), sā́, Greek ὁ, ἡ, Gothic sa, so, as contrasted with the neuter nominative tád, τό, þat-a, and the masculine and feminine accusative tám, tằm, τόν, τήν, þan-a, þo. Furthermore (cf. p. 186), the masculine accusative and the neuter nominative are formed identically in the -o-stems (e.g., Latin servum : oppidum). One may even suggest the possibility that the s of the active form *so(s) recurs in the -s which characterises the nominative singular and plural (cf. p. 183); and that the -t of the non-active pronominal base *tod is also seen in passive participles of the type of *mṇ'to- ' thought of ' (Sanskrit matá-, Greek αὐτό-ματος ' spontaneous ' [literally, ' self-thought '], Latin com-mentus ' devised ', Middle Irish der-met ' oblivion ', Lithuanian miñtas ' thought of '; Latin captus ' seized ', Middle Irish cacht ' maid-servant ', Gothic hafts ' seized ').

From the point of view of strict logic, there should be no neuter nominative; nor should there be a masculine or feminine nominative in connexion with a passive verb (cf. pp. 217–218). An inactive person or thing cannot, theoretically, have the active function implied by possession of an active (i.e., nominative) case; nor can a being normally active properly have an active case when that being does not act, but is acted upon. Such constructions as Latin *oppidum stat* ' the town stands ', *a filio pater amatur* ' the father is loved by the son ', are logically absurd, and *oppidum a Pompilio conditur* ' the town is founded by Pompilius ' is doubly so; only the types *filius patrem amat* ' the father loves the son ' and *oppidum condit Pompilius* ' Pompilius founds the town ' are logically possible. Nevertheless, as has happened often enough in realms other than linguistic, practical convenience and analogy (cf. pp. 106–114) have triumphed over logic and theory; and from the earliest historic period we find the neuter nominative enjoying good and regular standing in the Indo-European system of cases.

The close connexion here posited between the nominative and the accusative as contrasted with all other cases appears in language generally. The same form very frequently serves for both, their functions being sufficiently indicated by their position in the sentence, quite as in English *the son loves the father* as contrasted with *the father loves the son* over against Latin *filius patrem amat : pater filium amat*. This is true, for instance, of the Tibeto-Burman family, of Malay, Yenisei-Ostyak, Basque, African Māsai and Zande (or Nyamnyam), and many languages of the three Americas (e.g., Maidu, the extinct Mochika, and Tupi-Guaraní). In Eskimo the nominative and accusative are classed together as the *absolutive* case, whereas in Uralic the nominative has a place apart even from the accusative, appearing in its simple stem-form.

Besides its function as the non-active case, the accusative has a *terminative* or *illative* signification as denoting the end of motion toward which action proceeds, as in Latin *Italiam . . . Lavinia venit littora* ' he came to Italy . . . the shores of Lavinia ', *proficisci exilium* ' to depart into exile ', *sacrificatum ire* ' to go to sacrifice ' (similarly in Indo-Iranian, Greek poetry, Old Irish, Teutonic [except Old High German and Gothic], and sporadically elsewhere; cf. likewise Hebrew *ṣāφōnāh* ' to the north, northward '). Whether this terminative force is derived from the inactive value of the case, or whether the primary function of the accusative was itself to indicate the end of motion (so that, e.g., *filius patrem amat* originally meant, not ' the son loves the father ', but 'the son directs his love until it comes to the father '), or whether two cases primarily distinct have coincided in form, is a problem still unsolved.

Other linguistic families frequently show one or more forms corresponding to the Indo-European and Semitic accusative in its terminative aspect, as in the North Caucasian Chechen and in Burmese, where the terminative case has much the same force as that of the African *directive,* which indicates that action takes place in favour of some one or toward a specific end. The terminative finds further analogues in the Eskimo *allative,* denoting that toward which an action tends (e.g., *sawimmut* ' toward a knife ' for **sawik-mut);* in the Uralic *lative* and *illative,* the former indicating motion up to, and the latter motion to the interior of (e.g., Mordvin *kudo-s* ' as far as a house '; Cheremiss *nur-əško* ' to the interior of the forest '); and, in some measure, in the Yukagir, Samoyede, and Eskimo *prosecutive,* denoting motion along (e.g., Eskimo *sawik-kut* ' along a knife '). The Caucasian Ch'ak'ur even has a *superlative* case, indicating motion toward the top, a combination of the superessive (see p. 198) and the illative (e.g., *suwalk̑a* ' toward the top of the mountain ', a blend of *suwa-l* ' upon the mountain ' and *suwa-k̑a* ' into the mountain '). Nouns as well as verbs may take an accusative as their direct object, as in Latin *quid tibi hanc curatiost rem* ' why are you worrying about this matter? ' (cf. pp. 220–221).

The word ' accusative ' has its own history. It is borrowed from the Latin *accusativus* ' relating to a complaint or accusation ', so that the Latin grammarian Varro called it ' the case of accusing ' *(casus accusandi);* but this Latin term is only a clumsy translation of the Greek word for the case, αἰτιατική ' indicating the thing caused by the verb ', from αἰτία meaning both ' cause ' and ' accusation '. Although the Latin grammarian Priscian rightly gave *causativus* ' causal ' as an alternative rendering to *accusativus,* the false translation prevailed over the true, and has become too fixed to be overthrown. The reason for the designation ' causal ' was that the case was regarded philosophically as the cause of the action denoted by the verb, e.g., in our stock-sentence *filius patrem amat, patrem* ' father ' is the reason why the ' son ' *(filius)* ' loves ' *(amat).*

Turning to the *relational cases,* we may first consider the *dative,* which is conventionally defined as ' the case of the indirect object ', though it might equally well be termed ' *the to- or for-case* ', *its general meaning in Indo-European being that of advantage (or disadvantage)*. Its name means ' relating to giving ' (Latin *dativus* as a translation of Greek δοτική; cf. Varro's paraphrase by *casus dandi* ' case of giving '), doubtless derived from stock-phrases of the type of *pater filio librum dat* ' the father gives a book to the son '. It is, in essence, an inactive case (cf. Greek nominative ὁ, but dative τῷ; Gothic nominative *sa*, but dative *þamma;* see p. 175) ; and originally it may have been associated rather closely in formation with the locative (in Hittite, indeed, the same case serves as dative and as locative alike, e.g., *pēdi* ' to, or in, a place ' from **pede/oi)* and with certain types of the genitive. In Indo-European its termination was * *-ei* or * *-oi* (cf. Praenestine *Numasioi* = Latin *Numeriō* for *Numasio-oi ' for Numerius '; Oscan **p, pater, patereí** = Latin *patrī* ' for a father ') ; and this may have been the full grade (pp. 65–66) of a termination-base *ei or *oi whose reduced grade *ī* from *ₑi* is seen in the Latin genitive type of *virī* ' of a man ', and whose zero-grade *i* appears in Latin compounds like *belli-ger* ' war-waging ' and in the locative (cf. Sanskrit *áśmani* ' in a stone ', Greek οἴκοι ' at home '). If this be true, *we may class the dative, locative, and some types of the genitive together.*

Besides its use as the case of the indirect object, the dative occasionally has, in Indo-Iranian, Latin, Teutonic, and Slavic, a *lative* force denoting the place toward which, in contrast to the *illative* force of the accusative (pp. 193–194, as Latin *it clamor caelo* ' the shout goes towards the sky ' [but does not necessarily reach it] as contrasted with *Romam it* ' he goes to Rome ' [and reaches the city] ; Anglo-Saxon *he heofonum ástág* ' he rose heavenwards '; Old Church Slavic *stizaše vŭzrastu* 'he was attaining to maturity'). A similar use of the dative is common in Tibeto-Burman as well as in Georgian and other Caucasian languages; and in Georgian it may even serve as a direct object, a usage which reminds one of the Spanish type of *el hijo ama á su madre* ' the son loves his mother ' (see pp. 112, 246; for the so-called dative of agent see p. 228).

The next case to be considered is the *genitive*, whose primary meaning has been obscured by its prevailing functions of *possession (liber Petri* ' Peter's book '), of *material (virga lauri* ' twig of laurel '), and of *part (pars mundi* ' part of the world '; for the partitive genitive as subject or object see pp. 243–244). *It appears best definable as the generic case*, though its current name is derived from Latin *genitivus* ' relating to generation or birth ', an awkward rendering of its Greek designation γενική, which the Armenian and Syrian grammarians translated very accurately by ' generic ' *(serakan, gensānāyā,* the latter borrowed from Greek γένος = Latin *genus).*

In Indo-European, the termination of the genitive singular seems to have been **-es* or **-os* (cf. Latin *nominis* ' of a name ' for **nomen-es* beside Old Latin *nominus* for **nomen-os, Diovos* ' Iovis, of Jupiter '), to which **-io* (possibly connected with the relative pronoun seen in Sanskrit *yá-,* Phrygian ιος, and Greek ὅς ' who ') or the adjectival formative *-o-* may be added, as in Sanskrit *vŕkas-ya* ' of a wolf ', Homeric λύκοιο for **λυκοσ-ιο* beside Attic λύκον for **λυκοσ-ο* (perhaps a relic of a pre-inflexional stage [cf. pp. 153–154] ; for the suffixing of the uninflected relative **-io,* cf. the Celtic relative verb represented by Old Irish *berte* ' who carry ' from **'bheront-io,* Middle Welsh *yssyd* ' who is ' from **es'ti-io,* Gaulish *dugiiont-io* ' who make '). An ending *-ī* from **-ei* appears in Italic and Celtic genitives of the types of *virī* ' of a man ', Old Irish *fir* from **uirī,* Gaulish *Segomarī* ' of Segomaros '; and the zero-grade *-i* in such Latin compounds as *belli-ger* ' war-waging ' (cf. p. 195). This generic *-ī* is likewise seen in the types of Latin *aequī faciō* ' I make it the same, count it equal ', *serviō, servībam* ' I serve(d)' for **servī-iō, *servī-bam* (cf. the genitive *servī),* Sanskrit *mithunī-kar-* ' make a pair of ', and perhaps Lithuanian *sakýdavau* ' I was wont to say ' and Gaulish *logitoe* (if for **logītu)* ' he made a tomb ' (?) (cf. Gaulish *loka* [i.e., *loga]* ' grave '). It may even be suggested that the genitive termination **-es* or **-os* is ultimately identical with the neuter (i.e., vaguely generic; cf. p. 184) formation seen in such words as Sanskrit *jánas* = Greek γένος = Latin *genus,* so that the Greek genitives λύκον, λύκοιο would have meant originally ' relating to wolfness, wolfish ' derived from a neuter noun **λυκος* ' wolfness ', while such forms as Sanskrit *jánasas* = Greek γένους for **γενεσος* = Latin *generis* for **genes-es* would really be double genitives.

In any event, there would appear to be an almost indubitable trace of connexion between the genitive and the neuter in the old types preserved in Sanskrit *asmákam, yuṣmákam* : Latin *nostrum, vostrum* ' of us, of you ' (cf. such neuters as Sanskrit *yugám* : Latin *iugum* ' yoke '). The Latin genitive type of *quoius, cuius* 'of whom' may also fall within this category (cf. likewise the adjective *quoius);* and German *unser* ' of us ' (cf. Anglo-Saxon *úre)* was probably originally the nominative-accusative neuter singular of the adjective *unser* ' ours ' (Old High German *unsêr,* Anglo-Saxon *úre).*

From this generic basal signification, all the uses of the genitive seem derivable. Its employment as a *possessive case* is eminently generic and shades off into a purely adjectival connotation. The distinction between Latin *palatium regale* ' royal palace ' and *palatium regis* ' king's palace ' is essentially that between the generic and the specific, the former denoting the palace of kings generally, the latter that of an individual monarch; and the same is true of compounds as contrasted with a noun plus a genitive, as Sanskrit *deva-putra-* ' god-son, divine son ' (i.e., the typical son of any deity) : *devasya putra-* ' son of a (particular) god '.

The interpretation here suggested seems amply sustained by phenomena in many non-Indo-European languages. In Uralic, the genitive was originally a possessive adjective (e.g., Mordvin *škem-ən* ' mine, of me '), as it really is in Muṇḍā Santālī; while in Bunān, a complex pronominalised member of the Tibeto-Burman group, many adjectives appear to have been primarily genitives, and in Dravidian the genitive is in form an adjective. In some Tibeto-Burman languages, the adjective, if preceding the noun, is put in the genitive, and the pair form a quasi-compound, the postpositions indicating case being added only to the second component. Here the genitive sign itself seems to be, properly speaking, a demonstrative pronoun, so that Tibetan *mi-i khyim* ' man's house ' literally means ' man-that house ', a construction found also in Bantu and other African groups. In Melanesian and Indonesian, in Abk'az (of the North Caucasus), in some languages of Africa (Somali for instance) and of the Americas (e.g., Iroquois, Chikito, and Lule), the type of ' his-house the-boy ' for ' the boy's house ' is used, as Maya *una šibilpal.*

The position of the genitive and of the adjective in relation to the noun which they define is likewise highly significant. *Generally speaking, if the adjective precedes its noun, the genitive also precedes it; if the adjective follows its noun, the genitive also follows it, these statements likewise holding true of the order of the components of a compound word.* Sporadic instances where the genitive precedes while the adjective follows, as in Choctaw, Tupi-

Guaraní, Kunama, Mishmi, and Basque, or where the adjective precedes while the genitive follows, as in Efik, seem insufficient in importance to vitiate the principles of sequence as a whole. *In general, the tendency both of the genitive and of the adjective appears to be to precede, rather than to follow, the noun.*

The *genitive of material* and the *partitive genitive* seem to be eminently generic (e.g., Latin *virga lauri* ' twig of laurel, laurel-twig '; French *des hommes sont venus* '[indefinite beings of the general type of] men have come ' as contrasted with *les hommes sont venus* ' the [specific] men have come '). The generic force is apparently the origin of such adverbs as German *nachts* ' at night '; and it doubtless underlies such constructions as Latin *notus animi paterni* ' famed for paternal spirit ' and Oscan *aserum eizazunc egmazum* ' to make seizure involving these matters ', besides probably being the reason for the confusion of the genitive with the ablative (cf. p. 199; for the Slavic use of the genitive to denote the animate object see p. 188).

The locative is the ' in-case ', normally characterised by the termination *-i* (e.g., Old Latin *Romai* ' at Rome ', Latin *domī* ' at home ' for *domo-i*, Greek οἴκοι ' at home ', Sanskrit *udáni* ' in water '), though sometimes only the bare stem is used (e.g., Sanskrit *udán* beside *udáni;* the same phenomenon is seen in Āhom, a language of the Tai group). Semitic seems to show traces of a locative in *-ŭ* (e.g., Arabic *fawqu* ' above ', *qablu* ' previously ', Syriac *kaldū* ' enough, in sufficiency '). In many languages, the locative is represented by cases which indicate shadings not found in (or perhaps amalgamated into) the simple locative. Here belong the *inessive,* denoting ' in '; the *adessive,* ' at ' or ' near '; the *super-essive,* ' on '; and the *subessive,* ' under ' (e.g., Georgian *saxl-si* ' in the house ', Finnish *kaivo-ssa* ' in the well '; Votyak *atai-len* ' near the father '; Georgian *saxl-zed* ' upon the house '; Ch'ak'ur *diuwar-ik`* ' under the wall ').

The ablative is the ' from-case '. In Indo-European it is clearly distinguished only in *-o*-stems, where its sign is *-t* (e.g., Sanskrit *yajñát* ' from sacrifice ', Old Latin *Gnaivōd* ' from Gnaeus ', *facilumēd* ' most easily ' [cf. p. 170]; cf. also Delphic Greek ϝοικω [woiko:] ' from the house ' for *ϝoik̂ōt).* This *-t* was apparently augmented by the genitival *-os* (cf. p. 196), thus giving rise to the *-ts* from *-tos* shown by the Hittite ablatives of the type of *arunaz* (probably [arunats]) ' from the sea ' (cf. also Sanskrit

mukhatás ' from the mouth ', Greek ἐντός '[from] within ', Latin
funditus ' from the bottom ') ; and in Italic and Hittite this ablative in *-*tos* has been extended to other than -*o*-stems. For the
most part, however, the ablative coincides in form with the genitive
(e.g., Sanskrit *nāvás* ' of the boat ' or ' from the boat '), the syncretism (cf. pp. 201–202) being aided by the fact that the ideas of
' from ' and ' part of ' frequently overlap. In the Caucasian Chechen we find, beside the ablative, a *delative* and an *elative* (e.g.,
āmalgēra ' down from use ' — *āmalgē* itself being the allative [cf.
p. 194] of *āmal; āmalxī* ' out from use ' — *āmalx* being itself an
illative [cf. p. 194] ; cf. also Finnish *kala-sta* ' out from a fish ').

The remaining case in Indo-European is the *instrumental,* which
is essentially the ' *with-case* ' in all the senses of accompaniment,
instrument, and manner (e.g., Sanskrit *mṛgā mṛgaiḥ saṇgam
anuvrajanti* ' deer seek companionship with deer ', *paśubhiḥ
samānāḥ* ' like beasts ', *yajñais tu devān prīṇāti* ' by sacrifices he
propitiates the gods ', *bhrātṛsnehena kālo neyaḥ* ' time is to be
passed with brotherly love '). The case has a special form only
in Indo-Iranian, Hittite, Agnean, Armenian, Old Saxon, Old High
German (also in certain pronouns in other Teutonic languages),
and Balto-Slavic; but traces of it are found elsewhere, as in Greek
κρυφῇ ' secretly ', Latin *sacrō-sanctus* (?) ' sacrosanct ', and English *the* in the type of *the more, the merrier* (Anglo-Saxon ðý *mára,*
ðý *má* ' the more, the more ').

Agnean distinguishes between the instrumental and the *comitative (śolyo* ' by means of life ' : *śolaśśäl* ' together with life '), as
does the North American Maidu *(tsā'-ni* ' by means of a stick ' :
tsā'-kan ' together with a stick '). It is not wholly impossible that
Indo-European itself may once have differentiated between the
two, since one group (Indo-Iranian, Armenian, Greek, Italic, and
Celtic) has an instrumental formation in -*bh*- (Sanskrit *áśvābhis*
' by mares ', Armenian *mardov* ' by man ', Greek θεόφι[ν] ' by a
god, by gods ', Latin *deābus* ' by goddesses ', Old Irish *feraib* ' by
men '), whereas another group (Teutonic and Balto-Slavic) forms
the case in -*m*- (Gothic *wulfam* ' by wolves ', Lithuanian *rañkomis*
' by hands ', Old Churck Slavic *vlŭkomĭ* ' by a wolf '). It seems
at least possible to suggest that the forms in -*m*- were originally
true instrumentals, while those in -*bh*- were comitatives, the base
meaning of *bh apparently having been ' with '.

In Indo-Iranian, as well as in Caucasian and Dravidian, the

instrumental (often called *ergative* in grammars of the Caucasian languages) assumes a position of unusual importance. Here the active voice is in large measure supplanted by the passive (cf. pp. 168–169, 220), with the result that the objectival accusative becomes the subjectival nominative, while the old subjectival nominative becomes the instrumental or ergative, the type of *Peter strikes Paul* being replaced by *Paul is struck by Peter*. So far as Indo-Iranian is concerned, this use is found chiefly with perfect passive participles in the neuter singular, as Sanskrit *devena gatam* '(it was) gone by the god ' = ' the god went ', Hindī *ādmī-ne larkā mārā* ' by the man the boy (was) struck ' = ' the man struck the boy ' (also *ādmī-ne larkō-ko mārā*, literally ' a viro puerum [vel, puero] caesum '; so also, perhaps, in the Iranian Balōčī *thaf-á ma-na gipta* ' fever-by me caught ' = ' I have caught a fever '). In the Caucasian Avar, similarly, we have *dìca razì ha-v-ùla emèn* ' through-me contented makes-himself father ' = ' I make my father contented '. In Georgian, this usage is restricted to tenses not derived from the present, as also in Mingrelian, where ' I write a letter ' is *me ve'er c'eril-sa*, but ' I have written a letter ' is either *iman dac'era c'crili* ' by me (has been) written a letter ' or *c'erili da-mi-c'eria* ' a letter is-to-me-written (i.e., ' I have a letter written ').

In Kharosṭhī Prākrit this process has gone so far that the instrumental tends to supplant both the nominative as subject-case and the accusative as object-case, e.g., *Maharayaputra kala Pumña-balena lihati* ' Prince (?) Pumñabala, the Mahārāja's son, writes ' (*Maharayaputra kala* in the nominative, the appositional *Pumña-balena* in the instrumental), *śramana Caǵuṣenena viṣarjideṣi* ' thou didst send the monk Cagusena ' (*śramana* in the accusative, the appositional *Caǵuṣenena* in the instrumental). In Avestan, the sociative force of the instrumental results in its use as subject or object, as *kuθrā manō vahistəm kuθrā θwā xšaθrā* 'where (is) Best Mind, where (is) thy Kingdom? ' (nominative and instrumental side by side), *kva narąm ʲristanąm azdbīš barāma* ' where shall we carry the bones of dead men? '

It is not impossible that traces of yet another case, which we may term the *indefinite*, have survived in Greek, where the Indo-European vocalism is especially well preserved, in such forms as χαμαί ' on (or, to) the ground ', παραί ' beside ', and such infinitives as εἶπαι ' to say ', δόμεναι, Cyprian δοϝεναι = Attic δοῦναι ' to give '.

Usually these are regarded as datives or locatives, but if that were so, one would expect, rather, *χαμεί, *χαμοί, etc. (cf. p. 221).

At least twelve other cases are recorded sporadically. The *affective*, found in the Caucasian Ch'ak'ur and T'ush, denotes the object affected by the action of the verb (e.g., Ch'ak'ur *da:k'i-k'lä γež:dešod* ' the father does not see ' [because affected by blindness] ; T'ush *maik̦ nane-x ĵ̂xnas* ' I asked bread of the mother ' [thus affecting her]). The *caritive* denotes ' lack of ' (e.g., Abk'az *ĵ̂ika-dà* ' without salt '; T'ush *nan-c'ī* ' without a mother ') ; the *causative*, ' reason why ' (e.g., Udi *t'ur-ènk* ' because of a bone ') ; and the *comparative*, that one person or thing is greater or less than another (e.g., Chechen *āmal-al* ' more [or less] than custom '; Ḥürq'ili *ava-išir* ' more [or less] than a mother '). The *discriminative* denotes the performer of an act directed toward an object, i.e., it indicates the noun as a subject in sentences with a noun or pronoun as object (e.g., Siuslaw *cî'l·xūn qĩutc͏ᵘwa'nî* ' a woman [nominative *qĩutcū'nî*] shook him ') ; and the *equative* ' like, as ' (e.g., Georgian *katsi-vit'* ' like a man '; Ḥürq'ili *ava-cad* ' as a mother ').

The *factive* (sometimes termed *mutative* or *translative)* expresses the idea of becoming or being changed into something else (e.g., T'ush *nane-γ* ' to become, act like, a mother '; Finnish *silmä-ksi* ' turned into an eye '; Japanese *tori-to* ' turned into a bird ') ; the *identic*, sameness or identity with (e.g., Ḥürq'ili *ada-oan* ' same as a father ') ; the *modal*, manner (e.g., Mingrelian *cira-t'* ' girlishly ') ; the *potential* (only with pronouns), possibility (e.g., Ḥürq'ili *za:-sä* ' I possibly ') ; the *similative* or *conformative*, likeness, resemblance (e.g., Ḥürq'ili *dis-γuna*, Eskimo *sawittut* for *sawik-tut* ' like to a knife ') ; and the *subjective*, that which is used in the performance of an act (e.g., Chukchi *e'ce uwi'iᵉ* ' she cooked with fat ' = ' she cooked fat ').

In Indo-European, we find eight distinct case-forms in Sanskrit; Greek and Lithuanian have seven; Hittite and Old Church Slavic, six; Latin and Teutonic, five (Old French and Modern English, only two) ; Albanian, four; and Armenian and Old Irish, three. This reduction in the number of case-forms, with the result that some of them take over the functions of one or more others, gives rise to the linguistic phenomenon known as *syncretism*. The reason for this seems to be phonetic decay of the characteristic case-endings. Consequently, cases primarily unlike in form become outwardly identical, and their functions, originally distinct, are amalgamated, so that in the historic period what is superficially a single case has functions which are logically irreconcilable (cf. pp. 19–20).

In the singular, the nominative coincides in form with the vocative in Hittite and Albanian; with the accusative in Old Irish and Old Church Slavic; and with the vocative, accusative, and locative in Armenian. The accusative and vocative coincide in Teutonic. The instrumental coincides with the ablative in Greek; with the dative in Old Irish; with the dative and locative in Teutonic; with the dative, ablative, and genitive in Albanian; and with the dative, ablative, and locative in Latin consonant-declensions. The dative coincides with the locative in Hittite; and with the ablative and genitive in Armenian. The genitive coincides with the locative in Latin vowel-declensions; with the ablative in Sanskrit (except in vowel-declensions), Lithuanian, and Old Church Slavic; and with the ablative, locative, and vocative in Old Irish.

In the plural, the nominative coincides with the vocative in Sanskrit, Hittite, Armenian, Greek, Latin, Teutonic, Lithuanian, and Old Church Slavic; and with the vocative and accusative in Albanian. The accusative coincides with the vocative in Old Irish. The instrumental coincides with the dative and ablative in Greek; with the dative, ablative, and locative in Latin, Old Irish, and Teutonic; and with the dative, ablative, genitive, and locative in Hittite and Albanian. The dative coincides with the ablative in Sanskrit, Lithuanian, and Old Church Slavic; and with the ablative, genitive, and locative in Armenian.

Indo-European *numerals* (cf. p. 177) had case-forms only from ' one ' to ' four ', although Sanskrit inflects (except in the nominative, which shows simply the base-form) also from ' five ' to ' nineteen '. In this absence of declension we may, perhaps, see another survival of the pre-inflexional stage which has already been suggested in the case of certain prepositions, etc. (see pp. 171, 196).

Verbs, which are characterised by person, aspect, mood, tense, and voice (cf. p. 179), are either *active* or *stative,* terms which must not be confused with *transitive* and *intransitive,* or with ' active ' as the designation of a voice (see pp. 217–218). The basal meaning of an active verb is ' to perform an action ', whether directly affecting another person or thing (transitive) or not (intransitive), whereas the stative verb expresses ' the state of being in a certain condition ', whether such condition be complete in itself (intransitive) or incomplete (transitive). This distinction, though existing in Indo-European (e.g., Latin *currō* ' I run ' is active, and *dormiō* ' I am asleep ' is stative), is particularly clear in Semitic, where active verbs are characterised by *a*, and stative by *i* or *u* (Hebrew *ē*, *ō)*, e.g., Hebrew *qāṭal* ' kill ' (transitive), *kāzaβ* ' tell lies ' (intransitive) ; but *kāβēδ* ' be heavy ', *qāṭōn* ' be small ' (intransitive), *ḥāφēṣ* ' be pleased (with something), like ' (transitive).

As in the case of the pronouns (p. 173), the verb has three *persons* according as (1) the action or state which it denotes is regarded as performed or experienced by the person or persons speaking (first person; e.g., Sanskrit *bhárāmi, bhárāvas, bhárāmas;* Latin *ferō, ferimus;* English *I bear,* [*we two bear,*] *we bear); (2)* by the person or persons spoken to (second person; e.g., Sanskrit *bhárasi, bhárathas, bháratha;* Latin *fers, fertis;* English *thou bearest,* [*ye two bear,*] *ye bear);* or (3) by the person or persons (or thing or things) spoken of (third person; e.g., Sanskrit *bhárati, bháratas, bháranti;* Latin *fert, ferunt;* English *he* [*she, it*] *bears,* [*they two bear,*] *they bear).* The verb thus shares with the epithetologue the grammatical category of *number* (see pp. 179–183) ; and where the pronoun shows exclusive and inclusive forms (cf. p. 182), we find, if the verb is really inflected, a similar distinction in it as well (e.g., Fox *nenesāpen[a]* ' we exclusive have slain him ' : *kenesāpen[a]* ' we inclusive have slain him ').

As regards *tense* and *aspect,* the former indicates the *time* of the action or state *(he strikes, he struck, he will strike,* etc.), while the latter denotes the *kind* of action or state as *complete* or *incomplete in itself (telic : atelic);* as *instantaneous (momentary, aoristic)* or *durative (cursive, imperfective);* as *iterative, consuetudinal* or *usitative, terminative,* etc. *(he is in the state of having struck, he has struck; he is* [*was*] *striking; he strikes once and for all* as contrasted with *he keeps on striking; he strikes again and again; he strikes habitually; he strikes effectively).* In French *il écrivit* is instantaneous in aspect, but past in tense (' he wrote once ') ; *il écrivait,* though also past in tense, is durative or consuetudinal in aspect (' he was writing, he used to write '). For the English verb *to be,* Modern Irish employs three distinct bases according to the aspect to be expressed: ' the snow is cold ' (durative, since snow is always cold) is *is fuar an sneachta* [is fuːər ən ʃnæxtha] ; ' the day is cold ' (instantaneous, since some days are not cold), *tá fuar an lá* [thɔ: fuːər ən lɔː] ; ' the winter is usually cold ' (consuetudinal, since occasionally a winter is not cold), *bíonn fuar an geimhreadh* [biːʌn fuːər ən giːeːrə].

The meaning of many verbs in itself denotes their aspects; e.g., English *strike* is instantaneous, while *beat* is durative; *step* is instantaneous, but *walk* is durative, etc.; but for the most part, in Indo-European, only the context shows the aspect, so that the present tense, for instance, may be either instantaneous or durative. The use of a preverb in the so-called prepositional compounds frequently makes the verb instantaneous, whereas without such a preverb the verb is durative, as in Sanskrit *tar-* ' to be crossing ' : *san-tar-* ' to cross to, to traverse '; Greek θνήσκω ' I am dying ' : ἀπο-θνήσκω ' I die '; Latin *facio* ' I am making ' : *con-ficio* ' I complete '; German *denken* ' to be thinking ' : *ge-denken* ' to remember '; Gothic *swa rinnaiþ ei ga-rinnaiþ* ' so run that ye make the run ' (Revised Version, ' even so run, that ye may attain ', I Cor. ix. 24); English *fall* : *be-fall;* Lithuanian *darýti* ' to be making ' : *pa-darýti* ' to complete '; Old Church Slavic *mrěti* ' to be dying ' : *u-mrěti* ' to die '; Russian *'bitĭ* ' to be striking ' : *u-'bitĭ* ' to kill ' (cf. German *schlagen* : *er-schlagen*).

Except for certain modern innovations (p. 216), Semitic has no tense properly speaking, but only aspect. The Hebrew and Arabic atelic *yiqtōl* and *yaqtulu*, for example, do not mean ' he is killing ' or ' he will kill ', but simply connote that his act of killing is not yet completed; from the point of view of tense, the action is either now in progress or will take place in the future. Similarly, the telic *qāṭal* or *qatala* does not mean ' he has (or, had) killed ', but that his act of killing is completed, and the result of that act now exists. The difference between aspect and tense comes out very clearly in translations from Semitic into Indo-European. Thus, for instance, the Hebrew telic *YHWH mālāχ* of Psalms xciii. 1, etc., is translated by a perfect in the Latin Vulgate (' Dominus regnavit '), and by an aorist in the Greek Septuagint (' Κύριος ἐβασίλευσεν '), but, much more accurately, by a present in the English version (' the Lord reigneth '). On the other hand, the Hebrew atelic *bī məlāχīm yimlōχū* in Proverbs viii. 15, is rendered by a present in all three versions (' per me reges regnant ', ' δι ἐμοῦ βασιλεῖς βασιλεύουσιν ', ' by me kings reign '); but in Psalms cxlvi. 10, the same atelic in *yimlōχ YHWH lə-ʿōlām* is represented by a future in all three ('regnabit Dominus in saecula', 'βασιλεύσει Κύριος εἰς τὸν αἰῶνα', 'the Lord shall reign for ever'). In these examples, the aspectual force in the first is that Jehovah is now a king in that His kingship has been established, and, consequently, now exists; in the second, that the kingship of earthly rulers is now in force in so far as it is not yet finished; and in the third, that since Jehovah's kingship is not yet finished, it will continue into time to come. Each of the systems, the aspectual and the temporal, is clear in itself; but exact translation from the one to the other is very difficult, if not impossible.

Aspect rather than tense is characteristic not only of Hamito-Semitic, Sumerian, Uralic, and many African languages, but also of much of Indo-European, notably Old Indo-Iranian, Classical Greek, Armenian, and Balto-Slavic. In Latin, as the Roman grammarian Varro had already observed in the first century B.C., the tenses may be divided into two aspectual categories, *infectum* and *perfectum* as shown in the table on p. 206.

The aspectual force of the perfect tense in Indo-European is very evident in such forms as Sanskrit *véda*, Greek οἶδα 'I have perceived' and, hence, 'I know'; Latin *meminī* 'I have in mind' and, hence, 'I remember'; French *j'ai écrit une lettre* 'I have written a letter' (originally, 'I possess a letter [already] written', as is shown by relative clauses of the type of *la lettre que j'ai écrite*, literally, 'the letter which I have, written'); and Teutonic pre-terite-presents like German *ich weiss* 'I know' (Gothic *ik wait*, Sanskrit *véda)*, for which a new past, *ich wusste*, has been created, or English *I can*, with its new past, *I could*, cognate with the Latin perfect *(g)nōvī* 'I know' (i.e., I am in a state of possession of knowledge previously acquired). The diathesis (voice) of the per-fect seems originally to have been neutral (i.e., neither active, middle, nor passive; cf. pp. 216–220), and the distinctive medio-passive perfect of the type of Greek δέδομαι 'je me suit donné, j'ai été donné' is almost indubitably of late development. The primary meaning of such forms as δέδομαι for *δεδαι (cf. Sanskrit *dadé)* with medio-passive diathesis, when compared with their exact phonological Latin equivalent *dedī* 'I have given' (cf. also Latin *vīdī* 'I have seen' : Old Church Slavic *vědě* 'I know'), would seem to have been 'I am in a state of givenness', whence were developed the two polar shadings of 'I have given' and 'I have been given' (' j'ai donné, j'ai été donné').

	INFECTUM	PERFECTUM
Indicative	Present *dīcō* ' I am saying ' Preterite *dīcēbam* ' I was saying ' Future *dīcam* ' I shall (be) say(ing) '	*dīxī* ' I am in a state of having said ' = ' I have said ' *dīxeram* ' I was in a state of having said ' = ' I had said ' *dīxerō* ' I shall be in a state of having said ' = ' I shall have said '
Subjunctive	Present- future *dīcam* ' I may (be) say(ing) ' Preterite *dīcerem* ' I might be saying '	*dīxerim* ' I may be in a state of having said ' = ' I may have said ' *dīxissem* ' I might be in a state of having said ' = ' I might have said '

Besides these aspects, Indo-European possesses a number of others. The *ingressive* or *inchoative* indicates the beginning of an action or state (e.g., Gothic *wakan* : *ga-wak-nan* = English *wake* : *wake-n*); and the *terminative* (or *effective, perfective, transitional*), an action or state which is carried through to its conclusion (e.g., Latin *iu-n-gō* ' I fasten the yoke on ', Greek γι-γνώ-σκω, Latin *gnō-sc-ō* ' I come to know '); but the determinatives -*n*- and -*sk*- here functioning as terminative may also have ingressive force (contrast English *wake-n* with Latin *iu-n-gō* and *cale-sc-ō* ' I become warm '). It would seem that the ingressive and the terminative aspects are, in reality, identical, indicating, respectively, the beginning and the end of the action or state in question. The *iterative* or *frequentative* and the *intensive aspects* are similarly connected, the former denoting that the action or state is repeated or recurrent; the latter, that it is intensified in character (e.g., Latin *dic-t-it-ō* ' I keep saying ', Sanskrit *ji-gā-mi* = Greek βί-βη-μι ' I make step after step ' for the iterative; and Latin *iac-tō* ' I hurl ', Sanskrit *dardarīmi* ' I smash ' for the intensive). The *desiderative* expresses desire (e.g., Sanskrit *vi-vid-iṣ-ati* ' he wishes to know ' as contrasted with *véda* ' he knows '; Latin *ēsuriō* for **ed-suriō* ' I want to eat, am hungry ' as contrasted with *edō* ' I eat ') and may also be used as a future tense (e.g., Greek λύ-σ-ω ' I shall loose ', Lithuanian *dɨrb-s-iu* ' I shall work '); the *causative* denotes that one causes the action or state in question (e.g., English ' he *fells* the tree ' as contrasted with ' the tree *falls* ' [Anglo-Saxon *fellan* : *feallan*, Old Saxon *fellian* : *fallan*]; Latin *si-st-ō* ' I make to stand ' as contrasted with *stō* ' I stand '); and the *diminutive* indicates that the action or state is of minor degree (e.g., Latin *sorbillō* ' I sip ' : *sorbeō* ' I swallow '; German *lächeln* ' to smile ' : *lachen* ' to laugh ').

Non-Indo-European languages have yet other aspects, of which we may note the principal ones. Semitic has a *reflexive* or *reciprocal*, indicating that the action or state affects the agent primarily (e.g., Hebrew *ni-šmar* ' guard oneself ' : *šāmar* ' watch, keep '); and a *conative*, implying that the subject endeavours to perform an action (e.g., Arabic *qātala* ' he has tried to kill ' : *qatala* ' he has killed '). In Indo-European, this reflexive is represented by the *middle voice*, which, like the Semitic aspect itself, frequently functions as a passive (cf. pp. 217–220).

Outside these two great linguistic families, the *deteriorative* gives an evil connotation to the action or state (e.g., Taënsa [an extinct member of the Muskhogi stock, formerly spoken in Louisiana] *hāl-i-wove-r-i-jehōni* ' one speaks evil of me '); the *benefactive* (sometimes termed *accommodative, applicative, indirective*) implies that the state or action exists or is performed for the benefit of another (e.g., Tübatulabal or Kern River Shoshonean *wïcï-n-ana't* ' he is cooking it for him ' : *wïcï-'in't* ' he is cooking it '); the *comitative*, that an action is performed in association with someone or something else (e.g., Takelma [south-western Oregon] *lōᵘl-* ' play ' : *lōᵘl-agwa'ᵉn* ' I play with him '); the *distributive* or *mutual*, that the action or state is performed or experienced by more than one person or thing at the same time (e.g., Siuslaw [southern Oregon] *nīctc-* ' fight ' : *nï'ctcat'aᵘx-* ' fight side by side [against others]'); and the *necessitative* or *obligatory*, that an action or state must take place (e.g., Turkish *sev-* ' love ' : *sev-meli* ' he must love ').

The *apparitional* aspect denotes that an action or state seems to take place (e.g., Serer [African Senegal-Guinean] *bind-* ' write ' : *bind-adoχ-* ' act so that one seems to write '); the *potential*, that an action or state may take place (e.g., Angāmi [Nāgā sub-group of Tibeto-Burman] *tā-* ' go ' : *ā tā-lēto-we* ' I can go '; Taënsa *rewa* ' to love ' : *vō-rewa* ' to be able to love '); the *inferential* or *putative*, that the action or state is not postulated on the speaker's own authority, but on the statement of some one else (e.g., Takelma *hana'ᵉs* ' he stops ' : *ha'nᵉsk'* ' he stops [so one infers from another's words, or as circumstantial evidence implies]'); the *reservative*, that the action is brought to a certain stage, in which it remains for some further purpose (e.g., Santālī [Muṇḍā group] *dal* ' he will strike ' : *dal-ka* ' he will strike [e.g., so as to kill]'); the *cessative*, that the action or state ceases (e.g., Fox *pyä`wᵃ* ' he comes ' : *pō'ni-pyä`wᵃ* ' he no longer comes '); and the *negative*, that the action or state is not performed or does not exist (e.g., Turkish *sev-er* ' he loves ' : *sev-me-z* ' he does not love ').

The category of *mood*, as its name implies (cf. Latin *modus* ' manner, mode '), denotes the *manner* in which the action or state is performed or exists. It is virtually an aspect of the verb, and is formed, exactly like the aspects, by various determinatives (cf. pp. 156–159). The sole reason for speaking of mood rather than of aspect would seem to be that the Greek and Latin grammarians, from whose terminology the older grammars of the Indo-European and Semitic languages borrowed their own (cf. p. 166), recognised mood and ignored aspect.

The Indo-European languages have four principal moods: *indicative, subjunctive, optative,* and *imperative,* to which some scholars add a fifth, the *injunctive.* Of these, we may at once omit the imperative, which denotes a command (Latin *serpe!,* English *creep!),* since it is simply a base-form, and is to the verbal system just what the vocative case is to the nominal (Latin *serve!,* English *slave!;* pp. 150, 192). Strictly speaking, the imperative has but one person, the second singular active, and denotes only a *positive command.* The other persons are drawn, for the most part, either from the injunctive (e.g., Sanskrit *sárpatu* = Greek ἑρπέτω = Latin *serpitō* ' let him creep! ' [cf. the imperfects *ásarpat* = εἶρπε for *ἑhερπετ* from *ἐσερπετ*], Sanskrit *sárpata* = Greek ἕρπετε = Latin *serpite* ' creep ye! ' [cf. the imperfects *ásarpata,* εἴρπετε], Latin *sequere* ' follow thou! ' from *(e)seqᵘeso)* or from the subjunctive (e.g., Sanskrit *sárpāni* ' let me creep! ', cf. Greek ἕρπωμεν ' let us creep! '). Very frequently, *prohibitions* are expressed, not by the imperative, but by other moods (e.g., Latin *serpe* ' creep! ' is a real imperative, but *ne serpas* ' don't creep! ' is a subjunctive).

The *indicative,* broadly speaking, expresses *a fact or what is alleged to be a fact (I do, I live).* The *subjunctive* (which Dionysios Thrax termed ' hypotactic ', i.e., subordinate) denotes *a contingency which may or may not be realised because of dependence upon some factual condition.* Such a contingency may be regarded as desirable (e.g., Latin *serpat* ' may he creep '; *voluntative subjunctive);* or as possible under certain circumstances (e.g., Latin *gratias agam si dicas* ' I shall be grateful if thou may say '; *potential subjunctive);* or as deliberation as to the best course to pursue (e.g., Latin *eloquar an taceam?* ' should I speak, or be silent? ';*deliberative subjunctive);*or as consideration of what may take place in future (e.g., Latin *video quid sit ex hac re* ' I see what may come of this affair '; *prospective subjunctive);* or as dubiety (e.g., Latin *incertō quid peterent aut vitarent* ' since it was uncertain what they should seek or shun '; *dubitative subjunctive),* and the like. Not infrequently the subjunctive becomes a future (cf. p. 20), as in Greek δείξω ' I shall show ' (cf. the aorist subjunctive δείξω); Latin *dixō* ' I shall say ', *capiet* ' he will seize '; Old Irish *gi-g-s-e* ' I shall pray '; Armenian *beric̣* ' that I may carry, let me carry, I shall carry '; Sanskrit *prá bravā* ' I shall praise '.

The *optative* is essentially the mood of *wish*, and is found as a distinct category only in Indo-Iranian, Tokharian, and Greek. In Celtic it has vanished altogether; in Latin it is confused with the subjunctive *(agam* ' may I do ' and *amem* ' may I love ' are subjunctives, but *sim* ' may I be ' and Old Latin *duim* ' may I give ' are optatives) ; and in Slavic it has become semantically an imperative. In Classical Sanskrit and Middle Indian, on the other hand, it has almost completely superseded the subjunctive, as is also the case in Teutonic (e.g., Gothic *hugjaima* ' let us think ', Old High German *singêm* ' let us sing '; a trace of the subjunctive perhaps survives in the type of Gothic *qiþau* ' I may say ', with *-au* from *-ō-u [for *-u* cf. Latin *serpit-ō*, Sanskrit *sárpat-u*, p. 209]). Hittite has no subjunctive, though it may have traces of an optative, and the Albanian optative is of very doubtful origin, as is the Baltic conditional (e.g., Lithuanian *sùktumbiau* ' I would turn ').

The optative denotes especially either a desire (e.g., Vedic *prátheya paśúbhiḥ* ' may I become rich with cattle '; Greek ἴοιμεν ' may we go ', as contrasted with the subjunctive ἴωμεν ' let us go, eamus, allons '; *hortatory optative)* or a moral obligation or desirable possibility less strong than the potential subjunctive (e.g., Sanskrit *kāmáyeta rā́jā samrā́ḍ bhávitum* ' a king should desire to become an emperor '; Greek ἔλθοι ἄν ' he might [or, could, should] go '; *potential optative).*

The *injunctive*, found in full development only in Indo-Iranian, is held to express an *injunction*, i.e., a command or prohibition less strong than an imperative; and in form it is simply an imperfect or aorist tense (see pp. 212–213) without an augment (cf. p. 151), as in the Sanskrit injunctives *bhárat, bhār* contrasted with the imperfect *ábharat* and the aorist *ábhār* from *bhar-* ' carry ', cognate with Latin *ferō* and English *bear*. It was probably restricted at first to the aorist, which originally could express past, present, and future alike, and it may serve as a future tense (e.g., Sanskrit *naśat* ' it will befall ', Lithuanian *dìrb-s-k* ' he will work ') and as an imperative (p. 209). Its extension to the imperfect (and in the Vedas even to the pluperfect) would seem to have been by later analogy.

Semitic has, besides the indicative and the subjunctive (e.g., Arabic *yaqtulu, yaqtula)*, a *jussive* or *apocopated* and an *energetic* mood (e.g., Arabic *yaqtul, yaqtulan[na])*, while Hebrew shows, in addition, a *cohortative*. The jussive corresponds rather closely to the Indo-European injunctive; i.e., it is a mild command; the energetic denotes a strong asseveration (e.g., Arabic *yaqtulan[na]* ' I shall surely kill ') ; and the cohortative, normally restricted to the first person singular and plural, expresses an exhortation (e.g., Hebrew *'e-šmər-āḥ* ' let me keep! '). All these Semitic moods, significantly enough, are formed from the atelic (cf. pp. 204–205).

From a consideration of aspect and the closely kindred, if not identical, mood, we turn to the subject of *tense*. Modern European languages express *time of action* rather than *manner of action*, as in English *I do, I did, I have (had) done, I shall do, I shall have done*. At the same time, aspect is also present, as in English *I am (was) doing, I have (had, shall have) been doing, I shall be doing;* and a survey of the evidence as a whole would seem to imply that from the earliest ascertainable period tense has existed in Indo-European by the side of aspect, even though the latter was formerly predominant.

The tenses in English are given as *present, past, future, perfect, pluperfect*, and *future perfect;* in French, as *present, imperfect, definite past, future, perfect, pluperfect, past anterior*, and *future perfect (je donne, donnais, donnai, donnerai, j'ai donné, avais donné, eus donné, aurai donné)*. To the English past correspond not only the French imperfect and definite past, but also the Greek, Armenian, and Vedic Sanskrit imperfect and aorist (durative and instantaneous in aspect respectively).

The Romance languages, except for their new creation, the past anterior, correspond exactly to the earliest known stage of Indo-European, even though the linguistic evolution of the Romance forms is not the same as that of the Vedic Sanskrit or Greek. Confining ourselves to the actual meaning, which alone concerns us for the moment, and recalling the Latin division of tenses into infectum and perfectum (cf. p. 205), we have the scheme:

IMPERFECTIVE (DURATIVE)	PERFECTIVE (INSTANTANEOUS)	PERFECT
Some Presents	Some Presents	Perfect
Imperfect	Aorist	Pluperfect
Future		Future Perfect

These tenses may be defined as follows: *the present denotes a state or action now existing or being performed, whether durative or instantaneous in aspect (he exists, hits, is hitting); the imperfect, a state or action existing or performed continuously or repeatedly in the past (he existed, was hitting, used to hit); the future, a state or action not yet existent or not yet performed (he will exist, will hit); the aorist, a state or action which existed or was performed at a single time once and for all in the past (he loved once only, he hit once); the perfect, a state or action existing or performed in the past, with results that still continue in the present (he has existed [with consequent results for himself or others], he has hit [with like results]); the pluperfect and the future perfect, a state or action existing or performed or to exist or to be performed in the past or future respectively, and then completed or to be completed with permanent consequences for self or others (he had existed, he had hit; he will have existed, he will have hit).*

All this represents a relatively late development. A survey of the phenomena of the Indo-European verb-system as a whole seems to indicate that this linguistic family primarily had only three tenses, which had evolved semantically, not morphologically, from three aspects: imperfective into present, instantaneous into aorist, and perfect into perfect. With the later rise of feeling for time of action or state as distinct from manner, the aorist came to express, in the majority of cases, as we have just observed, ' a state or action which existed or was performed at a single time once and for all in the past '; and the present came to be used in an instantaneous as well as in an imperfective sense. The aorist developed, for the most part, into the past tense of an instantaneous or perfective verb; and the imperfect was created to serve as the past tense of an imperfective verb (cf. p. 214). The perfect retains its aspect unchanged. The future did not exist in the Indo-European period, but was created in different ways independently by various members of that linguistic family (cf. pp. 20–21, 210), after the dissolution of the primitive Indo-European linguistic unity; and the pluperfect and the future perfect (like the French past anterior) were developed still later.

If originally there were only three tenses, present, past, and perfect, it is evident that, when tense came to be combined with aspect, an imperfective present could not have for its past an aorist, which is instantaneous; nor could an instantaneous present have for its past an imperfect, which is imperfective. This fact explains many types of irregular verbs. Thus the Greek verb λείπω ['le:po:] 'leave' has as its present λείπ-ω, as its aorist ἔ-λιπ-ον ['elipon], and as its perfect λέ-λοιπ-α ['leloipa]. Here we have, in the first place, three grades (cf. pp. 65–67), *leip-, *lip-, and *loip-, indicative of the three aspects; and, in the second place, for each aspect we have a different personal ending, -ō, -on, and -a.

The vocalism of e for the imperfective and of o for the perfective seen in λείπω : λέλοιπα, τρέφω 'I nourish' : τέτροφα 'I have nourished' (cf. also Gothic giutan 'to pour' : gaut 'he poured', with Gothic iu, au from Indo-European eu, ou), seems to be found in nouns as well, as in Greek λόγος 'word' : λέγω 'I say'; τροφή 'nourishment' : τρέφω 'I nourish'; φόρος 'burden' : φέρω 'I carry'; Latin toga 'mantle' : tegō 'I cover' (cf. German Dach 'roof' : decken 'to cover', Decke 'covering'). Though usually explained as due to accent (cf. pp. 66–67), qualitative gradation may possibly represent aspect in the epithetologue (cf. Greek τέμνω 'I cut' : τόμος 'a cut, slice', τομός 'cutting, making a slice'), so that τροφή would properly mean 'the collectivity of that which creates a state of nourishment'; λόγος, 'the active force of what has been said and remains spoken'; φόρος, 'the active force of what has been and still is being carried'; and toga, 'the collectivity of what has been made, and still is, a covering'.

Many verbs which, being imperfective in aspect, can, properly speaking, have no aorist, indicate the instantaneous past by using a different verb. This phenomenon is known as suppletion. In English it has but two examples, I am, if I be, but I was; I go, but I went. Parallels to am : was are Latin sum : fuī; Sanskrit ásti : babhúva; Greek εἰμί : πέφυκα; Albanian jam : kjeshë; Agnean nas- : se- : tāk- (cf. pp. 230–231); for go : went, Gothic gagga [gaŋga] : iddja; Sanskrit éti : ágāt; Greek ἔρχομαι : εἶμι : ἦλθον; Old Irish tiagu : -lod : do-coad; Modern Irish téighim [ṭe:im] : raghad-sa [raədsə] : chuadhas [xʌəs]; Armenian ert'am : čogay [tʃhogai]; Agnean i- : kälk-. Other suppletive verbs are especially those meaning 'carry' or 'take', 'eat', 'see', and 'say' (e.g., for 'carry' or 'take', Greek φέρω : οἴσω : ἤνεγκα; Latin ferō : tulī; Armenian unim : kalay; Old Irish biru : ro-uiccius; Agnean pär- : kām; for 'eat', Greek ἐσθίω : ἔδομαι : ἔφαγον; Sanskrit átti ;

jaghása; Armenian *utem* : *keray;* for ' see ', Greek ὁράω : ὄψομαι : εἶδον; Sanskrit *páśyati* : *adarśat;* Albanian *shoh* : *pashë;* Old Irish *ad-cíu* : *ad-chon-dairc;* Modern Irish *chim* [çim] : *chonnac* [xʌnək] or *feacas* [fakəs]; Agnean *läk-* : *pälk-;* and for ' say ', Greek λέγω or φημί : εἶπον : εἴρηκα; Sanskrit *bráviti* : *ávocat;* Agnean *tränk-* : *wen-).*

The tense-system, probably evolved in early Indo-European, but found historically only in Vedic Sanskrit, Avestan, and Greek, soon decayed. In Classical Sanskrit, the aorist practically vanished; the pluperfect had always been weak; and the future perfect had never existed. In Armenian and Baltic, the old imperfect and perfect have disappeared; in Italic, the old imperfect is lost, and the aorist and perfect have merged into a single perfect (e.g., Latin *vidi* ' I have seen ' and *cecini* ' I have sung ' are true perfects, but *scripsi* ' I have written ' from **sqribh-s-i* is an old aorist in *-s-* with a perfect ending) ; Celtic has combined the aorist and perfect into a preterite, but has kept the imperfect in essence, and in its Brythonic (British) branch even has a pluperfect; Hittite has only a present and a past; in Tokharian and Teutonic, the perfect (with traces of the aorist) has become the imperfect; and in Slavic, the perfect has vanished (except for a few remnants), with the aorist as the sole past tense.

New tenses have been created by Armenian, Italic, Teutonic, and Balto-Slavic for the imperfect, and by Armenian, Modern Persian, Albanian, Modern Greek, Romance, Teutonic, and Balto-Slavic for the perfect. Thus, Latin *ferē-bam* ' I was carrying ' appears to have meant originally ' I became in carrying ', being compounded with the base **bheue-* ' become '; Gothic *habai-da,* English *ha-d,* to have denoted ' I put in having ', compounded with the base **dhē-* ' put ' (cf. perhaps Lithuanian *dìrb-davau* ' I was working ') ; and Armenian *berei* ' I was carrying ' to have signified ' I was in carrying ', compounded with the base **ese-* ' be ' (cf. possibly Old Church Slavic *nesě-axŭ* ' I was carrying '). This variety of ways of creating the imperfect gives further reason for believing that it was a relatively late formation (cf. p. 212). The old perfect has largely been supplanted by the type seen in English *I have written* (cf. p. 205) and in Armenian *cneal em* [tsəne'al 'em] ' I am born ' : Albanian *kam ljidhurë* ' I have bound ' = German *ich habe gebunden* = Modern Greek ἔχω δεμένο [Classical δέδεκα] ; Old Church Slavic *dalŭ jesmĭ* ' I am having given ' = ' I have given '. The future has already been discussed in several connexions (pp. 20–21, 207, 209, 210).

A survey of this material, particularly as regards the imperfect and the aorist, shows that even languages predominantly temporal in character cannot always dispense with aspect, and that they may create new tenses for the specific purpose of indicating it, as English *I am doing* : *I do;* French *je suis en train de faire* : *je fais;* Spanish *estoy haciendo* : *hago*. In this connexion, a comparison of the Romance (especially French and Spanish) tenses of the indicative and subjunctive with their Classical and Vulgar Latin originals (the latter marked by ! in the table on page 216) is not without interest.

Non-Indo-European languages show a multiplicity of tenses far transcending the relative simplicity of Indo-European. Thus Avar (of the North Caucasian Chechen group) has six presents (general, indefinite, inchoative, obligatory, intentional, and intentional iterative) and six perfects (general, general complete, inchoative, obligatory, intentional, and historical), one of which, the historical, has nine sub-divisions (putative, iterative, inchoative, inchoative putative, obligatory, obligatory putative, intentional, intentional putative, and intentional iterative), but only a single future. In Wiradyuri (South Australian), on the other hand, there are five futures (indefinite, proximate, indefinite of to-day, definite of to-day, and future perfect).

The Semitic languages, in course of time, came to feel a need for tense as distinguished from aspect. To accomplish this, especially in the present, they used the participle in a nominal sentence (see pp. 228, 230–232) ; e.g., Hebrew *hā-'ārōn wə-yiśrā'ēl w-īhūðāh yōšəβīm* ' the ark, and Israel, and Judah (are) abiding '; Syriac *'aryā gēr besrā 'āχel* ' for the lion (is always) eating meat '; Arabic *'as-samā'u munfaṭiruⁿ bi-hi* ' heaven (is) being reft asunder by it '; and in Modern Syriac and Modern Hebrew this is the normal mode of denoting a present tense. A future tense may be expressed in Classical Arabic by prefixing *sawfa*, or its abbreviation *sa*, ' in the end ' to the atelic, as *sawfa naṣlī-hi* ' we shall burn him ', *sa-yakfī-ka-humu 'llāhu* ' God will suffice thee against them '; a pluperfect is made by prefixing *qad* to the telic, e.g., *qad bakara* ' he had arisen early '.

The remaining characteristic of the verb proper is *voice*. In most modern Indo-European languages, e.g., English, this is

	LATIN	FRENCH	SPANISH
Present Indicative	cantō	chante	canto
Imperfect Indicative	cantāba(m)	chantais	cantaba
Preterite Indicative = Aorist and Perfect	cantāvī > cantāī	chantai	canté
Future Indicative (!)	cantāre habeō	chanterai	cantaré (Old Spanish also cantar . . . e)
Future Anterior Indicative (!)	cantāre habēba(m)	chanterais (conditional)	cantaría (conditional)
Perfect Indicative (!)	habeō cantātu(m)	ai chanté	he cantado
Pluperfect Indicative (!)	habēba(m) cantātu(m) cantāvera(m) > cantāra(m)	avais chanté (Old French avret chanté; preterite) Old Provençal cantera (conditional)	había cantado cantara (conditional)
Past Anterior Indicative (!)	habuī cantātu(m)	eus chanté	hube cantado
Future Perfect (!)	habēre habeō cantātu(m) cantāverō > cantārō	aurai chanté	O. S. cantaro (future subj.)
Conditional Perfect Indicative (!)	habēre habēba(m) cantātu(m)	aurais chanté	habría cantado
Present Subjunctive	cante(m)	chante	cante
Imperfect Subjunctive	cantāre(m)	Logudoresian morreret	
Perfect Subjunctive	cantāverī(m) > cantāri(m)		cantare (future subjunctive)
Pluperfect Subjunctive	cantāvisse(m) > cantāsse(m)	chantasse (imperfect subjunctive)	cantase (imperfect subjunctive)

216

either *active* or *passive*, i.e., the subject either acts or exists in a certain state *(I kill, I sit)*, or is acted upon *(I am killed)*. In certain older languages, notably Sanskrit, Greek, and Gothic, one finds, on the other hand, three voices, *active, middle*, and *passive*. The second of these, represented in Latin by the *deponent*, denotes that the action is either *dynamic*, indicating that the actor performs the action primarily for himself (e.g., Sanskrit *pácate* [middle] 'he cooks for himself' : *pácati* [active] 'he cooks for someone else '; cf. the native Indian grammatical terms for the active and middle, *parasmai padam* 'word for another' and *ātmane padam* 'word for one's self' respectively); or *reflexive*, meaning that the action affects primarily the actor (e.g., Sanskrit *vártate* 'he turns himself' : *vártati* 'he turns ' = Latin *vertitur* : *vertit);* or *reciprocal*, signifying that the action is performed by the actor in association with others (e.g., Sanskrit *vádante* 'they say one to another, converse' : *vádanti* 'they say ').

In all Indo-European there is only one distinctively *passive* formation, which is confined to Indo-Iranian and Armenian (e.g., Sanskrit *pacyáte* 'it is cooked', but *pácyate* 'it cooks itself, ripens '; Armenian *berim* 'I am carried ': *berem* 'I carry ' — both apparently denominative formations). All other passives may be traced directly to the middle; and many modern languages use the reflexive middle instead of the passive (e.g., French *il se trouve* 'it is found '; cf. p. 218). *Indo-European knew no passive, but only the active and middle; and the passive is a late development from the middle.* This evolution had taken place in the Proto-Indo-European period, for the Gothic passive type of *liuga-nda* 'they are given in marriage' (cf. French *ils se marient* 'they get married ') corresponds exactly in formation to the types of the Sanskrit and Greek middles *bhára-nte* and φέρο-νται 'ils se portent ', not to the Sanskrit and Armenian passive types *bhri-yante* and *ber-in* 'they are carried, ils sont portés '.

The exact point at which the passive diverged from the middle, and finally superseded it altogether, except in Modern Greek, is not wholly certain, but it would seem to have been the perfect and the aorist. These are, respectively, perfect and instantaneous in their aspect (pp. 211–212); and in their dynamic and (especially) reflexive senses, they readily pass from a middle to a passive connotation (e.g., for the aorist, Sanskrit *ábhrāji* 'it shone ', cf. Greek ἐφλέγη 'il se brûla' = 'il fut brûlé '; and for the perfect, Sanskrit *tistiré* = Greek ἔστρωται ' il s'est répandu ' = ' il est répandu). The passive is mostly either perfect or else instantaneous in aspect, just like the perfect and aorist, as is well illustrated by English and French, which have, strictly speaking, no imperfective present passive. *The house is built, la maison est bâtie* are clearly perfect, meaning ' the house is now in a state of completed building '; to form a true present one can say only *they are building the house, the house is being built; on est en train de bâtir la maison, on bâtit la maison.* Furthermore, a passive could come into existence only after the evolution of a non-active case (here to be construed as passive) as distinguished from the cases conventionally termed accusative and nominative (cf. pp. 192–193), the process being completed with the creation of the agential or instrumental case (cf. pp. 199–200).

The development of the passive from the reflexive middle survives not only in Romance (cf. French *il se trouve, ils se marient,* already quoted), but also in Scandinavian (e.g., Old Icelandic *finna-sk,* Swedish *finna-s* ' se trouver, to be found ') and in Slavic (e.g., Old Church Slavic *daite i dastŭ sę vamŭ* ' give, and it shall be given unto you '; Russian *gazéta citájet-sja* ' the newspaper is read '). Another very widespread mode of forming the voice is by the passive participle with or without an auxiliary verb meaning ' be ', as English *the house is built,* etc., a construction found in Teutonic (except Scandinavian), Baltic, Indo-Iranian, and Albanian, as well as in the perfect passive tenses of Latin, Romance, and Modern Greek.

Still another form of passive is seen in the type of Latin *amātur* ' he is loved ' as contrasted with *amat* ' he loves ', a type obviously identical with that of *vertitur* ' he turns himself ' as contrasted with *vertit* ' he turns '. This ending in *-r* appears in various Indo-European languages attached to all persons, numbers, and tenses; but when the evidence is taken as a whole, it would appear originally to have been neither active nor passive, and neither singular, dual, nor plural, but simply an impersonal termination of the third person attached directly to the verbal base. When, on the other hand, this *-r*-ending was added to the active inflexion, the result was the *deponent.* This distinction between the passive (i.e., impersonal) and the deponent (i.e., middle; cf. p. 217) is seen with special clarity in the Old Italic dialects of Oscan and Umbrian, and in Old Irish (e.g., Oscan **sakrafí-r** ' let one conse-

crate, let there be a consecration ' as contrasted with **sakarat-er**
' sacrifice is made ' = Latin *sacrāt-ur;* Umbrian *fera-r* ' let one
carry, let there be a carrying ' as contrasted with Latin *ferāt-ur*
' let it be carried '; Old Irish *berai-r* ' he is carried, one carries,
there is a carrying ' [cf. Umbrian *fera-r*] as contrasted with
midith-ir ' he judges ' = Latin *meditāt-ur).*

The impersonal meaning of *-r* is very evident in Vedic *vid-úr*
' they know ', a third plural, as contrasted with its exact phonological equivalent in Old Irish, *fit-ir* ' he knows ', a third singular
(i.e., originally, ' one knows, they know, it is known '; cf. also, for
the ending, Hittite *ese-r* ' they were '). It would seem that the
ending *-r,* primarily impersonal and attached to the verb-base,
was added, later in the Proto-Indo-European period, to the personal endings and became a *medio-passive* exactly like the Greek
type of φέρονται ' ils se portent ' or ' ils sont portés ' (cf. Latin *vertit*
' il tourne ' : *vertit-ur* ' il se tourne ' or ' il est tourné '). Similarly we have in Agnean *kälpnām-ār* ' let me attain ' beside *kalkam*
' let me go '; and in Phrygian αδδακετο-ρ ' he made (for himself ?)'
beside αδδακετ ' he made '. In Latin, where the impersonal type of
*ferar (represented by the Umbrian *ferar* already cited) is replaced by the medio-passive *ferāt-ur* (indicative *fert-ur* : active
fert; cf. also *fero-r* : *ferō,* etc.), the impersonal use survives in
phrases like *agitur* ' one discusses, it is discussed ', *itur ad astra*
' one goes to the stars ' (cf. also pp. 229–230).

In Modern Irish, where the impersonal type of Old Irish *berair*
has been superseded by the medio-passive type of *midithir,* the
old medio-passive is employed impersonally in the autonomous
form of the verb in *-tar* (e.g., *labharthar Gaedhilg annso* [lɔwɔrhər
gəe:lig ənsɔ] ' one speaks Gaelic here, Gaelic is spoken here, qui si
parla Ghelico '). Old Irish has no form even suggesting a passive
except in the third person singular and plural (e.g., *foilsigthir* ' he
is manifested ', *foilsigtir* ' they are manifested ' from the deponent
foilsigidir ' he manifests '; cf. *gaibthir, gaibtir* ' he is [they are]
taken ' : *gaibid* ' he takes ', *gaibit* ' they take ', but *berair, bertair*
' he is [they are] carried ' : *berid* ' he carries ', *berait* ' they carry ').
To express the other persons, the third person singular is used with
an objective pronoun of the logical subject, e.g., *no-m-berar* ' one
carries me ' = ' I am carried ', *no-n-berar* ' one carries us ' = ' we
are carried ', etc. In Hittite it is even possible that an inflexionless
verbal noun was used as the third person singular present of the

medio-passive, so that *esa* ' he sits ', *kisa* ' he becomes ', may have
meant originally ' there is a sitting, there is a coming into being '
(cf. p. 154). In passing, it may be noted that the two types generally recorded as true passives — Sanskrit *ákāri* ' it was made ',
Gāthā Avestan *srāvī* ' it was heard ', Old Persian *adāriy* ' he was
held ', and Greek ἐδόθη ' it was given ' — were really middle forms
in origin.

When once evolved, the passive sometimes shows an abnormal
development. This is particularly the case in Classical Sanskrit,
where such constructions as *mayā gamyate* ' it is gone by me ' =
' I go ' are common. Yet this type, in which only the third person
singular of the verb is used, is clearly impersonal in origin, so that
it really means ' there is a going by me ' (cf. Latin *itur ad astra*,
cited above; and also the type of Sanskrit *devena gatam* '[it was]
gone by the god ' = ' the god went '; cf. pp. 168–169, 199–200).

Outside Indo-European, the passive seems to present few new
types. We may note, however, for the sake of completeness, such
periphrases as Dhīmāl (of the eastern pronominalised group of
Tibeto-Burman) *yolla-sho dang-hai nēn-chā-hi-ka* ' brother-from
beating found-ate-I ' = ' I was beaten by my brother '; Pūrūm
(Kuki-Chin) *kai-ta wēl-e* ' me-concerning striking-takes-place ' =
' I am struck ' = Baltī (Tibetan) *ngā-ang t͜eang-ma song-s-et* ' me
striking-went '; Kanarese (Dravidian) *kareyal-paḍuttēne* ' I-
experience-calling ' = ' I am called '.

To the verb are conventionally attached certain forms which
are obviously nouns or adjectives, the former termed *infinitives*,
and the latter *participles*, *gerunds*, and *gerundives*. In inflexion,
these are distinctly epithetologic in character; and their basis lies
in the fact that epithetologues may, in virtue of their meaning,
govern the non-active (accusative) case. Thus we have in Sanskrit
mā́m kā́mena ' through love for me '; in Avestan, *kāmē dūtīm* ' in
longing for the message', *puθrəm varšta* ' begetter of a son '; in
Old Persian, *yaθā mām kāma āha* ' as was my desire '; in Greek,
θανόντα δεσπόταν γόοις ' with lamentations for the dead ruler ', τὰ
μετέωρα φροντιστής ' a meditator on things above '; in Latin, *quid
tibi hanc tactiost?* ' why do you touch her? ', *memores Platonis
sententiam* ' remembering Plato's opinion '; in Middle High German, *durch behalten den lîp* ' through keeping the body '; in Old
Lithuanian, *ant ischkalbeghima pasleptini Christaus* ' for speaking
the mystery of Christ '; and in Old Church Slavic, *po prijętiji mi*

THE GRAMMATICAL CATEGORIES

otŭ Boga velikyjĭ darŭ ' after my receiving a great gift from God '.
The *infinitive* (of which the Latin *supines* are merely species)
is usually a stereotyped case-form of a noun. Most frequently this
case is the dative, e.g., Sanskrit *dṛśé* ' to see '; Avestan *nəmōi* ' to
flee '; Old Persian *čartanaiy* = Modern Persian *kardan* ' to do ';
Hittite *harkana* ' to go to ruin ', *tawanzi* ' to take '; Kuchaean
nāktsi ' to blame ' (?) ; Latin (passive) *agī* ' to be done '; Lithuanian *dúoti*, Old Church Slavic *dati* ' to give ' (the Balto-Slavic
forms may also be locatives). Next in frequency comes the accusative, as Sanskrit *dhấtum* ' to place '; Avestan *snaθəm* ' to smite ';
Armenian *tal* ' to give '; Latin *habitūrum* (future), e.g., *bóna súa
habitūrum ómnia* ' to be going to have all his property ', *spectātum*
(supine), as *vēnit spectātum* ' he came to see '; Oscan *ezum*,
Umbrian *erom* ' to be '; Gothic *baíran*, Anglo-Saxon, Old High
German *beran* ' to bear '; Old Church Slavic *vidětŭ*, as *česo izidoste
vidětŭ* ' what went ye out for to see? '; Lithuanian *dúotų* ' to give '.
After the accusative comes the locative, as Sanskrit *neṣáṇi* ' to
lead '; Avestan *frāδati* ' to further '; Hittite *peskewan* ' to give '
(used as a supine, e.g., *peskewan dāēr* ' they began to give and continued to do so ') ; Greek *ἄγειν* ' to do ' (for *ἀγεσεν[ι]*), Homeric
θέμεν ' to place '; Latin *agere* ' to do ' (for *agesi*). The genitive
and ablative are very rare, e.g., Sanskrit *abhi-śríṣas* ' to attach ';
Avestan *darštōiš, darᵊsāṯ* ' to see '.

The instrumental as an infinitive occurs in Avestan *apa-yeⁱtī*
' to take away ', probably in Lithuanian *žinóte* ' to know ', and
in some uses of the Latin second supine, as *difficile dictŭ* ' hard to
say ', though this supine also represents an ablative, as *vēnātū
redíre* ' to return from hunting ' and a dative, as *lepida memorātuī*
' amusing to relate '. An indefinite case (cf. pp. 200–201) seems to
be found in Greek infinitives of the types of *δεικνύναι* ' to show ',
Homeric *δόμεναι*, Cyprian *δοϝεναι* = Attic *δοῦναι* ' to give '. In Celtic,
the infinitive so completely retains its noun-value that it may be
inflected (as is occasionally the case in Tokharian), and takes its
logical object in the genitive, e.g., Old Irish *dlegair dᵊcomalnad ind
huili rechto* ' he is bound to fulfil the whole law ' (literally, ' to
fulfilling of the whole law ').

The *participles* and *gerunds* (the latter also termed participles
of obligation) are simply adjectives which, like infinitives (and for
the same reason) may take a direct object in the accusative. It is
sufficient here to say that they may be either present, aorist, future,

perfect, or future perfect, and either active or medio-passive, e.g.,
Greek λῡοντ- ' loosing ' (nominative λῦων), λῦσᾱς, λῦσων, λελυκώς;
λῡόμενος, λῡσάμενος, λῡσόμενος, λελυμένος, λελῡσόμενος; special
passives λυθεντ- (nominative λυθείς), λυθησόμενος. Only Greek has
this wealth of participles. For the most part, there are only two,
present and perfect; the aorist is rare even in Sanskrit, and the
future, as in the verb proper (cf. pp. 20–21, 207, 209, 210), is everywhere a late formation. In Hittite we have the isolated phenomenon that the participle in *-e/ont-, elsewhere only active (cf.
Sanskrit bhárant-, Greek φεροντ-, Latin ferent-, Old High German
berant- ' bearing '), is active in meaning if formed from an intransitive verb, but passive in sense if formed from a transitive
verb (e.g., Hittite atanz ' eaten ' from the Indo-European base
*ede-, as contrasted with Latin edens ' eating ').

The participle of obligation, represented, for example, by Sanskrit janitavyà- (i.e., janitavía-) ' to be born ', karaṇīya- ' to be
done ', or Greek δοτέος from *δοτεϝιος ' to be given ', is especially
developed in Latin, where we have not only the adjectival gerun-
dive of the type of faciendus ' to be done ', but also the neuter
nominal gerund of the type of faciendī (genitive), faciendō (ablative or instrumental, rarely dative), faciendum (accusative), e.g.,
ars vera ac falsa diiudicandi ' the art of distinguishing true and
false '; ut spatium ad colligendum se homines haberent ' that the
men might have room to gather '; equites tegendo satis latebrosum
locum ' a place hidden enough for covering the cavalry '; óculi
spectandó dolent, manéndo medicum ' my eyes hurt with looking,
waiting for the doctor '. This last type became equivalent in Late
Latin to a participle, e.g. (Vulgate), qui pertransiit benefaciendo,
et sanando omnes oppressos a diabolo ' who went about doing good,
and healing all that were oppressed of the devil '; and it is the origin of the Romance types of French (en) venant, Italian venendo,
Spanish viniendo ' coming ' (the French type is carefully to be distinguished from the true participle venant = Latin veniente^m).
Similar gerunds are found in Sanskrit in the instrumental (pītvắ
' drinking '), dative (kr̥tvắya ' making '), locative (?) (kr̥tvî),
accusative (parikrāmam ' going around '), and indefinite (apparently uninflected; parikramya ' striding about ').

In the case of the participles, it will be observed that we have
distinctions of tense, and the same statement holds good for the
infinitives in Greek and Latin (Greek λῡειν, λῦσαι, λῦσειν, λελυκέναι;

Latin *tegere, tēxisse* ' to cover, to have covered '). With this phenomenon we may compare the past and future of nouns in certain American Indian languages, e.g., Hupa (Athapascan group) *xonta* ' house ' (now existing) : *xontaneen* ' house in ruins ' (i.e., one that formerly existed) : *xontate* ' house not yet built ' (i.e., one that will exist) ; Creek *miko* ' chief at the present time ' : *mikotati* ' former chief ' : *mikotaláni* ' future chief '.

CHAPTER VIII

Syntax: The Mutual Relation of Words

Definition of syntax — linguistic functions of syntax — the sentence as the speech-unit — prerequisites for syntactic investigations — studies of syntax at present available — classification of sentence-types — subject and predicate — monorrhemic sentences and impersonal verbs — the nominal sentence and the late development of the copula — word-order, fixed and free — word-order as influenced by accentuation: enclitics; accentuation of the verb; variation in word-order; the rôle of the verb in word-order; proclitics — effect of loss or absence of inflexion on word-order — emphasis on words as a factor in their order — literary sources for knowledge of word-order — study of idioms from the historical point of view — confusion of case-forms and their replacement by prepositions — varying cases after the same verb — the partitive genitive — Old French survivals in Modern French names of churches, streets, etc. — the origin of the Spanish type of *el hijo ama á su madre* and of the French *il y a* and *il fait chaud* — the source of French *on*, German *man*, and English *one* — contamination of cases in Late Latin.

SYNTAX considers the relation of words to each other as expressions of the conveyance of ideas from speaker to hearer, and the principles of their grouping into thought-units (sentences, clauses, etc.) ; and, like semantics, it is essentially psychological as contrasted with the physiological nature of phonology and morphology, or with the historical character of etymology (cf. pp. 8, 105). If phonology and morphology are the factors which make the outward forms of a genitive, an ablative, a third person singular present indicative, a perfect, etc., it is syntax which determines how and when such forms are used; and from empirical observation and comparison of syntactic phenomena in various languages and types of languages, one may, in the majority of cases, deduce the original meaning of a given form.

The unit of speech is neither the individual sound nor the individual word, but the sentence, i.e., a word or group of words expressing a complete concept, each word composed of individual sounds, and the meaning of the single word (when the sentence consists of only one word) or the combination of meanings of the group of words conveying a unitary idea. Since the sentence is the oral expression of a mental concept, the relationship of its constituent words is largely determined by psychological factors. The speaker speaks, and the hearer hears, sentences, not words (except when the single-word sentence conveys a complete concept), and still less sounds. The hearer, in particular, has his attention concentrated on getting the meaning of the sentence as a whole; he normally hears (i.e., specifically recognises) only those individual words or sounds which he feels necessary for understanding the force of the sentence collectively.

This is illustrated with particular clarity by almost any telephone-conversation. The telephone transmits certain sounds only imperfectly; and, consequently, words containing these sounds, though uttered distinctly by the speaker, are received by the hearer in more or less garbled form. Yet the hearer is, for the most part, quite unaware of this fact. He is thoroughly acquainted with the *langue* and, very often, with the *parole* of the speaker; he knows how the words ought to sound; and his acoustic image, in consequence of past stimulations, mechanically fills the gaps and faults of transmission so that he imagines that he hears exactly what the speaker says. Sometimes, especially in the case of unfamiliar or unknown proper names or foreign words, the acoustic stimuli may fail to operate by pure suggestion and recollection; and it may be necessary for the hearer to ask that a certain word or certain words be spelled. If even this does not suffice, the speaker may be obliged to resort to some such device as ' *w* in " William ", *i* in " Ida ", *n* in " Nellie ", *s* in " Samuel ", *h* in " Harry ", *i* in " Ida ", *p* in " Peter " ' for ' Winship '. Or, since only the supposedly important sounds or words are really heard, the meaning of the sentence may be misunderstood, so that, as a precaution, statements made over the telephone must be repeated or even rephrased.

The task of the syntactician is to deduce the exact meaning of the forms found in a language, whether written or spoken, and to see how analogous forms are used in other languages (especially in those which are cognate). Getting these meanings and uses firmly fixed in his mind, he must lay aside his own prepossessions and think himself into the mental and linguistic attitude of those speaking or writing the language or languages which he is investigating. In theory, this process is simple; in practice, it is not quite so easy. Phonology, morphology, and etymology may be studied with very fair adequacy with the help of tables of sound-correspondences, of paradigms of grammatical correspondences, and of dictionaries, especially those which contain under a single rubric many or all known cognate forms of words in languages related to the one under consideration. Thus, for instance, in a Latin etymological dictionary, the rubric *fortis* ' strong ' has all important words in Indo-European etymologically related to that Latin term; under the rubric *liegen* ' lie ', a similar German dictionary collects all important cognates of that German word; an Indo-European etymological dictionary, under the hypothetically reconstructed base *tere-* ' rub ' lists practically all words in the Indo-European languages which may be derived either from *tere-* or from that base plus such determinatives (see pp. 156–159) as *tere-u̯e-*, *ter-pe-*, *tre-ĝe-*, *tre-u-qe-*, etc.

While deep acquaintance with phonology, morphology, and etymology is an indispensable prerequisite for the study of syntax, a thorough reading and (wherever possible) speaking knowledge of the language or languages concerned is absolutely necessary, and the syntactician must have a real feeling for the texts which he reads or for the conversations in which he takes part. If the language or languages concerned have a history of sufficient length, it will be found that the syntax of one period differs more or less from that of another. The later period is seldom fully intelligible without knowledge of the earlier; and the syntax of the older stages can only rarely receive satisfactory explanation without examination of the syntax of cognate languages. Accordingly, just as we can, to a greater or less degree, reconstruct Proto-Teutonic, Proto-Italic, Proto-Indo-European, Proto-Semitic, Proto-Dravidian, etc., phonology or morphology (cf. pp. 30, 74, 360), so we may reconstruct, in great part, from the syntax of the various individual Teutonic languages (Gothic, Old Icelandic, Norwegian, Swedish, Anglo-Saxon, Middle and Modern English, Old Saxon, Frisian, Old, Middle, and Modern Dutch, Old, Middle, and Modern High German, together with the dialects of these languages), a Proto-Teutonic syntax; and, by similar processes, Proto-Italic, Proto-Indo-European, Proto-Semitic, Proto-Dravidian, etc., syntaxes.

Here also the theory is quite simple; the practice is the reverse of easy. The first requisite is to have a thoroughly adequate syntax, both synchronic and diachronic (cf. pp. 23–24), of the indi-

vidual languages of a given group, e.g., of Indo-European or of
Semitic, the literary productions in most of which are of very con-
siderable volume, although many of these languages have as yet
been explored only imperfectly from the syntactic point of view.
At present we have adequate syntaxes of relatively few, notably
of Greek and Latin, Osco-Umbrian, Romance, French, German,
Avestan, Afghān, Slavic, and Manx in Indo-European; and of
Semitic generally, as well as of Hebrew and Arabic particularly, in
Semitic. Fair syntaxes exist for the Indo-European Vedic Sanskrit,
Persian, Sindhī, Armenian, Old and Modern Irish, Lithuanian,
Lettish, and Old Church Slavic; and for the Semitic Syriac and
Mandaean. For Sanskrit in general, Spanish, Italian, Portuguese,
Rumanian, and Middle Irish, the existing treatises are scarcely
adequate. For Celtic generally (e.g., for Welsh and Breton), Anglo-
Saxon, and Old Icelandic they are quite unsatisfactory; a Hittite
syntax is announced as in course of preparation; and some languages, such as Tokharian, have not yet been sufficiently investigated to make syntactic discussion possible except in special
details.

Of the two complete treatises on Indo-European syntax generally, one (B. Delbrück, *Vergleichende Syntax der indogermanischen Sprachen,* three volumes, Strassburg, 1893–1900) is rather
antiquated; and the other (H. Hirt, *Syntax,* forming volumes vi
and vii of his *Indogermanische Grammatik,* Heidelberg, 1934–37)
is both cursory and governed somewhat too much by purely theoretical considerations. A further difficulty lies in the fact that
syntax is much more subject than either phonology or morphology
to influence from other languages, as when Swiss German uses such
phrases as *er ist kränker als du nicht denkst* (instead of *er ist
kränker als du denkst* ' he is more ill than you think ') because of
the French type of *il est plus malade que tu ne penses* (for the
origin of the latter cf. p. 257).

Although it is obviously not yet possible to discuss syntax with
the accuracy feasible in phonology, morphology, and etymology,
we can, with fair certainty, lay down general principles with which,
in all probability, special details of linguistic systems hitherto
insufficiently investigated will be found to agree.

A sentence may consist either of a single word or of a group of
words, e.g., Latin *pluit* ' (it) rains ', *equus currit* ' (the) horse runs ';
and it may be either *verbal,* if the predicate be a verb (e.g., *equus*

currit '[the] horse runs '), or *nominal,* if the predicate be an
epithetologue (e.g., *omnia praeclara rara* ' all splendid things [are]
rare '). It may also be *simple,* as the examples just cited; or *compound,* the latter consisting of a *main clause* (the sentence proper)
and one or more *subordinate* or *hypotactic clauses* whose sense
is incomplete by itself or themselves since its or their meaning
depends for completeness on the statement (or question, or exclamation) of the main clause. Such a sentence may be of any
length or complexity consistent with intelligibility. There are likewise *co-ordinate or paratactic sentences,* composed of simple sentences connected by such conjunctions as ' and ', ' but ', e.g., *he
came and stayed; he came, but did not stay.* Further types of sentences, such as *interrogative* (' what does he say? '), *exclamatory*
(' what things he says! '), etc., are of rhetorical and stylistic interest, but present no new problems to linguistics; and the same statement holds good for *conditional, temporal, characteristic, final,* and
relative sentences (e.g., ' if he were good, he would be happy ',
etc.).

The sentence consists essentially of two parts, the *subject,* or
theme; and the *predicate,* or statement concerning the theme.
These names are logical, not linguistic, in origin, and are translations of terms used by Aristotle (ὑποκείμενον ' underlying [part]' =
Latin *subiectum;* κατηγορούμενον, κατηγόρημα ' asserted [part]',
' assertion ' = Latin *praedicatum);* but that logical rather than
linguistic terms should be used with reference to syntax by so acute
a thinker as Aristotle is in itself significant. With regard to the
subject, we must distinguish between the *grammatical subject,*
which is in the nominative case (e.g., Latin *equus currit* '[the]
horse runs '), and the *logical subject,* where the doer of the action
or the experiencer of the state indicated by the verb is in a case
other than the nominative (e.g., Armenian *yaynžam matuçeal
ašakertaçn* [genitive plural] *nora asen çna* ' at that time [there
is a] coming of His disciples, they say unto Him ' [Authorised
Version, ' then came his disciples, and said unto him ']; Latin *haec
vobis* [dative plural] *provincia est defendenda* ' for you this is a
province to be defended ' = ' you must defend this province ',
mihi deliberatum et constitutum est ' for me it is [a thing] deliberated and resolved ' = ' I have deliberated and resolved ' [cf.
p. 195]; Sanskrit *devena* [instrumental singular] *gatam* '[it was]
gone by the god ' = ' the god went ' [cf. pp. 200, 220]; Old Irish

no-n- [accusative plural] *berar* ' one carries us ' = ' we are carried ' [cf. p. 217]).

While the sentence must contain both a subject and a predicate, it is by no means necessary that these be separate words, for the same word may contain the two components, e.g., Latin *currō*, Greek τρέχω, Sanskrit *dhā́vāmi*, Armenian *vazem*, Old Irish *rethim*, Russian *bjégaju* ' run-I '. Occasionally, this *monorrhemic* type of sentence may incorporate a noun in some case or an adverb, as in Latin *anim-advertō* ' I observe ' = *animum advertō; ven-dō* ' I sell ' = Old Latin *venum dō; pos-sum* ' I am able ' = *potis sum; nōlō* ' I will not ' = *ne volō;* Greek ἱππο-μαχέω ' I fight on horseback ', εὐ-λογέω ' I bless '; Avestan *yaož-daðā́ti* ' he purifies '; Modern High German *wahr-nehmen* ' to perceive ' = Old High German *wara nëman, lob-singen* ' to praise '. At least one such verb seems to be as old as the Indo-European period, Sanskrit *śraddadhāmi* (also as two words, *śrád dadhāmi),* Latin *crēdō,* Old Irish *cretim* (Modern Irish *creidim)* ' I believe ' (literally, ' I put trust ') ; and at least one compound noun is of equal antiquity, Sanskrit *nīḍá-* ' resting-place, abode, nest ', Armenian *nist* ' seat, abode ', Latin *nīdus,* Middle Irish *net,* Old High German, Modern German, Anglo-Saxon, English *nest* from **ni-zd-ós* ' sitting down ' (cf. Sanskrit *ní-sīdati* ' sits down ').

Another type of monorrhemic verbal sentence is seen in verbs expressing meteorological conditions, such as Latin *pluit,* Greek ὕει, Gothic *rignida,* Sanskrit *várṣati,* Armenian *anjrewē,* Lithuanian *lȳja,* Old Church Slavic *dŭžditŭ* as contrasted with English *it rains,* French *il pleut,* German *es regnet.* Since beside this type we have that of Sanskrit *devó varṣati* ' the god rains ', Greek Ζεὺς ὕει ' Zeus rains ', Lithuanian *lietùs lȳja* ' the rain rains ', it is often supposed that the subject of the sentence is omitted. When, however, we consider such constructions as Anglo-Saxon *mé sceamaþ,* Latin *pudet me,* Bulgarian *mŭrzi me* ' I am ashamed ', Sanskrit *kitavám tatāpa* ' the gambler is distressed ', Gothic *þana gaggandan du mis ni huggreiþ jah þana galaubjandan du mis ni þaúrseiþ hwanhun* ' he that cometh to me shall never hunger; and he that believeth on me shall never thirst ' = Anglo-Saxon *hingraþ ðone ... þyrst ðone* (cf. Old High German *mih hungerit, mih durstit* ' I hunger, I thirst '), but Modern German *es hungert mich, es dürstet mich* beside *mich hungert, mich dürstet,* it seems difficult to escape the conclusion that we here have further examples of impersonal verbs (cf. pp. **218–219**). Evidently the neuter personal pronoun, as *it rains, es schämt mich* ' I am ashamed ', has been added merely because certain languages have come to require the expression of a subject for every verb. Any idea of a true definite subject, as *devó* in *devó varṣati*, Ζεύς in Ζεὺς ὕει, or *lietùs* in *lietùs lỹja*, would seem to be only a late linguistic development.

A verb is the sole part of speech which can form a complete sentence, i.e., which can contain both a subject and a predicate in a single monorrheme. A noun cannot so constitute a sentence, for the same epithetologue cannot simultaneously be both subject and predicate. If, for instance, I say simply *the dog*, I do not make a complete predication; and my hearer, feeling my statement to be imperfect, does not understand it unless I add, or he supplies from the context, a predicate (normally a verb), such as *runs, barks, see!, beware of!*, etc., as occasion demands. Apparently monorrhemic sentences containing only a noun, such as *fire, murder,* are really elliptical, and require a verb to make their meaning complete, *there is, is being committed,* and the like. So, too, such commands as *attention!, eyes right!*, possess meaning solely because the verbs *pay!, turn!*, etc., are supplied by those to whom the orders are given. Much conversation, as a matter of fact, is carried on by elliptical sentences, as ' He's running '. ' Where (is he running)? ' ' There (he's running)'. ' Why (do you think he's running)? ' '(He's running because he wants) to catch his train '.

There is only one case in which the sentence does not require a verb, i.e., the nominal sentence of the type of the Latin *omnia praeclara rara* ' all splendid things (are) rare ' (cf. p. **228**). Contrary to popular opinion, the nominal sentence does not omit the copula, and none is to be supplied. Originally there was no such thing as a copula, equivalent to ' is '; and its creation and evolution are relatively late. The primary connotation of the most common verb of this type, **ese-* (e.g., Sanskrit *ásti*, Armenian *ē*, Hittite *eszi* from [esṭi], Greek ἐστί, Latin *est*, Old Irish *is*, Gothic, Old High German *ist*, English *is*, Lithuanian *ēst[i]*, Old Church Slavic *jestŭ)*, is uncertain, but seems to have been ' exist '. In Sanskrit it is noteworthy that the suppletive aorist and perfect of *as-* (cf. p. 213) are formed from the verb *bhav-* ' become ' *(bhávati* ' he becomes, il devient ' : *ábhūt* ' he was once, il fut ' [*ásīt* ' he was repeatedly, il était '] : *babhúva* ' he has become, he is, il est devenu, il est '). This *bhav-* is cognate with Greek φύομαι ' I grow, come into being ' (cf. ἔφῡν ' he was '), Latin *fuī* ' I have been ', *amā-bam, amā-bō* ' I was loving, shall love ' (cf. p. 214), Osco-Umbrian *fust* ' he will be ', Old Irish *bie(i)d, bói* ' he will be, was ', Modern Irish *bíonn* ' he is habitually ' (Anglo-Irish ' he does be '), Old High German *bim*, Modern High German *bin*, Anglo-Saxon *béo* ' I am ', English *be*, Lithuanian *búti*, Old Church Slavic *byti* ' to be '.

Other verbs which have become mere copulas are *st(h)ā-* ' stand ' (cf. Greek ἵστησι, Latin *sistit*, German *steht)* in Sanskrit *tísthati*, Spanish *estar*, Italian *stare* [occasionally also Latin *stāre*], Old Irish *attá*, Modern Irish *(a)tá* [from *ad-stāti*]); * u̯erte-* ' turn ' in Sanskrit *vártate* (literally, ' he turns himself '), Modern High German *werden* ' to become, be ' (e.g., *er wird gefangen* ' he is [literally, becomes] taken '); Indo-European *u̯ese-* ' dwell ' in Gothic *wisan*, Anglo-Saxon, Old High German *wesan* ' to be ', English *was, were;* and Indo-European *u̯ele-* ' see ' in Old Irish *fil* ' there is ' (cf. French [from the end of the twelfth century] *voi-ci, voi-là* ' here is, there is ' [literally, ' see here! see there! ']).

This Proto-Indo-European lack of any copula survived in great measure in Vedic Sanskrit, Old Persian, Avestan, Homeric Greek, Old Irish, and Balto-Slavic, and very frequently in Latin and Teutonic, but only rarely in Armenian (e.g., Vedic *etád vaí Sómasya rūpám* ' that, indeed, [is] the form of Soma '; Old Persian *manā pitā Vištāspa* ' my father [is] Vishtāspa '; Avestan *nōit mōi vāstā* ' for me [there is] no shepherd '; Armenian *lçēkʿ zi̯ursd or i covs* ' fill the waters which [are] in the seas '; Greek σοὶ τὸ γέρας πολὺ μεῖζον ' for thee the honour [is] much greater '; Old Irish *nem insin* ' venom [is] this ', *maic ni dosom* ' sons [are] we to Him '; Lithuanian *medùs saldùs* ' honey [is] sweet '; Russian *domŭ novŭ* ' the house [is] new '; Latin *quot hominum linguae, tot nomina deorum* ' as many as [are] the tongues of men, so many [are] the names of gods '; Middle High German *sō hōher berg, sō tiefer tāl* ' the higher the mountain, the deeper the valley '; Modern High German *Ende gut, Alles gut* ' all's well that ends well '). Modern Indo-European languages, excepting Balto-Slavic, for the most part employ the copula. The same construction of pure nominal sentences is found in other linguistic groups as well, e.g., Arabic *'Allāhu 'a'lamu* ' God (is) most wise ', Hebrew *zăhaβ hā-'āreṣ ha-hī ṭōβ šām hab-beδōlaḥ* ' the gold of that land (is) good; (there

is) bdellium there '; Hungarian *az ég kék* ' the sky (is) blue ';
Swahili *simba mui* ' the lion (is) bad '.

The psychological foundation of syntax comes very distinctly to
the fore in *word-order*, i.e., in the sequence in which words are
arranged in a sentence. Yet morphology, or the lack of it, also plays
a part, as does phonology in its special phase of accent (cf. pp.
63–66), since it is obvious that, at least in the earlier periods, the
accentuation or lack of accentuation of words would cause them
to take certain places in relation to other words in the sentence,
thus stereotyping their sequence to a greater or less extent. Broadly
speaking, some languages, Hittite, English, French, and German,
for instance, are said to have *fixed* word-order, and others, such as
Greek, Latin, Armenian, and Sanskrit, to have *free* order; although, as a matter of fact, fixed and free orders are found mingled
in widely varying proportions in the greater number of languages.

Taking up these factors of psychology and accent in reverse
sequence, we note that certain words are accented, and that others
have no accent whatever, but are either *proclitic* (pronounced as a
phonetic unit with the following accented word) or, more commonly, *enclitic* (pronounced as a phonetic unit with the preceding
accented word). To the enclitic class belong certain conjunctions
and particles, e.g., Indo-European *q^ue ' and ' (Sanskrit *ca*, Greek
τε, Phrygian κε, Latin -*que*); *$ĝ(h)e$, *$ĝ(h)o$, an emphasising particle (Greek ἐμέ-γε, Gothic *mi-k*, Old High German *mi-h*, Modern
High German *mi-ch*); certain forms of the personal pronouns (e.g.,
Sanskrit *me* ' me ' beside *máhyam, máma*; Greek μοι; cf. French
atonic *me* beside tonic *moi*); the vocative case (e.g., Sanskrit *deva*
' O god ! ' beside *devás* ' the god '); and especially, under certain
conditions, the verb.

In Vedic Sanskrit the finite verb is unaccented when it stands in
the main clause (e.g., *Agním īḷe puróhitam* ' I praise Agni, the
house-priest'; *eṣá me deváḥ Savitá cacchanda yáḥ samānáṁ ná
pramináti dháma* ' this hath seemed to me the god Savitr, who
diminisheth not the uniform creation '). In dependent clauses, as
the example just cited shows, the verb is accented; and this is also
the case with vocatives and verbs placed at the beginning of the
sentence or of a quarter-verse in Vedic poetry (e.g., *Ágne deván
ihá 'vaha* ' O Agni, bring the gods here!'; *śáye vavríṣ cárati
jihváyā 'dán rerihyáte yuvatím,* ' the covering lieth [there]; he
[Agni, the fire-god] moveth, eating with [his] tongue; he kisseth

the maiden '). If the vocative is thus accented, the accent always falls on the first syllable *(déva* ' O god ' beside the usual *deva* and contrasted with the nominative *devás)*. In verbs with preverbs (the so-called compound verbs), the preverb is accented in main clauses (the reverse holds for subordinate clauses), e.g., *gávām ápa vrajā́m vṛdhi* ' unclose the stable of the kine ! ', but *yáḥ samānā́m ná pramināti dhā́ma* ' who diminisheth not the uniform creation '.

Traces of the enclitic character of the verb still survive in several other Indo-European languages. In Greek, special developments, notably the three-syllable law (by which there must be an accent at least three syllables from the end of the word), have interfered, so that only the present indicative of φημι ' I say ' and of εἰμι ' I am ' (from *esmi) remain enclitic, whereas * ζυγόν φερετε, ' ye bear a yoke ' (Sanskrit *yugám bharatha)* became first * ζυγόν φέρετε, and finally ζυγὸν φέρετε. On the other hand, the type of Sanskrit *ápa-vṛdhi*, just cited, reappears in the Greek type of κάτα-σχε ' restrain ! ' beside κατέχετε ' ye restrain ' from * κάτεχετε. In Latin, only the forms associated with *sum* ' I am ' remain enclitic (cf. *in periclost* ' he's in danger ' and such English forms as *I'm, we're); but the type of *con'ficiō* ' I finish ' for * '*con-faciō* shows that, as in Sanskrit and Greek, the preverb, not the verb, originally bore the accent (cf. pp. 63–64).

While there are thus marked survivals of enclitic verbs, it must not be supposed that the verb is invariably enclitic; nor must Sanskrit be regarded as necessarily the standard for Indo-European word-order. Even in Sanskrit we find the three types represented by Latin *pater librum dat, dat pater librum,* and *librum dat pater* ' the father gives a book ', all present in examples already cited *(eṣá me deváḥ Savitā́ cacchanda; śáye vavrị́ṣ; Agním ḷe puróhitam)*, just as they occur in the simplest types of Greek sentences, e.g., in the Laconian and Thespian dedicatory inscriptions Αἰγλατας τοι Καρνειο[ι τ]οδ' ἀγαλμ' ἀνεθε̄κε ' Aigletes dedicated this statue to the Karneian ' (i.e., to Apollo) ; Φιλετηρος 'Ατταλω Περγαμευς ἀνεθεικε τ[α]ν γαν τοι Ἑρμη ' Phileteros, (son) of Attalos, the Pergamene, dedicated the land to Hermes '; ἀνεθε̄κε 'Εκεφυλος Νεαρεταν τοι Ποhοιδανι ' Ekephylos dedicated Nearetes to Poseidon '; ἀνεθηκε Αἰσχριον 'Απειρο̄τας τοι Ποhοιδανι 'Ηρακληιδαν ' Aischrion the Epirote dedicated Herakleides to Poseidon '.

The Vedic rule that the verb is unaccented in the main clause, but accented in the subordinate, is probably a late specialisation, particularly as it is generally agreed that the earliest stages of Indo-European knew only co-ordinating, not subordinating clauses, as is strikingly confirmed by Hittite, and as is still the case in colloquial speech (e.g., ' he came and saw the book and took it '). In Old Irish, the Vedic order is exactly reversed, so that the independent verb (in main clauses) is accented, but the conjunct (in subordinate clauses) is not (e.g., *asberid-si cid ar-ind epur frit* ' ye say, why do I say it to thee? '). In Modern German, on the contrary, just as in Vedic, the verb is unaccented in the main clause, but accented in the subordinate (e.g., *die grössten Schwierigkeiten liegen da, wo wir sie nicht suchen* ' the greatest difficulties lie there where we do not seek them ') ; but this is not necessarily true of Old High German (e.g., *oblâz uns sculdi unseero, sô uuir oblâzêm uns sculdîkêm* ' forgive us our debts, as we forgive our debtors '), so that the Modern German word-order is not a survival of any special Indo-European system, but merely a late development resulting in a purely chance coincidence. Indeed, we find in Teutonic precisely the same triple possibility (e.g., Modern German *der Vater giebt seinem Sohn das Buch* ' the father gives his son the book '; Old High German *holoda ina truhtin* = Modern German *es hohlte ihn der Herr* ' the Lord took him ', where *es* merely masques the initial verb as in the impersonal type of *es regnet* ' it rains ' [cf. p. 229]; Anglo-Saxon *se héah-engel to heofonum gewát* ' the archangel departed to heaven '), as also in Lithuanian (e.g., *devyni brólei turėjo tìk víeną sėserį* ' nine brothers had only one sister '; *aũgino bagóts tėvs víeninteli sũnų̀* ' a rich father brought up an only son '; *tà gaspadìnė taĩ pàdarė* ' the housewife did that ' [rare]).

Different members of the same linguistic family may favour one or other of these word-orders. Thus, in Slavic, Old Russian and South Slavic usually place the verb at the beginning of the sentence, though medial and final positions are also found; in Modern Russian and Polish, the medial position is more frequent (perhaps under French or German influence) ; in West Slavic (except in literary Polish), the final position is preferred. In Celtic, Gaulish, to judge from its few surviving sentences, had either medial or final position *(Ateknati Trutikni karnitu artuaš Koisis Trutiknos* ' of Ategnatos, son of Drutos, Koisios, son of Drutos, carved [?] the gravestones [?]'; *Nantonicn[os]* . . . *iorebe logitoe* ' Nantonicnos . . . for [his] nephews [?] a-tomb-made [?]') ; Irish and

Welsh have the order verb-subject-object (e.g., Old Irish *berid
cách brith for-arele* 'each passes judgement on the other'; Old
Welsh *gorgolches e greu y seirch* ' his blood stained the harness ') ;
Cornish and Breton tend to give the verb medial position (e.g.,
Cornish *in Polsethow ywhylyr anethow* ' in Polsethow [Glassiney]
shall habitations be seen ', *karenza whelas karenza* ' love seeketh
love '; Breton *leveriou brezoneka lennimp feteiz hag arc'hoaz e
skrivimp lizerou* ' we read Breton books to-day, and to-morrow we
shall write letters '). In the scanty dedicatory inscriptions in
Venetic and Messapic, we find both medial and final position (e.g.,
Venetic *meχo zoto Rehtiah Φukka Kolivhiila* ' Phukka Kolivhiila
gave me to Rehtia ' : *vzan Vhuχia Urklehna Rehtieh zonasto*
' Vhukhia Urklehna gave a pin [?] or, vow [?] to Rehtia ';
Messapic *Etθeta hipades Aprod[i]ta* ' Etheta dedicated [this] to
Aphrodite ' : *Daçta Moro Ana Aprodita hipades* ' Daçta Moro
dedicated [this] to Lady [?] Aphrodite '). In Phrygian, only final
position has thus far been found (e.g., αι νι κος σεμουν κνουμανει
κακουν αδδακετ ' if anyone does harm to this tomb ').

On the whole, the evidence thus far available seems to warrant
certain general conclusions. *The entire syntactic arrangement in
Indo-European appears to be conditioned by the position of the
verb in relation to its subject (and object); and this position may be
either initial, medial, or final. When initial, the verb is accented;
when medial or final, it is enclitic.* The underlying principle here
seems to be that *the most important concept is placed first* (e.g.,
Sanskrit *Agním īḷe puróhitam* ' Agni [not Indra, Varuṇa, or some
other god] I praise, the house-priest '; *eṣá me deváḥ Savitá
cacchanda* ' this one [not someone else] to me the god Savitṛ [not
some other deity] hath seemed '; *śáye vavríṣ* ' lieth [not moveth
about, etc.] the covering '). Verb, subject, and object are of primary importance; all other words are accessory. It would seem,
furthermore, that, since the verb may be unaccented (i.e., enclitic),
whereas the subject and object must always be accented, *the most
primitive position of the verb was either medial or final.* Accessory
words are connected in order of decreasing importance with respect
to those whose meaning they modify.

In this connexion, we must revert to the distinction (cf. p. 192)
between grammatical cases (nominative and accusative) and relational (dative, genitive, locative, ablative, and instrumental). If
we consider the accentuation of the oldest type of nouns (the so-

called consonantal stems), we find that the grammatical cases are very frequently accented on the semanteme, but the relational invariably on the morpheme, e.g., Sanskrit *pā́t* (for *'*pad-s*) ' foot ', *pā́dam* (by false analogy for *'*padam*), but *padé, padás, padí, padás, padá* (cf. Greek πούς, Doric πῶς [for *πόδ-ς], πόδα, but ποδός, ποδί; see pp. 108, 109).

The question arises (though no answer yet seems possible) whether the relational cases themselves may not originally have been enclitic, so that, instead of *padás, ποδός*, the earlier stages may have been *padas, *ποδος. The historical accent would then have been added later (perhaps through rhythmic considerations), as was demonstrably the case with the type of Greek Σωκράτης λέγει ' Sokrates says ' for *Σωκράτης λεγει (cf. p. 233). If such was the evolution, it is easy to see why, apart from purely psychological considerations, accessory words take subordinate positions unless, as in the case of the verb, they are placed first for purposes of emphasis (e.g., Sanskrit *diví vaí Sóma ā́sīd áthe 'há devā́h* ' in heaven [not on earth] Soma was, here [not in heaven] the gods '; Latin *tíbi darétur ílla* ' that to thee [not to someone else] she be given ').

Proclitics are much less frequent than enclitics. Among the more usual classes we may first cite the article, which is really only a demonstrative pronoun (cf. p. 173; e.g., Greek ὁ τόπος ' the place '; Old Irish *in-salm-so* ' this Psalm '; French *l'homme*, German *der Mann*, English *the man*). In Romance, the development of the masculine article into a proclitic is especially interesting, e.g., French *le*, Provençal *lo*, Portuguese *o*, as contrasted with Spanish *el;* Italian has both *il* and *lo*. All these are from Latin *ílle* ' that ', which, from the fourth century onward, tended to become weakened in force from a demonstrative pronoun to a mere article (cf. the similar weakening of the numeral for ' one ' to the indefinite article, e.g., Latin *unus* : French *un;* Modern German *éin* : *ein)*, seen, for instance, in an Old Latin version of the Bible *adducite vitulum illum saginatum* = φέρετε τὸν μόσχον τὸν σιτευτόν ' bring hither the fatted calf ' (the Vulgate omits *illum* here). Italian *il* and Spanish *el* point to an accentuation of their Latin original as *'ille*, as also in the personal pronouns Italian *egli*, French *il*, Provençal *el*, Spanish *él*, Portuguese *elle*. French *le* and the like show a loss of accent on the first syllable (cf. French *lui, leur* from Vulgar Latin *il'lui, il'loru*ᵐ*;* a Latin accentuation *il'le* is impossible). In Rumanian, on the other hand, the postfixed article (e.g., *pomul* ' the tree ' : *pom* ' tree '; *pîinea* ' the bread ' : *pîine* ' bread ') comes from Latin *ille* used enclitically (Vulgar Latin *pomus ille*, *panis illa*).

Some forms of the personal pronouns are proclitic (e.g., Sanskrit *utá bruvantu no nído* ' and let our enemies say '; Albanian *me tha* ' he said to me '; Old Irish *dar-far-cenn* ' on your head '; French *je vois, tu vois*, German *ich sehe, du siehst*, English *I see, thou seest*, etc.), as is the Irish copula (e.g., Old Irish *is hed do-moiniur* ' 'tis this [that] I intend ', Modern Irish *is fearr liom bainne* ' 'tis better with me milk ' = ' I prefer milk '). Prepositions before their cases are likewise proclitic, as in Greek προτοῦ ' before this ', ἐπιπολύ ' very much '; Old High German *aba uuege* ' from the way '; Old Irish *dar-far-cenn* ' on your head '. When, on the other hand, the preposition follows its noun, the original accent remains, as in Greek νεῶν ἄπο ' from ships ', where comparison with Sanskrit *ápa*, Latin *ab*, Gothic *af*, Anglo-Saxon *œf, of*, English *of* may indicate that the Greek type of ἀπὸ πολέμου ' from war ' is for *ἀπο πολέμου from *ἄπο πολέμου (Old High German *aba, ab*, Modern German *ab* ' from ' show an Indo-European variant *a'po*, so that Greek ἄπο and ἀπό may both date from the Indo-European period). Greek ἐκ, ἐξ ' out of ', ἐν ' in ', and ἐς or εἰς ' into ' (from *ἐνς; cf. Greek ἐνὶ δήμῳ beside δήμῳ ἔνι, Old Irish Ogam *ini-gena*, Modern Irish *ingean* ' daughter ', Gaulish *Eni-genos)* remained proclitic throughout their history, but even they were accented when they followed their nouns (e.g., κακῶν ἐξ ' out of evils ', αὔριον ἐς ' to the morrow '). If such a preposition as ἐνί was originally a locative (cf. p. 170), the accentuation ἔνι would appear to be of later date, perhaps influenced by such prepositions as the caseless ἄπο (cf. p. 171), whose accentuation ἀπό even in the Indo-European period may have been due to such other prepositions as περί ' around ', where the oxytone (accent on the last syllable) is historically correct.

Loss of inflexion, or lack of it, may also affect word-order. In Latin, one may say *pater filio librum dat*, or *filio librum pater dat*, or *librum filio pater dat*, or even *dat pater filio librum*, but in English only *the father gives the son a book; the son gives the father a book* or *a book gives the father the son* would mean totally different things. In Chinese, as in English, both of which are characterised by *deflexion* (loss of inflexion; pp. 155, 301, 390), the word-order is very largely fixed. The position of an adjective with reference to its noun may be determined by certain conventions, so that if the adjective precedes, the combination has one meaning, but quite another if it follows (e.g., French *mes propres mains* ' my own hands ', but *mes mains propres* ' my clean hands '; Old Irish *maith fer* ' a man [is] good ', but *fer maith* ' a good man ' = Hebrew *ṭōβ īš : īš ṭōβ).*

Apart from the phonological and morphological factors just cited, syntax is largely determined by psychology. The Latin sentences just cited for varying word-order are normally rendered in English, not by the sequence of words, but by stressing the word on which importance is laid by the speaker: ' the *father* (not the mother, etc.) gives the son a book ', ' the father gives the *son* (not the daughter, etc.) a book ', ' the father gives the son a *book* (not a pencil, etc.)', ' the father *gives* (not sells, etc.) the son a book '. Similarly, the Modern Irish sentence *tá Conn ag dul go Doire indiu* ' Conn is (a) going to Derry to-day ' may have such variants as *is é Conn atá ag dul go Doire indiu* ' 'tis *Conn* (not Art, etc.) that is (a) going to Derry to-day ', *is go Doire atá Conn ag dul indiu* ' 'tis to *Derry* (not to Sligo, etc.) that Conn is (a) going to-day ', *is indiu atá Conn ag dul go Doire* ' 'tis *to-day* (not to-morrow) that Conn is (a) going to Derry ', *is ag dul go Doire atá Conn indiu* ' 'tis *(a) going to* (not coming from) Derry that Conn is to-day '.

If we exactly follow in English the first few lines of Caesar's *Gallic War*, we shall get, even though we violate the normal English word-order in some measure, a fair idea of the psychology underlying and determining the sequence of the original: *Gallia est omnis divisa in partes tres, quarum unam incolunt Belgae, aliam Aquitani, tertiam qui ipsorum lingua Celtae, nostra Galli appellantur. Hi omnes lingua, institutis, legibus inter se differunt. Gallos ab Aquitanis Garumna flumen, a Belgis Matrona et Sequana dividit. Horum omnium fortissimi sunt Belgae, propterea quod a cultu atque humanitate provinciae longissime absunt —* ' Gaul is all divided into parts three, of which one inhabit the Belgians, another the Aquitanians, the third (they) who in their own language Celts, in ours Gauls are called. These all in language, institutions, laws among themselves differ. The Gauls from the Aquitanians the Garonne river, from the Belgians the Marne and the Seine divide. Of these all, the bravest are the Belgians, because from the culture and refinement of the province furtherst are they away '.

It is possible that *rhythm* plays more or less part in word-order, but our knowledge of this subject is still too inadequate to make discussion profitable. When we have discounted the phonological and morphological factors, including the accentual, practically only the psychological element remains to explain the arrangement of the words of the sentence so as best to bring out the meaning of the speaker or writer. This is especially evident in languages with free word-order, notably, Greek, Latin, Sanskrit, and Armenian. But what are we to say of groups like Slavic and Celtic, where, with presumably free word-order in Proto-Slavic and Proto-Celtic, South Slavic and Irish-Welsh prefer one sequence, but West Slavic and Cornish-Breton another (cf. pp. 234–235)? The answer we can thus far give would seem to be that, for some reason as yet unknown, one group preferred one, and another another.

In Semitic, in exactly the same way, Arabic normally has the fixed word-order of verb-subject-object (e.g., *ḍaraba Zaydu^n rajula^n* ' Zayd struck a man '); Akkadian puts the verb in medial or final position (e.g., *úqu attû'a idûkû ana úqu ša Umizdâti* ' my army smote the army of Vahyazdāta '; *šumma în warad awêlim uḫtappid . . . mišil šimi-šu išaqal* ' if he puts out the eye of a man's slave, . . . let him pay half his value '); Hebrew usually has the Arabic word-order of verb-subject-object *(way-yišlaḥ 'Aβrāhām 'eθ-yāδō* ' and Abraham stretched forth his hand '), though other sequences also occur: subject-verb-object *(wǝ-Nōaḥ māṣā ḥēn bǝ-'ēynēy YHWH* ' and Noah found grace in the eyes of YHWH '), object-verb-subject *(wǝ-hak-kǝšāβīm hiɸrīδ Ya'ăqōβ* ' and Jacob did separate the lambs '), verb-object-subject *(wǝ-χāθaβ 'eθ-hā-'ālōθ hā-'elleḥ hak-kōhēn bas-sēɸer* ' and the priest shall write these curses in the book '), subject-object-verb *(ū-qǝšāθōθ nǝ'ārīm tǝrattašnāḥ* ' bows also shall dash young men to pieces '), and object-subject-verb (very rare, e.g., *wǝ-horǝβōθ mēhim gārim yōχēlū* ' and the waste places of the fat ones shall strangers eat '). In Syriac, the order is essentially free.

In any investigation of word-order, especially in languages of which only written records remain, much caution is necessary in selecting material. Generally speaking, prose is here a better source than poetry, for in poetry the sequence may be affected by considerations of metre. Thus, in Sanskrit, the *Śatapathabrāhmaṇa* is a safer guide than the Rigveda; in Greek, the history of Herodotos than Homer; in Latin, Livy than Plautus or Vergil; in Anglo-

Saxon, King Alfred's original compositions than *Béowulf*. An original text is better than a translation, which may be influenced by the language from which it is rendered. One must, therefore, consider with care the evidence of Armenian, which is largely translated from Greek or Syriac, and of Gothic, which is practically a version from Greek. The Anglo-Saxon *Chronicle*, for example, is preferable to Alfred's rendering of Saint Gregory's *Pastoral Care*.

A text of simple style is better for a study of word-order than one which is ornate, since in fine literature the sequence is apt to be modified for purely aesthetic effect. One would here prefer, for instance, Xenophon's *Anabasis* to the orations of Demosthenes, or Caesar to Cicero's oratorical or philosophical writings. In this connexion, however, one should not forget that education very often modifies the word-order of a speaker or writer. The *Letters* of Cicero are preferable to his orations for syntactic study, but even in his correspondence he could scarcely avoid fine writing; even Greek and Latin inscriptions often endeavour to be literary; and literary tradition must frequently be suspected even in such Vulgar Latin works as the *Historia Francorum* by Gregory of Tours and Aetheria's *Peregrinatio ad loca sancta*.

Many syntactic phenomena which are not only puzzling but often inexplicable from the synchronic point of view, i.e., from that of a given period in a language, become fully intelligible and perfectly natural when considered diachronically, i.e., historically (cf. p. 23).

School-grammars of Latin state that the subject of an infinitive is in the accusative. On the face of it, this is absurd. The accusative cannot possibly serve as the subject of anything, but, unless terminative in force, can be only a direct object; and the infinitive itself is but a case-form of a noun (see pp. 192–194, 221). It thus becomes evident that such a sentence as *dicit eos agere* ' he says that they do ' originally meant ' he says them in doing '; i.e., *eos* is not the subject of *agere* (an old locative of the verbal noun *ages-i), but the direct object of *dicit*.

In Latin, again, the ' place where ' is apparently indicated in the first and second declensions by the genitive, and in the third by the ablative (e.g., *Romae* ' at Rome ', *Lanuvī* ' at Lanuvium ', *premit altum corde dolorem* ' he presses the pain deep in his heart '). On investigation, however, we find that in Old Latin *Romae* is *Romai;* that the equivalent of *Lanuvī* is *Delei* ' in

Delos '; and that *corde* is for an older **cordi*. When we compare these types with those of Avestan *grīvaya* ' on the neck ' (for **grīvā-i-ā̆)*, Greek Θηβαι-γενής ' born in Thebes ', Elean 'Ολυνπιαι ' in Olympia ', Oscan **víaí** ' in the road ' (genitive *eituas* ' of money '), Lithuanian *rañkoj-e* ' in a hand '; Sanskrit *áśve* ' in a horse ' (from Indo-European **ek̥u̯o-i)*, Greek οἴκοι ' at home ', Oscan *comenei* ' in the assembly ' (genitive **sakarakleís** ' of the shrine '), Lithuanian *namiẽ* ' at home ', Old Church Slavic *rodě* ' in birth '; Sanskrit *hr̥dí* ' in a heart ', Greek πέρυσι ' in the previous year ', we see that *Romae, Lanuvī*, and *corde* were originally case-forms ending in *-i*. Primarily they were not genitives or ablatives, but locatives (cf. p. 198) which, through weakening of the final vowel, came to coincide with the usual forms of genitives and ablatives respectively (cf. p. 202). The old forms lingered on in the case of proper names like *Romae*, and in a few stereotyped phrases such as Greek οἴκοι ' at home ' or Latin *domī bellīque* ' in peace and in war ', and occasionally in poetry, which is inherently conservative (cf. also the origin of the so-called Latin ' dative of agent ', p. 228).

With the progress of syncretism, involving more or less loss of feeling for the original functions of the case-forms, and, often, the disappearance of the old case-endings (cf. pp. 19–20, 201–202), it became necessary to indicate the old case-functions in some other way. This was accomplished by using prepositions (cf. pp. 170–171), a device which began, for Latin, even in the Classical period, and which was widely extended in Vulgar Latin, whence it was carried into the various Romance languages. Thus, the locative (the in-case) was indicated by using the preposition *in* ' in ' with the ablative *(in insula* ' in an island ', *in Gallia* ' in Gaul ') ; the instrumental (the with-case), by. *cum* ' with ' with the ablative *(cum telo* ' with a weapon ', cf. Italian *percuotere col piede* ' to strike with the foot, to kick ') ; the ablative proper (the from-case), by *ab* ' from ', *ex* ' out from ', etc. *(a proposito* ' from the point ', *ex civitate* ' away from the state ', an Old Latin version of John xix. 29, *vas de aceto plenum* ' a vessel full of vinegar ' beside the Vulgate *vas . . . aceto plenum)*.

The dative (the for-case) gradually yielded to the accusative with *ad* ' to ' *(filiae librum dat* ' he gives his daughter a book ' became *ille dat* [*donat*] *unum librum ad suam filiam* = French *il donne un livre à sa fille,* a construction found also in early colloquial Latin, as *hunc ad carnuficem dabo* ' I'll give this fellow to the hangman ' [Plautus]; cf. Vulgar Latin *dicens ad eum* ' saying to him ', and even *ad Dei officio paratus* ' ready for God's service ' and *hic requiiscunt membra ad duus fratres Gallo et Fidencio* ' here rest the limbs of two brothers, Gallus and Fidentius '; cf. p. 245). The genitive (the generic case) was replaced by *de* ' from ' (developing in meaning to ' of ', exactly like English *of* as contrasted with Sanskrit *ápa*, Greek ἀπό ' from ') with the ablative (cf. *expers partis . . . de nostris bonis* ' without a share of our property ' [Plautus]; *pauci de nostris* ' a few of our men ' [Caesar]; *conscientia de culpa* ' consciousness of guilt ' [Sallust]; cf. also *securus futuri* ' certain of the future ' beside *securus de ea re* ' certain of that matter '; Vulgar Latin *fundamenta de palacio* ' foundations of the palace '), a phenomenon which not only recalls, but may be a reminiscence of, the wide confusion between the genitive and the ablative in Indo-European generally (cf. p. 199).

This replacement of case-forms by prepositions is likewise found in English and Modern Persian; and even in languages which retain the old forms, the use of prepositions in addition to case-forms is very common and tends steadily to increase (cf. Latin *in oppidum ire* ' to go to the town ' as contrasted with *Romam ire* ' to go to Rome '). The decay of the force of case-forms, and their replacement by prepositions, is particularly well illustrated in Vulgar Latin inscriptions (e.g., *ab hostem . . . occissus* ' killed by the enemy ' [for *ab hoste occisus*], *cum libertos meos* ' with my freedmen ' [for *cum libertis meis*], *ex donationem* ' from the gift ' [for *ex donatione*], *hec iacet in tenebras* ' she lies [here] in darkness ' [for *haec iacet in tenebris*], *pro salutem meam* ' for my welfare ' [for *pro salute mea*], *sine alteritrum animi lesionem* ' without grievance on either side ' [for *sine alterutra animi laesione*], *ante ara* ' before the altar ' [for *ante aram*], *inter eis* ' between them ' [for *inter eos*], *ob meritis eius* ' for his merits ' [for *ob merita eius*], *per ultimo fato* ' by final doom ' [for *per ultimum fatum*], *post eorum excessu* ' after their death ' [for *post eorum excessum*]). Some of this confusion may have been more apparent than real, as when, e.g., *salutem meam* [salu:tē meã] was pronounced [salu:te mea]; but in any event it is clear that one was already on the course that was eventually to lead to the Romance system of one case for the subject (cas sujet) and another for all the rest (cas régime; cf. p. 245).

Frequently a verb or an epithetologue may govern various cases. Thus we have, in Latin, *donat coronas suis* ' he presents wreaths to his men ' (accusative and dative) beside *donat suos coronis* ' he presents his men with wreaths ' (accusative and ablative) ; *mulier eximia pulchritudine* ' a woman with extraordinary beauty ' (ablative) beside *vir summae virtutis* ' a man of highest courage ' (genitive) ; *animus meminit praeteritorum* ' the soul is mindful of things past ' (genitive) beside *suam quisque homo rem meminit* ' every man remembers his own affair ' (accusative) ; *adulatus est Antonio* ' he flattered Anthony ' (dative) beside *Neronem adulatus est* ' he flattered Nero ' (accusative). In Greek one finds τῶν ἡδονῶν ἐκράτει ' he was master of his pleasures ' (genitive) beside τοὺς Θρᾷκας κρατήσαντες ' having mastered the Thracians ' (accusative) ; οὐκέτι ἡμῖν ἡγήσεται ' he will no longer be a guide for us ' (dative) beside ἡγήσατο λαῶν ' he was leader of the men ' (genitive) and ἅρματα ἡγεῖσθαι ' to drive chariots ' (accusative).

Sanskrit shows *grāmam gacchati* ' he goes to the village ' (and reaches it) (accusative) beside *grāmāya gacchati* ' he goes toward the village ' (but does not necessarily reach it) (dative) and *grāme gacchati* ' he goes in the village ' (i.e., goes to it and stays in it) (locative) ; *anena sadṛśo loke na bhūto* ' (there has) not been one like him in the world ' (instrumental) beside *simhasya mukhasya sadṛśam mukham* ' a face like a lion's face ' (genitive) ; *harṣeṇa naṣṭā 'syāḥ kṣun na rogataḥ* ' her hunger is destroyed by joy (instrumental), not from illness ' (ablative). The construction *grāme gacchati* ' he goes (to and stays) in the village ', just noted, is termed *pregnant,* i.e., in the logical process of the action, the mind jumps over a step which is readily supplied by the hearer or reader, e.g., Greek ἐν τῷ ποταμῷ ἔπεσον ' they fell (into and remained) in the river '; αἱ ξύνοδοι ἐς τὸ ἱερὸν ἐγίγνοντο ' the synods took place in (to) the temple ' (i.e., those who held them went into the temple, and there conducted them).

How carefully such syntactic alternants must be considered, each on its own merits, is clearly shown by the French constructions *les hommes sont venus* ' the (specific) men have come ' as contrasted with *des hommes sont venus* ' (some) men have come '; *je vois les hommes* ' I see the (specific) men ' as contrasted with *je vois des hommes* ' I see (some) men '. This construction, a subdivision of the partitive genitive (see pp. 195, 198), is widespread in Indo-European. It is found both in Early Latin (e.g., Plautus, *hic tecum filius negoti gessit* ' my son carried on [some] business with you here ') and in Umbrian (e.g., **revestu** ... **eru emantur herte** ' let him see [whether some] of them should be taken '; **struhçlas** ... **kumaltu** ' let him grind [some] sacrificial cake '). For Greek one may cite ἔπιπτον ἑκατέρων ' (some) of both sides fell ', πέμπει τῶν Λυδῶν ' he sends (some of) the Lydians ' (cf. Homer's αἵματος ὄφρα πίω ' that I may drink of the blood ', but πίεν αἷμα κελαινόν ' he drank the dark blood ' two lines later).

In Vedic Sanskrit, we find such examples as *dádāta no amŕtasya prajáyai* ' give ye of immortality to our offspring ', but *dádāsi dāśúṣe vásūni* ' thou givest good things to the pious man '; and in Avestan, *yaṯ hē stārąm baγō-dātanąm aᵢwi-raočayǻnte* ' that (some) stars (des étoiles), God-created, may shine for him ', *yō sūne ... astanąm ahmarštanąm daδāᵢti* ' who gives a dog ... (some) un-broken bones '. The construction likewise occurs in Teutonic, e.g., in Gothic, *taujiþ þiuþis* ' (if) he doeth any good ' (' s'il fait du bien '; the Greek original here has the accusative, ἐάν τι ποιήσῃ ἀγαθόν); in Anglo-Saxon, *híe him woldon óðerra wera céosan* ' they would choose them (some) other husbands ' (' d'autres maris '); in Old High German, *hiaz sie bringan thero fisgo* ' he bade them bring (some) of the fish ' (in the Greek original ἐνέγκατε ἀπὸ τῶν ὀψαρίων); and in Swiss German, *de(r) zīt hā* ' to have (some) time ' (' avoir du temps '). It also occurs in Balto-Slavic, as in Lithuanian, *šiañdien žmonių̃ pàs manè ateĩs* ' today (some) people (' des gens ') will come to me ', *atnèšk mán vandeñs* ' bring me (some) water ' (' de l'eau '); in Old Church Slavic (rare), *prijętŭ že chlĕbŭ* ' he takes of the loaves ' beside *prijętŭ že chlĕby* ' he takes the loaves ' (the Greek original has ἔλαβεν οὖν τοὺς ἄρτους); in Russian, *kup'iti chlj'ĕva* ' to buy (some) bread ' (' acheter du pain '), *naj'ĕchalo gost'ej* ' (some) guests (' des invités ') came '; and in Polish, *daj mi wina* ' give me (some) wine ' (' donne-moi du vin ').

Proper names frequently preserve archaic features which elsewhere have disappeared. This phenomenon comes very interestingly to the fore in certain Modern French idioms. Here it is a rule that churches, streets, etc., named after individuals do not have *de* unless a common noun intervenes. Thus one finds in Paris *église Saint-Gervais*, but *église de la Trinité; rue Jacob*, but *rue du Temple, rue du Général Lambert; île Saint-Louis*, but *île de la Cité; hôtel-Dieu*, but *hôtel des Monnaies;* and the plural of family-names has no final -s, e.g., *les Rinfret* ' the Rinfrets, the Rinfret family '. This finds its explanation in the history of the language. In Old French we have such constructions as *un dent saint Piedre et del sanc saint Basilie* = Modern French *un dent de saint-Pierre et du sang de saint-Basile* ' a tooth of Saint Peter and (some) blood of Saint Basil '; *la niece le duc* = *la nièce du duc* ' the duke's niece ', the possessive *de* being used in Old French only with words denoting animals or things, or designating a class of individuals (cf. p. 188).

In Vulgar Latin, we find, beside the type of *ecclesia sancti Gervasii, dens sancti Petri,* the constructions represented by *Ursiniano subdiacono sub hoc tumulo ossa quiescunt* ' the bones of Ursinian the subdeacon rest beneath this tomb ', *in curte duci* ' in the duke's court ', and also *hic requiiscunt membra ad duus fratres Gallo et Fidencio* ' here rest the limbs of two brothers, Gallus and Fidentius ' (whence the Old French type of *la fille a emperëor* ' an emperor's daughter ', *li oncles au buen chevalier* ' the uncle of the good knight '; Modern French *c'est à moi* ' it's mine ', colloquial *la maison à M. Grandet* ' Monsieur Grandet's house '; cf. also in the Old French *Prose of Saint Eulalie li Deo inimi* ' the enemies of God ', *lo Deo menestier* ' the service of God '; the type is likewise found in other Romance languages). It would seem that in the type of *dent saint Piedre* we have a survival of the Latin *dens sancti Petri,* and in that of *la niece le duc* of *neptis duci,* i.e., we have a contamination (cf. p. 257) of two case-forms of identical outward termination and of similar meaning. The type of *les Rinfret* becomes clear when we consider the Old French nominal inflexion:

	LATIN	OLD FRENCH	MODERN FRENCH		LATIN	OLD FRENCH	MODERN FRENCH
Singular nominative	*murus*	*murs*	*mur*	Plural nominative	*muri*	*mur*	*murs*
Singular oblique	*muru^m*, etc.	*mur*		Plural oblique	*muros,* etc.	*murs*	

In other words, it is simply the Old French nominative plural form retained.

History likewise explains the distinction in Spanish between the types of *leo un libro* ' I read a book ' and *el hijo ama á su madre* ' the son loves his mother ' (cf. pp. 112, 188). The oldest known instance of this construction is from the early eleventh century: *decepit ad suo germano* = Modern Spanish *engañó á su hermano* ' he deceived his brother '. We have just noted the confusion between the Classical Latin dative and *ad* with the accusative; and in this Hispano-Latin example we have the complete contamination of *ad* with a dative. Many Latin verbs which normally govern an accusative occasionally govern a dative, and *vice versa*, e.g., *imperō* ' I command ' (e.g., *num quid aliud imperas?* ' do you order anything else? ' : *imperare liberis* ' to rule children '), *maledicō* ' I revile ' (e.g., the Vulgate version of Exodus xxii. 28, *principi populi tui non maledices* ' thou shalt not curse the ruler of thy people ', but quoted in Acts xxiii. 5, as *principem populi tui non maledices), serviō* ' I serve ' (e.g., *servit ipse nulli cupiditati* ' he himself serves no desire ' : Old Latin *eius serviat cupidines* ' she should serve his desires '), *vitō* ' I avoid ' (e.g., *ut omnes suspiciones vitet* ' that he may avoid all suspicions ' : *vitent infortunio* ' let them avoid misfortune '; cf. also an Old Latin version of Galatians v. 7, *quis vobis impedivit?* ' who did hinder you? ' as contrasted with the Vulgate *quis vos impedivit?).*

In this Spanish idiom we have the following contaminations (denoted by ⌣) : *suam matrem* ⌣ *ad suam matrem* ⌣ *suae matri* ⌣ *ad suae matri* > *á su madre*. Gradually this type became specialised to denote the animate object, the inanimate object being retained in the old accusatival form (e.g., *leo un libro* = Latin *lego unu^m libru^m;* cf. also p. 188). Semitic has what is at least superficially the same mode of expression, especially in Syriac, which frequently employs *lə* ' to ' (cf. for meaning Latin *ad)* with definite nouns of the direct object, as *man da-mə'īq lə rūḥeh da-Məšīḥā* ' he who (hath) distressed the spirit of the Messiah ' beside *man da-məqakkel rūḥeh da-Məšīḥā* ' he who (hath) received the spirit of the Messiah '.

Such French idioms as *il y a* ' there is ' (cf. Old French *n'at tant bel chevalier* ' there is not so fair a knight ') and *il fait chaud* ' it is hot ' find their origins in Vulgar Latin phrases like *in arca Noe habuit homines* ' there were men in Noah's ark ' (literally, ' one had men in Noah's ark '), *habebat de civitate forsitan mille quingentos passus* ' it was about fifteen hundred paces from the

town ', *habebat ibi silvam* ' there was a forest ' (' il y avait une
forêt ', literally, ' one had a forest there '), *numquam fecit tale
frigus* ' it was never so cold ' (' il n'avait jamais fait tellement
froid '), *gravem eo anno hiemem fecit* ' there was a severe winter
that year '. In like manner, *es giebt*, the German equivalent of the
French *il y a* and the English *there is*, seems to have meant primarily ' one gives ', i.e., the verb was originally impersonal, just
as in the type of *es regnet, il pleut, it rains* (cf. p. 229).

Translation of Vulgar Latin *habebat* by ' one had ' brings up
the question of the origin of this phrase, as well as of its French
and German equivalents, *on avait (on eut), man hatte*. It is usually
regarded as evolved from negatives of the type of Latin *nēmō* ' no
one ' from **ne-hemō* ' not a man, nobody ' (cf. Old Latin *hemō*),
and its distribution is rather curious. It is found sporadically in
Anglo-Saxon, Middle and Modern English, Scandinavian, Old
Saxon, Old and Middle High German, Spanish, Portuguese, and
Italian, but not in Gothic (except with a negative, *ni manna-hum*)
or in Old Frisian, Rhaeto-Romanic, or Rumanian; it is extremely
frequent in all periods of French and in Modern German; and
analogues occur in Albanian *(njer)* and in Malay *(orang)*. On the
other hand, *one* in this sense finds parallels in Latin *unus*, Spanish
uno (rare), and in some Italian dialects, as well as in Plattdeutsch
and certain German dialects. The type of English *one had* may
be a contamination of English *one* with French *on*, rather than a
development parallel to that of *unus, uno*, etc.

In Classical Greek, ἀνήρ and ἄνθρωπος ' man ', and in Classical
Latin, *homo* ' man ', appear in rare instances as indefinite pronouns.
In the Vulgate, *homo* sometimes serves to render the Hebrew
'*ādām* or '*īš* ' a man ' (and, hence, ' anyone '), as in Job v. 7:
'*ādām lə-'āmāl yullāδ* = ἄνθρωπος γεννᾶται κόπῳ = *homo nascitur
ad laborem* ' man is born unto trouble '. It is this use of *homo* (in
reality a Semitism, like the corresponding Septuagint employment
of ἀνήρ, ἄνθρωπος) which seems to have given rise to the use of *on*
and *man* ' one ' as an indefinite. This usage was then extended to
passages which were not literally translated, as in the Anglo-
Saxon version of Matthew xiv. 11: *and man brohte ðá his heafod
on ánum disce* = Vulgate *et allatum est caput eius in disco* ' and
his head was brought in a charger '. In Luke iv. 17, where the
Greek, Vulgate, Anglo-Saxon, and English versions have a passive
(ἐπεδόθη αὐτῷ βιβλίον τοῦ προφήτου Ἠσαΐου = *traditus est illi liber*

Isaiae prophetae = *him wæs geseald Isaias bóc* ' there was delivered unto him the book of the prophet Esaias '), the Old High German translation of Tatian has *man (salta man imo then buoh des uuizagen Esaies)*.

Finally, we may note the type represented by a Britanno-Roman inscription, *Vitaliani emereto* '(the tomb) of Vitalian, (the soldier) emeritus ', a type which finds many parallels in documents of the Merovingian period in France. This represents a contamination of the genitive of the possessor with the dative of the possessor. It is not, strictly speaking, what it superficially seems to be, a mere blundering of cases, but a confused blending of the functions of two cases fundamentally distinct, ' the tomb of Vitalian ' and ' the tomb for the soldier emeritus '.

CHAPTER IX

Semantics: The Changing Meanings of Words

Definition of semantics — loss of linguistic consciousness of original meaning of words — development of connotations from base-meanings — homonyms — evolution of meanings from general or vague to specific — English *deer* and cognates from the Indo-European base **dheṷe-* 'blow' — metaphor the basis of semantics — polysemy, restriction, and extension of meanings — contamination — replacements and doublets in vocabulary — evolution of meanings as affected by the development of civilisation — pejoration and melioration — reasons for displacement of words — linguistic tabu: names of divine beings and 'power of the Name'; clipped oaths; tabued words retained in addressing the Deity or as terms of familiarity; replacement of real names of dread or uncanny beings — euphemism — isolation in specialised senses causes survival of old meanings otherwise lost — multiplicity of terms for objects or beings of diverse functions; the words for 'horse' — transfers of meanings in words for parts of the body — popular etymology — place-names changed by popular etymology — transformation of proper names into epithetologues — changes of meaning in words borrowed from another language — onomatopoeia.

SEMANTICS, the second of the predominantly psychological aspects of linguistics (cf. p. 145), deals with the evolution of the meanings of words and with the reasons for their survival, decay, disappearance, and, sometimes, revival, as well as with the causes of creation of new words. It seems safe to affirm that very few words, if any, excepting those recently coined, exactly retain their original meanings; and in countless instances their connotations have so changed that only patient and often intricate research can reveal their primary significations.

No speaker is conscious, unless linguistically trained, that English *beaver*, Anglo-Saxon *befer*, Old Icelandic *bjórr*, Old High German *bibar*, Modern German *Biber*, Cornish *befer*, Latin *fiber*, Lithuanian *bēbras*, Russian *bobrŭ*, Bulgarian *béber*, and Avestan *bawri-* originally meant simply ' deep-brown ' (Sanskrit *babhrú-),* and that primarily it did not designate any animal whatsoever, even though in Sanskrit it sometimes signifies ' ichneumon '. Still less does he realise that ' brown ' was originally the name of the animal called in English *bear,* in Anglo-Saxon *bera,* in Old Icelandic *björn,* in Old High German *bëro,* or in Modern German *Bär* (contrast Lithuanian *bëras* ' brown ', especially of horses) ; or that *beaver* and *bear* are etymologically akin not only to each other, but to English *brown,* German *braun* (Anglo-Saxon, Old High German *brūn,* Old Icelandic *brúnn);* or that the English poetic term *bruin* is simply borrowed from the Modern Dutch form of the same word for ' brown '. Even less does the speaker know why he calls the animal ' bear ', and the Russian is equally ignorant of why he terms the bear ' honey-eater ' *(mëdvëdi),* or the Middle Welshman ' honey-pig ' *(melfochyn),* or the Lithuanian ' licker ' *(lokỹs;* cf. Lithuanian *làkti* ' to lick '), or the Old Prussian ' grunter ' *(clokis;* cf. Lithuanian *kriōkti* ' to grunt ').

Except for the semantic principle termed euphemism (cf. pp. 265–267), all these peoples might equally well have called the bear by some name etymologically equivalent to its Indo-European term (cf. p. 306), which survived in French *ours,* Latin *ursus,* Middle Irish *art,* Albanian *arí,* Greek ἄρκτος, Armenian *arǰ,* Avestan *arəša-,* Sanskrit *ŕkṣa-,* the speakers of all these language-groups being at best only dimly aware that they were, in reality, bluntly calling the beast a ' harmer ' (cf. Sanskrit *rákṣas-* ' demon ', Avestan *raš-* ' injure ', Greek ἐρέχθω ' rend, break '). They must have been still less cognisant of the fact that originally this ' harmer ' had been specified as a ' harmer of men ' or ' of cattle ', and the like. The accent of *ŕkṣa-* can be explained only as secondary, i.e., as a rhythmic accent falling on the zero-grade of a base (cf. pp. 65–66), whereas the primary accent had fallen on the first member of some such compound as **'nero-ˌr̥k̂p̄o-* ' man-harmer ', **'peku-ˌr̥k̂p̄o-* ' cattle-harmer '. Hence, when the first component vanished with its accent, the second remained with its theoretically impossible accentuation; the ' 'man-harmer ', the ''beast-harmer ' had become the ''harmer ' in general.

The English word *constable* denotes in ordinary parlance ' a policeman, a subordinate official who helps keep the peace and who serves legal papers in minor cases ', but in the mediaeval period, it designated a man of very exalted rank. Originally he was, literally, only a ' stable-companion ' *(comes stabuli).* Similarly, French *maréchal,* Old French *mareschal* (borrowed in English *marshal),* and Old Italian *mariscalco* connote both an official of (usually) high rank and a farrier; while Engadine *marescal* and Catalan *menescal* mean 'veterinary surgeon', the *marascalz* of the Friulian of Belluna signifies 'servant', and the Italian *mascalzone* connotes 'knave'. All these are derived from Old High German *marahscalh* 'horse-boy'; and *marahscalh* itself is simply a translation of the Latin *comes stabuli*, and thus is virtually a loan-word (cf. p. 132), so that *constable* and *marshal*, however different in meaning now, originally meant one and the same occupation and position in society.

The Middle English version of Genesis and Exodus (about 1250) prays that Joseph may find joy 'among engeles & seli men' ('among angels and blessed men'), and the story of Havelok the Dane (before 1300) has the line, 'ful sori was that seli knaue' ('full sorry was that simple boy'), whereas 'silly men' and 'silly knave' would now imply something very different indeed. In the Authorised Version of the Bible (Psalms cxix. 147), the Psalmist says, 'I prevented the dawning of the morning'; and the Book of Common Prayer has a Collect which begins, 'Lord, we pray thee that thy grace may always prevent and follow us', where 'prevent' certainly does not mean 'forbid' or 'hinder', but 'go before, precede' (in the passage from the Psalms, the Vulgate has *praeveni;* and in the Collect, the Latin Rites have *praeveniat).*

Generally speaking, *the connotations of individual words develop from basal meanings just as the forms of words evolve from base-forms* (cf. pp. 150–151). Since, however, meanings are developed psychologically, whereas forms are evolved essentially by physiological processes, semantics, like the equally psychological syntax, is far less capable of being reduced to systems of regular correspondences than are phonology, morphology, or etymology. Here one can do no more than lay down certain wide categories in broad outline. Nevertheless, just as the form of a word cannot be fully understood without tracing it back historically as far as data permit, and considering all its cognates, so *its meaning becomes clear only when the word's history is studied from the semantic point of view together with the history of all its cognate words.* We may go still further, and may affirm that no word can be exclusively investigated from any single point of view, whether phonologically, morphologically, syntactically, semantically, or etymologically; it must, indeed, be considered under each of these aspects, but *the conclusions of all five separate investigations must be in harmony if the result is to be deemed scientifically exact.* Even if four agree, and only one is irreconcilable with the rest, the whole problem must either be studied anew with consideration of additional factors, or it must be abandoned.

From the semantic point of view, this comes clearly to the fore in *homonyms,* words of identical sound, form, and function, but of totally different meanings. Thus, the English word *host* has three irreconcilable significations, though their sound, form, and function (noun) are the same. If I say, ' I see the host ', my hearer does not know, without some aid of sight or context, whether I see a large number of people, some one who will make us welcome under his roof, or the wafer of unleavened bread used in the Mass. These three connotations cannot be reconciled; and only when the history of the words is investigated, does one find that, although now alike, they come from three separate sources. As meaning ' a large number of people ', *host* is developed from Old French *ost,* from Latin *hoste^m* ' stranger, enemy ', and, in Vulgar Latin, ' army '; as ' one who gives hospitality ', from Old French *oste* (Modern French *hôte,* also meaning ' guest ') from Latin *hospite^m* ' guest, host ', and this for **hosti-pote^m* ' guest-master ' (cf. Old Church Slavic *gospodĭ* ' lord, master '), so that ultimately it is cognate with *hostis* ' stranger ', the stranger being regarded from one point of view as a dangerous alien, and from the other as one to whom hospitality should be shown; and as ' the Wafer consecrated in the Mass ', from Latin *hostia^m* ' victim, sacrifice '.

For the most part, the meanings of words, at first general, and perhaps vague, tend to become more and more specific. Let us take, for example, the English word *deer,* studying it in connexion with its etymological cognates, and tracing the whole group back to its base. These cognates show superficially no family-meaning whatever, but, at the same time, both *deer* and they derive their significations, however divergent now, by entirely rational developments from the connotation of their common Indo-European base. The English noun *deer* now means only a certain type of wild animal represented by the elk, reindeer, fallow-deer, stag, caribou, wapiti, roebuck, musk-deer, etc.; and this is also the signification, as a hunting-term, of its German cognate *Tier.* In Anglo-Saxon, however, *déor* meant any wild animal, as in the translation of Genesis i. 25, *God geworhte ðære eorþan déor æfter hira hiwum,*

where the Authorised Version has, ' God made the beast of the
earth after his kind '; and as late as Shakespeare we read of ' mice,
and rats, and such small deer '. The corresponding Gothic word
dius means ' wild beast ', and the same is true of Old High German *tior* (Modern German *Tier)*, Dutch *dier*, Old Saxon *dior*,
Old Frisian *diar*, Old Icelandic *dýr*, and Swedish *djur*. The reason why English *deer* has thus become specialised in signification
is because it is *par excellence* the wild beast pursued in the chase
in England.

The connotation of ' wild animal ' for *déor*, *Tier*, *dius*, etc., is
itself a specialisation, for the Indo-European base **dheuese-*, from
which they are all derived, means ' breathe ', so that the group of
déor, *deer*, which is neuter in gender, signifies ' the breathing ',
thus being quite parallel in semantic development to Latin *animal*
as compared with *anima* ' breath, breeze, life ' (cf. Greek ἄνεμος
' wind ', Sanskrit *an-* ' breathe '). If **dheuese-* has thus been
specialised in the direction of ' what is (merely) breath ', i.e., ' animal ', and thence to the animal *par excellence* of the chase, the
' deer ', it would seem also to have evolved, by another semantic
development, into the concept of the gods as spirits rather than
as mere corporeal beings like men, as in Greek θεός ' god ' (cf. p.
99), for ' God (is) a Spirit ' (John iv. 24) ; and certainly into a
connotation of the dead as spirits without bodies, as in Middle
High German *ge-twās* ' ghost '. Similarly we use *spirit* (literally,
' breath '; cf. Latin *spīrō* ' breathe ') in the sense of ' ghost ', and
ghost still denotes ' spirit ' in the stereotyped phrases ' Holy
Ghost ' (alongside of ' Holy Spirit ') and ' give up the ghost '
(' die ') as compared with Anglo-Saxon *gást*, Old Saxon *gêst*,
German *Geist* ' spirit '.

The development of the meaning ' spirit ' from ' ghost ', we may
remark in passing, is the reverse of that of Middle High German
getwās from ' breathe ', for the base-meaning of the group of *ghost*
seems to have been ' terrify ' (cf. Anglo-Saxon *gǣstan* ' terrify ',
English *aghast)*. This same base **dheuese-* may also evolve the
connotation ' soul ', as in Lithuanian *dūšià* and Lettish *dvēsele* (also
meaning ' life, breath '), or ' spirit ', as in Old Church Slavic *duchŭ*,
or even ' air ', as in Lithuanian *daũsos*, while the English phrase
' give up the ghost ' finds a quasi-parallel in Lithuanian *dvẽsti*
' die' (of animals). To this same group belong, further, Greek
θυιάς ' Bacchante, woman possessed by a deity ' and Gaulish *dusios*

' unclean spirit, incubus ', Cornish *dus, diz* ' devil ', while its connexion with the spirits of the departed reappears in Latin *fērālis*
' relating to the dead ' (cf. pp. 99–100).

We have said that the base *dheuese-* meant ' breathe '; but this
seems itself to have been a specialisation from a still more primitive signification ' whirl, storm, blow, gasp ' (originally, in all
probability, simply ' blow '), with yet another semantic development to ' dust(y), dark ', whether physically or mentally. So we
have Sanskrit *dhūsara-* ' dust-coloured, grey ', Greek θεῖον (for
dhues-iom) ' brimstone ', Latin *fuscus, furvus* ' dark ' (for *dhus-
qos,* *dhus-[u]uos),* *furō* ' rage, rave ', Old Irish *dásacht* ' mad-
ness ', Anglo-Saxon *dosc* = English *dusk,* Anglo-Saxon *dysig* =
English *dizzy,* Old High German *tusig* ' stupid ', Modern High
German *Tor* ' fool ' (from *dhouso-).*

Even yet we are not at the end of the quest, for *dheuese-* is
formed, by the determinative *-s-* (cf. pp. 156–159), from an older
base *dheue-,* which also receives the determinatives *-m- (*dheue-
me-)* in Sanskrit *dhūmá-,* Latin *fūmus,* Lithuanian *dúmai* ' smoke ',
Greek θῡμός ' soul, spirit ', Middle Irish *dumacha* ' mist, fog ';
-l- in Sanskrit *dhūli-* ' dust ', Latin *fūlīgō* ' soot ', Lithuanian
dúlis ' smudge ', Gothic *dwals* ' foolish ', Anglo-Saxon *dwola* ' error,
heresy ', Old Irish *dall* ' blind ', Anglo-Saxon *dol* = English *dull,*
Old High German *tol,* Modern German *toll* ' mad '; *-i-* in Greek
θύω for *θυ-i-ω* ' sacrifice ' (especially with burnt offerings), Latin
suf-fiō ' fumigate ', Russian *duti* ' blow '; *-k-* in Sanskrit *dhūka-*
' wind ' (recorded only by native lexicographers), Lithuanian
dvėkúoti ' sigh '; *-dh-* in English *dodder, dud; -bh-* in Greek τῦφος
' smoke, mist, cloud ', Middle Irish *dub* ' black ', Gothic *daub-,*
Anglo-Saxon *déaf,* English *deaf,* Old High German *toub,* Modern
German *taub* ' deaf ', Gothic *dūbo,* Anglo-Saxon *dúfe,* English
dove, Old High German *tûba,* Modern German *Taube* ' dove ';
-mbh- in Gothic *dumbs,* Old High German *tumb,* Anglo-Saxon,
English *dumb; -p-* in Sanskrit *dhūpa-* ' incense, perfume ', Old
High German *tûbar, tûvar* ' stupid '; *-r-* in Greek θοῦρος ' rushing,
impetuous, furious '; and *-n-* in Sanskrit *dhvaṁs-* ' fall in pieces,
perish ', Avestan *dunman-* ' mist, cloud ', Greek θάνατος ' death ',
θνητός ' mortal ', Lettish *dvans* ' vapour, steam ', Old High German
tun(i)st ' storm ', Modern German *Dunst* ' vapour ', Anglo-Saxon
dust = English *dust.*

This discussion of a single base with its wide range of meanings all specialised from one very general sense is but a specimen, taken almost at random, of a study which would prove equally profitable and interesting in investigating countless words, whether in English or in any other language belonging to a linguistic group which presents sufficient data for such research. Even in our discussion of *dheue- and its derivatives, we have cited only a relatively small number of the words evolved from it.

A survey of the significations derived from a common base-meaning will reveal the very simple principle which underlies all semantics. This is, in essence, *selection by the speaker of that one of various possible meanings of a base or word which seems to him best to meet his needs.* Such choice is based, in turn, upon analogy between a specialised connotation of the base in the speaker's mind and the idea which he desires to express; and it is essentially metaphorical in character, so that we may say that *metaphor is the chief cause of semantic change.* Whether the reason for this selection of meaning be true or false, whether exact or highly fanciful, matters little so long as both speaker and hearer readily grasp the connotation to be conveyed. Thus, to revert to the base *dheue- ' blow ', the wind blows; breath is a sort of wind; without breath, man cannot live, whence breath may be regarded as the indispensable vital part of man, his spirit; this spirit is held to survive his bodily death, and so may become his ghost; or, on the other hand, he may breathe out his spirit, and so die. From a totally different point of view, the blowing of the wind raises dust; but dust is dark, so that darkness and dark-coloured objects (e.g., the dove) may be denoted by derivatives from the same base-meaning ' blow '; and since darkness may affect the senses and the mind, words for ' deaf ', ' dumb ', or ' dull ' may likewise come from this same base.

Thus, words are very frequently *polysemantic;* i.e., the same word may possess several meanings, often widely different, yet all derived from the same basal idea by more or less intricate specialisations. On the other hand, a mental process directly opposed to specialisation (or restriction) of meaning may be at work, so that a word which has been specialised may receive an extension of connotation. Though the outward results may be absolute antitheses — *restriction* in the one case, and *extension* in the other — they are identical in origin: *both restriction and extension of meanings spring from analogies and metaphors, whether true or false.*

As an example of such an extended or polysemantic term, let us take, again almost at random, the English word *crown*. This comes from a base **qere-* or **sqere-* ' turn, bend ', the parent of a family at least as numerous, and superficially as involved, as that of **dheye-*. One of these derivatives is the Greek κορώνη ' anything hooked or curved ', e.g., a door-handle, a bow-tip to which the bow-string is attached, the tip of a plough-pole on which the yoke is fastened, the coronoid process of the ulna or of the jaw, some sort of crown (recorded only by the lexicographer Hesychios), the culmination of a festival. This Greek word was borrowed in Latin as *corōna* in the sense of ' garland, wreath, crown '; and since victors received crowns, it came to mean ' fame '. It might also denote other things of a circular or quasi-circular character, such as a circle of men (e.g., a judicial assembly, a host of besiegers), a cornice, an elevated ridge of land as a boundary, the hairy crown above a horse's hoof, and a halo around the sun. In Mediaeval Latin, *corōna* also signified the clerical tonsure, the nimbus about the head of a saint, a piece of money stamped with a crown, and a chandelier (cf. German *Kronleuchter* ' chandelier ', literally, ' crown-light ').

In its turn, *corōna* was borrowed by Romance, Teutonic, Celtic, Albanian, and Balto-Slavic (e.g., Old French *corone*, French *couronne*, Old Icelandic *krúna*, German *Krone*, Middle Irish *coróin*, Albanian *kunorë, kurorë*, Old Church Slavic *kruna*, Lithuanian *karūnà)*. From Old French *corone*, in the reign of William the Conqueror, Middle English borrowed *coroune, krúne, croune*, etc., Modern English *crown;* and *crown* is now eminently polysemantic. It denotes the head-covering worn as a symbol of sovereignty (the King's crown), the monarch himself (the Crown decrees), royal power (to seek the crown), any garland or wreath (a crown of flowers), any high reward or distinction (' a virtuous woman is a crown to her husband '), culminating glory (the crown of martyrdom), the highest part (the crown of a hat), the top of the head (to break one's crown), the acme (the very crown of falsehood), the clerical tonsure, the part of a tooth which appears above the gum, the area enclosed between two concentric circles, a circle of appendages on the throat of the corolla, a sort of sailor's knot, and a coin marked with a crown or with a crowned head.

Which of these special meanings is intended must be determined by the context or by attendant circumstances; and in actual use, their kinship is often quite unrealised. One does not feel precisely kingly while a dentist is drilling the crown of one's tooth; and when a tradesman tells me that the price of such-and-such a thing is ' half a crown ', I do not associate the term with anything circular, still less with semi-perfection, but merely with a coin worth two shillings and six pence. Similarly, when he says, ' a florin ', I have no immediate thought of the Italian city of Florence, where such money was first struck in 1252, or of the fact that it was originally stamped with a lily (Italian *fiore* ' flower ', from Latin *florem*), but simply of a certain coin, so that I mechanically hand him two shillings. Neither does one think, when one speaks of a ' dollar ' (from Low German *daler*), of Joachimstal in Czecho-Slovakia, which furnished the silver from which the coins were first made towards the end of the fifteenth century; the average person knows nothing whatever of the origin of the term.

When a word has become specialised, it tends, if much used, to acquire a variety of meanings by analogical or metaphorical association of ideas. Some of these may, in turn, become so highly specialised that in one branch of science they may acquire a connotation wholly unlike that which they possess in another, so that the word *operation*, for instance, connotes by no means the same ' working ' in the technical vocabularies of theology, surgery, mathematics, and strategics. In ordinary parlance, *contamination* denotes ' pollution, defilement, taint '; but to the historian of literature or to the linguist a contaminated plot is merely one combined from two or more plots by some other author; and a contaminated word, form, or construction is simply a combination of two or more others, as when French *rendre* ' restore, give back ' is a contamination of Latin *reddere* ' give back ' with *prendere* ' take '; or *je me souviens* ' I remember ' of *je me rappelle* ' I recall to myself ' with *il me souvient* ' it occurs to me '; or *je sortirai avant qu'il n'entre* ' I shall go out before he enters ' of *je sortirai avant qu'il entre* ' I shall go out before he enters ' with *il n'entrera (pas) avant que je sorte* ' he will not enter before I go out '.

When a word is used with extreme frequency, it very often tends to lose its force, and, especially if it has become highly poly-semantic, speakers may feel obliged to substitute for it some cognate term of more exact and specific meaning. Such *replacement* frequently causes the creation of doublets (cf. pp. 134–135). Thus, Latin *fragilis* means ' breakable, brittle ', whether literally *(fra-*

gilis ramus ' brittle branch ') or figuratively *(fragile corpus* ' frail body ') ; and the naturalised English *frail* has the same connotations *(frail support, frail health)*. Since, however, *frail* increasingly tends to be used figuratively, the necessity for definite expression of the literal meaning has led to the creation of the alien *fragile* in the strict sense of ' brittle ' (cf. the French doublets *frêle* : *fragile)*. This word, in turn, is gradually acquiring a figurative sense, so that one may speak not only of a ' fragile boat ', but also of ' fragile health ', with the result that still another alien word, *frangible*, has been coined in English as in the Romance languages (no Latin *frangibilis* seems to occur). This is used only in its literal sense *(frangible glass*, but scarcely *frangible health); and* another alien, *fractable* (Latin *fractabilis),* is in use as a technical term in architecture. If *frangible* and *fractable* go the way of *frail* and *fragile*, it will probably be necessary to create yet another synonym, perhaps *fractitious* (Vulgar Latin *fractitius); and* in reserve will still remain *euclastic* (cf. Greek εὔκλαστος ' easily broken ').

The principle of analogy or metaphor in polysemantism (or *polysemy)* also appears when the name of a well known historical or literary character is extended to persons supposed to resemble that character, as when we speak of *a Galahad, a Judas, a Machiavelli, a Hercules, a Mr. Micawber, an Aspasia, a Messalina, a Sary Gamp, a Florence Nightingale,* and the like. Other changes of meaning are still more interesting as showing how entirely the primary connotation has vanished from consciousness. Originally, for instance, as its Latin source, *penna*, shows, the *pen* was a ' feather '; then it became a feather used for writing; and, finally, any instrument for writing, so that we now speak, without any sense of absurdity, of a ' steel pen ', a ' gold pen ', or a ' fountain pen ', whereas the French and German equivalents *plume* and *Feder* still mean both ' feather ' and ' pen '. One can also ' arrive ' at a place far from any body of water, quite oblivious (usually, indeed, utterly ignorant) of the fact that, literally, *arrive* means ' to reach the bank ' of a river, ocean, or the like (Mediaeval Latin *arrivāre* from *ad-ripāre),* a connotation still retained in Spanish and Portuguese *arribar* and Luccan Italian *arripare*, but now lost in English (though occasionally found in Middle and early Modern English) and in most Romance dialects (e.g., French *arriver).*

Not infrequently, evolution of meaning is connected with some development in the history of civilisation. Thus, in Latin, *pecus* meant ' cattle ', just like its cognates, e.g., Sanskrit *páśu-*, Old High German *fëho, fihu,* Modern German *Vieh,* Old Prussian *pecku,* though some of these (e.g., Kurdish *pez,* Ossetic *fus,* Portuguese *pego)* have been specialised to denote ' sheep '. Since cattle were the chief property in the early Roman period, the derivative *peculium,* originally meaning ' herd of cattle ', came to denote ' private property ', and its adjective *peculiaris* ' relating to private property ' acquired the connotations of ' relating to one's self, individual ', and so of ' extraordinary ', and, for example in its English derivative *peculiar,* ' odd, strange '. On the other hand, another Latin derivative, *pecunia,* primarily ' wealth in cattle ', developed the meaning of ' property in general ' and, ultimately, of ' money '; so that its adjectives *pecuniarius* and *pecuniaris,* like the English *pecuniary,* which is borrowed from the former, denotes only ' monetary ' and has lost all association with cattle. Some Teutonic cognates of *pecus,* Old Saxon *fehu,* Old Frisian *fiā,* Anglo-Saxon *feoh,* and Old Icelandic *fé,* mean both ' cattle ' and ' money ' or ' property '; in Old Icelandic, the ' cattle ' denoted by *fé* were especially sheep; and the meaning ' cattle ' is occasionally found in Middle English, as in the fourteenth-century *Cursor Mundi (ne for vr fee* ' nor for our cattle '). In Gothic, on the contrary, *faíhu* denotes only ' money ', while in Modern English *fee* usually connotes a sum of money paid for a specific service or purpose *(a lawyer's fee, an initiation fee).*

Words, like the human beings who use them, often manifest an unhappy tendency to ' go to the bad '. So far as words are concerned, their degeneration (technically termed *pejoration;* cf. pp. 266–267, 273–274) is often due to a selection and specialisation of some ethically lower connotation which may be implied in them. Since, for example, animals possess certain traits which are regarded as ignoble when contrasted with the higher qualities ascribed to man, such words as *animalism, brutal,* and *bestial,* or even the nouns *animal, brute,* and *beast,* may have evil implications. A certain cynicism and worldly wisdom often lead words to degenerate in meaning. We have already mentioned (p. 251) the Middle English word *seli* (Modern English *silly).* Originally, this meant ' blessed ' (Anglo-Saxon *sǽlig,* Modern German *selig,* etc.), but now is a synonym of ' foolish '. Since ' the children of this world are in their generation wiser than the children of light ', and since the good will not stoop to the tricks of the evil, the latter regard them as lacking in intelligence and as mere fools to have such scruples, as, in short, ' blessed idiots '. So the French *crétin* ' idiot ' is derived from Latin *christianus* ' Christian ', and the German *albern* ' foolish ' originally meant ' true, kindly, friendly ' (cf. Old High German *alawāri*).

On the other hand, words may change in meaning for the better *(melioration)*, as in the case of the English adjective *smart* in contrast to the noun *smart* (cf. German *Schmerz* ' pain ') from a base * *(s)mer-de-* ' rub '. This adjective originally meant ' sharply stinging, painful ', and such is still the only connotation of its cognates; but it came to have the force of ' vigorous, brisk, quick ' *(smart skirmish, smart breeze;* cf. Richard Rolle of Hampole [about 1340], *now er we smert, now er we slawe* ' now are we quick, now are we slow '), ' acute, intelligent, witty, impertinent, flippant ' *(smart repartee, smart business-man, you're too smart)*, ' fashionable, stylish ' *(smart frock, the smart thing to do)*. Or, again, we may consider such words as English *count* from Old French *conte, comte*, from Latin *comite^m*, literally ' companion ', but specialised to mean ' companion (i.e., assistant) of a proconsul, propraetor, or emperor ', and, finally, ' a nobleman of high rank '; or English *duke* from French *duc* from Latin *duce^m*, primarily designating any ' leader ', and then especially the leader of an army, but now only a certain high rank of nobility.

Occasionally a word which has suffered pejoration in most senses retains its original connotation in technical languages or in stereotyped phrases. Here belongs, for instance, the *knave* in a suit of playing-cards, representing the ' servant ' (literally, ' boy ') of the king and queen (cf. French *valet* ' servant ', Italian *fante* ' manservant ' for *knave* in this sense). The original signification of the group is ' boy ', and hence ' servant ' (cf. French *garçon* in the same double sense) ; but since servants are often dishonest and insincere, the English word has become a synonym of ' scoundrel ', just as German *Bube* connotes ' boy, rascal, knave in a deck of cards '.

If one word for ' boy ' has suffered pejoration in the case of *knave*, in that of *knight* another has found melioration. Originally the English *knight* meant only ' boy, youth, attendant, servant ', and Anglo-Saxon *cniht* only rarely signified ' knight ', quite as Old High German *kneht* ' boy, attendant, slave, vassal ' only occasionally denoted ' soldier '. In Modern German, as in all other Teutonic languages except English, *Knecht* connotes ' servant '; although the Danish *knegt*, like the Swedish *knekt* (borrowed from Dutch or German), may indicate the knave in cards. The English *knight* was originally a lad of noble birth who began his career in arms as a page, and then became a squire, to the sovereign or to some lord; and *knight* is still a title of minor nobility.

Just when words undergo pejoration, and when melioration, is difficult to say; perhaps, generally speaking, we may agree with the Dutch linguist, Mgr. Schrijnen, that *ethical concepts tend toward pejoration; whereas in modifications of meaning based upon social transformations, pejoration and melioration show approximately equal frequency.* As an instance of the retention of an old meaning in a stereotyped phrase, we may cite the English *Holy Ghost* (translating Latin *Spiritus Sanctus*, Greek Πνεῦμα Ἅγιον, Hebrew *Rūaḥ haq-Qōdeš)* as synonymous with *Holy Spirit.* Elsewhere in English *ghost* has come to signify an ' apparition of the dead ', though the old connotation still survives in a few archaic formulae, such as *ghostly father* ' spiritual father ' and *give up the ghost* ' die ' (cf. p. 253).

Changes in the meanings of words very often lead to their *displacement,* with the result that other words are substituted for them, while they themselves may vanish entirely, or may survive only in special connexions or in dialects. The reasons for this are various. Their connotation may have become so vague or, at the other extreme, so specialised that another term must be adopted or coined to meet the need which the old word no longer supplies, as when *animal, beast,* and the like replace *deer,* or when *foolish,* etc., are substituted for *silly* (cf. pp. 251, 259–260).

In other cases, a word may be so altered in form, and so shortened by phonetic decay or by the loss of inflexional endings, that it becomes obscure, and may then disappear, being replaced by another, perhaps quite unrelated, term. Thus, Latin *avis* ' bird ' survives in Romance only in Logudoresian *ae* (with the specialised meaning of ' bird of prey, eagle '), Old Catalan *au,* and Spanish and Portuguese *ave.* It has vanished in French, where it would have become * *oi* (liable to confusion with *oie* ' goose ' from Vulgar Latin *auca* from * *avica,* itself formed from *avicula,* * *aucula* ' little bird ') ; and it has been replaced by what was originally a diminutive, Latin * *avicellus, aucellus,* whence French *oiseau,* Italian *uccello,* etc., so that French *oie* and *oiseau* both ultimately mean ' little bird '. The specialisation of the meaning ' duck ' from that of ' little bird ' in the case of *auca* and *oie* suggests that of *deer* from ' wild animal in general ' (cf. pp. 252–253) ; and in Romance all recollection of the original diminutive connotation of *oiseau,* etc., has entirely disappeared, so that one speaks of *un grand oiseau* with no consciousness that it literally means ' a big birdie '.

Similarly, Latin *os* ' mouth ' has vanished from Romance and has been replaced by derivatives from Popular Latin *bucca* (French *bouche,* Italian *bocca,* Spanish, Portuguese, Catalan, and Provençal *boca),* very possibly because it would be confused with derivatives from Latin *os,* Late Latin *ossum* ' bone ' (French, Catalan, and Provençal *os,* Italian and Portuguese *osso,* etc.). For Latin *equus* ' horse ' has been substituted the more resonant and popular *caballus* (French *cheval,* Italian and Portuguese *cavallo,* Spanish *caballo,* Albanian *kal,* etc.; cf. pp. 131, 269, 306) ; while *equa* ' mare ', though surviving in Spanish *yegua,* Portuguese *egua,* Logudoresian *ebba,* and Old French *ive,* has yielded in Modern French to *jument* from Latin *iumentum* ' beast of burden ', since mares were used for heavy work, and stallions or geldings for the hunt, racing, and warfare. In French, the word *jument,* originally neuter in gender, has become feminine because of the sex of the animal which it denotes, while Italian *giumento* (masculine) and Catalan *jument* mean ' ass ', and Provençal *jumen* signifies ' beast of burden '.

Words originally used only by the lower classes, especially when employed in a more or less humorous sense, may be taken over by the higher strata of society, and may replace words previously regarded as of irreproachable dignity. Thus, Latin *caput* ' head ' retained in Italian *capo,* Spanish *cabo,* Provençal, Catalan, and Rumanian *cap,* survives in Modern French *chef* only in the sense of its English derivative *chief.* Its original meaning ' head ' has received a substitute in *tête* (Old French *teste)* from Latin *testa* ' jar, pot, shard, shell, skull ' (the latter connotation only in Late Latin) ; and, in its turn, *tête* is replaced in popular speech by such words as *caboche* (cf. Italian *capocchio* ' stupid fellow '), *fiole* ' phial ', *bobine* ' spool ', and the like (cf. pp. 31–32).

Native words are often replaced by terms borrowed from languages regarded as belonging to higher levels of civilisation (cf. pp. 130–131). In such cases, the word displaced tends to vanish in favour of the term supplanting it unless it is retained in special connotations, as when in English one calls the flesh of the calf *veal* (Old French *veël*, Modern French *veau* ' calf '), of the swine *pork* (Old French, French *porc* ' pig '), of the sheep *mutton* (French *mouton* ' sheep '), and of cattle *beef* (French *bœuf* ' ox ').

A very frequent reason for the displacement of words is that they often acquire a connotation regarded as too sacred for ordinary speech, or as dangerous, sinister, or indecent. Here we come into contact with a religious and ethical aspect of language, and with the principle of *linguistic tabu*. To the first category of these tabus belong, notably, names of divine beings, whether benevolent or malevolent, perhaps the most generally known instance being the name of God in the Old Testament. In this text, whose Hebrew script, like all Semitic alphabets except Akkadian and Ethiopic originally indicated only consonants (cf. p. 359), the sacred name never has vowel-points, but is written simply *YHWH*, whose meaning is uncertain (cf. p. 420). Instead of this word, orthodox Jews read (and still read) *'Ăδōnāy* ' Lord ' (a word of unclear origin, possibly Canaanite or even non-Semitic, which is borrowed in the Greek "Aδωνις, etc.), the antithesis of the heathen Semitic *ba'al* ' lord '; and they substituted the vowels of *'Ăδōnāy* for those of *YHWH*, thus giving the familiar *YᵃHᵒWᵃH*, anglicised as *Jehovah*. The actual pronunciation of *YHWH* is uncertain, but is commonly supposed to have been something like [jahwe] (cf. its transliteration by 'Iaβϵ, where β has its Late Greek value [v]).

Very frequently the real name of a deity was kept secret, and was made known to the initiate alone, with the result that the divinity was called only by some descriptive epithet. His true appellation might thus actually be forgotten, so giving rise to a category of deities much more numerous than is commonly supposed, and who may be termed amnestonymous. The reason for such subsbtitution must be sought in the widespread belief in ' the power of the Name '. To know a name was to have real power over the person or thing possessing it, for the name and the person or thing bearing it were one and the same. Knowledge of the name brought with it magic potency which might be used either for good or for evil; and the operation of this power was mechanical.

All this is well illustrated in the familiar story of ' 'Alī Bābā and the Forty Thieves ', where knowledge and utterance of the words ' open, sesame ', cause the doors of a secret cave to open alike to the thieves who store their loot there and to 'Alī Bābā who takes it from them; but forgetfulness of the spell caused the death of his brother Qasīm, who said ' open, barley '. In Mediaeval Hebrew, *ba'al šēm* ' master of the Name ' meant that its possessor knew the secret Name of *YHWH,* and so could exercise supernatural power. A change of name means a change of personality. Popes and those who enter certain religious orders often receive new ' names in religion ' to indicate that they are no longer the persons they originally were.

Such popular sayings as ' speak of angels, and you hear their wings; speak of the devil, and he's sure to appear ', were once meant absolutely literally; and the belief survives in such substitutes for ' devil ' as ' Old Nick ', ' Old Harry ', ' the deuce ', and the like: the devil, not knowing these nicknames, but only his own proper designation, will not answer to them. Similarly, to primitive peoples, curses are very real: ' damned scoundrel ' actually means that the unhappy person so addressed is doomed to eternal torment. The ' power of the Name ' is likewise the underlying reason for reluctance to address or be addressed by one's personal name, as distinct from one's family name, by any but close friends or relations, or by social superiors, use of the personal name giving its user power over its possessor.

Reverence leading to more or less tabu, as in the case of the Hebrew *YHWH,* or in the frequent reluctance to utter the personal name of the Second Person of the Trinity, and the feeling that divine names must not be used carelessly (' Thou shalt not take the name of the Lord thy God in vain ', i.e., frivolously, idly), lead to *clipped oaths,* such as *by gad, by Jove, zounds* (God's wounds '), *parbleu, sacrebleu* (for *par Dieu* ' by God ', *sacré Dieu* ' holy God '), *nom d'un nom* (for *nom des noms* ' Name of Names ', i.e., God's holy Name), *potztausend* (in the seventeenth century, *potzsiebenschlapperment* = [bei] Gottes sieben Sakramenten ' by God's Seven Sacraments ', with seven raised to a non-existent thousand Sacraments for further deformation) ; and to such abbreviations as *(by) thunder* (' God's thunder '), *potzblitz* (for *Gottes Blitz* ' God's thunder '), *strike me dead* (i.e., ' may God strike me dead '), *ods-bodikins* (' God's little Body ', probably referring to the Host in the Sacrament), *drat it* or *od rot it* (' may God rot it '), and the like.

On the other hand, words tabued as too exalted or too debased for ordinary use may be employed as terms of familiarity. Here belong the widespread tabu of the pronoun of the second person singular and its replacement by the second person plural (e.g., English *you*, French *vous* instead of *thou, tu*) or even by the third (e.g., German *Sie*), or by substitutes of wholly different origin (e.g., Spanish *usted* for *vuestra merced* ' your worship '); polite Modern Persian *bandah guft* ' the slave says ' instead of *guftam* ' I say '; *Your Grace, Your Highness, Your Eminence, Your Majesty will be pleased* instead of ' you will be pleased ' in formal address to a duke or archbishop, a prince, a cardinal, a sovereign, etc.) ; so that French has the special verb *tutoyer* ' to thee-and-thou, address familiarly '. In all these cases, the true second person is employed only in addressing the Deity or, at the other extreme, children, intimate friends, and relatives, or servants and others of much lower social rank.

Terms of abuse may even be used as terms of endearment, such as English *little rascal, little devil, little scamp*, French *petit coquin* ' little rogue ', *petit polisson* ' little blackguard ', *vieille canaille* ' old riff-raff ', German *du Schelm* ' thou scoundrel ', and the like. Some of these, however meaningful in their native speech, cannot be translated into another language without becoming absurd. I may address a child of whom I am very fond as *mon chou* in French, but ' my cabbage ' cannot claim rank as an endearing term in English; and while a German mother may affectionately call her young son *kleiner Lausbube*, an English mother would scarcely be pleased to hear her child termed ' lousy little brat '!

In keeping with the principle of ' the power of the Name ', the name of a dangerous or malignant being is often replaced by some epithet of a harmless or even complimentary character. Thus, the Greek goddesses of revenge, the Erinyes (' the Furious Ones '; cf. their Latin translation *Furiae* ' Furies ') were called Eumenides (' Gracious, Kindly '), Semnai (' August '), and the like. They knew both their real and their replacement-names; but, naturally, they would be flattered by the compliment shown them and, one might hope, would be appeased and spare the guilty. For a like reason, animals regarded as dangerous or uncanny often receive substitute-names, as we have already seen in the case of the words for ' bear ' (cf. pp. 249–250).

Thus, the weasel (Anglo-Saxon *wesle*, Old High German *wisala*, Modern German *Wiesel*), whose name may originally have meant 'stinking' (cf. Latin *vis*[*s*]*io* 'stench'), receives such euphemistic appellations as 'little lady' (Italian *donnola;* cf. Old Prussian *mosuco)*, 'pretty lady' (Danish *kjönne)*, 'pretty little lady' (French *belette,* Breton *kaerell,* Albanian *bukël)*, 'pretty little beast' or 'pretty little thing' (Bavarian *Schöntierlein, Schöndinglein)*, 'bride' (Modern Greek *νυμφίτζα)*, 'godmother' (Spanish *comadreja)*, and 'white-breasted' (Welsh *bronwen)*, etc. The Mandaeans, a syncretistic religious sect living along the lower Euphrates, believe that Satan will be restored to Divine favour at the Last Day, so that it is unwise to offend him; hence they are said to avoid words beginning with [ʃ], the initial phoneme of Arabic *šaytān* 'Satan'. In Polynesia, the tabu attaching to words employed during their lifetime by those who had died, and so regarded as ill-omened, caused them to be disused by the living, with necessary replacement by other terms, the result often being material modification of the vocabulary within a relatively short period of years.

With this type of replacement, we enter upon the wide field of *euphemism,* where words of unpleasant or obscene connotation tend to fall out of polite usage. Unfortunately, the words substituted for them often share their fate and are, in their turn, displaced as their meaning becomes specialised into an offensive implication; but sometimes euphemisms become so stilted and affected that their formerly tabued equivalents are reinstated. Euphemism seems to be, in the main, a question of taste and convention; and it is very doubtful whether what seems to us egregiously improper in, for instance, the comedy of the English Restoration was any more indecent to the audiences of that day than are the innuendoes of the comedies of our own time to us.

An excellent illustration of the euphemistic principle is seen in the various terms for 'death' and 'grave': 'to pass (or, be) away', 'to be called', 'to fall asleep', 'to join the great majority', 'to expire', 'to end one's days', 'to be gathered to one's fathers', 'to go west'; 'cemetery' (literally, 'sleeping-room'), 'churchyard', 'God's acre', 'long (or, last) home', etc. It is, in all probability, to this wholly natural desire to veil unpleasant facts by pleasant words that we must ascribe the development whereby words often suffer pejoration (cf. pp. 259–260).

Thus, Latin *periculum,* from which, through French *péril,* comes English *peril,* originally meant 'experiment, trial, attempt, proof' (e.g., Terence, *fac periclum in litteris* ' try writing!'); but soon, because attempt is attended by risk, and even by danger, it acquired the connotation which we now associate with *peril* (e.g., Plautus, *res in periclo vortitur* ' the affair becomes dangerous '). If we speak of ' a valetudinarian ', we mean ' a sickly man ' or, in euphemistic phrase, ' a man of delicate health '. As a matter of fact, Latin *valetudo* signified any bodily condition, whether good or bad (e.g., Caesar, *Caesaris exercitus optima valetudine . . . utebatur* ' Caesar's army enjoyed the best of health ' as contrasted with *affectum valetudine filium* ' his son suffering from ill health '); but from such phrases as *curatio valetudinis* ' care for [preserving] health ' it came to connote ' weakness of health ', the precise opposite of its primary signification (cf. Latin *valeō* ' be strong, be worth, be well ').

In like manner, παθ- in Greek means ' to experience something from without, whether good or bad ', so that εὖ πάσχω (πάσχω from *παθ-σκ-ω) signifies ' I am in good condition, fortunate ', etc., and κακῶς πάσχω ' I am in a bad state '. But even Greek has the euphemism εἴ τι πάθοιμι, almost exactly equivalent to the English ' if anything [bad] should happen to me '; and the noun πάθος, properly ' event, experience ', again whether good or bad, came to denote ' disease ', as in the English learned word *patho-logical*. On the other hand, *sym-pathy* and *a-pathy* are still applied in English, as in their Greek originals, to feelings good and bad alike, so that one may have sympathy with or apathy toward another's highest ideals and joys or toward his deepest misfortunes and lowest vices; but *pathetic*, not having the neutral connotation of *sympathetic* and *apathetic*, has suffered pejoration, and now means only ' sad, pitiable '.

In specialised and restricted senses, as in *sym-pathetic* and *a-pathetic* in contrast to *pathetic*, the old meanings of words may survive after those connotations have vanished in common usage, this phenomenon being known as *isolation*. Here belongs such a word as *meat*, now denoting almost exclusively ' flesh of animals used for food ', but meaning food of any kind as late as the time of the Authorised Version of the Bible (e.g., Matthew iii. 4, ' his meat was locusts and wild honey '; Genesis i. 30, ' every green herb for meat '), a signification which still survives in the phrase *meat and drink* and in the compound *sweetmeats*. Similarly, *board* in the sense of ' table ' (cf. Anglo-Saxon *bord* ' plank, table, shield, deck or side of a ship ') is still used in such phrases as *bed and board* (translating the legal Latin *mensa et torus)* and *board and lodging,* while the old meaning ' ship's deck ' is retained in *on board* (Anglo-Saxon *on borde), board and board* ' side by side ' (of ships), etc. Again, words once widely used may survive solely in highly specialised meanings, such as French *traire* from Latin *trahere* ' draw ' (its connotation in Old French as well), which now means only ' to milk '; while French *pondre,* Provençal *ponre,* from Latin *ponere* ' lay down ', now signifies simply ' to lay eggs '. Similar isolation is found in morphology, e.g., in the retention of the old genitive in German *nachts* ' at night ', *heimwärts,* English *homewards, Ladyday* (the feast of the Annunciation of the Blessed Virgin, 25 March; cf. p. 110).

Another general principle in semantics is that *objects or beings normally capable of very restricted functions tend to preserve the same designation throughout a linguistic family; whereas those whose functions are, or may be, very diverse are likely to have a multiplicity of terms, often unrelated, to denote them.* The cow has practically only one designation throughout Indo-European (cf. pp. 132–133), since her one special function is to give milk. The horse, on the other hand, is used for many purposes and, like the dog, has been artificially evolved into a large number of breeds, each for a distinct employment. There is, it is true, a general Indo-European term for ' horse ', whose basal meaning is uncertain: Sanskrit *áśva-,* Old Persian, Avestan *aspa-,* Agnean *yuk,* Kuchaean *yakwe,* Greek ἵππος (Tarentine and Epidaurian ἴκκος; one would expect *ἵππος),* Latin *equus,* Gaulish *epo-,* Old Irish *ech,* Gothic *aíhwa,* Anglo-Saxon *eoh* (especially ' war-horse ') ' horse ', archaic Lithuanian *ašvà* ' mare '. The group is explained by some as originally meaning ' swift ' (cf. Sanskrit *āśú-* ' quick ' and, occasionally, ' horse ', Greek ὠκύς ' swift ', Latin *ōcior* ' quicker ', Old Welsh *di-auc,* Modern Welsh *di-og* ' lazy '), but the differing vowel-lengths render this etymology dubious.

Vedic Sanskrit has several terms for ' horse besides *áśva-:* he is ' the runner ' *(átya-, sápti-),* ' the swift ' *(árvant-),* ' the strong ' *(vājín-),* ' the speedy ' *(háya-);* and in Classical Sanskrit, he is ' the quick-goer ' *(turaga-)* and ' the tawney ' *(ghota-,* Hindūstānī *ghorā).* In Armenian, he is ' the speedy ' *(ji* [dzi] = Sanskrit *háya-);* in Modern Greek, he is ' the animal ' *par excellence* (ἄλογο, literally, ' the thing without reason '). In Latin, besides *equus* and *caballus* (for the latter, see pp. 131, 262, 306), we find *verēdus* ' post-horse ', borrowed from Gaulish *ve-rēdos* ' under the chariot ' and represented by archaic Welsh *gorwydd* ' horse '; while Late Latin has, in addition, *paraverēdus* ' extra post-horse ', a hybrid compound of *verēdus* and the Greek preposition παρά ' beside ', and the source not only of Old French *palafreid, palefroid*, Modern French *palefroi* (borrowed in English *palfrey)*, but also of Old High German *parafrid, pfarifrit, pfar(fr)it*, Modern German *Pferd*, and Middle Low German *palefroot*, Dutch *paard*.

Celtic has still another group whose base-meaning is unknown, represented by Gaulish μαρκα, Irish *marc*, Welsh *march*, Breton *marc'h*, and appearing also in Old High German *mar(a)h*, Anglo-Saxon *mearh*, and English *mar-shal* (pp. 250–251), as well as Old High German *mer(i)ha*, Modern German *Mähre*, Anglo-Saxon *mere, myre*, and English *mare*. Teutonic itself has the group represented by Old High German *(h)ros*, Modern German *Ross*, Middle Low German *ros, ors*, Old Icelandic *hross* (rarely *hors)*, Old Frisian *hars, hers, hors*, Swedish, Anglo-Saxon *hors*, English *horse*, etc., borrowed, in all likelihood, in French *rosse*, Italian *rozza* ' miserable horse ', the base-meaning of the entire group apparently being ' the springer, jumper ' (cf. Sanskrit *kūrd-* ' leap ').

Two other Teutonic groups are represented respectively by Dutch *guil* ' mare that has never foaled ', Middle High German *gūl* ' monster, boar, male animal ', Modern German *Gaul* ' wretched horse ', possibly from the base *ĝheu̯e-le- ' pour ' (cf. the meaning ' stallion ' for *Gaul* in Bavarian German) ; and by Old Icelandic *hestr*, Norwegian *hest*, Swedish *häst*, probably connoting ' the leaper ' and found in its superlative form in Anglo-Saxon *hengest* ' gelding ', Old High German *hengist* ' horse, gelding, eunuch ', and Modern German *Hengst* ' stallion ' (cf. Lithuanian *šókti* ' spring, jump ', *šankus* ' quick ').

In Baltic, Lithuanian calls the horse ' the plougher ' *(arklỹs;* cf. *árklas* ' plough ', Latin *arō* ' I plough '), its other term — Old Prussian *sirgis*, Lithuanian *žìrgas*, Lettish *zirgs* — being of uncertain origin. Slavic, besides the group of Russian '*lošadĭ*, Polish *łoszak*, borrowed from Turkish *alaša*, has another represented by Russian *konĭ*, etc., perhaps connected in some way with Old Russian '*komonĭ*, Ruthenian *kom'on*, Old Prussian *camnet*, Lithuanian *kumelỹs*, and Lettish *kumelš*, all of which are obscure in origin. Finally, one need think only of such specialised English words for ' horse ' as *steed, nag, charger, courser, racer, hunter, barb, roan, jade, hack, pony,* and the like.

In some cases, notably in names for parts of the body, derivatives of the same base show curious transfers of meaning. Thus, Sanskrit *kákṣa-* means ' armpit, girth ', but its Latin cognate *coxa* denotes ' hip ' and, later, ' thigh ' (Italian *coscia,* French *cuisse,* etc.) ; its Old Irish kindred *coss* signifies ' foot ', but in Modern Irish *cos* is the word for ' leg '; and its Teutonic representative (Old High German *hahsa,* Modern German *Hechse)* means ' hough '. Similarly, Sanskrit *hánu-* denotes ' jaw ', like Agnean *śanwe-m;* Greek γένυς, like Armenian *cnawt,* is both ' jaw ' and ' cheek '; and Latin *gena* is ' cheek ' or, occasionally, ' eyelid, eye '. Old Irish *gin* and Old Cornish *genau* mean only ' mouth ', though Welsh *gan* denotes either ' jaw ' or ' chin ', while Middle Breton *guen* is ' cheek ', and Modern Breton *genou* is ' mouth '. Gothic *kinnus,* Old Icelandic *kinn,* and Swedish *kind* mean only ' cheek ', and Anglo-Saxon *cin,* Modern English *chin,* and Modern German *Kinn* only ' chin '; but Old High German *kinni* denotes both ' chin ' and ' jaw ', and Old Saxon *kin* is both ' chin ' and ' cheek '. Lithuanian *žándas* is ' jaw ', but Lettish *zuôds* is ' chin '.

Semantics is concerned, further, with *popular etymology,* whereby a foreign word or an obsolete native term of unfamiliar sound or meaning is replaced by one which is familiar or by a compound of more or less similar sound and with a signification which is generally intelligible, though usually widely different from that of the word displaced. Here belong such words as English *sparrowgrass* for *asparagus,* though the plant is neither a grass nor favoured by sparrows; *crayfish* or *crawfish,* which is not a fish and has nothing to do either with the craw or with the obsolete English *cray,* a disease of hawks (from Old French *craye,* Modern French *craie,* and ultimately Latin *crēta* ' chalk '), but is simply borrowed from French *écrevisse,* itself a loan-word from Old High German *krebiz* (Modern German *Krebs)* ' crab '; and *demijohn,* which does not mean ' half-John ' any more than its immediate source, French *dame-jeanne,* means ' Lady Jeanne ', but which is probably derived, through sailors and merchants, from the name of the Persian city of Damghān, noted for its fine pottery.

For French, one may cite such words as *contredanse* ' quadrille ', which is not a ' counter-dance ', but a popular etymology for its

English original, *country-dance;* and *jeu de l'âne salé,* which is not a ' game of the salted ass ', but simply an attempt to reproduce the English *game of Aunt Sally;* while *pomme d'amour* ' tomato ', translated into English as *love-apple* and into German as *Liebesapfel,* is scarcely associated with any tender romance, but is probably a corrupted borrowing from Italian *pomo dei Mori* ' Moors' apple' (possibly influenced also by Song of Sol. ii. 5: ' comfort me with apples: for I am sick of love ').

German has a wealth of popular etymologies, from which we may cite as examples *Sündflut* ' Noah's flood ', supposed to mean ' sin-flood' since the Deluge was sent in Noah's day because of a sinful world, but really denoting, as the Old High German form *sin(t)vluot* shows, ' universal deluge' (cf. Old High German *singruoni,* Modern German *Singrün* ' periwinkle-plant' [literally, ' ever-green']) ; *Hängematte* ' hammock ', felt to denote ' hanging mat' (cf. *Hängebrücke* ' suspension-bridge ') from Karib *hamaca* (Spanish *hamaca,* French *hamac,* English *hamack, hammock);* *Ohnmacht* ' weakness ', construed as ' without strength' *(ohne Macht),* but really derived from Old High German *âmaht* ' strengthlessness '; *Seehund* ' seal ', interpreted as ' sea-dog' (cf. English *sea-dog* ' harbour-seal, sea-calf '), but actually meaning ' seal-dog' (Old High German *sëlah, sëlho,* Middle High German *sële,* Old Icelandic *selr,* Anglo-Saxon *seolh,* English *seal;* cf. Middle Low German *selhunt,* Danish *sœlhund);* and the phrase *Maulaffen feil haben* ' stand gaping, loaf ', which looks as though it meant ' to have mouth-apes for sale ', but which is, as a matter of fact, from dialectic German *mūl apen (feil) haben* ' have the mouth open '.

Place-names frequently suffer change through popular etymology, as we have already noted in the cases of the rue Saint-Yves-à-l'Argent at Senlis and of the rue Gît-le-Cœur at Paris (pp. 123–124). Paris possesses, besides, the name *Montmartre,* which, from at least the ninth century, has been supposed to mean ' Martyrs' Mount' *(Mons Martyrum)* because Saints Denis, Rusticus, and Eleutherius were martyred there in the third century; but which actually was, in all probability, the ' Mount of Mars ' *(Mons Martis),* who, in the Roman period, must there have had a temple, of which four columns still preserved in the twelfth-century church of Saint-Pierre-de-Montmartre may have formed part. For a short time, because of the similarity of sound, Montmartre was even called *Mont-Marat* in commemoration of the revolutionist of that name.

For England, one may mention the *Dane John* at Canterbury, which, as a glance from the city wall shows, is a popular etymology for a long-vanished *donjon*, the great tower in the innermost bailey of a castle. Since this donjon often contained a subterranean cell or cells for prisoners, the word *dungeon* now means ' prison-cell ', though the original signification of the group was simply '(protective) covering, room (especially underground)' as seen in Old Icelandic *dyngja* ' lady's bower ', Anglo-Saxon *dung* ' prison ', Old High German *tunc* ' underground chamber, women's apartment, weaving-room '; the English *dungeon* is borrowed from French *donjon*, which, in turn, is an augmentative taken from Low Teutonic. In Cornwall, the name of the town of *Marazion* or *Market Jew* (there is also a *Market Jew Street* in Penzance) has no connexion either with Zion or with Jews, but is probably a popular etymology of the Cornish plurals *mar(g)hasow, mar(g)-hazow, mar(g)hasiow, mar(g)haziow, mar(g)hasion, mar(g)hazion*, of *mar(g)has, mar(g)haz, mar(c)has, mar(c)haz, maras, maraz* ' market '. So also the Romano-British name of York, *Eburācon* (cf. p. 123), because of the resemblance of the first part to Anglo-Saxon *eofor* ' boar ', was called in Anglo-Saxon *Eoforwíc* ' Boar-Town '.

Proper names may also be transformed into epithetologues, often in such mutilated forms that their originals are utterly forgotten. Here belongs, for instance, English *tawdry*, originally in the phrase *tawdry lace* for **Saint Audry's lace*, i.e., lace bought at Saint Audry's fair, held in June at Saint Ethelreda's shrine in the Isle of Ely; but since cheap and flashy wares are only too often sold at fairs, the word, which primarily had no sinister meaning whatever, has suffered pejoration (cf. pp. 259–260, 266–267). Other English terms of this type are *maudlin* ' tearful, foolishly sentimental ', corrupted from Saint Mary *Magdalene*, who washed our Lord's feet with her tears (cf. the pronunciation of Magdalen College, Oxford, and of Magdalene College, Cambridge, as contrasted with that of Saint Mary Magdalen's Church at Oxford); and *bedlam* ' wild noise and confusion ', derived from the name of a thirteenth-century London priory, subordinate to the Church of the Nativity at *Bethlehem*, which, a little more than a century later, became an asylum for the insane and which still exists, though on a different site, as the Bethlem Royal Hospital. Of not dissimilar origin is the French term for ' go on strike ', *faire la grève*, from la Grève (' the Strand ') in Paris, the name, up to the Revolution, of what is now the Place de l'Hôtel-de-Ville, where executions took place and where idlers loitered.

Place-names are the now-forgotten origin of many common nouns, such as *copper*, ultimately from Latin *cyprium (aes)* ' Cyprian (bronze)'; *muslin* (French *mousseline)* from the city of Mōṣul in Kurdistān; *milliner* (older *millaner)* from Milan in Italy, so that the word originally meant ' merchant of Milan ' or ' dealer in goods from Milan ' (cf. Scottish *Italian warehouseman*, who is not an Italian, and whose wares — groceries, etc. — come only in small part from Italy) ; *peach* (French *pêche*, Old French *pesche*, Spanish *pérsico, pérsigo, prisco*, Italian *persico, pesca*, German *Pfirsich)* from Latin *persicum (malum)* ' Persian (apple)'; *indigo* from Spanish *indigo, indico* ' Indian '; *spruce*, with a non-original *s*, from Old French *Pruce* (Modern French *Prusse)*, Mediaeval Latin *Prussia*, the original home of the Prussian fir *(spruce-fir)* and a land noted for the meticulousness of its inhabitants in dress and manner *(spruce dress)*; and *argosy* (earliest English form, *ragusye)* from Italian *ragusa* '(vessel of) Ragusa ', a famous commercial city on the eastern coast of the Adriatic.

We must also observe that when a word is borrowed by another language, it may come to diverge widely in meaning from its earlier sense. This is particularly patent in many English loan-words from French, as English *agree* ' be in harmony ' : French *agréer* ' accept ' (cf. Old French *a gre* ' at pleasure ') ; English *altered* ' changed ' : French *altéré* ' thirsty '; English *attend* ' accompany, be present at ' : French *attendre* ' await, expect ' (so also in archaic English, e.g., Shakespeare, ' thy intercepter . . . attends thee at the orchard end '; Latin *attendere* ' stretch toward ', Mediaeval Latin also ' guard, await ') ; English *cave* ' cavity in the earth ', archaic also ' cellar ' : French *cave* ' cellar '; English *chair* : French *chaire* ' pulpit ' (with the doublet *chaise* ' chair ', originally a dialectic pronunciation, adopted in Standard French by the fifteenth century). An especially interesting instance is found in English *curate* ' clergyman attached to a parish to assist the rector or vicar ' : French *curé* ' parish priest ', both having the *cure* (i.e., care) of souls; in older English, *curate* may denote any person (Modern English *parson)* having the cure of souls, e.g., English Book of

Common Prayer ' all Bishops and Curates ' = American Book
' all Bishops and other Ministers '. Both *curate* and *curé* come from
Mediaeval Latin *curatus* ' put in charge of the cure of souls '; but
the meanings of the terms are exactly reversed in dignity in the
Roman and Anglican Communions: in the former, the *curé* is the
superior of the *vicaire;* in the latter, the *vicar* is the superior of the
curate; in both, the *vicaire* or *vicar* (Latin *vicarius* ' substitute,
proxy ') takes the place of an absent *curé* or *rector* respectively
(in Brittany, *recteur* is used instead of *curé* as the designation of
the parish priest).

As additional examples we may cite English *editor* ' one who
superintends or prepares a book, journal, etc., for publication ' :
French *éditeur* ' publisher ' (English *editor* = French *rédacteur);*
English *injure* ' harm ' : French *injurier* ' insult ' (Post-Classical
Latin *iniuriare,* literally, ' swear against ', may have the same
meaning) ; and English *journey* ' travel ', in Middle English also
' day's work or day's travel ' : French *journée* ' space of a day '
(Mediaeval Latin *diurnata, iornata* ' day's work, day's journey '). An interesting semantic development is seen in English *mercy* ' compassion ' : French *merci* ' thanks ' from Latin
merces ' pay, price, reward ', in Vulgar Latin also ' pity, gracious gift, grace ' (cf. the Old French *Prose de sainte Eulalie,*
qued avuisset de nos Christus mercit ' that Christ have mercy
upon us '; Old French *Chanson de Roland, cist champs est*
vostre la mercit Dieu ' this field is yours by the grace of God ').
The evolution of meaning here is that one gives thanks for a gracious gift or for compassion shown (cf. Mediaeval Latin *mercedem*
referre = *gratias agere* ' give thanks '), the meaning ' thanks ' still
surviving in the archaic English *gramercy* (the *graunt mercy* of
Chaucer and Gower) from Old French *grant merci* ' great thanks '.
Finally, mention may be made of English *travel* ' journey ' :
French *travail* ' labour, toil ' (this connotation also found in
Middle English, e.g., Robert of Gloucester [1298], *uor eld & uor*
trauail bigan to febli vaste ' for age and toil began to feeble fast '),
the old meaning still surviving in the archaic English *travail* (with
retention of the French spelling) ' pangs of childbirth ' (cf. the
English translation by *labour* in the same sense).

Identical semantic developments may arise independently in
different languages, as in English *be-fall* ' happen ' (in this sense
in Middle English by 1300, but not in Anglo-Saxon), Sanskrit

ā-pat-, Greek προσ-πίπτω, Latin *ac-cidere*, ' fall to ', Welsh *di-gwydd*, German *Zu-fall* ' happening '. Here we have, first, translations in Welsh *di-gwydd*, German *Zu-fall*, and (perhaps) English *be-fall* : Latin *ac-cidere*; and second, independent developments in Sanskrit *ā-pat-* and Greek προσ-πίπτω (whether the Latin *ac-cidere* is modelled on προσ-πίπτω is not certain).

Onomatopoeia, or imitation of sound (cf. p. 40), is far less common than one would expect, and many of its demonstrable instances are reduplicated formations indicative of repetition of the sound imitated. Here belong such words as English *baa-baa* ' sheep ' (Greek βηβήν); Sanskrit *kāka-* ' crow '; *barbara-* ' stammering, foreigner ' (Greek βάρβαρος ' barbarian ', literally, '[saying] bar-bar '); *balbalā-kar-* ' stammer, stutter ' (Latin *balbus* ' stammering, stuttering ', German *babbeln*, French *babiller*, English *babble;* cf. the Hebrew popular etymology of *Bābel* ' Babylon ' [literally, ' Gate of the God '; Akkadian *Bāb-ilu*] as ' babble ' in Genesis xi. 9; pp. 419–420) *gárgara-* ' eddy ' (Latin *gurges* ' whirlpool ', *gurguliō* ' gullet ', Spanish *gárgara* ' gurgling ', French *gargouille* ' water-spout, gargoyle ', English *gargle, gurgle*, etc.) ; *marmara-* ' rustling, murmuring ', *múrmura-* ' burning chaff ' (Greek μορμύρω ' roar and boil ' [of water], Latin *murmur*, German *murmeln*, English *murmur);* *kṣav-* ' sneeze ' (Old High German *niosan*, Modern German *niesen*, English *sneeze*, Lithuanian *čiáudėti);* English *grunt* (Greek γρύζω ' grumble, mutter, growl, grunt ', Latin *grundiō, grunniō*, German *grunzen* ' grunt ') ; *clang, klink* (Greek κλαγγή ' twang ', Latin *clangor* ' clang ', German *klingen* ' clink '). This type of words, as the examples just cited indicate, frequently violate the regular systems of correspondences (cf. pp. 74–83), thus showing that they have been formed independently from imitative base-sounds common to the Indo-European area. *In terming a word onomatopoetic, the utmost caution must be observed; and in every case the criterion must be, not whether the word in a late form may seem to be onomatopoetic, but whether its Indo-European base may fairly be considered as imitative of the sound which its meaning implies.*

If this principle be observed, some words which do not now seem to be onomatopoetic probably had that character in the beginning. Thus English *laugh* (Anglo-Saxon *hlehhan*, Gothic *hlahjan*, Old High German *(h)lahhan*, Modern German *lachen)* scarcely suggests sound-imitation; but investigation of its history shows that it is from the same base as that which gives the Latin *clangor*, etc., just cited, and so is very distantly related to *clang* and *klink*. On the other hand, words which might readily appear at first glance to be onomatopoetic are seen, when examined by the same method, not to fall within this category. Thus, English *flow* (Anglo-Saxon *flówan*, Old Icelandic *flóa*, Old High German *flewen)* might superficially so be construed because of its initial *fl;* but its Indo-European base is **pleu̯e-* (cf. Sanskrit *plav-* ' float, swim ', Kuchaean *plewe* ' boat ', Armenian *luanem* ' wash ', Greek πλέω (for **πλεϝω)* ' go by boat ', Latin *pluit* ' it rains ', Lithuanian *pláuti* ' wash ', Old Church Slavic *pluti* ' flow, go by ship '), which neither in sound nor in meaning suggests either the motion or the sound of ' flowing '. Any idea that words of the type of *flow* are at all connected with the sounds of the action or state which they designate is due merely to a late association between sound and sense of a purely superficial character devoid of any linguistic value. The whole subject of onomatopoeia has been so mishandled by unscientific guesses that it urgently needs an impartial and technical examination to determine how large (or how small) a part imitation of sounds has actually played in the development of vocabulary.

CHAPTER X

Etymology and Linguistic Method: The Historical Aspect of Words

Definition of etymology — history of the term — pre-scientific etymology — etymology in relation to phonology — importance of strict scientific method — formulation of correspondence-tables — ambiguity of alphabets and spellings — influence of alien scripts on orthography — methods and principles of transcription — the method of etymologising: analysis of a word into its components; study of the base, of inflexion, and of every phoneme of the word etymologised — why some words are said to have no etymology — base-meanings sometimes doubtful or unknown — ambiguous etymologies: the Umbrian word *pelso-* — the requirements of scientific etymology — the necessity of bibliographical knowledge.

I. ETYMOLOGY

ETYMOLOGY, which is essentially historical in character, may be defined as that branch of linguistics which traces words to their earliest ascertainable base in the language-group to which they belong. It then either demonstrates their affiliation with other words similarly traced to this same base; or shows that words supposed, whether by the scientific investigator or by the layman, to have come from the base in question cannot have done so, but must have evolved from some other base, seeking, in such case, to determine from what one or ones they have developed, either certainly or with more or less probability. *The etymology of a word is essentially its history;* and when we speak of the derivation of a word as synonymous with its etymology, we are quite within the bounds of scientific accuracy.

Semantically the term etymology has, like most other words, travelled far from its earliest signification. Just when it was first used, we do not know; but we do know that the Stoic philosopher Chrysippos (about 280–206 B.C.) wrote a work, now lost, concerning τὰ ἐτυμολογικά (' Etymologics '). What he meant by this term was not what it connotes to us, but the establishment of the ' true ' meaning of a word (Greek ἔτυμος ' true ' and λόγος ' word '; cf.

Cicero's translation of ἐτυμολογία by *veriloquium* and its Armenian rendering, in the version of the grammar of Dionysios Thrax [cf. p. 166], by *stugabanut'iwn)*; and by ' true ' he understood, as a good Stoic, the connotation which a word possessed by its inherent nature *(φύσει;* pp. 14, 423, 427–428), implying the exclusion of all meanings which might later be attached to it. Similarly, an anonymous Greek writer of unknown date defines etymology as ' an unfolding of words whereby the truth is made clear '; and the Sanskrit term for it, *vyutpatti-* (also denoting, in non-grammatical senses, ' production, derivation, origin '), literally signifies ' off-production, offshoot ' (cf. *ut-patti-* ' production, origin ', *vi-pad-* ' fall asunder '). To the Greek and Roman grammarians etymology would seem to have been part of what we now term semantics; to them, its object was to determine the original *meaning* of a word, not the *origin* of the word itself; and derivatives of a base (as we would call it) were studied from the point of view of signification only, not, as now, to determine the affiliation or lack of affiliation of words.

The general principles of pre-scientific etymology are fairly well summarised by Saint Isidore of Seville (about 570–639; *Origines* i. 28) :

' Etymology is the origin of words, since the force of a verb or noun is gathered by interpretation. . . . For when thou seest whence the noun has arisen, the more quickly dost thou understand its force, for all investigation of a thing is clearer when its etymology is known. All nouns, however, were not established by the ancients according to nature *(secundum naturam = φύσει)*, but some also according to prescription *(secundum placitum = θέσει)*. . . . Furthermore, the etymologies of nouns have been given either from their matter, as *reges* (" kings ") from *recte agendo* (" acting rightly "); or from their origin, as *homo* (" man "), because he is made *ex humo* (" from earth "; cf. Genesis ii. 7); or from their opposites, as *lutum* (" mud ") from *lavando* (" washing "), because mud is not made clean [by washing].'

He also notes (correctly in principle) the derivation of words from other words or from names of places and rivers, and by borrowing from other languages.

The method of etymologising from opposites was carried to mad extremes, a classic instance being the famous *lucus a non lucendo* ' a grove (originally " bright place ") because it is not bright '. Since we now know that *lūcus* primarily meant ' a clearing ' (cf. Latin *collūcō* ' thin a forest ', *interlūcō* and *sublūcō* ' prune a tree '), we can emend the old derivation simply by dropping the negative and saying, ' lucus a lucendo '. One quaint gem may be added from Aulus Gellius (second century A.D.; *Noctes Atticae* x. 4) to the effect that when the Romans said *vos* (' ye, you '), they fitted the meaning to the word by projecting their lips as well as their thoughts towards the persons addressed; but when they said *nos* (' we, us '), they restrained both lips and thoughts within themselves — an argument which would seem to need reversal in the case of English *we* and *you*, where Gellius would probably have argued, had the language then existed, that English is egoistic and haughty, while Latin, Italian, etc., are altruistic and humble.

Etymology, though indissolubly bound up with morphology, syntax, and semantics, finds its closest link with phonology. *Without an exact knowledge of phonology and of phonetic correspondences* (pp. 74–83), *no etymology of any scientific validity can be made;* and, on the other hand, *unless we know the precise etymology of a word, we can do no more than guess at its original meaning or, in many cases, understand its semantic development.* Phonetic correspondences are usually established by observing the phonetic relations between words of identical or closely related meaning in different languages; and if such correspondences are found to be regular, i.e., to hold in all instances of the sound or sounds in question, one may then proceed to use the results obtained to make further etymologies. *Etymology and phonology stand in reciprocal relation to each other; and they are the prime factors in proving or disproving the relationship of languages, and their grouping with or separation from linguistic families* (cf. pp. 295–303).

II. METHOD

In discussing the terms for ' ten ', ' god ', ' house ', ' cow ', and ' deer ' (see pp. 74–75, 99–105, 132–133, 252–255), we have had occasion to consider the elements of etymological procedure; and we may now take up the actual method in some detail. One cannot emphasise too strongly the cardinal principle that *establishment of strict scientific method is the absolute* sine qua non *of all exact investigation.* Paradoxical though it may seem, it is better to arrive at a wrong result by a correct method than at a correct one by a wrong method. In the one case, there may be a mere mechanical error (as when one makes a mistake in adding a column of figures), or some essential factor may be omitted, which, on being taken into account, gives the correct result (as when a set of figures should give a certain sum, but refuses to do so, the error lying, not in the method of addition, but in the absence of some item or items which, when included, make up the total required). In the other case, one is reduced to mere guesses which, by the laws of probability and chance, may occasionally be correct, but in the overwhelming majority of cases will be wrong.

There is little place for guesses in etymology, or, indeed, in any department of linguistics; and the results of guessing often leave the linguist uncertain whether to laugh or to weep at the folly of the guesser. The author has read a statement, made in all seriousness, that the symbol of the Papacy is the bull because the Pope issues bulls; whereas the most elementary investigation would have shown that *bull* as the name of an animal is a real Teutonic word, while *bull* in the meaning of a Papal pronouncement is a specialisation of the Latin *bulla* in its ecclesiastical connotation ' seal '. Another sciolist, claiming to have found a word *ski* ' dog ' in Kwakiutl, solemnly compared it with the English *skye-terrier*, which takes its name from the Isle of Skye in Scotland!

The only scientifically permissible approximation to anything which in the least resembles a guess is the tentative formulation of a working hypothesis to be tested by the method of trial and error. Confronted by a problem either yet unsolved or not yet satisfactorily solved, the linguist, already equipped with sound method, may, like any other scientist, legitimately say to himself, ' Perhaps such-and-such an hypothesis will help '; and he may then proceed on the basis of such hypothesis. Once seriously embarked upon the problem, he must, in a sense, forget his hypothesis except as a mere possibility to be tested out; he must not seek to prove that he personally is right, or that some other investigator is wrong; and still less dare he distort, suppress, or manufacture evidence either in behalf of his hypothesis or against some other theory. He must be an impartial and impersonal judge, not an advocate for either side; and he must be ready at any moment to revise or discard any solution, whether formulated by himself or by others, if new data or increased knowledge demand it.

What, then, is the scientific method to be pursued in studying the etymology of a given word or group of words? First of all, the investigator must have a thorough knowledge of the phonetic correspondences involved in his problem. Tables of such correspondences are to be found in many scientific grammars, particularly in those dealing either with linguistic families as a whole (Indo-European, Semitic, etc.) or with individual language-groups (Greek, Italic, Teutonic, Romance, Slavic, etc.). For the beginner, an excellent method is to make his own tables of the sounds found in the particular language or group of languages which he is studying, and to equate these, with the help of tables in more general scientific grammars, with their correspondences in such other language-groups as he may find important in his special problem, the chief of these for the beginner in Indo-European being Sanskrit, Greek, Latin, Gothic, Lithuanian, and Old Church Slavic. In passing, we must emphasise the fact that *the methods here laid down for etymology are equally valid in the investigation of morphology*, with which etymology is indissolubly linked.

Suppose, for instance, that the student wishes to study the English word *ten* and its cognates (cf. pp. 74–75). He should first draw up a table somewhat as follows, taking it, if need be, from a good comparative grammar of Teutonic and Indo-European in general: English t = Anglo-Saxon t = Old Saxon t = Old Frisian t = Dutch t = Old Icelandic t = Swedish t = Gothic t = Old High German z [ts] = Proto-Teutonic *t = Italic-Romance d = Celtic d = Greek δ [d] = Albanian d = Balto-Slavic d = Armenian t = Indo-Iranian d = Afghān l = Indo-European *d. It is then well to make a reverse-table, perhaps in abbreviated form, showing what a given Indo-European phoneme becomes in the language or group which he is investigating, e.g., Indo-European *d = Proto-Teutonic *t = Low Teutonic (English, etc.) d = High Teutonic (German) z [ts]; and similar tables may be constructed for the e in *ten*.

Quite a different phenomenon will confront him when he seeks to compare *ten* with Anglo-Saxon *tíen, týn* (from **tehan)*, Old Saxon *tehan*, Old Frisian *tian*, Dutch *tien*, Old Icelandic *tío*, Gothic *taíhun (ai* is here merely a *façon d'écrire* for the phoneme [e], borrowed from the later Greek pronunciation of αι as [e]), Old High German *zehan*, Latin *decem*, Greek δέκα, Armenian *tasn*, Old Church Slavic *desę-tŭ*, Sanskrit *dáśa*, etc. In the English word, as in its counterparts in Old Frisian, Dutch, and Old Icelandic, a Teutonic h (retained in the Old Saxon, Gothic, and Old

High German cognates) = Indo-European $\hat{k}$ has vanished, though in Modern High German *zehn* the *letter* (not the *sound*) acts as a sign of a long vowel (Old High German [tsehan] : Modern German [tseːn]). Finally, he will observe, by the same method of comparison, that the *n* itself can be explained only as derived from an Indo-European nasal sonant [m̥], which becomes [n̥] in Teutonic when final.

If, on the other hand, he compares Anglo-Saxon *tíen* from **tehan*, Old Saxon *tehan*, Old Frisian *tian*, Dutch *tien* [tiːn], Old High German *zehan* with Gothic *taíhun* and Old Icelandic *tío*, he will find, by consulting or making analogous correspondence-tables, that the final. *-an* and *-un* are not of the same origin, but that the former comes from Indo-European *-om* and the latter from *-m̥* [m̥]. He will then be able to reconstruct the hypothetical Proto-Teutonic pre-forms **tehom-* and **tehm̥-*. By similar operations with the kindred words for ' ten ' in all known Indo-European languages, he will finally reach the hypothetical Indo-European pre-forms **'dekom-* and **'dekm̥-* as the sources from which all the historic words for ' ten ' in the Indo-European languages may be derived, although some scholars hold that these forms should be **'dekomt-* and **'dekm̥t-* because of Old Church Slavic *desętŭ*, Greek τριάκοντα, Latin *triginta* ' thirty ', etc.

Throughout this process, the operation of vowel-gradation must be observed (cf. pp. 63–67), as well as the fact that a phoneme may be represented in one way when initial, and in other ways when it is internal or is a final; and the treatment may also differ according as a group of phonemes is original (i.e., dating from the Indo-European period) or has developed later. Thus, an original final *-ns* becomes *-ss* in the Old Italic dialect Oscan, but *-f* in the kindred Umbrian, as Oscan **feíhúss** ' walls ', Umbrian **turuf** ' bulls ' : Latin *murōs, taurōs* (cf. Cretan ἐλευθερονς ' freemen ', Argive υίονς ' sons ', Sanskrit *tā́ms ca* ' and those ', Gothic *wulfans* ' wolves '; p. 72); but a secondary *-ns* arising from a syncope of vowels remains unchanged in both, as Oscan **Púmpaiians** ' relating to Pompeii ', Umbrian **Ikuvins** ' relating to Iguvium ' = Latin *Pompeianus, Iguvinus.* Again, in **'dekm̥-*, where the accent precedes the $\hat{k}$, $\hat{k}$ becomes *h* in Teutonic; but when it follows, as in **de'ku-* ' decade ', it becomes *g* by Verner's Law (pp. 72–82), as in Gothic *fidwor-tigjus*, Old Icelandic *fjórer-tiger*, Old Frisian *fi(ū)wer-tich*, Old Saxon *fi(ū)war-tig*, Anglo-Saxon *féower-tig*,

English *for-ty*, Old High German *fior-zug*, Modern German *vier-zig*. Besides all this, one must bear in mind the general principles of such phenomena as assimilation, dissimilation, metathesis, epenthesis, prothesis, and sandhi (cf. pp. 68–73).

In making his tables and in attempting to etymologise, the beginner will perhaps do well to restrict his attention, so far as the vowels are concerned, to those in accented syllables; for, *generally speaking, unaccented vowels show, in many languages, a tendency first to become blurred, and then wholly to disappear* (cf. p. 63). Thus we have, for example, Oscan **húrz** [horts] = Latin *hortus* (with *u* blurred from *o)* = Greek χόρτος ' enclosed place '; Old French nominative *murs* ' wall ' = Latin *mūrus* : accusative *mur* = Latin *mūru*ᵐ; Gothic *akrs* ' field ', Old Icelandic *akr* for *akrr, Anglo-Saxon *œcer*, English *acre*, Old High German *achar*, Modern German *Acker*, etc., from Proto-Teutonic **'akraz*, Indo-European **'aĝros* (cf. Latin *ager* for **'agr̥* from **'agr̥r* from **'agr̥s* from **'agrs* from **'agros);* Armenian nominative singular *kin* ' woman ' from **'gu̯enā* (cf. Gothic *qinō* from **gu̯enōn*, Old Prussian *genna*, Old Church Slavic *žena)*, but instrumental singular *knaw* from **gu̯en'ābhi;* Old Prussian *wi(j)rs*, Lettish *vīrs*, colloquial Lithuanian *výrs* ' man ' beside literary Lithuanian *výras* (cf. Latin *vir*, Old Irish *fer* ' man ' from **u̯ir(o)s* : Sanskrit *vīrá-* ' hero ').

We must always remember that we are dealing with *sounds,* not with *letters;* and although, in the nature of the case, we have only letters to guide us in any language that we cannot actually hear spoken, we must endeavour, so far as data permit, to recover the true pronunciation. Very often the actual writing is misleading or ambiguous; and the same sign or group of signs frequently stands for wholly different phonemes in different languages. Thus the letter *z* in English is [z], as in *zeal* [ziːl]; in Spanish it is now [ð] in Castilian, as in *mozo* [moːðo] ' boy ', but [s] in Andalusian and in American Spanish, as in *mozo* [moːso], and in Old Spanish it was [dz], as in *mozo* [moːdzo] or in *pezuña* [pedzuɲa] ' solid hoof ' from Latin *ped(i)s ungula* ' nail of the foot '. In German it is [ts], as in *zehn* [tseːn] ' ten '; and in Ancient Greek, though transcribed *z*, it must have had at least three values: [zd], as in Ἀθήναζε [a'θeːnazde] ' to Athens ' from *Ἀθηνασ-δε; [dz], as in πεζός [ped'zos] ' on foot ' from *πεδ-ι̯ος; and, from the fourth century B.C. to the present time, [z], the value [dz] perhaps going back to a still earlier [dʒ] from [ɟ], as in vulgar English [dʒuːk]

for [d̨uːk] 'duke', palatalised from [duːk] (cf. Latin *dūcem*
[duːkem]), which still survives as a vulgarism.

The combination of letters *ch* is equally ambiguous. In English
it represents [tʃ], as in *church* [tʃəːtʃ]; in German, [x] or [ç],
as in *Loch* [lox] 'hole' and *ich* [iç] 'I'; in Italian, [k], as in *che*
[keː] 'what'; and in French [ʃ], as in *char* [ʃar] 'waggon'.
Variants in spelling often help to indicate the pronunciation, as in
Lesbian ὔσδος 'branch' beside Attic ὄζος and inscriptional Attic
Σευς 'Zeus' (340 B.C.) beside Ζεύς, Rhodian and Boeotian Δευς from
*δͷευς (cf. Sanskrit *Dyaú-*); and sometimes linguistic comparison
is an aid, as in Oscan **húrz** 'garden', which was evidently [horts]
because of Latin *hortus*, or in the Hittite ablative singular, e.g.,
arunaz 'from the sea', which must have been something like
[arunats] because of such identical formations as Sanskrit
mukhatás 'from the mouth', Greek ἐντός '[from] within', Latin
funditus 'from the bottom' (cf. pp. 198–199).

Alphabets and spellings cannot be trusted blindly; and spellings
in particular are often misleading unless their origin is known.
Modern Irish spelling, for instance, is largely etymological and by
no means reproduces the present pronunciation. A tourist, on seeing
the name *Dún Laoghaire* on the railway-station at the port of
Dublin, might be pardoned if he did not at once pronounce it
[dhʌːn liːri] (cf. p. 65), or if, hearing the modern pronunciation
for the first time, he should fail to spell the name correctly. French
spelling is also full of pitfalls for the unwary; and English orthography is notoriously misrepresentative of English pronunciation.
How, for instance, would Aristotle, however learned, have spoken
such a phrase as *tough though he was, he was caught by his
daughter through a cough when he laughed,* had he possessed only
a printed text and an exact knowledge of English grammar, but
no guide to English pronunciation? Of one thing we may be quite
sure: he would not have said [tʌf ðou hiː wəz, hiː wəz kɔːt bai
hiz dɔːtə θruː ə kɔːf wen hiː laːft].

In ancient languages, spelling is not infrequently influenced
by the alphabets or spellings of other languages from which they
have borrowed their script or their orthography. Thus, in Gothic,
ei, *ai*, and *gg* were pronounced [iː], [e], and [ŋg] respectively
because such were the values of Greek ει, αι, and γγ by the time
of Ulfilas (fourth century A.D.). In Old Irish, *g*, *d*, and *b* between
vowels were 'aspirated' (i.e., spirantised) into [ɣ], [ð], and [β]

respectively (e.g., *tige* [tiɣe] 'of the house', written *tighe* in Modern Irish, and now pronounced [tiːə]); but if they were to have the values [g], [d], and [b], they were written *c, t,* and *p* (e.g., *ocus* [ogus] 'and', now written *agus).* In Armenian, the phonemes [u] and [uː] are written *ou* because such were the values of *ου* in Greek, to distinguish them from [y], the sound which the Greek *υ* had developed from its original force of [u] or [uː], and which is still retained in the Modern Greek dialect of Tsaconian, a descendant of the ancient Doric (cf. pp. 29, 329), whereas elsewhere in Modern Greek it has become [iː].

Particularly interesting is the transcription of one language in the alphabet of another when this script is inherently unfitted to be the vehicle for such transcription. Thus, Greek, Spanish, Persian, and German have been and still are written in Hebrew characters, Greek and Turkish in Armenian (cf. pp. 313–314). A long inscription in the Cyprian dialect of Greek of about 450 B.C. is in the native Cyprian alphabet, which not only was syllabic (cf. p. 148), but had no characters for voiced or aspirated plosives, so that *p,* for instance, stood for [p], [b], or [ph] indiscriminately, as in *potolise* = πτολις [ptolis] 'city', *pasileuse* = βασιλευς [basileus] 'king', *pilokuporone* = φιλοκυπρον [philokuproːn] 'Cypros-loving'.

Occasionally, such transcriptions are our only source for even a guess at the pronunciation of certain extinct languages. Here we may cite, as an outstanding instance, the evidence to be drawn for the phonetic values of Hebrew vowels from the representation of Hebrew words (especially proper nouns) in the Greek Septuagint, the Latin Vulgate, and the *Hexapla* of Origen (A.D. 185–254), since all of these are much earlier than the indications of the pronunciation in the Masoretic text, which began only about the sixth century A.D., a thousand years after Hebrew had ceased to be a vernacular. Even here, however, as the divergent transcriptions of the same word in the same passage by different manuscripts indicate, we must proceed with the utmost caution. Our one source for a knowledge of the pronunciation of Punic (cf. pp. 362, 425), apart from a few scattered glosses, is thirty-two lines of the Latin comedy *Poenulus* by Plautus (about 250–184 B.C.); but his evidence is quite inadequate for exact judgement on the matter (cf. p. 359).

Since one is dealing with sounds or phonemes rather than letters, the linguist will do well to acquaint himself from the very first with the principles of the *International Phonetic Alphabet* (see Fig. 6, pp. 58–59) in order that he may be able to reproduce at least the approximate pronunciation, whether actually heard or inferred from linguistic evidence, of the characters found in the documents which he studies. Such transcription may, as circumstances require, be either ' broad ' (i.e., approximate) or ' narrow ' (i.e., exact) ; and transcriptions in this alphabet are conventionally placed in square brackets, as French *cent* [sẽ] ' hundred '. Many languages written in non-Roman scripts have received conventional transcriptions which the linguist must learn. Here belong, for instance, Sanskrit, Avestan, Armenian, Greek, Russian, Sumerian, Hittite, Georgian, and all the Semitic and Dravidian languages (Hebrew, Telugu, etc.) ; and some of these (e.g., Sanskrit and Avestan) have had several transcriptions, all of which have enjoyed more or less favour. In such cases, the most generally accepted conventional transcriptions should, practically speaking, be retained for broad use; if for some reason a narrow transcription be desirable, the conventional representation can readily be transmuted into the International Alphabet.

The underlying principle of transcription is quite simple: each character of the original script should be represented by a single character of the Roman alphabet, with diacritical marks if necessary, and supplementation by italics or by Greek letters when occasion demands. In practice, considerable confusion exists, as when the Sanskrit word for ' and ' is written *ca*, but the Avestan equivalent appears as *ča*, both being in the International Alphabet [tʃa]. All this, however, is more vexatious than serious. On the other hand, certain characters in some alphabets are of doubtful or unknown phonemic value, such as the Umbrian letter transcribed ř in reproducing texts originally in the native alphabet, but appearing as *rs* in Umbrian inscriptions written in Latin script, e.g., **teřa** : *dersa* ' let him give ' (for **dedet*, cf. Vestinian *didet* ' gives '; the native Umbrian alphabet does not distinguish between *t* and *d)*. Here all that we can now say is that ř and *rs* have developed from [d] ; they are supposed to have had somewhat the value of [rʒ], represented by the Czech ř (whence the transcription), but more than this we do not know as yet.

The first work of importance on the problem of transcription was C. R. Lepsius's *Standard Alphabet for Reducing Unwritten*

Languages and Foreign Graphic Systems to a Uniform Orthography in European Letters (second edition, London, 1863) ; and the next noteworthy exhaustive study of the question was Father W. Schmidt's *Die Sprachlaute und ihre Darstellung in einem allgemeinen linguistischen Alphabet* (both in German and French, *Les Sons du langage et leur représentation dans un alphabet linguistique général*, Salzburg and Vienna, 1907, reprinted from *Anthropos* ii [1907], 282–329, 508–587, 822–897, 1058–1105). The history of alphabets is in itself a study of much value, interest, and complexity, and has been thoroughly investigated in such works as I. Taylor's *History of the Alphabet* (two volumes, London, 1899), P. Berger's *Histoire de l'écriture dans l'antiquité* (second edition, Paris, 1892), and H. Jensen's *Geschichte der Schrift* (Hanover, 1925) ; but it scarcely falls, strictly speaking, within the sphere of linguistics proper.

Since a word consists of a base and an inflexion, whether with or without one or more determinatives, and since the base ramifies not merely in meanings, but also in forms, through the addition of such determinatives to it (cf. pp. 150–159), we must, in the actual process of etymologising, begin by splitting the word into its components of base, determinative or determinatives, and inflexions, and must then study each part separately by the methods and principles of etymology, which are identical for them all. Thus, for example, we must analyse Latin *amābimus* ' we shall love ' into *amā-bi-mus* and Arabic *taktubu* ' thou wilt write ' into *ta-ktub-u*. Having made this segregation of the components of the word, we must next consider its foundation, the base, whether in its simple form or as enlarged by determinatives, paying especially careful attention to its grade according to the principles of vowel-gradation (pp. 65–67).

Thus, the base $*\hat{g}hele/o-$ ' shine, bright, yellow, green, blue, grey ', when accented on its first syllable $(*'\hat{g}hele/o-)$, assumed the forms $*'\hat{g}hel\partial-$, $*'\hat{g}hel_{e/o}-$, $*'\hat{g}hel-$, as seen historically, for example, in Sanskrit *hári-* '(reddish) brown, tawney, (pale) yellow, fallow, green ', Phrygian ζελκια ' garden-herbs ', Greek χόλο-ς ' bile, anger ', Latin *hel-vus* ' light bay ', Old Irish *gel* ' white ', Anglo-Saxon *geolo*, English *yellow* (from $*'\hat{g}hel-\mu o-$), Anglo-Saxon *gealla*, English *gall* (from $*'\hat{g}hol-no-$), Lithuanian *žélti* ' grow green ', Old Church Slavic *zele-nŭ* ' green '. When the first syllable was unaccented, $*\hat{g}hele/o-$ assumed the form $*\hat{g}hle/o-$, as in Greek χλω-ρός ' greenish-yellow ', χλό-η ' young verdure ', Old Icelandic glá-mr ' moon ', Anglo-Saxon gló-wan, English glow, Old Church Slavic zla-to ' gold '. If neither syllable was accented when determinatives were added, the forms were *ĝhlə-, *ĝhlₑ-, or *ĝhl-, as in Old Irish glan ' pure ', Old Icelandic glan ' brilliancy ' (from *ĝhlə-'no-), Anglo-Saxon, English gold (from *ĝhl̥-'to-), Lettish žults ' gall ' (from *ĝhl̥-'ti-), Old Church Slavic zlŭči ' gall ' (from ĝhl̥-'qi-). This base also has many extensions by determinatives into which we need not enter here. Suffice it to say that through them it has given rise to such English words as glad, glass, gleam, glisten, glint, gloat, glower, glare, and the obsolete glout ' stare, pout '.

Remembering that the normal grade is found under the original, or Indo-European, accent, while the reduced and zero-grades are seen only in syllables originally unaccented (cf. the relation of Greek χόλος, χλόη, Old Icelandic glan, English gold to *ĝhel-, ĝhlo-, ĝhlə- or *ĝhlₑ-, and ĝhl- respectively), we can very frequently restore the Indo-European accentuation where in historic times the accent of Latin, Celtic, Teutonic, etc., no longer shows it, since these groups have substituted fixed for free accent (cf. p. 64), particularly valuable help for Teutonic being given by Verner's Law (cf. pp. 79–82).

In dealing with inflexion, zero-inflexion (cf. p. 151) must count just as much as plus-inflexion; e.g., English foot is to be analysed as *foot-0 from *fōt-s (cf. Latin pēs ' foot ' for *ped-s, Anglo-Saxon fót for *fót-s), and the plural feet as *feet-0 from *fōtiz from *fōtes (cf. Latin pedes ' feet ', Anglo-Saxon fét).

In all these operations, each and every phoneme in the word under investigation must be accounted for in detail; and if a patent irregularity is found, one must consider whether the apparent violation of phonetic correspondences may not be due to dialect-mixture, analogy, borrowing, onomatopoeia, and the like, or to the presence of some factor hitherto unobserved (cf. pp. 79–83, 106–114, 126, 128, 275–276). The prudent investigator will use such factors, however, only when necessity drives; and then he will defend his employment of them by the most convincing parallels that he can adduce. He will also do well to explain phenomena so far as possible from within the language in which they occur. French sounds, forms, vocabulary, and syntax, for example, should be elucidated from within Modern, Middle, and Old French wherever possible. Interpretation of these phenomena, if not explicable from French itself, should next be sought in the other Romance languages (Italian, Spanish, etc.) and in Latin (including Vulgar, Classical, and Archaic). Only when these fail, should one look for explanations from Italic (Oscan, Umbrian, and minor non-Latin dialects), from Celtic (Gaulish, Welsh, Breton, Cornish, Irish, and Manx), from Teutonic (especially Gothic and Old High German), or from Greek, and other Indo-European families; only in the last resort, when all else proves unavailing, should one seek an elucidation in Proto-Indo-European or in the theory of sub-strata (cf. pp. 84, 136–137). If an explanation becomes laboured and unduly involved, it may well be regarded with some suspicion; although an interpretation is by no means necessarily correct because it is superficially self-evident.

One cannot hope to find an etymology for every word, or an explanation of every form; and it is not merely rare words, but some of those most commonly used in a language, which have thus far defied even plausible etymologising, as in the groups of English *drink* (cf. p. 133), *sheep*, etc. Just what do we mean when we say that no etymology can be found? If I can reconstruct hypothetical Indo-European bases *$dhre(n)g(h)e$- and *$(s)k\bar{e}be$- for *drink* and *sheep* by precisely the same processes as those by which I reconstruct *$dheu̯e$- ' breathe ' or *$dek̑m̥$- ' ten ' (pp. 252–255, 281–282), why do I say that *$dhre(n)g(h)e$- and *$(s)k\bar{e}be$- have no etymology, while *$dheu̯e$- and *$dek̑m̥$- have? Simply because the groups derived from *$dhre(n)g(h)e$- and *$(s)k\bar{e}be$- are, so far as our present evidence goes, restricted to a single language-family (perhaps even to a single language) of the Indo-European stock, while those from *$dheu̯e$- and *$dek̑m̥$- are not so isolated. If, at some future time, sure cognates of the groups of *drink* and *sheep* are found (i.e., words which may be reduced to the bases *$dhre(n)g(h)e$- and *$(s)k\bar{e}be$- by observation of phonetic correspondences, and which will be semantically in harmony with the meanings of those bases), then *drink* and *sheep* will have etymologies.

A group may be derivable from a base, and still we may not know its original meaning. We seem fully justified in affirming that *$dek̑m̥$ denoted ' ten '; but why ' ten ' was so designated we cannot yet certainly say. Some have held that *$dek̑m̥$ was really *$de-k̑m̥(t)$- ' two hands ' (i.e., the ten fingers), and so was ultimately cognate with the group of Gothic *handus,* German and English *hand,* just as English *five* (Anglo-Saxon *fíf,* German *fünf,* Gothic *fimf,* Old Irish *cóic,* Old Welsh *pimp,* Latin *quinque,* Greek πέντε, Sanskrit *páñca,* Indo-European *'peɳqᵘe-; pp. 68–69) has been very plausibly connected with *finger* (Gothic *figgrs,* Old Icelandic *fingr,* German *Finger,* Indo-European *peɳqᵘ'ros).

In our present state of knowledge, it seems most prudent, while by no means denying the possibility of such speculations, to observe an extremely cautious attitude toward them. They are ingenious and possible, at least in the case of *five* (in the case of *de-ḱm̥[t]-,* however, we should expect, rather, *du̯e-ḱm̥[t]-,* since the Indo-European base of the numeral ' two ' begins with *du̯-,* not with *d);* but they cannot be regarded as cogent demonstrations and must, accordingly, be considered unproved. With equal probability one might connect English *three* (Anglo-Saxon *þrí,* Gothic *þreis,* Old Icelandic *þrír,* Old High German *drî,* Modern German *drei,* Old Irish *trí,* Latin *trēs,* French *trois,* Greek τρεῖς, Lithuanian *trỹs,* Old Church Slavic *trije,* Sanskrit *tráyas,* Indo-European *trei-)* with the base *tere-* ' pass beyond ' (Sanskrit *tar-* ' pass beyond ', Greek τέρμα, Latin *terminus* ' boundary, end '; Sanskrit *tirás* ' through, beyond ', Latin *trans* ' beyond ', Old Irish *tar* ' over ') as being the number next beyond the dual (cf. p. 183), for which a parallel might be sought in Old Welsh *trim-uceint* ' thirty ', i.e., '(the decade) beyond twenty '. Perhaps the best that can be said for this bit of ingenuity is that it is less bad than a connexion once seriously sought with the base *tere-* ' rub ' because the third finger is often used for rubbing or erasing.

A very real difficulty is presented by *ambiguous etymologies,* i.e., by those which may with equal probability be traced to entirely different bases, particularly to those which are homonymous and have different meanings, or which rhyme (pp. 113–114) and possess synonymous connotations. Here we may take as an example a word whose signification, despite all the study devoted to it, remains uncertain, so that a somewhat detailed consideration of it presents an excellent specimen of linguistic method in etymology. In the Iguvine Tables, an Umbrian ritual text found at Gubbio in Italy and dating from before the Christian Era (cf. pp. 333–334), the word *pelso-* occurs seven times, an instance being **unu erietu sakre pelsanu fetu** ' let him have a ram ? (as) a sacrifice ' (II a, 6). This *pelso-* may come equally well, from the purely phonological point of view, and with assumption of a determinative -*s*-, from any of the Indo-European bases *pele- ' sell ', *pele- ' move to and fro ', *pele- ' flow, pour ', *pele- ' fall ', *pele- ' drive ', *pele- ' burn ', *spele- ' speak loudly ', **sp(h)ele*- ' split ', **sp(h)ele*- ' shine ', *qᵘele- ' turn ', and *sqᵘele- ' ripple, wash '; and if we suppose, to exhaust all possibilities, that we are dealing with a denominative verb, we may add to this list *pele- ' grey ', *pele- ' marsh ' (*pele- ' butterfly ' occurs only in reduplicated forms), *pele- ' vessel, container ', *pele- ' skin ', *pele- ' meal ', **pel(e)s*- ' rock ', *qᵘele- ' afar ', *qᵘele- ' multitude '.

Here are no less than twenty distinct phonological possibilities, to which we must add the view, held by excellent scholars, that *pels*- is cognate with Latin *sepeliō* ' bury ', interpreted as for *se-pel-ịō. Since, however, *sepeliō* is more probably akin to Sanskrit *sápati* ' strives after, honours ', *saparyáti* ' serves, honours ', Greek ἕπω ' busy one's self with ', its original meaning would seem to have been ' honour the dead with proper rites '. Connexion of *pels*- with *sepeliō* thus seems improbable, although one must grant the possibility that *pels*-, if for *pel-s-, may be cognate with the Teutonic group of Gothic *filhan* ' hide, bury ' from *pel-qe-, in which case its primary meaning would seem to have been ' hide, cover ', and then ' hide underground, bury ' (cf. Old Icelandic *fela* ' hide ', Old High German *ga-felhan* ' hide, bury ', and, probably, Old Prussian *pelkis* ' mantle ', Lithuanian *plēkis* ' handful of wool '). In any event, it would appear that we must assume that *pels*- comes from an Indo-European base **(s)p(h)ele*- or **(s)qᵘele*- plus a determinative -*s*-.

We have now satisfied phonological and morphological conditions; and when we read the seven passages in which the word occurs, we find that syntactic obligations are also met. But we have not yet considered the meaning, the semantic requirements. Since the text which we are especially considering speaks of a sacrificial ram, we may exclude all possibilities except that it was sold, moved about, poured upon, felled, driven, burned, split, turned, washed, buried, or skinned; it can scarcely have been made to shine or made a marsh, etc. Thus our possibilities are reduced from twenty-two to eleven.

At this point, we must depart from linguistics proper to see what evidence we can gain from other sources; in this particular instance, from what we know of the Iguvine ritual (for which our only document is these same Tables) and from comparative religion in general. Having read the Tables through, and having found that they already have terms for ' drive ', ' burn ', and ' pour ', thus reducing our possibilities to eight, we next examine anew all the passages containing *pels-* with attention to the meaning of the text as a whole, and with reference to the principles of ritual, especially, in the present instance, the rituals of Rome and of Greece, including the latter since Greek religion profoundly influenced that of ancient Italy.

These passages, besides the one (II a, 6) already cited, are as follows: *pesondro sorsalem (staflare) persome . . . ife endendu pelsatu* (VI b, 39, 40) ' let him there stretch into the trench [and] ? a pig-effigy (a stall-beast-effigy)'; *habina trif . . . pelsana fetu* (VI b, 22 = I a, 24–26 ' let him have three lambs ? '; **katel asaku pelsans futu** (II a, 43) ' let the puppy be ? at the altar '; and **uvem . . . pelsanu feitu** (III, 31–32) ' let him have a sheep ? '. Having now not merely accumulated a number of phonologically possible bases, but having also studied all their semantic developments and the relevant religious and ritualistic requirements, we find that certain derivatives of the base *q^uele-* ' turn ' have evolved into a connotation of ' serve deities, make things proper for deities ', a general sense which seems to fit all conditions better than any of the significations of the other bases.

In support of the meaning thus chosen, we make such comparison of derivatives from the base *q^uele-* as the following: Greek τέλειος '(ritually) perfect' (e.g., Argive hῖ κα τôι Μαχανει θυōμες τους ϝεξέκοντα τελεονς οϝινς ' where we sacrifice the sixty [ritually] perfect sheep to Machaneus '), τελεσμός ' consecration-ceremony ' (e.g., συντελοῦντες τὸν τελεσμὸν καὶ τὴν θυσίαν τῷ 'Ασκληπιῷ ' completing the consecration-ceremony and the sacrifice to Asklepios '), τελέω ' perform sacred rites ' (e.g., Euripides, τὰ δ' ἱερὰ νύκτωρ ἢ μεθ' ἡμέραν τελεῖς; ' dost thou perform the sacred rites by night or by day? '), τέλος (in the plural) ' divine services or offerings ' (e.g., Aischylos, δαίμοσιν θέλουσα θῦσαι πέλανον, ὧν τέλη τάδε ' desiring to sacrifice a mixture [of meal, honey, and oil] to daimons, whose offerings those are '), θεο-πολέω ' I minister in things divine ', θεο-πόλος ' priest ' (cf. Cicero, *hos deos et venerari et colere debemus* ' these gods we should both venerate and serve ', Latin *colō* also being a derivative of the base *q^uele-)*. This same base is found with the determinative -*s*-, though with a different semantic development, in Greek τέλσον 'turning-point' (of the plough at the end of a furrow) and in the Hesychian gloss τέλσας (accusative plural) 'turnings, ends'.

Taking all accessible evidence into account, impartially weighing all available material from every point of view, and considering all the interpretations and explanations previously advanced, we seem not unjustified, on the whole, as the author's former pupil, Mr. William B. S. Smith, first pointed out to him, in inferring that the Umbrian *pels-* may have meant something like 'make (ritually) perfect, consecrate', and in translating our passage **unu erietu sakre pelsanu fetu** by 'let him have a ram made (ritually) perfect (i.e., consecrated) (as) a sacrifice. It is quite possible that *pels-* may be a literal translation of the Greek τελέω, especially as Osco-Umbrian shows several instances of such translated loanwords (cf. pp. 135–136). The usual translation of *pels-* is 'bury', but, as we have seen, of the only two words cited as etymological cognates, the Latin *sepeliō* is scarcely akin, and the group of Gothic *filhan* means 'bury' only as 'hiding something in the ground'. Even after all this, we can regard our solution simply as that which seems most likely (or least unlikely) in the light of our present evidence, and as subject to modification or rejection if cogent arguments or additional data so require.

To make a scientific etymology, all the data, phonological, morphological, syntactic, and semantic, both for and against, must be weighed; and evidence must be sought from non-linguistic sources wherever possible. It is not enough merely to consult grammars and dictionaries, but the actual texts, wherever they exist, must be read in their original languages or dialects. Since grammars and dictionaries are not always infallible, and since scholars only too often quote blindly from their predecessors (sometimes with such excessive fidelity that they repeat the errors of those predecessors), and are not invariably correct in their statements and solutions, one should, after having examined every previous serious linguistic explanation strictly on its merits and without prejudice, take up the problem anew as though it had never been discussed before, and with fresh study of the original evidence.

It is absolutely essential, furthermore, to have a thorough knowledge of the bibliography of the subject, since without it the investigator runs the risk of mere reduplication of effort and useless rediscovery of what is already known. Some indication of the chief linguistic bibliographies and of the principal works both on linguistics in general and on individual language-groups and languages will be found in the chapters on the various language-families and on the history of linguistics. Many earlier studies, even though now more or less antiquated, contain material still of value; and some old theories, once discarded or ignored, possess elements whose worth and true implications, then unrealised, are only now beginning to receive the recognition which they have always deserved. A book or a theory is not necessarily worthless simply because it is old; nor is it inherently of value merely because it is new.

CHAPTER XI

Classification of Languages: The Indo-European Languages

Criteria of linguistic relationship — difficulties of classification — psychological, typical, and genealogical classifications of languages — isolating, juxtaposing, agglutinative, polysynthetic or incorporating, inflexional or synthetic, and analytic types as a basis of classification — genealogical classification — possible connexions of language-groups now regarded as unrelated — underlying principle of genealogical classification — the twenty-six language-groups of the world — the Indo-European group — its name and possible evolution — the original home of Indo-European; linguistic evidence from words for 'snow', for fauna and flora, and for 'copper' and 'iron' — the date of the end of Indo-European unity — dates of Chalcolithic, Copper, Bronze, and Iron Ages — earliest known homes and migrations of principal members of the Indo-European linguistic group — Indo-European home probably in Central Europe, and dispersal by 2500 B.C.; Indo-European migrations — *centum-* and *satem-* languages — the twelve divisions of Indo-European; bibliography — Indo-Iranian: general characteristics; difficulties of Avestan transcription; migrations; Indian and Iranian languages; bibliography — Tokharian — Hittite and Luian — Armenian — Thraco-Phrygian — Greek: general characteristics; nature of its records; dialect-groups; Tsaconian and other Modern Greek dialects; bibliography; Macedonian — Albanian — Illyrian: Venetic and Messapic — Italic: oldest records; Latin, Faliscan, etc.; Osco-Umbrian; Sabellian; Osco-Umbrian and Sabellian as contrasted with Latin and Faliscan; characteristics of Latin; Italo-Celtic affinities; Sicel, etc.; bibliography — Romance descendants of Italic; possible influence from other linguistic groups; special linguistic interest of Romance; Romance outside Europe; creolisations; bibliography — Celtic: *q*- and *p*-groups; Goidelic and Brythonic; Pictish; bibliography — Teutonic: East, North, and West Teutonic; Anglo-Saxon dialects and origin; Middle English and its dialects; Modern English; American English; creolised English; the three divisions of German; origin of Dutch and Modern literary German; characteristics of Teutonic; creolised Teutonic; problem of the origin of the Teutonic sound-shift; the Teutonic vocabulary; bibliography — Balto-Slavic: the Balto-Slavic languages; characteristics; bibliography.

THE relationships of languages are determined chiefly by regular correspondences between their phonology and morphology (cf.

pp. 74–75) and, in minor degree, by similarities in the arrangement of words in clauses and sentences, but only in small measure by similarities or identities in vocabulary. Languages showing such correspondences are said to be related, and the linguist is thus led to determine and delimit various language-groups. Some of these groups will be found to possess regular correspondences with certain other groups, the closeness or remoteness of such resemblance being, to all intents and purposes, constant, so rendering it possible to combine a larger or smaller number of such groups into a single major group termed a linguistic family, all members of which are considered to be related.

Certain other languages and groups of languages will be seen, on investigation, to show no such correlations with the group or groups already found to be related within itself or within themselves; their individual phonologies have no mutual relation that can be reduced to a system of regular correspondences (cf. pp. 76–77) with that group or with those groups; the methods of inflexion are totally unlike theirs, and are often based on entirely different and irreconcilable principles; they possess no words in common with other groups save such as may perhaps be due to borrowing on one side or the other, or may be drawn from a common third source (cf. pp. 130–137); and their rules for arranging words in sentence-groups may be wholly divergent. Such languages and language-groups we regard as unrelated with other languages and language-groups. So complicated may be the systems of correspondences, and so obscure the significant differences, that even the trained linguist may be at a loss to determine definitely whether a given language is related to a given other language, and, if so, in what degree; for a layman to express an opinion here does more credit to his daring than to his wisdom.

Dubieties as to linguistic relationship may arise from one or both of two factors. First, the material may be too scanty to admit of precise judgement. Many languages are known only from a few words recorded in a manner the reverse of accurate. Here belong, for instance, numerous glosses in Greek lexicographers, notably Hesychios (cf. p. 425), and foreign words quoted by Greek and Latin writers both in the Classical and in the mediaeval period, the problem here being further complicated by corruptions and attempted emendations of the transmitted text. Other languages are known only from scanty inscriptions or brief documents, often corrupted by ignorant stone-cutters or taken down by men with but an imperfect knowledge of the language in which they were endeavouring to write, as, for instance, the Venetic and Messapian inscriptions, or the Old Prussian translations of two versions of a *Catechism* of 1545 and of Luther's *Short Catechism (Enchiridion)* (cf. pp. 332, 353). Or a language may be known only from a few coins and from words preserved in names of persons, places, rivers, mountains, and the like, as in the case of Iberian (cf. p. 377) ; or its former existence may be inferable solely from the presence, in the vocabulary of a given language, of words clearly borrowed by that language from some unknown source, as in the ' Alpine ' words surviving in some Romance dialects (cf. p. 128) ; and some languages are still undeciphered, such as Etruscan, whose alphabet we can read with ease, but whose meaning is, for the most part, unknown (cf. pp. 383–384).

The host of languages which have vanished is incalculable. Of a vast number we have lost even the names and the nature, as of the languages spoken throughout Europe before the invasions of peoples speaking the tongues we call Indo-European, their traces apparently surviving only in place-names (cf. pp. 121–123) and perhaps in words borrowed and naturalised (cf. pp. 130–132, 133–136) by in-comers. Some have died out within the historic period, such as Old Prussian, which was still known by at least one old man as late as 1677; or Cornish, which lingered on in the mouths of a very few till late in the eighteenth century, or perhaps even into the early nineteenth (cf. p. 341) ; or Dalmatian, whose last speaker, Antonio Udina, was killed by an explosion in a mine in 1898; or the Beothuk of Newfoundland, which was very inadequately recorded in 1829 (cf. p. 32). We may even witness languages dying before our eyes, particularly in the case of North American Indian tongues, some of which have disappeared within recent years, while others are now spoken only by the merest handful, yielding place to the vernaculars of their more powerful neighbours.

The second great barrier to a fully accurate classification of languages lies in the very uneven distribution of our knowledge of their history. Our oldest documents are in Sumerian, from about 4000 B.C.; next comes Egyptian, about half a millennium later; the Semitic group is known from about 2800 B.C.; Chinese from the first half of the second millennium B.C.; and Indo-European from, perhaps, 2000 or 1850 B.C. (cf. pp. 378, 365, 360, 391, 323). All the rest are much later: Dravidian possibly from the fifth century of our era, and South Caucasian (Georgian) certainly from that century; Tibeto-Burman from the ninth; Turkic from the eighth; and Uralic from the thirteenth (cf. pp. 386–387, 375, 392, 371, 368). Leaving out of account languages more or less isolated, though of fairly old literary record, such as Japanese (cf. p. 373), a number of groups, e.g., Australian, Malayo-Polynesian, African, and American Indian, have been reduced to writing only within the last few centuries, so that their history is practically unknown.

Within the groups, the distribution is equally irregular. Thus, in Indo-European, linguistically the best studied, the situation is as follows for its principal members: Indo-Iranian from between 2000 and 1500 B.C. (dates only estimated); Hittite from about 1850 B.C.; Greek from about 800 B.C.; Italic from the seventh century B.C.; Teutonic from the third century A.D. (excluding words cited by Classical authors and those borrowed by Finnish); Armenian from the fifth; Tokharian from the seventh; Celtic from the eighth (exclusive of Gaulish fragments and Ogam inscriptions); Slavic from the ninth; Albanian from the fifteenth; and Baltic from the sixteenth (cf. pp. 314, 323, 327, 332–333, 345, 325, 322, 341, 355, 331, 353). In Semitic, we have Akkadian from about 2800 B.C.; Hebrew from the second millennium B.C.; Rās Shamrah from at least the fourteenth century B.C.; Phoenician from the thirteenth; Old West Aramaic and South Arabic from the eighth; Old East Aramaic from the seventh; Biblical and Egyptian (Elephantine) Aramaic from the fifth; North Arabic from the second or first; Syriac and Samaritan from the third century A.D.; Classical Arabic from A.D. 328; and Ethiopic from the fourth century A.D. (cf. pp. 360–364).

It thus becomes obvious that if, say, Indo-Iranian and Greek be akin to Albanian and Baltic, the latter pair recorded only some three millennia after the first records of the former, a vast amount of evolution must have taken place during so long a period, particularly when we remember that internal linguistic factors were by no means the sole influences at work, but that events of military, economic, religious, and political nature, and the like, were also operative. There is little cause for wonder that linguistic affinities are often thickly veiled. Armenian, because of its mass of words borrowed from Iranian, was long supposed to be an Indo-

Iranian dialect (cf. pp. 127, 320, 324, 439); the precise source from which Albanian is derived is still not absolutely settled (cf. p. 331); and Hittite has formed a subject for sharp debate ever since its discovery, some holding that it is a sort of cousin to Indo-European, and not a full member of that group, so that we should speak, not of Indo-European, but of Indo-Hittite (cf. p. 323). Despite all these dubieties in detail, the main principles may be regarded as established: there are certain groups of languages which are, to all intents and purposes, surely akin; and we are justified in speaking of linguistic families.

Classifications of the languages of the world have been essayed in various ways, especially psychological, typical, and genealogical. While it is of interest to find that language conforms to the general rule that under similar conditions (e.g., approximately the same general level of civilisation) man shows similar modes of expression in areas widely distant, the psychological system of classification appears to afford no evidence of actual kinship between languages psychologically similar; it seems merely to indicate resemblances independently evolved in regions far apart, supposing that these similarities are as real as they appear to be, an hypothesis which may not invariably be assumed without more profound knowledge of the languages concerned than we now possess.

The second proposed method of classification, that according to outward linguistic type, has enjoyed long popularity, and at first glance seems to afford a good basis for grouping languages. The conventional division here is into isolating, juxtaposing, agglutinative, polysynthetic (or incorporating), inflexional (or amalgamating, synthetic), and analytic, the inflexional type sometimes being termed formal, and all the others formless.

The classical example of an *isolating* language is Chinese, which has, properly speaking, no distinction between verb, noun, adjective, or any other part of speech, so that the same combination of phonemes may signify, for instance, ' great, greatness, greatly, grow, be great ', etc., according to its position in the sentence. On the other hand, in view of our almost complete ignorance of the history of the Chinese language, we cannot be sure whether this condition represents an early linguistic stage, or the result of a long evolution (cf. pp. 151–152, 390).

Juxtaposing languages are defined as those which indicate accessory concepts or grammatical relations by prefixing certain elements ('classifiers', apparently corresponding roughly to Indo-European determinatives; cf. pp. 156–159) to the word denoting the main concept, a notable example being the African Bantu, this name itself, meaning 'men', being formed by the personal classifier *ba* prefixed to the word *ntu* 'man' or 'men' (cf. p. 404).

Agglutinative languages are held to be marked by agglutination into a single word of various elements, each with a fixed connotation, each preserving its own individuality, and each mechanically added to or separated from the complex used as a word. The stock illustration of this type is regarded as Turkish. Here, for instance, *sev* means 'love' in its pure base-sense (cf. p. 150), but *sev-mek*, 'to love'; *sev-er*, 'lover, he loves' ('[is] a lover'); *sev-er-im*, 'I love' ('I [am] a lover'); *sev-me-mek*, 'not to love'; *sev-dir-mek* 'to cause to love'; *sev-ish-mek*, 'to love each other'; *sev-ish-dir-mek*, 'to cause to love each other'; *sev-in-mek*, 'to love one's self, to rejoice'; *sev-in-dir-mek*, 'to cause to rejoice'; *sev-il-mek*, 'to be loved'; *sev-il-dir-mek*, 'to be caused to be loved', etc., through some thirty-six types. Similarly, in Turkish declension, we have *ev* 'house', *ev-ler* 'houses', *ev-den* 'from a house', *ev-ler-den* 'from houses', etc. (cf. p. 370).

Polysynthetic (or *incorporating*) languages are considered those which make the sentence co-extensive with the word, subject, object, verb, etc., being combined into a single unit, no member of which has a separate existence, e.g., Eskimo *takusar-iartor-uma-galuar-nerp-â* 'do you think he really intends to go to look after it?' (literally, 'he busies himself with that + he goes to + he intends to + he does so + but + do you think he' + third personal interrogative) or Oneida *g-nagla'-sl-i-zak-s* 'I search for a village' (literally, 'I + live' + abstract noun + verbal characteristic + 'search' + continuative particle); but in this last example, for instance, one cannot say *g-zak* 'I search' — one must search for something; nor can one say merely *sl* 'village' — something must be done to the village, happen in it, etc.

The *inflexional* (or *amalgamating, synthetic*) type is regarded as distinguished from the agglutinative in that the components making up the inflexion of nouns, verbs, etc., while originally independent, have now become so amalgamated with the stem-forms that they can no longer be separated mechanically from the complex constituting a word. To this type the Indo-European and

Semitic languages are held to belong, e.g., Sanskrit *ás-mi* ' I am ', Armenian *e-m*, Greek εἰ-μί, Latin *su-m*, Old Irish *a-m*, Gothic *i-m*, English *a-m*, Lithuanian *es-mì*, Old Church Slavic *jes-mĭ;* Arabic *ya-qtubu, 'a-qtubu, ya-qtubū-na, na-qtubu* ' he, I, they, we will write '. When, in the course of development of a language, *deflexion* (loss of inflexion; cf. pp. 155, 237) takes place, with substitution of prepositions, auxiliary verbs, etc. (cf. p. 155), as in French and English *au père, to the father,* or *j'ai fait, I have done,* as contrasted with Latin *patrī, fēcī,* the language in question is supposed to change its type from synthetic to *analytic.*

These schemes of classification break down when scrutinised at all closely. Of the ' isolating ' languages we know too little to express any definite opinion; the ' juxtaposing ' and ' polysynthetic ' groups are too rare and scattered to afford a basis for judgement; and there are no real lines of demarcation between the ' agglutinative ', ' synthetic ', and ' analytic ' types. The same language may show more than one of these supposed types. Thus, all Indo-European languages are regarded as synthetic (i.e., as inflexional), but in French and English one finds the analytic *j'ai fait, I have done,* beside the synthetic *je fais, je fis, I do, I did;* in Classical Armenian, the agglutinative *ban-kʿ* ' words ', *baniw-kʿ* ' with words ' beside the synthetic singulars *ban, baniw* (cf. *berem-kʿ* ' we bear ' beside *berem* ' I bear '), and in Modern West Armenian, the agglutinative *pan-er* ' words ', *pan-er-ov* ' with words ' (Classical Armenian *ban-kʿ, baniw-kʿ)* beside the synthetic singulars *pan, panov;* and in Old Irish the incorporating *no-m-berar* ' one carries me, I am carried ' beside the synthetic *berar* ' one carries ' (cf. p. 219).

The only system of classification of languages which seems possible is none of these, but the *genealogical,* founded on the genetic and historical connexion between languages as determined by phonological and morphological correspondences, with confirmation, wherever possible, from history, archaeology, and kindred sciences. We may, therefore, adopt, as less exposed to serious objection than any other view thus far advanced, Meillet's definition of language-groups: ' Two languages are termed related when they both result from two different evolutions from a single language previously spoken '. Consideration of geography, which must constantly be borne in mind, will show that related languages are usually contiguous. When this is not the case, as when Romance

Rumanian is far separated from its cognates, French, Italian, Spanish, and Portuguese, or when Uralic Hungarian is at a great distance from any of its kin, or when Celtic is found in Galatia in Asia Minor, or when Indo-European languages are seen to be ousting American Indian, we must look for the reason in historic migrations, conquests, and the like.

In theory, it is by no means impossible that great language-groups of the world now regarded as unconnected (Indo-European, Hamito-Semitic, Uralic, etc.) may yet be found to be genealogically related. Affinities of Indo-European with Hamito-Semitic, and even with Uralic, have been argued with much skill (cf. pp. 366–367, 369). The great Bantu group of Africa has been connected with Egyptian, and thus with Hamito-Semitic (pp. 366–367, 406). The Muṇḍā group in India is, it has been argued, akin to certain languages of Farther India and the Nicobars (the so-called South-East Asiatic family; cf. pp. 392–393); and these have been linked to the Malayo-Polynesian family under the common name of Austric (cf. pp. 392–393, 399); while, on the other hand, the Muṇḍā languages have been separated from them all, and have been connected with the Uralic group (cf. pp. 369, 393). The kinship of Basque with South Caucasian, and perhaps with a vanished Mediterranean family, whose partial reconstruction seems not wholly impossible, has been strongly urged (cf. pp. 375–376, 378–379). In such problems it seems most prudent to hold that no genetic relationship has yet been demonstrated, and to maintain an attitude of reserve without denying the possibility of such kinship.

If we find that in a certain group of languages ‘ he has killed ’ is represented by qǝṭal (Aramaic), qāṭal (Hebrew), qatala (Arabic and Ethiopic), and ‘ he will kill ’ by yiqṭul, yiqṭōl, yaqtulu, and yeqatel respectively, and if we also find similar correspondences throughout the verb, noun, and pronoun, besides regular correspondences of sounds between these languages, we are amply justified in considering them cognate. If, however, we find that in another group ‘ he beat ’ is avan aḍittān (Tamil), avan aḍichchu (Malayalam), and that ‘ he will beat ’ is avan aḍippān, avan aḍikkum; and in yet another that ‘ he carries ’ is bhárati (Sanskrit), bara'ti (Avestan), berē (Armenian), φέρει (Greek), fert (Latin), berid (Old Irish), bairiþ (Gothic), birit (Old High German), bereti (Old Russian), we may fairly assume that we here have two groups cognate within themselves, but unrelated to each other, always provided that the correspondences in question are observed to occur with regularity.

In this manner one reaches a classification of languages according to the twenty-six following genealogical groups: Indo-European, Hamito-Semitic, Uralic or Finno-Ugric, Altaic, Japanese and Korean, Eskimo-Aleut, Caucasian, Ibero-Basque, Near-Eastern and Asianic, Hyperborean or Palaeo-Asiatic, Burushaskī, Dravidian, Andamanese, Sino-Tibetan, La-Ti, South-East Asiatic or Austroasiatic, Malayo-Polynesian or Austronesian, Papuan, Australian, Tasmanian, Sudano-Guinean, Bantu, Hottentot-Bushman or Khoiń, North American, Mexican and Central American, and Antillean and South American. Certain of these groups are purely geographical, notably Australian and American, both of which include many different linguistic families whose precise inter-relation is still far from clear.

INDO-EUROPEAN

This group, which, through special circumstances, has given the model and the method for the linguistic investigation of all others (cf. p. 459), has been called by several names. It has been termed Aryan, though this epithet is more accurately restricted to the Aryans proper, the Indo-Iranians dwelling in northern India and in the Iranian Plateau. A more common term is Indo-Germanic, because of the fact that members of the family are spoken from the northern half of the Indian Peninsula to Iceland. This name, based on the linguistic groups at the two extremes of its area, seems less good than one implying almost the entire geographical region in which the languages concerned have been or are spoken; and it accordingly appears wisest to adopt the French designation Indo-European. No term hitherto proposed is wholly exact, and all exclude Tokharian, once spoken in Chinese Turkistān; but since a perfectly accurate designation can scarcely be devised without being too cumbrous, we may hold to Indo-European as being the least objectionable thus far proposed.

The evolution of Indo-European (and, *mutatis mutandis*, of the other language-groups) would seem to have been somewhat as follows. A certain nucleus of individuals whom we may conventionally call Indo-Europeans, without implying that they had the racial or geographical affinities which this term might suggest, developed a form of speech which may be designated as hypothetical Proto-Indo-European. This language evolved dialects (cf. pp. 24–30), from which were selected, for political or for other reasons, the languages actually found in history, such as Vedic Sanskrit, Armenian, Greek, etc. These languages themselves possessed dialects, as is shown by traces in Vedic itself, to say nothing of the various historic Greek dialects, and of Oscan, Umbrian, etc., beside Latin. Gradually the dialects disappeared, except for scattered traces in individual sounds or words, before the dominance of the languages (or standard dialects); but, in their turn, the languages again gave rise to dialects of greater or less extent and importance, some one of which, for one reason or another, might rise to the dignity of a language, and might even acquire such prestige as to be spoken far outside its original borders.

This process we have traced (p. 29) in the case of Greek; and in Italic it is perhaps even more detailed. Here we can observe how Proto-Italic (cf. pp. 332–339) had already been broken up, before our earliest historic records, into Oscan, Umbrian, Faliscan, Paelignian, Marrucinian, Volscian, Sabine, Latin, etc.; how Latin gained supremacy over all the rest; how it absorbed elements from them as well as from Etruscan and, later, from Greek, Gaulish, etc.; how it passed through a series of changes from the archaic period to the close of the Empire; how its old models, despite every effort, were compelled to yield to a Latinity which became ever more and more popular. This Latin we see transformed into Romance languages, each influenced by earlier tongues into whose areas Latin had entered — Celtic in Gaul, Iberian or Celto-Iberian in the Iberian Peninsula, Ligurian in northern Italy, Thracian (or perhaps Illyrian) in Rumania, etc. In each of these areas we find many dialects which, though often surviving to-day, have given place to standard dialects which for some reason have become supreme — the dialect of Paris and the Île de France in France, of Castile in Spain, of Tuscany in Italy, etc. Finally, we perceive how the local dialects tend to disappear through the influence of commerce, common systems of instruction in the schools, military conscription, etc., and, sometimes, through deliberate intention on the part of the authorities of State.

The *original home* of Proto-Indo-European is a problem on which no agreement has yet been reached. The earliest investigators were quite certain that it was in Asia, the continent which was the source of the oldest civilisation, the traditional site of the Garden of Eden, and where Sanskrit was spoken. Later, the consensus of opinion shifted to Europe. The home has been localised in a narrow strip from France across Central Europe and the Kirghiz Steppes to the Iranian Plateau; in the wide steppes of South Russia north of the Black Sea between the Volga and the mouth of the Danube; along the Baltic; in Lower Saxony, i.e., the area between the frontier of Holland and the Oder, and between southern Scandinavia and Thuringia; and on the northern slopes of the Caucasus.

So far as linguistics is concerned in approaching this problem, we can reckon only with cognate words for definite things (particularly, in the nature of the case, for trees, animals, metals, and phenomena of nature) found in the principal Indo-European language-groups, especially in those widely separated, and, specifically, in those at the extreme east and the extreme west of the area now occupied by those groups, Indo-Iranian and Italo-Celtic respectively (cf. p. 453). This principle would appear to be obvious; but, as semantics shows (Chapter IX), words may change their meanings either by extension or by specialisation (as in the American use of *corn* for *maize*, the proper meaning of the former, still so used in British English, being ' grain ' in general, and then, in particular, the special grain of a country) ; or may be replaced by others in consequence of metonymy or of linguistic tabu (as in English *bear*, properly ' the brown one ', Russian *mĕdvĕdĭ* ' honey-eater '; cf. pp. 249–250). These possibilities considerably restrict the number of terms which give cogent proof; and we must be on our guard against the ' argument from silence ' — the absence of a common Indo-European word does not necessarily mean that the object which would have been denoted by it did not actually exist (cf. p. 99).

When we have made all such allowances, we find, from purely linguistic evidence, that the Indo-European home knew of *snow* (Avestan *snaēž-*, Greek νίφα [accusative], Latin *niv-* [nominative *nix*], Old Irish *snechta*, Gothic *snaiws*, Lithuanian *sniēgas*, Old Church Slavic *snĕgŭ;* Sanskrit *himá-* ' cold, frost, snow ' is connected with a group meaning ' winter ': Greek χεῖμα, Latin *hiems*, Lithuanian *žiemà*, Old Church Slavic *zima*, or ' snow ': Armenian *jiwn*, Greek χιών).

Of *trees,* the home must have had the *birch* (Sanskrit *bhūrja-,*

Ossetic *bärz*, Dacian place-name *Bersovia*, Latin *fraxinus* [here meaning ' ash '], Old High German *bircha*, Modern German *Birke*, Anglo-Saxon *birce*, English *birch*, Lithuanian *béržas*, Russian *berëza)*; the *willow* (Avestan *vaētay-*, Greek ἰτέα, Latin *vītis* [here meaning ' vine '], Old High German *wîda*, Modern German *Weide*, Lithuanian *výtis)*; and, probably, the *pine* (Sanskrit *pīta-dāru-* [recorded only by native lexicographers], Greek πίτυς, Albanian *pishë*, Latin *pīnus)*.

Of *animals*, the most important, from our present point of view, were the *horse* (Sanskrit *ásva-*, Tokharian *yakwe*, *yuk*, Greek ἵππος, Venetic *ecu-peθaris* ' charioteer ', Latin *equus*, Old Irish *ech*, Anglo-Saxon *eoh*, Lithuanian *ašvà* ' mare ') ; the *bear* (Sanskrit *ŕkṣa-*, Avestan *arəša-*, Armenian *arĵ*, Greek ἄρκτος, Albanian *arí*, Latin *ursus*, Middle Irish *art)*; the *hare* (Sanskrit *śaśá-*, Afghān *sōya*, *sōe*, Welsh *ceinach*, Old High German *haso*, English *hare*, Old Prussian *sasins)*; and the *wolf* (Sanskrit *vŕka-*, Avestan *vəhrka-*, Armenian *gayl*, Greek λύκος, Latin *lupus*, Gothic *wulfs*, English *wolf*, Lithuanian *vil̃kas*, Old Church Slavic *vlŭkŭ)*. It is significant, on the other hand, that there is no common Indo-European word for ' sea '.

As regards *metals*, the Indo-Europeans knew of gold and silver; but the only terms from which any deductions of prehistoric value can be drawn are those for *copper* and *iron*, **aios-* and **roudho-*, the meanings of both words shifting between ' copper ', ' iron ', and ' ore '. Of the derivatives from **aios-*, Sanskrit *áyas-*, Avestan *ayah-*, Gaulish *īsarno-*, Middle Irish *iarn* (?), Gothic *eisarn*, Old High German *îsarn*, *îsan*, Modern German *Eisen*, Anglo-Saxon *îren*, and English *iron* (?) mean ' iron '; Latin *aes*, Gothic *aiz*, Old High German *êr*, Anglo-Saxon *ár*, and Old Icelandic *eir* mean ' copper '; the third signification is represented in this group only by English *ore*. As regards the derivatives from **roudho-*, Sanskrit *lohá-*, Middle Persian *rōd*, and Latin *raudus* (?) signify ' copper ' (the Sanskrit word later denotes ' iron ' as well) ; Old Icelandic *rauði* means ' haematite '; and Old Church Slavic *ruda*, ' metal '.

The base-meaning of **roudho-* seems to have been ' red ', so that the metal designated by it would appear to have been ' copper '; the original connotation of **aios-* is quite unknown, but may possibly have been ' ore ', in which case archaeological evidence suggests that it was especially ' copper ore '. Whether the group represented by English *iron* belongs here is problematical; it seems to have been borrowed from the Celtic group of Gaulish *īsarno-*, which it is difficult to derive from *aios-;* and Latin *raudus* is best explained as borrowed from Celtic **roudo-* ' red ' (cf. Old Irish *rúad).* On the other hand, **roudho-* has been interpreted as borrowed from Sumerian *urud* ' copper ' (Basque has *urraida),* and **aios-* as taken from *Ayasya,* a name appearing in Egyptian texts for the island of Cyprus or for some place on the mainland (cf. Latin *cuprum,* English *copper,* from Greek Κύπρος ' Cyprus '). Neither of these derivations from non-Indo-European sources has yet been established scientifically. In their favour may be alleged the archaeological evidence that copper and iron are known in the Orient earlier than in the Occident; against this may be the possibility that both metals were discovered independently in Asia and in Europe. On the whole it seems most prudent, in our present stage of knowledge, to consider the problem as yet unsolved. For ' bronze ', ' brass ', and ' tin ', no Indo-European terms have thus far been found.

With the evidence at our disposal, it seems safe to infer that Indo-European unity came to an end after copper had become known, but before the Bronze Age, i.e., during the Chalcolithic (Copper-Stone) Age; and since the use of bronze was established in Europe by 1700 B.C., Indo-Europeans must have begun to migrate in various directions from their original home previous to that date. Copper itself had become known in Egypt by the fifth millennium B.C., in Cyprus by the beginning of the fourth, in the Danube area by at least 2600, and in Italy by 2500, but in South Russia perhaps not before the ninth century B.C. *It would seem, on the whole, that the unity must have ceased sometime in the third millennium* B.C.

In discussing archaeological ages, one must bear in mind that all dates are more or less approximate, and often vary widely in the estimates of equally qualified authorities. With these reservations, the following dates may be given: *Chalcolithic* — Egypt, early predynastic (?) ; Susa, 4500 (?) ; Panjāb, before 3000 (?) ; Eastern Anatolia, around 2900; Thessaly, 2800; Troy, 2500–2000; Catalonia, 2000; Danubian area, 1600. *Copper* — Egypt, 4000 (?) ; Cyprus, 3000; Danubian, 2600; Italy, 2500; Russia, ninth century B.C. (?). *Bronze* — Egypt, 3000–2800; Mesopotamia, before 3000; Anau (in Turkistān), before 2200; Cyprus, 2200; Thessaly, Bohemia, and Britain, 2000; North Italy, Catalonia, and France,

1600; South Scandinavia and Denmark, 1600–1400; Troy, 1200; South Russia, ninth to seventh century B.C. *Iron* — Anatolia, 1300–1200; Egypt, 1250; Crete, Aegean area, and Thessaly 1200–1100; Syria, Palestine, and Mesopotamia, 1100; Italy, 1000; Central Europe and France, 900; Britain, 500–450 B.C.

Further light on this complicated problem may possibly be gained from what we know or may reasonably infer regarding the earliest habitats of the principal members of the Indo-European group of which we have any archaeological or linguistic evidence, even though by that time considerable migrations had clearly taken place. The first home of the *Teutons* of which we possess any such evidence seems to have been in Denmark, southern Scandinavia, and along the German coast between the Elbe and the Oder. The *Celts* were already divided into Goidels, Belgae, and Brythons: the first on the seaboard between the Rhine and the Oder; the second in the valley of the middle Rhine and along its right bank to the Main; the third in southern Germany. The *Italic* peoples were somewhere on the middle Danube, perhaps in Bohemia, Moravia, and western Hungary, and had, like the Celts, already become divided into the *q-* and the *p-* speakers (Goidels and Belgae-Brythons in the one case, and Latins and Osco-Umbrians in the other; cf. pp. 335, 340). The *Illyrians* (later represented by the Venetic and Messapic peoples) were perhaps likewise in this general region; while the *Greeks*, in two divisions subsequently to become Achaeans and Dorians, were apparently in the South Balkan area.

From Central Europe also came, it would appear, the *Hittites* and perhaps the *Tokharians*. The former of these had migrated to the centre of Asia Minor by the second millennium B.C.; the latter, though not known in history until the seventh century A.D., would seem, from their habitat in Turkistān, to have journeyed there, probably from Europe, and by a very circuitous route through China, at a still earlier period than the Hittites. The basis for these inferences is the fact that both Hittite and Tokharian are *centum*-languages (cf. pp. 310–311); and the retention of an original guttural, instead of changing it to a sibilant, as in the *satem*-group, would seem to imply an older stage than the families characterised by an *s* developed from a *k̂*.

Of the *satem*-group, the northernmost division was the *Baltic*, occupying roughly the area of eastern East Prussia and Lithuania.

South of them were the *Slavs* in what is now eastern Poland, the south of White Russia (with the middle course of the Beresina and the courses of the Sozh and Isput), and the north of Little Russia (Podolia, Volhynia, and the district of Kiev). Then came the *Albanians* in the area north of the Carpathians, whence they migrated to their present home on the eastern coast of the Adriatic. Somewhere in this same Carpathian region must have been the *Phrygians,* who established a kingdom in western Asia Minor about 1100 B.C.; and the *Armenians,* who, later crossing to Asia Minor, arrived in the region of Lake Van towards 600 B.C.

To the east of these *satem*-peoples was yet another division, the *Indo-Iranians,* whose line of migration is far from certain, whether they came to Mesopotamia and Iran across the Caucasus or, by a longer but less difficult route, round the north of the Caspian Sea. In any event, we find Indian (not Iranian) proper names among the Kassites, who had established a dynasty at Babylon about 1760 B.C. (cf. p. 380), and also in a Mitanni-Hittite treaty of 1360 B.C., while other Mitannian documents of about this latter date (cf. p. 380) contain a few Indian epithetologues (e.g., *aika* ' one ', *satta* ' seven '; cf. Sanskrit *éka-, saptá-* [Prākrit *satta-*] as contrasted with Avestan *aēva, hapta-).*

The main body of Indians, however, pressed on, probably through eastern Afghānistān, into the Pañjāb, which they must have reached some centuries before 2000 or 1500 B.C., the dates conventionally assigned to the earliest portions of the Rigveda. They were, it would seem, driven on by a wave or waves of Iranians, who came to dominate the entire Iranian Plateau (Īrān, Balōčistān, and Afghānistān), and whose later linguistic stage, as contrasted with Indian, is shown by their change of Indo-European *s* to *h* (e.g., Avestan and Old Persian *had-* ' sit ' : Sanskrit *sad-,* Latin *sedeo,* English *sit).* The first certain mention of Iranians is in 835 B.C., when an inscription of Salmanassar III speaks of Medes in the region of Lake Urmī, while about a century later Hakhāmaniš (Achaimenes) founded the Persian Empire. Finally, towards the end of the eighth century B.C., there was a reflux of Iranians (Scythians, Sauromatians, and Sarmatians [the latter two identical?]) westward into southern Russia as far as the Don.

The migrations here outlined may be represented very roughly by the diagram on the following page, which is anything but exactly geographical.

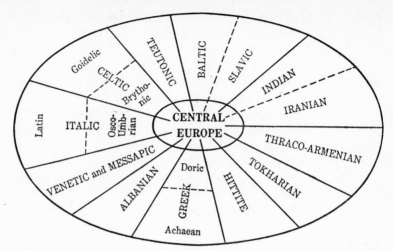

FIG. 9. Hypothetical Contiguity of Languages in Central Europe just after the End of Indo-European Unity.

On the whole, we seem to have reason to suppose that *the Indo-European home was somewhere in Central Europe, and that the division of the Indo-European linguistic family into the groups found in historic times had taken place at least as early as 2500* B.C. About 2000 B.C., when the Hittites had already reached Asia Minor, the Indo-Iranians began to enter the Iranian Plateau, and the Goidels, already separated from the Brythons, made the first Celtic invasion of Britain, though the Brythons did not follow them until the sixth century; the Belgae arrived there only in the middle of the second century B.C., and the Goidels seem to have begun to colonise Ireland about the seventeenth century B.C. Around 1500 the Achaeans appear to have invaded Greece, and the Latins Italy; about 1200 came the Dorian invasion of Greece, with the Umbrian invasion of Italy a couple of centuries later. In the centuries immediately preceding the Christian Era, the first Teutonic sound-shifting seems to have taken place, the second evolving between that time and our first written documents in Old High German in the eighth century A.D. (cf. p. 82).

Indo-European languages are conventionally divided into two groups according as the Proto-Indo-European guttural $\hat{k}$ is represented by a guttural or by a sibilant; and these are termed *centum*- and *satem*-languages respectively from the Latin and Avestan words for ' hundred '. The first division comprises, of the great groups, Greek, Italic, Celtic, and Teutonic in the west, with Tokharian and Hittite in the east; the second, Indo-Iranian, Armenian, Albanian, and Balto-Slavic (cf., for the *centum*-group, Greek ἑ-κατόν, Latin *centum*, Old Irish *cét*, Gothic *hund*, English *hund-red*, Kuchaean *ḵant*[*e*]; for Hittite, cf. *kita* ' lies ' : Sanskrit *śéte;* and for the *satem*-group, cf. Sanskrit *śatám*, Avestan *satəm*, Lithuanian *šiṁtas;* for Armenian, cf. *asełn* ' needle ' : Latin *acus;* for Albanian, *vis* ' place ' : Latin *vīcus* ' village '; and for Old Church Slavic, *desętĭ* ' ten ' : Latin *decem)*.

This classification is very convenient, but it is doubtful whether it should be taken too seriously; after all, it is only one, though a very important one, of many isoglots (cf. pp. 25–26). If we consider it rigidly, it might be supposed that the Tokharians and Hittites migrated from the west, and the Albanians and Balto-Slavs from the east (we have reason to believe that the Armenians did so). On the other hand, it is equally possible that Tokharian and Hittite, like the western group, simply preserved the old guttural, whereas the eastern division palatalised it into a sibilant.

The evidence at our disposal appears to show quite conclusively that the Indo-European group once had more languages than is now the case. We have scanty remains of some, such as Old Sakian, Old Sarmatian, Phrygian, Thracian, Illyrian, Vandal, Burgundian, Old Low Franconian, and Lombard (cf. pp. 320, 326, 332, 345, 346, 349); and if these have well-nigh vanished, we may justifiably suppose that others have disappeared without leaving a trace behind. The language-groups of this linguistic family of which we have actual remains, sometimes most abundant and distributed over many centuries, sometimes lamentably fragmentary and represented only for a brief period, may be regarded at present as some twelve in number: Indo-Iranian, Tokharian, Hittite, Armenian, Thraco-Phrygian, Greek, Albanian, Illyrian, Italic, Celtic, Teutonic, and Balto-Slavic, this sequence being in no wise genetic or historical, but based merely on a rough geographical order running (except for Tokharian, which lies far to the east of any of the others) from east to west, to north, and to east.

For the linguist, the most important of these are Indo-Iranian, Greek, and Lithuanian for morphology; Indo-Iranian for consonantism; and Greek for vocalism, for which Oscan and Lithuanian are also of much value. Next come Teutonic and Slavic; Italic and Celtic represent interesting combinations of extremely archaic features with most intricate and difficult special evolutions (Celtic is easily the hardest and most obscure of all the Indo-European family); Hittite and, to an even greater degree, Tokharian are still in the early stages of study; Armenian and Albanian are less vital for the general Indo-Europeanist; and the remains of Thraco-Phrygian and Illyrian are too meagre for any but highly specialised researches.

The best studies of Indo-European as a whole are K. Brugmann's *Grundriss der vergleichenden Grammatik der indogermanischen Sprachen* (second edition, two volumes in seven parts, Strassburg, 1897–1916), with an abridged *Kurze vergleichende Grammatik der indogermanischen Sprachen* (Strassburg, 1904; French translation by J. Bloch, A. Cuny, and A. Ernout, *Abrégé de grammaire comparée des langues indo-européennes*, Paris, 1908), and A. Meillet's *Introduction à l'étude comparative des langues indo-européennes* (seventh edition, Paris, 1934). H. Hirt's *Indogermanische Grammatik* (seven volumes, Heidelberg, 1921–37) is very stimulating, but should be used with caution. The one modern etymological dictionary of the group is A. Walde's *Etymologisches Wörterbuch der indogermanischen Sprachen* (edited by J. Pokorny, three volumes, Berlin and Leipzig, 1930–32); and much of value may be found in O. Schrader's *Reallexikon der indogermanischen Altertumskunde* (second edition by A. Nehring, two volumes, Berlin and Leipzig, 1917–29) and in such works as H. Hirt's *Die Indogermanen* (two volumes, Strassburg, 1905–07) and S. Feist's *Kultur, Ausbreitung und Herkunft der Indogermanen* (Berlin, 1913).

Indo-Iranian

The Indo-Iranian group of the Indo-European family is by all odds the oldest for which we have documentary evidence; and in their earliest known periods Indian and Iranian are so similar that much may readily be translated mechanically from the one to the other. The main distinctions are as follows: Sanskrit *s* = Iranian *h;* in Iranian, plosives become fricatives before most other consonants while aspirated voiced sounds are deaspirated initially and become fricatives intervocalically (e.g., Sanskrit *saptá* ' seven ' : Avestan *hapta;* Sanskrit *krátu* ' plan ' : Avestan *xratav-;* Sanskrit *bhávati* ' becomes ' : Avestan *bavaᵗti;* Sanskrit *aghá-* ' bad ' : Avestan *aγa-).* Both branches are characterised by a rich morphological development equalled only by Greek and (for the epithetologue) by Baltic-Slavic, though after the Vedic period Sanskrit verbal inflexion became relatively scanty. The consonantism (especially in Sanskrit) is, on the whole, much more representative of Indo-European conditions than that of any other member of that linguistic family; but the vocalism is decidedly meagre, having only *ă*, *ĭ*, and *ŭ*, the coalescence of Indo-European *a*, *e*, and *o* into Indo-Iranian *a* being a phenomenon which caused much error in the earlier Indo-European linguistics (cf. pp. 439–440, 442–443); and the Indo-European diphthongs *ai*, *ei*, *oi*, *əi*, and *au*, *eu*, *ou*, *əu* are represented in Sanskrit by *e* and *o* respectively, in Old Persian by *ai* and *au*, and in Avestan by *aē* and *aō*.

It is true that *e* and *o* appear as vowels in Avestan, but as new developments, not as representatives of Indo-European *e* and *o* (e.g., Avestan *yeze* 'I honour' : Sanskrit *yájāmi* 'I sacrifice', Greek ἅζομαι for *ἰαγ-ἰο-μαι 'I stand in awe of '; Avestan *vohu-* 'good ' : Sanskrit *vásu-*, Greek ἐΰς for *ϝεσύς, where Indo-Iranian [a] is palatalised to [e] after [j] and labialised to [o] after [v] respectively; cf. also Avestan *yasnəm* ' sacrifice ' : Vedic *yajñám*, where a shift of accent, such as occurred also in Classical Sanskrit *'yajñam* [cf. p. 315], evidently dulled *a* to *ə*). The present Avestan script shows infection-vowels analogous to those in Irish or to the Teutonic umlaut (cf. pp. 69, 349; e.g., Avestan *bavaⁱti* ' becomes ' : Sanskrit *bhávati*; Avestan *haᵘrva-* ' whole ' : Sanskrit *sárva-*; cf. Old Irish *fer* ' man ' : *fir* ' of a man ' : *fiur* ' to a man ' = Latin *vir* [for *ụiros*], *virī*, *virō*; German *Gast* ' guest ' : plural *Gäste* = Old High German *gast* : *gesti* = Gothic *gasts* : *gasteis* [gasti:s] from Proto-Teutonic *gasts* : *gastiụiz* from Indo-European *ghostis* : *ghosteịes* [cf. Latin *hostis* : *hostēs*]).

The Avesta was transcribed into its present vocalised alphabet in the third century A.D. from an older unvocalised script, presumably that in which the Pārsīk (Sāsānian Pāhlavī) inscriptions were carved (twenty-two characters), scarcely from that of ' Book Pāhlavī ', or Middle Persian (fourteen letters, most of which have several values and are complicated by a vast number of ligatures; cf. p. 319). This transcription is so faulty that it is unsafe to use Avestan linguistically without close examination. The Avestan equivalent of Sanskrit *devá-* ' god ', for instance, is written *daēva-* (Indo-European *deiụos;* cf. p. 99), although the evidence of Modern Persian *dēv*, *dīv* (the older and present pronunciations respectively), of Avestan metre, and of the borrowed Armenian *dew* indicates that it was pronounced [de:va], the Armenian form being taken from a North Iranian *dēva-*, and the corresponding Syriac loan-word *daywā* from Old Persian *daiva-*. Again, the present Avestan text has a form *hū* ' of the sun ', which is linguistically impossible from every point of view, and which, the metre shows, was a disyllable. This has clearly arisen from misinterpretation of a Pārsīk combination which may be read *HVR, HRV, HRR,* or *HVV,* the reading *HVV = hū* having been taken instead of *HRV = h(ū)rō* (cf. Vedic *sū́rō* ' of the sun '), which is actually found elsewhere in the Avesta, and which should here be substituted for the meaningless Vulgate *hū*.

The first wave or waves of Indo-Iranian-speakers that entered the Iranian Plateau (cf. pp. 308–310) represented the Indo-European guttural *k̂* by the sibilant *ś* (originally, probably, [ş] as in the Polish *ś)*, and thence passed southwards into the north-east of India (the Pañjāb) through the compulsion of waves of kindred language-speakers who changed *k̂* into *s* instead of into *ś* (cf. Sanskrit *śatám* ' hundred ' : Avestan *satəm* : Latin *centum)*.

(1) *Indian.* — Indian is older than Iranian both linguistically and in historic record. It is true that its earliest dated texts are inscriptions of King Aśoka in the middle of the third century B.C., but its first documents are, in reality, the hymns of the *Rigveda.* This collection of one thousand and seventeen (or one thousand and twenty-eight) poems is conventionally dated between 2000 or 1500 and 500 B.C.; its composition doubtless covered several centuries; and it shows traces of various dates as well as of more than one dialect. It is marked by a language of great complexity, but also of remarkable clarity, in nominal and verbal formations; and it is likewise important as preserving the earliest known system of accent in Indo-European, this accent, as the statements of the native grammarians show, having been tonic, not expiratory, until at least about 400 B.C. (cf. pp. 63–64). The other three Vedas *(Sāma, Yajur* — in several recensions — and *Atharva)* are also accented, as are certain somewhat later texts (the *Taittirīya* and *Śatapatha Brāhmaṇas,* the *Taittirīya Āraṇyaka,* part of the *Aitareya Āraṇyaka,* and the *Suparṇādhyāya).*

The Vedas are mostly in metrical form; but about 500 B.C., prose makes its formal appearance in the Brāhmaṇas, devoted to exposition of the religious ritual, and important for us as showing sentence-structure unhampered by metrical requirements. In the Brāhmaṇas the verb is becoming simplified, a process carried almost to an extreme in *Classical Sanskrit, or Sanskrit* proper, which seems to have begun to receive literary cultivation about the third century B.C.

Sanskrit is not a direct descendant of the Vedic language, but is derived from some lost dialect closely akin to it. In Sanskrit, the old tonic accent has disappeared in favour of one of stress; and this tonic accentuation, which is like that of Classical Latin, except that the stress may go back to the fourth syllable if the penultimate and antepenultimate are short (e.g., 'brāhmaṇayos ' of two Bhāhmans '; cf. Latin con'ficiō ' I finish ' from *'confaciō, p. 335), may be a survival of Indo-European conditions. No Classical Sanskrit text is accented graphically, but information may occasionally be gleaned from certain phonological phenomena in Middle and Modern Indian equivalents of Classical Sanskrit words. There seems to be no reason to doubt, as some scholars have done, that Sanskrit was actually a spoken language, and not a mere learned figment; and, as a matter of fact, it is still spoken in India by the learned, and literary works are composed in it to-day, so that in these respects its use much resembles that of Latin in the Roman Catholic Church.

Besides Sanskrit, there were a number of other vernaculars called *Prākrits,* two of which received voluminous literary cultivation as the religious languages of Buddhism and Jainism respectively: *Pāli,* possibly a dialect of the region of Malva, north of Indore, though its localisation is not at all certain; and *Jaina Māgadhī,* which arose in Magadha. Several other Prākrits are known from literary specimens in the Indian drama, etc., but they have been so ' edited ' and are so artificial in their present form that they are of relatively small value for linguistic purposes except as controlled by the not invariably trustworthy statements of native grammarians. In addition to them, there were vernaculars called *Apabhraṁśa* (' Break-Down '), in which a fair amount of literature still preserved was written. Our surest Prākrit records are the inscriptions of King Aśoka (third century B.C.), which exist in several dialects.

The precise number of Prākrits is uncertain. Some native authorities list as many as thirty-eight, but all agree that the most important of them were four: Māhārāṣṭrī, Śaurasenī, Māgadhī, and

Paiśācī, spoken respectively in the Godāvarī country, the Bihārs, and adjoining territory; in the Middle Gangetic Dōāb and its neighbourhood (around Muttra) ; in South Bihār (around Patna) ; and in the extreme north. To these must be added *Ardhamāgadhī* ('Half-Māgadhī') between Māgadhī and Śaurasenī. This list seems to be sustained by the groupings of the *Modern Indian* languages. Śaurasenī, centring in the Dōāb, is now represented by Standard (Western) Hindī, Pañjābī, Sindhī, Gujarātī, Rājasthānī, Pahārī, Bhīlī, Khāndeśī, etc.; Māgadhī by Bengalī, Bihārī, Assamese (not to be confused with Tibeto-Burman Assamese dialects; cf. p. 389), and Oṛiyā; Ardhamāgadhī by Eastern Hindī; Māhārāṣṭrī by Marāṭhī and Siṁhalese (spoken in the southern half of Ceylon) ; and Paiśācī (for which we have little but the statements of native grammarians) by the Dardic group of Pashai, Kāfir, Khōwār, Kāśmīrī, Kōhistānī, Shiṇā, etc., these apparently forming a transition between the Indian and the Iranian divisions.

It must be understood, however, that the Modern Indian languages are not derived directly from the Prākrits, but from the Apabhraṁśas based upon them. The immediate Apabhraṁśa predecessors of the modern languages would seem to have been as follows: Auḍra or Autkala for Oṛiyā; Gauḍa for North Bengalī and Assamese; Ḍhakkī for East Bengalī; Ardhamāgadhī (of which Āvantī and Cāṇḍālī were apparently dialects) for East Hindī; Śaurasenī (of which Prācyā and Dākṣiṇī seem to have been dialects) for Western Hindī; Māgadhī (of which Śākārī and Śābarī were apparently dialects) for Bihārī; Āvantya for Rājasthānī; Gaurjara or Nāgara for Gujarātī; Ṭākka and Upanāgara for Pañjābī; Vrācaḍa for Sindhī and Lahndā; and Vaidarbha or Dākṣiṇātya for Marāṭhī. Sir George Grierson classifies these languages into three groups: Outer Sub-Branch (Bihārī, Assamese, Bengalī, Oṛiyā, Marāṭhī, Sindhī, and Lahndā), Inner Sub-Branch (Pañjābī, Western and Central Pahārī, Khas-Kurā [Eastern Pahārī or Naipālī], Western Hindī, Rājasthānī, Bhīlī, and Gujarātī), and Mediate Sub-Group (Eastern Hindī). The dialects of Modern Indian run into the hundreds; and there are, besides, dialects of uncertain classification, as well as the widespread group spoken by the Gypsies of various countries, which go back to an Indian original, doubtless once spoken in the north-west (cf. p. 38).

The best descriptive grammar of Sanskrit as a whole is W. D.

Whitney's *Sanskrit Grammar* (third edition, Boston, 1896); for Vedic, A. A. Macdonell's *Vedic Grammar* (Strassburg, 1910; his *Vedic Grammar for Students*, Oxford, 1916, contains additional material of value); for Classical Sanskrit, L. Renou's *Grammaire sanscrite* (Paris, 1930); for the purposes of comparative linguistics, the best work is A. Thumb's *Handbuch der Sanskrit-Sprache* (second edition, edited by H. Hirt, Heidelberg, 1930); the *Altindische Grammatik* of J. Wackernagel (assisted now by A. Debrunner), of which three volumes (Göttingen, 1896 sqq.) have thus far appeared, will be, if ever completed, by all odds the most exhaustive discussion of Sanskrit in all its periods. For syntax as a whole, we have only the *Sanskrit Syntax* (Leyden, 1886) and the *Vedische und Sanskrit-Syntax* (Strassburg, 1896) of J. S. Speijer (or Speyer). The only complete etymological dictionary thus far is C. C. Uhlenbeck's *Kurzgefasstes etymologisches Wörterbuch der altindischen Sprache* (Amsterdam, 1899); a new one, on a very large scale, is in course of preparation by W. Wüst *(Vergleichendes und etymologisches Wörterbuch des Alt-Indoarischen [Altindischen]*, Heidelberg, 1935 sqq.).

For the Prākrits we have R. Pischel's *Grammatik der Prākrit-Sprachen* (Strassburg, 1900), purely descriptive and linguistically weak; W. Geiger's *Pāli Literatur und Sprache* (Strassburg, 1916); and T. Burrow's *Language of the Kharoṣṭhi Documents from Chinese Turkestan* (Cambridge, 1937).

For Modern Indian the *Comparative Grammar of the Modern Aryan Languages of India* by J. Beames (three volumes, London, 1872–79) and the *Comparative Grammar of the Gaudian Languages* by A. F. R. Hoernle (London, 1880), though now antiquated in method, are occasionally worth consulting; volumes v-ix, xi of *The Linguistic Survey of India* (Calcutta, 1903–22) contain specimens and brief grammars of a vast number of languages and dialects; for individual languages we have model treatments in J. Bloch's *La Formation de la langue marathe* (Paris, 1920) and J. Sampson's *The Dialect of the Gypsies of Wales* (Oxford, 1926; with a valuable etymological dictionary); the Gypsies are also considered by F. Miklosich, in his *Ueber die Mundarten und die Wanderungen der Zigeuner Europa's* (twelve parts, Vienna, 1872–80), and Simhalese by W. Geiger, in his *Literatur und Sprache der Singhalesen* (Strassburg, 1900); for etymology, practically the only works besides Sampson's are Geiger's *Etymologie des Singhalesischen* (Munich, 1897) and R. L. Turner's *Comparative and Etymological Dictionary of the Nepali Language* (London, 1931), though these are necessarily restricted to words having cognates in Siṁhalese and Nepalī respectively; and Turner is also preparing a *Comparative Dictionary of the Indo-Aryan Languages* as the final volume (i, part 3) of the *Linguistic Survey of India*. A particularly valuable survey of the entire development of Indian is given in J. Bloch's *L'Indo-aryen du Veda aux temps modernes* (Paris, 1934).

(2) *Iranian.* — This division, spoken in the Iranian Plateau and in a small area of the Caucasus, falls, like Indian, into Ancient, Middle, and Modern. In the ancient period it appears in two distinct forms, the latter of these having two varieties which may represent two different stages of the same dialectic development. The first of these is *Old Persian,* found in the inscriptions of the Achaemenian Dynasty (521–338 B.C.), written in a simple style of cuneiform alphabet of thirty-six signs. The language betrays the influence of another Iranian dialect, and was spoken in the southwestern part of the plateau, the region anciently known as Persis and now called Fārs, the Arabic pronunciation of the Iranian name Pārs. The second form of Old Iranian is *Avestan,* the language of the sacred texts of the Zoroastrian religion. This language, whose value for linguistics is hampered by the alphabet in which it is written (cf. pp. 313–314), falls into two strata: the older of these is the *Gāθā* (' Song ') dialect, which approaches Vedic Indian in the antiquity of its phonology and morphology; the second, conventionally termed *Younger Avestan,* represents a more recent stage, though not without ancient survivals. In the later parts of this dialect, grammatical decay, e.g., in the confusion and misuse of case-forms, is so manifest that it would appear that these portions were written in a dead and learned language only imperfectly understood.

The dates of Avestan are quite uncertain. According to Iranian tradition, the *Gāθās* were composed by Zoroaster himself, whose date is set by the same tradition at 660–584 B.C. When Avestan ceased to be spoken is not wholly clear; and we have no cogent evidence as to its area. Some have considered its closest modern representative to be Afghān; but it seems more likely that its nearest cognates to-day are the Persian dialects of the north-west, this agreeing with the native tradition which associates Zoroaster's activities with Media and the region corresponding to the modern Azarbayjān. We may perhaps regard Avestan as Median; and in this connexion we may note that the two most important ancient Iranian peoples were the Medes and Persians (cf. Esther i. 3, 14, 18, 19; x. 2; Daniel v. 28; vi. 8, 12, 15; viii. 20), just as the later division, as shown by the inscription of Pāīkūlī, was between Persians and Parthians.

Avestan has left no descendants. Old Persian, on the contrary, was directly continued by *Middle Persian* or *Pāhlavī*, whose earliest datable document is a short papyrus from Āvramān (13–12 B.C.), though coins of the Śaka Dynasty show Middle Persian forms between 163 and 116 B.C. The numerous Persian loan-words in the Bible (especially in Esther, Ezra, and Daniel) fail to help in solving the problem of the date when Old Persian passed into Middle, since they may be interpreted either as Middle Persian or as Semitised forms of Old Persian, the latter possibility being rendered the more likely because of similar borrowed Old Persian words in Babylonian and Aramaic documents of the Achaemenian periods. On the whole, it would seem that both Old Persian and Avestan had ceased to be spoken by 400 B.C.

Middle Persian appears in several types: the inscriptional Middle Persian, whose chief document is the great inscription of Pāīkūlī (late in A.D. 293 or early in 294) in two dialects closely similar (Pāhlavīk and Pārsīk, northern and south-western respectively in provenance, and possibly implied by the ' Parthians ' and ' Medes ' of Acts ii. 9); the Middle Persian of the manuscripts found at Turfān in Chinese Turkistān; and the Middle Persian of the numerous books dealing with Zoroastrian matters during the Sāsānian Dynasty (A.D. 224–651). This ' Book-Pāhlavī ' (cf. p. 313) again falls into two types: *Huzvarišn*, in which Semitic (Syriac) words are written, but with Iranian inflexions (e.g., *yemalelūnd* ' they say ' [cf. Aramaic *məlal* ' says '] = Iranian *guft-and)*; and *Pāzand*, which uses only Iranian. In this connexion it should be noted that the inscriptions likewise employ Semitic words, whereas the Turfān manuscripts show only Iranian. Arabic writers state that words written as Semitic were pronounced as Iranian (e.g., the word for ' bread ' was written *laḥmā*, but pronounced *nān)*; and this is borne out by the fact that the metre of hymns written in Huzvarišn, while impossible if read as Semitic, becomes good poetry when read as Iranian.

Besides Middle Persian proper, we have a fair amount of material in some other Middle Iranian dialects, notably *Middle Parthian* north of Persia (the source, rather than Middle Persian, of the majority of the older Iranian words borrowed by Armenian) ; *Middle Sogdian* in the north-east of Irān; and Khotanese or *Middle Sakian* (termed North Aryan by its first investigator, E. Leumann) in the southern part of East Turkistān. The literatures of these dialects are chiefly translations of Buddhist and Christian documents from Sanskrit and Syriac respectively; and they seem to have flourished especially in the eighth and ninth centuries of our era. *Old Sakian* ('Scythian') and *Old Sarmatian* are preserved only in a few proper names and glosses recorded by Greek and Latin authors.

Pārsīk Middle Persian is the direct ancestor of *Modern Persian*, whose first great author was the poet Firdausī in the tenth century A.D. Modern Persian differs from Middle only in minor respects, notably in the weakening of final consonants, the systems of inflexion being virtually the same in both. As contrasted with Ancient Iranian, the noun has lost all cases but two, the nominative and the oblique, mere fragments of the nominative now surviving. The verb is equally simplified. Little but the old present is retained; the perfect is formed by combining the neuter perfect passive participle with the oblique (e.g., *kard-am* ' I have done ' is really '[the thing]done of [or, by] me '; cf. Old Persian *manā kartam* ' mei factum '; cf. p. 168) ; and precise tense-relations are obtained by using various prefixed particles and auxiliary verbs. Compared with Old Persian, Modern Persian presents a most remarkable parallel to Modern Romance (e.g., French) as compared with Latin, or to English as compared with Anglo-Saxon. Excepting in Firdausī, the vocabulary is overloaded with Arabic words, this double vocabulary, though here carried to an excess, again recalling the similar richness of English; but with the intense nationalism now sweeping Iran, a determined effort is being made to purify the language of any but Iranian words. Modern Persian has a large number of dialects, which fall into three main groups: *Caspian, Central,* and *Pāmir,* the first perhaps related to Avestan, and the last forming a transition to the Dardic group of India (cf. pp. 316, 318–319).

Besides Persian, the Modern Iranian dialects are *Kurdish* (with several sub-dialects), *Balōčī* and *Afghān* or Puštū, each with two principal sub-divisions, and, to the east of Vladikavkaz in the Caucasus, *Ossetic* (with two main sub-divisions), this latter perhaps the descendant of Old Sakian. While considerable work has been done in Modern Iranian dialects, much still remains to be accomplished, particularly in view of the mass of new material in Middle Iranian, of which only part has as yet been made accessible.

For Old Iranian, the standard treatment is C. Bartholomae's ' Vorgeschichte der iranischen Sprachen ' and ' Awestasprache und Altpersisch ' in the first part of volume i of the *Grundriss der iranischen Philologie* (Strassburg, 1901), pp. 1–248; for Avestan alone, A. V. W. Jackson's *Avesta Grammar in Comparison with Sanskrit* (Stuttgart, 1892) and H. Reichelt's *Awestisches Elementarbuch* (Heidelberg, 1909) ; and for Old Persian, A. Meillet's *Grammaire du vieux-perse* (second edition, by E. Benveniste, Paris, 1931). For Middle Persian, the best books are E. Blochet's *Études de grammaire pehlvie* (Paris, no date) and H. S. Nyberg's *Hilfsbuch des Pehlevi* (two volumes, Upsala, 1928–31; J. Darmesteter's *Études sur la grammaire historique de la langue persane* in the first volume of his *Études iraniennes,* Paris, 1883, is still often worth consulting) ; for Sogdian, R. Gauthiot's *Essai de grammaire sogdienne* (completed by Benveniste, two volumes, Paris, 1914–29) ; for Khotanese, the *Saka Studies* of S. Konow (Oslo, 1932) ; for Modern Persian and its dialects, the only strictly linguistic discussions are P. Horn's ' Neupersisch ' and W. Geiger's studies in the second part of the first volume of the *Grundriss der iranischen Philologie,* pp. 1–200, 287–423, for which Geiger has also written on Afghān and Balōčī (pp. 201–230, 231–248; further material is given in volume x of *The Linguistic Survey of India,* Calcutta, 1921), while Modern Persian dialects have been synchronically described by A. Christensen in his *Contributions à la dialectologie iranienne* (two volumes, Copenhagen, 1930–35), *Les Dialectes d'Awromān et de Pāwä* (Copenhagen, 1921), and *Le Dialecte de Sämnān* (Copenhagen, 1915).

For Ossetic we have the study of W. Miller in the supplementary volume of the *Grundriss der iranischen Philologie* (Strassburg, 1903) ; and for the languages on the Indo-Iranian frontier, G. Morgenstierne's *Indo-Iranian Frontier Languages* (two volumes, Oslo, 1929–38). For Kurdish, the only linguistic grammar is still F. Justi's *Kurdische Grammatik* (St. Petersburg, 1880) ; for Afghān, a work of much value is D. L. R. Lorimer's *Syntax of*

Colloquial Pashtu (Oxford, 1915). As regards etymology, we have, for Old Iranian, Bartholomae's *Altiranisches Wörterbuch* (Strassburg, 1904) ; for Modern Persian, Horn's *Grundriss der neupersischen Etymologie* (Strassburg, 1894; to be checked by H. Hübschmann's *Persische Studien*, Strassburg, 1895) ; for Afghān, Geiger's *Etymologie und Lautlehre des Afghānischen* (Munich, 1893) and Morgenstierne's *Etymological Vocabulary of Pashto* (Oslo, 1925) ; for Balōčī, Geiger's *Etymologie des Balūčī* (Munich, 1890) ; and for Ossetic, Hübschmann's *Etymologie und Lautlehre der ossetischen Sprache* (Strassburg, 1897) and R. von Stackelberg's *Beiträge zur Syntax des Ossetischen* (Strassburg, 1886).

Tokharian

Early in the present century, explorations in Chinese Turkistān revealed the existence of a language belonging to an Indo-European group hitherto unknown, recording a literature of medical and Buddhist works strongly influenced by, and in part translated from, Sanskrit. The language falls into two dialects, one centring in the east around Karashar, and the other in the west around Kucha; and they may perhaps best be termed *Agnean* (other designations being Tokharian A, Turfanian, and Karasharian) and *Kuchaean* (also called Tokharian B) respectively. Since the texts of the eastern dialect term the language *Tokhrī*, thus connecting its speakers with the Tokharoi of the Greeks, the Tukhāra of the Indians, and the Tu-hu-la of the Chinese, the group as a whole is called Tokharian. The earliest document yet known is dated in the reign of King Suvarnata in the seventh century A.D., and none is later than the tenth century. A considerable amount of Agnean has been made available, but relatively little of Kuchaean is yet accessible.

Tokharian possesses all five short vowels in addition to an indeterminate sound transcribed *ä* ($=$ [ə]), but has only the voiceless plosives *k, p, t*, which it modifies in some manner before the indeterminate vowel; and it represents the Indo-European $\hat{k}$ by *k* (e.g., *kant*[e] ' hundred ' : Latin *centum*, as contrasted with Avestan *satəm),* so that it alone of the Asiatic division belongs to the *centum*-group (cf. pp. 310–311). Verbal inflexion has a present, an imperfect, and a narrative past; but, on the other hand, it distinguishes between the subjunctive and the optative, and has preserved the highly archaic medio-passive type characterised by *-r-,* as in Hittite, Italo-Celtic, and Phrygian (cf. pp. 218–219). The inflexion of the epithetologue, which has, properly speaking, only a nominative and an oblique, is largely by postpositions instead of by case-endings. The language would seem to have formed part of a group (perhaps including Hittite) bounded by Balto-Slavic on the one hand and by Greek, Armenian, and Thraco-Phrygian on the other, originally dwelling in the area between the Dnieper and the Ural Mountains.

For Agnean, a *Tocharische Grammatik* has been written by W. Schultz, E. Sieg, and E. Siegling (Göttingen, 1931), purely descriptive, and without phonology, comparative material, or syntax; for Kuchaean, we have only studies on the noun, verb, and numerals by S. Lévi and A. Meillet in volumes xvii–xix of the *Mémoires de la société de linguistique de Paris* (1912–16), and a brief survey by the latter in the first volume of the *Indogermanisches Jahrbuch* (1914, pp. 1–19), though G. Bonfante is preparing a comparative grammar of it.

Hittite

Preliminary excavations in 1893, followed by intensive explorations from 1905 to 1907, led to the discovery at Boghaz-köi, some one hundred and fifty kilometres east of Ankara (Angora) in Asia Minor, of a mass of cuneiform texts in a language hitherto unknown; and in 1917 the Czech scholar B. Hrozný, after exhaustive study, established the Indo-European character of the tongue in his *Die Sprache der Hethiter*. The language, whose records are chiefly ritualistic and historical in nature, is usually termed Hittite, since the earliest known name of the capital of the classical Hittite period was Ḥatti; but since a passage in one of the texts speaks of a ' singer of Kanes ' (earliest known as Kusar) as contrasted with one ' of Khattu ' (the Hittites proper), it has also been called Kanesian, though some prefer to designate it as Nāsili ' the language of Nēsas '.

The linguistic structure of Hittite is clearly Indo-European in type, although some investigators regard it as standing in a sort of sister-relation to that group, and speak of the Indo-Hittite language-family (cf. p. 299), while affinities have been sought between it and Lycian and Lydian (cf. pp. 382–383). Its texts date between the nineteenth century and the thirteenth B.C., and are characterised by a linguistic decay astonishing in a language of such early date, unless one is to suppose that it represents a stage more primitive than the highly developed system of Indo-European generally. It has no aspirates, only masculine-feminine and neuter genders (perhaps better termed animate and inanimate; cf. pp. 183–190), and two conjugations, one in -*mi* and the other in -*hi* (e.g., *etmi* ' I eat ' : *sakhi* ' I know '), each with a present and a preterite, the -*hi*-conjugation apparently being a perfect in origin; and several of its case-forms are by no means easy to explain. On the other hand, it possesses the vowels *a, e, i, u* (but no *o)* and a medio-passive in -*r* (cf. pp. 218–219), and is clearly a *centum*-language (cf. *kita* ' lies ', Greek κεῖται, as contrasted with Sanskrit *śéte).*

Hittite phonology is marked by a phoneme transcribed *h* which is otherwise unknown in Indo-European except as a sound of secondary development. This *h* apparently represents a voiceless velar fricative [x] or, more probably, a voiceless pharyngal fricative [ħ]; and the discovery of this stop, for whose existence in Indo-European additional evidence has been found in Greek and Armenian, will oblige us to make certain revisions in the Indo-European phonological scheme (cf. pp. 66, 445–446). The vocabulary contains a large percentage of words of non-Indo-European origin.

Besides the cuneiform texts, there are also Hittite inscriptions in pictographic or hieroglyphic characters. Hrozný and P. Meriggi, among others, are deciphering these texts, and are in fair agreement that their language may be akin to that seen in the thus far scanty fragments of *Luian* or *Luvian,* closely related to Hittite, and regarded by some as cognate with Lycian and Carian (cf. p. 382). For the study of Hittite we possess the admirable *Comparative Grammar of the Hittite Language* of E. H. Sturtevant (Philadelphia, 1933). Since 1930, the *Revue hittite et asianique,* published at Paris, has dealt with this language as well as with the Asianic group generally and H. Pedersen has published a valuable study on *Hittitisch und die andern indoeuropäischen Sprachen* (Copenhagen, 1938).

Armenian

This language, once supposed to belong to the Indo-Iranian division because of the large number of Iranian (Parthian) words borrowed in its vocabulary (cf. pp. 127, 320), has long been recognised as constituting an independent branch of Indo-European. The Proto-Armenians appear to have migrated from east of the Caspian Sea, passing north of the Black Sea into Asia Minor, leaving colonies among the Thracians, Phrygians, etc., and settling in the Hittite Empire in the region of Lake Van, whence they have been driven, in the course of their tragic history, to their present centre in the southern Caucasus area. Greek tradition makes them offshoots from the Phrygians, which may, indeed, have been the case. Except for a few lines of poetry, their literature begins with a highly important translation of the Bible in the fifth century A.D.; and the bulk of their writings are versions of theological and historical works from Greek or Syriac originals, some of which are no longer extant. Only one dialect of *Classical Armenian* (Grabar) is known, this probably being that spoken in the district of Tarawn on the shores of Lake Van.

Armenian possesses all five vowels and a rather complex system of consonants which shows strong (but apparently only fortuitous) resemblance to that of the South Caucasian languages; it has no grammatical gender; and is characterised by a heavy stress-accent (cf. pp. 63–64) which, resulting in the loss of short vowels in unaccented syllables, has much changed the appearance of its words. One of its most remarkable features is a consonant-shift even more thorough-going than in Teutonic itself (cf. pp. 79–82), whereby, for instance, Indo-European *d* becomes *t*, and Indo-European *t* becomes *t'* (e.g., Armenian *tasn* ' ten ' : Latin *decem;* Armenian *t'otum* ' endure ' : Latin *tollō* ' bear '). In the Eastern dialects of *Modern Armenian* (e.g., that of Tiflis) this condition still holds, but in the Western (as that of Constantinople) the shift has been reversed, so that Eastern and Old Armenian *t* and *d* have become *d* and *t* respectively (for example, Old and Eastern Armenian *Tigran* from the Old Persian proper name found in Classical writers as Τιγράνης = Western Armenian *Dikran)*. The verb has lost the perfect, but retains the aorist, and has a passive (e.g., *sirem* ' I love ' : *sirim* ' I am loved ') analogous to the Sanskrit type of *pácati* ' he cooks ' : *pacyáte* ' it is cooked ' (cf. p. 217); and the inflexions of both the verb and the epithetologue show, on analysis, a remarkable piling-up of inflexional endings strongly suggestive of a late stage of linguistic development.

The dialects of Armenian, which begin to be known from the twelfth century, seem to be, as in the case of those of Modern

Greek (cf. p. 29), deviations from the Classical language rather than descendants of ancient dialects which doubtless once existed. They show wide transformation in the inflexion of the verb and great simplification in that of the epithetologue, while their syntax is much modified under the influence of Turkish; and they fall into three broad groups according to their mode of forming the present indicative (e.g., Classical *sirem* ' I love ' : *sirum em* ' I am in loving ', *sirem gə* [indicative plus a particle; cf. Mediaeval Cilician Armenian *gu sirem*], *sirel im* ' I am to love ').

The old and purely descriptive grammars by J. J. Schroeder *(Thesaurus linguae Armenicae antiquae et hodiernae*, Amsterdam, 1711) and J. Ch. Cirbied *(Grammaire de la langue arménienne*, Paris, 1823) are still of value for their exhaustive collection of material; but the only linguistic treatment is A. Meillet's *Esquisse d'une grammaire comparée de l'arménien classique* (second edition, Vienna, 1937, with the collaboration of Father L. Mariès; Meillet's *Altarmenisches Elementarbuch*, Heidelberg, 1913, is descriptive). For Middle Armenian, we have J. Karst's *Historische Grammatik des Kilikisch-Armenischen* (Strassburg, 1901) ; the relation between Ancient and Modern Armenian is given consideration in A. Abeghian's *Neuarmenische Grammatik* (Berlin and Leipzig, 1936) ; and the modern dialects are grouped in H. Adjarian's *Classification des dialectes arméniens* (Paris, 1909). The single etymological dictionary thus far is H. Hübschmann's *Armenische Grammatik*, volume i (Strassburg, 1897; no more published) ; and the question of the relationship of Armenian to South Caucasian is well discussed by G. Deeters in his *Armenisch und Südkaukasisch* (Leipzig, 1927).

Thraco-Phrygian

This group, conventional rather than certain, comprises the scanty remains of ancient Thracian and of Old and New Phrygian. The former is known only from proper names and glosses (especially names of plants), and from a single brief inscription on a gold ring, found in 1912 near Ezerovo in Bulgaria and dating from the fifth or fourth century B.C., which still awaits satisfactory interpretation. For Old Phrygian we have nineteen inscriptions of the eighth century B.C., likewise imperfectly understood, and eighty-eight in New Phrygian from the early centuries of our era, in addition to a number of glosses. It is possible that *Bithynian*, of which a half-dozen glosses survive, as well as *Dacian* and *Getic* (in which the Roman Ovid tells us that he wrote some poems long since vanished), may have belonged to this same group; but its further affinities are uncertain, some considering it akin to Illyrian, while others place it midway between Armenian and Tokharian. It is at least clear that Phrygian possessed the vowels *ă, i, ĕ, o (ō* becomes *ū,* and *u* apparently *i); and* it probably belonged to the *satem*-group (New Phrygian σεμον[ν] ' to this one ' : Old Church Slavic *semu,* contrasted with Greek κεῖνος ' that one ', Latin *ce-do* ' give here ').

For Thracian, we have materials by W. Tomaschek *(Die alten Thraker,* two parts, Vienna, 1893–94; to be used with great caution) ; and for New Phrygian, J. Fraser's ' Phrygian Studies, I ' *(Transactions of the Cambridge Philological Society,* volume vi, part 2, Cambridge, 1913) ; the Phrygian inscriptions are most conveniently collected, together with the remains of other languages of the Near East, by J. Friedrich in his *Kleinasiatische Sprachdenkmäler* (Berlin, 1932) ; and the collection of glosses of this same area in the *Arica* (Halle, 1851) of P. de Lagarde (earlier named P. Bötticher), reworked in great part in his *Gesammelte Abhandlungen* (Leipzig, 1866), may still be consulted with profit.

Greek

Generally speaking, Greek is the most important of all the Indo-European languages for determining the primitive vowel-system of the family, its only rivals here being Oscan and Lithuanian; but its consonantism shows considerable deviation from the original scheme. Its fidelity to the old verbal system is closer than that of any other language except Vedic Sanskrit; but its inflexion of the epithetologue is marked by much syncretism (cf. pp. 201–202), the earlier stages here being essentially retained by Sanskrit, Baltic, and Old Church Slavic. Although its accentuation has been rather seriously modified by the ' three-mora law ', which prevents the accent from being further than three syllables from the end of a word, it has otherwise retained the Indo-European accentual system to a degree which makes it rival Vedic Sanskrit, this accent having been tonic until about the fourth century A.D., since which time it has been expiratory (cf. pp. 63–64).

Greek is further noteworthy in that it has had a continuous literary record from the eighth century B.C. to the present day. In historic form it is thus older than the Italic group, which is really known only five centuries later; and we are particularly fortunate in having a large mass of inscriptions in many dialects over a long period and a wide area. The sole rival of Greek in this respect is Italic, where, however, the non-Latin remains are relatively scanty. These inscriptions are more important linguistically than the strictly literary remains in their representation of the language as actually spoken, although their value is only too often impaired by masons' errors, by attempts to be learned or literary, and, particularly in texts of later date, by mixture of dialects. The literatures in Attic and in such Ionic writers as Herodotos are accurate documents, but the literary remains in other dialects (e.g., the Doric of the bucolic poems of Theokritos, Bion, and Moschos, and of the lyrics in the dramas; the Aeolic of Sappho; etc.) are of less worth, for not only are they based on a learned and literary tradition, but they have also been seriously ' emended ' by editors both ancient and modern, to say nothing of blunders made by ignorant scribes. An additional source for a knowledge of Greek dialects is found in the lexicographers, especially Hesychios, though here also faulty manuscript transmission has led to many errors; and some information (though much less than one would expect) may be gleaned from the old Greek grammarians.

The exact mutual relations of the *Greek dialects* have been much debated, the question being complicated by the uneven distribution of their outstanding features, so that any attempt to group them according to the co-existence of this or that particular phenomenon in various dialects is extremely hazardous, and any endeavour to draw isoglottic lines upon a map would be most confusing. The least objectionable classification seems to be into Western, Central, Arcado-Cyprian, and Attic-Ionic. The *Western group* comprises Doric (including Laconian, Messenian, Argolic, Cretan, and the various Doric colonies), Achaean, Elean, and North-Western (Epirote, Acarnanian, Aetolian, Locrian, Phocian, and Phthiotic in southern Thessaly); the *Central* (also termed Aeolic), consisting of Boeotian, Thessalian, and Lesbian; the *Arcado-Cyprian* with the divisions of Arcadian, Cyprian, and probably, though with much dialect-mixture, Pamphylian in Asia Minor; and *Attic-Ionic* falling into Attic and Ionic, the two dialects in which almost all Greek literature is written. Another dialect of historical and literary, rather than of strictly linguistic, importance is found in the epics associated with the name of *Homer* (probably dating, in kernel, from before the ninth century B.C.), where one evidently has an Aeolic foundation revised by Ionians, so that the ' epic ' dialect is essentially Aeolo-Ionic.

In another connexion, we have already outlined the history of the Greek language (p. 29), noting that the old dialects have long since vanished excepting for a single descendant in *Tsaconian*, spoken in a small area along the Gulf of Nauplia, and retaining marked evidences of its Doric origin. With the Turkish conquest in the fifteenth century, the old supremacy of Attic (with its minor modifications) was crushed, and dialects again began to evolve. One of the earliest monuments of *Modern Greek* is a version of the Pentateuch published in Hebrew characters at Constantinople in 1547 (transcribed into Greek letters by D. C. Hesseling, *Les cinq livres de la loi*, Leyden, 1897) ; but the beginnings and evolution of the language still need much investigation. The actual vernaculars of Modern Greek fall into a large number of local dialects, which may very roughly be divided into a northern and a southern group, the former characterised by a heavier stress accent than the latter, thus leading to the loss of vowels in unstressed syllables, with considerable resultant change in the appearance of words. Just as Ancient Greek contains many allogenous words, so Modern Greek has a large alien element in its vocabulary, particularly Turkish, Slavic, and Italian.

The principal scientific grammars of Ancient Greek are G. Meyer's *Griechische Grammatik* (third edition, Leipzig, 1896; largely antiquated, but still of value for its collection of material), H. Hirt's *Handbuch der griechischen Laut- und Formenlehre* (second edition, Heidelberg, 1912), and K. Brugmann's *Griechische Grammatik* (fourth edition, Munich, 1913), the latter to be replaced by E. Schwyzer's work of the same name, of which the first volume has appeared (Munich, 1939). For the Greek dialects we have O. Hoffmann's *Die griechischen Dialekte in ihrem historischen Zusammenhange* (three volumes, Göttingen, 1891–98), a number of special grammars in the fourth volume of the *Sammlung der griechischen Dialektinschriften* by F. Bechtel and H. Collitz (Göttingen, 1884–1915), Bechtel's *Griechische Dialekte* (three volumes, Göttingen, 1921–24; skeleton grammars of the individual dialects — all these works purely descriptive), and E. Boisacq's *Les Dialectes doriens* (Paris, 1891) ; while general surveys are given in A. Thumb's *Handbuch der griechischen Dialekte* (Heidelberg, 1909; first volume of a thorough revision by E. Kieckers, 1932) and C. D. Buck's *Introduction to the Study of the Greek Dialects* (revised edition, Boston [1928]).

P. Kretschmer's *Einleitung in die Geschichte der griechischen Sprache* (Göttingen, 1896) is of great value for the pre-history of Greek; for the general history of the language the best work is A. Meillet's *Aperçu d'une histoire de la langue grecque* (fourth edition, Paris, 1935); and the later periods are treated in Thumb's *Die griechische Sprache im Zeitalter des Hellenismus* (Strassburg, 1901), K. Dieterich's *Untersuchungen zur Geschichte der griechischen Sprache* (Leipzig, 1898), E. Mayser's *Grammatik der griechischen Papyri* (two volumes, Berlin and Leipzig, 1923–34), J. H. Moulton's *Grammar of New Testament Greek* (completed by W. F. Howard, two volumes, Edinburgh, 1908–29), S. B. Psaltes's *Grammatik der byzantinischen Chroniken* (Göttingen, 1913), G. N. Hatzidakis's *Einleitung in die neugriechische Grammatik* (Leipzig, 1892), and Thumb's *Handbuch der neugriechischen Volkssprache* (second edition, Strassburg, 1910; English translation, *Handbook of the Modern Greek Vernacular*, Edinburgh, 1912), individual dialects being studied, for instance, in R. M. Dawkins's *Modern Greek in Asia Minor* (Cambridge, 1916) and H. Pernot's *Introduction à l'étude du dialecte tsakonien* (Paris, 1934). The older etymological dictionaries of G. Curtius *(Grundzüge der griechischen Etymologie,* fifth edition, Leipzig, 1879), L. Meyer *(Handbuch der griechischen Etymologie,* four volumes, Leipzig, 1901–02; antiquated even before it appeared, but still of some value for its references to Greek literature), and W. Prellwitz *(Etymologisches Wörterbuch der griechischen Sprache,* second edition, Göttingen, 1905) have been entirely superseded by E. Boisacq's *Dictionnaire étymologique de la langue grecque* (Paris, 1916; third reprinting, with index of words, Paris, 1938).

The relation of *Macedonian* to Greek is uncertain, some scholars regarding it as a Greek dialect, while others consider it closely akin to Illyrian, if not, indeed, a mere Illyrian dialect (cf. p. 332). It is known only from glosses and proper names, some of which, though recorded as Macedonian, may not really belong to it. Its only reasonably certain characteristic is its deaspiration of old aspirated voiced plosives (e.g., δανος ' death ' : Greek θάνατος from Indo-European *dhu̯enⱥtos; Βερενίκη = Greek Φερενίκη, cf. Sanskrit *bhar-* ' bear ') ; and it would seem to have belonged to the *centum*-group (cf. ακρουνοι ' boundaries ' : Old Latin *ocris* ' rugged mountain ' as contrasted with Sanskrit *aśri-* ' sharp edge '). The one special work on the language is O. Hoffmann's *Die Makedonen* (Göttingen, 1906; to be used with caution, but of value for its collection of material).

Albanian

The oldest documents of Albanian thus far known are a short baptismal ritual of 1462 and a Bible translation of 1555, preserved in the Uniate Seminary at Palermo and still unedited; but the greater part of its early literature dates from the seventeenth century, its most valuable records consisting of folk-songs. The language falls into two groups, each with a number of sub-dialects: *Geg* (with colonies in Dalmatia) to the north and *Tosk* (with colonies in Greece, Italy, and Sicily) to the south of the Shumbi River.

Long before its appearance in writing, Albanian underwent such radical changes both in phonology and in morphology that profound further study must be made before its full value for Indo-European linguistics can be determined; while as a result of successive domination by Venetians and Turks, and in consequence of its proximity to Greece, its vocabulary is so mixed with foreign words that the native element forms only a small minority (cf. p. 126). The language belongs to the *satem*-group, but its further affinities are much debated; and at present it is best considered as forming a group by itself. It is often supposed to represent ancient Illyrian; but since the latter appears to have been a *centum*-group (cf. p. 332), the view that Albanian was akin to the Thraco-Phrygian division (cf. pp. 326–327) seems somewhat more probable.

There are many purely descriptive grammars of Albanian, notably G. Meyer's *Kurzgefasste albanesische Grammatik* (northern Tosk; Leipzig, 1888), G. Pekmezi's *Grammatik der albanesischen Sprache* (both dialects; Vienna, 1908), A. Leotti's *Grammatica elementare della lingua albanese (dialetto tosco)* (Heidelberg, 1915), G. Weigand's *Albanesische Grammatik im südgegischen Dialekt* (Leipzig, 1913), A. Feizi's *Grammatica della lingua albanese* (Geg; Naples, 1929), and S. E. Mann's *Short Albanian Grammar* (central dialect; London, 1932) ; but we have as yet no scientific and comparative grammar, though we possess an excellent etymological dictionary in G. Meyer's *Etymologisches Wörter-buch der albanesischen Sprache* (Leipzig, 1891).

Illyrian

Although once spoken over a wide area, Illyrian has left behind it only a brief inscription of three words discovered near Scutari in Albania, and a fairly large number of personal and geographical names. It is generally agreed that it was a *centum*-language, and that it was connected with at least two ancient Italic dialects: *Venetic*, in the area corresponding approximately to the modern Venezia, and represented by some two hundred short inscriptions; and *Messapic*, in the heel of the Italian boot, of which we have about one hundred and eighty equally brief texts; and to these we may perhaps add *Raetic*, with some sixty fragments. The remains of all these are still too inadequate for very definite statements; but if Venetic and Messapic belong to the *centum*-group, and if they are akin to Illyrian, the latter cannot, as is maintained by good authorities, be the ancestor of Albanian, which is a *satem*-language. The remains of Illyrian are collected (only too probably with an admixture of allogenous elements unavoidable in our present state of knowledge) by H. Krahe in his *Die alten balkanilly-rischen geographischen Namen* (Heidelberg, 1925) and *Lexikon altillyrischer Personennamen* (Heidelberg, 1929), and the Venetic, Raetic, and Messapic inscriptions, with all the grammar now possible, by R. Conway and J. Whatmough in their *Prae-Italic Dialects of Italy* (three volumes, Cambridge, U. S. A., 1933).

Italic

The oldest record of Italic is a Praenestine fibula of the seventh century B.C., *Manios med fhefhaked Numasioi* ' Manius me fecit Numerio '; and the earliest Latin text is a very fragmentary in-scription on the *lapis niger* in the Roman Forum from the sixth century B.C. About 300 B.C., we have inscriptions on coins, mirrors, cups, etc.; but little of value has been preserved older than the second half of the third century.

The Italic dialects fall into three groups: Latino-Faliscan, Osco-Umbrian, and Sabellian, of which the most important, both his-torically and in wealth of material, is the *Latin*. This may be divided into several periods: Old Latin until the first Civil War

(82 B.C.) ; Classical Latin from the time of Caesar and Cicero to the death of Augustus (81 B.C.–A.D. 14) ; Silver Latin from Tiberius to Trajan (A.D. 14–117) ; Archaistic Latin (A.D. 117–180) ; and Vulgar Latin from A.D. 180 until its disappearance as a vernacular. It must be borne in mind that while Old Latin (as seen, for instance, in the comedies of Plautus) and Classical Latin (notably as illustrated by Caesar) doubtless represented, fairly closely, the current speech of the day, Silver Latin and all subsequent periods were artificially influenced by Classical norms, except for such frankly colloquial documents as the *Peregrinatio Aetheriae* (fourth century), the writings of Gregory of Tours (sixth century), and the documents of the Merovingian period in France from the fifth to the eighth century. One must also remember that, along with the more or less artificial written language, there was likewise a vernacular, which has left practically its sole literary remnant in parts of the *Satyricon* of Petronius (first century A.D.; notably in the amusing account of Trimalchio's dinner) ; and that this vernacular was constantly changing, doubtless with dialectic peculiarities. Our surest source for knowledge of the language as actually spoken is the inscriptions, which number thousands, scattered throughout the Empire and covering many centuries, but to be used with caution analogous to that requisite in studying Greek epigraphic remains (cf. p. 328) ; but, on the other hand, surprising though it be, the inscriptions appear to show no dialectic differences whatever, but present one and the same language regardless of their geographical positions in the Empire.

The other member of this sub-division, *Faliscan*, is represented by several inscriptions, glosses, and proper names; and to the group also belonged the closely similar *Hernician* and *Praenestinian*.

The second division, *Osco-Umbrian*, has left an abundance of epigraphic evidence which enables us to draw up a fairly complete grammar of both its dialects, of which Oscan is the more retentive of old forms, especially as regards its vocalism, which is much more primitive than Latin, even rivalling Greek and Lithuanian. Oscan has some one hundred and seventy-five inscriptions, but only a few (the Bantine Tablet, the Cippus Abellanus, the Agnone Tablet, and the Curse of Vibia) are of any considerable length. The one great document of Umbrian is the long ritual contained in the Iguvine Tables found at Gubbio in Italy, containing between four and five thousand words in four hundred and forty-nine lines, of which seventy-nine are repetitions. They are written in two alphabets, one native and the other Roman, the tablets in Umbrian script apparently dating from between 200 and 120 B.C. (conventionally printed in black-faced type), and those in the Latin alphabet from between 150 and 70, both sets from tablets of the third century B.C.

The third group, conventionally termed *Sabellian*, occupies a position midway between Oscan and Umbrian, but its remains are lamentably scanty. Here belong Paelignian, Marrucinian, Vestinian, Volscian, Marsian, Aequian, and Sabine; but the eight inscriptions called Old Sabellian are not Italic, being of very uncertain affinities, though some connect the language with the Illyrian group (cf. p. 332).

The chief differences between Osco-Umbrian and Sabellian as contrasted with Latino-Faliscan are that the former groups represent Indo-European q^u by a labial instead of by a guttural, and Indo-European medial *bh* and *dh* by *f* instead of by *b* and *d* (e.g., Oscan *petiro-pert* ' four times ' : Latin *quater;* Umbrian *tefe* ' to thee ' : Latin *tibi,* cf. Sanskrit *túbhyam;* Oscan **mefiaí** ' in the middle ' : Latin *mediae,* cf. Sanskrit *mádhya-).* It also goes without saying that Latin itself contains not only words of unknown origin, but also those of dialectic source (cf. p. 128), such as *rūfus* ' red ' beside the genuinely Latin *ruber* (cf. Umbrian **rufru** ' rubros ' : Sanskrit *rudhirá-);* and similar traces of non-Latin dialects may be found in Romance, e.g., probably, French *siffler* ' to whistle ' : Latin *sibilare;* Late Latin *cofea,* French *coiffe,* English *coif* from an Osco-Umbrian **cŭfea* = Latin **cŭbea,* cognate with Greek κεύθω, Indo-European **qeu-dhe-* ' hide '.

The special characteristics of Latin are the monophthongisation of Indo-European diphthongs (e.g., Old Latin *oinos* ' one ' : Latin *ūnus,* cf. Greek οἴνη ' ace on dice ', Gothic *ains;* Latin *ĭt* ' goes ' : Greek εἶσι, Lithuanian *eĩti);* the change of aspirated voiced plosives to voiceless fricatives, which become voiced plosives intervocalically (e.g., Latin *fuĭ* ' I have been ', *amā-bō* ' I shall love ' : Sanskrit *bhávati* ' becomes ') ; the amalgamation of the aorist with the perfect (e.g., *dīxī* ' I have said ', for **dīc-sī,* is an -*s*-aorist; *de-dī* ' I have given ' is a true perfect) ; the creation of new compound imperfects and futures from the Indo-European base **bheu̯e-* ' become ' (e.g., *amā-bam, amā-bō);* and the surrender of the free accent of Indo-European (cf. p. 64) for a fixed stress-

accent on the first syllable with consequent weakening or loss of
vowels in unstressed syllables, this later being modified by a
'three-mora law' analogous to that in Greek (cf. p. 327; e.g.,
am'āmus 'we love' = [in morae] **am'aamus*, but '*dīcimus* 'we
say '; *am'īcō* ' to a friend ' = [in morae] **ami'icoo)*, though traces
of the earlier system still survive, notably in compound verbs (e.g.,
'*faciō* ' I make ', but *con'ficiō* ' I finish ' for **'conficiō*, from a still
earlier **'confaciō;* cf. pp. 63–64, 315).

Italic shows such close affinities with Celtic that many scholars
assume a prehistoric period of Italo-Celtic unity. Here belong, for
instance, the representation of Indo-European *qᵘ* by *k (c)* in Latin
and Goidelic, but by *p* in Osco-Umbrian and Brythonic (e.g.,
Latin *quatuor* ' four ' : Oscan *petiro-pert* ' four times ' = Old Irish
cethir : Old Welsh *petguar)*; superlatives in **-(i)sṃmo-* (e.g.,
Oscan **nessimas-** ' next ' : Middle Irish *nessam)*; genitives in *-ī*
(e.g., Latin *virī* ' of a man ' : Old Irish *fir* for **uirī*, Gaulish
Trutikni ' Drutei f[ilii], of the son of Drutios ') ; subjunctives in
-ā- (e.g., Latin *feram* ' that I may carry ' : Old Irish *bera);* and
the great development of the passive and deponent in *-r* (cf. pp.
218–219).

Besides the Italic dialects proper, mention must also be made of
Sicel, of which a few glosses and an inscription of three lines have
been preserved, and which seems to have belonged either to this
group or to Ligurian. Two inscriptions, with a total of fifteen lines,
found at Novilara, near Pesaro in Umbria, are written in a language sometimes called Pre-Sabellian, Liburnian, or Picenian,
concerning whose affinities no opinion can yet safely be expressed.
In the extreme north of Italy, in the general area of Lago Mag-
giore, some seventy-two inscriptions, chiefly sepulchral or dedicatory, and containing about fifty different words (chiefly proper
names), have been discovered. These are conventionally called
Lepontine, and their language may well represent the sole known
remnants of *Ligurian,* which would seem to have stood midway
between Italic and Celtic.

For Latin, the chief scientific grammars are W. M. Lindsay's
The Latin Language (Oxford, 1894), F. Sommer's *Handbuch der
lateinischen Laut- und Formenlehre* (second and third editions,
Heidelberg, 1914), and, especially, the *Lateinische Grammatik* of
F. Stolz and J. H. Schmalz (fifth edition by M. Leumann and J. B.
Hofmann, Munich, 1928). For the later period, one has such works

as C. Grandgent's *Introduction to Vulgar Latin* (Boston, 1908), A. Carnoy's *Le Latin d'Espagne d'après les inscriptions* (second edition, Brussels, 1906), J. Pirson's *La Langue des inscriptions latines de la Gaule* (Liége and Paris, 1901), and M. Pei's *Language of the Eighth-Century Texts in Northern France* (New York, 1932). The entire development of the language is outlined by A. Meillet in his *Esquisse d'une histoire de la langue latine* (third edition, Paris, 1933), and the possible relation of Italic to Celtic by A. Walde in his *Über älteste sprachliche Beziehungen zwischen Kelten und Italikern* (Innsbruck, 1917).

For the non-Latin Italic and ' Pre-Italic ' dialects we have the collections of R. Conway, *The Italic Dialects* (Cambridge, 1897; a comparatively small number of inscriptions have since been discovered) and *The Prae-Italic Dialects of Italy* by Conway, J. Whatmough, and S. E. Johnson (three volumes, Cambridge, U. S. A., 1933) ; and for grammars, R. von Planta's *Grammatik der oskisch-umbrischen Dialekte* (two volumes, Strassburg, 1892–97) and C. D. Buck's *Grammar of Oscan and Umbrian* (revised edition, Boston [1928]). For etymology one has A. Walde's *Lateinisches etymologisches Wörterbuch* (third edition, by J. B. Hofmann, Heidelberg, 1930 sqq.), F. Muller's *Altitalisches Wörterbuch* (Göttingen, 1926), and the *Dictionnaire étymologique de la langue latine* of A. Ernout and A. Meillet (Paris, 1932), which supplement each other; and Ernout's *Les Éléments dialectaux du vocabulaire latin* (Paris, 1909) is also of value in this connexion.

From the Italic group, especially from Latin, the *Romance* languages are derived. These, each with many dialects, often of great interest, are French, Spanish, Portuguese, Provençal, Catalan, Italian, Sardinian, Rhaeto-Romanic, Rumanian, and Dalmatian. The Latinity underlying all of them was doubtless the vernacular of the periods of the colonisation of the countries in which they came to be spoken, even though the inscriptions from these areas show no dialectic differences (see p. 333). In each region this Latinity would seem to have been modified by the languages of the peoples among whom the colonists and soldiers came: in Gaul and Portugal by Celtic (e.g., commencing with a phrase by a copula in French [an unnatural arrangement outside French and Celtic], e.g., Old Irish *is i persin Críst d-a-gníu-sa-sin* = French *c'est dans la personne du Christ que je fais celà); in Spain, by Iberian (perhaps in the change of Italic *f* to *h*, except before *o* [e.g., *hija*

' daughter ' = Latin *filia^m* as contrasted with *fuego* ' fire ' = Latin *focu^m* but cf. p. 83) ; in North Italy, very possibly by Ligurian; and in Rumania, equally possibly, by Illyrian. The Romance vocabulary contains many words from non-Indo-European languages, as well as a large number of Indo-European stock which are neither represented in Italic nor explicable as mere borrowings (cf. pp. 127–128).

The entire group is of particular linguistic interest as representing, in actual historic form, the evolution of dialects from a common stock carried to areas populated by peoples speaking other tongues, so that both the similarities and the divergencies of the individual Romance languages are of value to the student of linguistics. Although Vulgar Latin shows many approximations in phonology, morphology, and syntax to the various Romance languages, the actual lines of transition from Latin to Romance have vanished. The first documents in the Romance dialects are already distinct linguistic entities — for French, the Strasbourg Oaths of 842; for Italian, in 964; for Provençal, at the beginning of the eleventh century; for Spanish, in 1145; for Catalan, in 1171; for Portuguese, in 1192; for Rumanian, in the sixteenth century; and for the rest, even later. No agreement has yet been reached as to when Vulgar Latin ceased to be vernacular and when Romance began actually to be spoken; but the language of the Strasbourg Oaths would seem to have required a considerable period for its evolution from any form of Latin.

The principal dialectic divisions of the Romance languages are as follows: (1) *French:* Île de France (which has become the standard language), Champenois, Burgundian (not to be confused with the extinct Teutonic Burgundian; cf. p. 345), Lorrainese, Walloon, Picard, Norman (historically important as the source of the Anglo-Norman dialect which has so profoundly affected English; e.g., English *castle* from Norman *castel* = Old Île de France *chastel,* Modern French *château,* from Late Latin *castellu^m* ' castle, town '), Poitevin, and Berrichon; the south-eastern dialects of southern Franche-Comté, northern Dauphiny, and Savoy, and those of French Switzerland form a Franco-Provençal group; (2) *Spanish:* Aragonese, Asturian, Leonese, Andalusian, and Castilian (the standard language, whereas Andalusian is the basis of the American Spanish-speaking areas); (3) *Portuguese:* Portuguese proper, with several sub-dialects, and Gallego; (4) *Proven-*

çal: Provençal proper, Langue d'Oc, Auvergnese, Limousine, and Gascon; (5) *Catalan,* so closely akin to Provençal that many scholars class them together; (6) *Italian:* Gallo-Italian (Emilian, Lombard, Piedmontese, and Ligurian, with interesting connexions with Provençal on the one hand and with Italian proper on the other) and Italian proper (Tuscan [the standard language], Roman, Umbrian, Neapolitan, Tarentine, Calabrian, Abruzzian, Sicilian, and Venetian); (7) *Sardinian:* Campidanese, Logudoresian, Gallurese; remarkable as the sole Romance group which preserves the Latin distinction between $\bar{e}, \breve{\imath}$ and $\bar{o}, \breve{u}$ (e.g., Latin *tēla* ' web, cloth ' : Campidanian *tela* : Italian *tela* : French *toile; pīlus* ' hair ' : *pilu* : *pelo* : *poil; vōx* ' voice ' : *boži* : *voce* : *voix; bŭcca* ' mouth ' : *bukka* : *bucca* : *bouche);* (8) *Rhaeto-Romanic:* a large number of dialects which may roughly be grouped as those of Grisons, Tyrol, and Friuli; (9) *Rumanian:* Daco-Rumanian in Rumania itself, Macedo-Rumanian in scattered areas of Greece and Turkey, and Istro-Rumanian in some parts of Istria; and (10) the extinct *Dalmatian,* formerly spoken from the island of Veglia to Ragusa, Ragusan having become extinct in the fifteenth century, while the last speaker of Veglian was killed by a mine-explosion in 1898.

Through colonisation, the Romance languages have become vernacular far outside Europe, notably French in the Province of Quebec, and in parts of Louisiana; Spanish in Mexico, Cuba, and Central and South America, except in Brazil, where Portuguese is spoken. These colonial languages show many interesting variations from the parent stocks. Thus, the French of the Province of Quebec and the closely similar Acadian of parts of Nova Scotia, New Brunswick, and Louisiana are based essentially on the dialects of northern France as spoken in the seventeenth century, and preserve a certain number of words and pronunciations obsolete or only dialectic in the mother country (e.g., *an* [ɛ̃] ' fish-hook ' : Old French *aim,* Latin *hamus;* [lwɛ] for *loi* [lwa] ' law '; *je suis après manger* ' I am eating ' for *je suis en train de manger ');* the Spanish of Chile has been influenced to a striking degree by the South American Araucanian; and Judaeo-Spanish and Judaeo-Portuguese have been affected by Hebrew, etc. Such developments must not be confused with the creolised debasements (cf. p. 37) of Negro-French in Mauritius, Louisiana, Haiti, Martinique, and Cayenne, of Annamito-French in Cochin-China, of Malayo-Spanish in the

Philippines, of Negro-Spanish in St. Domingo and Trinidad, of Negro-Portuguese in Cape Verde and Senegambia, of Malayo-Portuguese in Java, and of Indo-Portuguese in Cochin, Ceylon, etc. For studies of the Romance languages as a whole, we have, notably, W. Meyer-Lübke's *Grammatik der romanischen Sprachen* (four volumes, Leipzig, 1890–1902; French translation, *Grammaire des langues romanes*, by E. Rabiet and A. and G. Doutrepont, Paris, 1890–1906) and *Einführung in das Studium der romanischen Sprachwissenschaft* (third edition, Heidelberg, 1920), E. Bourciez's *Éléments de linguistique romane* (third edition, Paris, 1930), A. Zauner's *Romanische Sprachwissenschaft* (two volumes, fourth edition, Berlin and Leipzig, 1921–26), and P. Savj-Lopez's *Le origini neolatine* (Milan, 1920), while the first volume of the *Grundriss der romanischen Philologie* (second edition, Strassburg, 1906) contains seven studies on the pre-Romance languages in the Romance areas, and seven on the individual old and modern Romance tongues. For etymology, one has the *Romanisches etymologisches Wörterbuch* of Meyer-Lübke (third edition, Heidelberg, 1935), which supersedes G. Körting's *Lateinisch-romanisches Wörterbuch* (third edition, Paderborn, 1907), both to be used with caution when dealing with Romance words from non-Latin sources.

Descriptive grammars and dictionaries of all the Romance languages and of many of their dialects abound, but the number of special diachronic and scientific grammars and of etymological dictionaries is surprisingly small. For French, we have, in particular, K. Nyrop's *Grammaire historique de la langue française* (six volumes, Copenhagen, 1914–30), Meyer-Lübke's *Historische Grammatik der französischen Sprache* (two volumes, Heidelberg, 1913–21), A. Ewert's *The French Language* (London, 1933), and Mildred Pope's *From Latin to Modern French* (Manchester, 1934); for the dialects, E. Herzog has a convenient collection in his *Neufranzösische Dialekttexte mit grammatischer Einleitung* (Leipzig, 1906); and for etymology, the *Französisches etymologisches Wörterbuch* of W. von Wartburg (Bonn, 1928 sqq.), E. Gamillscheg's *Etymologisches Wörterbuch der französischen Sprache* (Heidelberg, 1928), and, for the French-Canadian of Quebec, the *Glossaire du parler français au Canada* (Québec, 1930), giving the dialectic sources in France. For Walloon, M. Valkhoff has published a general survey in his *Philologie et littérature wallonnes* (Groningen and Batavia, 1938).

For Spanish, the chief works are the *Gramática histórica de la lengua castellana* of F. Hanssen (Halle, 1913; the German original, *Spanische Grammatik auf historischer Grundlage*, Halle, 1910, is much inferior), R. Menéndez Pidal's *Manual de gramática histórica española* (fifth edition, Madrid, 1929) and *El idiom español en sus primieros tiempos* (Madrid, 1927), and W. J. Entwistle's *The Spanish Language, together with Portuguese, Catalan, and Basque* (London, 1936). For Portuguese, we have J. J. Nunes's *Compêndio de gramática histórica portuguesa* (Lisbon, 1919) and J. Leite de Vasconcellos's *Esquisse d'une dialectologie portugaise* (Paris, 1901), as well as E. B. Williams's *From Latin to Portuguese* (Philadelphia, 1938) and A. Epiphânio da Silva Dias's *Syntaxe histórica portuguesa* (second edition, Lisbon, 1933); for Italian, C. H. Grandgent's *From Latin to Italian* (Cambridge, U. S. A., 1927) and G. Bertoni's *Italia dialettale* (Milan, 1916); for Rumanian, D. Densusianu's *Histoire de la langue roumaine* (two volumes, Paris, 1901–32); and for Dalmatian, M. Bartoli's *Das Dalmatische: altromanische Sprachreste von Veglia bis Ragusa und ihre Stellung in der apennino-balkanischen Romania* (two volumes, Vienna, 1906).

Celtic

The Celtic group falls into two divisions, in one of which Indo-European q^u is represented by a guttural, while in the other it appears as a labial, a distinction which recurs in Latin as contrasted with Osco-Umbrian (cf. p. 335; e.g., Old Irish *cethir* ' four ' : Gaulish *petru-decametos* ' fourteenth ', Old Welsh *pet-guar*, Modern Welsh *pedwar*, Cornish *peswar*, Breton *pevar* ' four '; cf. Latin *quater*, Oscan *petiro-pert* ' four times ', Greek τέσσαρες, Sanskrit *catvāras*, Indo-European *q^uetuor* ' four '). The q-group, consisting of Irish (including Scots Gaelic) and Manx, is conventionally called *Goidelic;* the p-group, comprising Gaulish, Welsh, Cornish, and Breton, is similarly termed *Brythonic,* although Gaulish, for geographical reasons, is often classed by itself as Continental.

The oldest of the Celtic languages, so far as historical records are concerned, is *Gaulish,* represented by a host of names of persons and places, glosses, and some seventy-eight brief inscriptions, written in Greek or Roman letters, and ranging from the third century B.C. to the second A.D. (?), besides a large number of *graffiti,* found chiefly at La Graufesenque (Aveyron) and collected by F. Hermet *(La Graufesenque (Condatomago),* two volumes, Paris, 1934) ; but the only document of any length is the very fragmentary and obscure Calendar of Coligny. From all this material we get a fair idea of the inflexion of the noun, but only a few forms of the verb. After the Roman conquest of Gaul, the language became moribund (cf. pp. 32, 33), yet Saint Jerome (about 331–420) could still say that the Galatians of Angora spoke essentially the same language as the Gauls of Trèves, so that Gaulish must still have survived both in Asia Minor and in Gaul even at that late date.

Between Gaulish and the Brythonic of Britain, Tacitus tells us, there was little difference; but our earliest Brythonic glosses do not appear until about 800 for *Welsh* and *Breton,* and not until the twelfth century for *Cornish.* The oldest literary records, which constitute the middle periods, are still later: for Welsh, from the twelfth century; for Cornish and Breton, from the fifteenth, Middle Welsh literature consisting chiefly of short poems, and Cornish and Breton of dramas on Biblical themes and on lives of the saints respectively. The modern periods begin for Welsh in the middle of the sixteenth century, and for Breton from the beginning of the nineteenth. Cornish, after its great dramas of the fifteenth century, steadily gave place to English until it vanished in the early nineteenth century (the stock story that Dolly Pentreath of Mousehole, who died in 1777, was the last to speak it is now abandoned). Breton, which is not a survival of Gaulish, but which was carried from Britain to Armorica by immigration in the fifth and sixth centuries, is, it would seem, more closely related to Cornish than to Welsh.

Of Cornish, we have no evidence of dialectic fissure; but Modern Welsh falls into Northern (Anglesey, Carnarvon, and Merioneth) and Southern (Cardigan, Carmarthen, and Glamorgan) ; and Breton has four main dialects: Trégorois, Léonard, Cornouaillais, and Vannetais, centring at Tréguier, St-Pol-de-Léon, Quimper, and Vannes respectively, three of which are closely alike, while the fourth (Vannetais) shows marked divergencies. Both Welsh and Breton are flourishing, though the latter is handicapped by at least passive resistance on the part of the French Government (cf. p. 117). Efforts are being made to combine Trégorois, Léonard, and Cornouaillais into a unified literary language, and some attempt is even under way to revive Cornish as a vernacular, though scarcely with prospect of success.

By far the most important Celtic language is *Irish*, represented by about three hundred inscriptions (mostly brief epitaphs) in Ireland and some sixty in Great Britain, mostly of the fifth and sixth centuries, and chiefly in Ogam characters, a script from the same source as the Teutonic ' secret runes ', if one be not actually derived from the other; a large body of glosses on the Bible and Latin authors, with one composition, the *Cambrai Homily*, of some length (Old Irish, from the eighth century to the eleventh) ; a very abundant literature of high intrinsic merit and interest, including much re-edited pagan material in which marked linguistic traces of Old Irish survive (Middle Irish, from the twelfth century to the early part of the seventeenth) ; and a rapidly increasing amount of Modern Irish from the early seventeenth century to the present day.

Of early Irish dialects, we have little knowledge; but the modern language has four great dialectic divisions: Munster, Leinster, Connacht, and Ulster, of which, Munster has been chosen by the Government of Eire to serve as the basis of the standard dialect. A line drawn from Dublin to Galway leaves the dialects of Munster and Leinster to the south, and those of Connacht and Ulster to the north, the former pair marked by greater conservatism in phonology than in morphology, and the latter by tenacity in morphology rather than in phonology. In the early part of the nineteenth century, Irish was still the vernacular of four-fifths of the population, but it then declined rapidly in favour of English until it is now spoken almost only in the ' Gaeltacht ' along the western coast, though the Government of Eire is making strenuous efforts to revive it as a vernacular throughout its entire area (cf. p. 117).

An off-shoot of Irish is *Scots Gaelic*, carried to Scotland from Ireland from the fifth century onward, likewise divided into several dialects, and with an unexpectedly large representation in Nova Scotia and Cape Breton Island, thanks to Scottish immigrants. The remaining Goidelic language, *Manx*, whose earliest literary record is a translation of the Book of Common Prayer between 1625 and 1630, which was not printed until 1895, is now spoken only by a few hundred people in the Isle of Man, and is rapidly becoming extinct.

The Brythons evidently once occupied large parts of Britain later conquered by Goidels and English, as is clear from such place-names as the Brythonic *Aberdeen* (' mouth of the Dee ') in contrast with the Goidelic name of the neighbouring town of *Inverurie* (' mouth of the Urie '; cf. p. 122) ; and it seems likely, on the whole, that *Pictish*, of which only proper names, a very small number of glosses, and (apparently) six practically unintelligible Scottish inscriptions have survived, was also a Brythonic dialect.

Celtic is the most difficult and obscure of all the Indo-European family from the linguistic point of view because of its excessively complicated phonology, which thus far seems to defy reduction to any system of correspondences, and which has led to a deformation of words which often renders them unrecognisable except after the most painstaking analysis. Its syntax also is highly intricate; and the group has even been supposed to have a non-Indo-European (Iberian or Berber) sub-stratum (cf. pp. 136–137), an hypothesis which as yet has not been conclusively established.

The remains of Gaulish are collected (though with certain omissions and with inclusion of some allogenous material, both unavoidable in the nature of the case) in A. Holder's *Alt-celtischer Sprachschatz* (three volumes, Leipzig, 1896–1913; the author's death stopped the work abruptly in the addenda to the letter *C*, and there is no prospect of its completion), and are scientifically discussed in G. Dottin's *La Langue gauloise* (Paris, 1920) and L. Weisgerber's *Die Sprache der Festlandkelten* (in *Berichte der römisch-germanischen Kommission des deutschen archäologischen Instituts*, xx [1930], 147–226).

For Old Irish, we have the comparative discussion in R. Thurneysen's *Handbuch des Altirischen* (Heidelberg, 1909; the *Grammaire du vieil-irlandais* of J. Vendryes, Paris, 1908, rich in material, is purely descriptive, as is the *Manuel d'irlandais moyen* of Dottin, two volumes, Paris, 1913) ; and for Modern Irish, the descriptive *New Era Grammar of Modern Irish* by G. O'Nolan (Dublin, 1934) and T. F. O'Rahilly's *Irish Dialects Past and Present* (Dublin, 1932). Goidelic etymology is treated in A. Mac-Bain's *Etymological Dictionary of the Gaelic Language* (second edition, Inverness, 1911; to be used with caution).

Welsh has a scientific discussion in the *Welsh Grammar, Historical and Comparative* of Sir J. M. Jones (Oxford, 1913; not without faults), who died before completing his *Welsh Syntax* (Cardiff, 1931; only the epithetologue is treated fully), and in J. Baudiš's *Grammar of Early Welsh*, of which only the part dealing with phonology appeared (Oxford, 1924) ; and Breton, of which W. B. S. Smith is preparing an historical and comparative grammar, has a very fair etymological dictionary in V. Henry's *Lexique étymologique des termes les plus usuels du breton moderne* (Rennes, 1900), while E. Ernaut has appended a *Dictionnaire étymologique du breton moyen* to his edition of *Le Mystère de sainte Barbe* (Nantes, 1885).

For the remaining languages, we have only descriptive grammars, e.g., for the Irish of the Isles of Aran, F. N. Finck's *Die Araner Mundart* (two volumes, Marburg, 1899) ; for Scots Gaelic, G. Calder's *Gaelic Grammar* (Glasgow [1923]) ; for Manx, J. J. Kneen's *Grammar of the Manx Language* (Oxford, 1931) ; for Cornish, H. Jenner's *Handbook of the Cornish Language* (London, 1904) ; and for Breton, J. Le Gonidec's *Grammaire celto-bretonne* (new edition, Paris, 1838), J. Hingant's *Éléments de la grammaire bretonne* (Tréguier, 1868), L. Le Clerc's *Grammaire bretonne du dialecte de Tréguier* (second edition, Tréguier, 1911), the *Grammaire bretonne du dialecte de Vannes* of A. Guillevic and P. Le Goff (second edition, Vannes, 1912), A. Sommerfelt's *Le Breton parlé à Saint-Pol-de-Léon* (Rennes, 1920), and L. Vallée's *La Langue bretonne en quarante leçons* (seventh edition, St. Brieuc, 1926).

For the Celtic family as a whole, we have the masterly *Vergleichende Grammatik der keltischen Sprachen* of H. Pedersen (two volumes, Göttingen, 1909–13), replacing the pioneer *Grammatica Celtica* of J. K. Zeuss (second edition, Berlin, 1871) and abridged by Pedersen and H. Lewis as *A Concise Comparative Celtic Grammar* (Göttingen, 1937). The only etymological dictionary of Celtic generally is W. Stokes's *Urkeltischer Sprachschatz* (Göttingen, 1894), which is wholly antiquated.

Teutonic

The Teutonic languages, more usually called Germanic, a term which, from the specific connotation of ' German ' in English, is apt to suggest an unduly limited geographical area, are conventionally divided into Eastern, Northern, and Western, a classification which is geographic and convenient rather than historic and accurate. The oldest traces of Teutonic are proper names recorded by Classical writers, words borrowed by Finnish, and about a hundred archaic Runic inscriptions, found especially in Scandinavia and Denmark, ranging in date from the third century to the eighth, and consisting chiefly of proper names, with relatively few common nouns or verbs.

The earliest literary remains are in *East Teutonic* or *Gothic* — translations of parts of the Bible by the Arian bishop Wulfila (Ulfilas) in the fourth century, a commentary *(Skeireins)* on the Fourth Gospel, a fragment of a calendar, signatures to a couple of legal documents, and a vocabulary of some sixty words in Crimean Gothic, recorded by the Fleming Ogier Ghislain van Busbecq, envoy of Charles V from the Low Countries to Constantinople in the sixteenth century. Wulfila's see was in Dacia, whither a wave of Gothic migration had spread, and he himself was a Visigoth; but the language belongs, in reality, to the North Teutonic division in Scandinavia, where the island of Götland and the areas of Öster-götland and Vestergötland still perpetuate the memory of the Goths. Because of its primitive form and the amount of its fragments, Gothic is essentially the foundation of all Teutonic linguistics, and a knowledge of it is requisite for every student of Indo-European. It perhaps finds cognates in *Vandal* and *Burgundian*, of which little survives but proper names and some words long since naturalised in Romance.

Besides the Runic inscriptions and the Vandal and Burgundian just mentioned, *North Teutonic* falls into a western and an eastern group. To the former belong *Icelandic, Norwegian,* and *Faroese,* the most important linguistically being Icelandic, whose oldest documents date from the twelfth century. Thanks to the wide extent of its literature, which, like that of Middle Irish, possesses real intrinsic interest, it is the chief source of knowledge of all North Teutonic. Norwegian has records almost as old as Icelandic, and Iceland was, indeed, but a Norwegian colony. The Norwegians also went as far as Scotland and Ireland, besides controlling the Shetlands, Orkneys, Hebrides, and the Faroe Islands.

To the eastern division belong *Swedish, Danish,* and *Gothlandic* (Jutnian), the earliest remains of the two first dating from the thirteenth century, and of Gothlandic a hundred years later. The Danes occupied Schleswig, set up a brief dynasty in England, crossed to Ireland, and put their stamp on Normandy (' Land of the Northmen '), where Danish was spoken in Bayeux as late as the twelfth century, and where a few Danish place-names still survive (e.g., *Daubeuf* = *Dal-búð* ' Valley-Booth '; *Harfleur* = -*flóð* ' flood ' both modified by popular etymology with French *bœuf* ' ox ' and *fleur* ' flower ' respectively; *Le Torp*[*t*] = *þorp* ' village '). The Swedes spread into Finland, Esthonia, Livonia, and even into Russia, to which they gave its name (cf. p. 125) and where they held Novgorod until about 1300. Norwegian died out as a literary language in the Middle Ages, when it gave place to Danish, which, under the appellation of *Riksmaal*, served as the standard speech until the nineteenth century and, indeed, still so functions to a considerable extent. The *Riksmaal* is now yielding place to a truly national *Landsmaal*, based upon indigenous Norwegian dialects, after a struggle analogous to that in modern Greece between the *Katharévousa* and the *Dhēmotikế* (cf. p. 29).

Western Teutonic is conventionally divided into Low and High, these terms referring to the different altitudes above sea-level, running from north to south; and it would seem that we should also speak of a *Middle* group in German proper. The basis of classification is the divergent consonantism (the so-called sound-shift; cf. pp. 79–82), e.g., Low Teutonic *t* = High Teutonic *z* [ts] (English *ten* : German *zehn)*, while Middle German stands midway between the two (e.g., English *God* : Middle German [standard High German] *Gott* : Bavarian *Kot)*.

It is not easy to give a systematic grouping of this Western division. Perhaps one may begin with *Old Saxon*, whose chief monument is the *Hēliand* (' Saviour '), a poem of some six thousand lines, composed about A.D. 830. This language was spoken between the Rhine and the Elbe, the North Sea and the Harz Mountains, from the ninth century to the twelfth, and then merged into *Middle Low German*, represented by *Plattdeutsch* in northern Germany. *Old Low Franconian*, or *Old Dutch*, preserved only in fragments of a glass, is the principal forerunner of *Modern Dutch;* and Old Saxon survives in the *Saxon* vernacular of the north-east.

Old Frisian, the ancestor of *Modern Frisian*, was spoken between the Scheldt and the Weser, and by A.D. 800 had become so closely akin to Anglo-Saxon that the two are often regarded as constituting a special Anglo-Frisian sub-group of Teutonic. Its oldest documents date only from the thirteenth century. *Anglo-Saxon* itself had several dialects, spoken from the Thames southward, of which

West Saxon was the most important in view of its wealth of documents, beginning with the ninth century. *Kentish* was the dialect of Kent; *Northumbrian* (itself divided into Northern and Southern, represented respectively by the Lindisfarne Gospels and by the Rushworth Gospels from Mark ii. 15 onward) and *Mercian* were *Anglian* dialects; but their remains, however important for comparison with West Saxon, are relatively scanty.

According to the Venerable Bede (675–735), the Teutonic invaders of England came from Jutland, Angulus (an area in eastern Schleswig which is still called Angeln), and Old Saxony (meaning by this the territory between the Elbe and the Weser or Ems); but however true this may have been as regards their earliest known habitats, the three peoples seem to have been amalgamated both racially and linguistically on the Continent. The three main Anglo-Saxon dialects, then, are not to be traced to three separate Continental languages, but to one single origin which became differentiated into three in England itself, the bulk of their distinctive variations probably being later than A.D. 500. The most that can safely be said is that resemblances between Old Frisian and Kentish may indicate a close relationship between Jutes and Frisians, or a Jutish settlement in Frisian territory before the invasion of England; while similar connexions between Anglian and Scandinavian may point to a proximity of Angles to Scandinavians on the Continent.

Anglo-Saxon passes over into *Middle English,* from 1150 to 1400, ending with such authors as Chaucer and Gower. Its three main divisions, *Northern, Midland,* and *Southern,* broadly characterised by their forms of the third plural present indicative (e.g., *hop-es, hop-en,* and *hop-eth),* represent the older Northumbrian, Mercian, and West Saxon respectively; and to these must be added the continuance of *Kentish* in Kent. *Modern English* likewise has a large number of dialects, which thus far seem unsusceptible of exact classification even on the basis of Anglo-Saxon or Middle English predecessors, and which are of much value for phonology and as preserving words which have disappeared from standard English.

Through colonisation, English has spread far outside England; and in the United States especially the language has so changed that one is fairly justified in speaking of *American English.* Here we find three chief types, each with many subdivisions: *New England* (' Yankee '), *Southern,* and *General American* (the latter covering about four-fifths of the United States and spoken by about two-thirds of their population), due, in the main, to Puritan and Pilgrim and to Cavalier colonists, all from England, and to later migrations of these elements after the Colonial Period. The pronunciation of the first is relatively flat and sharp, often with a nasal twang; that of the second is softer and more drawling, and more musical, and tends to sonantise or even to drop plosives; and the third is characterised by the retention of [r], which inclines to vanish in the other two. All are essentially based on a mixture of English dialects, further complicated by migrations within the United States themselves, and show the independent evolutions normally found in languages cut off from their sources. In part this evolution has been consciously stimulated, e.g., by Noah Webster, through a nationalistic desire to be independent of the mother-country in language as well as in government, sometimes with unfortunate results, as in spelling *honour*, etc., *honor*, etc., thus implying that the word is derived directly from Latin *honor-* instead of from Anglo-French *honur, honour* (cf. Modern French *honneur)*. On the whole, American English is more drawling, and its pitch lower and more monotonous than British. In vocabulary, there is considerable difference between American and British, the former retaining a number of words and meanings which have become obsolete in the latter, e.g., American *sick* ' ill ' : English *nauseated;* American *fall* : English *autumn;* and accentuation frequently differs, as American *'laboratory* : English *la'boratory.*

English also has certain creolised forms (cf. pp. 36–37), notably *Pidgin English (pidgin* being itself a ' pidgin ' corruption of *business)*, a mixture of English and Chinese used as a means of communication especially in China; *Beach-la-mar*, a combination of English and Malay similarly employed in certain islands of the Pacific; *Ningre-Tongo* or *Taki-Taki*, spoken by the descendants of slaves along the coast of Surinam in Dutch Guiana; and *Jew-Tongo*, the vernacular of the Bush Negroes on the Saramakka River in the same colony; to which one may add the extinct *Chinook Jargon*, an amalgam of English and American Indian Chinuk formerly current on the north-west coast of the United States.

The *German* division of the Western Teutonic group is divided into three broad types: (1) *Franconian*, (2) *Hessian* and *Thuringian*, and (3) *Alemannic, Bavarian*, and *Lombard*. Of these, Franconian shows three forms: *Lower, Middle,* and *Upper,* the distinction between them being the extent to which they are affected by the Teutonic sound-shifting. Lower Franconian is essentially Low Teutonic of the type represented by Flemish, Frisian, Old Saxon, and Plattdeutsch; and has combined with Frisian and Saxon to produce Dutch. Middle Franconian appears in two sub-forms: *Ripuarian* in the north, and *Moselle* in the south; while Upper Franconian is divided into *Eastern* and *Rhenish.*

Middle and Upper Franconian have united with Hessian and Thuringian to form *Middle German,* which is the basis of the modern German literary language. Alemannic and Bavarian, together with Lombard, which seems to have become extinct about A.D. 1000, and which survives only in words preserved in mediaeval Latin documents, proper names, and reconstructions from forms borrowed from it by Romance, constitute *High German* in the strict sense of the term. Here the sound-shifting has been carried to its furthest extent, whereas Middle German represents a stage midway between Low German (Dutch, English, etc.) and High German (e.g., Old Franconian *beran,* English *bear* : Old Alemannic *peran;* Old Franconian *gast,* English *guest* : Old Alemannic *kast*).

The earliest records of German are glosses of the eighth century, but literature proper begins in the ninth. Chronologically, Old High German literature runs from the eighth century to the end of the eleventh, and Middle High German from the twelfth to the fifteenth, when the Modern High German period begins.

The principal characteristics of the Teutonic group as a whole are (1) sweeping transformation of much of the consonantism by the sound-shifting; (2) weakening of unaccented vowels because of the strong stress-accent; (3) modification of the vowels of accented syllables by those of unaccented syllables following (umlaut; a similar phenomenon is seen in Celtic, where it is termed infection, and in Avestan; cf. pp. 69, 313); (4) employment of vowel-gradation (ablaut; see pp. 65–68) to indicate functions, notably to mark tense in the strong verbs, as in English *sing* : *sang* : *sung);* and (5) the great simplification of the verb, which retains only the present and preterite (cf. p. 214).

The two chief forms of creolised languages of the Teutonic group, in addition to those already noted for English (cf. pp. 36–37, 348), are *Afrikaans,* spoken among the Boers in South Africa, i.e., Dutch profoundly modified by contact with the native African languages and with English, French, and Malayo-Polynesian immigrants; and *Yiddish*, or *Judaeo-German*, based upon a Franconian German dialect of the fourteenth century with many Hebrew words, and spoken by Jewish communities in Lithuania, Poland, Russia, and parts of Rumania as well as by Jewish emigrants from those areas. The dialect has almost disappeared from its original home, Germany, as it has from Alsace and Lorraine.

While Teutonic shows a number of affinities with Slavic and Italo-Celtic, these are scarcely sufficient to warrant assumption of a period of earlier unity. The chief problem here is the origin of the sound-shifting (cf. pp. 79–82, 310), for which several explanations have been advanced. Some hold that it was the result of more strenuous vocal effort in high altitudes; others, that it was due to purely physiological causes; others still, that its cause was imposition of Indo-European speech upon earlier inhabitants of the area, who spoke some non-Indo-European language or languages. The question is still open; but it would seem that we may at once discard the first theory; the opinion of the majority of scholars now inclines toward the third, though it would appear that the second may have some arguments in its favour; in all probability, it is the result of more than one factor.

The vocabulary of Teutonic is as mixed as that of other Indo-European groups (cf. pp. 126–128). Out of 1165 of its word-groups, it has been estimated that 504 (.4326%) are restricted to the Teutonic dialects, while 661 (.5674%) are found in other Indo-European languages. Some of the groups thus far known only in Teutonic may yet be found to be Indo-European; but many of them are doubtless of allogenous origin, as is the case with the word-stocks of all other members of this linguistic family (cf. pp. 133, 136).

The following sections of the first volume of the *Grundriss der germanischen Philologie* (second edition, Strassburg, 1901) are important for a knowledge of Teutonic linguistics: *Urgermanisch*, by F. Kluge (third edition, Strassburg, 1913); *Geschichte der gotischen Sprache*, by M. H. Jellinek (Berlin and Leipzig, 1926, replacing Kluge's work of the same title); *Geschichte der nordischen Sprachen*, by A. Noreen (third edition, Strassburg, 1913); *Geschichte der deutschen Sprache*, by O. Behagel (fifth edition, Berlin and Leipzig, 1928); *Geschichte der niederländischen Sprache*, by J. te Winkel (pp. 781–925); *Geschichte der englischen*

Sprache, by F. Kluge (pp. 926–1151) ; *Geschichte der friesischen Sprache,* by T. Siebs (pp. 1152–1464) ; and treatments of various Teutonic dialects (pp. 1465–1537).

For the group in general, the principal works are A. Meillet's *Caractères généraux des langues germaniques* (fourth edition, Paris, 1930), W. Streitberg's *Urgermanische Grammatik* (Heidelberg, 1896), H. Hirt's *Handbuch des Urgermanischen* (three volumes, Heidelberg, 1931–34), R. Loewe's *Germanische Sprachwissenschaft* (fourth edition, two volumes, Berlin and Leipzig, 1933), the *Laut- und Formenlehre der altgermanischen Dialekte* edited by F. Dieter (Leipzig, 1900), E. Prokosch's *Comparative Germanic Grammar* (Philadelphia, 1939), the etymological dictionary of A. Torp and H. S. Falk, *Wortschatz der germanischen Spracheinheit* (Göttingen, 1909), and, for early Teutonic loan-words in Finnish, V. Thomsen's *Den gotiske sprogklasses indflydelse på den finske* (Copenhagen, 1869; reprinted, with additional material, in his *Samlede Afhandlinger* ii, Copenhagen, 1920, pp. 51–264; German translation by E. Sievers, *Über den Einfluss der germanischen Sprachen auf die finnisch-lappischen,* Halle, 1870), T. E. Karsten's *Germanisch-finnische Lehnwort-Studien* (Helsingfors, 1915) and *Fragen aus dem Gebiet der germanisch-finnischen Berührungen* (Helsingfors, 1922), and B. Collinder's *Urgermanische Lehnwörter im Finnischen* (Upsala, 1932).

For Gothic, the best linguistic discussion is by E. Kieckers, *Handbuch der vergleichenden gotischen Grammatik* (Munich, 1928), and the best dictionary, S. Feist's *Vergleichendes Wörterbuch der gotischen Sprache* (third edition, Leyden, 1939). The Scandinavian languages have practically been treated only descriptively, but H. S. Falk and A. Torp have made an excellent *Norwegisch-dänisches etymologisches Wörterbuch* (Heidelberg, 1910–1911). For Danish, we have also V. Dahlerup's *Det danske sprogs historie* (second edition, Copenhagen, 1921). For Dutch, one may mention M. Schönfeld's *Historiese grammatica van het Nederlands* (second edition, Zutphen, 1921) and J. Franck's *Etymologisch woordenboek der nederlandsche taal* (second edition, by N. Van Wijk, The Hague, 1912; supplement by C. B. van Haeringen, The Hague, 1938) ; the creolised forms of Dutch are discussed by D. C. Hesseling in *Het Afrikaans* (second edition, Leyden, 1924), and *Het Negerhollandsch der Deense Antillen* (Leyden, 1905), as well as by J. P. B. de Josselin de Jong, in his *Het huidige*

Negerhollandsch (Amsterdam, 1926), while Low German generally is treated by H. Grimme, in his *Plattdeutsche Mundarten* (second edition, Berlin and Leipzig, 1922).

Perhaps the best histories of English are R. Huchon's *Histoire de la langue anglaise* (two volumes, to the introduction of printing, Paris, 1923–30) and H. C. Wyld's *Short History of English* (third edition, London, 1927), other works being, for example, O. Jespersen's *Growth and Structure of the English Language* (fourth edition, London, 1929) and *Modern English Grammar* (four volumes, Heidelberg, 1927–33), O. F. Emerson's *History of the English Language* (New York, 1912), A. G. Baugh's book with the same title (New York, 1935), and K. Luick's *Historische Grammatik der englischen Sprache* (only the first volume, dealing with phonology, has appeared, Leipzig, 1929). For American English we have G. P. Krapp's *The English Language in America* (two volumes, New York, 1925) and H. L. Mencken's *The American Language* (revised edition, New York, 1936; of value chiefly for its collection of material). The outstanding features of English dialects are presented in J. Wright's *English Dialect Grammar* (Oxford, 1905).

For English etymology perhaps the best work is *The Century Dictionary* (eight volumes, New York, 1895; the new edition is very meagre in this respect), together with E. Weekley's *Etymological Dictionary of Modern English* (London, 1921) and *Concise Etymological Dictionary of Modern English* (London, 1924). W. W. Skeat's *Etymological Dictionary of the English Language* (revised and enlarged edition, Oxford, 1910) is largely antiquated, while the *English Etymology* of F. Kluge and F. Lutz (Strassburg, 1898) and the *Etymologisches Wörterbuch der englischen Sprache* of F. Holthausen (second edition, Leipzig, 1927), like his *Altenglisches etymologisches Wörterbuch* (Leipzig, 1934), are too brief to be of much value. For English dialects, the one work is J. Wright's *English Dialect Dictionary* (six volumes, Oxford, 1898–1905).

For German, mention may be made of H. Hirt's *Geschichte der deutschen Sprache* (second edition, Munich, 1925) and of S. Feist's *Die deutsche Sprache* (second edition, Munich, 1933), while syntax is treated by O. Behagel in his *Deutsche Syntax* (four volumes, Heidelberg, 1923–32), and the dialects are briefly summarised by H. Reis in his *Die deutschen Mundarten* (Berlin and Leipzig,

1912). The two chief works on German etymology are F. Kluge's *Etymologisches Wörterbuch der deutschen Sprache* (eleventh edition, by A. Götze, Berlin, 1934) and H. Hirt's *Etymologie der neuhochdeutschen Sprache* (second edition, Munich, 1921).

Balto-Slavic

As the designation implies, this group falls into two main divisions: Baltic and Slavic. Some investigators maintain that they should be considered distinct families, their correspondences being due to independent, though parallel, development; but in our present state of knowledge it is perhaps more prudent to retain the old view that, like Indo-Iranian (cf. pp. 312–322), they form essentially a single division of Indo-European.

(1) *Baltic.* — This sub-group comprises Old Prussian, Lithuanian, and Lettish (or Latvian). *Old Prussian* is represented by two versions of Luther's *Catechism* (both printed in 1545), the *Enchiridion*, or Short Catechism, of Luther (1561), eight hundred and two words in the Elbing Glossary of the early fourteenth or even thirteenth century, and one hundred words recorded in the early sixteenth century by the Dominican friar Simon Grunau. The Catechisms show the existence of two dialects; but the value of the documents is much diminished by the fact that either the translator, Abel Will, was imperfectly acquainted with Old Prussian, or that the language had reached a stage of grave linguistic decay; and the work of Grunau is seriously inaccurate. Old Prussian became extinct by the end of the sixteenth century; and though M. Praetorius records some ' Prussian ' words in his *Preussische Schaubühne* in the seventeenth century, these are probably Lithuanian.

If Old Prussian has vanished, Lithuanian and Lettish are still spoken, and have been made the official languages of the new States of Lithuania and Latvia, with a considerable and growing literature which includes a large mass of folk-songs of more than usual interest. In *Lithuanian*, which linguistically is by far the most important member of the Baltic group, the earliest records date from 1547; and the language falls into two main divisions, each with several dialects: *Žemaitish* or *Low* in the north, and *High* in the south, the latter being the source of the standard literary dialect. *Lettish*, whose earliest extant documents were written in 1586, is an off-shoot from Lithuanian, considerably modified because of the migration of the Latvians into a Finnish-speaking area which still survives in Esthonia, to the north of Latvia (cf. p. 369). Lettish is divided into three main dialect-groups: *Tahmian* or *Low* in western Kurland and part of western Livonia; *Middle*, the basis of the standard dialect; and *High* in south-eastern Livonia, the highlands of Kurland, and the arrondissements of Dünaburg, Rositten, and Ludsen. Of these, Middle Lettish is the most conservative as regards phonology, while Tahmian and High are more retentive of the old system of morphology.

Lithuanian and Lettish alike (cf. p. 311) are characterised by conservatism in phonology and in the inflexion of the epithetologue, the vowel-system of Modern Lithuanian being, like that of Greek and Oscan, nearer to the Indo-European stage than is Vedic Sanskrit; and the epithetologue still retains seven cases and the dual number, though the latter survives only in stereotyped fragments in Lettish. Furthermore, Lithuanian and, to a much less degree, Lettish have kept in principle the early triple system of accent represented in Greek by the acute, grave, and circumflex, which are distinguished by different intonations (cf. p. 63); but, because of special and often mutually contradictory developments, Baltic accent can be used only with caution in determining Indo-European accent, for which the chief sources must remain Vedic and Greek.

The whole Balto-Slavic group is considered in R. Trautmann's *Baltisch-slavisches Wörterbuch* (Göttingen, 1923), and the much-disputed problem of accentuation in such works as N. van Wijk's *Baltische und slavische Akzent- und Intonationssysteme* (Amsterdam, 1923), while the relationship of the family to other linguistic stocks is studied in H. Arntz's *Sprachliche Beziehungen zwischen Arisch und Balto-Slawisch* (Heidelberg, 1933), C. C. Uhlenbeck's *Die lexicalische Urverwandtschaft des Baltoslavischen und Germanischen* (Leyden, 1890), and V. Thomsen's *Beröringer mellem de finske og de baltiske (litauisk-lettiske) Sprog* (Copenhagen, 1890). Old Prussian is linguistically studied in R. Trautmann's *Die altpreussischen Denkmäler* (Göttingen, 1910); and Lettish in J. Endzelin's *Lettische Grammatik* (Heidelberg, 1923), this language also having an admirable dictionary, with etymological material, in K. Mühlenbach's *Lettisch-deutsches Wörterbuch* (completed by Endzelin, four volumes, Riga, 1923–32). Lithuanian, on the other hand, has received as yet no adequate linguistic grammar, for the

Leišu valodas rokas grāmata of J. Plāka (in Lettish; Riga, 1926) is quite meagre; and E. Fraenkel's *Syntax der litauischen Kasus* (Kaunas, 1928) considers only the epithetologue.

(2) *Slavic.* — This division of the Balto-Slavic family falls into three great groups: Southern, Northern (Russian), and Western. The oldest of these is the *Southern,* represented since the second half of the ninth century by translations of the Bible and other theological writings in the dialect then spoken in the region of Saloniki and known as *Old Bulgarian* or (perhaps better) as *Old Church Slavic,* a language which maintained its position in the liturgy long after it had ceased to be a vernacular. The modern representatives of Southern Slavic are *Bulgarian,* based on Macedonian Slavic dialects; *Serbo-Croatian,* with three dialects conventionally named according to the way in which they form the word for ' what ': *Štokavian* (the basis of the literary language), *Čakavian,* and *Kaykavian;* and *Slovenian,* spoken in the Alpine regions of the Slavic area. Of these, Serbian, especially in its Čakavian dialect, is of particular interest because of its preservation (with certain regular mutations) of the Proto-Slavic accent.

The *Northern* group has three main divisions, none of which is older than the twelfth century: *Great Russian* (Russian *par excellence), White Russian,* and *Ruthenian* or Little Russian, Russian being the most important of this group for a knowledge of Slavic accent. The *Western* group consists of *Polish* (closely connected with *Kashubian* and *Slovincian), Sorbo-Wendic,* and *Czecho-Slovak* (formerly called Bohemian).

From the linguistic point of view, the chief Slavic languages are Old Church Slavic, Štokavian Serbian, and Russian. The Slavic group as a whole is more homogeneous and far less differentiated than any other Indo-European linguistic family. It has preserved the ancient inflexion of the epithetologue (including the dual); and though it has lost the perfect (except for a few fragments), it has retained both the root- and the -s-aorist, here being more primitive even than Baltic. It is particularly characterised by the principle of the open syllable, all plosives and spirants disappearing in final position, and being retained only when beginning a syllable. For the study of Indo-European, Balto-Slavic ranks third in importance, being outranked only by Vedic Sanskrit and Greek.

The chief comparative Slavic grammars are F. Miklosich's *Vergleichende Grammatik der slavischen Sprachen* (four volumes,

Vienna, 1874–79; the first and third volumes in a second edition; of great value for its collection of material, though antiquated in its point of view) ; W. Vondrák's *Vergleichende slavische Grammatik* (second edition, two volumes, Göttingen, 1924–28), and especially A. Meillet's *Le Slave commun* (second edition, aided by A. Vaillant, Paris, 1934). The group has two etymological dictionaries: Miklosich's *Etymologisches Wörterbuch der slavischen Sprachen* (Vienna, 1886; now in considerable part antiquated) and E. Berneker's *Slavisches etymologisches Wörterbuch* (Heidelberg, 1913 sqq.; the work stops abruptly in the middle of the word *morŭ*, and there is little hope that it will be completed) ; and Berneker also discussed an important syntactic problem in his *Wortfolge in den slavischen Sprachen* (Berlin, 1900). The phonology of the group is studied in O. Broch's *Slavische Phonetik* (Heidelberg, 1911), and the phonology and accentuation in J. J. Mikkola's *Urslavische Grammatik*, i (Heidelberg, 1913; no more published).

For the individual languages one has only historical and descriptive grammars, notably N. van Wijk's *Geschichte der altkirchenslavischen Sprache* (Berlin and Leipzig, 1931; the volume on syntax has not yet appeared; the fullest descriptive grammar is Vondrák's *Altkirchenslavische Grammatik*, second edition, Berlin, 1912), S. Mladenov's *Geschichte der bulgarischen Sprache* (Berlin and Leipzig, 1929), A. Leskien's *Grammatik der serbo-kroatischen Sprache* (Heidelberg, 1914; the volume on syntax is lacking), K. H. Meyer's *Historische Grammatik der russischen Sprache* (Bonn, 1923; the volume on syntax has not yet appeared), S. Szober's *Gramatyka języka polskiego* (two volumes, Warsaw, 1931, also lacking syntax), F. Lorentz's *Slovinzische Grammatik* (St. Petersburg, 1903) and *Geschichte der pomoranischen (kaschubischen) Sprache* (Berlin and Leipzig, 1925), K. Mucke's *Historische und vergleichende Laut- und Formenlehre der niedersorbischen (niederlausitzisch-wendischen) Sprache* (Leipzig, 1891), and J. Gebauer's *Historická mluvnice jazyka českého* (four volumes, completed by F. Trávníček, Prague, 1894–1929). Etymological dictionaries are represented by A. V. Preobražanskij's *Etimologičeskij slovarĭ russkago jazyka* (Moscow, 1910–16; only to the word *suleja)* and A. Brückner's *Słownik etymologiczny języka polskiego* (Cracow, 1927).

CHAPTER XII

Classification of Languages: The Non-Indo-European Languages

Hamito-Semitic: Semitic (migrations and characteristics; East, North-West, and South-West Semitic); Hamitic; suggested connexions with other language-families — Uralic: migrations and characteristics; groups of Uralic; suggested connexions with other language-families — Altaic: characteristics; groups of Altaic — Japanese and Korean — Eskimo-Aleut — Caucasian: North and South Caucasian; suggested connexions with other language-families — Ibero-Basque — Near Eastern and Asianic: Lower Mesopotamian, Peripheral, and Asianic groups — Hyperborean — Burushaskī — Dravidian: Tamil-Kurukh, Kui-Gōṇḍī, Telugu, Brahui; literature and characteristics; suggested connexions with other language-families — Andamanese — Sino-Tibetan: Yenissei-Ostyak, Tibeto-Burman, Tai-Chinese; characteristics and literatures; suggested connexions with other language-families — La-Ti — South-East Asiatic: Muṇḍā, Mon-Khmēr, Annam-Muong; difficulty of classification within the group; characteristics — Malayo-Polynesian: area and general characteristics; Indonesian, Melanesian, and Micronesian — Papuan — Australian: Northern and Southern groups; characteristics — Tasmanian — Sudano-Guinean: difficulty of classification; sources; general character of Negro-African; divisions of the group — Bantu: general characteristics; divisions of the group; suggested connexions with other language-families — Hottentot-Bushman — North American: difficulty of classification of American languages; divisions of North American — Mexican and Central American — Antillean and South American — question of number of languages in the world.

HAMITO-SEMITIC

SECOND in importance only to the Indo-European linguistic family comes the Hamito-Semitic group. Spoken in the fifth century B.C. throughout Africa north of the Sahara, in the Nile valley and east of the Blue Nile as far as the Equator, in all Arabia, and in Asia from the easternmost shore of the Mediterranean between Africa and Asia Minor to Mesopotamia, it still retains practically the same area, though some languages belonging to it (e.g., Akkadian) have vanished, only to be replaced by tongues of cognate stock, especially by Arabic. Excepting Sumerian (pp. 378–379), its literary remains are the oldest known, Egyptian being recorded as early as 3400 B.C., and Akkadian by 2800.

The group as a whole is composed of Semitic and Hamitic, the latter sub-divided into Egyptian, Libyco-Berber, and Kushitic; and a special society is devoted to its study, the Groupe linguistique d'études chamito-sémitiques, established at Paris in 1931. A notable feature of the entire family is the form of the base, which is predominantly triliteral in Semitic (e.g., *KTB* ' write '), though very frequently biliteral in Egyptian and Berber, and regularly so in Kushitic. A somewhat daring discussion of the family in connexion with Indo-European has been made by A. Cuny in his *Études prégrammaticales sur le domaine des langues indo-européennes et chamito-sémitiques* (Paris, 1924).

(1) *Semitic.* — The Semitic sub-group is divided into East Semitic (represented only by Akkadian) and West Semitic, the latter sub-divided into North-West (Canaanite and Aramaic) and South-West (Arabic, South Arabic, and Ethiopic). The original home of the Semites is as problematic as that of the Indo-Europeans (cf. pp. 304–310) ; but the consensus of opinion at present tends to place it in Arabia, even though ultimately, in view of the connexion of Semitic with Hamitic, the entire group may well have arisen somewhere in North Africa. From Arabia, wave after wave of Semitic migrations would seem to have set forth. The earliest of these migrants, and those who went farthest from the homeland, were the Akkadians, who, journeying along the Fertile Crescent through Palestine and Syria, and crossing over into the Mesopotamian Valley, reached the junction of the Tigris and Euphrates before 3000 B.C. The Aramaeans would appear to have followed as far as Syria about 2500, and the Canaanites as far as Palestine about 1400, while the Ethiopians migrated to Africa some centuries before the beginning of the Christian Era. It seems premature to decide on the linguistic affinities of *Palaeo-Sinaitic*, recorded in inscriptions dated between 2000 and 1500 B.C., and ascribed by some to the Semitic Hyksos, who ruled Egypt for more than a century before they were expelled to Palestine; or of *Amorite*, known only from proper names in Akkadian texts.

Linguistically, Semitic is often regarded as characterised by triliteral bases (as *KTB* ' write ', *TMM* ' end ', *KWM* ' stand ') and by an inflexional rôle of the vowels (e.g., Arabic *kataba* ' he has written ', *kutiba* ' it has been written '; *yaktubu* ' he will write ', *yuktabu* ' it will be written '; *kātaba* ' he has corresponded with someone ', *'aktaba* ' he has made someone write '; *kitābu^n* ' writing, book ', *kātibu^n* ' writer, scribe ', *katbu^n* ' act of writing ', etc.) ; but the real proof of its unity, as in the case of all linguistic groups, lies in the regular phonetic correspondences between its members which delimit it and contrast it over against all other language-families (cf. pp. 74, 302–303).

Semitic possesses, at least so far as its scripts show, a relatively poor vowel-system, having only *ă*, *ĭ*, and *ŭ* (the rich development of Hebrew according to the Masoretic vocalisation, reduced to writing thirteen centuries after Hebrew had ceased to be a vernacular, can scarcely be taken into consideration for determining the original conditions). The situation is rendered still more difficult by the fact that, outside Akkadian and Ethiopic, only consonants are written, except in the texts of the Bible and of the Qur'ān, where it was felt necessary to retain the exact traditional pronunciation; and in special cases, as in spelling foreign words, so that, for instance, Arabic *KTB* may be read *kataba, kutiba,* or *katbu^n* as the context seems to require. Our only source for even an approximate knowledge of Old Semitic vocalism (except for the special cases just noted) is the transcription of Semitic words by foreign authors, e.g., in glosses, in the Septuagint and Vulgate (the Greek and Latin versions of the Bible), in the *Hexapla* of Origen (A.D. 185–254), and in thirty-two lines in the *Poenulus* of Plautus (about 250–184 B.C.), etc. (cf. pp. 285, 425). The consonantal system is highly developed, especially as regards fricatives (glottal, pharyngal, uvular, palatal, emphatic, interdental, and labial) ; and the evolution of some of these, particularly of the interdentals and emphatics, is peculiarly intricate in the individual languages.

In the historic period, Semitic possesses two genders (masculine and feminine) ; three cases (nominative, genitive, and accusative, with traces of a locative) ; three numbers (singular, plural, and dual, the latter, as in Indo-European, in great part moribund or dead) ; separate forms for masculine and feminine in the second and third persons of the verb; moods ranging in number from five or six in Classical Arabic to five in Akkadian and Hebrew, four in Biblical Aramaic, three in Ethiopic, and two in Syriac and Modern Arabic; and two aspects (telic and atelic, commonly called perfect and imperfect; cf. pp. 203–208), to which Akkadian adds a permansive (e.g., *šakânu* ' to make ', *iškun* ' he has made ' [' his

making is finished '], *išakan* ' he makes ' or ' will make ' [' his
making is unfinished '], *šakin* ' he is [was, will be] making ' [as
a continuous procedure]) ; and both nouns and verbs are formed
not only by suffixing determinatives, but also by prefixing them
(cf. pp. 156–157). Generally speaking, the various Semitic dialects
closely resemble one another, their relative positions being roughly
analogous to those of the Romance languages among themselves,
or to the close mutual relations within the Slavic group. As contrasted with the intricate developments in Indo-European, reconstruction of Proto-Semitic, however difficult in details, is relatively
simple.

East Semitic is represented only by *Akkadian* (formerly, and
still popularly, called *Assyrian, Babylonian,* or *Assyro-Baby-
lonian)* with a rich literature of inscriptions and clay tablets.
These texts, whose subjects are historical records, legal codes,
letters and business documents, linguistic matters, omens, formulae of conjuration, hymns and prayers, rituals, epics and myths,
astronomy, astrology, and medicine, run from about 2800 to the
closing centuries B.C., the period from 2800 to 650 being termed
Old Akkadian (or Assyrian), and that after 650 being called New
Akkadian (or Babylonian). Although its documents are the oldest,
Akkadian is by no means the earliest linguistically (cf. p. 21), for
its speakers had not only travelled farthest of all the Semites, but
in their migrations they had passed through lands populated solely
by peoples whose languages were non-Semitic. Even when the
Akkadians reached the region which was to be their home, they
came in contact with a race not merely of alien speech, but also of
higher civilisation, the Sumerians (cf. pp. 378–379), with the result
that Akkadian as written contains many Sumerian logograms, i.e.,
words written as Sumerian but pronounced as Akkadian, somewhat as we write £ (for *libra*[*e*]*)* but read ' pound(s)', or write
10 d. (for *decem denarii)* but read ' ten pence ', or write *&, etc.*
(for *et cetera)* but read ' and ', ' and so forth '.

Linguistically, Akkadian shows considerable decay, particularly
in its loss of the uvular, pharyngal, palatal, and bilabial fricatives
and the glottal fricative [h], all of which have become a simple
glottal stop [ʔ] ; and in New Akkadian the cases of the noun
(-u for the nominative, *-i* for the genitive-dative, and *-a* for the
accusative) are confused, foreshowing the stage seen in Hebrew,
Syriac, and Modern Arabic, where they have wholly disappeared.

In the fifteenth century B.C., Akkadian was the language of commerce and diplomacy throughout the Near East; but from the eighth century onward, Aramaic replaced it in ever increasing measure, until, by the time of Alexander the Great, it practically vanished as a vernacular, though it continued to be written as a learned tongue as late as the first century B.C. One corrupt Middle Akkadian dialect, *Nuzi*, is known, dating from the middle of the second millennium B.C., and strongly influenced in phonology, syntax, vocabulary, and even morphology by the totally non-related *Khurrian* (cf. p. 380).

Of the two divisions of *North-West Semitic*, *Canaanite* is much the older, *Old Canaanite* words and glosses being found in Tell-el-'Amārnah tablets as early as the fifteenth century B.C. Excavations begun in 1929 at *Rās Shamrah*, a mile inland from Minat-al-Baydah, north of Latakia (the ancient Laodicaea ad Mare) on the coast of northern Syria, have brought to light a number of tablets dating from at least the fourteenth century B.C., written in a cuneiform consonantal script of some thirty characters, and containing, besides ritual and other religious material, poems concerning a vegetation-deity 'Aleyan. The phonology is on an earlier stage than that either of Phoenician or of Hebrew, and the old case-endings still survive, while the syntax presents some interesting phenomena. The exact position of the language, called Ugaritic, and one of the North Canaanite group, is not yet precisely determined, though the suggestion has been made that it was the dialect of the Amurrites (the Amorites of the Bible).

Phoenician, whose earliest documents (inscriptions of the Kings of Byblos) date from the thirteenth century to the tenth B.C., is closely akin to Hebrew. It is written in a consonantal alphabet of twenty-two letters, running from right to left, and each letter is named acrophonically, i.e., from a word beginning with that letter, e.g., the character for [b] is called *bēθ* ' house ' (whence Greek *βῆτα)*, on the principle of the old nursery-rhyme ' A is for Archer ', etc. The alphabets of practically the entire Western world, as well as of India and of all the Semites except the Akkadians and the Rās Shamrites, are, in all probability, ultimately derived from the Phoenicians, though whence they obtained their script is not yet absolutely certain; but the history of the alphabet, though of much interest, importance, and complexity, scarcely falls within the domain of linguistics proper.

The greater number of texts in Phoenician are dated between the fifth century and the second B.C., but it continued to be spoken, in its western form of *Punic*, as late as the time of Prokopios, who died about A.D. 565. The language, with dialectic variations in Byblos, Zinjīrli, and Cyprus, is divided into Phoenician proper in the east (Old Phoenician, from the thirteenth century to the ninth; Middle, from the eighth to the sixth; and New, from the fifth century to the Christian Era) and Punic in the west (Old Punic, from the fifth century to 146 B.C.; and New, from 146 B.C. to at least the sixth century A.D.; cf. pp. 285, 359, 425).

Of *Moabite* we possess little but an inscription of thirty-four lines of King Mēša' in the middle of the ninth century B.C.; but in *Hebrew* we have by far the most important member of the Canaanite group, and the only one which has survived as a spoken language to the present time. Old Hebrew, in which all the Old Testament is written, excepting Genesis xxxi. 47, Jeremiah x. 11, Daniel ii. 4b–vii. 28, and Ezra iv. 8–vi. 18, vii. 12–26, which are in Aramaic, was vernacular from the second millennium B.C. (Song of Deborah and Barak = Judges v.) until about the fourth century B.C., the greater part dating from between the ninth and seventh centuries, though it continued to be written as a learned language as late as A.D. 100. There are also a couple of inscriptions of the ninth and eighth (or seventh) centuries and some shards of the ninth, as well as seals, coins, weights, etc. Dialects existed (cf. Judges xii. 5–6; p. 128), and the Old Testament itself contains traces of dialectic differences. When the Jews returned from the Exile in 536 B.C., Aramaic had become the chief vernacular of Palestine; but, despite this, Hebrew survived and became the foundation of Talmudic Hebrew (also called Rabbinical Hebrew), which was the language of the Mišnā and of the Hebrew parts of the Talmuds and Midrashes, etc., until the rise of Islām in the seventh century A.D. As Mediaeval Hebrew, it was the vehicle of a copious religious literature; and with the development of Jewish nationalism, it is being revived as a vernacular (Modern Hebrew, Neo-Hebrew), especially in Palestine.

Aramaic falls into Western and Eastern. To the former group belong (1) *Old Aramaic* inscriptions (Ḥamā and Zinjīrli, early eighth century B.C.; Palmyrene, from the first century B.C. to the third century A.D.; Nabataean, from the first century B.C. to the fourth century A.D.; and Sinaitic, from the first to the fourth century A.D.); (2) *Biblical Aramaic* (often incorrectly termed *Chaldaean)*, the dialect of the non-Hebrew portions of the Bible just mentioned, as well as of an important collection of papyri found in Egypt; (3) *Judaeo-Aramaic,* employed in the Targums and in the Palestinian Talmud; (4) *Christian Palestinian Aramaic* of the fifth and sixth centuries A.D. (portions of the Bible and translations from Greek); and (5) *Samaritan* (translation of, and commentary on, the Pentateuch; third and fourth centuries A.D.). Formerly the *lingua franca* throughout Palestine, Syria, etc., and the language of Christ (cf. *talitha cumi* = ταλειθα κουμει ' damsel, arise '; *ephphatha* = εφφαθα ' be opened ', Mark v. 41; vii. 34), Western Aramaic was supplanted by Arabic in the ninth century A.D., and now survives only in and near Ma'lūla in the Anti-Libanus.

Eastern Aramaic, recorded in the Akkadian region as early as the ninth century B.C. and frequently employed on Akkadian dockets in the seventh, spread far and wide to the Upper Indus, Cappadocia, and Western China. Its chief dialects are (1) *Judaeo-Aramaic,* the language of the Babylonian Talmud (from about the fourth century to the sixth A.D.); (2) *Mandaean,* spoken along the Euphrates from the seventh century to the ninth A.D., the vehicle of the literature of the highly interesting syncretistic sect of Mandaeans, and syntactically the most valuable of all non-Jewish Aramaic dialects since its texts are original, whereas the documents of all the rest are translations; (3) *Syriac,* from the third century to the thirteenth A.D., spreading from the region of Edessa to Persia, but divided in the fifth century by political and ecclesiastical conditions into Jacobite and Nestorian, and possessed of a very rich theological literature and of some inscriptions, the earliest dating from the first century A.D.; (4) *Harrānian,* recorded only in a few glosses; and (5) modern dialects spoken in Mōṣul and Ṭūr 'Abdīn in Mesopotamia and in the Persian area of Urmī.

In the *South-West Semitic* group, *North Arabic* is first recorded in Liḥyānian and Thamūdian inscriptions (the former between the second or first century B.C. and the fourth or sixth A.D.; the latter of wholly uncertain date) and in Ṣafāitic *graffiti* (probably of the first centuries A.D.). By all odds the most important member of the group is *Arabic,* famous as the language of the Qur'ān (based on the dialect of Mekkah), and the vehicle of one of the greatest literatures of all the East, first recorded in an inscription of A.D. 328, and spreading wherever Muḥammadanism has gone. It was divided into several dialects, of which only that of Mekkah has survived, this being the parent of a large number of modern vernaculars, notably Arabian (Hijāz, Najd, Yemen, Ḥaḍramaut, Dathīna, Oman, Muskat), Irāqian (Baghdādh, Mōṣul, Mardīn), Syro-Palestinian (Aleppo, Beirut, Damascus, Lebanon; Jerusalem, Syrian desert), Egyptian, Maltese, Libyan and Tripolitan, Tunisian, Algerian (Constantine, Algiers, Oran), Moroccan, Ḥassānī (from Mauritania to Timbuktu), and the extinct Andalusian (from the eighth century to the sixteenth A.D.; cf. p. 430).

South Arabic is known only from inscriptions (Minaean, Sabaean, Qathabānian, and Ḥaḍramautian) ranging, perhaps, from the eighth century B.C. to the sixth A.D., and by the modern dialects of Mahrī, Qarawī or Garwī, and Soqoṭhrī.

The most important member of the Ethiopic group is *Ethiopic* proper (also called Geʻez), which finds its closest cognate in South Arabic, so that it serves as an imperfect representative of an older South Arabic-Ethiopic family. It is first known from Aksūmite inscriptions of the fourth century A.D., and not only possesses a fairly abundant literature from the fifth century to the tenth, but still serves as a learned language, though its true linguistic successor is *Tigriña* or *Tigray*, which is written by few except officials of the Italian colony of Eritrea. The other members of the group are *Tigrē* (with no written literature), *Amḥaric* (from the fourteenth century A.D. onward; strongly influenced by Kushitic), *Gāfāt, Argobba, Hārārī,* and *Gurāgē.*

The chief modern works on Semitic as a whole are C. Brockelmann's *Grundriss der vergleichenden Grammatik der semitischen Sprachen* (two volumes, Berlin, 1908–13), abbreviated in his *Kurzgefasste vergleichende Grammatik der semitischen Sprachen* (Berlin, 1908; replacing H. Zimmern's *Vergleichende Grammatik der semitischen Sprachen,* Berlin, 1898) and summarised in his *Semitische Sprachwissenschaft* (Berlin and Leipzig, 1906; French translation, *Précis de linguistique sémitique,* Paris, 1910; only the *Grundriss* contains a discussion of the syntax), and L. H. Gray's *Introduction to Semitic Comparative Linguistics* (New York, 1934; an attempt to apply Indo-European methods to Semitics); M. Cohen's *Le Système verbal sémitique et l'expression du temps* (Paris, 1924); and for Hebrew, the *Historische Grammatik der hebräischen Sprache* of H. Bauer and P. Leander, of which only

the first volume has appeared (Halle, 1922). The word ' Semitic '
as a technical linguistic term appears to have been coined by
A. L. Schlözer in an article in the eighth volume of J. G. Eichhorn's
Repertorium für biblische und morgenländische Literatur (Leipzig, 1781).

(2) *Hamitic.* — Historically, the most important member of this
group is *Egyptian,* with records from about 3400 B.C. to about the
third century A.D., and divided into Old (3400–2200 B.C.), Middle
(2200–1580 B.C.), and New (1580 B.C. to the third century A.D.),
after which it is known as Coptic. It is the vehicle of a rich literature of religious, didactic, epic, amatory, and secular poetry, of
tales, and of epistolary, medical, and incantational writings, and
the like. Old Egyptian is written in an elaborate system of hieroglyphs, some six hundred in number, representing consonants only,
and was first deciphered in 1822 by J. F. Champollion by the help
of the famous Rosetta Stone, which has a text both in hieroglyphic
and demotic script, together with a version in Greek. This hieroglyphic system, practically the only one employed in Old Egyptian, was simplified in Middle Egyptian into hieratic (used in the
papyri), and in New Egyptian still further into demotic (' popular '), the latter giving some indication of the vowels.

In its long recorded history, the language underwent much
change; and this continued when it entered its final stage of *Coptic,*
written in an alphabet of twenty-four letters based on Greek, with
seven supplementary characters borrowed from demotic. Possessed of a literature exclusively Christian and religious, Coptic
had several dialects, notably Bohayric (the literary and liturgical
language of all Christian Copts after the eleventh century),
Saʻīdic, Fayūmic, and Akhmīmic; but by the seventh century it
began to feel the opposition of Arabic, and though still generally
spoken by Egyptian Christians in the fifteenth century, two centuries later it was used only by the aged, and now survives solely
as a religious language.

The *Libyco-Berber* division is represented in ancient times only
by some hundreds of brief *Libyan* inscriptions, ill-deciphered, and
scattered from Sinaï to the Canary Islands, none datable with
certainty earlier than the fourth century B.C. The majority of them
are found within the area known in Classical times as Numidia
(the modern Algeria) ; and to them, one may add *graffiti* (provisionally termed *Saharan)* of uncertain date and in a script which

marks them off from ancient Libyan and from modern Tuareg alike.

The modern *Berber* group, distinguished by differences in phonological correspondences sufficient to render the languages mutually unintelligible, appears to fall into two divisions, each of whose dialects has sub-dialects. To one of these belong Shluh in southern Morocco, Tuareg in the Sahara, Zenaga in Mauritania, and Kabyl in the mountains of Algiers and Tunis; to the other, Zenete, a group of dialects scattered through the north and east. To these must be added the *Guanche* of the Canary Islands, which became extinct in the seventeenth century A.D., and which is known only from some inscriptions in Libyan characters and from words recorded by Europeans from the fourteenth century onward.

Of all the Berber group, only Shluh possessed written documents of the twelfth century A.D.; but these have disappeared, so that our earliest religious texts and poems in it now date from the eighteenth century. Berber has fewer pharyngals than Semitic, but more emphatics; and it presents the curious phenomenon of repeating personal and nominal endings both at the beginning and at the end of words, e.g., *töqqīmöδ* ' thou shalt remain ' as contrasted with the equivalent Arabic *taqūmu*. For the group one may refer to R. Basset's *Études sur les dialectes berbères* (Paris, 1894), and for Hamitic as a whole, to C. Meinhof's *Die Sprachen der Hamiten* (Hamburg, 1912). Attempts have been made to connect Berber with ancient Iberian, and Hamitic with Sumerian.

The *Kushitic* sub-division occupies part of the western coast of the Red Sea and of Ethiopia, and the eastern corner of Africa. Scarcely anything is known concerning it before the second half of the nineteenth century, and none of its members possesses any written literature. As yet, it seems hardly possible to classify its dialects satisfactorily. Running from north to south are the Beja (of whom the ancient Blemmyes doubtless once formed part, and of whom inscriptions found at Meroë may be an early record; cf. p. 401) and the dialects of the Bishari, Hadendoa, Halenga, and Beni 'Amer; the closely related Afar and Saho (the latter the dialect of the Danakil), Somali, and Galla; mixed with Ethiopic-speakers are the Agaw dialects (Bilin, Khamir, and Khamta, Quara, etc.); and in the south-west are the Sidama (Gudella, Kaffa, Kullo-Walamo, Bambala, etc.).

Despite many attempts to prove relationship between Hamito-

Semitic and Indo-European, a relationship which seems by no means impossible in principle, no cogent evidence of genetic connexion appears yet to have been produced; and affinity with Basque, which has likewise been suggested, must be deemed scarcely probable. On the other hand, it may well be that the African Bantu group is genealogically akin to Egyptian, and thus, ultimately, to the Hamito-Semitic family as a whole (cf. pp. 404–406). Relationship between Hottentot-Bushman and the Kushitic Beja has also been proposed.

URALIC

The Uralic or Finno-Ugric linguistic family falls into four main divisions: Finnish, Permian, Ugric, and Samoyede, spoken in northern Sweden, in Finland, Esthonia, and Hungary, on both sides of the Ural Mountains, and as far east as the Tunguska River. The original home of the stock has been sought in the forests and plains north of the Caucasus, but seems more probably to have been in the middle Volga region. Here they were in contact with Indo-Europeans, and especially with Indo-Iranians, from whom they borrowed words at a very early date, notably the term for ' hundred ' (Finnish *sata*, Mordvin *śada*, Vogul *sāt*, Ostyak *sat*, Hungarian *száz*, etc. : Avestan *satəm*, Sanskrit *śatám)*.

The first to migrate from the homeland were the Ugrians, who journeyed to the Urals, whence their most important component historically, the Hungarians (or Magyars), re-migrated westward, reaching their present area of Hungary about A.D. 900. By the beginning of the Christian Era, the Finns had come to the vicinity of the Baltic coast, as is shown by numerous words which they borrowed both from Baltic and from Teutonic in forms older than any recorded historically in either branch, some of them, in all probability, having been taken over before the first sound-shift (cf. p. 82). Among these terms we may mention Finnish *armas* ' dear ' : Gothic *arms* ' miserable ', Old Icelandic *armr* ' poor, wretched, wicked ', Anglo-Saxon *earm*, Modern German *arm* ' poor ', Proto-Teutonic **armaz;* Finnish and Esthonian *kuningas* ' king ' : Old High German *kuning*, Anglo-Saxon *cyning*, English *king*, Proto-Teutonic **kuningaz* (Lithuanian *kùnigas* ' priest, pastor ' is borrowed from Teutonic); Finnish *reipas* (genitive *reippaan)* ' quick ' : Old Icelandic *rífr* ' munificent, abundant ', Anglo-Saxon *rífe*, English *rife*, Proto-Teutonic **reipaz*. The Permians went to the east and north-east after the seventh century A.D.; of the early history of the Samoyedes we know nothing.

The oldest written records of the family are Hungarian words found in Arabic and Byzantine writings of the ninth and tenth centuries A.D. and in Latin documents of the eleventh, but the first actual text is a funeral oration of some three hundred words from the first quarter of the thirteenth century. Manuscripts of religious content begin in the first half of the fifteenth century and increase in number in the sixteenth, while the first printed text appeared in 1527. Syryenian is recorded in religious texts of the fourteenth century; Finnish and Esthonian began their literary existence with translations of the Bible in 1548 and 1632 respectively, and the former is famous for its *Kalevala,* a collection of folk-songs gathered by Elias Lönnrot in the nineteenth century.

Uralic was originally characterised by an alternation of plosives within a word according as they appeared after an accented or after an unaccented syllable, the former condition being termed strong and the latter weak. This phenomenon is now practically restricted to Finnish and Lapp, e.g., Finnish *kukka* ' flower ' : *kukan* ' of a flower '; *tapa* ' custom ' : *tavan* ' of a custom ' (original accentuations '*kukka* : *ku'kan,* etc.) ; and we have, accordingly, such series as '$kk : k'$; '$tt : t'$; '$pp : p'$; '$k : [\gamma]' > 0$; '$t : [\eth]' > d'$; '$p : [\beta]' > v'$, etc. Vowel-harmony (cf. p. 69), where a palatal vowel in the base-syllable must be followed by a palatal vowel, and a non-palatal by a non-palatal (e.g., Finnish *vesi* ' water ' : *mato* ' worm '), is frequent; gender is lacking, but Vogul, Ostyak, Lapp, and Samoyede have a dual as well as a plural; the cases range from eight in Lapp to twenty-two in Hungarian, though most of the case-endings really correspond to the adverbial periphrases, prepositions, etc., of Indo-European (cf. pp. 152–153, 170–171) ; and in the first and second persons the verbs are essentially epithetologic in character (e.g., Finnish *koira-mme* ' our dog ' : *sano-mme* ' we say ' [literally, ' our saying ']; cf. p. 152).

In syntax, neighbouring languages have exercised much influence on the Uralic languages of advanced civilisations, Finnish, Esthonian, Lapp, and Hungarian. Thus, Finnish has developed a perfect on the Teutonic model (e.g., *minä olen tullut* = Swedish *jag är kommen* = German *ich bin gekommen* = English *I am come* = French *je suis venu),* and Esthonian employs the verb *sāma* ' become ' on the model of German *werden* to form a future and a passive (e.g., *ta sāβ tulema* = *er wird kommen* ' he will come '; *sē sāβ tehtuδ* = *es wird getan* ' it is done ').

The languages of the Uralic family are as follows: (1) *Finnish* group: Finnish proper or Suomi (Eastern and Western), Karelian (four main dialects), Olonetzian, Ingrian, Lüdish, Vepsian, Votian, Esthonian (dialects of Reval and Tartu [Dorpat]), Livonian (moribund), Lapp (six main dialects), Cheremiss, and Mordvin (each with two dialects); (2) *Permian* group: Syryenian and Votyak; (3) *Ugric* group: Hungarian or Magyar (with eight dialects), Vogul, and Ostyak (the former with four dialects, and the latter with eight); and (4) *Samoyede* group: Yurak, Yenisei-Samoyede, Tagvy, Ostyak-Samoyede, and Kamassin (or Southern, or Sayan, Samoyede).

Linguists of high repute have sought to connect Uralic genetically with Indo-European, calling attention to such phenomena as the nasal termination of the accusative singular (e.g., Finnish *kodan* ' hut ' : Sanskrit *áśvam* ' horse ') and aorists in -*s*- (e.g., Vogul *minsəm* ' I went ' : Sanskrit *ávakṣam* ' I said '). Such connexion seems not wholly impossible, but much further investigation is necessary before it can be regarded as either proved or disproved. Affinity with Altaic has frequently been postulated, but as yet can scarcely be considered demonstrated; and the hypothesis that Uralic is related to the Muṇḍā family of India (cf. pp. 392–393) seems very doubtful, as is a proposed connexion of Ural-Altaic with Sumerian.

The group has several journals devoted especially to it, notably the *Journal de la société finno-ougrienne* (Helsingfors, 1886 sqq.) and the *Mémoires* of the same society (Helsingfors, 1890 sqq.), the *Keleti Szemle* (Budapest, 1900 sqq.), and the *Finnisch-ugrische Forschungen* (Helsingfors, 1901 sqq.); and besides the works mentioned on p. 455, we may note Károly Jenö Ujfalvy's *Étude comparée des langues ougrofinnoises* (Paris, 1875), A. Ahlquist's *Forschungen auf dem Gebiete der ural-altaischen Sprachen* (three parts, St. Petersburg, 1861–80), O. Donner's *Die gegenseitige Verwandtschaft der finnisch-ugrischen Sprachen* (Helsingfors, 1879), and his incomplete *Vergleichendes Wörterbuch der finnisch-ugrischen Sprachen* (three volumes, Helsingfors, 1874–88), M. A. Castrén's *Grammatik der samojedischen Sprachen* (St. Petersburg, 1854), and the brief comparative *Finnisch-ugrische Sprachwissenschaft*, by J. Szinnyei (second edition, Berlin and Leipzig, 1922).

ALTAIC

The Altaic group consists of at least three sub-groups: Turkic, Mongol, and Manchu or Tungus, spoken in Turkey, in European Russia from the Volga eastward, and throughout Asiatic Russia, Chinese Turkistān, Mongolia, and Manchukuo, as well as in parts of north-western Iran and northern Afghānistān. It shows such resemblances to Uralic that the two families are often classed together as Ural-Altaic, among these striking similarities being vowel-harmony (e.g., Turkish *ev-ler* ' houses ' : *quš-lar* ' birds '; cf. Finnish *vesi* ' water ' : *mato* ' worm '); but at present it seems most prudent to regard them as wholly separate in view of their differences of inflexion (e.g., Turkish *ev-ler* ' houses ' : Finnish *kala-t* ' fishes ') and the lack of geminated consonants in Altaic as contrasted with their frequency in Uralic (cf. p. 368). Even within the Altaic group, the resemblances are chiefly in syntax and vocabulary, both of which are peculiarly subject to borrowing. Although morphemes traceable to a common Proto-Altaic are relatively few, notably a locative in *-dä*, often with a suffixed *-ki* (e.g., Turkish *yär-där-ki*, Mongol *gadzar-da-ki* ' who is in [or, on] the earth ', Tungus *bira-du* ' in the river '), the personal pronouns are evidently akin, and the group shows a high degree of agglutination (cf. p. 300), as in Turkish *tšat-* ' strike, play a musical instrument ', *tšat-gi* ' musical instrument ', *tšat-gi-dži* ' musician '; *sev-* ' love ', *sev-mek* ' to love ', *sev-dir-mek* ' to make to love ', *sev-il-mek* ' to be loved ', *sev-me-mek* ' not to love ', *sev-il-eme-mek* ' to be impossible to be loved ', *sev-il-dir-eme-mek* ' to be impossible to be made to be loved ', etc. The problem of affinity is rendered still more difficult by the obscurity of the peoples speaking Altaic, by their extreme mobility and readiness to change their vernaculars, and by the close similarities of the languages within each sub-group. Whether Turkic, Mongol, and Manchu really form a single family, or are actually separate groups, is best left an open question. Japanese and Korean, as well as Eskimo and Aleut, have also been regarded as Altaic.

The *Turkic* group may be divided into four sub-groups, each with sub-divisions: *Eastern* or *Altaic proper* (Altaï, Baraba, Abakan, Soyonian, Karagas, and Uighur); *Western* (Kirghiz, Bashkir, Chuvash, and Irtysh); *Central* (Chagataï, Kashgar, Yarkand, Taranchī, Sart, and Uzbeg); and *Southern* (Osmanlī Turkoman, Kumik, Balkar, Azarbayjānī, and Anatolian). Of all these, only Chuvash shows striking divergencies from the rest. In popular terminology, ' Turkish ' means Osmanlī, and it alone of the Turkic family has received extensive literary cultivation. This literature is based essentially on Persian and Arabic, and its vocabulary is largely borrowed from those languages, though a determined effort, inspired by a strong nationalistic sentiment, is being made to exclude these alien elements, and to employ only Turkish, while Roman script has recently been substituted for Perso-Arabic, which is ill-fitted to represent Turkish phonology.

The oldest documents of the group are quasi-runic inscriptions of A.D. 734 or 735, of which the most important are found near the Orkhon River, south of Lake Baikal *(Kökturkish)*. A Turko-Arabic dictionary of about 1074, by Mahmūd of Kashgar, shows the language already divided into Western and Eastern; and another record of importance is the *Codex Cumanicus*, dated in 1303 (edited by G. Kuun, Budapest, 1880; facsimile edition by K. Grønbech, Copenhagen, 1936), containing a Latin-Persian-Coman, a Coman-Latin, and a Coman-German glossary, riddles, penances and other Christian religious texts, and some hymns, one of which seems to be original, the rest being translated from Latin. The oldest literary document dates from 1069, the didactic *Qutadgu Biliq* of Yussūf in Chagataï, and the first important poem was the *Gharīb-nāmah* by the Ṣūfī 'Āshiq Pasha, who died in 1332. An important feature of this group is the strong influence exercised by the noun on the inflexion of the verb, although only a very few words may function as both.

The *Mongol* group is spoken throughout Mongolia and by the Buryats to the north of it. Its internal resemblances are even closer than in Turkic, and it falls into *Western* or *Kalmuk; Northern* or *Buryat;* and *Eastern,* sub-divided into Khalkha, Shara, and Tangut, to which may be added the moribund Afghān Mongol and, according to many, Yakut, spoken in the north-east of the area, though others classify this, rather, with the Turkic family. If this latter grouping is correct, Yakut and Chuvash, which have points in common as against all the rest of Turkic, might be considered the peripheral languages (cf. p. 43) of the Turkic division. The oldest record is an inscription of five lines on granite found near Nerchinsk on the Onon, mentioning the nephew of Genjhiz Khan (1154–1227) ; the most important early work is the *Secret History of the Mongols,* beginning in 1240 and written phonetically in

Chinese characters; and there are many translations of Buddhist and Shamanist texts, didactic, juridical, and medical writings, and folk-tales.

The *Manchu* or *Tungus* division, with Yakut and Yukagir (cf. p. 385) to the north, and Turkic and Mongol to the south, falls into Manchu proper (in Manchukuo) and Tungus, the latter subdivided into a large number of dialects, such as Oroch, Kile, Olcha or Mangun, Lamut, Orochon, Oroq, Yenisei Tungus, Chapogir, and Shibä. Under the Manchu dynasty in China, Manchu had a considerable literary development, and a number of polyglot dictionaries were made, e.g., one of Manchu, Mongol, Chinese, and Tibetan in ten volumes, and another of the same languages in thirty-six.

Among the many works devoted to Altaic, mention may be made of H. Vambéry, *Etymologisches Wörterbuch der turko-tartarischen Sprachen* (Leipzig, 1878), E. Büge, *Über die Stellung des Tungusischen zum Mongolisch-Türkischen* (Halle, 1887), W. Bang, *Uralaltaische Forschungen* (Leipzig, 1890), and J. Grunzel, *Entwurf einer vergleichenden Grammatik der altaischen Sprachen nebst einem vergleichenden Wörterbuch* (Leipzig, 1895) ; and for Turkic, J. Deny, *Grammaire de la langue turque* (Paris, 1921), V. Thomsen, *Inscriptions de l'Orkhon déchiffrées* (Helsingfors, 1896) ; W. Radloff, *Phonetik der nördlichen Türksprachen* (Leipzig, 1883), V. Grønbech, *Forstudier til tyrkisk lydhistorie* (Copenhagen, 1902), and K. Grønbech, *Der türkische Sprachbau*, i (Copenhagen, 1936). Attempts to connect Altaic with Indo-European or with Elamite must be deemed unsuccessful.

JAPANESE AND KOREAN

The classification of these languages is quite uncertain, and their relation to each other is equally dubious. Of *Japanese* itself no adequate historical study has yet been made, and its dialects, which retain features lost in the standard language, have thus far received insufficient investigation. Its homeland would seem to have been the Asiatic continent; and, on the whole, the theory which holds it to be akin either to the Manchu or to the Mongolian division of Altaic not only seems at present the least unlikely, but also appears much less improbable than the connexion proposed between it and Malayo-Polynesian. Its one certain kin is the language of the Riu-Kiu Islands. The noun has neither gender nor number, and may, as in Mongol, be used as a verb; the verb itself is impersonal, stress being laid on the fact of action or state, not upon the performer of the action nor upon the person or thing existing in the state in question. The adjective may be either uninflected, in which case it is essentially an epithetologue, or inflected, when it functions as a verb. Japanese literature begins with two historical works, the *Kojiki* and the *Nihongi* (A.D. 712 and 720 respectively), which contain archaic poetry from at least the fifth century, and with rituals *(norito)*. The classical period runs from 794 to 1186, with a Chinese influence on vocabulary and style which finally becomes analogous to that of French on English. This period was followed by one of decline (1186–1600), after which came a literary renaissance and a wealth of popular literature (1600–1868).

In its inflexion and syntax, *Korean* closely resembles Japanese, but the post-positions which serve to indicate cases differ widely (e.g., Korean *son-eui* ' of a hand ' : Japanese *te-no)*. The question of the connexion of the two languages has been discussed (not wholly conclusively) by M. S. Kanazawa, *The Common Origin of the Japanese and Korean Languages* (Tokio, 1910); and an attempt has even been made to connect Korean with Indo-European.

Eskimo-Aleut

This group is spoken by the Aleut in the Aleutian Islands and by the Eskimo in the western and northern parts of Alaska, in a belt along the entire Arctic coast of North America, the western, eastern, and northern shores of Hudson's Bay, the Labrador coast, and the habitable shores of Greenland, in addition to a small area on the extreme north-eastern tip of Asia (Yuit). It falls into three divisions: *Eastern* (the Labrador dialect forming the literary language), *Central*, and *Western*. The noun possesses three numbers, but gender exists only in the interrogative pronoun *(kina* ' who? ' : *suna* ' what? '); the verb has no tense, but four moods, and distinguishes between subjective and objective conjugations (e.g., *tusarpo-q* ' he hears ' : *arnap qimmeq takuwâ* ' the woman sees the dog ', literally, ' of the woman the dog sight of him of her '). Perhaps its most striking feature, though not restricted to this group, is its extreme development of incorporation (cf. p. 300), so that a single word may denote what we express by a phrase e.g., *takusariartorumagaluarnerpâ* ' do you think that he really intends to set about busying himself with that? ', to be analysed as *takusar[pâ]* ' he busies himself with that ', *iartor[poq]* ' he goes to ', *uma[voq]* ' he intends to ', *[g]aluar[poq]* ' he does so, but ', *ner[poq]* ' do you think he? ', *â* interrogative of the third person. Eskimo-Aleut has been regarded by highly competent authorities as ultimately cognate with Altaic, although the connexion cannot yet be regarded as demonstrated. Among works dealing with the family, mention may be made of C. C. Uhlenbeck's *Ontwerp van eene vergelijkende vormleer der Eskimotalen* (Amsterdam, 1907). A suggested relationship with Indo-European must be considered highly improbable.

CAUCASIAN

The term Caucasian is applied to all languages spoken in the Caucasus area which are neither Indo-European (Ossetic and Russian) nor Turkic (Azarbayjānī, Kumik, Balkar, etc.) ; but the appellation is geographic rather than linguistic, for we here have two families, North Caucasian and South Caucasian, whose affinity, though often postulated, has not yet been satisfactorily demonstrated.

North Caucasian is characterised by an extremely rich consonantism, including labialised consonants and lateral affricates (Avar, for instance, has no less than forty-three consonants), but all consonant-groups except the simplest (e.g., liquid plus plosive) are avoided. The vocalism, on the other hand, is relatively scanty ; and a distinction is drawn between the ergative case as the logical subject of a transitive verb and the patient case as the subject of an intransitive verb or the logical object of a transitive, as in Avar *dicà razì ha-v-ùla emèn* ' through-me contented makes-himself father ', i.e., ' I make my father contented ' (cf. p. 200). The group falls into two main divisions: Checheno-Lesghian or Eastern Caucasian; and Abasgo-Kerketian or Western. Of these, *Checheno-Lesghian*, spoken in the territory bounded by the Caspian on the east, the Terek on the north, and the Berbere-Chaï on the south, possesses a rich development of noun-classes (cf. pp. 189–190) and of cases, of which Avar has no less than thirty, and Lak' even fifty (cf. p. 201); and the verb has separate forms for durative and instantaneous aspects. The group is composed of eight subgroups: Chechen (Ingush and T'ush or Bats') ; Avaro-Andi (Avar,

Andi, Dido, K'varshi and Qaputsi) ; Lak' or Kazikumyk'; Dargva (of whose dialects, Ḥürq'ili, the most studied, best preserves the multiplicity of durative and punctual aspects) ; Samurian (K'üri, Aghul, T'abarasan, Buduk', Jek, Rut'ul, and Ch'ak'ur) ; Artshi, Udi; and K'inalugh.

Abasgo-Kerketian contrasts with Checheno-Lesghian in possessing complicated consonant-groups, labialised alveolo-palatal sibilants ([∫v]), and labial vibrants, a definite article (postfixed in Qabardi), and a strong predilection for compounds (e.g., Qabardi *na-p'e* ' eye-nose ' = ' face '; *ne-p's* ' eye-water ' = ' tear '). It falls into three divisions: Adyghe (Qabardi and Cherkess or Circassian, the majority of whose speakers migrated to Asia Minor and Syria after the Russian conquest of the Caucasus), Ubyk' (with two sub-dialects, both now almost extinct), and Abk'az (with several dialects, and phonetically the most difficult and harshest of all Caucasian languages). No North Caucasian dialect possesses either a national script or a written literature.

South Caucasian, or *K'art'velian,* consists of four languages: Georgian or Grusinian, with several dialects (Imeric, Guric, Mt'iulic, K'evsur, Pshav, and Ingiloïc), Mingrelian, Laz, and Svanian or Svanetian. Of these, Georgian is by far the best known, and it alone possesses a real literature beginning with a translation of the Bible in the fifth century, of which only fragments have survived, the standard Georgian version being of later date. Until the middle of the eighth century, the literature was deeply influenced by Syriac and Armenian; from then until about 1000, the spirit was essentially Georgian; and after that, Byzantium exercised predominance for a century and a half. Throughout these centuries, the literature was theological; but with the Golden Age in the twelfth century, secular writings appeared, notably the romance of *The Man with the Tiger-Skin.* From the thirteenth century to the seventeenth, there was a linguistic decline, followed by a revival in the next two centuries, largely inspired by Roman Catholic missionaries. In the nineteenth century, Occidental influence gained supremacy. The phonology of South Caucasian, whose inflexion is highly complicated, so strikingly resembles that of Armenian that it has frequently been supposed that the latter was affected by the former, but this hypothesis seems open to some doubt.

Attempts have been made to connect Caucasian with many other language-groups: with Elamite (Ch'ak'ur being supposed to be nearest akin), with Khattian (Ubyk' here regarded as the closest cognate), with Mitannian, with Khaldic, with Lycian, with Lydian, with Hittite, and with Basque. Even more daring was the theory advanced by the Georgian N. Marr, who held that Caucasian was related to the pre-Indo-European languages of all Europe, and that it was cognate with Basque, Etruscan, Pelasgian, and other ' Mediterranean ' tongues, as well as with Sumerian, Elamite, and Asianic, to which entire congeries he gave the name ' Japhetic ' (for another use of this term cf. p. 433). For the propagation of this theory, a special *Jafetičeskij Sbornik* was established under Soviet auspices at Petrograd in 1922; a series of *Materialy po jafetičeskomu jazykoznaniju* (' Materials for Japhetic Linguistics ') has been published (St. Petersburg, 1910 sqq.) ; and Marr issued a general summary of his views under the title *Der japhetische Kaukasus und das dritte ethnische Element im Bildungsprozess der mittelländischen Kultur* (Berlin, 1923; cf. also A. Braun's *Die Urbevölkerung Europas und die Herkunft der Germanen*, Berlin, 1922). The theory, at least partly inspired, it would seem, by Marxian ideology, deserves scant credence in its present form, even though adopted in essence in the ' Japhetic ' or ' Nostratic ' family of Father W. Schmidt. This alleged family has four sub-groups, characterised respectively by a sibilant (e.g., [s] in Georgian, [ʃ] in Mingrelian), a spirant plus a sibilant (e.g., plus [s] in Abk'az and Basque, plus [ʃ] in Svanian and Etruscan), a spirant (e.g., in Cherkess, Ubyk', Chechen, Avar, Lesghian, and Udi), and a spirant plus a sonant (e.g., in Khaldic, Elamite, and Sumerian).

The best works on Caucasian as a whole are A. Dirr's *Einführung in das Studium der kaukasischen Sprachen* (Leipzig, 1928; a series of skeleton grammars), G. Dumézil's *Études comparatives sur les langues caucasiennes du nord-ouest* (Paris, 1932) and *Introduction à la grammaire comparée des langues caucasiennes du nord* (Paris, 1933), and G. Deeters's *Armenisch und Südkaukasisch* (Leipzig, 1927). The principal journal here is *Caucasica: Zeitschrift für die Erforschung der Sprachen und Kulturen des Kaukasus* (Leipzig, 1925 sqq.).

IBERO-BASQUE

The *Basque* language, called Euskara, Eskuara, etc., by its speakers, stands in complete isolation in Europe, where it is vernacular in the entire Spanish province of Guipúzcoa and in parts of those of Vizcaya, Alava, and Navarra, and in the French arrondissements of Bayonne and Mauléon; but the name of the old French province of Gascony shows that at one time it extended much farther north. It has a large number of dialects, whose classification is extremely difficult; but two great divisions may be made: Biscayan in the west; and Guipúzcoan, Navarrese, Labourdine, and Soulean in the centre and east. Its earliest records are place-names, some of which go back to the eighth century, but the oldest texts of any extent date only from the sixteenth, the first book being the *Linguae Vasconum primitiae,* a collection of poems by a priest named Dechepare (Bordeaux, 1545). Until about 1880, most Basque literature consisted of translations of religious works, but since that time, other subjects have received attention, and there is, besides, a wealth of oral tradition both in poetry and in prose.

Basque phonology is extremely rich, especially in plosives, spirants, and palatalisations; and its morphology is essentially suffixational. The verb is much less complicated than is generally supposed, but has no active voice (e.g., ' the man sees the dog ' is represented by the equivalent of ' by the man is seen the dog '; cf. p. 200), and though not originally periphrastic, has now become so (e.g., ' I am in sight ' = ' I see '). The great difficulty of the language is its highly intricate syntax.

Basque would seem to be the descendant of *Aquitanian,* known only from some two hundred names of men and deities, and the language of a people already recognised by Caesar as forming one of the three great ethnic divisions of Gaul. Aquitanian, in its turn, was a dialect of *Iberian,* once spoken throughout the Iberian Peninsula (modern Spain and Portugal), and known from place-names, such as *Iliberis* ' New Town ', now Elvira (cf. Basque *ili-beri),* as well as from words recorded by Classical authors and surviving in Spanish and Portuguese (e.g., *baluc* ' gold dust ' : Spanish *baluz; paramus* ' barren land ' : Spanish and Portuguese *páramo; sarna* ' mange, itch ' : Spanish and Portuguese *sarna; sarralia* ' wild lettuce ' : Spanish *sarraja,* Portuguese *sarralha* ' sow-thistle '), or on coins and inscriptions. Of Iberian grammar we know little, though it would seem to have an inert case in -*s*, -*c*, an agential in -*c*, a recipient in -*i*, -*e*, an instrumental in -*š*, -*s*, a possessive in -*n*, -*m*, and an adjectival in -*co*.

Nothing definite can be affirmed regarding the affinities of Iberian, despite attempts to connect it with Hamitic (especially Berber), with the Nilo-Chad group of the Sudano-Guinean family (particularly Nuba), or with Caucasian, 'Mediterranean', or Ligurian. The name Iberia was applied in ancient times not only to the Iberian Peninsula, but also to an area in the southern Caucasus; but what inferences, if any, may be drawn from this fact are quite uncertain.

For the group, reference may be made, for the ancient period, to A. Luchaire, *De lingua Aquitanica* (Paris, 1877) and *Origines linguistiques de l'Aquitaine* (Pau, 1877), E. Hübner, *Monumenta linguae Ibericae* (Berlin, 1893), and H. Schuchardt, *Die iberische Declination* (Vienna, 1907); for Basque, to H. Winckler, *Das Baskische und der vorderasiatische mittelländische Völker- und Kulturkreis* (Breslau, 1909), and C. C. Uhlenbeck, *Over een mogelijke verwantschap van het Baskisch met de palaeo-kaukasische talen* (Amsterdam, 1923). The best special journal is the *Revue internationale des études basques* (Paris, 1907 sqq.).

NEAR-EASTERN AND ASIANIC

Under this designation, geographic rather than linguistic, are grouped, quite arbitrarily, a number of extinct languages (formerly often termed Alarodian), some of which have no genetic relationship one with another, and none of which can as yet be connected with any of the linguistic families within or around them. We may most conveniently consider them in the geographical order of Lower Mesopotamian, Asianic (the mountainous peripheral areas and the peninsula of Asia Minor), and their extensions in the Mediterranean world.

(1) *Lower Mesopotamian.* — The one language here is *Sumerian*, the speech of a once-powerful empire stretching from Babylon to the Persian Gulf. Its tablets and inscriptions begin about 4000 B.C., and even after 2000 it served for a time as an official language; but gradually it was more and more restricted to literary and liturgical use until it finally became extinct in the third century B.C. Its records deal with many subjects: economics, law, administration, history, religion, astrology, myth, poetry, grammar, etc. Sumerian

does not distinguish genders, and its inflexion of the epithetologue is rudimentary, prefixes, infixes, and postfixes being employed to denote syntactic relationships. It indicates the plural either by doubling the singular or (more frequently) by affixing -*(e)ne* to the singular (e.g., *kur-kur* 'mountains', *dingir-ene* 'gods'); it has three tenses (telic, atelic, and aoristic; e.g., *in-gar* 'il a fait', *in-gar-e* 'il fait, il fera', *mu-gar* 'il fit'), and four moods (indicative, imperative, subjunctive, and optative or precative). The verb is really a verbal noun and does not ordinarily indicate the person, so that *mu-gar* may mean ' he made, thou madest, I made ' (literally 'his made-ness', etc.), and *mu-gar-ene* 'they, ye, we made' (cf. p. 152).

Attempts have been made to connect Sumerian with Ural-Altaic, with Burmese, with Kanuri or Bornu of the Nilo-Chad division of Sudano-Guinean, with Hamitic, with Malayo-Polynesian, with Khattian, with Caucasian, and even with Indo-European; but for the present we must regard Sumerian as an isolated language with no known cognates.

(2) *Peripheral and Asianic.* — Here we may first consider *Elamite* (also termed *Anzanite* or *Susian)*, spoken in the area corresponding to the modern Lūristān and Khūzistān in Iran, and recorded in inscriptions from about 2500 B.C., the earliest being in a national script accompanied by an Akkadian version. A second group, in a cuneiform alphabet adapted from Old Babylonian, dates from the sixteenth century to the eighth B.C.; and a third, with translations in Old Persian and Akkadian, from the Achaemenian period (fifth and fourth centuries B.C.), though it would appear from Acts ii. 9, that Elamite was still spoken to some extent in the first century A.D. In conformity with these three groups of texts, the language is chronologically divided into Old, Middle, and New Elamite, Old Elamite sometimes being called Anzanite in a restricted sense and New Elamite being termed Ḥōzī.

Elamite distinguishes between animate and inanimate gender, the latter having no special plural form; inflexion may be by aid of postpositive particles or may be entirely lacking, so that syntactic functions are indicated by the position of the word in the sentence; and animate nouns may have deictic suffixes of the first or third person (e.g., *sūki-k* '[I] the King ', *sūki-k sūki-me-k* '[I] the King of [my] kingdom ' : *sūki-r* '[he] the King ', *sūki-r sūki-me-r* '[he] the King of [his] kingdom '). In the verb, Old Elamite distinguishes between singular and plural, but in New Elamite this faculty is lost; there are transitive and intransitive voices, the latter apparently serving as a passive, four tenses (present, perfect, aorist, and future[?]), and four moods (indicative, imperative, optative, and subjunctive). Attempts have been made to connect the language with Altaic, with the North Caucasian Ch'ak'ur, with Kassite, and with Carian, or through Brāhūī, with Dravidian; but, like Sumerian, it is thus far best regarded as isolated.

The language of the *Kassites* (or *Cossaeans*), whose centre was the Zagros Mountains, where they were an important power in the seventeenth century B.C., and where they were finally conquered by Alexander the Great, is known only from a scanty glossary giving the Semitic equivalents of a few words appearing as components of proper names (e.g., *dakaš* ' star ', *šīr* ' bow ', *šàribu*, ' hang ', *uzīb* ' protest '). All that can safely be said at present is that the language was neither Indo-European nor Semitic; it may possibly have been cognate with Mitannian and Khaldic, though connexion with Elamite has also been suggested.

Northern Mesopotamia was the home of the *Subaraean* group, so named from Subartu, the ancient designation of the region, and divided into Mitannian and Khurrian (or Kharrian), which were very similar, if not identical. Of *Mitannian* we possess, besides proper names, only one text, which is, fortunately, of considerable length — a letter discovered at Tell-el-'Amārnah in Egypt, of the Mitannian King, Tušratta or Dušratta (about 1410–1375 B.C.), to the Pharaoh Amenophis III, regarding boundaries and the marriage of Tušratta's daughter, Daduhepa, to the Egyptian monarch. The documents of the *Khurrians* (the Ḥōrites of the Bible) from Bhogaz-köi, about one hundred and fifty kilometres east of Ankara, deal with invocations to the gods, conjurations, and mythology. Additional inscriptions are being discovered all the way from Boghaz-köi to Tell-el-'Amārnah, and from Kirkūk beyond the Tigris to Rās Shamrah; while Nuzi tablets (cf. p. 361) contain many Khurrian words and are strongly affected by Khurrian grammar. The Subaraean personal pronouns have separate forms for active and inactive cases (singular active, *šu-š, we-š, -š*; inactive, *suene, anni, n;* cf. pp. 175, 192) ; the singular and the plural frequently have the same form in the epithetologue; and the verb possesses no special plural. Subaraean may be cognate with Kassite and Khaldic, though some have regarded it as related to Caucasian, to Elamite, to Carian, or even to Dravidian; and it has been suggested that it stood to Indo-European in a relation similar to that of Hamitic to Semitic (cf. p. 358).

Khaldic (also called *Urarṭaean* or *Vannic)*, the language of a kingdom which flourished between 900 and 600 B.C. in the region which the Assyrians named Urarṭu (Ararat), with its capital at Turušpā or Ṭušpā on the site of the present city of Van, is known from nearly two hundred inscriptions in Akkadian cuneiform of the ninth and eighth centuries B.C., dealing chiefly with history and royal buildings. Despite the abundance of material, our knowledge of the language is still too scanty to admit of definite statements concerning it, although we can determine some of its forms and vocabulary by comparison with parallel versions in Akkadian. Its affinities are uncertain, but it may be cognate with Subaraean and Kassite, while some have endeavoured to affiliate it with Caucasian.

The speech of the inhabitants of the land later occupied by the Hittites, with their capital at Khattušaš on the site of the present Bhogaz-köi, is known as *Khattian* or *Proto-Khattian,* and would more properly be termed Hittite had not this appellation been usurped even in linguistic usage by a totally different language (see pp. 323–324). The texts, which date from before 2000 B.C., consist chiefly of hymns and invocations embedded in Hittite documents. The language is as yet very imperfectly known, but its inflexion was evidently marked by prefixes rather than by suffixes (e.g., *binu* ' child ' : *le-binu* ' children '). Connexions between Khattian and Ubyk' of the North Caucasian group have been sought, as well as with Sumerian and even with African. Still less is known of *Palāwi* (or *Palāian, Balāian)*, the language of Palā (in the region of the modern Kastamuni), recorded in fragmentary bits in Hittite texts.

Turning to the south, a bilingual vocabulary in Sumerian and in an unknown language with uncertain resemblances to Subaraean was discovered at Rās Shamrah in 1930 (the latter discussed by F. Bork, *Das Ukirutische, unbekannte Sprache von Ras Schamra: Grundlagen der Entzifferung,* Leipzig, 1938) ; and at Ördek-burnu, south of Zinjīrli, has been found a text of ten lines in a Semitic script of between the tenth and eighth century B.C., badly weathered and as yet uninterpreted. *Pisidian* is perhaps represented

by sixteen epitaphs at Sofular in the area of ancient Pisidia. Of
Lycian, we have no less than one hundred and fifty inscriptions,
mostly epitaphs, and sometimes with Greek texts, which, however,
only rarely correspond to the Lycian documents, and frequently
are entirely different from them. Written in a form of the Greek
alphabet, the Lycian inscriptions are, for the most part, from the
fifth and fourth centuries B.C.; one of them, the Xanthos-Stele
(412 B.C.), contains two hundred and forty-three lines on its four
sides, but cannot yet be translated, although we know that it contains two distinct dialects. From the accompanying Greek texts
we learn the meaning of some Lycian words and declensional
forms, but very little about the verbs. Certain inflexions closely
resemble Indo-European, such as nominative singular *lada* ' wife '
(cf. the Greek myth, of Asianic origin, of Zeus and Leda [Ionic
and Attic for Doric *Λᾱδα]*), accusative *ladā,* dative *ladi,* genitive
singular *pulenjdah* ' of Apollonides '; *prñnawatē* ' he made ',
prñnawātē ' they made '; but, in view of the overwhelming majority of forms which seem to have no correspondents in Indo-
European, these similarities are thus far most safely regarded as
chance coincidents. Nevertheless, Lycian has been considered to
be cognate with Hittite, and even to be the direct descendant of
Luian (cf. p. 324), while others think that it is related to Caucasian; and a short inscription on a disk found at Phaistos in Crete
may also be akin. Of *Carian,* we have only seventy-five short
inscriptions, mostly made by Carian soldiers in Egyptian service
about the seventh century B.C. No pronouncement can yet safely
be made concerning its affinities, which have been sought in
Lydian, in Elamite, in Luian, or in Subaraean.

Fifty-three inscriptions, from the fourth century B.C. so far as
dated, now constitute our records of *Lydian.* Some are of fair
length; one, of only three words, is accompanied by a Greek version, and another, of eight lines, by one in Aramaic. We have some
evidence of the inflexion of the epithetologue and of the verb:
nominative singular *vañaś* ' grave ' (the phonetic value of this *ś*
is unknown), accusative *vañań* (the value of *ń* is also unknown),
dative *artimuλ* ' to Artemis '; third singular present *fénsńibid* ' he
destroys ', third plural present *vqbahēnt* ' they abolish ', and a
third singular imperative in -*pi,* *ἰωπι* '(come) hither '. The affinities
of the language are disputed, some connecting it with Lycian,
Hittite, or Caucasian, others regarding it as Indo-European or a

very early form of Etruscan, particularly in view of the statement of Herodotos that the Etruscans came from Lydia. Of *Mysian* we may have a scanty inscription of the fourth or third century B.C., consisting of five lines and found in 1926 at the village of Uyujik on the Mysio-Phrygian boundary. We can as yet say nothing about it, and can only refer to the statement of Xanthos (fifth century B.C.), as cited by Strabo, that Mysian was a mixture of Lydian and Phrygian.

In addition to our epigraphic sources, Classical authors have recorded glosses in Carian, Lycian, Cilician, Cappadocian, Pontic, Paphlagonian, Mariandynian, Bithynian, Lydian, Isaurian, Cataonian, and Gergitho-Solymian. From Acts ii. 9–11, it would appear that Elamite, ' Mesopotamian ', Cappadocian, Pontic, ' Asian ' (West Asianic [?]), Cretan, and Pamphylian (these scarcely the Greek dialects of those two areas [cf. p. 328], which would probably have been termed simply Greek) were still spoken in the first century A.D., as we know was the case with Lycaonian (Acts xiv. 11 [10]).

Leaving Asia Minor, we find in Cyprus twelve inscriptions in *Eteocyprian*, one with a Greek text of seven words which does not reproduce the Cyprian text. From the Greek characters of this inscription, the texts would seem to date from the fourth century B.C.; but the language, studied by F. Bork in his *Die Sprache von Alasija* (Leipzig, 1930), is still unknown. In Crete, *Eteocretan* is represented by three inscriptions, found at Praisos, in a hieroglyphic alphabet still undeciphered, as well as by four brief texts in the Greek alphabet and a few words in a conjuration in a London medical papyrus. Of the language we can say nothing, our only possible clue being the statement of Herodotos that the pre-Greek inhabitants of Crete were akin to the Lycians. The texts of the most of these peripheral and Asianic languages (except Elamite) are collected in J. Friedrich's *Kleinasiatische Sprachdenkmäler* (Berlin, 1932), and many glosses are to be found in the *Arica* of P. Bötticher (later P. de Lagarde) (Halle, 1851). Important discussions of the group are given in Friedrich's *Hethitisch und " kleinasiatische " Sprachen* (Berlin and Leipzig, 1932), P. Kretschmer's *Einleitung in die Geschichte der griechischen Sprache* (Göttingen, 1896), and K. Oštir's *Beiträge zur alarodischen Sprachwissenschaft* (Vienna and Leipzig, 1921).

To the Asianic group belongs, finally, *Etruscan*, of which we have around nine thousand inscriptions, mostly very brief, though a few are of some length, notably a clay tablet from Capua (fifth century B.C.), the *Cippus Perusinus* (much later), a lead tablet from Magliano, a *pulena*-roll from Tarquinii, and especially the *Liber Linteus*, a linen roll of the first century B.C., torn in strips to wrap a mummy now at Zagreb (Agram), together with a very few bilinguals in Etruscan and Latin. We know the meanings of several words, such as *clan* ' son ', *puia* ' wife ', *tiv* ' moon ', *usil* ' sun ', *avil* ' year ', *ril* ' age ', and *tular* ' boundary ' (borrowed in Umbrian as *tuder* and preserved in the Italian city-name *Todi*); we can tell something of its phonology, thanks to its representation of Greek and Latin words; and we have a little knowledge of its inflexions (e.g., genitive singular *clen-ś* ' of a son ', dative [-genitive] *clen-si*, *clen-śi* ' of [or, to] a son ', nominative plural *clen-ar* ' sons ', dative [-genitive] *clen-ar-aśi* ' of [or, to] sons ', locative singular *śpur-eri* or *śpur-eθi* ' in a city ', and perhaps a genitive-ablative singular *laris-al* ' of Laris '; *ama* ' he is ', *am-ce* ' he was ') ; but of Etruscan as a whole we can say practically nothing.

The oldest records date from the eighth century B.C., though the majority are from the reign of Augustus; and the language was employed by soothsayers as late as the fourth century A.D. The Etruscans would seem to have come from northern Asia Minor, perhaps from Lydia, and to have reached Italy about the end of the eleventh century B.C. Their language is very probably akin to that of an inscription of ten lines, in a Greek alphabet of the sixth century B.C., on a stele found on the island of Lemnos in 1885; further than this, it is at present unsafe to go. One would naturally suppose it to be cognate with Lydian, and the Raetian of Italy has also been regarded as akin; but until a bilingual text of sufficient length is found (if such happy event ever should occur), it would appear that we must add Etruscan to the list of languages which we can read, but cannot understand. The history of the study of Etruscan and its present status are summarised by Eva Fiesel in her *Etruskisch* (Berlin and Leipzig, 1931), and the subject has its special journal *Studi etruschi* (Florence, 1927 sqq.), while the Asianic languages, with Hittite, have theirs in the *Revue hittite et asianique* (Paris, 1930 sqq.).

HYPERBOREAN

The term Hyperborean, or Palaeo-Asiatic, geographic rather than linguistic, is applied to a small group of languages in the extreme north-east corner of Asia, Yukagir, Chukchi-Kamchadal, and Aïnu, whose genetic connexion, if any, has not yet been demonstrated. *Yukagir* is spoken in the northern and western part of this area; *Chukchi-Kamchadal* consists of Chukchi in the extreme north-east, Koryak (Eastern, Western, and Kerek) from the Anadyr River to the peninsula of Kamchatka, Kamchadel or Itelmic (Western and the extinct Southern and Eastern) in the peninsula of Kamchatka and the Kurile Islands, and Gilyak in northern Saghalien and on the lower Amur; while *Aïnu* (Yezo, Saghalien, and Kurile) is spoken in the islands of Yezo, southern Saghalien, and Shikotan. The cases in these languages are formed by postpositives (e.g., Aïnu *aïnu-kot tši* ' of-the-man house ', Gilyak *mu-rox* ' boat-to ') ; and in the verb Aïnu distinguishes aspects and tenses by auxiliaries (e.g., *ku kik* ' I beat ', *ku kik nisa* ' I beat have '), while Gilyak uses infixes (e.g., *ni vind* ' I go, went ', *ni v-i-ind* ' I am going, shall go '). Aïnu numerals are interesting as showing a combination of the decimal with the vigesimal system (e.g., *ara-wan* ' three [from] ten ' = ' seven ', *re-kašima-wan* ' three plus ten ' = ' thirteen ', *ine-hotne* ' four-twenty ' = ' eighty, quatre-vingt ').

BURUSHASKĪ

Burushaskī (also called Khajuna or Kunjūtī) is spoken in Hunza, Nagar, the Ghizr Valley, and a portion of Yāsin in the extreme north-west of India, where it is completely surrounded by Turkic, Tibeto-Burman, and Indo-Iranian. Although it has been regarded as cognate with Dravidian or with Muṇḍā, it appears to be wholly isolated; and is of particular interest as representing the sole surviving remnant of what once must have been an important linguistic family of India. A thorough study of it has been made by D. L. R. Lorimer, *The Burushaski Language* (three volumes, Oslo, 1935–38).

DRAVIDIAN

Of the three great language-groups spoken in India, Indian, Muṇḍā, and Dravidian, the only one which can be considered aboriginal is Dravidian, spoken chiefly in the southern half of the peninsula and in the northern half of Ceylon, with various linguistic islands (Kōlāmī, Gōṇḍī, Kui, Kurukh, and Malto) in the north of India, and one (Brāhūī) in the mountains of eastern Balōčistān. Originally, it would seem, it was the vernacular of a much larger region, and before the Indian invasions (cf. p. 309), it apparently shared supremacy with Muṇḍā. It falls into four great divisions, the first of which is *Tamil-Kurukh*, comprising Tamil or Kāliṅgī, spoken in the greater part of South India between the Eastern Ghats and the Coromandel Coast, from Madras to Cape Comorin, and in the northern half of Ceylon; Malayāḷam, in reality a comparatively late dialectic development of Tamil, spoken on the Malabar coast; Tuḷu in the Mangalore area on the west coast; Koḍagu or Coorg, south-east of Tuḷu; Kanarese, including Toda, Kōta, and Baḍaga, in Mysore and the south-western portion of the Nizam's Dominions, with the western coast from Karvar to Mangalore; and Kurukh, consisting of Kurukh or Orāōn in the western part of the Bengal Presidency and the neighbouring parts of the Central Provinces, and Malto in the Rajmahal Mountains of Bengal.

The second group of Dravidian is *Kui-Gōṇḍī*, composed of Kui or Khond, on both banks of the Mahānādī in the province of Orissa, and Gōṇḍī (Gōṇḍī, Kōlāmī, Naikī, and Bhīlī) in the Central Provinces and Berar. The third division is *Telugu* on the east coast from Madras to Mount Mahendragiri; and the fourth is *Brāhūī*, geographically far isolated from the rest, whether by migration or as a surviving outpost of the original Dravidian territory.

Some of these languages have received extensive literary cultivation, this being especially true of Tamil, whose literature is richer than that of any other language of India except Sanskrit. Its age is disputed, but one of its oldest works, the grammatical *Tolkāppiyam* ('Ancient Poem'), must have had a long series of predecessors. Though largely dependent on Sanskrit models, Tamil contains much that is original and of high literary merit, especially in gnomic poetry, and notably in the distichs of the *KuRal*, ascribed to the Pariah Tiruvaḷḷavar. Classic literary Tamil is extremely archaic as compared with the modern vernacular. Malayāḷam literature, dating from the twelfth or thirteenth century A.D., is based mainly on Tamil or Sanskrit.

The oldest monument of Kanarese is a brief inscription from the end of the fifth century A.D.; its earliest literary production, on the art of poetry, dates from the ninth century; and one distinguishes the three periods of Old Kanarese (until about 1250), Middle (about 1250–1500), and Modern (since 1500). The earliest known Telegu works are a grammar and a translation of the Sanskrit *Mahābhārata* of the eleventh century A.D., and its literature seems to have been inspired by Sanskrit and Kanarese alike. The word recorded in the Old Testament for ' peacock ' *(tukkī;* I Kings x. 22; II Chronicles ix. 21) may be of Dravidian origin (cf. Kanarese *tōke* ' tail ', Malayāḷam *tōge,* Tamil *tōgai* ' feather, tail ', especially of the peacock) ; and certain words ostensibly Indian in a Greek farce of the second century A.D., preserved in an Oxyrhynchos papyrus, have been regarded as Kanarese, although the equivalents proposed are not very satisfactory.

In consonantism, Dravidian possesses not only the retroflex phonemes found in Indian, but also, in Tamil, a plosive *T* (voiceless), *R* (voiced), *N*, and *L; R* and *L* also occurring in Old Kanarese, and *R* in Old Telugu. Their precise values are uncertain, but they would seem to have been palatalised (i.e., [ṭ], [ṛ], [ṇ], [ḷ]), though *R* is now practically [r], and *L* has become [ʒ] and even [j] in North Tamil, while in the south it is fused with the retroflex lateral [ḷ]. Morphology is based entirely on the inflexion of the noun, which is dominated by a classification according to castes (cf. p. 189), the formations of the plural differing according to the caste to which the word in question belongs. There are two numbers, singular and plural; and inflexion is by means of postpositions, the original values of some of which are still evident, as when Tamil *il* ' house ' means ' in ' when affixed to a noun like *ūr* ' city ', as *ūr-il* ' in the city ', and has a conditional force when affixed to a base of verbal connotation, as *seyy-il* ' in doing ' = ' if one does '. These affixes may be added either to the subjective or to the oblique case (for example, Tamil *kal* ' stone ', oblique *kalliN,* instrumental *kall-ōḍu* or *kalliN-ōḍu* ' with a stone ', *-ōḍu,* *-uḍaN* properly meaning ' aid, union ') ; and both the oblique case and the case with an affix may have an adjectival value as well as a case-force (e.g., *kalliN* and *kalliN-uḍeya* mean either ' of a stone ' or ' stony ', *-uḍei[ya]* signifying ' possession, possessing ').

In the pronouns, modern Tamil, Telugu, Kui, and Kurukh distinguish between inclusive and exclusive plurals in the first person (cf. p. 182) ; Kanarese, Gōṇḍī, and Brāhūī do not; but whether Proto-Dravidian had the two types is quite uncertain (in any event, Muṇḍā influence [cf. pp. 392–394] seems highly improbable). The Dravidian verb makes its moods, voices, aspects, and tenses by means of auxiliaries; the personal forms tend to approximate to the pronominal declension; and the third person looks like a noun in the subjective case (e.g., Tamil *sey-v-āN* 'maker' or 'he will make' [cf. the Sanskrit periphrastic *kartā́* meaning either 'maker' or 'he will make' [p. 21], *sey-v-ār* 'makers' or 'they will make', *sey-d-āN* 'he made', *sey-d-ēN* 'I made': Old Tamil oblique case *ēN* 'me, my', so that *sey-d-ēN* would literally be 'my having made, mon fait' = 'I have made, j'ai fait'). Certain isolated forms, indeclinables, and imperfect assimilations, however, suggest that this nominal aspect of the verb is a later development, so that Proto-Dravidian may very possibly have made a clear distinction between the verb and the epithetologue.

The sentence is essentially of the nominal type (cf. pp. 230–232) with a sort of inflected participle at the end of the clause as a predicate; and it has neither subordinate clauses nor relative pronouns. Thus, 'I see that a large house exists' would be in Tamil *periya vīṭṭei und eNDu kaṅgiRēN* 'large house existing having-said my-seeing', a construction which may have affected the syntax of Classical Sanskrit in such sentence-types as *mahā gṛho vartata iti dṛśann aham* 'large house exists so *(iti* equivalent to quotation-marks) seeing I'.

The Dravidian family seems to be isolated within India, all attempts to connect it either with Uralic, Altaic, Elamite, Subaraean, Burushaskī, Andamanese, Australian, or Papuan having proved unsuccessful. The chief works on the group as a whole are Bishop R. Caldwell, *Comparative Grammar of the Dravidian or South-Indian Family of Languages* (second edition, London, 1875; the third edition, 1913, is merely an abridgement), J. Vinson, *Le Verbe dans les langues dravidiennes* (Paris, 1878), and S. Konow in the *Linguistic Survey of India*, iv (Calcutta, 1906), 277–681; while F. Kittel's *Kannaḍa-English Dictionary* (Mangalore, 1894) carefully distinguishes between the Dravidian and the Sanskrit components of Kanarese.

ANDAMANESE

This isolated group is confined to the Andaman Islands in the Bay of Bengal, and falls into *Great Andamanese* (northern sub-group with two divisions: Chari, Kora, Ba, and Yeru; and Kede, Kol, Juwoi, and Puchikvar; and southern sub-group: Bale and Bea) and *Little Andamanese* (Yärava on South Andaman, and Önge on Little Andaman). In phonology, *s* and all fricatives are lacking; but the system of prefixes and suffixes is highly elaborate, and the base often vanishes, the prefix alone being employed. Animate and inanimate gender are distinguished, the former classified into human and non-human living beings. The human body is divided into seven parts, and this division is extended to inanimate things associated with the human parts in question, so that the class-system becomes very intricate. Separate numerals exist only for ' one ' and ' two ', the digits up to nine being indicated by raising the requisite number of fingers with the word *anka* ' and this ', and ten being expressed by showing both hands with the exclamation *ordura* ' all '. Beyond ten, no counting is possible. The chief work on the group is M. V. Portman's *Notes on the Languages of the South Andaman Groups of Tribes* (Calcutta, 1898).

SINO-TIBETAN

South of the Altaic language-group, the Sino-Tibetan family, originally situated much further north, extends over China, Tibet, Burma, and a great part of Siam and Annam, with an islet of *Yenisei-Ostyak* (including the probably extinct Kottish on the Agul) on the upper Yenisei. The group falls into three great divisions: Yenisei-Ostyak, Tibeto-Burman, and Tai-Chinese. *Tibeto-Burman* is divided into *Tibeto-Himalayan*, consisting of Tibetan (standard literary language, Baltī, etc.) ; and of Himalayan, with several dialects (Sunvār, Gurung, Lepcha or Róng, Ṭōṭō, etc.), *North Assamese* (Aka, Daflā, and Abor-Miri; and Mishmi, the latter with three dialects), *Middle* and *South Assamese* (Bodo or Bārā with ten dialects, Mech, Kāchārī, Chutiyā, etc.; Nāgā-Bodo, including Mikir, Ēmpēō, etc.; Nāgā, with Angāmi or Tengimā, Semā, etc., in the west, Lhōtā, etc., in the centre, and Tableng, etc., in the east; Kachin or Sing-phō; and Nāgā-Kuki, including Sopvomā or Māo, etc.; these Assamese dialects not to be confused with the Modern Indian Assamese; p. 316), and *Arakan-Burmese*, comprising Kuki-Chin (Meithei, Thādō, Shunkla or Tashōn, Lai, Lushēi, Pūrūm, etc.), Old Kuki (Rānkhōl, Shö or Khyang, Khami, etc.), and Burmese (Burmese proper or Maghī, Arakanese, Mrū, etc.).

Tai-Chinese has four great divisions. The most important of these is *Chinese*, divided into a large number of dialects which are often mutually unintelligible though falling into the broad categories of Northern and Southern. The standard dialect is that of Peiping (often termed Mandarin) of the Northern group, while Cantonese is the most important of the Southern. The literary language is divided into Archaic (from the earliest records in the first half of the second millennium B.C. to the sixth century A.D.), Old (from the sixth century to the tenth), Middle (from the tenth century to the thirteenth), and Modern (from the thirteenth century onward) ; and much light is cast upon the ancient pronunciation by transcriptions of Chinese words in Annamese, Korean, and Japanese. The other members of the Tai-Chinese family are Si-lo-mo (Lolo, etc.), Karen (Sgaw, Pwo and Taungthu, and Bghai), and Tai, the latter sub-divided into south-eastern, eastern, and northern. To the south-eastern division belong Siamese, Lao, Lü, and Khün; to the eastern, Li, Dioi, etc.; and to the northern, Miao, Yao, Khāmtī, the extinct Āhom, etc.

Just how far this classification is exact is not wholly certain; and as yet it is impossible to reconstruct an hypothetical Proto-Sino-Tibetan or even a Proto-Chinese, despite the combined evidence of ancient lexicons and modern dialects. Some authorities would add to the Tibeto-Himalayan sub-groups Kirāntī and Dhīmāl; and to Tai, Annamese and Muong, which others classify with Muṇḍā and Mōn-Khmēr respectively. It seems very probable that Sino-Tibetan words were once longer than they now are, and possessed not only affixes, but also inflexions; yet such had been the wear and tear before their written records began that we cannot be sure whether even the bases can be distinguished from the putative amalgamation of the base with prefixes, postfixes, and inflexions. Āhom still had an abundance of non-syllabic prefixes, and some Tibetan dialects possess syllabic prefixes of the types *ba, da,* etc., standard Tibetan showing only the non-syllabic *b, d,* etc.; but Chinese had almost completely lost prefixes by the beginning of the Old Chinese period.

Archaic Chinese would seem at one time to have possessed a certain measure of inflexion, e.g., **nguo* ' I ', **nga* ' me '; **ńžḙᵂo* ' thou ', **ńžiḁ* ' thee ' (Modern Chinese only *wo²*, *nin²*), as compared with Burmese *nga-ga, nga-go; nin-ga, nin-go;* and in some Tibetan verbs one finds at least a quasi-distinction of tense (e.g., *gaṅ* ' full ', present *'geṅs* ' fill ', perfect *b-kaṅ,* future *d-gaṅ,* imperative *k'oṅ),* whereas in Chinese and Siamese the verb has the same form, whatever be its tense or mood. In Tibetan, the verb tends to be replaced by the epithetologue, so that one says, ' struck by me ' rather than, ' I strike ' (cf. pp. 199–200). From Old Chinese onwards, a word may be any part of speech, its function being indicated by its position in the sentence, by the use of determining particles, by the context, etc., somewhat as in English *I will go, I will my will,* where *will* is, respectively, an empty word (cf. p. 155), a verb, and a noun.

A further noteworthy characteristic of Sino-Tibetan (though by no means restricted to it; cf. pp. 62–63) is its elaborate system of tones, which distinguish what would otherwise be homonyms. Thus, Mandarin has four tones, indicated in romanised transcription by superior numbers, e.g., fu^1 ' man, husband ', fu^2 ' fortune, happiness ', fu^3 ' prefecture ', fu^4 ' rich ', or in musical notation by 茾,茾.굴.ₐₙ 茾 respectively. The lack of inflexion receives compensation in the use of empty words, e.g., $tsə^3$ ' son, child ' *(dzə³* in composition) and $ər^2$ ' child ' serve as diminutive elements and lose their tone, as tao^1 ' knife ', tao^1 *dzə* ' little knife ', $l\ddot{u}^2$ ' ass ', $l\ddot{u}r^2$ (for $l\ddot{u}^2$ *ər)* ' little ass '. Such compounds are relatively late in Chinese, as are those formed by a combination of synonyms, e.g., $čan^4$ ' stand ' and li^4 ' stand ' combined into $čan^4$ li^4, a process rendered necessary because of the fact that li^4 has other connotations expressed in writing by different characters.

Some languages of the Sino-Tibetan family possess literatures. Of these, the best known is Chinese. Archaic and Classical Chinese literature (from 1500 B.C. to the second century A.D.) begins with characters on bones and tortoise-shells used for purposes of divination, and includes the ' Classics ' ascribed to Confucius (K'ung-fu-tzŭ; 551–479 B.C.), i.e., *Shih-ching, Shu-ching, I-ching, Li-ki,* and *Chun-chiu* (' Books of Odes, of Annals, of Changes, of Rites ', and ' Spring and Autumn '), all containing much older material; early poetry, and the works of the philosophers Lao-tzŭ (about 600 B.C.) and Mêng-tzŭ (Mencius; fourth century B.C.). From the third century to the sixth A.D. was a period of transition, followed by a bloom of the lyric under the T'ang Dynasty (A.D. 618–907) and by Neo-Confucianism and a stereotyped style (philosophy, encyclopaedias, dramatic and lyric poetry, and even romances) from the eleventh century onwards.

The oldest important Tibetan record is a Sino-Tibetan treaty of A.D. 822, inscribed on a bilingual pillar at Lhasa; the earliest Burmese inscription dates from A.D. 1084 (?) on a pillar at Mya-zedi, written in Burmese, Pāli, Mōn, and Pyu (the latter also known from about fifteen inscriptions, some of which may be as old as the seventh century of our era); the first known Siamese inscription was carved in A.D. 1293, and the oldest Assamese in the fourteenth century. The literatures of all these languages are mainly Buddhist, and have little originality.

Some scholars hold that the entire Sino-Tibetan family results from a blending of the Altaic group with some language close to one of the South-East Asiatic dialects, but final judgement on this question cannot yet be rendered. Attempts to connect Burmese with Sumerian have been unsuccessful. Among works dealing with the group, mention may be made of W. W. Hunter, *Comparative Dictionary of the Languages of India and High Asia* (London, 1868), C. J. F. S. Forbes, *Comparative Grammar of the Languages of Further India* (London, 1882), A. Conrady, *Eine indochinesische Causativ-Denominativ-Bildung und ihr Zusammenhang mit den Tonakzenten* (Leipzig, 1896), E. Kuhn, *Über Herkunft und Sprache der transgangetischen Völker* (Berlin, 1883), *Linguistic Survey of India*, ii (three parts, Calcutta, 1903–09), L. F. Taylor, *Linguistic Survey of Burma* (Rangoon, 1917), A. Castrén, *Versuch einer jenissei-ostjakischen und kottischen Sprachlehre* (St. Petersburg, 1858), and B. Karlgren, *Philology and Ancient China* (Oslo, 1926).

LA-TI

This language, apparently wholly isolated, is spoken only by a small group, numbering about 450 in 1906, on the borders of Yun-nan and Tongking, north-west of the city of Hagiang.

SOUTH-EAST ASIATIC

The term South-East Asiatic (Austroasiatic, as strictly meaning ' South Asiatic ', is less exact) is applied to a group of languages spoken in Annam, Cambodia, and Cochin-China, in scattered areas of Siam, in the non-Malay portions of the Malay Peninsula, in India as far as the plain of Chota-Nagpur, and in the Nicobar Islands. It falls into three main divisions: Muṇḍā (also called Kōl or Kōlarian) in the west, Mōn-Khmēr in the centre, and Annam-

Muong in the east. *Muṇḍā* has two sub-divisions: Northern or Himālayan (the less important), consisting of Manchāṭī or Paṭnī, Kanāwᵃrī, Bunān, Limbū, Dhīmāl, etc.; and Southern or Chota-Nagpur, including Santālī, Muṇḍārī, Bhumij, Kōḍā, Asurī, etc., in the east, and Kūrkū, etc., in the west. Originally, this division would seem to have been spoken throughout north-eastern India from the Himālayas to the Bay of Bengal, and to have been concentrated in their present areas by invasions of Tibeto-Burmans from the north, of Indians from the west, and of Dravidians from the south.

Mōn-Khmēr has six sub-divisions: Central (Mōn or Talaing, Khmēr or Cambodian, Bahnar, etc.); Eastern (Cham, Sedang, etc., all profoundly influenced by Malay); Malaccan (Semang, Sakai, and Yakun); Nicobarese; Salwen Basin (Palaung, Wa, etc.); and Khāsī (in Annam). *Annam-Muong* consists of the two sub-divisions of Annamese (Upper Annamese, Tongkingese, and Cochin-Chinese) and Muong (Northern, Central, and Southern). Of these, Kanāwᵃrī, Dhīmāl, and Annam-Muong are grouped by some with the Sino-Tibetan family; and the entire South-East Asiatic group has been combined, notably by Father W. Schmidt, with Malayo-Polynesian into a single ' Austric ' family, while Annamese has been considered predominantly Tai with a South-East Asiatic admixture. This supposed Austric family has been linked, further, with Sino-Tibetan as a whole, as well as with Burushaskī; while at least one investigator would connect Muṇḍā with Uralic, and another suggests an affinity of Muṇḍā with Australian. Toward all these hypotheses it seems wisest at present to adopt an attitude of reserve.

The possible survival, as sub-strata (cf. pp. 136–137), of remnants of languages spoken before the arrival of the present linguistic stocks, as well as the obvious influence of Indian, Malay, Chinese, Tibetan, etc., upon them, combined with the lack of historic data for the majority of the dialects of the group, render it difficult to decide whether South-East Asiatic really constitutes a unitary linguistic family. Nevertheless, such phenomena as the use of the infix -*n*- throughout to denote nouns of instrument, adjectives, and abstracts, and an apparently constant relation between certain finals and certain semantic groups (possibly arising from old determinatives fused with the base), may be significant in determining genetic relationship. While there is some reason to suppose that morphemes played a considerable part at an earlier stage, the order of words in the sentence now replaces the loss of inflexion, as is so largely the case in English. At present the sub-groups differ widely in this regard, Muṇḍā even now being essentially agglutinating (cf. p. 300), while Annamese is predominantly monosyllabic. Again, Mōn-Khmēr (excepting Nicobarese) employs only prefixes and infixes; Muṇḍā has suffixes as well as prefixes and infixes; modern Annamese has only infixes, though the older language, like Muong to-day, possessed prefixes. Annamese and Muong have tones, unlike either Muṇḍā or Mōn-Khmēr. Muṇḍā, like many Mōn-Khmēr dialects, distinguishes singular, dual, and plural numbers; and both, as well as Annamese, have animate and inanimate genders. The pronominal system in Muṇḍā is highly complicated (indeed, the dialects of the Himālayan sub-group are often classed together as 'complex pronominalised languages'; cf. p. 182), and the pronouns may even stand between the morpheme and the base (e.g., Santālī *hâpân-iñ-e dal-ket'-ta-ko-tiñ-a* ' my son has struck theirs ', literally, ' son-of-me-he [*hâpân-iñ-e*] has-struck [*dal-ket'-a*] of-them [*ta-ko*] of-me [*tiñ*]'). In all three groups, the pronouns have both inclusive and exclusive forms, and present in general very archaic features.

Only a few of the South-East Asiatic languages possess literary records. The oldest Khmēr inscriptions thus far known date from the first half of the seventh century A.D.; the earliest Mōn inscription is of 1084 (?) (cf. p. 392), and the earliest Cham of A.D. 813; while the first Annamese book appeared in the fifteenth century. The principal works on the group are Father W. Schmidt's *Die Mon-Khmer Völker, ein Bindeglied zwischen Völkern Zentralasiens und Austronesiens* (Brunswick, 1906) and the *Linguistic Survey of India*, ii, 1–57; III, i, 273–567; iv, 1–175 (Calcutta, 1904–1909).

MALAYO-POLYNESIAN

The Malayo-Polynesian linguistic group, so named from the sub-groups at its western and eastern extremes (cf. the analogous use of Indo-Germanic, p. 303), and also termed Austronesian by some scholars, extends over the Pacific area from Madagascar in the west to Easter Island in the east, and from Formosa in the north to New Zealand in the south, including, besides, part of the

Malacca Peninsula on the continent of Asia, but excluding New Guinea (except along the coast), Australia, and Tasmania. Generally speaking, the base in this group is now a disyllable accented on the first syllable, though analysis shows that it is really a monosyllable extended by a determinative; the noun has neither inflexion, number, nor gender; and verbs are distinguished as transitive, intransitive, passive, causative, reciprocal, potential, relative, frequentative, etc., by a great variety of morphemes prefixed, infixed, or suffixed. The same form may serve, especially in Melanesian, either as a verb or as an epithetologue (e.g., Malay *tidor* ' sleep ', Fiji *vosa* ' discourse '), the function being determined by the accompanying words (e.g., Malay *tidor iya* ' he sleeps ' : *tidor na* ' his sleep '; Fiji *ausa sa vosa* ' I discourse ' : *a vosa* ' the discourse '). The group is divided into Indonesian, Melanesian, Micronesian, and Polynesian, classifications which are geographically convenient rather than linguistically accurate. As a whole, the languages possess a system of regular phonetic correspondences and a fairly homogeneous morphology and syntax.

The *Indonesian* area, so called because of its extensive colonisation from India, probably in the fourth or third century B.C., may be divided into eight insular groups: Formosan, Philippine, and Sangir (Favorlań, etc.; Tagalog, Bisaya or Visaya, Bontok-Igorrot, Ibanag, Magindanao, etc.); Celebes (Tombulu, Tontemboan, Gorontalo, etc., in the north; Western and Eastern Toradža, each with many dialects, in the centre; and Bugi and Makassar in the south); Borneo (Dayak and its dialects); Java (Sunda, Javanese, and Madura); Sumatra and islands to the west (Atšeh or Atšin, Batak, Malay on the east coast, etc.; Nias, etc.); southern Malacca (Malay); Madagascar (Antankára, etc., on the east coast; Sakaláva, etc., on the west coast; Mérina or Hova, etc., in the interior); and islands to the east of Java (Bali, Lombok, Sumbawa, Flores, Rotti, Timor, Letti, Babar, Tanimbar or Timorlaut, Aru, Banda, Amboina, Ceran or Seran, Moluccan Archipelago, etc.). Of all these some two hundred languages and dialects, only Javanese can boast of an old literature, dating from about A.D. 800, inspired by Sanskrit models, filled with Sanskrit words, and significantly called by a Sanskrit name, *kavi-* (' poet '). At Kota Kapur, on the Sumatran island of Banka, is an inscription of the seventh century A.D., perhaps written in Old Malay; but wherever literature exists, as in Tagalog, it is of comparatively recent date.

The Indonesian verb may be either simple or compound, the connotation of the former being expressed by the bare base, while the latter requires a morpheme (e.g., Nias *moi* ' go ' : *mu-ra'u* ' seize '). Certain dialects have a sort of classification for the plural, as Malay *oraṇ* ' person ' for human beings and angels; *ikor* ' tail ' for animals; *buah* ' fruit ' for fruits, houses, cities, boats, islands, and lakes; *bidži* ' grain ' for small objects more or less round; *bataṇ* ' trunk, branch ' for long things; and *kepiṇ* ' flat ' for planks, coins, leaves, etc. (e.g., *buda' dua oraṇ* ' child-two-person ' = ' two children ', *kuda dua ikor* ' horse-two-tail ' = ' two horses ', *rumah dua buah* ' house-two-fruit ' = ' two houses '). The article has seven forms: personal, relative, definite, indefinite, collective, ligative, and partitive (for the ligative article cf. Tagalog *aṇ aso ṇ malaki* ' the dog the big ' = ' the big dog ', a parallel development being seen, for instance, in the corresponding Greek ὁ κύων ὁ μέγας and Hebrew *hak-keleß hag-gāδōl).*

The *Melanesian* group, with about thirty-five languages, is spoken in the Solomon, Santa Cruz, Torres, Banks, New Hebrides, and Loyalty Archipelagos (e.g., Mare), and in Rotuma and Fiji. The pronoun has exclusive and inclusive forms for the first person plural (for the so-called trial number cf. pp. 181–182). There is no passive, but there are four tenses, aorist-present, definite past, perfect, and future (e.g., Fiji *au lako, au sa lako, au a lako, au na lako* ' je vais, j'allai, je suis allé, j'irai ') ; and the article has one form for common nouns and another for proper names, as Fiji [*n*]*a su* ' the basket ' : [*k*]*o Filipe* ' Philip '.

Micronesian, with some eight languages, is spoken in the Gilbert or Kingsmill, Marshall, Caroline, and Marianne Archipelagos, and on the island of Yap. In phonology, morphology, and syntax it closely resembles Melanesian, except in its extremely complicated system of pronouns.

Polynesian, with about twenty languages, is vernacular east and south of Melanesia, i.e., in the Samoa Islands, Cook's Archipelago or Hervey Islands (Rarotonga), Society Islands (Tahiti), Paumotu or Tuamotu Islands, Tonga Islands (Tongatabu), Gambier or Mangareva Islands, Easter Island, New Zealand (Maori), the Chatham or Moriori Islands, the Marquesas Archipelago, the Hawaiian Islands, and in a number of islands which, geographically, form part of Melanesia (Uea of the Loyalty Islands; Futuna, Three Hills, and some of the Sheppard Group in the New

Hebrides; Tikopia and several islets of the Swallow Group in the Santa Cruz Archipelago; Rennel and Bellona south of the Solomon Islands; and Onton Java near Ysabel Island in the same archipelago). Polynesian possesses no consonant-groups, diphthongs, or final closed syllables, and has a strong tendency to eliminate consonants, so giving a large number of homonyms. Thus, in the Marquesas, *ua* means ' rain, two, lobster, grotto, to vomit, to warm ', and also indicates the past tense, the homonyms being derived respectively from *uha* or *usa, rua, uka, rua,* **rua, ura,* and *kua.* The verbs may be transitive, intransitive, passive, causative, desiderative, reciprocal, etc., formed by various prefixes or suffixes added to the base; and the pronoun of the first person has both an exclusive and an inclusive plural.

The principal works on the group are D. Macdonald, *Oceanic Languages, their Grammatical Structure, Vocabulary, and Origin* (London, 1907), R. H. Codrington, *The Melanesian Languages* (Oxford, 1885), S. H. Ray, *A Comparative Study of the Melanesian Island Languages* (Cambridge, 1926), A. Thalheimer, *Beiträge zur Kenntnis der Pronomina personalia und possessiva der Sprachen Mikronesiens* (Stuttgart, 1908), H. Jensen, *Studien zur Morphologie der polynesischen Sprachen* (Kiel, 1923), J. L. Brandes, *Bijdragen tot de vergelijkende klankleer der westersche afdeeling van de malaiisch-polynesische taalfamilie* (Utrecht, 1889), and especially a long series of monographs by R. Brandstetter under the general title of *Malayo-polynesische Forschungen* (Lucerne, 1893 sqq.). Attempts to connect Malayo-Polynesian with Sumerian cannot be deemed successful; and relationship between Malayo-Polynesian, Australian, and American has also been sought. Since 1892 the Polynesian Society has published at Wellington, New Zealand, a *Journal,* and since 1910 *Memoirs,* in which Polynesian linguistics is studied.

PAPUAN

This group, again geographic rather than linguistic, and including some hundred and thirty-two languages (e.g., Mafōr), is spoken in most of New Guinea, in Halmahera and the islands of Rau, Tolo, Ternate, and Tidore, in the southern part of Bougainville Island and in Savo (both in the Solomon group), and in a portion of New Britain. So little is known of these languages that no classification can yet be made; but it would seem that they have no connexion with either Indonesian, Melanesian, or Australian.

AUSTRALIAN

This group also is geographic, not linguistic. The Australian languages, considerably more than a hundred in number, may be divided into Northern and Southern, which seem to have no genetic connexion. In the north, the mutual relationships are as yet unknown; in the south, some degree of affinity would appear to exist. To the *Northern* group belong three sub-divisions characterised initially by vowels or consonants, by vowels or sonants, and by only vowels respectively (e.g., the dialects of Catherine River, Caledon Bay, and Aranta). The *Southern* comprises the Victoria (Kulin-Kurnai, etc.), Yuin-Kuri, and Narrinyeri groups; mixed languages on the upper Murray River (Bangerang, etc.) ; eastern, western, and southern (Murrawari, Yungar, Parnkalla, Kabi, Mamburra, etc.) ; and Wiradyuri-Kamilaroi.

The Australian languages, like the tribes who speak them, are steadily vanishing. The oldest group in the north appears to be that marked by initial vowels or consonants; that with only vocalic initials is seemingly later; and that with initial vowels or sonants must be considered a transition-stage between the other two. In the south, the Victoria group is the oldest; and the ancestors of the Australians as a whole would seem to have entered the island-continent at Cape York, the nearest point to New Guinea, even though no linguistic affinity can yet be traced between Australian and Papuan.

In some languages, as in the South Narrinyeri dialect, the plural is essentially a trial (cf. pp. 181–182; e.g., *korni* ' man ', dual *korneṇk*, plural *kornar;* cf. *niñeṇk* ' two ', *nepaldar, maltaiar* ' three '), while North Narrinyeri has a true plural *(meru* ' man ' : *mera;* with the ending of the dual *merakul* cf. *taṇkul* ' two '). Many languages have numerals only for ' one ', ' two ', and ' three ', higher numbers up to twenty being expressed by additions, such as Yungar *gud'al-gud'al* ' two-two ' = ' four '; *mard'in baṇga gud'ir gań* ' hand-half and one ' = ' six '; *mard'in belli belli gud'ir d'ina baṇga* ' hand side-side and foot-half ' = ' fifteen ' (cf. also North Australian Daly River *nanyilk yenak* ' hand-one ', *nanyilk veren* ' hand-two ', *mad'an yenak* ' hand-two-foot-one ', *nanyilk veren mad'an veren* ' hand-two-foot-two ' for ' five ', ' ten ', ' fifteen ', and ' twenty '). In South Narrinyeri, everything beyond three is *rūwar* ' many ', or such additions as *kukko kukko kukko ki* ' pair-pair-pair-one ' = ' seven '.

Inclusive and exclusive forms for the first person dual and plural are frequent (e.g., Wiradyuri ɒ*ad*[*z*]*u* ' I '; dual ɒ*alli*, ɒ*alliguna;* plural ɒ*eani*, ɒ*eaiguna*, where the exclusive forms are obviously based on the inclusive). In Saibalgal (Torres Strait Islands) we even find separate masculine and feminine pronouns for the first person singular *(*ɒ*ai*, ɒ*atu* ' I ' masculine; ɒ*azo*, ɒ*ŏzo* ' I ' feminine; the first used in intransitive, and the second in transitive sentences) ; and in Daly River the third person has four forms for male, female, animate, and inanimate respectively (singular [*y*]*i*, *nin, mun, vun;* dual *yugot, nogot, mogot, vogot;* plural *yogöt, nogöt, mogöt, vogöt)*. The verb in Dieri (South Central division of the South Australian Central group) has distinct forms for the indefinite and definite present; proximate, indefinite, definite, remote, and more remote preterit; future; imperative; optative; conditional; and prohibitive (cf. p. 216).

Attempts have been made to connect Australian with African (more particularly with the Nilo-Chad or Nilo-Abyssinian subgroups), Malayo-Polynesian and Papuan, Andamanese, and Dravidian; but the group is best regarded as wholly independent. The one study of the linguistic area in its entirety is Father W. Schmidt's *Die Gliederung der australischen Sprachen* (Vienna, 1919), and A. Sommerfelt has made a valuable study of the linguistic structure of the Central Australian Aranta in relation to the social organisation in his *La Langue et la société: caractères sociaux d'une langue de type archaïque* (Oslo, 1938). Other works of importance here are W. Ridley's *Kamilaroi, Dippil and Turrubul: Languages Spoken by Australian Aborigines* (second edition, Sydney, 1875), Sir B. Spencer, *Native Tribes of the Northern Territory of Australia* (London, 1914), and Spencer and F. J. Gillen, *The Native Tribes of Central Australia* (London, 1899) and *The Northern Tribes of Central Australia* (London, 1904). The journal here is *Oceania: A Journal Devoted to the Study of the Native Peoples of Australia, New Guinea, and the Islands of the Pacific Ocean* (Sydney, 1930 sqq.).

TASMANIAN

Of this group, consisting of some five extinct languages, three in the east and two in the west, little definite can yet be said. The family would appear to be isolated, though it seems not impossible that affinities may some time be found with the Kulin-Kurnai division of the South Australian Victoria group. The material on the family is best collected in E. M. Curr's *The Australian Race,* iii, 593–675 (Melbourne and London, 1886–87), and in H. Ling Roth's *The Aborigines of Tasmania* (second edition, Halifax, 1899, pp. i-lxxxiii and 178–190).

AFRICAN

South of the Sahara Desert, the language-groups of Africa fall into three great divisions: Sudano-Guinean, bounded on the west by the Atlantic and the Gulf of Guinea to a point between the Cross River and Duala, on the east by Hamito-Semitic stocks, and on the south by an irregular line to Mombasa; Bantu, south of the Sudano-Guinean family; and Hottentot-Bushman scattered in the north-western part of the Province of the Cape of Good Hope and the southern part of South-West Africa.

Negro-African, generally speaking, is marked by an elaborate division of the epithetologues into classes (cf. p. 190) of human beings, liquid or liquefiable substances, woods and vegetables, earth and its products, the seasons, etc., indicated by pronominal forms or by prefixes or suffixes. Even where these do not now exist, there seems to be reason to believe that they were once employed; and the usage varies widely from language to language. When these elements fall into disuse, the epithetologue and the verb have the same form; only the meaning or the position in the sentence distinguishes the one from the other, so that word-order becomes of prime importance. The verb has no real tense, but only aspect (cf. pp. 203–208), notably telic, atelic, and contingent, the latter denoting that the action or state of the verb is not absolute, but dependent upon some condition exterior to itself. On the other hand, there are quasi-tenses for such relative aspects as pluperfect (really a telic-telic), imperfect (atelic-atelic), etc.

Not only is the general structure of Negro-African very similar throughout, but the bases and prefixes or suffixes seem to be traceable to a common Proto-Negro-African source. Many languages have tones (cf. pp. 62–63) ; others within the same sub-group do not possess them. In short, while the fundamental characteristics appear to be the same, their developments are manifold. In view of the absence of any historical data regarding the evolution of the phonology, and the probability of the influence of the phonetic systems of neighbouring peoples one on the other, the best criteria for classification thus far seem to be the modes of making the plural and the forms assumed by the personal pronouns.

Sudano-Guinean

The classification of the *Sudano-Guinean* group is much disputed. The system here adopted is that of M. Delafosse in *Les Langues du monde* (Paris, 1924, pp. 463–560) ; and A. Drexel has made another, radically different, in his ' Die Gliederung der afrikanischen Sprachen ' *(Anthropos* xvi-xvii [1921–22], 73–108; xviii-xix [1923–24], 12–39; xx [1925], 210–243, 444–460), which is followed by Father W. Schmidt *(Die Sprachfamilien und Sprachenkreise der Erde,* Heidelberg, 1926, pp. 92–116) and by E. Kieckers *(Die Sprachstämme der Erde,* Heidelberg, 1931, pp. 153–168). Delafosse holds that Sudano-Guinean and Bantu constitute a larger unity of Negro-African (the Hamito-Semites, north of the Sahara, are not Negroes; cf. pp. 365–367), united by similar characteristics of phonology, morphology, and syntax, as well as by the formative elements of their vocabularies. Sudano-Guinean shows a chaos which, he thinks, can be reduced to some sort of order only by assuming at least sixteen separate families, whereas Bantu presents a distinct homogeneity. The wide divergence between the systems of Delafosse and Drexel is at once evident from the fact that for Sudano-Guinean the former lists four hundred and thirty-five languages, the latter only one hundred and seventy-one.

Our sources for a knowledge of Sudano-Guinean are almost without exception of comparatively recent date. Whether the inscriptions of Meroë are in the language of the Blemmyes (perhaps represented by the modern Kushitic Beja; cf. p. 366), or in that of the Nobades (the supposed ancestors of the modern Nilo-Chadian Nuba), is uncertain; the former seems more likely. The Carthaginian traveller Hanno (sixth century B.C.) records one word, and Arabic authors list some twenty-five; the older grammars and translations by Europeans are often very faulty. Our only source of any value for ancient Sudano-Guinean is *Old Nubian,* recorded in *graffiti,* inscriptions, and written texts from the middle of the eighth century to the beginning of the eleventh. Of many languages we know nothing but the names, and there are doubtless others still to be discovered. Any classification and comparison, then, must be regarded only as tentative.

The divisions of *Sudano-Guinean,* according to Delafosse, may now be enumerated:

(1) *Nilo-Chad* (thirty languages) with traces of classes, but no class-pronouns or tones, and including Nuba, Kunama, Tubu, Kanuri, etc.

(2) *Nilo-Abyssinian* (fifteen languages) with evident traces of classes and class-pronouns and tones, and including Shiluk, Dinka, etc.

(3) *Nilo-Equatorial* (twenty-six languages) with very obvious classes and tones, and including Bari, Suk, Māsai, etc.

(4) *Kordofanian* (ten languages) with a high development of classes but no tones, bearing a general close resemblance to Bantu, and including Tumeli, etc.

(5) *Nilo-Congolese* (nineteen languages) with traces of classes, and including Mangbetu, Mbuba, etc.

(6) *Ubangi* (twenty-five languages) with classes but only vestiges of class-pronouns, apparently with tones, and including Mittu, Mungu, Zande, Banda, etc.

(7) *Shari-Wadi* (twelve languages) with neither classes nor class-pronouns, and including Sara and Barma.

(8) *Shari* (fifteen languages), relatively little known.

(9) *Nigero-Chad* (thirty-one languages) presenting many varieties of evolution of the underlying principles of Sudano-Guinean, and having in Haussa (regarded by some as an isolated language) a *lingua franca* for the western and southern Sudan.

(10) *Nigero-Camerun* (sixty-six languages) with classes and tones, and including Fi or Efik, Bo or Ibo, Yoruba, etc.

(11) *Lower Niger,* having only one language, Jo (or Ijo, Bonny, New Calabar) with several dialects and with tones and classes, but, apparently, no class-pronouns.

(12) *Voltaic* (fifty-three languages) with tones, classes, and (in some of the group) class-pronouns; apparently possessing inclusive and exclusive pronouns for the first person plural, and including Gurma, Mô or Mossi, Kuruma, Senufu, etc.

(13) *Ivory Coast-Dahomian* (forty-eight languages) with classes in various degrees of preservation, sometimes with tones, and including Fon or Dahomian, Ehue or Ewe (which has developed a literature and serves as a *lingua franca* over a considerable area), Gã, Chi, Fanti, etc.

(14) *Nigero-Senegalese* (thirty-six languages) with only vestigial remnants of classes, and including Songoï, Dogon, Sarakolle, Mandingo, Vaï, Mende, etc.

(15) *Ivory Coast-Liberian* (twenty-four languages) with vestiges of classes and tones, having two systems of conjugation according as the verbs are simple or accompanied by a separable particle, and including Gre or Grebo, Kra, Bassa, etc.

(16) *Senegal-Guinean* (twenty-four languages) with classes and remnants of class-pronouns, with tones in the south, and including Peul or Fula, Wolof, Serer, etc.

Besides these, one may mention small groups of Negrillos scattered in the Sudan from the Upper Nile to the Cameruns, whose speech is little known, though it may prove to be connected with Hottentot-Bushman in the south-west of the continent. There are also a number of creolised languages (cf. p. 37) in Africa, notably Negro-Portuguese, Negro-English, and Negro-French; and descendants of slaves in the Antilles (especially in Haiti), as well as in the Guianas and in Brazil, still retain survivals of African, particularly, it would seem, from the Ivory Coast-Dahomian stock. Haussa, here classified with the Nigero-Chad group, has been regarded by some as isolated or as cognate with Hamitic, Bantu, or even Akkadian. The proposed affinity of Nuba with Iberian, and of Kanuri with Sumerian, is highly improbable.

Among the comparative studies dealing with this linguistic area, mention may be made of S. W. Koelle, *Polyglotta Africana* (London, 1854), J. T. Last, *Polyglotta Africana Orientalis* (London, 1885), H. Steinthal, *Die Mande-Negersprachen* (Berlin, 1867), C. Meinhof, *Die Sprachen des dunklen Erdteils* (Stuttgart, 1909) and *Die moderne Sprachforschung in Afrika* (Berlin, 1910; English translation, *Introduction to the Study of African Languages*, London, 1915), D. Westermann, *Die Sudansprachen* (Hamburg, 1911), F. W. Migeod, *The Languages of West Africa* (two volumes, London, 1911–13), F. Ll. Griffith, *The Nubian Texts of the Christian Period* (Berlin, 1913); E. Zyhlarz, *Grundzüge der nubischen Grammatik* (Leipzig, 1928), H. Schuchardt, *Kreolische Studien* (nine parts, Vienna, 1882–91), K. Lentzner, *Colonial English* (London, 1891), and L. Adam, *Les Idiomes négro-aryen et maléo-aryen* (Paris, 1883). The principal journals are the *Zeitschrift für Eingeborenensprachen* (formerly the *Zeitschrift für Kolonialsprachen*, Berlin, 1910 sqq.), the successor of the *Zeitschrift für afrikanische, ozeanische und ostasiatische Sprachen* (Berlin, 1895–1903), as that was of the *Zeitschrift für afrikanische Sprachen* (Berlin, 1887–90), the *Bibliotheca Africana* (Innsbruck, 1924 sqq.), the *Journal of the African Society* (London, 1901 sqq.), and *Africa: Journal of the International Institute of African Languages and Cultures* (London, 1928 sqq.).

Bantu

Possibly cognate with Sudano-Guinean, Bantu is spoken, except for linguistic islets of Hottentot-Bushman, throughout South Africa below an irregular line running roughly from the boundary between Nigeria and Camerun on the west to Mombasa in the east, passing north of Uganda and approaching the Congo. Native tradition would seem to indicate that the Bantu came from the region of the Upper Nile. A few words are recorded by mediaeval Arab sources; F. Pigafetta noted others in 1591; and in 1659 Hyacinthus Brusciottus a Vetralla published at Rome his *Regulae quaedam pro difficillimi Congensium idiomatis faciliori captu ad grammaticae normam reductae*, following a Catechism of 1624, all these showing that the languages were then very nearly the same as now.

Every Bantu syllable ends in a vowel, and the only consonant-groups allowed are a nasal plus a consonant or a consonant plus *w* or *y* (e.g., *puga* ' blow ', *bwato* ' boat ', *otyikombo* ' broom ', *ba-ntu* ' men '). While tones have been observed in some languages, they do not seem to possess semantic value as in many Sudano-Guinean dialects. Inflexion is by prefixes and suffixes, the former indicating the method of employment and syntactic relations, and the latter modifying the connotation of the base. Thus, the prefix *ku-* denotes the infinitive, and *u-* the second person singular of the aorist; while the suffix *-a* indicates duration (e.g., *ku-tand-a* ' to be loving ', *u-tand-a* ' thou wert and art loving '). All nouns are grouped in classes (cf. p. 190), and the prefix characteristic of the class in question is repeated before all morphemes or words standing in relation to the noun (e.g., Swahili *m-thu m-zuri* ' handsome man ', *wa-tu wa-zuri* ' handsome men '; *ki-su ki-kali* ' sharp knife ', *vi-su vi-kali* ' sharp knives ').

Separate prefixes mark the singular and the plural of human beings, of diminutives, of collectives and unities, of things, of implements, of animals, etc. (e.g., Sotho *ho-lael-a* ' to be commanding ', *mo-lael-i* ' commander '; Swahili *ku-f-a* ' to be dying ', *ki-f-o* ' place of death '; *ku-tum-a* ' to be sending ', *m-tum-e* ' one sent, messenger '; *mu-ntu* ' man ', *ba-ntu* ' men ', *ka-ntu* ' little man ', *tu-ntu* ' little men '; *ma-naka* ' horn ' collectively, *le-naka* ' single horn '; Sotho *mo-sot^{h}o* ' Sotho man ', *ba-sot^{h}o* ' Sotho men ' [whence the generic name *Basuto*], *se-sot^{h}o* ' Sotho thing, Sotho language ', *bi-sot^{h}o* ' Sotho things '; Nyamwezi *ki-neneko* ' cup ', *fi-neneko* ' cups '; Herero *om-bua* ' dog ', *ozom-bua* ' dogs '). Derivative verbs are formed by suffixes, as Sotho *ho-lul-a* ' to be sitting ', *ho-lul-el-a* ' to be sitting for someone, to be waiting ', *ho-lul-is-a* ' to be making someone sit ', *ho-lul-ol-a* ' to be ceasing to sit '; *ho-hlomp^h-a* ' to be honouring ', *ho-hlomp^h-eh-a* ' to be honourable, honoured '; *ho-op-a* ' to be striking ', *ho-op-an-a* ' to be striking one another ', etc. There is no declension, properly speaking; and moods and tenses are formed by suffixes, particles, or auxiliaries.

The number of Bantu languages and their classification is far from settled. Mlle. L. Homburger *(Les Langues du monde,* Paris, 1924, pp. 579–587) gives eleven groups with eighty-three principal languages; Father Schmidt, following Drexel, seven groups with ninety-three languages; and Sir H. H. Johnson, three hundred and sixty-six Bantu and eighty-seven Semi-Bantu languages. Mlle. Homburger's classification is as follows:

(1) *Ganda,* north-east of Lake Victoria Nyanza: Ganda, Nyoro, and Kerewe.

(2) *Ruanda,* north-east of Tanganyika: Ruanda and Rundi.

(3) *North-Eastern,* in the Kilimanjaro chain: Kikuyu, Kamba, Chagga, etc.

(4) *Northern group* on the east coast: Taveta-Taita, Shambala, Comoros, etc., and especially Swahili, with a written literature for some centuries, and the *lingua franca* of a wide area.

(5) *East African,* bounded by Lakes Tanganyika, Victoria Nyanza, and Nyasa, and by the Indian Ocean: Nyamwezi, Nyaturu, Kaguru, Hehe, Yao, etc.

(6) *South-East African* in Portuguese East Africa with two subgroups, coastal and Chuana, the former including Makua, Ronga

or Thonga, etc., and the latter comprising Sotho, Kololo, Chuana (whence the name of Bechuanaland), etc., with Venda as a transition-dialect between the two sub-groups.

(7) *Zulu:* Zulu, Kafir or Xosa, Tebele (whence Matabeleland), etc.

(8) *Central,* north of the Zambezi and west of Lakes Nyasa and Tanganyika: Bemba, Bisa or Wisa, Lala-Lamba, Senga, Subiya, etc.

(9) *Western,* west of the Zambezi and the Kalahari Desert: Herero, Umbundu or Nano, etc.

(10) *Congolese:* Congo, Lolo Nkundu, etc.

(11) *North-Western,* along the coast between the Congo and Duala and inland to the north: Bangui, Mpongwe or Galoa, Duala, Bube, etc.

It seems by no means impossible that Mlle. Homburger's endeavour to establish an ultimate genetic relationship between the Bantu family and Egyptian (cf. pp. 365, 367), and so, in the last analysis, a connexion with Hamito-Semitic as a whole, may prove successful; but the hypothesis of an affinity between Bantu and Ural-Altaic, proposed by J. F. van Oordt, cannot be accepted.

Among the works dealing with the family as a whole are W. H. Bleek's *Languages of Mozambique* (London, 1856) and *Comparative Grammar of South African Languages* (London, 1869), L. Homburger's *Phonétique historique du bantou* (Paris, 1913), Sir H. H. Johnson's *Comparative Study of the Bantu and Semi-Bantu Languages* (two volumes, London, 1919–22), C. Meinhof's *Grundriss einer Lautlehre der Bantusprachen* (second edition, Berlin, 1910) and *Grundzüge einer vergleichenden Grammatik der Bantusprachen* (Berlin, 1906), W. H. Stapleton's *Comparative Handbook of Congo Languages* (Yakusu, 1903), J. Torrend's *Comparative Grammar of the South African Bantu Languages* (London, 1892), and A. Werner's *The Bantu Languages* (London, 1919).

Hottentot-Bushman

Of the Hottentot-Bushman or Khoiń group, spoken in scattered areas in south-west Africa by pygmies of a very low grade of civilisation, relatively little is known. It falls into two main divisions: *Hottentot* (more properly Nama) with four dialects, and *Bushman* (more properly San) with two. They are characterised by inspirated consonants (clicks; see p. 57; the South-East Bantu group also possesses clicks, apparently borrowed from Hottentot-Bush-man), which are employed only initially, San having seven, and Nama four. Three tones (cf. pp. 62–63) are found, and there are three numbers, with inclusive and exclusive duals and plurals for the pronouns of the first persons. Verbal forms are obtained by means of morphemes to denote simple, negative, stative or con-suetudinal, causative, reciprocal, diminutive, desiderative, poten-tial, and passive aspects, as well as moods and tenses, suffixed par-ticles also being used to express case-relations. Connexions have been sought between this group and Hamitic, especially with Beja of the Lower Kushitic sub-division.

AMERICAN

When one turns to the Americas, one finds a multitude of lin-guistic families which are wholly unrelated, at least so far as one can tell from their brief history, dating only from the early years after the discovery of the continents. To give any general charac-terisation of them is quite impossible (see p. 168) ; and even their classification is not entirely certain, as may be seen from the divergencies of the lists given by P. Rivet *(Les Langues du monde,* Paris, 1924, pp. 597–712) and by Father W. Schmidt *(Die Sprach-familien und Sprachenkreise der Erde,* Heidelberg, 1926, pp. 163–267), who is followed by E. Kieckers *(Die Sprachstämme der Erde,* Heidelberg, 1931, pp. 169–230). For purposes of convenience, an arbitrary division may be made into the languages of North America (Canada and the United States), Mexico and Central America, and the Antilles and South America; and the best that we can do here is simply to record the linguistic families in alpha-betic sequence, noting some of the most important dialects of each, following the order given by Rivet, and indicating by a * lan-guages now extinct, but, for the sake of brevity, omitting their geographical positions.

North American

In *North America,* twenty-five linguistic families are listed:

(1) *Algonkin,* with six divisions and fifty-one languages, com-prises Blackfoot (Piegan, Kaina or Blood, and Blackfoot or Siksika) ; Cheyenne (Cheyenne and *Sutaio) ; Arapaho (Gros-Ventre and Arapaho) ; Central (Cree-Montagnais, Menomini, Sauk, Fox, Kikapu, Ojibway or Chippewa, Algonkin, Potawatomi,

*Kahokia, Kaskaskia, Peoria, Miami, *Natik, Delaware or Leni-Lenape, *Mahikan or *Mohikan, Pequot, etc.); Eastern (Mik-mak, Abnaki, Penobscot or Pennakuk, Passamaquoddy, and Malesit; the precise position of several languages within the group is uncertain, such as *Massachusett, *Narraganset, *Wampanoag, Montauk, *Nipmuk, *Nantikok, Powhatan, *Sekotan, etc.); and Californian or Ritwan (Wiyot or Wishokan and Yurok or Weit-spekan).

(2) *Beothuk, formerly spoken in Newfoundland (cf. p. 32).

(3) Chimakum: *Chimakum and Kwileut.

(4) Hoka with forty-two languages: Shasta, *Chimariko, Karok, Yana, Pomo or Kulanapan, *Esselen, Yuma with three sub-divisions (Havasupai, Walapai, Tonto, and Yavapai in the east; Mohave, Yuma, Marikopa, Diegueño, and Kokopa in the centre; and Kiliwi, Santo Tomás, and *Kochimi in Lower California), *Salina, *Chumash, Seri, Washo, Tekistlatek, and *Koahuiltek with some seven dialects.

(5) Iroquois with seven languages: Huron or Wyandot, Five Nations (Cayuga, Mohawk, Oneida, Onondaga, and Seneca), *Konestoga, *Susquehanna, Tuscarora, Cherokee, and perhaps *Kori.

(6) Kaddo with three sub-groups: Northern (Arikara), Central (Pawnee), and Southern (Kaddo, Wichita, and Kichai).

(7) Keresan with two dialects.

(8) Kiowa.

(9) Klamath or Lutuamian.

(10) Kutenai or Kitunahan.

(11) Muskhogi with three divisions and sixteen languages: Seminole, *Apalachi, Alabama, Choctaw, etc.; Muskhogi or Creek; and Natchez (*Taënsa, etc.); to which may perhaps be added *Kalusa, *Paskagula, etc.

(12) Na-Dene with forty-seven languages and three sub-groups formerly considered independent: Athapascan, Haida, and Tlingit. Athapascan has the three sub-divisions of Tinneh or Dene in the north (Tatsanottine or Yellow-Knives, Thlingchadinne or Dog-Ribs, Chippeway, etc., in the east; Kuchin, Ahtena, and Khotana in the north-west; and Nahane, Carriers or Takulli, etc., in the south-west); Pacific (*Kwalhiokwa, Shastakosta, Hupa, Whilkut, Mattole, Wailaki, etc.); and Southern (Lipan, Navaho, Apache, with many tribes, etc.). Haida or Skittagetan consists of Haida

and Kaigani, the principal dialects being Skidgate and Masset; and *Tlingit* or Kolushan comprises Tlingit proper and Tagish.

(13) *Penutian*, with thirty-one languages, may be divided into four groups: Californian, Oregon, Chinuk, and Tsimshian. To the *Californian* sub-group belong Wintun or Copehan with four main dialects; Maidu or Pujunan with three; Yokuts or Mariposan; and Miwok or Miwa or Moquelumnan with four dialects; and to the *Oregon* sub-group, Takelma with two dialects: Coastal (Coos, Siuslaw, Yakona, Yakina, and Alsea) and Kalapuya. *Chinuk* comprises Wasko, Wishram, Kathlamet, Klakamas, *Klatsop, etc.; and *Tsimshian* consists of Tsimshian proper, Niska, and Gyitkshan.

(14) *Shahaptin* with eight languages: Klikitat, Nez Percé, Wallawalla, Yakima, etc.

(15) *Salish* with sixteen languages: Lilluet, Shuswap, Flathead, Skitswish or Cœur d'Alène, etc., in the interior; and Bellakula, Komoks, Songish, Tillamuk, etc., on the coast.

(16) *Sioux* with twenty-four languages in seven sub-groups: Dakota-Assiniboin (Mdewakanton, Wahpeton, Yankton, Teton, Assiniboin, etc.); Dhegiha (Omaha, Ponka, Kwapaw, Osage, and Kansa); Chiwere (Iowa, Oto, Missouri, and Winnebago); Mandan; Hidatsa (Hidatsa and Crow); Biloxi (Biloxi and *Ofo); and Eastern (Katawba and *Tutelo, with some extinct and dubious dialects).

(17) *Tano*, consisting of Tiwa (and perhaps *Piro), *Towa, and Tewa.

(18) *Timukua.

(19) *Tunika* with twelve languages: *Tunika, *Atakapa, Chitimasha, etc.

(20) *Uto-Aztek* with sixty-five languages in three groups, formerly supposed to be independent: Shoshon, Pima-Sonora, and Nahuatl. *Shoshon*, with twenty-four languages, is sub-divided into four groups: Plateau (Shoshoni-Comanch, Ute-Chemehuevi, and Mono-Paviotso or Mono-Bannok, each with a number of dialects); Southern Californian (Serrano, Luiseño-Kahuilla, and Gabrieleño, each with dialects); Kern River (Tübatulabal); and Pueblo (Hopi or Moki). *Pima-Sonora*, with thirty-two languages, and extending far into Mexico, consists of Upper Pima (Pima, Pápago, *Sobaipuri, and *Potlapigua); Lower Pima; Ópata or Teguima with two dialects; Kahita or Yaqui, Cinaloa, or Sinaloa (Yaki, Mayo,

Tehueco, Vakoregue, etc.); *Tepahue; *Zoe and *Baimena; *Nio; Tarahumare with four dialects; *Koncho; *Laguneros or *Irritila; *Akaxee and kindred tribes; *Zakatek; Huichol (descendants of the *Guachichile); Kora; and Tepekano. *Nahuatl*, with nine languages, and spoken in Mexico and Central America, has six subgroups: Nahuatl or Aztek, Pipil (probably akin to *Alaguilak), *Nikarao or *Olomega or *Nikiran, Tlaskaltek, *Sigua, and *Kazkan.

(21) *Waiilatpu:* *Kayus and Molala.

(22) *Wakash* with seven languages: Nutka and Kwakiutl, with the dialects of the latter.

(23) *Yuki* with four dialects.

(24) *Yuchi* or Uchean.

(25) *Zuñi*.

Among the great number of works dealing with North American languages in general, we may mention especially the *Handbook of American Indian Languages North of Mexico*, edited by F. Boas (three volumes, Washington, 1911–39; incomplete; a collection of grammars), D. G. Brinton, *The American Race: A Linguistic Classification and Ethnographic Description of the Native Tribes of North and South America* (New York, 1891), and J. W. Powell, *American Linguistic Families North of Mexico* (Washington, 1891). The special journals on the subject are the *International Journal of American Linguistics* (New York, 1917–35) and the *Journal de la société des américanistes de Paris* (Paris, 1904 sqq.).

Mexican and Central American

Besides languages of the North American groups of Uto-Aztek, Na-Dene, and Hoka spoken in Mexico (Pima, Ópata, Kahita, Tarahumare, Huichol, etc., and the entire Nahuatl division; part of the southern division of Tinneh or Dene; Yuma, Seri, Tekistlatek, etc.), and excluding Chibcha and Karib, which are primarily Antillean and South American, the *Mexican and Central American* languages may be classified into twenty families.

(1–4) *Amusgo; Chinantek; Kuikatek;* and *Kuitlatek*, the first and third formerly considered to be Mixtek, and the fourth Nahuatl.

(5) *Lenka* with seven dialects: Guaxikero, Opatoro, Chilanga, *Intibukat, *Kakaguatike, etc.

(6) *Maya*, the most important of the specifically Central American families, with twenty-seven members falling into two main divisions, Huastek and Maya proper. *Huastek* consists of Huastek proper and its dialect Chikomuseltek; *Maya* has the two subgroups of Tzental-Maya and Pokonchi-Kiche-Mam. Tzental-Maya includes Tzotzil (Chontal, Tzental, Tzotzil, Chañabal, Chol, Chortí, *Subinha, etc.) and Maya (Maya, Lakandon, Itza or Peten, and Mopan); and Pokonchi-Kiche-Mam comprises Pokonchi (Pokonchi, Kekchi, and Pokomám), Kiche (Kiche, Kakchikel, Tzutuhil, and Uspantek), and Mam (Mam, Ixil, Aguakatek I, and perhaps *Achis).

(7) *Miskito-Sumo-Matagalpa* with five languages: Mískito or Muskito or Moskito, Úlūa or Sumo (sub-divided into Úlūa proper, Sumo-Táuaxka, and Yósko), and Matagalpa or Chontal.

(8) *Mixe-Zoke* with nine languages: Mixe, Zoke, *Tapachultek, *Aguakatek II, Huave, etc.

(9) *Mixtek*.

(10) *Olive*.

(11) *Otomí* with twenty languages, including Otomí, *Serrano, *Meko or *Xonaz or *Tonaz, Tepehua, Pame, Mazahua, Pirinda or Matlaltzinko, and probably Mazatek (sub-divided into Trike, Chocho or Chuchon, and Mazatek with three dialects) and Chipanek, formerly considered to be independent and consisting of Chipanek proper, Mangue or Cholutek, *Diriá, and Orotina.

(12) *Paya*.

(13) *Subtiaba* with three languages: Tlappanek-Yopi, Subtiaba proper, and *Maribichikoa.

(14) *Tarask*.

(15) *Totonak* with several dialects.

(16) *Waïkuri:* *Waïkuri proper and *Perikú.

(17) *Xanambre:* *Pisone and *Xanambre proper.

(18) *Xikake* or Jicaque with three dialects.

(19) *Xinka* or Jinca or Sinca with three dialects, to which *Pupuluka should perhaps be added.

(20) *Zapotek* with four languages: Zapotek proper, Soltek, Chatino, and Papabuko.

The two chief works on the area are C. Thomas and J. R. Swanton, *Indian Families of Mexico and Central America* (Washington, 1911), and W. Lehmann, *Die Sprachen Zentral-Amerikas* (two volumes, Berlin, 1920; a collection of skeleton grammars).

Antillean and South American

Of all the linguistic areas of the world, that of the Antilles and South America is the least known; but we may say that it comprises at least seventy-seven distinct linguistic stocks, although Father W. Schmidt lists only thirty-six.

(1) *Alakaluf* with seven languages: Alikulip or Alakaluf, *Chono, *Lecheyel, *Adwipliin, etc.

(2) *Al'entiak:* *Al'entiak or *Huarpe and *Mil'kayak.

(3) *Amuesha,* possibly to be classed with Arawak.

(4) *Araukan* with nine languages: Mapuche, Pehuenche, Kunko or Huil'iche, Taluhet or Taluche, Leuvuche, Rankel, *Pikuntu or *Pikunche, etc.

(5) *Arawak* with one hundred and thirty languages (including twenty-nine now extinct), perhaps the most important of all South American groups and once spoken not only in South America, but throughout the Antilles, and even in south-western Florida. Both in the Little Antilles and in Venezuela, however, the Arawak were conquered, shortly before the arrival of the Spaniards, by the Karib of Guiana, with the result that, the Arawak men having been massacred or driven into the hills, and their women taken by the conquerors, women and children continued to speak Arawak, while adult males spoke Karib (cf. p. 37). The enormous family appears to be divisible into seven groups: North Amazon and Orinoco (*Maipure, Goaxiro, Yaulapíti, Mehinakú, Kustenaú, Waurá, Paressí, etc.); Prae-Andean (Ipuriná, Piro-Chontakiro-Kuniba-Kushitíneri, Kanamari, Maniteneri, Inapari, Kampa, Palikur-Marawan, etc.); Bolivian (Baure, Moxo, Paikoneka, Paunaka, etc.); Araua (Pama, Pamana, Pammari, Purupurú, Yuberi, Araua, Yamamadi, Kulina, Guaná-Tereno-Layaná, etc.); Guianian (Taruma, Atoraí, Mapidian, Wapishána, etc.); Uru-Pukina; and Takana (Araona, Kavina, Mabenaro, Tiatinagua, Toromona, Guakanahua or Guarayo, Takana proper, Maropa, etc.).

(6) *Arda.*

(7) *Atakama.*

(8) *Atal'an* with four languages, all extinct.

(9) *Auaké.*

(10) *Aymará* with eleven languages: Kol'a, Pakase or Pakaxe, Charka, Kil'agua or Kil'aka, etc.

(11) *Bororó* with eight languages: Bororó or Coroados, *Otuke, *Korabeka, *Tapii, etc.

(12) *Chapakura* with fifteen languages: Chapakura or Huachi, Pawumwa or Huanyam, Turá, Arikem, *Rokorona, *Okoróno, etc.

(13) *Charrúa* with seven dialects: *Charrúa proper, *Bohane, *Chaná-Beguá, etc.

(14) *Chibcha* with seventy-three languages in four sub-divisions: Talamank-Barbakóa, Dorask-Guaymi, Chibcha-Aruak, and Paez. *Talamank-Barbakóa* includes four groups: Guatuso, descended from the ancient *Korobisí; Talamank proper (*Güetare and *Kepo, Kabekar and *Suerre, Bribri, Térraba and Tíribi, and Boruka [the latter descended from the ancient *Koto], *Turukaka, and *Burukak); Kuna; and Barbakóa (*Barbakóa proper, Kayápa, *Kara, *Kixo, etc.). *Dorask-Guaymi* consists of *Murire or *Bukueta or *Sabanero, *Move or *Valientes or *Norteños, *Changina, *Dorask, Chimila, etc. To *Chibcha-Aruak* belong *Chibcha proper, *Muysca or *Moska, Rama, Melchora, Aruak, Tunebo or Tame, *Betoi, Andakí, etc.; and to *Paez,* Paez proper, Totoró, *Pixao, etc.

(15) *Chikito* with six languages: *Manasika, Piñoka, Churápa, etc.

(16) *Chirino.*

(17) *Choko.*

(18) *Cholona* with two dialects.

(19) *Chon* with thirty-nine languages in two groups, Patagonian and Fuegian. To the former belong Tehuelche or Tsoneka with two tribes, and Téuesh; to the latter, Ona with two sub-divisions.

(20) *Diagit* or *Katamareño: *Diagit proper or *Kalchaki and *Lule.

(21) *Enimaga:* Towothli, *Enimaga, *Guentuse, and *Lengua.

(22) *Esmeralda.*

(23) *Guahibo* with nine languages: Kuiva, Chirikoa, Katarro, Churoye or Bisanigua or Guaigua, etc.

(24) *Guarauno.*

(25) *Guató.*

(26) *Guaykurú* with ten languages: *Mbayá-Guaykurú, *Guachí, Payaguá, Toba, Mokoví or Mbokobí, *Abipon, etc., and perhaps *Kerandí.

(27) -*Het:* *Chechehet and part of *Diuihet.

(28) *Huari.*

(29) *Itonama.*

(30) *Kahuapana* or Mayna: Xébero, Mayna, and Kahuapana.

(31) *Kaliána.*

(32) **Kañari.*

(33) *Kanichana.*

(34) *Karajá:* Shambioá, Žawažé or Žavahé or Shavayé, and Karayá.

(35) *Karib* with seventy-four languages, including seventeen now extinct, and divisible into six groups: Akawaí, Arekuna, Makushí, Sapará, Seregóng, Ipurukotó, etc.; Trio, Umáua, Pianokotó, Makiritáre, etc.; Kumanagoto, Guaikerí, Chaima, Upurui, etc.; Bakaïrí, Arára, Parirí, etc.; Bonari and Yauaperý; and Peba, Yagua, and Yameo.

(36) *Karirí:* Karirí proper and Sabuyá.

(37) *Katukina* with eight languages: Tukundiapa or Tukanodyapá, Tawari or Kadekilidyapá, Kanamari, Katukina with two sub-groups, Katawishi or Hewadie, etc.

(38) *Kayuvava.*

(39) *Kichua* or Runa-simi, notable as the only one of all South American families able to boast of a pre-Columbian language of civilisation and extended, largely by missionary zeal, far beyond its original borders. Divisible into the five geographic groups of Inka, Chinchasuyu, Kiteño, Bolivian, and Argentine, it has eight principal dialects: Kiteño, Lamaño or Lamista, Chinchasuyu or Chinchaya with three sub-dialects, Huancayo, Ayacucho, Kuskeño, Bolivian, and Argentine or Tukumano or Kuzko.

(40) *Koche* or Mokóa.

(41) **Kófane.*

(42) *Leko.*

(43) *Máku.*

(44) *Maskoi* with six languages: Maskoi, Lengua or Gekoinlahaǎk, Angaité or Enslét, Sanapaná, Sapukí, and Guaná.

(45) *Mashubi.*

(46) *Matako-Mataguayo* with twelve languages: Mataguayo proper, Vexoz or Aiyo, Matako, Noktén, etc.

(47) *Mobima.*

(48) *Moseten:* Moseten proper and Chimáne.

(49) *Múra.*

(50) *Nambikuára* with four languages: Kôkôzú in the south-east, Anunzê in the north-east, Uaintasú or Uáinjê or Kabishí in the south-west, and Tagnanís, the latter with four sub-divisions, in the north-west.

(51) *Otomak.*

(52) *Pano* with forty-three languages divided into three groups: Kulino or Kurina, Mayoruna or Maxuruna or Pelados, Kapanahua, Katukina, Kashibo or Kachibo or Kahibo, Amahuaka or Maspo or Impetineri, Yaminawa, Shipinaua, *Itukale or *Urarina, *Maparina, etc.; Arasaire or Arasa, Yamiaka, and Araua; Pakaguara, Karipuna, etc.

(53) *Puelche* with two dialects.

(54) *Puináve:* Puináve and Makú.

(55) *Puruhá.*

(56) *Sáliba:* Sáliba proper, Piaróa, and Máku.

(57) *Samuku* with sixteeen languages: Chamakoko, Morotoko with six sub-divisions, Ugaraño, Chírakuá, etc.

(58) *Sanaviron,* of which *Komechingon was probably a dialect.

(59) *Sek:* Katakao, *Kolan, and *Sechura.

(60) *Shavanté* or Eoshavanté.

(61) *Shirianá:* Shirianá proper or Shirishána, and Waíka.

(62) *Timote* or Muku with ten languages: Timote proper, Mukuchi, Eskaguey, Kuika, Tostó, Xaxó, etc.

(63) *Trumaí.*

(64) *Tukáno* or Betoya with thirty-nine languages in three divisions. To the eastern group belong Tukáno proper or Daxseá, Uásöna, Uaíkana, Dätuana, Kueretú, etc.; to the western, Amaguaxe, Makaguaxe, Pioxe, etc.; and to the northern, Tama and Ayriko.

(65) *Tupi-Guaraní,* with sixty-eight languages, of which fourteen are extinct, seems originally to have centred in the region between the Paraná and the Paraguay, and Guaraní or Abañeême is still the dominant language of the Republic of Paraguay. Before the discovery of the continent, however, Guaraní tribes had migrated to the Brazilian coast as far as the mouth of the Amazon, though few of them now remain there, and then had ascended the river almost to its source, settling along many of its affluents as well, particularly to the south. Just as the southern branch of the family, Guaraní, became vernacular in Paraguay, so its northern member, Tupi or Ñeêngatu, serves as a *lingua geral* in all the Amazon basin, and even throughout Brazil. Among the many languages of the family, we may mention, in Paraguay, *Paranaé, Guayakí, Kainguá, etc.; in Brazil, Aré, *Tapé, *Tupinamba,

*Kaité, Manažé, Anambē, *Yurimagua or *Zurimagua, Miránya or Boro, Paikipiranga, Tapirapé, Yuruná, Parentintin or Kawahíb or Kawahíwa, Rama-Rama, Apiaká, etc.; and in the west, Chiriguano or Aba or Kamba or Tembeta, Guarayo, Sirióno, etc.

(66) *Tuyuneiri.*

(67) *Vilela-Chulupí* or Lule with nineteen languages, divided into *Lule (*Lule proper, *Oristiné, etc.) and Vilela (Vilela proper, Atalalá, Ipa, Teket, etc.).

(68) *Witóto:* Witóto proper, Miraña-Karapaná-Tapuyo, Orejones, and perhaps *Koëruna.

(69) *Xíbaro* or Shiwora or Shuāra with ten languages: Xíbaro proper, Makas, Aguaruna, Miazal, *Palta, etc.

(70) *Xiraxara:* Xiraxara proper, Ayamán, and Gayón.

(71) *Yahgan.*

(72) *Yaruro.*

(73) *Yunka:* *Morrope, *Eten, *Chimu, *Mochika or *Chincha, and *Chanko.

(74) *Yurakáre.*

(75) *Yuri.*

(76) *Záparo:* Záparo proper, Konambo, Gae, Andoa, and Ikito. All resemble Miránya lexicographically.

(77) *Že* or Ge or Kran with fifty languages, and the single group of South American which has been thoroughly investigated from the modern point of view. It falls into four divisions: Eastern, Northern, Central, and Southern. The *Eastern* group comprises Botokudo or Burung or Borung or Borun, Kamakan or Mongoyó or Monshokó, and perhaps *Pañamé, *Mashakalí, *Malalí, *Purí, etc.; the *Northern*, Timbira, Sakamekran, Makamekran or Karaôu or Kraô, Purekamekran, etc.; the *Central*, the sub-groups of Kayapó (Suyá, etc.) and Akuä (Sherénte, Shavánte Opaié or Araē, *Shikriabá, *Akroá, etc.); and the *Southern* or Guayanā has eastern and western sub-groups, the former consisting of Kaingáng, and the latter of Ingain and Guayaná or Waiganna.

The principal works dealing with South American and Antillean as a whole are D. G. Brinton's *The American Race* (New York, 1891) and *Studies in South American Languages* (Philadelphia, 1892); and there are four volumes of a comparative character: L. Adam's *Matériaux pour servir à l'établissement d'une grammaire comparée des dialectes de la famille tupi* (Paris, 1896) with similar treatises for Carib (Paris, 1893) and Guaykurú (Paris,

1891), and S. A. Lafone-Quevedo's *Las Lenguas de tipo guayacuru y chiquito comparadas* (Buenos Aires, 1910). Connexion of American with Malayo-Polynesian and Australian has been suggested, especially by Rivet.

The question is often asked, ' How many languages are there? ' To this, no reply can be given which is in the least satisfactory. In the first place, how is language in this sense to be defined? We may fairly say that Modern French, German, and English are three languages; but are Old and Middle French, and Old, Middle, and Modern High German, which in their standard forms show such regular and obvious developments that one may pass, with relatively little difficulty, from the earliest known records to those of the present day, to be considered five languages, or only two? So, too, the transition from Middle to Modern English is fairly simple; that from Anglo-Saxon to Middle English is quite the reverse. How, again, are we to regard the three great dialectic divisions of Anglo-Saxon, or the multitudinous dialects of Modern English, French, Italian, and German, which are often mutually unintelligible to those who know only the standard languages or only certain dialects of English, French, Italian, or German? Again, of many languages we possess nothing but the names, or have at best but a few words; and it is very possible that languages now unknown may yet be discovered (cf. pp. 296–297). In the second place, in many areas, notably in Africa and in the Americas, languages still await definite classification; and investigators of equally high standing differ widely, not merely in enumerations, but even in the names of the languages which they list. For Sudano-Guinean, one authority gives four hundred and thirty-five, and another one hundred and seventy-one; for Bantu, one has eighty-three, another ninety-three, and a third three hundred and sixty-six; for North American, one has three hundred and fifty-four, and another two hundred and forty-seven; for all the languages and dialects spoken in India (Indo-Iranian, Dravidian, Tibeto-Burman, Muṇḍā, etc.), the *Linguistic Survey of India* has a total of some three hundred and sixty-eight.

The French Academy has recently decided that the number of languages in the world is two thousand seven hundred ninety-six; the lists followed in the present volume, made independently and including extinct languages known once to have existed, as well as many whose names alone are recorded, but excluding hosts of

minor dialects, give exactly the same total, divided according to
the linguistic groups here adopted:

Indo-European	132	Sino-Tibetan	115
Hamito-Semitic	46	La-Ti	1
Uralic or Finno-Ugric	32	South-East Asiatic or Austroasiatic	52
Altaic	34	Malayo-Polynesian or Austronesian	263
Japanese and Korean	2	Papuan	132
Eskimo-Aleut	24	Australian	96
Caucasian	26	Tasmanian	5
Ibero-Basque	2	Sudano-Guinean	435
Near-Eastern and Asianic	29	Bantu	83
Hyperborean or Palaeo-Asiatic	12	Hottentot-Bushman or Khoiń	6
		North American	351
Burushaskī, Khajuna, or Kunjūtī	1		
Dravidian	26	Mexican and Central American	96
Andamanese	12	Antillean and South American	783
		Total	2,796

None of the totals proposed is of any real scientific value; the
number of languages in the world, both living and dead, is but
one more of the many linguistic questions which may legitimately
be asked, but can as yet receive no answer, however approximate;
between two thousand five hundred and three thousand five hundred may be given as a very rough estimate, an estimate so rough
as to be practically worthless.

CHAPTER XIII

The History of the Study of Language

Etymological attempts in the Bible and in Sanskrit — early guesses at an original language — Indian, Greek, and Latin grammarians — influence of Christianity on the study of languages — the mediaeval period — the Renaissance — grammatical treatises from the eleventh century through the seventeenth; comparisons of languages, collections of specimens, and essays at classification and etymology in these centuries — the eighteenth century: von Leibnitz; principal linguistic works and grammars of the period — Sanskrit becomes known in Europe — the beginnings of scientific linguistics and its first period: Rask, Bopp, Grimm, Holtzmann, Schleicher, Fick, Steinthal, Max and Friedrich Müller, etc. — the second period: Verner, Ascoli, Thomsen, de Saussure, Brugmann and the Neo-Grammatical school, etc. — the period from 1890: the theory of the consonantal shwā; the Hjelmslev-Uldall theory — specific activities during this period: phonetics; syntax and semantics; psychology of language; social linguistics; the Indo-European problem; linguistic geography; study of names of places and of persons; classification of languages and the peripheral theory; treatises on general linguistics — question of the relationship of Indo-European to other linguistic families — linguistic journals — linguistic bibliographies — question of the original Indo-European home — works on the history of linguistics — the method of Indo-European linguistics the model for studying all other language-families — the needless cleavage between Indo-European and Classical and Romance linguistics.

At a very early period man began to interest himself in problems of language and in the riddle of its origin, a question which modern linguistic science considers so hopeless of solution that it refuses even to discuss it (pp. 38–41). The eleventh chapter of Genesis preserves a tradition that originally ' the whole earth was of one language, and of one speech '; but that when men began to build the Tower of Babel (a reminiscence of a Babylonian *ziggurat,* or tower attached to a temple), the Lord, fearing lest humanity should become too mighty, ' confounded their language, that they might not understand one another's speech ', the name of Babel (' Babylon ') itself being given ' because the Lord did there confound the language of all the earth '. Here we have not only a legend to account for the diversity of languages, but also an

419

attempt to explain the meaning of *Bāβel*, Akkadian *Bāb-īlu*, 'Babylon' by a fanciful connexion, through popular etymology, with the Hebrew verb *bālal* 'confuse, confound, mingle, mix', whereas it really signifies 'Gate of the God' (cf. p. 275). The Bible gives several other examples of such etymologies: 'woman' (Hebrew *'iššāḥ)* was so called 'because she was taken out of man' (Hebrew *'īš)*; Eve (Hebrew *Ḥawwāḥ)*, 'because she was the mother of all living' (Hebrew *ḥāy)*; Cain (Hebrew *Qayin)*, because Eve had 'gotten (Hebrew *qānāḥ)* a man from the Lord'; Seth (Hebrew *Šēθ)*, because he was 'appointed' (Hebrew *šīθ)* to replace the murdered Abel; Ishmael (Hebrew *Yišmā'ēl)*, because the 'Lord had heard' (Hebrew *yišmā' 'Ēl)* his mother's affliction; Jacob (Hebrew *Ya'ăqōβ)*, because he 'followed on the heel' (Hebrew *'āqaβ)* of his brother Esau; and *YHWH*, the sacrosanct name of God ('Jehovah'; cf. p. 263), because 'I am that I am' (Hebrew *'ehyeḥ)*, etc. Place-names also receive explanation: the Well of Beer-lahai-roi (Hebrew *bə'ēr laḥay rō'ī)* was so called because the Lord there 'saw' (Hebrew *rā'āḥ)* Hagar; Bethel (Hebrew *bēyθ 'Ēl*, 'House of God'), because there God appeared to Jacob; Mahanaim (Hebrew *maḥănāyim* 'two camps'), because the 'camp' *(maḥăneḥ)* of God's angels there met Jacob; Peniel or Penuel (Hebrew *pənī'ēl, pənū'ēl* 'face of God'), because there Jacob saw God face to face; Allon-bachuth (Hebrew *'allōn bāχūθ* 'oak of weeping'), because Rebekah's nurse was there buried beneath an oak *('allōn)* with weeping *(bāχūθ)*, etc.

Similar attempts at etymology are to be found in Sanskrit, e.g., the proper name *Nārāyaṇa* 'descendant of Nara' ('Man') is interpreted as 'he who has his going *(ayana-)* in the waters *(nāra-)*'. To these simple and naïve etymologies no scientific value can be attached, whether they are obviously correct, such as Bethel, Allon-bachuth, or are plainly popular etymologies (cf. pp. 270–272) like Eve, Nārāyaṇa, or whether the traditions underlying them be authentic or not.

The notion that some one language was the parent of all the rest was by no means confined to the Hebrews, who doubtless thought that this primal language was Hebrew, a view which found many defenders in much later times for obvious supposed theological reasons. On the other hand, the Egyptian King Psammitichos held the parent speech to be Phrygian (p. 39); the Jains of

India considered it to be Ardhamāgadhī Prākrit, while the Bud-
dhists gave this honour to Māgadhī (cf. p. 315); the Dutch scholar
Goropius Becanus (1518–72) very patriotically made it Dutch
(which he called Cymbrian); Johannes and Olaus Magnus, who
died in 1544 and 1568 respectively, thought that it was Gothic;
and the Swede Andreas Kemke, who died at Hamburg in 1689,
seriously maintained that in the Garden of Eden God spoke Swedish, Adam Danish, and the serpent French.

Linguistic speculation and investigation in the true sense of the
term did not begin until philosophy and the analytic study of
language had become well developed. It is noteworthy, therefore,
that it was precisely the two great thinking peoples of antiquity,
Indians and Greeks, who independently evolved not only philosophical systems of high acuteness and intellectuality, but also
grammatical studies of much profundity; and one of these peoples,
the Greeks, made an impress upon grammar, especially in its
nomenclature and classifications, which endures to the present day.
In India, the term for ' grammar ', *vyākaraṇa-*, literally means
' separation, analysis ', while its Greek equivalent, γραμματική
whence *grammar*, etc.), denotes '(the art) relating to written
characters '. For both peoples alike, the primary motive was practical: How was one to understand the great religious and literary
works of antiquity (the Veda and the Homeric poems respectively), whose languages had become archaic, but which must be
explained and made intelligible to later generations?

The oldest linguistic treatise preserved to us in India is the
Nirukta (' Explanation ') of Yāska (fifth century B.C.), brief
explanations of Rigvedic words which had already become obscure.
The work which here overshadowed all others, however, was the
Sūtras of Pāṇini (end of the fourth century B.C.), who gave a
marvellously detailed analysis of the Sanskrit language which remained authoritative for all succeeding generations. This first
formal grammar of which we have any knowledge consists of some
four thousand very brief statements of linguistic phenomena, most
of them designated by arbitrary sounds or complexes of sounds
used as code-words. Thus, *l* indicates all personal endings of the
verb; *ṭ* the primary tenses (present, perfect, and future); *ṅ* the
secondary tenses (imperfect and aorist); *a* the indicative; *e* the
subjunctive, etc.; so that *laṭ* means present indicative, *laṅ*, imperfect indicative; *leṭ* present subjunctive, etc. Other code-words,

some of them at least as old as Yāska, possess obvious meanings which are of value as indicating the linguistic philosophy underlying the Pāṇinian system, such as *dhātu-* ' base ' (literally, ' constituent '), *kṛt-* ' primary determinative ' (literally, ' making '), *taddhita-* ' secondary determinative ' (literally, ' put to that '), etc.

In themselves, these *sūtras* are practically unintelligible without a knowledge of the tradition underlying them; and for an understanding of them we are dependent upon their elucidation in the *Mahābhāṣya* (' Great Commentary ') of Patañjali (probably in the second half of the second century B.C.). With Patañjali, Indian linguistic science reached its definite form, for all later Indian treatises on the subject are little more than further commentaries on his work. The system thus established is extremely detailed as to phonology (including accent) and morphology; syntax it scarcely touches; etymologies are very frequent, in obvious words usually with success, but in obscure words frequently almost ludicrous; and these etymological attempts naturally lead to semantic explanations. How weak these often are is seen in the great canonical commentary of Sāyaṇa on the Rigveda, where, to fit the supposed meaning of a passage, the same text-word is frequently interpreted in several different ways. In all this, we find practically no discussion of linguistic philosophy; but some of the purely philosophical treatises of India touch upon linguistic problems, and it is obvious that much thought had been devoted to the philosophy of language even though only sporadic traces have survived, at least from an early period.

All in all, we may say that Indian linguistic speculation was almost wholly analytic and descriptive; and such is also the character of the grammars of the various Middle Indian dialects, or Prākrits, as exemplified in the greatest of them all, the eighth book of the *Siddhahemecandra* of Hemacandra (A.D. 1088–1172), and in the *Vyākaraṇa* of the Pāli grammarian Kaccāyana (after the seventh century A.D.). Besides these works, we have a number of dictionaries *(kośas)* both for Sanskrit and for the Prākrits, notably the *Nighaṇṭavas* (' Vocabularies ') for the Veda (before Yāska's time), the *Amarakośa* of Amara (apparently about A.D. 500) for Classical Sanskrit, and the *Deśīnāmamālā* (' Garland of Country-Words ') of Hemacandra for Prākrit.

Unlike the linguistic investigations of the Indians, which were mainly analytic, those of the Greeks were very largely speculative and philosophical in character. It is highly significant that the earliest extant document of Greek speculation of this type, which in itself presupposes a long period of concentration on the subject, is the *Kratylos* of Plato (429–347 B.C.). This contains little of real grammatical importance, but in it its author propounds certain etymologies which are more naïve than exact, and which, on the whole, he seems to have taken seriously, such as ἐνιαυτός 'year' from ἐν ἑαυτῷ 'in itself', Διόνυσος for *Διδοινυσος = διδοὺς τὸν οἶνον 'wine-giving', and ἀήρ 'air' because it 'raises' (αἴρει) things from the ground or because it 'always flows' (ἀεὶ ῥεῖ). However obscure this Dialogue, Plato seems to favour, in the large, the views of his predecessors Pythagoras (sixth century B.C.) and Herakleitos (576–480 B.C.) that language had arisen by some inherent necessity, 'by nature' (φύσει; cf. p. 14), a conclusion which he was obliged to reach in conformity with his basal theory of 'ideas', borrowed, it would seem, from the Sumero-Babylonian doctrine that all things on earth are but counterparts of their prototypes in heaven.

A far more important figure in the early history of linguistics was Aristotle (384–322 B.C.), who may practically be regarded as the father of grammar in the Occidental world. In conformity with Demokritos (fifth century B.C.), but in opposition to Herakleitos, to Pythagoras, and, apparently, to Plato, he maintained that language had arisen by 'convention' or 'agreement' (θέσει, συνθήκη); and in addition to his philosophical observations on linguistics, he investigated the parts of speech (cf. pp. 166–167), distinguishing nouns, verbs, and conjunctions (σύνδεσμοι, here meaning, not conjunctions in our sense of the term [cf. pp. 171–172], but all words neither nouns nor verbs), as well as cases and genders, and simple and compound nouns.

In linguistics as in philosophy, the conflicting and irreconcilable systems of Plato and Aristotle were to dominate investigation and speculation for centuries to come. Broadly speaking, the Stoics followed Plato, and the Epicureans agreed with Aristotle (cf. p. 14). The situation was further complicated by controversy between the analogists and the anomalists. The former, represented by the greatest grammarians, notably by Aristarchos (third or second century B.C.), held that language is a coherent system governed by law and indicating like categories by like forms. The anomalists, on the other hand, headed by the Stoic Krates of

Mallos (about 120 B.C.), who opposed Aristarchos in a work now lost, maintained that language is marked by irregularities ungoverned by laws or systems. Analogy meant to the analogists essentially what we term phonetic correspondences (cf. pp. 74–83); and it is their school which in modern linguistics has triumphed over the anomalists, even though the latter can boast of such distinguished representatives as the Romance scholars Hugo Schuchardt (1842–1927) and Karl Vossler (1872–   ).

The next great linguistic name after Aristotle was that of the Stoic Chrysippos (280–206 B.C.), the author of many works, of which only fragments have survived, on language and its philosophy. It was, indeed, the Stoics who now became pre-eminent in grammar. Building upon Aristotle, however much they differed from him in philosophical theory, they elaborated the system of linguistics, giving the cases names still found in Latin translated forms (cf. pp. 190–191, 194, 195, 196), and devoting intensive study to the verb. Linguistics was still inextricably confused with philosophy of language; but since it is scarcely possible to develop a sound philosophy of language (i.e., of *langage*) on the basis of any individual language (i.e., on *langue*), or, indeed, without wide knowledge of many languages of entirely different stocks, the results attained by the Greeks were of very minor permanent worth.

In the Alexandrine period, lasting from Zenodotos (fourth or third century B.C.) to Apollonios Dyskolos (second century A.D.) and his son Herodian, grammatical study was carried still further. One of the greatest figures here was Aristarchos, grammarian and interpreter of Homer (cf. p. 423); but even he was overshadowed by Apollonios Dyskolos, who wrote on almost every phase of language as then known, though of his voluminous studies only scattered fragments have survived. He it was who laid the foundations of Greek syntax, to which Indian grammarians never evolved a counterpart; and he also studied the characteristic features of the literary dialects of Greece: Doric, Ionic, Aeolic, and Attic. The first formal grammar of Greek, however, which has come down to us intact is that of Dionysios Thrax (second century B.C.; cf. pp. 166, 167, 177–178). This is a book of less than four hundred lines in ordinary Greek type, but its influence upon all subsequent grammar has been incalculable. Summarising in categorical fashion all that the Greeks had thus far done, it was translated into Armenian in the fifth century of our era (one of the earliest versions, next to the Bible, to be made in that language) as well as into Syriac; and it shaped conventional Greek grammar (and, consequently, Latin, Armenian, and Syriac) into the form which it retains to-day.

After grammar came lexicography, dealing especially with rare and obsolete words found in Homer and other great works of Greek literature, notably the *Etymologicum Magnum* and the *Etymologicum Gudianum* (both of uncertain date), and, most important of all for our purposes, the dictionary of Hesychios (fifth century A.D. ?), who cites words not only from Attic Greek, but from the Greek dialects and Latin, and from many non-Classical languages, such as Egyptian, Akkadian, Galatian, Indian, Lydian, Persian, Phrygian, Phoenician, Scythian, and Parthian.

Greek grammar and lexicography were, like Sanskrit, practically self-contained; besides the standard language, they considered only dialects of Greek or of Middle Indian (Prākrit). Yet the Greeks, even more than the Indians, came in touch with peoples speaking other languages; the conquests of Alexander the Great, the voyages of Greek explorers, and the journeys of Greek merchants all brought extra-Hellenic contacts. But in these Greek mentality as a whole took no interest — why bother with the jargon of barbarians? The loss which this indifference has caused to linguistics is incalculable, and it was to be the same with Rome. Sallust drew on Punic sources for his account of the Roman conquest of Jugurtha; Ovid in exile wrote a eulogy of Augustus in Getic (cf. p. 327); but of the Punic and Getic languages they tell us nothing, though Ovid's lost Getic poem would be worth to the linguist thousands of lines of his too-facile erotic verse, and the only bit of Punic that has survived, aside from inscriptions, is thirty-two lines (counting the two divergent versions) in Plautus's comedy *Poenulus* (cf. pp. 285, 359, 362). The one exception which Greece condescended to make was in favour of her conqueror, Rome: Tyrrhanion the Younger (first century B.C.) wrote a work, now lost, to prove that Latin was derived from Greek; and Philoxenos of Alexandria (beginning of the Christian era) also devoted to Latin a volume which likewise has vanished.

In linguistics, as in most things other than practical, Rome was dependent upon Greece. Here the beginning was made by Varro (116–27 B.C.) in his *De lingua Latina* in twenty-four books, of which only six (v-x) have come down to us. Though basing his work largely on the Stoics and the analogist Aristarchos, he showed considerable independence of judgement, and acutely observed the Latin tense-distinction between perfectum and imperfectum (cf. pp. 205–206). The rhetorician Quintilian (about A.D. 35–95) has linguistic observations of interest; but the political conditions of Rome and the decline of the Empire were unfavourable to intellectual pursuits, and linguistics languished with the rest, although in the middle of the fourth century Aelius Donatus wrote his little *Ars minor*, which was authoritative for two hundred years.

After Rome, Byzantium became a refuge, and there, in the reign of Justinian, Priscian (512–560) wrote his eighteen books of 'Grammatical Commentaries', which, based on Apollonios Dyskolos and Herodian, were to be the standard work on their theme for the Middle Ages, when they were divided into the *Priscianus maior* (the sixteen books dealing with the parts of speech) and the *Priscianus minor* (the two books on syntax). In this same period, etymology was studied in the twenty books of *Origines sive Etymologiae* of Saint Isidore of Seville (about 570–639), a Latin analogue to the Greek *Etymologicum Magnum* and *Etymologicum Gudianum* (cf. p. 425); and many glossaries were drawn up, such as the *Glossae Latinograecae et Graecolatinae* between the second and sixth centuries (edited by G. Goetz, *Corpus glossariorum Latinorum*, ii, Leipzig, 1888); the brief list of seventeen Gaulish words known as 'Endlicher's Glossary', dating from the fifth century; the Anglo-Saxon-Latin Epinal, Erfurt, Corpus, and Leyden glossaries of about 700 (edited by H. Sweet in his *Oldest English Texts*, London, 1885, pp. 35–117 = *Early English Text Society*, lxxxiii); Old High German-Latin glosses from the middle of the eighth century (edited by E. Steinmeyer and E. Sievers, *Die althochdeutschen Glossen*, three volumes, Berlin, 1879–95); and the Romance-Latin glossaries of Reichenau and Cassel of the eighth and ninth centuries (edited in great part by W. Foerster and E. Koschwitz, *Altfranzösisches Uebungsbuch*, sixth edition, Leipzig, 1921, pp. 1–43), to say nothing of the glosses of Hesychios (cf. p. 425).

Meanwhile, a new force had entered which was to affect all things, even the attitude toward language and its study — Christianity. Christianity did not speak solely to the mighty, the learned, and the proud, but to the lowly, the unlearned, and the humble as well; and to win all men to Christ, they must be

addressed in their own tongues. The liturgies might indeed remain
in Greek or in Latin; but the words of Holy Writ must be interpreted in the various vernaculars, and if inculcation of the Faith
was to be successful, it must be presented in the languages of the
people. This was an independent recognition of a truth which
Buddhism and Jainism had already recognised in India when they
had discarded the learned Sanskrit, unintelligible to the vulgar,
for the Prākrits which the common people could understand.
Buddhist works were soon rendered into Tokharian, Tibetan, and
Chinese; and in Christianity likewise an abundant translation-
literature sprang up. The great monument of the Golden Age of
Armenian is the version of the Bible (fifth century) from the
Greek Septuagint text of the Old Testament and the original Greek
of the New. In like fashion, in the fourth century, the Arian
Bishop Wulfila made a Gothic version of the Bible whose fragments are still almost our only source for a knowledge of that
language (cf. p. 345); and in the ninth century, Saints Cyril and
Methodius gave us the oldest documents of Slavic in their Bible-
translations.

The need for practical knowledge of the languages of those to
whom Christianity was carried brought with it the necessity of
compilation of grammars and dictionaries of those vernaculars for
the use of missionaries and of the learned generally. It is no accident that it is missionaries who have given us so much of our
knowledge of less-known languages, particularly, in modern times,
of those of the Americas, Africa, and Polynesia. That their works
are often faulty, and too frequently forced into the mould of
Graeco-Roman models, is true; but their authors were not trained
linguists — indeed, linguistics in the modern sense of the term did
not then exist; and even the work of trained scientific linguists of
the present day in these fields occasionally leaves somewhat to
be desired.

Regarding the Patristic age of the Church Fathers from the
second century to the fifth, and the Scholastic period of the great
mediaeval philosophers from the eleventh century to the fifteenth,
we may say in general, so far as the philosophy of language was
concerned, that the Fathers adhered to Plato and the Stoics, and
the Schoolmen to Aristotle. The Patristic writers (e.g., Saints Basil,
Jerome, Augustine, and John Chrysostom) were practically obliged
to maintain that language had had its origin φύσει, since God had

given it directly to man, though after the fall of the Tower of Babel it had been divided into seventy-two varieties, the number of the three sons of Noah and their descendants (Japheth fourteen, Ham thirty-two, and Shem twenty-six; Genesis x.). In this period little linguistic advance was made; every available energy must be bent to establish the truths of Christianity, to convert the heathen, and to refute heresy.

Scholasticism was less hampered. The Faith was firmly founded, and there was time for thought for thought's sake. With the reestablishment of philosophy, grammar was accorded a place in the *trivium*, the triple course of studies (the other two being rhetoric and logic) which every man with any pretensions to learning must know. Language, both in itself and in its relation to philosophy, was intensively studied, although, by force of circumstances, practically only in Latin. The old controversies as to whether words existed φύσει or θέσει were revived as component parts, respectively, of realism (the theory that things are, as the Platonists taught, actual counterparts of ' ideas ', or superterrestrial prototypes; cf. p. 423) and of nominalism (the theory that things are, as the Aristotelians maintained, only names arbitrarily assigned by man).

For the most part, Scholastic linguistic speculations must be laboriously disentangled from the philosophical discussions in which they are embedded, although from this period we have two special treatises on grammar, the *De grammatica* of Saint Anselm (1033–1109) and the *De modis significandi, sive grammatica speculativa* ascribed to Duns Scotus (1274–1308; cf. p. 187). Formal grammar as such was based essentially on Priscian (cf. p. 426) or on abridgements of his work, notably the *Graecismus* of Eberhard of Béthune (early thirteenth century) and especially the great school-grammar of the Middle Ages, the *Doctrinale puerorum* of Alexander de Villa Dei (i.e., Villedieu in Normandy), composed in 1199. This was revised successively by N. Perottus in the late fifteenth century (with examples in French and German) and by J. Despauterius (1460–1520) in a series of writings from 1510 to 1528; but by this time the revival of Greek learning had brought the old period to an end.

It is the fashion to regard all these early investigations with more or less of scorn; yet a sympathetic study of them would seem to show that Greeks and Schoolmen alike recognised many of the problems which actually underlie the nature of language, and that some of the solutions which they reached are essentially those agreed upon in principle by modern linguistic science, working with different methods and with infinitely richer material. There is far more reason to marvel at what they accomplished than to jest at their errors.

Outside the current of Graeco-Roman linguistic study, with its elaboration in the Middle Ages, there is little to detain us. We may regret the loss of the orations, histories, and tragedies composed in Greek by the Parthian prince Artavasdes of Armenia (first century B.C.); but we could wish much more that something had survived written by him in Armenian long before our oldest extant documents in this language (cf. p. 325) or in Parthian, of which we have no literary records whatsoever (cf. p. 320). The Syrians, the Arabs, and the Jews wrote voluminously on grammar, but the Syrians drew their linguistics from the Greeks, the Arabs from the Syrians, and the Jews from the Arabs, just as in India all non-Sanskrit grammatical work, whether in Prākrit or in the Dravidian languages of the South, was wholly based upon Pāṇini, Patañjali, and their successors.

During the Middle Ages, knowledge of Greek, though never quite lost, was very scanty; but with the decline of the Byzantine Empire and the fall of Constantinople in 1453, a new spirit and a veritable rebirth were brought to Western Europe, exercising a profound influence upon linguistics as upon all else. However unpopular it may be to-day, the thesis that *true education, as contrasted with the mere acquisition of facts and ' practicality ' which now passes for it, is impossible without knowledge of the Greek language and love of its literature*, seems to the author of this book too obvious to need discussion. The Renaissance was almost wholly due to revival of the study of Greek and of its literature; and a further impetus in this period was the discovery of new lands with their languages, which had to be mastered by the missionary, the coloniser, and the explorer.

At first, grammatical work on languages, whether long known or only just discovered, was purely descriptive. As early as the eleventh century, Ælfric had written a *Grammatica latino-saxonica;* in the thirteenth, Ederyn the Golden-Tongued composed his Welsh *Dosparth Ederym Davod Aur* (edited and translated by J. Williams ap Ithel, Llandovery, 1856); the anonymous Irish *Auraicept na n-éces* (' The Scholar's Primer '; edited by G. Calder,

Edinburgh, 1917) is of uncertain date; and *Snorri's Edda* includes four treatises on Old Icelandic from the twelfth, thirteenth, and fourteenth centuries. In this latter century, the dignity of vernacular languages over against the learned Latin received its earliest formal recognition from no less an authority than Dante himself in his *De vulgari eloquentia*, though formal rules for Tuscan Italian were first laid down by P. Bembo (1470–1547) in his *Prose*.

Without attempting to be exhaustive, it may be worth while to list the first formal grammars of some of the more important languages from the fifteenth century to the seventeenth as showing the active interest taken in them. In the fifteenth and sixteenth centuries we have for German the anonymous *Tractatus dans modum teutonisandi casus et tempora* (written at Münster in Westphalia in 1451 and published soon after); for Greek, the *De octo orationis partibus* by K. Laskaris (Milan, 1476, and frequently re-printed); for Spanish, the *Gramática ... sobre la lengua castellana* by Aelius Antonius Nebrissensis (António de Lebrixa; Salamanca, 1492); for Spanish Arabic, the *Arte para ligeramente saber la lengua aráviga* by Pedro de Alcalá (Granada, 1505; our only source for knowledge of this extinct dialect; reprinted by P. de Lagarde, Göttingen, 1883); for Hebrew, the *De rudimentis Hebraicis* by J. Reuchlin (Pforzheim, 1506); for Old Church Slavic, the anonymous *Grammatica Slavonica* (Vilna, 1516). For Hungarian, we may mention, from this period, the *Grammatica Hungaro-Latina in usum puerorum* by J. Erdösi (J. Sylvester, Vissigath, 1539); for Latin, the *De causis linguae Latinae libri tresdecim* by J. C. Scaliger (Lyons, 1540); for Ethiopic, the *Chaldaeae sive Aethiopicae linguae institutiones* by M. Victorius (Rome, 1548); for Mexican, Totonak, and Huastek, the *Grammatica et lexicon linguae Mexicanae, Totonacae et Huaxtecae* by A. de Olmos (two volumes, Mexico, 1555–60); for French, the *Traicté de la grammaire françoise* by R. Étienne (Paris, 1569); for Syriac, the *Institutiones linguae Syriacae, Assyriacae atque Thalmudicae, una cum Aethiopicae atque Arabicae collatione* by A. Caninius (Paris, 1554); for Kichua, the *Grammatica o arte de la lengua general de los Indios de los reynos del Peru* by Domingo de San Tomás (Valladolid, 1560); for Welsh, the *Dosparth byrr ar y rhann gyntaf i ramadeg Cymraeg* by G. Roberts (Milan, 1567); and for Basque, the *De la antigua lengua, poblaciones y comarcas de las Españas* by A. de Poza (Bilbao, 1587).

In the seventeenth century we find grammars for Tagalog, the *Arte y reglas de la lengua Tagala* by S. Joseph (Bataam, 1610) ; for Turkish, the *Institutionum linguae Turcicae libri quatuor* by H. Megiser (Leipzig, 1612) ; for Malay, the *Spieghel van de maleysche taal* by A. C. Ruyll (Amsterdam, 1612) ; for Arabic, the *Grammatica Arabica* by T. Erpenius (Leyden, 1613) ; for Persian, the *Rudimenta grammatices Persicae* by J. B. Raymundus (Rome, 1614) ; for Armenian, the *Grammaticae Armenae libri quatuor* by F. Rivola (Milan, 1624) ; for Huron, the *Grand voyage du pays des Hurons* by G. Segard (Paris, 1632) ; for Modern Greek, the *Grammatica linguae Graecae vulgaris* by S. Portius (Paris, 1638; also edited by W. Meyer, Paris, 1889) ; for Irish, the *Grammatica Latino-Hibernica nunc compendiata* by P. F. O'Molloy (Rome, 1642) ; for Finnish, the *Linguae Fennicae institutio* by A. Petraeus (Abo, 1649) ; for Lithuanian, the *Grammatica Lituanica* by D. Klein (Königsberg, 1653) ; for English, the *Grammatica linguae Anglicanae* by J. Wallis (Oxford, 1653) ; for Chinese, the *China illustrata* by A. Kircher (Amsterdam, 1667) ; for Tamil, the *Arte tamulica* by B. da Costa (Verapoli, 1680) ; for Russian, the *Grammatica Russica* by H. W. Ludolf (Oxford, 1696) ; for Amharic, the *Grammatica linguae Amharicae* by J. Ludolf (Frankfort, 1698) ; and for Moxo (in South America), the *Arte y vocabulário de la lengua morocosi* by P. Marban (Madrid, 1699).

Meanwhile interest in the comparison of languages was arising, i.e., comparative linguistics was coming into being. The first real attempt here seems to have been made by the Norman G. Postel (1510–81), who proposed to write ' on the affinity of languages and the excellence of Hebrew ', though he never carried his project to its conclusion. Travellers began to collect words from various languages, e.g., A. Pigafetta, who accompanied Magellan on his voyage around the world in 1519–22, although his *Primo viaggio intorno al globo terraqueo* was first published at Milan in 1800. P. Sassetti, who lived in India (chiefly at Goa) from 1583 to 1588, made observations on Sanskrit and its resemblances to Italian (cf. p. 436), but his *Lettere* likewise remained unpublished until the nineteenth century (Florence, 1855) ; and in 1589 O. G. van Busbecq printed at Paris, in the fourth of his *Legationis Turcicae epistolae quatuor* a list of words in Crimean Gothic, our only record of this dialect (cf. p. 345). Collections of specimens from various languages were made by W. Lazius in his *De gentium aliquot migrationibus* (Basel, 1557), by H. Megiser in his *Specimen quadraginta diversarum et inter se differentium linguarum et dialectorum* (Frankfort, 1592; the second edition, in 1603, had fifty), and by B. Vulcanius in his *De literis et lingua Getarum sive Gothorum* (Gothic, Old High German, Anglo-Saxon, Persian [which he supposed to be closely related to German], Basque, Frisian, and Gypsy).

Guesses at the classification of languages had already been made by Postel; and this work was continued by T. Bibliander (i.e., Buchmann) in his *De ratione communi omnium linguarum et literarum commentarius* (Zurich, 1548), by C. Gesner in his *Mithridates: De differentiis linguarum tum veterum tum quae hodie apud diversas nationes in toto orbe terrarum in usu sunt observationes* (Zurich, 1555), and by J. J. Scaliger in his *Diatriba de Europaeorum linguis*, written in 1599, but first printed in his *Opuscula varia antehac non edita* (Paris, 1610).

Etymology also found representatives, as in the *Etymologicum Teutonicae linguae* of C. Kilianus (Antwerp, 1588), the *Etymologicum Latinae linguae* of G. J. Vossius (Paris, 1662), and the *Dictionnaire étymologique, ou origines de la langue françoise* of G. Ménage of Angers (Paris, 1650), who also wrote *Origini della lingua italiana* (Paris, 1669). How naïve some of this etymologising was appears in E. Guichard's *Harmonie étymologique des langues hébraïque, chaldaïque, syriaque, grecque, latine, françoise, italienne, espagnole, allemande, flamende, angloise* (Paris, 1606), in which its author held that words may be derived by adding, subtracting, transposing, and inverting letters, ' the which is not hard to believe when we consider that the Hebrews write from right to left, and the Greeks and others from left to right '. However absurd this argument now seems, many years were to pass before scholars were to realise that letters are only symbols for sounds, and that linguistics must deal with *sounds*, not *letters* (cf. pp. 283–285). We may also note that T. Hobbes discussed the unprofitable question of the origin of language in the tenth chapter of the second section of his *Elementa philosophiae* (Amsterdam, 1668).

The eighteenth century saw much linguistic activity, but little real progress. At its very opening (1702), J. Ludolf recognised that the affinities of languages must be determined by grammatical (i.e., morphological) correspondences, not by mere resemblances in vocabulary; and held that in vocabulary, only correspondences of

simple words, such as names for parts of the body, should be taken
into account in establishing linguistic relationships. About this
same time, H. Reland published three volumes of *Dissertationes
miscellaneae* (Utrecht, 1706–08) in which he discussed Old Indian,
Old Persian (both on the basis of words preserved by Classical
writers), Malay, Javanese, Chinese, Annamese, Oceanic, American, and African.

The great figure in this period was that of G. W. von Leibnitz
(1646–1716), who, in his *Brevis designatio meditationum de ori-
ginibus gentium ductis potissimum ex indiciis linguarum* (published
in the Proceedings of the Berlin Academy in 1710), derived all
languages, not from any historically recorded source, but from a
' proto-speech ', so being the first to advance an hypothesis which,
in much modified form, is now a cardinal doctrine of linguistics
(cf. pp. 30, 74, 226). To this proto-speech he traced the ' Japhetic '
and ' Aramaean ' languages; and ' Japhetic ' he divided into
' Scythic ' and ' Celtic ', the first corresponding roughly to Indo-
European, the second to Ural-Altaic (cf. pp. 369–370). He recognised the affinities of Turkish, Mongol, and Manchu, as well as of
Finnish, Lapp, Esthonian, Livonian, Samoyede, and Hungarian;
and he saw that Basque was unlike any other language in Europe.
An entire book of his *Nouveaux essais sur l'intendement humain*
(written in 1704, but not published till long after his death, e.g.,
at Paris in 1886) was devoted to language, especially in its philosophic aspects; he knew the importance of linguistic maps (cf. pp.
120–125, 449–451) ; and he urged Peter the Great to order studies
of the many languages of the Russian Empire, reducing them to
writing, and making provision for dictionaries of them as well as
for translations into them of the Ten Commandments, the Lord's
Prayer, the Apostles' Creed, etc. He likewise had the idea of a
universal alphabet, and realised the necessity of comparing the
newer stages of a language with the older.

At Oxford, in 1707, E. Lhuyd wrote on the Celtic languages the
first (and only) volume of his *Archaeologia Britannica*, which is
still of value; J. Ihre attempted a Swedish etymological dictionary
in his *Glossarium Suiogothicum* (Upsala, 1769) ; in 1770, the Jesuit
P. Saijnovics showed the relationship of Hungarian and Lapp in
his *Demonstratio idioma Ungarorum et Lapponum idem esse*, published at Copenhagen, while at Göttingen, in 1799, S. Gyármathi
did the same for Hungarian and Finnish in his *Affinitas linguae*

Hungaricae cum linguis Fennicae originis grammatice demon-
strata; and at Berlin, in 1796, D. Jenisch issued his *Philosophisch-*
kritische Vergleichung und Würdigung von vierzehn ältern und
neuern Sprachen Europas.

Works on general linguistics had already been inaugurated at
Paris in 1660 by the famous ' Port Royal Grammar ', the work of
several collaborators, notably C. Lancelot and A. Arnauld: *Gram-*
maire générale et raisonnée contenant les fondamens de l'art de
parler, expliqués d'une manière claire et naturelle. Les raisons de
ce qui est commun à toutes les langues et des principales diffé-
rences qui s'y rencontrent; et plusieurs remarques nouvelles sur la
langue françoise. In 1751, J. Harris published at London his
Hermes, or a Philosophical Inquiry concerning Universal Gram-
mar; at Paris, in 1767, N. Beauzée his two volumes of *Grammaire*
générale, ou exposition raisonnée des éléments nécessaires du
langage pour servir de fondement à l'étude de toutes les langues;
and in 1786–1805, at London, J. H. Tooke his Ἔπεα πτερόεντα, or the
Diversions of Purley, in which he advanced the theory that ' all
those common terminations in any language, of which all nouns
or verbs in that language equally partake (under the notion of
declension or conjugation), are themselves separate words with
distinct meanings. . . . These terminations are all explicable, and
ought all to be explained ', so that, for example, Latin *ībō* ' I shall
go ' contains three words: two verbs and a pronoun, *ī* ' go ', *b*
' shall ', *[eg]ō* ' I '.

Much energy and ink were again wasted on the origin of language, as in J. B. Drouet de Maupertuys's *Dissertation sur les*
différents moyens dont les hommes se sont servis pour exprimer
leurs idées (Paris, 1754), J. J. Rousseau's *Discours sur l'origine*
et les fondaments de l'inégalité parmi les hommes (Amsterdam,
1754), C. de Brosses's *Traité de la formation méchanique des*
langues et des principes physiques de l'étymologie (two volumes,
Paris, 1765), J. P. Süssmilch's *Versuch eines Beweises dass die*
erste Sprache ihren Ursprung nicht vom Menschen, sondern allein
vom Schöpfer erhalten habe (Berlin, 1766), J. G. Herder's *Abhand-*
lung über den Ursprung der Sprache (Berlin, 1772), and the *On the*
Origin and Progress of Language by James Burnett, Lord Mon-
boddo (six volumes, Edinburgh, 1773–92).

Among the languages which first received grammatical discussion in the eighteenth century we may mention Dutch, in the

Nederduytsche spraakkonst of W. Séwel (Amsterdam, 1708); Tarask (in Central America), in the *Arte de la lengua tarasca* of N. de Quixas (Mexico, 1714); Hindūstānī, in the *Lingua Hindostanica* of J. J. Kelelaer (about 1715; first published by D. Mill in the second edition of his *Dissertationes selectae*, Leyden, 1743); Bengalī, in the *Vocabulario em idioma bengalla e portuguez* of M. da Assumpçam (Lisbon, 1743); Eskimo, in the *Grammatica Grönlandico-Danico-Latina* of P. Egede (Copenhagen, 1760); Scots Gaelic, in the *Analysis of the Gaelic Language* of M. Shaw (Edinburgh, 1778); and Kurdish, in the *Grammatica e vocabulario della lingua kurda* of M. Garzoni (Rome, 1787).

Attempts were also made to collect specimens of all known languages. Thus, two hundred and eighty-five selected words and forms in two hundred languages and dialects (the latter number increased by seventy-two in the second edition) were recorded in P. S. Pallas's *Linguarum totius orbis vocabularia comparativa* (two volumes, St. Petersburg, 1786–89; enlarged edition by T. J. de Miriewa, 1791); the *Catálogo de las lenguas de las naciones conocidas* of the Spanish Jesuit L. Hervas y Panduro (six volumes, Madrid, 1800–05) dealt with more than eight hundred languages; and the *Mithridates, oder allgemeine Sprachenkunde* of J. C. Adelung (four parts, Berlin, 1806–17; completed after the author's death by J. S. Vater) contained the Lord's Prayer in some five hundred languages and dialects.

Shortly before the close of the eighteenth century, the linguistic importance of Sanskrit had been realised; and with this recognition, the science of linguistics really began. All that had gone before from the days of Plato and Yāska had prepared the way: much was now known of a large number of languages; many attempts had been made to discover the relationships of languages and to classify them; and these gropings, however naïve they now seem, had made the minds of men ready for, and receptive to, the new science. Henceforth, linguistics was to proceed not by mere guesses, brilliant and, at times, surprisingly accurate though they might be, but in accord with principles tested by ever severer criticism and formulated with ever greater exactness.

Modern linguistics had its germ in sentences penned in 1786 by Sir William Jones, Chief Justice at Fort William in Bengal, and justly quoted in many books dealing with the science of language:

' The *Sanscrit* language, whatever be its antiquity, is of a wonderful structure; more perfect than the Greek, more copious than the Latin, and more exquisitely refined than either; yet bearing to both of them a stronger affinity, both in the roots of verbs and in the forms of grammar, than could possibly have been produced by accident; so strong, indeed, that no philologer could examine all three without believing them to have sprung from some common source which, perhaps, no longer exists. There is a similar reason, though not quite so forcible, for supposing that both the Gothick and the Celtick, though blended with a very different idiom, had the same origin with the Sanscrit; and the old Persian might be added to the same family, if this were the place for discussing any question concerning the antiquities of Persia'.

It is quite true that Sir William's discovery was not wholly novel. Certain principles still valid had already been announced, though the time had not yet come to recognise their true significance or to give them the importance which they deserved, such as the necessity of classifying languages, the determination of affinity by grammatical, not lexicographical, correspondences (J. Ludolf), the theory of an hypothetical original language (von Leibnitz), and the linguistic establishment of the relationship of Hungarian to Lapp and Finnish (Saijnovics and Gyármathi).

In the last quarter of the sixteenth century, P. Sassetti (cf. p. 431) had observed that Sanskrit shows certain affinities with Italian (he lists Italian *sei, sette, otto, nove, dio, serpe* : Sanskrit *ṣás, saptá, aṣṭaú, náva, devá-, sarpá-);* and about 1620, the Jesuit missionary Robertus de Nobilibus (Roberto de Nobili; 1577–1656) had acquired so thorough a knowledge of Sanskrit that Indian tradition ascribes to him (apparently incorrectly) the authorship of a pseudo-Veda in that language which, in its French translation *(Ezour-Veda,* two volumes, Yverdon, 1778), helped arouse linguistic interest. Between 1630 and 1647, the Dutch missionary A. Roger translated two hundred verses of the Sanskrit poet Bhartṛhari into his native language in his *Open-Deure tot het verborgen heydendom* (Amsterdam, 1651; soon translated into French and German; new edition by W. Caland, The Hague, 1915); and in 1664, a German missionary, H. Roth, had learned Sanskrit to be able to dispute with the Brāhmans. In the first quarter of the eighteenth century, the German Jesuit J. E. Hanxleden wrote the first European Sanskrit grammar which, itself unpublished, was used in part by Paulinus a Sancto Bartholomaeo in the first printed grammar of the language, *Sidharubam seu grammatica Samscrdamica* (Rome, 1790). The German missionary B. Schultze (1725), like many others, was well acquainted with Sanskrit; and in 1768, the French Father Cœurdoux noted such correspondences as Sanskrit *dāna-* 'gift', *vidhávā* 'widow', and *ásmi* 'I am' with Latin *dōnum, vidua,* and Greek εἰμί.

In the opening years of the nineteenth century, F. von Schlegel had gone to Paris to study Sanskrit manuscripts, and there had learned Sanskrit from Alexander Hamilton, who had acquired a knowledge of it in India, and who was then interned at Paris in consequence of the Napoleonic War. In 1808, von Schlegel published at Heidelberg his little *Ueber die Sprache und Weisheit der Inder,* which contains the following remarkable sentence:

' The decisive point which will illuminate everything here [i.e., the relationship of Sanskrit to other languages] is the inner structure of the languages, or the comparative grammar [*vergleichende Grammatik*], which will give us information wholly new on the genealogy of language just as comparative anatomy has shed light on higher natural history. '

Thus for the first time we hear of ' comparative grammar ', and of the true principle for determining the ' genealogy of language '.

The actual beginning of ' comparative grammar ' (i.e., of comparative linguistics) dates from 1814, when R. K. Rask wrote his *Undersögelse om det gamle nordiske eller islandske sprogs oprindelse* (' Investigation of the Origin of the Old Norse or Icelandic Language '), which was published at Copenhagen in 1818. In this work, as his distinguished compatriot H. Pedersen justly says, ' we find the whole kernel from which modern methods have developed ': the necessity of a regular system of phonetic correspondences (cf. pp. 74–76) ; a classification of the Indo-European languages surprisingly accurate for its time; and a clear recognition of the Teutonic sound-shifts later formulated by J. L. C. Grimm, and still known as Grimm's Law (cf. pp. 79–82). Two years after Rask had written his *Undersögelse,* but also two years before it appeared in print, F. Bopp published at Frankfort his *Ueber das Conjugationssystem der Sanskritsprache in Vergleichung mit jenem der griechischen, lateinischen, persischen und germanischen Sprache,* a work with scarcely a word about phonology, but showing much acuteness as regards verb-inflexion, though marred by a desire to prove that all endings with *s* contain the base **es-* ' be ' (e.g., Latin *amās* ' thou lovest ' = ' thou art loving ' : *es* ' thou art ').

In 1819 there appeared at Berlin the first edition of the first

volume of Grimm's *Deutsche Grammatik,* ' deutsch ' meaning to
him what we now term Teutonic or Germanic. Here again phonology was lacking, but in the second edition (1822), doubtless
influenced by the work of Rask, some six hundred pages were
devoted to this subject (revised edition in 1840), and his famous
Law was fully developed. Three more volumes followed (1826,
1831, 1837). In his *Geschichte der deutschen Sprache* (Berlin,
1848; third edition, 1867), Grimm was the first scientifically to
discuss the phenomena of ablaut (vowel-gradation) and umlaut
(cf. pp. 65–67, 69). These he erroneously regarded as due to
semantic reasons, whereas, in fact, the semantic differentiations,
as in English *sing, sang, sung* (cf. p. 67), are later developments;
and the true cause of vowel-gradation was destined to be discovered by another and less famous scholar (cf. p. 439). Although
Grimm wrote at length on phonology, he was still possessed by
an almost superstitious reverence for letters (cf. p. 432), failing
to see that if the letter changed, as in Old Latin *dacruma* ' tear ' :
Classical Latin *lacrima* : Anglo-Saxon *téar,* English *tear* : Old
High German *zahar,* Modern German *Zähre,* it was because the
sound had changed.

Despite these faults, which were those of Grimm's day, his
work marked a very great advance in linguistics; and it is particularly noteworthy, from the historical point of view, as being
the first truly scientific treatment of one of the chief branches of
the Indo-European family. The example of Grimm for Teutonic
was followed for Romance by F. Diez in his *Grammatik der
romanischen Sprachen* (three volumes, Bonn, 1836–44; third edition, 1882), for Slavic by F. Miklosich in his *Vergleichende Grammatik der slavischen Sprachen* (four volumes, Vienna, 1874–79),
and for Celtic by J. K. Zeuss in his *Grammatica Celtica* (Berlin,
1853; second edition, 1871).

In 1821, a remarkable little essay was published at Copenhagen
by one of Rask's followers, J. H. Bredsdorff, *Om aarsagarne til
sprogenes forandringer* (' On the Causes of Change in Language ') ;
but, partly because of the language in which it was written, and
partly because linguistic science was not yet ripe for it, it failed
to win the attention which it merited until other investigators had
advanced far beyond it.

Remarkably soon, all things considered, a comparative grammar
of Indo-European could be written; and this task was performed

by Bopp in his *Vergleichende Grammatik des Sanskrit, Zend, Griechischen, Lateinischen, Lituanischen, Gothischen und Deutschen* (three volumes, Berlin, 1833–52; third edition, 1868–70; in the course of the first edition, Old Church Slavic was added to the title). Celtic, Albanian, and Armenian were omitted here; but Bopp still regarded Armenian as a ' Zend ' (i.e., Iranian) dialect (cf. pp. 320, 324); Albanian he later placed in its true setting as an independent branch; and in Celtic he subsequently explained one of the features most puzzling to a beginner, the so-called aspiration and eclipsis in such combinations as Modern Irish *a talamh* [ə thɔlɔw] ' her land ' : *a thalamh* [ə hɔlɔw] ' his land ' : *a dtalamh* [ə dɔlɔw] ' their land ' = Sanskrit *asyās talam* : *asya talam* : *esām talam*. He was still almost silent on phonology, but extremely detailed as to morphology, though dominated by the theory that the personal endings of the verb were remnants of the personal pronouns, an hypothesis devoid of validity (cf. p. 153). He even extended this explanation to the epithetologues, so that, for example, he connected the determinative $*qo$-, $*\hat{k}o$- with the interrogative pronoun $*q^{u}o$-, seen in Sanskrit *ká-* ' who ? ', Greek πό-τε ' when ? ', Latin *quod* ' what ? ', Gothic *hwas* ' who ? '.

Simultaneously with Bopp, A. F. Pott was publishing his *Etymologische Forschungen auf dem Gebiete der indogermanischen Sprachen* (Lemgo, 1833–36; new edition in ten volumes, 1859–76), in which he emphasised the importance of phonology and, for the first time, drew up formal tables of phonological correspondences. Accent likewise now began to receive attention. As early as 1844, A. Holtzmann, in his *Ueber den Ablaut,* published at Carlsruhe, perceived that accent conditioned vowel-gradation (cf. pp. 65–66), and thus explained changes of the type of German *singen* : *sang* : *gesungen* = English *sing* : *sang* : *sung*, his work being followed at Paris, three years later, by L. Benloew's *De l'accentuation dans les langues indo-européennes tant anciennes que modernes*. Holtzmann was, moreover, the first to see that accent also underlay the so-called ' grammatical change ' *(grammatischer Wechsel)* exemplified, for instance, in Gothic *þarf* ' I need ' : *þaúrbum* ' we need ', and later fully explained by Verner (see pp. 78, 79–82).

Up to this time, in the first enthusiasm of comparative linguistics, Sanskrit had been regarded as the most primitive of all Indo-European languages. In some respects, this is quite true, but not in all (cf. p. 313); and the failure to recognise that certain of its phenomena are relatively late actually retarded, to a considerable extent, the progress of linguistic science. This was notably the case as regards its vowel-system. Sanskrit has only three short vowels — *a*, *i*, and *u* (*e* and *o* are diphthongs, not simple vowels) ; and Gothic, the oldest form of Teutonic then known, likewise has only the same short vowels (here *e* and *o* are only long). It was taken for granted, accordingly, that Indo-European had but the three vowels *a*, *i*, and *u*, and that *e* and *o* were late innovations, as in Anglo-Saxon *etan*, Latin *edō* as contrasted with Gothic *itan*, Sanskrit *ádmi* ' eat '; Greek ὀκτώ, Latin *octo*, Old Irish *ocht*, Old Church Slavic *osmi* as contrasted with Gothic *ahtau*, German *acht*, Lithuanian *aštuo-nì*, Sanskrit *aṣṭaú*. So far as the Western languages were concerned, it was now admitted that they had the five vowels, *e* and *o* having ' split off ' from *a*. This new tenet was defended by G. Curtius, whose chief work was his *Grundzüge der griechischen Etymologie* (Leipzig, 1858; fifth edition, 1879), and who laid much stress on phonetic correspondences, though he continued to regard many sound-changes as sporadic, i.e., as occurring without reason and merely by chance.

In 1861, the second summary of Indo-European appeared at Weimar in A. Schleicher's *Compendium der vergleichenden Grammatik der indogermanischen Sprachen* (fourth edition, 1876). Here we find increasing accuracy in phonetic correspondences, but many faulty statements in morphology; and he adhered to the doctrine of the three original vowels *a*, *i*, and *u*. On the other hand, he introduced the method of reconstructing hypothetical forms from which the historical forms were (we would now say, may be [cf. p. 150]) derived, indicating them, as we still do, by an asterisk (*). Such forms he seems to have regarded as once possessed of a real existence, whereas we now make them to serve merely as formulae representing our present state of knowledge, to be modified or discarded as further information may dictate. He even wrote a fable of ten lines in this hypothetical language on ' the sheep and the horses ' (**avis akvāsas ka*, which we would make **oṷis eḱṷōs qᵘe; Beiträge zur vergleichenden Sprachforschung*, v [1868], 206–208) : and to account for the divergence of the Indo-European languages from a parent stock, he proposed the pedigree-theory *(Stammbaumtheorie)*, to which J. Schmidt, in his *Die Verwantschaftsverhältnisse der indogermanischen Sprachen* (Weimar, 1872), successfully opposed his wave-theory *(Wellentheorie;* cf. pp. 41–43), the foundation of the genealogical classification now generally adopted (cf. p. 301).

The last great name in the first period of modern linguistics is that of A. Fick, who in 1868 published at Göttingen the first edition of his *Wörterbuch der indogermanischen Grundsprache in ihrem Bestande vor der Völkertrennung.* In the second and third editions (1870–71, 1874–76), this was much enlarged with the title of *Vergleichendes Wörterbuch der indogermanischen Sprachen;* and in 1890, a fourth edition was begun to which W. Stokes contributed a Celtic volume in 1894, and H. Falk and A. Torp one on Teutonic in 1909 (the *Baltisch-slavisches Wörterbuch* of R. Trautmann, Göttingen, 1923, is practically another volume in this series); but the work remained a torso, and can now be used only with caution. In this same period we should also mention H. Steinthal's *Classification der Sprachen* (Berlin, 1850) and *Charakteristik der hauptsächlichsten Typen des Sprachbaues* (Berlin, 1860; second edition, 1893), in the latter of which he divided languages according to their outward form into incorporating, isolating, juxtapositional, agglutinative, and inflexional (cf. pp. 299–301), a work followed in principle by F. N. Finck's *Haupttypen des Sprachbaues* (Leipzig, 1910), giving the structure and specimens of Chinese, Greenlandic, Subiya (of the African Central Bantu group), Turkish, Samoan, Arabic, Greek, and Georgian.

The study of physiological phonetics also began in this period, notably in J. Müller's *Handbuch der Physiologie* (two volumes, Coblenz, 1834–40); and the principles of transcribing alphabets of languages written in non-Roman scripts and of indicating sounds in languages not yet reduced to writing received attention, particularly in the *Standard Alphabet* of R. Lepsius (second edition, London, 1863).

In 1861 and 1864, F. Max Müller published at Oxford his *Lectures on the Science of Language,* which did much to make linguistics generally known in the English-speaking world. Müller deserves all praise as the editor of the Rigveda with Sāyaṇa's commentary (six volumes, Oxford, 1849–74; second edition, four volumes, 1890–92; text only, second edition, two volumes, London, 1877) and of the important series of *The Sacred Books of the East* (fifty volumes, Oxford, 1879–1910), and as a populariser; but as a serious linguist he was scarcely successful, and his work in this field no longer merits consideration. He was assailed with somewhat unbecoming acerbity by an author also more distinguished as a Sanskritist than as a linguist, W. D. Whitney, in his *Language and the Study of Language* (New York, 1867) and *The Life and Growth of Language* (New York, 1874). A work, on the other hand, not yet entirely superseded is R. Caldwell's *Comparative Grammar of the Dravidian or South Indian Family of Languages* (London, 1856; second edition, 1875; the third edition, 1913, is drastically abridged); and in 1858, W. H. Bleek published at London his *Comparative Handbook of Australian, African, and Polynesian Languages*, following it with his *Comparative Grammar of South-African Languages* (London, 1869). To this category belongs in spirit, though in date it runs over into the next period, F. Müller's *Grundriss der Sprachwissenschaft* (Vienna, 1876–88), a collection of skeleton-grammars of languages from all parts of the world, which is still indispensable to the student of general linguistics as a convenient source of material.

The second period of comparative linguistics may be said to have begun in 1875 with Karl Verner's article (published in 1877) ' Eine Ausnahme der ersten Lautverschiebung ' in the *Zeitschrift für vergleichende Sprachforschung auf dem Gebiete der indogermanischen Sprachen*, xxiii, 97–130 (for a statement of Verner's Law, see pp. 79–82) ; and, in 1876, K. Brugmann, in his article ' Nasalis sonans in der indogermanischen Grundsprache ' *(Curtius' Studien zur griechischen und lateinischen Grammatik,* ix, 287–338), established the existence of the nasal sonants $m̥$ and $n̥$, as well as of $r̥$ and $l̥$ (cf. p. 54).

About this same time, there was an increasing realisation that the phonology of Sanskrit was less primitive than had formerly been supposed. In 1870, G. Ascoli perceived, in his *Corsi di glottologia* (i, Turin and Florence; no more published; German translation, *Vorlesungen über der vergleichenden Lautlehre des Sanskrit, des Griechischen und des Lateinischen*, by J. Bazzigher and H. Schweizer-Sidler, Halle, 1872), that Sanskrit *k* and *ś* both arose from original gutturals (e.g., Sanskrit *kravís-* ' raw flesh ', Lithuanian *kraũjas* ' blood ' : Greek κρέ(ϝ)ας ' flesh ', Latin *cruor*, Middle Irish *crú* ' blood ', Anglo-Saxon *hréaw*, English *raw*, Old High German *(h)râo*, Modern German *roh;* but Sanskrit *śatá-*, Lithuanian *šim̃tas* : Greek ἑ-κατόν, Latin *centum*, Old Irish *cét*, Welsh *cant*, Old High German *hunt*, Modern German *hund-ert*, Anglo-Saxon, English *hund-red).* In 1877 (though his study was first pub-

lished in his *Samlede afhandlingar*, ii, Copenhagen, 1920, 305–327),
V. Thomsen announced the palatal law, which established the fact
that Indo-Iranian had once possessed an *e*-vowel, as exemplified in
Sanskrit *ka-* ' who? ' : Greek πό-τε ' when? ', Latin *quod* ' which ',
Old Irish *cá-ch* ' anyone ', Gothic *hwas* ' who? ', Anglo-Saxon
hwæt, English *what*, Old High German *hwaz*, Modern German
was, Lithuanian *kàs*, Old Church Slavic *kŭ-to* ' who ' from Indo-
European *$q^{u}o$-; but Sanskrit *ca* [tʃa] ' and ' : Phrygian κε, Greek
τε, Latin *-que*, Lepontine *-pe* ' and ', Old Irish *na-ch*, Old Bulgarian
če ' but, and ' from Indo-European *$q^{u}e$.

This discovery now seems so obvious that one wonders why it
had not been made long before. The explanation must be that
everyone was hypnotised by the idea that, since Sanskrit was the
oldest Indo-European language known, and was extremely primitive in many respects, it must be the most primitive in all regards
without exception. Finally, in the year after Thomsen's discovery,
the theory of Indo-European vocalism was placed on a firm foundation by F. de Saussure's *Mémoire sur le système primitif des
voyelles dans les langues indo-européennes* (Leipzig, 1878), written
when its author was only twenty-one.

At this point, a bitter linguistic quarrel broke out. Brugmann's
article on the nasal sonant had appeared in a series edited by him
in collaboration with his teacher Curtius; but Curtius, absent on
a journey at the time, had not seen it in manuscript and declined
to assume any responsibility for its statements. It would seem
that he thought himself affronted by an unruly pupil who presented
views at variance with his own, while Brugmann may have felt that
his investigations were hampered when he justly considered himself able to stand on his own feet. In any event, scientific research
was unhappily entangled with personal animus; and in 1878 Brugmann, with his friend H. Osthoff, established his own series of
Morphologische Untersuchungen (six volumes, Leipzig, 1878–
1910).

In the preface to this series appear the words: ' All sound-change,
in so far as it proceeds mechanically, takes place in accordance
with laws which know no exceptions ' (' nach ausnahmslosen
gesetzen '). The idea in itself was scarcely new. Verner, in 1872,
had already observed that every exception to phonetic correspondences must have a cause: ' there must be a rule for irregularity;
the problem is to find it '; and he had brilliantly established the

truth of his statement by his discovery of the Law which still bears his name. A. Leskien had spoken to the same effect in the introduction to his *Declination im Slavisch-Litauischen und Germanischen* (Leipzig, 1876); but the statement of Brugmann and Osthoff, under the conditions of conscious opposition to Curtius which prompted it, and in consequence of the polemic tone which they adopted, was nothing short of a declaration of war on the older school. They, like other pupils of Curtius who had not been wholly satisfied with his teachings, had jestingly been called ' Neogrammarians ' (' Junggrammatiker '); and since their preface also spoke of endeavouring to further the ' " junggrammatische " Richtung ' (note the use of quotation-marks by Brugmann and Osthoff themselves), the term was construed as a further mark of hostility. The result, absurd and needless as it now must seem, was a division into the Leipzig School, represented by Brugmann and Osthoff, as against linguists like J. Schmidt and A. Bezzenberger of the Berlin and Göttingen Schools.

In the end, the Leipzig School, with its more exact principles, prevailed, though the contributions of its rivals were in many respects in no way inferior to its own; and the unhappy cleavage no longer exists. In 1886, Brugmann and B. Delbrück began their great *Grundriss der vergleichenden Grammatik der indogermanischen Sprachen* (three volumes in six parts, Strassburg, 1886–1900), Brugmann dealing with phonology and morphology (two volumes in three parts) and Delbrück with syntax (one volume in three parts). In 1897–1916, a second edition, which Brugmann did not live to complete (one more volume should have been added to finish the syntax, which is here completely rewritten from Delbrück), appeared, completely revised and much enlarged, in three volumes (seven parts). Though already antiquated in details, but still valid, on the whole, for principles, the *Grundriss* must be in the library of every advanced student of linguistics, just as its abridgement, the *Kurze vergleichende Grammatik der indogermanischen Sprachen* (Strassburg, 1904; French translation by J. Bloch, A. Cuny, and A. Ernout, *Abrégé de grammaire comparée des langues indo-européennes*, Paris, 1905), is still indispensable for the beginner.

Meanwhile, de Saussure had been teaching along slightly different lines, and may be regarded as the founder of the Swiss-French School, although his *Cours de linguistique générale*, edited after his death by two of his pupils, first appeared at Geneva in 1916 (second edition, Paris, 1922). Apart from his work on the vowels (p. 443), his *De l'emploi du génitif absolu en sanscrit* (Geneva, 1881), and his posthumous *Cours*, de Saussure published relatively little. This little, however, was of exceptionally high value; and through his pupils, especially A. Meillet, equally distinguished as a Slavist, an Armenist, an Iranist, and a general linguist, who likewise wrote brilliantly on Greek, Latin, Tokharian, and Teutonic, he exercised a profound influence on French linguistic science. Meillet himself, a prolific writer, was the author, among many other works, of an *Introduction à l'étude comparative des langues indo-européennes* (seventh edition, Paris, 1934), which, supplementing and correcting Brugmann's work, and written from a different point of view, is also a book which must be studied by each and every student of linguistics.

The period from 1890 onwards has been one of intense investigation in specific problems of linguistics. In 1900, H. Hirt published at Strassburg his *Indo-germanischer Ablaut* (completely revised in his *Der indogermanische Vokalismus*, Heidelberg, 1921, the second volume of his *Indogermanische Grammatik)*; and this book was supplemented by H. Güntert's *Indogermanische Ablautsprobleme* (Strassburg, 1916). Very recently a pupil of Meillet's, J. Kuryłowicz, has begun to develop a new possibility in Indo-European phonology with his theory of the 'consonantal shwā' (cf. p. 65), the germs of which may be found in de Saussure's *Système*, as well as in the writings of H. Pedersen, H. Möller, and others.

According to this theory, which seems destined to solve many problems of the Indo-European sound-system which have hitherto defied explanation, there would appear to have been three (perhaps four) of these shwās; and the present position of Kuryłowicz in his *Études indoeuropéennes*, i (Cracow, 1935), may be summarised as follows: all original long vowels (i.e., those resulting neither from prolonged grades [cf. p. 66] nor from contraction of two short vowels) arise from combination of a short vowel with a consonantal shwā, i.e., $\bar{e}$ from $e + ə_1$; $\bar{a}$ from $e + ə_2$; $\bar{o}$ from $e + ə_3$; $\bar{a}$ from $e + ə_4$; e from $ə_1 + e$; a from $ə_2 + e$; o from $ə_3 + e$; a from $ə_4 + e$; $eə_1e$, etc., become first e-$ə_1e$, then e-e, and finally $\bar{e}$, etc.; every $ə$ vanishes between consonants except for surviving traces in Greek and Armenian; all Indo-European words beginning with a

vowel have lost an initial ə except in Hittite, where it appears as
h (e.g., Hittite *hanti* ' before ' : Sanskrit *ánti*, Greek ἀντί, Latin
ante from *ə₂enti); ə₂ appears as *hh* in Hittite (e.g., Hittite *dehh-i*
' I place ' from *dheə₂-* : Greek τί-θη-μι, Latin *fēc-ī); ə₃* voices
voiceless plosives (e.g., Sanskrit *píbati* ' he drinks ', Old Irish *ib*
from *'pi-pə₃e-ti)* and, like ə₄, it aspirates plosives in Indo-Iranian
(e.g., Sanskrit *prthú-* ' broad ' : Greek πλατύς ' broad ', Lithuanian
plõtis ' breadth ' from *prtə'u-*; Sanskrit *ahám* ' I ' : Latin *ego*
from *egə'o)*.

Attempts to determine the phonetic values of these consonantal
shwās, whose true order seems to have been ə₁, ə₄, ə₂, ə₃, have been
made, with fair accord in principle, by E. Sapir, E. Sturtevant,
W. Couvreur, and the author. The latter regards the second pair
(which he writes ə₁ and ə₂) as probably the voiceless and voiced
laryngal spirants [ħ] and [ʕ]; and the first pair (written by him
ҏ₁ and ҏ₂) as the voiceless glottal plosive [ʔ] and the voiceless
glottal spirant [h]. His chief divergency is that he believes at
present that *a* + ə₁ (the ə₂ of Kuryłowicz) becomes *ā; e* + ə₁
becomes *ē; o* + ə₁ becomes *ō* (cf. Hittite *newahhun* ' I renewed ' :
Greek νεᾶν from *νεϝaə₁-εσεν*, Latin *novāre;* Hittite *dehhi* ' I place ' :
Greek τί-θη-μι, Latin *fēc-ī;* Hittite *dahhi* ' I take ' : Greek δί-δω-μι
' I give ', Latin *dō-num* ' gift ').

An endeavour to establish linguistics as an exact science (cf.
p. 4) is being made by the Danes L. Hjelmslev and H. J. Uldall
on the basis of immanent method and objective analysis. Convinced that the nature of an object can be understood solely when
studied from within, they hold that language has been considered
hitherto practically exclusively from a combination of the physical, physiological, and psychological points of view which is essentially transcendental, and has led to an analysis which is merely
subjective, so that no theory has yet been evolved which gives a
complete and unambiguous explanation of linguistic phenomena.
The theory advanced by these scholars, which is nothing short of
revolutionary in its implications for the whole foundation of linguistics, has not yet been formulated definitely by them; but it
seems highly probable that, when fully developed, it may prove
to be of great value.

The importance of physiological phonetics has likewise received
increasing recognition. The first specific work on this subject was
E. Brücke's *Grundzüge der Physiologie und Systematik der*

Sprachlaute (Vienna, 1856), which was superseded by E. Sievers's *Grundzüge der Lautphysiologie* (fifth edition, Leipzig, 1901). Among later treatises on this theme we may mention Abbé P. J. Rousselot's *Principes de phonétique expérimentale* (Paris, 1897–1909), E. W. Scripture's *Elements of Experimental Phonetics* (New York, 1902), G. Panconcelli-Calzia's *Experimentelle Phonetik in ihrer Anwendung auf die Sprachwissenschaft* (second edition, Berlin, 1924), and D. Jones's *Outline of English Phonetics* (fourth edition, Cambridge, 1935); but all these have been superseded for the linguist by M. Grammont's *Traité de phonétique* (Paris, 1933). A good elementary introduction to the subject is G. Noël-Armfield's *General Phonetics* (third edition, Cambridge, 1924). Likewise essentially phonological in bearing are E. Hermann's *Die Silbenbildung im Griechischen und in den andern indogermanischen Sprachen* (Göttingen, 1923), R. Gauthiot's *La Fin de mot en indo-européen* (Paris, 1913), and E. H. Sturtevant's *Linguistic Change* (Chicago, 1921); while the theory of determinatives (cf. pp. 156–159) has been developed with acumen and daring by P. Persson in his *Studien zur Lehre von der Wurzelerweiterung und Wurzelvariation* (Upsala, 1891) and *Beiträge zur indogermanischen Wortforschung* (Upsala, 1912).

Syntax and semantics have had fewer general discussions of importance, though we may mention particularly H. Jacobi's *Compositum und Nebensatz* (Bonn, 1897) for the former; and M. Bréal's *Essai de sémantique (science des significations)* (seventh edition, Paris, 1922; English translation by Mrs. H. Cust, *Semantics: Studies in the Science of Meaning*, London, 1900), H. Falk's *Betydningslære* (Christiania, 1920), and A. Carnoy's *Science du mot: traité de sémantique* (Paris, 1938) for the latter. On the psychology of language, many books have been written, notably H. Paul's *Principien der Sprachgeschichte* (fifth edition, Halle, 1920; English translation of the second edition by H. A. Strong, *Principles of the History of Language*, London, 1890), J. van Ginneken's *Principes de linguistique psychologique* (Paris, 1907), H. G. C. von der Gabelentz's *Sprachwissenschaft: ihre Aufgaben, Methoden und bisherigen Ergebnisse* (second edition, Leipzig, 1901), and W. Wundt's *Die Sprache* (the first part of his *Völkerpsychologie*, third edition, Leipzig, 1911–12).

This latter work provoked a lively controversy with Delbrück (cf. p. 444); but since Wundt knew little linguistics, and Delbrück little psychology, their logomachy profited neither side. More recently, the German philosopher E. Cassirer has taken up the subject in the first volume of his *Philosophie der symbolischen Formen* (Berlin, 1923), and F. Mauthner wrote three volumes of *Beiträge zu einer Kritik der Sprache* (third edition, Leipzig, 1923); but the best book here known to the author is H. Delacroix's *Le Langage et la pensée* (second edition, Paris, 1930), where a really serious attempt is made to evaluate both linguistic and psychological data without pre-conceived theories (cf. p. 93). The thankless subject of the origin of language (cf. pp. 38–41) has also attracted attention, as in O. Jespersen's *Language: Its Nature, Development, and Origin* (London, 1922). Two excellent popular presentations of these aspects of linguistics have been made by A. Dauzat in his *La vie du langage* (Paris, 1910) and *La Philosophie du langage* (Paris, 1917).

A work of unusual linguistic value was P. Kretschmer's *Einleitung in die Geschichte der griechischen Sprache* (Göttingen, 1896), which inspired intensive study of the languages of Asia Minor; and about this time began a series of archaeological investigations which have given us a knowledge of Hittite and other Asianic tongues and of Tokharian, Khotanese, Parthian, and Sogdian in the general region of Chinese Turkistān. The problem of the relation of language to civilisation (social linguistics), first seriously taken up in 1845 by A. Kuhn in his *Zur ältesten Geschichte der indogermanischen Völker* (second edition, Berlin, 1877), was carried further in A. Pictet's *Les Origines indo-européennes, ou les Aryas primitifs* (second edition, three volumes, Paris, 1877); but material and method were then scarcely adequate, and the picture drawn was far too ideal. In 1870, V. Hehn reacted vigorously against this romanticism in his *Culturpflanzen und Hausthiere in ihrem Übergang nach Griechenland und Italien sowie in das übrige Europa* (eighth edition, Berlin, 1911); and he was followed by Otto Schrader in his *Sprachvergleichung und Urgeschichte* (third edition, Jena, 1907) and, especially, in his *Reallexikon der indogermanischen Altertumskunde* (Strassburg, 1901; completely revised and enlarged by A. Nehring, Berlin and Leipzig, 1917–29).

The Indo-European problem itself was treated by H. d'Arbois de Jubainville in his *Les premiers habitants de l'Europe* (second edition, two volumes, Paris, 1889–94), by G. Dottin in his *Les anciens peuples de l'Europe* (Paris, 1916), and especially by H. Hirt in his *Die Indogermanen* (Strassburg, 1905–07) and by S. Feist in his *Kultur, Ausbreitung und Herkunft der Indogermanen* (Berlin, 1913). The most recent summaries of our knowledge of these subjects are the relevant articles in M. Ebert's *Reallexikon der Vorgeschichte* (fifteen volumes, Berlin, 1924–32). The actual combination of social with comparative linguistics has been especially furthered by A. Meillet, as in his *La Méthode comparative en linguistique historique* (Oslo, 1925) and his *Linguistique historique et linguistique générale* (two volumes, Paris, 1926–36; collections of studies originally published in technical journals, etc.), as well as in the chapters on vocabulary in his volumes on Teutonic and Slavic and on general linguistics. A careful study of the relation of language to society, based on an examination of the very primitive Australian Aranta has been made by A. Sommerfelt *(La Langue et la société: caractères sociaux d'une langue de type archaïque*, Oslo, 1938). In his incomplete posthumous *Languages in History and Politics* (Oxford, 1938), A. C. Woolner planned a comprehensive study of the influence of language on historical and political developments.

Linguistic geography (cf. pp. 120–125) practically began with G. Wenker's *Das rheinische Platt* (Düsseldorf, 1877), and its principles have been discussed by K. Jaberg in his *Sprachgeographie* (Aarau, 1908) and *Aspects géographiques du langage* (Paris, 1936), by E. Gamillscheg in his *Sprachgeographie* (Bielefeld and Leipzig, 1928), and others, and has been popularised by A. Dauzat in his *La Géographie linguistique* (Paris, 1922).

Investigation here has borne fruit in a large number of linguistic maps and atlases, of which easily the most elaborate yet published is the *Atlas linguistique de la France* (Paris, 1902–10) by E. Edmont and J. Gilliéron, with more than two thousand and forty-eight sheets for six hundred and twenty-nine communes throughout France. This formed the model for their *Atlas linguistique de la Corse* (Paris, 1914), O. Bloch's *Atlas linguistique des Vosges méridionales* (Paris, 1917), P. Le Roux's *Atlas linguistique de la Basse-Bretagne* (Rennes, 1924 sqq.), A. Griera's *Atlas linguistic de Catalunya* (Barcelona, 1923 sqq.), K. Jaberg and J. Jud's *Sprach- und Sachatlas Italiens und der Südschweiz* (Zofingen, 1928 sqq.), E. Blanquaert's *Dialect-Atlas van Klein-Brabant* (Antwerp, 1925), H. Vangassen's *Dialect-Atlas van Zuid-Oost-*

Vlaanderen (two volumes, Antwerp, 1931), and *Dialect-Atlas van
Nord-Oost-Vlaanderen en Zeeuwsch-Vlaanderen* (Antwerp, 1935),
A. Bennike and M. Kristensen's *Kort over de danske folkemål*
(Copenhagen, 1898–1914), the *Deutscher Sprachatlas* of F. Wrede
and his collaborators (Marburg, 1926 sqq.), the projected linguistic atlas of the United States and Canada by H. Kurath and his
staff, of which the three volumes for New England appeared at
Providence in 1939 with a handbook, and C. Weigand's *Linguistischer Atlas der dacorumänischen Sprachgebietes* (Leipzig, 1898–
1909).

Perhaps the best general maps for Europe are Stanford's *Sketch-Map of the Linguistic Areas of Europe* (London, 1917), D. Schäfer's *Karte der Länder und Völker Europas* (eighth edition, Berlin,
1918), A. Haberlandt's *Karte der Völker Europas nach Sprache
und Volksdichte* (Vienna, 1927), *L'Europa etnico-linguistica*
(Novara, 1916), various maps in L. Dominian's *Frontiers of Language and Nationality in Europe* (New York, 1917), and an
excellent *Linguistic Map of Europe* (never published) prepared
in 1919 for the American Commission to Negotiate Peace.

Linguistic maps for special areas are to be found in many works
dealing with the regions in question. The whole world is covered
in the series given in *Les Langues du monde*, edited by A. Meillet
and M. Cohen (Paris, 1924), in the atlas of Father W. Schmidt's
Sprachfamilien und Sprachenkreise der Erde (Heidelberg, 1926),
and in A. Drexel and R. Wimpissinger's *Sprachen, Völker und
Rassen der Erde* (Innsbruck, 1934), and the *Atlas linguisticus*
of the same cartographers, aided by a staff of collaborators (Innsbruck, 1934).

We may also note for ancient Greek the map in C. D. Buck,
Introduction to the Study of the Greek Dialects (revised edition,
Boston [1928]; also in H. Pedersen's *Linguistic Science in the
Nineteenth Century*, Cambridge, U. S. A., 1931); for Italic, the
map in J. Whatmough's *The Foundations of Roman Italy* (London,
1937); for Irish, the maps giving the proportions of Irish-speakers
in 1911 and 1925 in the *Report of the Coimisiún na Gaeltachta*
(Dublin, 1925); for Romance, the map in the first volume of G.
Gröber's *Grundriss der romanischen Philologie* (second edition,
Strassburg, 1904; reprinted in H. Hirt's *Die Indogermanen*, ii,
Strassburg, 1907); for Teutonic, three maps in the first volume of
H. Paul's *Grundriss der germanischen Philologie* (second edition,

THE HISTORY OF THE STUDY OF LANGUAGE 451

Strassburg, 1901) ; for Poland and the Baltic area, *Poland: Ethno-graphical Map* and *Baltic Provinces (Ethnographical Map) (Geo-graphical Section of the General Staff, 3703ᵃ* and *Geographical Section of the Peace Congress*, no. 133) ; and for Uralic and Altaic the *Map of Eurasia showing the Distribution of Turanian Peoples* in *A Manual on the Turanians and Pan-Turanianism* (London, 1921).

For the Caucasus, we have the maps by N. von Seidlitz in *Peter-manns Mitteilungen*, xxvi (1880), Tafel 15, and H. Schuchardt, ib. xliii (1897), Tafel 6, and especially the *Ethnografičeskaja karta kavkazkago kraja* (Tiflis, 1909) ; for Modern Armenian, the map in H. Adjarian's *Classification des dialectes arméniens* (Paris, 1909) ; for Indian, the extremely detailed series in the *Linguistic Survey of India* (Calcutta, 1903 sqq.) ; for North America, J. W. Powell's *Linguistic Families of American Indians north of Mexico* (most conveniently accessible in the *Handbook of American Indians*, i = *Bulletin of the Bureau of American Ethnology*, no. 30, Washington, 1907) ; and for Central America, the map in *Indian Languages of Mexico and Central America* by C. Thomas and J. R. Swanton (= *Bulletin of the Bureau of American Ethnology*, no. 44, Washington, 1911) and especially the *Übersichtskarte der Sprachen Mexikos und Mittelamerikas, Nordwest-Südamerikas und West-indiens* in the second volume of W. Lehmann's *Zentral-Amerika*, part i, *Die Sprachen Zentral-Amerikas* (Berlin, 1920). Many others are scattered through scientific books and journals, and some may be ignored as open to the suspicion that they have been made for purposes of propaganda. A full cartography of linguistic and ethno-logical maps is much to be desired.

Closely connected with linguistic geography is the study of place-names, which, by their survival, often show that certain languages were once spoken in areas from which they have long since vanished. Such names are not merely of linguistic interest, but are also highly important for the historian as being the sole evidence, apart from archaeological indications, for many migra-tions of peoples in pre-historic periods (cf. pp. 120–125). One must bear in mind, however, that research in place-names (includ-ing, in practice, the names of peoples and rivers, and even of streets, farms, and fields) is beset by even greater difficulties than etymology in general. If, for example, one did not have actual record of the original form of the name of *York*, one could scarcely trace it back to *Eborācom;* and while the names of *Vienne* in France and of *Vienna* on the Danube are now identical in form, they come from totally divergent and unrelated origins (see p. 123).

An excellent popular book on this subject is A. Dauzat's *Les Noms de lieux* (Paris, 1926); and among the soundest scientific treatments for special areas one may mention the *Introduction to the Survey of English Place-Names* (two parts, Cambridge, 1924), followed by a series of volumes on the place-names of individual counties; E. Ekwall's *Concise Oxford Dictionary of English Place-Names* (Oxford, 1926), W. J. Watson's *History of the Celtic Place-Names of Scotland* (Edinburgh, 1926), P. Joyce's *Origin and History of Irish Names of Places* (three volumes, Dublin, 1869–1913), E. Hogan's *Onomasticon Goedelicum* (Dublin, 1910), A. Longnon's *Noms de lieu de la France* (Paris, 1920–29); E. Muret's *Les Noms de lieu dans les langues romanes* (Paris [1929]), M. Olsen's *Farms and Fanes of Ancient Norway: The Place-Names of a Country discussed in their Bearings on Social and Religious History* (Oslo, 1928), and H. Krahe's *Die alten balkanillyrischen geographischen Namen* (Heidelberg, 1925). This branch of linguistics has as its special journal the *Zeitschrift für Ortsnamenforschung* (Munich and Berlin, 1925 sqq.).

Personal names have likewise received scientific investigation, but here the results have been less satisfactory. Popular works of merit, which indicate the principles to be followed, are Dauzat's *Les Noms de personnes* (Paris, 1925) and E. Weekley's *Surnames* (third edition, London, 1937) and *The Romance of Names* (third edition, London, 1917). The general structure of the Indo-European system of nomenclature is given in the first edition of A. Fick's *Die griechischen Personennamen* (Göttingen, 1874; the second edition by F. Bechtel, in 1894, deals only with Greek), and most of the Indo-European groups have special treatises on the subject, such as A. Hilka, *Die indischen Personennamen* (Bonn, 1910); F. Justi, *Iranisches Namenbuch* (Marburg, 1895); F. Bechtel, *Die historischen Personennamen des Griechischen bis zur Kaiserzeit* (Halle, 1917); W. Schulze, *Zur Geschichte der lateinischen Eigennamen* (Berlin, 1904); H. Krahe, *Lexikon altillyrischer Personennamen* (Heidelberg, 1929); E. Förstemann, *Althochdeutsches Namenbuch*, i (second edition, Bonn, 1900); M. Schönfeld, *Wörterbuch der altgermanischen Personen- und Völkernamen* (Heidelberg, 1911); R. Trautmann, *Die altpreussischen Personennamen* (Göttingen, 1925); and F. Miklosich, *Die Bildung der slavischen Personennamen* (Vienna, 1860); while F. Solmsen's *Indogermanische Eigennamen als Spiegel der Kulturgeschichte* (edited by E. Fraenkel, Heidelberg, 1922) is of particular interest in this connexion. Outside Indo-European, special mention should be made of G. B. Gray's *Studies in Hebrew Proper Names* (Oxford, 1896). The classification of languages has been studied by F. N. Finck in his *Klassification der Sprachen* (Marburg, 1901), by Meillet in his *Dialectes indo-européens* (second edition, Paris, 1922), and by H. Pedersen in his *Groupement des dialectes indo-européens* (Copenhagen, 1925); while their distribution in Europe has been discussed by L. Dominian in his *Frontiers of Language and Nationality in Europe* (New York, 1917) and by Meillet in his *Les Langues dans l'Europe nouvelle* (second edition, much enlarged and with a statistical appendix by L. Tesnière, Paris, 1928).

In considering classification, Meillet later advanced a highly interesting *peripheral theory*. Observing that the language-groups at two extremes of the Indo-European area, Italo-Celtic in the west and Indo-Iranian in the east, possess certain points in common which are not found in the areas between them (e.g., the Italo-Celtic genitive in -ī, as in Latin *virī* ' of a man ' = Old Irish *fir* from *ụirī*, compared with such Sanskrit formations as *stambhī-bhavati* ' he becomes a post ', *upahārī-kariṣyati* ' he will make an offering '; cf. the type of Latin *vīvi-ficō* ' I vivify, make alive '), he suggested that these extreme linguistic groups broke away from the primitive Indo-European language-speakers before any others of their kin. Though this hypothesis has not escaped criticism, it seems sound in principle and is apparently confirmed by certain minor, though cumulatively important, evidence which he himself did not note. Meillet also discussed Indo-European metrics in his *Origines indo-européennes des mètres grecs* (Paris, 1823), an older and now antiquated work on this subject being R. Westphal's *Allgemeine Metrik der indogermanischen und semitischen Völker* (Berlin, 1892).

Surveys of the various language-families of the world have been made in *Les Langues du monde* (Paris, 1924), edited by A. Meillet and M. Cohen; by Father W. Schmidt in his *Die Sprachfamilien und Sprachenkreise der Erde* (Heidelberg, 1926), with rich bibliographical material and an excellent linguistic atlas; and by E.

Kieckers in his *Die Sprachstämme der Erde* (Heidelberg, 1931).
L. Hjelmslev, in his *Principes de grammaire générale* (Copenhagen, 1928), followed by his *La Catégorie des cas,* i (Aarhus, 1935),
has begun, in collaboration with H. J. Uldall, a fresh investigation
of language and a new classification of linguistic phenomena which
give promise of being of much value (cf. p. 446).

In discussion of language and of linguistics in general, volumes
of importance have been written (passing over the antiquated *La
Linguistique* of A. Hovelacque, fourth edition, Paris, 1888) by
L. Bloomfield, *Introduction to the Study of Language* (second
edition, practically re-written, New York, 1933); E. Sapir, *Language* (New York, 1921); J. Vendryes, *Le Langage: introduction
linguistique à l'histoire* (Paris, 1921; English translation by P.
Radin, *Language,* London and New York, 1925); J. Marouzeau,
La Linguistique, ou science du langage (Paris, 1921); and W. L.
Graff, *Language and Languages: an Introduction to Linguistics*
(New York, 1932), Marouzeau being also the author of a very
serviceable little *Lexique de la terminologie linguistique* (Paris,
1933). H. Hirt wrote a new *Indogermanische Grammatik* (seven
volumes, Heidelberg, 1921–37), marked by great ingenuity and
deep learning, but so daring that caution is frequently advisable
in using it; and Kieckers has published the first volume of an
Einführung in die indogermanische Sprachwissenschaft (Munich,
1933). The useful *Handleiding bij de studie der vergelijkende indo-
germaansche taalwetenschap vooral met bestrekking tot de klas-
sieke en germaansche talen* by Mgr. J. Schrijnen (second edition,
Leyden, 1924; German translation, *Einleitung in das Studium der
indogermanischen Sprachwissenschaft,* by W. Fischer, Heidelberg,
1921) deals only with the history and the general principles of
linguistics, and with Indo-European phonology. In his volumes
L'unità d'origine del linguaggio (Bologna, 1905) and *Elementi di
glottologia* (two volumes, Bologna, 1922–23), A. Trombetti
gathered an immense amount of material, but was led by superficial resemblances and ill-founded theories to conclusions incommensurate in value with the labour expended; and a similar verdict
must be rendered on H. Koppelmann's *Die eurasische Sprach-
familie, Indogermanisch, Koreanisch und Verwandtes* (Heidelberg,
1933).

During this recent period of linguistics, very special attention
has been paid to etymology. The principal etymological diction-

aries and chief grammars of individual languages have already been listed in Chapters XI and XII. Here we need add only that the scientifically unjustifiable, though pedagogically practical, comparison of Greek and Italic has received discussion in accordance with linguistic principles in the *Traité de grammaire comparée des langues classiques* of A. Meillet and J. Vendryes (second edition, Paris, 1924) and in the *Comparative Grammar of Greek and Latin* of C. D. Buck (Chicago [1933]).

The possible relation of Indo-European to other linguistic families has naturally received much study, although stress has too often been laid on lexicographical coincidences rather than on phonological and morphological correspondences, which alone can be considered decisive for establishing genetic relationship (cf. pp. 301–303). Attempts have been made to connect Indo-European with Semitic on the one hand, and with Uralic on the other. To the advocates of the first theory belong, notably, H. Möller with his *Semitisch und Indogermanisch* (Copenhagen, 1907) and his *Vergleichendes indogermanisch-semitisches Wörterbuch* (Göttingen, 1911), and A. Cuny with his *Études prégrammaticales sur le domaine des langues indo-européennes et chamito-sémitiques* (Paris, 1924); while the hypothesis of the affinity of Indo-European with Uralic, first suggested by V. Thomsen in 1869, is defended, to mention only a single name, by B. Collinder in his *Indouralisches Sprachgut* (Upsala, 1934).

The words borrowed by Uralic from Indo-European were studied by H. Jacobsohn in his *Arier und Ugrofinnen* (Göttingen, 1922); and Thomsen wrote two standard works on the relations of Uralic to Teutonic and to Baltic; *Den gotiske sprogklasses inflydelse på den finske* (Copenhagen, 1869; reprinted in his *Samlede afhandlinger*, ii, 51–264, Copenhagen, 1920; German translation by E. Sievers, *Ueber den Einfluss der germanischen Sprachen auf die finnisch-lappischen*, Halle, 1870) and *Beröringer mellem de finske og de baltiske (litauisk-lettiske) sprog* (Copenhagen, 1890). More recent discussions are T. E. Karsten's *Germanisch-finnische Lehnwortstudien* (Helsingfors, 1915) and *Fragen aus dem Gebiete der germanisch-finnischen Berührungen* (Helsingfors, 1922), and Collinder's *Urgermanische Lehnwörter im Finnischen* (Upsala, 1932).

How far implications of this character may go is clearly expressed by H. Pedersen, who lends to them the favouring weight of his authority in the words *(Linguistic Science in the Nineteenth*

Century, Cambridge, U. S. A., 1931, p. 338): ' If we accept relationship, we are led yet farther afield, not only to Samoyed, which cannot be separated from Finno-Ugrian, but throughout all of Northern Asia and across Bering Strait, because similar, though fainter, resemblances like those here cited are found also in Turkish, Mongolian and Manchu, in Yukaghir, and even in Eskimo. If, on the other hand, we agree in the matter of relationship with Semitic, then we must also accept relationship with the far-flung Hamitic family, and perhaps with Basque. And squarely in the midst between our supposed Northern and Southern relatives stand the Caucasian languages, which we cannot ignore, and various extinct languages in Asia Minor and thereabout. It is not impossible that some of the non-Indo-European languages of antiquity in Asia Minor were once the most closely related of all to the Indo-European family '.

The number of periodicals devoted to linguistics is far from small. Here belong, notably, the *Zeitschrift für vergleichende Sprachforschung auf dem Gebiete des Deutschen, Griechischen und Lateinischen* (Berlin, 1852–74), continued as *Zeitschrift für vergleichende Sprachforschung auf dem Gebiete der indogermanischen Sprachen* (Berlin, 1877 sqq.; generally abbreviated as *KZ* = *Kuhn's Zeitschrift)*, the *Mémoires* and *Bulletin de la société de linguistique de Paris* (Paris, 1868 sqq.; *MSLP* and *BSLP* respectively), the *Archivio glottologico italiano* (Rome, Turin, and Florence, 1873 sqq.; *AGI)*, the *Beiträge zur Kunde der indogermanischen Sprachen* (Göttingen, 1877–1906; *BB* = *Bezzenberger's Beiträge)*, the *Indogermanische Forschungen* (Strassburg, now Berlin and Leipzig, 1891 sqq.; *IF)*, *Glotta: Zeitschrift für griechische und lateinische Sprache* (Göttingen, 1907 sqq.; especially important for linguistics in the Mediterranean area), *Wörter und Sachen: kulturhistorische Zeitschrift für Sprach- und Sachforschung* (Heidelberg, 1909 sqq.; dealing particularly with social linguistics), the *Rivista indo-greca-italica* (Naples, 1916 sqq.; *RIGI)*, *Language* (Baltimore, 1925 sqq.), and *Emerita* (Madrid, 1933 sqq.).

Phonetics has its special journals, such as *Le Maître phonétique* (Bourg-la-Reine, 1889 sqq.), *Vox: internationales Zentralblatt für experimentelle Phonetik* (Berlin, 1891–1922), and *La Revue de phonétique* (Paris, 1911 sqq.). Since 1928, international linguistic congresses have been held; and the first international congress for toponymy and anthroponymy met at Paris in 1938. Studies of much value on Asiatic, Oceanic, Australian, African, and American languages frequently appear in *Anthropos: internationalle Zeitschrift für Völker- und Sprachenkunde* (Mödling-bei-Wien, 1906 sqq.) ; and many journals which are primarily philological, ethnological, or archaeological often contain articles of linguistic value.

To control this mass of material, of all grades of importance, the linguist, like every other specialist, must have bibliographies. From 1891 to 1913, books dealing with linguistics were listed and reviewed especially in the *Anzeigerblatt* which forms a supplement to the volumes of the *Indogermanische Forschungen;* and something may also be found in the *Orientalische Bibliographie* (Berlin, 1888–1922; *OB).* Since 1913, the linguist has had the *Indogermanisches Jahrbuch* (Strassburg, now Berlin and Leipzig; *IJ),* which lists both books and articles, often with illuminating criticisms; the ' compte-rendus ' of the *Bulletin de la société de linguistique de Paris* are invaluable; and most linguistic journals contain reviews and bibliographical material which should be consulted. The exhaustive character of the bibliography of the *Indogermanisches Jahrbuch* is indicated by the rubrics in the volume for 1936 (published in 1938) : general linguistics, phonetics, grammar, and etymology; linguistic sociology; linguistic philosophy, psychology, pedagogics, and physiology; Indo-European linguistics and archaeology; Tokharian; Indo-Iranian; Armenian; Albanian; Greek; Italic (including the non-Indo-European and prae-Italic languages of Italy) ; Celtic, Teutonic; Balto-Slavic; and Asianic (Hittite, etc.). Of bibliographies for individual groups not exhaustively covered by the *Jahrbuch,* the most important are, for Classics, the *Bibliotheca philologica classica* (Berlin, 1875 sqq.) and J. Marouzeau's *Dix années de bibliographie classique, 1914–1924* (Paris, 1927–28) and *L'Année philologique* (Paris, 1928 sqq.) ; and for Teutonic, the *Jahresbericht über die Erscheinungen auf dem Gebiete der germanischen Philologie* (Dresden and Leipzig, 1879 sqq.).

The question of the original home of Indo-European (cf. pp. 304–310) has been exhaustively discussed not only by O. Schrader in his *Reallexikon,* by H. Hirt in his *Indogermanen,* and by others (e.g., R. G. Latham, in his *Elements of Comparative Philology,* London, 1862), but also in special volumes by M. Much, *Die Heimat der Indogermanen im Lichte der urgeschichtlichen For-*

schung (second edition, Berlin, 1904), and E. Michelis, *L'origine degli Indo-Europei* (Turin, 1903). The linguist would do well also to consult such works as M. Ebert's *Reallexikon der Vorgeschichte* (fifteen volumes, Berlin, 1924–32), V. Gordon Childe's *The Aryans* (London, 1926), A. Jardé's *La Formation du peuple grec* (Paris, 1923; English translation, *The Formation of the Greek People*, London, 1926), L. P. Homo's *L'Italie primitive et les débuts de l'impérialisme romain* (Paris, 1925; English translation, *Primitive Italy and the Beginnings of Roman Imperialism*, London, 1926), J. Whatmough's *The Foundations of Roman Italy* (London, 1937), H. Hubert's *Les Celtes* (two volumes, Paris, 1932; English translation, *The Rise of the Celts* and *The Greatness and Decline of the Celts*, two volumes, London, 1934), T. E. Karsten's *Germanerna* (second edition, Stockholm, 1927; German translation, *Die Germanen*, Berlin, 1928; French translation, *Les anciens Germains*, Paris, 1931), L. Niederle's *Manuel de l'antiquité slave* (two volumes, Paris, 1923–26), etc.

The history of linguistics has received special discussion in T. Benfey's *Geschichte der Sprachwissenschaft* (Munich, 1869; now of value only for the period before the nineteenth century and for its bibliographical material), H. Steinthal's *Geschichte der Sprachwissenschaft bei den Griechen und Römern* (Berlin, 1863), S. K. Belvarkar's *Account of the Different Existing Systems of Sanskrit Grammar* (Poona, 1915), C. Thurot's *Notices et extraits de divers manuscrits latins pour servir à l'histoire des doctrines grammaticales au moyen âge* (Paris, 1868), J. Bäbler's *Beiträge zu einer Geschichte der lateinischen Grammatik im Mittelalter* (Halle, 1885), P. Rotta's *Filosofia del linguaggio nella patristica e nella scolastica* (Turin, 1909), V. Thomsen's *Sprogvidenskabens historie* (Copenhagen, 1902; reprinted in his *Samlede afhandlinger*, i, 3–106, Copenhagen, 1919; German translation by H. Pollak, *Geschichte der Sprachwissenschaft bis zum Ausgang des neunzehnten Jahrhunderts*, Halle, 1927), and H. Pedersen's *Sprogvidenskaben i det nittende aarhundrede* (Copenhagen, 1924; English translation by J. W. Spargo, *Linguistic Science in the Nineteenth Century*, Cambridge, U. S. A., 1931).

Since 1916, a series of histories of linguistics, with very full bibliographical references, has been appearing at Strassburg (now at Berlin and Leipzig) under the title *Grundriss der indogermanischen Sprach- und Altertumskunde*. Of this, the following parts have thus far been published: *Griechische Sprache* by A. Thumb, *Italische Sprachen* by A. Walde, *Vulgärlatein* by K. R. von Ettmayer, *Keltische Sprachen* by R. Thurneysen (1916); *Germanisch*, part i (general and phonology), by W. Streitberg, V. Michels, and M. H. Jellinek (1936); *Slavisch-litauisch* by A. Brückner, *Albanisch* by N. Jokl (1917); *Indisch* by W. Wüst (1929); *Iranisch* by H. Reichelt, *Armenisch* by H. Zeller (1927); *Hethitisch und 'kleinasiatische' Sprachen* by J. Friedrich (1931); *Tocharisch* by E. Schwentner (1935); and *Etruskisch* by Eva Fiesel (1931).

Valuable linguistic material is also contained in the first volumes of the *Grundriss der iranischen Philologie* and its appendix (on Ossetic) (Strassburg, 1895–1903), the *Grundriss der romanischen Philologie* (second edition, Strassburg, 1904–06), and the *Grundriss der germanischen Philologie* (second edition, Strassburg, 1901; cf. pp. 321, 339, 350–351). A general survey of the state of linguistics at the time, and of the problems then confronting it, appeared at Heidelberg in 1924 under the title *Stand und Aufgaben der Sprachwissenschaft: Festschrift für Wilhelm Streitberg*, followed by two volumes of studies in honour of H. Hirt, edited by H. Arntz, *Germanen und Indogermanen* (Heidelberg, 1936).

It will be observed that our account of the history of linguistics has dealt almost solely with Indo-European. For this, there are very good reasons. From the days of Yāska and Plato through the Classical period and the Middle Ages to the present time, linguistic interest has centred about Indo-European. Semitic linguistic studies were derived from Greece (cf. p. 429); and Sir William Jones, with whom the modern science may be said to begin (cf. pp. 435–436), was a Sanskritist. The Indo-European languages were the only ones sufficiently known, sufficiently divergent, and sufficiently complete in records to stimulate interest in the initial stages of linguistics. Their sole possible rival at that time was Semitic; Dravidian, the one remaining group with early remains, was then practically unknown. It has been only natural that linguistic study and linguistic method should have been built up on Indo-European, and every step in this study and method has been scrutinised with merciless and often hostile criticism. The result has been that a method of increasing severity and exactitude has gradually been constructed. That it is perfect, no one claims; that it needs much further development, all admit. Yet, however great its faults and however wide its lacunae, it has, by force of circumstances, become the model for all linguistic work in non-Indo-European families of speech; there the method must be modified at most only in detail, scarcely in principle.

Two branches of Indo-European are, most unfortunately for all concerned, relatively unsympathetic to, and unaffected by, linguistics: Classics and Romance. While there are honourable exceptions, the average Classicist is interested solely in philology; he seems to feel (perhaps often unconsciously) that linguistics is in some way a profanation of the beauty of the languages of Greece and Rome, and appears to inherit the out-worn feud of Curtius with Brugmann (pp. 443–444). The average Romance scholar, again with honourable exceptions, seems hypnotised by Latin and seldom thinks of going outside the Italic field; whereas the Slavist, for example, whose languages are more like each other than are those of his Romance colleague, would not dream of ignoring Indo-European linguistics. This state of affairs is the more lamentable because it is utterly unnecessary; but, on the other hand, the average Indo-Europeanist is culpably and inexcusably ignorant of Romance, though never of Classics. One can only hope that all sides will see the error of their ways, and amend them to their mutual profit and to the advancement of science.

INDEX

A

ABASGO-KERKETIAN, 374, 375
ABK'AZ, 375, 376
caritive case in, 201
genders in, 189
genitive in, 197
word cited, 201
Ablative case, 192, 198–199
apparently formed in Sanskrit,
Hittite, and Italic by compound-
ing genitive and ablative, 191,
198–199; as supine in Latin, 221;
formation of, in Āhom, 153;
Latin, as illustrating a single
form with several functions, 19–
20; Latin locative often has
form of, 202, 240–241; singular,
as source of adverbs, 170; syncretism of, with other cases, 202;
with prepositions replaces genitive, locative, and instrumental
in Latin and Romance, 241,
242
Ablaut: *see* Vowel-gradation
Abnormalities of vocal or auditory
apparatus of interest to linguists, 6–7
Absolutive case, 193
Abuse, terms of, used for endearment, 265
Accent, 63–67, 213, 288
a factor in Teutonic sound-shifts,
78, 79, 439
Armenian, 325
Baltic, 354
early works on, 439
effect of, on word-order, 232
Greek, 63, 327
Indo-European, Vedic Sanskrit,
Greek, and Baltic as sources for
determining, 354
Indo-Iranian, 313, 315
Latin, 63–64, 288, 334–335

Accent *(Cont.)*
Lithuanian, 63, 354
of grammatical *vs.* relational cases,
235–236
of Latin demonstrative pronoun in
evolution into definite article,
236–237
of prepositions, 237
of verb, 232–234, 235, 236
of vocative in Vedic Sanskrit, 232–
233
primary, sometimes created from
secondary, 236, 250
Proto-Slavic, best preserved in
Čakavian Serbian, 355
syllabic, 147
Accent-shift in Greek, 233
in Latin, 63–64, 233, 335
Accessory words, subordinate position of, in sentence, 235, 236
Accommodation, type of assimilation, 68
Accommodative Aspect: *see* Benefactive Aspect
Accusative case, 192–194, 218
and nominative differ in base in
pronouns of the first person, 173;
as alleged subject of infinitive
in Latin, 240; as gerund in Sanskrit, 222; as infinitive, 221; as
logical subject in Old Irish, 228–
229; as non-active or passive,
186, 192; may be governed by
verbal epithetologue, 194, 220–
221; neuter singular, as source
of adverbs, 170; often supplanted
by instrumental in Kharoṣṭhī
Prākrit and Avestan, 200; singular, formation of, in Modern
Persian, 153; singular masculine,
identical in form with nominative singular neuter in -*o*-stems,
186, 192; syncretism of, with